THE SECONDARY MOD

DICK STROUD

CONTENTS

PROLOGUE

When I told friends about *The Secondary Mod* their first comment was, 'But you vowed never to write another book', closely followed by, 'What does Stella [my wife] think?' Only then did they enquire what it's about and why I was breaking my 'I am finished with writing books' vow.

In the past I have always known the scope of the topics I wanted my books to cover and what I hoped to achieve from writing them. Normally it was to support some new business venture.

My first book documented the transformative effect of the internet on business and society. Most recently I have written about population ageing and its effects on business and society.

Everything about *The Secondary Mod* was different. Before beginning I had planned less than half of the content and done less than 20% of the research, and had only the sketchiest idea about the conclusions. As for why I was writing the book, the answer was complicated and not a set of reasons that makes for a single, pithy sentence. To be honest, I am not sure I fully understood all the reasons myself. Financial gain certainly wasn't one of them.

Let me try and explain. For the past decade, probably longer, I have had a low-grade irritation about the way that secondary modern schools are discussed. They are invariably referred to as the inevitable (and unwanted) result of educating a minority of children in grammar schools.

It is like the subject of positive discrimination. Any mention of its benefits is immediately countered by arguments about the negative outcomes and unfairness for those it penalises. This might be a valid argument, but it polarises any debate into a simplistic argument about 'winners' and 'losers'. It is the 'zero-sum game' argument of game theory in which one person's gain is equivalent to another's loss.

Secondary modern schools and the millions of children who attended them are always described as the 'losers' who were sacrificed for the minority of 'winners' attending grammar schools. The 'winners', allegedly, got the better teachers and school facilities and had the expectation of success. The implicit assertion, which is sometimes made explicit, is that secondary modern children had a second-rate education that limited them to second-rate life chances.

These schools are now a footnote in the history of British secondary education. They were last counted in government education statistics in 2011, when there were 137 remaining. The intervening years have done nothing to improve their reputation.

If you want to silence a debate about selective schools, then look thoughtful and say the magic words, 'But look at the unfairness of secondary moderns.' Your audience is likely to nod in approval while concocting their own interpretation of the statement usually focusing on failure, poor teaching, unfairness, scarred for life, second-class citizens etc.

This simplistic dismissal of the schooling system that educated the majority of children for 23 years always annoys me. Let's be frank – it pisses me off.

I went to a secondary modern and it was nothing like this received wisdom. Don't worry – this is not going to be a tale about how I fought against the odds to succeed. I have recounted my personal experiences, only because I know the facts are accurate, thanks to my parents who dutifully kept all my school records.

I think that this disconnect between my experience and the universally accepted story of the awfulness of secondary modern schools was what made me write this book. Perhaps it is even more of a personal mission, to provide a balanced story for the sake of the teachers and headmaster to whom I owe such a debt of gratitude.

However, it was also at this point that my uncertainty about the book's content began. Maybe I was blessed with a one-off secondary modern experience, and maybe the criticisms of the schools were correct. I found that difficult to believe, but it was a possibility that I couldn't discount. Only by doing a lot of research would I know the answer. For an author, this uncertainty was both daunting and exciting, and it's not something I had experienced before. I hope you, the reader, are comfortable with a book whose storyline evolved as the writing progressed.

My best attempt at a single-sentence description of the book goes something like this: 'It is the story of secondary modern schools in England and Wales based on facts, not prejudice.' My motivation for writing it, other than as a token of thanks to my teachers, was to provide an alternative narrative to the establishment's simplistic notion that these schools were a scar on the country's educational history. However, I had to be prepared for the possibility that the establishment's view was correct.

I was on much firmer foundations in knowing what *The Secondary Mod* was not about. It is not a defence of selective education and a diatribe about bringing back grammar schools. Neither is it a commentary on teaching techniques and schools' curriculum. Above all, it is not a chronicle about the 'good old days' of schooling and an attack on all that is wrong with today's way of educating the young. It touches on these topics, of course, but they were not my primary interest.

A cursory study of the subject reveals that many of the arguments against secondary moderns are either rehashed versions of previous critical reporting or based on the selective use of information. I can easily recognise these mistakes, having made them myself on an embarrassingly large number of occasions. I did my very best not to repeat the error.

To help me avoid this problem and as a prism to illustrate how others have fallen into the trap, I start by explaining how individual and collective views about events and subjects become distorted by the selective filtering of information. I researched and wrote this book at the height of 'fake news' hysteria and witnessing the media reporting of events polarising in an extraordinary way. This was the time of Brexit, Donald Trump and Covid-19.

If we can create such differing views about what is happening today – just think of how we might distort the truth about events that occurred over half a century ago?

The story begins with an account of my own experience of failing the 11-plus and finding myself at George Gascoigne, a secondary modern in East London. I had assumed that this chapter would be easy to write, but it proved surprisingly difficult. Memories that had always seemed crystal clear become distinctly fuzzy when you try to summarise them into a succinct readable form. I had always been immensely grateful to my teachers and writing this section made me even more so, having studied the difficulties they overcame to give us a good education.

Next I look at the most common stories about the 11-plus and what happened to those who failed the exam. I think the technical term for this is the 'dominant narrative'. I was astonished at how often the subject is still discussed by politicians, media commentators, academics and 'celebrities'. In almost all cases their views are negative and worryingly consistent. This section concludes with a summary of the most common arguments and 'facts' that are used to damn these schools.

By this stage, you will have read my personal account of attending a secondary modern school and the very different viewpoint given by the media and the self-appointed commentators about education history. So, what is the truth? The only way to answer this question was to look at the evidence. I began by thinking this could be found from reading the books that have been written about the schools, supplemented by academic papers. How wrong and naïve I was. Most of what I read was variations on the dominant narrative with little objective thinking and would have resulted in me compounding the error of simplifying the story of the schools. To do the job properly I needed to access the original sources of information – the numerous government reports, papers and acts. This involved many visits to the National Archive.

When I began, I thought I was writing a critical appraisal of the history of secondary moderns. I concluded by writing both the appraisal and their history, which stretches from the First World War (WWI) to the early 2000s. For readers with only a peripheral interest in their plight, Chapter 4 ('A condensed history of secondary moderns') provides an overview of the characters, politics and economic and social changes that determined the type and quality of children's education.

I am not a historian, nor do I have a background in education (other than having been a child). But, I am somebody who has spent most of their life needing to understand new subjects rapidly, to extract the salient facts and then to make decisions and recommendations. A cursory look at the subject revealed that recounting its history could become a story about the succession of Parliamentary committees and reports that shaped the schooling system. Obviously, the top-down decisions about the organisation of schooling are important, but I have no reason to believe that those responsible for delivering education back then paid any more attention to government diktats than they do now. I did my best to assemble the facts of what actually happened and to review the results in the context of the time, not through today's eyes. Above all I tried to suspend my own prejudices and to tell the story as it was, not how I would have liked it to be.

Although it is much shorter than the history, Chapter 8 ('Much maligned or monstrous mistake?') is the crux of the book. Having understood why secondary moderns are portrayed as being such a mistake and then having created my own account of their story, I was able to answer – well, attempt to answer – the question posed in the chapter's title. When I began I had no idea what those conclusions would be. My instinct was that 'much maligned' was a more likely outcome than 'monstrous mistake'. As you might guess, there was not a black-and-white conclusion but one that contained lots of shades of grey.

The final chapter of the book, 'Half a century on – what lessons can we learn?', does exactly 'what it says on the tin'. Having been immersed in reading and thinking about the subject, I have formed some strong opinions. I have had the luxury of travelling through the history of a subject, seeing educational policies created and implemented, and picking over their resulting successes and failures. With depressing regularity the same mistakes kept being made. Each new generation of politicians was certain they had the solution to their predecessors' problems. Sometimes they had; more often their dreams ended in failure.

I don't think for an instant that I have the answers to these perennial problems, but I know that repeating the same flawed solutions and expecting the results to be different doesn't work. Hopefully by describing the deep-seated weaknesses in the political administrative system that determines and implements education policy I have shed some light on what needs to change.

In my last book (*This I Know*[1]) the context was a train journey in which I met the reader and explained, in a couple of hours, the fundamentals of a subject on which I am something of an expert. I think the context of *The Secondary Mod* is also a journey, but it's a much longer one – more a voyage of discovery. We start during WWI and end during Tony Blair's second term as prime minister. Along the way I find the answers to my questions about secondary moderns but discover much, much more that is relevant to today's school children.

CHAPTER 1

THE TRUTH IS WHAT WE WANT
IT TO BE

I t couldn't have been easier to access the knowledge and data that I needed for this book. Living in the Wiltshire countryside and blessed with a fast broadband connection and Google, I could access information on every conceivable facet of secondary modern schools. Those publications that have yet to be digitised are available from Amazon or in the Newsroom at the British Library. Days spent at the National Archive allowed me to study the original documents detailing the torturous process that resulted in the landmark decisions that determined our educational history.

Despite the simplicity of the research process I am apprehensive – in all honesty, I am scared stiff – about whether I have produced a true and fair account of the secondary modern school's history and legacy.

You might well wonder why I am starting the book with my worries about discovering the truth about such a well-documented subject. Let me explain. At the risk of sounding conceited, I am something of a subject expert about population ageing and its effect on business. This is not due to innate ability but, rather, having spent the past 15 years steeped in researching, writing and consulting about the subject.

The deeper I delved the more my concerns grew, as I discovered factual inaccuracies and biases in how the subject was reported and discussed. It was terrifying to watch the speed with which errors and omissions rapidly became the accepted narrative, and were then endlessly repeated in the media. The advent of social media exacerbated the problem.

I have no reason to believe that the written accounts of secondary education are less susceptible to this problem of biased and inaccurate reporting. Having done the research, my hunch is that it could be far worse. Much of the history of these schools took place over half a century ago and by now the details have become distilled into a few summary sentences of explanation. Worse still, any mention of secondary moderns immediately raises the emotive subject of academic selection and grammar schools, topics that still polarise the discussion of education into extremes of opinion. Perhaps the rights or wrongs of public schools is the only topic that generates more heated debate.

By making the following observations I am aware that I might be committing the error that I am anxious to avoid. I have no way of 'proving' the statement but commentators and writers about education seem to come from one part of the political spectrum – the left – and hold similar views about education. Sometimes their affiliations are well known. Brian Simon, perhaps the most-quoted educational historian, was a Marxist and a member of the Communist Party. Sometimes their views become clear by the language they use and their hostility to 'the market' and all things associated with the Conservative Party. In a perfect world personal views shouldn't affect the neutrality of academic scholarship – but we don't live in a perfect world.

Before plunging into the research phase of the book, about a subject of which I knew very little, I wanted to understand whether, how and why the accounts of events and facts had become distorted. I felt that I needed the tools and discipline to enable me to interpret my research correctly and to prevent my own biases from distorting how I relate the story.

Let me begin by showing how easy it is to create a biased version of the truth. Maybe I am being too harsh using the word 'biased' – perhaps 'slanted' is a more accurate term. These examples are all taken from my most recent book about the ageing business.[1]

Since the 2008 recession economists and media pundits have talked about the increasing unfairness that exists in society between the old and young. Older people, especially those in their 60s and 70s, are portrayed as having benefited from generous pension schemes and the huge increase in property prices. Among a long list of problems, young people are portrayed as suffering from the high costs of housing, stagnant wage growth and debts from funding their university education. If this was not bad enough, most older people voted to leave the EU, unlike the majority of people their children's and grandchildren's age. This has been seen to illustrate the disregard that the old have for the young's future. The high turnout of young voters in the June 2017 general election was portrayed as their revenge on the older generation. Most of these observations are more or less true. It is what is not said that distorts the accuracy of this account.

There is another set of facts, which are equally true, but which convey a very different message. Young people have educational opportunities that were denied to most of their parents. In 1971, the year I graduated, only 6% of school leavers went to university.[2] In 2018 the figure was just over 50%.[3] For over a decade, interest rates have been at, or below, 0.5%. Older people have received less interest income and seen the value of their pension savings eroded. The interest rate for young people buying a house has never been lower. Retired people are expected to survive on a basic state pension that in 2019 was ranked 'worst in the developed world' by the OECD.[4] In the 2017 presidential elections in France, the majority of young people supported politicians with policies for France to leave the EU. Again, these individual facts are correct, but they aggregate to convey a very different message.

This simple example shows how easy it is to create two totally different versions of the truth by selecting the facts that support an argument and ignoring those that don't.

When this selective use of the facts is endlessly repeated in the media, and not contested, it soon becomes the dominant narrative. Very quickly the details and nuances of the arguments get lost and all that is left is a one-dimensional, simplistic stereotype. The zillions of different types of young people become grouped together and labelled the 'snowflake generation'. Older people who are in hospital, for whatever reason, are referred to as 'bed blockers'. Young people are assumed to be highly technologically literate, the 'digital native' generation, whereas their grandparents are depicted as finding the simplest of electronic devices beyond their comprehension.

It is not surprising that when *The Guardian* newspaper writes about intergenerational unfairness[5] its account of the young is gloomy and portrays them as victims.

> *Too many young people face a bleak lifetime of economic realities: a poorly paid job offering few progression prospects, little hope of getting on the housing ladder, decades of paying off their student loan, and an utterly inadequate pension when they hit retirement.*

In fairness to *The Guardian*, the article does explain that this account is an incomplete story and that the high level of inequality within generations is just as destructive as that between them. In my experience, this partially balanced reporting is the exception, not the rule. Opposing arguments and data are either excluded or given little prominence.

I call this selective and simplistic reporting of events and situations the 'Christmas tree' effect. The subject, be it secondary moderns or ageing, is the undecorated Christmas tree. The 'facts' and opinions are the decorations that are selected to adorn the tree to the best effect, to support whatever argument is being proposed. At the base of the tree, locked away in a box and well out of sight, is any information that conveys a different message.

The selective use of facts, which are correct, is bad, but when the data is incorrect it is far worse. Let me put my hand up and admit to being the source of incorrect data about the ageing business. It was never my intention to mislead, but that might well have been result. When I first started studying the subject I needed to understand how much of the UK's wealth was owned by older people. There were no official statistics that provided this information so I was forced to calculate the number using indirect measures. I arrived at an approximate – a very approximate – figure that 80% of wealth was owned by people aged over 60. In my writings, conference speaking and blog posting I used this number.

Whenever I used this figure, I qualified its accuracy by listing my caveats and concerns about its accuracy. Very soon, 80% wealth ownership was being quoted by the media and used in government and company reports. But my qualifying comments soon disappeared when others quoted my conclusions and all that was left was the single figure of 80%. Most of the time the origin of the figure was not referenced. In the great scheme of things, I doubt if I caused any catastrophe by my mistake. I later discovered that the figure is less than 80%, depending on the interpretation of official statistics. I learnt a lot from this experience. First, be careful not to assign credibility to 'facts' just because they are regularly reported. Second, whenever possible look at the original source of the data to understand the conditions that were associated with its accuracy.

The final lesson from my time working in the ageing business is the undue importance that is ascribed to the most recent event or development, at the same time devaluing, even forgetting, what went before. A good example of this condition is the importance that many companies give to 'doing things digitally'. I am totally convinced about the importance of the internet and computing and the huge changes they have made to the way companies and consumers behave. The fact that I wrote a book on the subject[6] and spent most of my life working in the computer industry are evidence that I am not some reactionary old luddite. But, I also know that its impact has not been as great as has been claimed and for many older people 'doing things digitally' is of zero importance.

We are in the crazy position where companies claim that they intend to spend more of their budgets on digital communications while simultaneously admitting they don't have the analytical evidence to justify the decision. The wealthiest group of consumers is the older cohort and they place the least importance on digital communications. Quaint old habits like reading newspapers and magazines, watching TV and even responding to direct mail and buying from paper catalogues are hugely important to this group. Mark Ritson,[7] a professor of marketing and regular contributor to *Marketing Week* magazine, believes there is a simple explanation for this behaviour.

> *Most marketers will continue to switch more and more of their budget to digital marketing and away from so-called traditional channels. They will do that not because traditional media is losing share or engagement or because digital media metrics actually make sense or impress anyone. They will do it, quite simply, because it is in their nature to favour the new over the old. The digital over the traditional.*

I am sure Mr Ritson is right, although the effects of Covid-19 will have altered the balance between digital and traditional media.

Unfortunately, I don't think the greater valuing of the most recent news and development is limited to marketers and people in business. I believe politicians and policy makers are just as susceptible to the weakness and I am equally certain that education professionals and those who write about education behave the same way.

There is a human condition that in my view helps explain these very different examples. As somebody who suffers from the 'condition' more than many, I feel well-equipped to comment on its effect. I am talking about laziness. Whenever possible, I would prefer a simple explanation to a complex one, because it means I have less to think about. I would prefer to use easily accessed information, rather than spending time and energy seeking out hard-to-find data sources. Again, it saves time and energy.

It is so much less work to simplify the description of a group of people to a single stereotype than having to explain their variations and complexities. It is even easier and more likely to get attention if the stereotype is given a memorable name. Those older people who drink more alcohol than the official NHS guidelines become 'Saga louts'. Parents who try to get their children into the best local schools become the 'sharp-elbowed' middle class.

The latest development always seems more interesting and exciting than what happened last month, last year or, heavens forbid, last century.

One of the first things I learnt when I worked for IBM was the 'KISS rule'. This means to 'keep it simple, stupid'. We were taught to minimise complexity in the way we worked and how we communicated. The term was first used by the US Navy in the 1960s and soon became popular with large US companies, where it is still used today. In retrospect, I think the concept is too 'simple' and can result in horrible mistakes. Had the rule had the caveat that accuracy and completeness must never be sacrificed for simplicity, it would have been much better, but then it wouldn't be a 'simple rule'.

My business experience has convinced me that very few events, ideas or groups of people can be neatly explained and described by a couple of pithy sentences. Invariably, there are exceptions, counter-arguments, unknowns and complexity that challenge the KISS principle.

I fear that in our drive to reduce everything to a few lines of memorable narrative, to minimise any cognitive dissonance and to 'keep it simple', we don't just lose the fine detail of the argument – we can completely misrepresent the truth. The widespread use of Twitter and its limitation on the length of content has amplified the problem of 'simplicity'.

The danger of only talking among ourselves

Hopefully, this tale about a subject that I understand well explains my trepidation about trying to understand what really happened during the era of secondary modern schools. My only 'expert' knowledge on this subject is what happened to me. I readily admit to having been ignorant of all other aspects of the story. As we will see in Chapter 3 ('A Consistently Negative Image'), the details about these schools, the pupils and those who taught in them have all but disappeared. All that remains is a simple, consistently negative narrative that is decorated with equally negative personal recollections.

I didn't want to keep it simple. I wanted to resurrect the detail and to understand the complexity and conflicting arguments.

There was another personal experience that made me want to understand how events, ideas and people are represented – perhaps I should say 'misrepresented'. The original draft of this chapter was written in May 2017 when the US election and the British decision to leave the EU still dominated the news agenda.

As a Grade-A news junkie, I regularly read multiple current affairs publications, from both countries, along with numerous online news sources. It felt like I was reading about little else.

The rights and wrongs of Mr Trump and the decision for the UK to leave Europe are hugely important, but not the subject of my concern. What shocked and scared me was the reporting of the events by the media. The reasons why US and UK voters came to their decisions were rapidly simplified to a short list of arguments. Stereotypes of the Trump and Brexit voter soon appeared. Those who voted Democrat and to remain in the EU suffered the same fate.

During the US presidential and EU referendum campaigns, the media seemed to jettison objective reporting and instead recounted news stories through the narrow prism of their prejudice. If I wanted to read a 'remain' newspaper and wanted the reassurance of news reporting skewed to this viewpoint, I knew where to look – most conspicuously, the *Financial Times*. The same applied to the opposing position – *The Daily Telegraph* led the way, ably supported by the *Daily Mail*. I knew if I was reading the *New York Times* it would be wall-to-wall anti-Trump. Watching Fox News would give me an opposite, but equally partisan, viewpoint. I am editing this chapter a month after the start of 'lockdown' caused by Covid-19. Much the same seems to be happening again. After a short spell of 'we are all in this together', journalists' prejudices soon reappeared, treating the virus-related traumas as a Christmas tree to be decorated with their pet political and economic hang-ups.

You might say 'that's the way it has ever been', but I am certain that these events illustrate a worrying polarisation and distortion of the news. It is impossible to prove that the reporting of events has become more partisan. What can be said for certain is that social media, especially Facebook and Twitter, have provided a way of enveloping individuals in content that reinforces their own view of reality. There has been much discussion of the 'echo chamber' effect of social media. The Wikipedia explanation of the term is as good as any.[8]

> *In news media, the term echo chamber is analogous with an acoustic echo chamber, where sounds reverberate in a hollow enclosure. An echo chamber is a metaphorical description of a situation in which information, ideas, or beliefs are amplified or reinforced by communication and repetition inside a defined system. Inside a figurative echo chamber, official sources often go unquestioned and different or competing views are censored, disallowed, or otherwise underrepresented.*

The Facebook pages of my friends during the Brexit campaign, the US elections and now the Covid-19 emergency mirror their political and social viewpoints. I totally understand the nice warm feeling that results from reading and watching material that massages our ego about having made the right decision – I do it all the time. But, I realise the danger of insulating myself from things that challenge my view of the world.

Dangers of framing, schemas and heurists

I hope you now understand my apprehension about the task of finding out about and recounting the complete story of secondary modern schools. To be honest, the process of writing this chapter made me highly suspicious when reading and listening to all types of commentators on any subject.

Over the years, I have encountered bits and pieces of theory about how we distort information and make faulty decisions, but none of these ideas really 'stuck', until now. Writing this book has been the catalyst for me to become more disciplined in how I research and review the research of others. It is sad that it has taken me so long to reach this point. Having now celebrated my 71st birthday at least shows that you are never too old to change.

Around the time I began researching this book I had a fantastic stroke of luck. Michael Lewis, one of my favourite authors, published *The Undoing Project,*[9] in which he tells the story of two Israeli professors of psychology. He interweaves the tale of their extraordinary friendship with an account of their research that has forever changed our understanding of the way people think and make decisions. All of the examples that I have recounted are explained by the work of these academics. As I read, I kept thinking how much more effective I would have been had I used their insights in my professional work. They might also have been handy in my personal life. I cannot rewrite history but at least I could apply their thinking in the writing of this book.

It would be crazy for me to try and summarise Michael Lewis's book. Whatever I wrote would be a pale reflection of the original – what's more, much of his story, although fascinating, isn't relevant to our needs. Instead, I will detail the insights from the heroes of the book, Tversky and Kahneman, that will help give greater clarity and accuracy to the story of secondary moderns.

The New Yorker magazine[10] captured the essence of what these two academics achieved when it reviewed Lewis's book: 'they changed how people think about how people think'.

Before their work, it was thought that our thinking and decision making were rational. Problem-solving was a logical process in which we would amass the evidence, weigh the options and choose the solution that was statistically most likely to succeed. Tversky and Kahneman demonstrated that this was nonsense. We behave in muddled, often contradictory, imperfect ways.

What pains me is that so many of their ideas have been published for 30–40 years and yet outside a small section of academia they are little understood and rarely discussed.

Like all events in our history, the story of the secondary modern school involved numerous instances of people defining a problem: collecting information to evaluate the possible solutions and then deciding what to do. I hadn't realised the likelihood of making errors at each stage of this process. Reading Michael Lewis's book was something like swallowing the red pill in *The Matrix*. Unlike Neo in the film, I didn't discover the truth about the Matrix but I certainly had my eyes opened to how easy it is to make mistakes and arrive at a manipulated version of the truth.

'It all depends how you ask the question' seems an innocuous statement but its power to influence decisions is immense. Tversky and Kahneman showed that altering how a situation is described (framed) results in people making different, often diametrically opposite, choices. 'People do not choose between things. They choose between descriptions of things.'[11]

For example, in questioning the success or failure of secondary modern schools, the answer will be different if the question was: 'did the 60% of the country's children they educated leave school with the skills they needed to succeed?'[12] rather than 'did those children who failed the 11-plus suffer because of the education they received?' The questions are essentially the same, but one defines the schools by the fact that they educated the majority of children and is framed in a positive context, and the other defines the schools by their intake (those who didn't pass the 11-plus) and anticipates a negative outcome by using the words 'failed' and 'suffer'. I should have paid more attention when I heard market researchers comment 'if you tell me the answer you want I will tell you the question to ask'.

Let's assume that we are capable of 'framing' issues in a neutral way, something that is not as easy as you might think. The next test is collecting the facts, arguments and ideas to make a decision. It would be nice to think this is done systematically by searching for the relevant data and investigating all the possibilities. If only we worked in such a methodical and unbiased way. The pressures of life and our human fallibility mean that we try to simplify this process. We take shortcuts by using our past experience of tackling similar problems and use a schema, a mental model, to organise and prioritise the information.

In the context of secondary moderns, maybe we have already formed a mental picture of a typical pupil and instead of starting from first principles we use this image to augment an existing stereotype that we have of the child. This might simplify the research process, but it runs the risk of disproportionately valuing the evidence that supports our preconceived notions. For subjects that are regularly reported in the media it is very difficult to ignore the stereotypes that they create. For instance, it is a 'well-known fact' that Trump voters were poorly educated, older and fearful of globalisation and immigration. Those who voted to remain in the EU are portrayed as being younger, better educated, living in urban areas with a liberal and progressive outlook. It is frightening to think that these are the schemas, the stereotypes, that have taken root in the general consciousness. The more they are repeated the more entrenched they become. Hopefully, you don't need me to tell you that these are gross simplifications.

So far, this ultra-brief outline of the work of Tversky and Kahneman shows that both the way a question is framed and how the information is processed to answer it (the schema) are packed with opportunities to introduce bias and inaccuracy.

This brings us to the final concept of 'heuristics'. These are the 'rules of thumb' that we all use when making decisions. Definitions of heuristics often include the idea that they allow us to substitute an easy question for a difficult one. My layman's view would see this as being an excuse to be lazy. Heuristics might be an instinctive human way of coping with the complexity of the world but, like the packaging on prescription drugs, they should come with a long list of health warnings.

There are numerous types of heuristic, each with its own set of potential problems, but I am only going to mention those that I have used and now wish I hadn't.

I must admit that I used the 'conditionality heuristic' in numerous consultancy reports. I never called it that but it was implied in the caveat that my decision relied on 'all other things being equal'. Either I couldn't be bothered, or found it too difficult, to factor into my decision how other conditions can drastically change. In the context of secondary moderns, the conditionality heuristic would be attempting to compare the performance of schools in different eras without taking account of how the styles of teaching and children's respect for authority had changed over time. Another example is passing judgement on events that took place in the past without accounting for the way that social norms have changed – let alone the rise in education spending. In 2014–2015 the amount spent on education was nearly three times more than when I left school.[13]

Another mistake that I am sure I have made is 'anchoring' – the difficulty in changing our views once they have become established. I know I have used information to substantiate my position even though it was irrelevant to the question being asked. Once we have something in our mind it is hard to ignore it and move on. This quote from Lewis's book is a lovely way of explaining how our opinions become anchored to the past. Turning on its head the famous lines about the importance of history:

> *Those who cannot remember the past are condemned to repeat it.*
> *What people remember about the past is likely to warp their judgment of the future.*

As we will see, a lot of people criticise secondary moderns because of their historically poor record of pupils passing General Certificates of Education (GCE) 'A' levels. This includes the well-known information source Wikipedia.[14] The fact that most secondary moderns didn't offer 'A' level exams but instead encouraged pupils to transfer to other secondary schools or technical colleges to take these exams is rarely, if ever, mentioned. This illustrates how a statistic from the past, which is correct but unrelated to evaluating the schools' performance, has a disproportionate influence today.

Very few of us would know how to calculate a 'statistically significant sample size' but we regularly feel confident in drawing conclusions from spotting patterns in the results of a few events. This is known as the 'law of small numbers'. The very worst example of this mistake is when we place an undue importance on our own experience. In this instance, we take a sample of one and treat it as if it has some universal importance. The next chapter in this book is about my experiences of going to a secondary modern. I recognise it for what it is – one person's experience. As I explain, my account does have value but it provides few insights that can be applied to the other 733,000 pupils who were in my age cohort.[15]

I have left discussing the 'availability heuristic' to the end because I want it to be fresh in your mind when you read about the consistently negative image that secondary moderns have throughout the media and with politicians. When making a decision or forming an opinion we are disproportionately influenced by the most recent information we have encountered, even if it has less relevance and accuracy than older, harder-to-recall data. So, if the facts being published about secondary moderns are consistently negative they will have a cumulative influence on our opinions.

The negative and dangerous effects of the availability heuristic on our perception of events and decision making were identified and explained in a seminal paper published in the *Chicago Law Review*.[16] The authors believed that this heuristic, when reinforced by certain social traits, can result in 'availability cascades'.

Availability Cascades trigger chains of individual responses that make expressed perceptions appear increasingly plausible through their rising availability in public discourse.

The resulting mass delusions may last indefinitely, and they may produce wasteful or even detrimental laws and policies.

The paper explained that there are two types of cascades – the informational and reputational. I believe both might be relevant to how secondary moderns are perceived and discussed.

An informational cascade occurs when people with incomplete personal information on a particular matter base their own beliefs on the apparent beliefs of others. In response to their communications, other individuals, who lack reliable information, may accept that belief simply by virtue of its acceptance by others.

In a reputational cascade, individuals do not subject themselves to social influences because others may be more knowledgeable. Rather, the motivation is simply to earn social approval and avoid disapproval. In seeking to achieve their reputational objectives, people take to speaking and acting as if they share, or at least do not reject, what they view as the dominant belief.

Using today's language, the informational cascade becomes the 'establishment of the dominant narrative'. The reputational cascade is a perfect example of 'virtue signalling' and its dangers. Combined, these 'cascades' become a powerful mechanism to create a false memory of the past.

Despite being aware of the pitfalls, I am certain that I have made mistakes of the type I have described in this chapter. What I can say is that there are fewer than if I hadn't tried to understand how we think and make decisions. I am equally certain that I will not forget the concepts of framing, schemas and heuristics.

Finally, my apologies to the academics whose works I have quoted. My summaries are probably a crude account of their work but I hope to have captured the essence of their ideas.

CHAPTER 2

GEORGE GASCOIGNE SECONDARY MODERN – A PERSONAL VIEW

I am beginning the book by talking about myself. This isn't a sign of my egotism or my claim to any unique knowledge about the subject. By recounting my own experience of attending a secondary modern school, I can be sure the facts are correct. My school-day memories may have dimmed but my mum was dutiful in collecting my school reports, exam results, school speech day programmes and clippings from the local press.

The other reason for recounting my experiences is that it will help explain to me, as much as you the reader, why I am writing this book.

I have no idea if my experiences were the norm or the exception. We will find out as the book unfolds. The same applies to any universal lessons that can, or cannot, be derived from my school days. I know these memories were formed through the eyes of a child and here I am, interpreting them as an adult. But you must start somewhere and a personal account of my school experiences seemed a good point.

I was born into a typical working class family, living in Walthamstow, a predominantly working class East London borough. By 'typical', I mean my family was not particularly poor, but certainly not wealthy. Both sets of grandparents were born in London. My dad's parents had five children; my mum came from a family of eight. I had a lot of cousins. A couple of my uncles had progressed into the middle class but most were very much like my mum and dad. I guess in today's parlance we would have been called a 'hard-working family'. Maybe the term 'JAM' (just about managing) is more appropriate.

From a child's perspective, we seemed like all the other families living in the neighbourhood. My dad was a sign-writer and my mum a housewife. My friends' parents were builders, printers, clerks and railway staff. I don't remember any friends having parents who were teachers, doctors, solicitors or any other member of the professional class. This is not a gripe, just a fact.

I know my mum and dad valued education. There were lots of self-improvement books in the house and at weekends there was often the sound of opera – my dad loved all types of music, but especially opera.

Like my sister, I learnt to play the piano and for a while had 'elocution lessons' to try and pick up my dropped 'H's and to encourage me to use 'th' instead of 'f', along with removing the other worst excesses of my East London accent. My writing and spelling were (and still are) a weakness and for a year or so I had weekly lessons with a private tutor. Like most parents, they wanted my life to be better than they had and would do whatever they could, within their limited means, to make sure that happened.

My older sister (Jill) went to the local junior school and then to a secondary modern. Jill must have inherited my dad's artistic talents. On leaving school she went to art college and eventually became a children's clothes designer.

I followed Jill to the same junior school and, like her, I failed the 11-plus. I went to a different secondary school – George Gascoigne Secondary Modern. All the schools I attended were within a 10-minute walk. I guess these days we call them neighbourhood schools.

And so to the secondary modern

In 1961 I took the 11-plus exam. In my class of 28 children I was positioned 14th – average arithmetically and in all other respects. My school reports described me as a cheerful boy who rushed his work, was good at sports and, how shall we say, unremarkable. I think it is all summed up by the headmaster's comment on my leaving report: 'Richard has ability but can never give himself enough time.' My mum knew the school secretary, who told her that in going to the secondary modern I would be a 'big fish in a small pond'. I think she was trying to be kind, but it annoyed the hell out of my mum. In truth, I was about to become an average fish in a small but choppy pond.

I never expected to pass the 11-plus, my parents never expected me to pass the 11-plus and I am certain my teachers didn't expect me to do anything other than fail the exam.

Taking the 11-plus was not a traumatic event. To be honest, I have the dimmest of memories of sitting the exam. My main concern, on leaving junior school, was to attend the same school as my friends. I certainly didn't feel any stigma about failing and, if my parents did, they never ever told me about it. Viewing the situation from today's perspective, you could say that my parents should have pushed me more to pass the exam, maybe by using the age-old incentive of promising a prize for success? I doubt if that would have worked. Their attitude was that as long I did my best, they couldn't ask for more.

Two boys and one girl passed the exam, about 10% of the class. One of the boys went to the local grammar school and then on to Cambridge, the others attended a technical school. The other boy went to university, I think it was the London School of Economics, but I have no idea of what happened to the girl. Even though all three had been friends and lived near my home we immediately drifted apart.

As you can see, failing was the norm; passing was the exception.

Like most children, I was apprehensive about going to the grown-up school. I had heard stories about nasty things happening to first-year children. My great fear involved the older boys pushing my head into the toilet. Fortunately, this didn't happen – or any of the other initiation ceremonies. What came as nasty shock was my form teacher's punishment of making me 'write lines', for not paying attention and fidgeting. I am sure my behaviour justified her actions and it probably helped improve my handwriting and attention span. During the writing of this book I discovered that this teacher had taken a cine-film of my class, the first year I was at the school (aged 11). One of my classmates, who has created an extremely active Facebook presence for the school, has transcribed the film to video and uploaded it to YouTube. Here you can see the first form at George Gascoigne Secondary Modern hard at work.[1] I look at myself in the video and cannot believe it was taken nearly 60 years ago.

George Gascoigne Secondary Modern had, so I remember, a reputation as a tough school. I don't know if that was true; maybe I wanted to think of it as that sort of place. What it did have was an inspirational headmaster called James Dixon. Talking among ourselves, he was either 'Jimmy' or 'Taffy' Dixon, but always Mr Dixon when in his presence. He was a very short Welshman who naturally commanded respect. As I progressed through the school I realised what an amazing man he was. As some small act of thanks, I have dedicated this book to him and my teachers.

Not all my school days were blissful. There was some bullying, but as a reasonably tall child, who was OK at sports, I never had too many problems. Like my junior school, it was mixed-sex. Coming to terms with girls was by far my biggest challenge.

There was no corporal punishment at the school, although I do remember a very large boy, the archetypical bully, being pushed and pulled around the playground by the games master, much to the delight of us onlookers. Nobody ever got expelled from the school; if anything, it was the school where 'difficult' children were sent.

Class discipline was normally good. I guess like all schools, there were some teachers who had problems holding a class together and others where there was never any thought of misbehaving. Most of my teachers were in the latter category. When you are 13, anybody over the age of 21 looks ancient. That said, I do remember a lot of teachers who were 'old'. From looking at school photos it appears that many male teachers were in their 40s, maybe 50s.

I cannot remember much about what I was taught during the first three years. From my school reports I seemed to do OK, but not brilliantly. There was the occasional A- but mostly C+ and B- marks. During these years we studied English language, English literature, history, geography, maths, science, religious education, arts & crafts, wood-work (needlecraft and housecraft, if you were a girl) and physical education. For a short time, we had a German language teacher, but that didn't last long. There was some homework, but nothing that got in the way of me playing with my mates, mainly kicking a football about and playing in the street.

There were lots of after-school activities. I was only interested in the sporting ones, but for the more artistic there was a production of Gilbert & Sullivan's *The Mikado* and pottery and wood-work classes. I have dim memories of a chess club, too.

For those who did well academically, there was an opportunity to transfer to another secondary school. I remember that a couple of my class-mates, both girls, moved to a technical school when we were 13. Maybe we took a 13+ exam or maybe their transfer resulted from our teachers' belief that they were in the wrong type of school. Whatever occurred didn't change my schooling, other than robbing my class of its prettiest girl.

You might be thinking that this ramble through my early education is all jolly interesting but it doesn't tell us very much about secondary modern schools. It sounds very traditional and unexceptional. Well that is the point, that is exactly what it was, the sort of school years most children have. The school was called a secondary modern but it was providing a typical educa-tion that I expect would be familiar to today's parents.

What should be clear from the story is that failing the 11-plus, for me and my friends, was not a surprise or a crisis. Most of us had brothers and sisters who had failed and were doing OK in life. The three classmates at my junior school who passed were always at the top of the class, were always the ones with the handfuls of gold stars. It seemed like the natural order of things that they would go to the grammar school or technical school.

I am sure our parents cared what happened to us, but failing the 11-plus wasn't seen as an insurmountable barrier to our future life opportunities. OK, I can only make this comment from my own experience, I cannot speak on behalf of my classmates' parents. Maybe when our parents were talking together, something that rarely occurred, they had concerns about our future. I cannot be certain, but I very much doubt it.

I was about to move on to the period where school life became a lot more serious and provided me with a life-changing opportunity.

At the end of my third year, I was nearly 15 years old and reaching the school-leaving age. My days of playing football and generally having a good time were coming to end. I could leave school or stay on for the 'Extended Course'. This could lead to me taking exams and whatever happened after that.

In retrospect, I think the decision was greatly influenced by my lack of artistic skill and physical dexterity. The school provided technical drawing classes that my dad encouraged me to take. I think he thought that if I had any of his artistic skills I could earn a living by becoming a draughtsman. It was soon clear to him, and to me, that this was not going to be a career in which I would shine.

I had no idea what I would do if I left school and neither did my mum and dad. Remaining at school, in form 4PR, and starting George Gascoigne's Extended Course seemed like the best, probably the only, decision. Passing some exams seemed like my best way forward as well as delaying making the decision about finding a job. Some of my classmates couldn't see the point and left as soon as possible.

The letter that my parents received about the Extended Course, and a description of what it involved, is shown in Appendix A. I have no recollection of reading the document. I assume my parents understood its contents and talked to me about what was involved, but I cannot recall what was said. I just knew I was going to have to work hard and 'get some exams'. I cannot be certain how many of my classmates took the course. It was certainly the majority; my best guess is about three-quarters.

There are many things that stand out when you read the document. First, it is a bit of a 'ramble' and the use of English, especially the capitalisation, is, to say the least, unusual. Mr Dixon must have realised this because he wrote: 'These thoughts are given in sketchy form, in some parts even as "notes".'

What jumps out of the document, to me, is the genuine belief that the school could make a difference to a child's life, irrespective of their academic ability. It is full of hope, but with the continually repeated caveat that success is dependent on the child's hard work and commitment.

For those wanting to take external exams the opportunities existed.

In this respect a good boy or girl (good academically) with really hard personal work, could gain 5 passes, which is considered by most professional boards a good GCE result. (Over the past few years, passes in 6, 7 and even 8 subjects have not been uncommon – thanks to the VERY hard work by the students and the heavy sacrifices of many teachers.)

If you achieved success with your GCE 'O' levels, there was a gateway to take GCE 'A' levels'. I can now see that the school staff had taken a conscious decision not to provide a 6th form for these exams.

On the completion of our two-year Extended Courses we can transfer children who have gained at least 4 'O' levels to appropriate grammar schools and technical schools or colleges.

For those wanting to expand their education, before starting work, even though that didn't result in a handful of GCEs, the opportunity was there.

Most importantly of all, individual opportunity to develop to the fullest of one's abilities and attitudes – the less academic making good gaps gaining confidence and poise, the academic, by hard personal studies, to gain examination successes.

Laudable as success itself is, it cannot be too strongly emphasised that examination successes are by no means the greatest achievements to be gained from a good education.

The school's Extended Course was not a programme of education handed down from central or local government. It was something started, maintained and implemented by the school's teachers. This is a striking difference from today's centrally organised system of education.

What I didn't understand at the time was the pressure on the headmaster and his staff. In the document, there are comments about the uncertainty of the course being available.

Until very recently we felt that Gascoigne's numbers and staffing might mean a severe readjustment in our schemes, because of the administrative difficulties. The picture is now clearing and it is now clear that we should be able to provide for the many needs of our pupils. One thing is most certain. The loyalty of those who form the backbone of the Gascoigne team can be relied upon in the interests of its pupils. Given reasonable Ministry support, therefore, it should be possible for Gascoigne to offer benefits as here recorded.

I cannot be certain, but I think these comments refer to the fact that the school was closing at the end of the school year when we took our GCE 'O' levels. Walthamstow was in the process of 'going comprehensive' and ceased using the 11-plus in 1965, when selection was done using teachers' reports from each pupil's junior school. All forms of selection were abolished in 1967.[2]

George Gascoigne was one of the many casualties as local authorities changed from selective to comprehensive education. As an adult, I can appreciate the strain on our teachers, who were simultaneously trying to get us to pass exams and worrying about their own careers.

Unaware of any of these difficulties, I began my final two years at the school. Much to my surprise, I was selected to take an 'O' level in economic history a year early. Little did I know that this was the beginning of a period of studying and taking exams that would last for the next six years. I passed the exam, along with three or four of my classmates. I was surprised; my parents were astonished. For some unaccountable reason, I got it in my head that 'doing sciences' was the way forward. This required me to pass 'O' level maths and physics. By the end of my fifth form I had gained six 'O' levels.

I was by no means the only child to pass 'O' levels. The 31 children in my year passed 79 'O' levels and achieved 104 passes in the Royal Society of Arts (RSA) exams. I will talk more about the RSA exam later in the book.

The median pass rate, for my class, was three 'O' levels. To put this into context, the same measure for the best grammar school in Walthamstow was six passes. You could argue that the pass rate for my school was lower, because some children declined to stay beyond the age of 15. As the description of the Extended Course makes clear (many times), the opportunity to stay beyond the statutory leaving age was open to all children, not just those who were expected to take exams. For this reason, I think the way I have calculated the median pass rate is reasonable.

Life after George Gascoigne Secondary Modern

To be able to go and study for 'A' levels you needed to have passed four 'O' levels. Eleven of my class achieved this pass rate and could have continued their education, six boys and five girls. As it was, only three of us went to the grammar school and took 'A' levels, enabling us to go to university. This school (George Monoux), was soon to change and became a comprehensive senior high school for children aged 14-plus.

I attended Sussex University to read physics, the other two read electronics at Salford University and economics at Manchester University.

I don't know why my other eight classmates didn't continue with their education. It may have been that their parents couldn't afford for them to remain at school or that they thought that getting a job was the best career path. I know that some of them went to jobs arranged at their fathers' employers. This was the era before nepotism was a despised practice and it was commonly employed by the working class.

The most notable member of my class left to work for the local council. I think his parents were keen for him to pursue a political career as they were committed members of the Labour Party. After a period of being a councillor he was elected as the local MP, where he remained for the next 27 years. His period of office, like many others, came to a crashing halt with the 'expenses scandal' of 2009.

Thanks to Facebook and the now-defunct Friends Reunited, I have been able to see what happened to some of the others in my year at George Gascoigne. A couple of them continued their education, at a later stage in their life, and became college lecturers.

There were a few in my year who I had thought would struggle in life. They left school at the earliest opportunity and were the 'rough' boys in the class. Much to my surprise and delight, they seem to have had a good life. One of them had joined the navy, where he stayed for 25 years, and another had done well in his own business.

Let me highlight the weakness of generalising from the commentary on social media. The contributors will always be a sub-set of the universe of people. In this case, only those who were positive about school days. As we will see, where the context is critical of secondary moderns, there are lots of people wanting to recall their bad experiences.

Maybe I was fortunate in being in an unusually academically successful age cohort? Looking at speech day programmes from previous years, I found that in 1963 the school achieved 103 'O' level passes, with a median of three passes per student. In that year, 11 of the class went on to grammar and technical schools to take 'A' levels.

In 1965, the year before I took the exams, the numbers staying for the

Extended Course were lower and only 50 'O' level passes were achieved. Even so, nine children went to other secondary schools to study for 'A' levels.

So, what is to be made of the recollections of my childhood? What does this tell us about secondary modern schools?

By now you will appreciate that I have positive memories of my secondary education and the opportunities provided to me by the school. In truth, I owe an immense debt of gratitude to my teachers and especially the headmaster. I have tried to explain these five years of my life in a summarised, analytical way. What I haven't listed is the day-to-day encouragement and kindness provided by the school's staff. You don't want to read pages of reminiscences, but it was these things that made all the difference to our schooling.

The facts I have recounted show that the opportunity was available to achieve exam passes that could lead to a better job or be the stepping-stone to higher education. The Extended Course enabled those who wanted to fill in gaps in their education or to learn specific skills.

Hopefully, you can now understand why I am writing this book. Secondary moderns are universally portrayed as representing all that was bad with UK education, as an emblem of failure that stunted the life chances of children. When, in addition, secondary modern teachers are labelled as second-rate, you can understand my annoyance. This was not my experience and, from the facts I have presented, it was not the experience of my classmates.

At this point in writing the book, I have no idea if we were unbelievably lucky to have attended George Gascoigne; maybe it was a one-off example of a successful secondary modern. We will soon find out.

CHAPTER 3

A CONSISTENTLY NEGATIVE IMAGE

Your age is what most influences your reaction when you hear the words 'secondary modern'. If you are in your 50s or older then you might have attended one; if not, it's likely you are related to or know somebody who did. I expect you have shared with them personal experiences of schooling in the 1940s through to the late 1960s and have read stories about the schools.

Unfortunately, and understandably, I don't have the resources to research the views of the tens of millions of children, now adults, who attended these schools. If such research was possible, I am sure I would find a spectrum of views ranging from those thinking it was 'the best years of my life' to 'I am still in therapy trying to recover'. I expect I would find a similar range of emotions about any system of schooling. My friends who attended a public school seem evenly spread between these two ends of the spectrum.

I might not be able to research the views of past pupils but I can access the archives of the media, to understand how it has told the story of the schools. I can, metaphorically, take the temperature of the millions of words that have been written about the subject. This diagnostic gives a simple and incontrovertible conclusion. The subject (excuse the pun) had a deathly chill and a welcomed death. Echoing the title of this chapter, secondary moderns have a consistently negative image.

I am an instinctive contrarian, although my friends would probably use more emotive words to describe how I view the world. If everybody thinks something is good or bad, I start by thinking the opposite. Eventually, I might agree with the majority view, but I get a queasy feeling in my stomach when so many people think the same thing, especially if the 'thing' is so intertwined with and conditioned by political and sociological dogma. I wish I had been the originator of the saying 'where all think alike, no one thinks very much' – it encapsulates how I feel.[1]

Having studied the research of Tversky and Kahneman (see Chapter 1, 'The truth is what we want it to be') I am even more suspicious of the testimony of experts and the memories of a small, but vocal, group of people. These critical voices might be right, but I want to dig deeper into the evidence. I want to conduct an autopsy to understand what was thought to be ailing the subject and the facts that were offered to support the diagnosis.

Let's assume that your opinions and knowledge of secondary moderns are determined solely by what you read and hear in the media. I know it is difficult to put aside your personal experience or the stories you have heard from older friends and relatives. To be brutally honest, personal reminiscences are priceless to the individual but worthless in building our understanding of the schools. For every positive story, I am sure I can find one that is negative, and vice versa. Personal recollections add colour and texture to a subject but no substance in describing a system of schooling that stretched over more than 30 years and at its peak was educating 1.7 million pupils in 3,900 schools.

Because there are no simple models for measuring the media's attitudes, I needed to invent one. No doubt the methodology could have been more exhaustive and precise but I feel confident that my primary conclusions are correct. When 99% of the results say the same thing then further research to determine if the answer was 98.5% or 99.5% seems worthless.

I selected six high-circulation publications that provide the facility to search, by keywords, their archives of past stories. As we will see, the views about secondary moderns have always been and still are interminably linked with political and social beliefs – a subject I will be returning in later chapters. To achieve a balanced view, my choice of publications needed to reflect the range of political opinion. Details of the publications and why I selected them are shown in the table.

Publication	Publication frequency	Reason for selecting
The Guardian	Daily	Views to the left
The New Statesman	Weekly	Views to the left
The Daily Telegraph	Daily	Views to the right
The Spectator	Weekly	Views to the right
The Economist	Weekly	Global and centrist
Tes	Weekly	Specialist publication for teachers

| The publications I analysed and the reason for selecting them

Accessing the articles is the easy bit; how to make sense of what they are saying, without introducing personal prejudices, is the difficult part of the process. To guard against this problem I searched each publication for the term 'secondary modern'. I decided to view the search results in the order of the 'most relevant' rather than the 'most recent'. I was concerned that using the most recent results would unduly bias the outcome by featuring the latest news events.

Having identified and accessed the articles, I analysed the top 15 from each publication. To do this I again searched for the term 'secondary modern'. In each article I extracted the sentences that contained 'secondary modern', as well as the preceding and subsequent sentences. My reason for doing this was that these three sentences would include the words used to describe the school.

The articles varied in length and style, from those discussing education policy to obituaries, where the person had been educated at a secondary modern. Some of the articles had a single mention of the search term; others had multiple mentions. One article referenced 'secondary modern' over 30 times. If the term appeared in the readers' comments that were associated with the article, I treated it in the same way as those in the main body of the article.

You might wonder why I decided on analysing 15 articles from each publication? It was an arbitrary decision, as was selecting only one preceding and subsequent sentence. As we will see, the results of the analysis are so decisive, I don't believe a greater sample size would have materially changed the conclusions.

This process produced hundreds of sentences, for each of the publications. Now came the really difficult part of the analysis – to extract from these thousands of words the sentiment they were expressing about the schools. This was achieved using software that counted the words, excluding common words and phrases, and then presented the results as a word cloud. To declutter the results and to improve the visual representation, I excluded all words that were not directly associated with describing the schools; whenever the term '11+' appeared I replaced it with '11-plus'.

The word clouds are the most graphic result of my analysis, but the process also provided the main facts and arguments appearing in each publication. These results are summarised in Appendix B. I was surprised, very surprised, by the consistency in the sentiment expressed by all of the publications. Those publications favouring the left were more extreme and forceful in their comments, but the essence of the message was the same in the right-leaning publications – secondary moderns were a sad and inevitable result of selective education and best forgotten. Several of the articles commented that considering their influence on so many peoples' lives, little is known about the schools. I hope to rectify that deficiency.

Going beyond this simple message, what more can we understand about the facts and arguments about these schools?

The first place to start is to study a composite word cloud that was created by amalgamating the results of all the publications (shown below).

| The word cloud created by amalgamating the results from all six publications

Three words jump out of the word cloud. The process of determining a child's school – 'selective' education. The exam used to evaluate children – either called '11+' or '11-plus'. The school attended by those who passed – the grammar school.

Although they never educated more than 27% of children, politicians devoted a disproportionate amount of time to discussing the role, worth and fate of grammar schools. A measure of this is seen by analysing the frequency that words were used during debates in Parliament. Throughout the period 1944–2004, grammar schools were mentioned, in every year, more than secondary moderns.

For most of the time the same applied to comprehensive schools, other than the period 1966–1981.

The ability of grammar schools to generate so much Parliamentary discussion is graphically demonstrated in the following chart.[2]

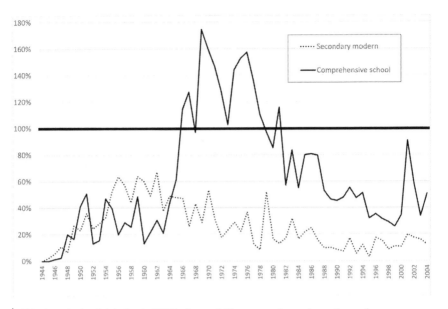

Word analysis of debates in UK Parliament. The percentage of mentions of secondary modern and comprehensive schools compared with that of grammar school

The dominant theme in the media was about the rights and wrongs – overwhelmingly the wrongs – of selecting children by exam and sending those who were successful to a different school from those who failed. Most of the commentary was about the social fairness and, to a lesser extent, the educational usefulness of this process.

If the media was your only source of knowledge, then you could only conclude that the schools were a terrible mistake and that they achieved very little. What you will not find in the media are many facts about the schools; very little commentary about their variation in size, scope and success, little discussion about what they did achieve and almost nothing about the constraints of the social and economic conditions during the time they educated the majority of the UK's children.

All of their history has been condensed into a few, much-repeated, story-lines: that while grammar schools might have benefits, although that is disputed, secondary moderns were uniformly 'bad news' and everything must be done to ensure they are never resurrected.

Many of the articles were written by past pupils of the schools. If the writer didn't attend one themselves, their account is about relatives or friends who did. The similarity in the authors' life story is surprising. The tale begins with an account of how they were cheated by the education system. Perhaps they hadn't been prepared for the 11-plus, unlike their peers. Maybe the primary school staff cheated the system by ensuring a less academically able child was awarded their grammar school place. Sometimes their parents didn't want, or couldn't afford for, them to take their grammar school place. There are many variants on the unfairness of 'the system', often involving tales of siblings who failed the 11-plus but later made good.

Next come details of how they received, at best, a third-rate education. The school had poor facilities, the teachers didn't care and the kids felt they were on the conveyor belt to a low-status, low-paying job.

Finally, their luck changed and against all the odds they triumphed. Very often they went on and studied at university and then became a teacher, doctor or some other combination of academic achievement and professional job. Despite their success, most of them resent, with a passion, the unfairness of their secondary modern experience and believe it has left them emotionally scarred.

If this isn't the story of the article's author then an account like it often appears as an online comment or a letter responding to the article.

I found this same storyline when looking at other content about the schools. A website that was established to record the memories of ex-secondary modern pupils contains many similar tales.[3] The sentiment of all but one of the posts to this blog was distinctly negative. It was clear, from the length of the blog postings – many are over a thousand words – that the contributors were deeply affected by their secondary education.

I am sure that the people writing these accounts are genuine and their stories are truthful, or at least truthful recollections of their memories. However, the intensity of the feelings they express makes me wonder if their schooling was but one factor contributing to their anger and unhappiness. But, it is not my right or intention to question their sincerity and accuracy, but to understand the accusations they made about the schools.

What facts, rather than feelings, can be filtered from the thousands of words of online and offline commentary about the schools? What is the rationale of the criticism? I had hoped to find much more detail. I didn't. I can only recount what exists and that isn't much.

From distilling the media coverage, listed in Appendix B, the commentary from other media sources, websites and books, it seems there are nine arguments why secondary moderns are thought to have failed to provide an adequate education, which limited their pupils' academic and employment potential.

When a 'fact' was provided to substantiate an argument, I have tried my best to identify the original source containing the data. As you might expect, Wikipedia was one of the websites that I researched. Its account of the schools was, without exception, negative and critical of their achievements. Surely, these schools did something right?

This final part of this chapter lists the 'facts' and often-repeated arguments about the schools. We will be returning to this section, later in the book, when I evaluate their accuracy, compared with my brief history of the schools.

The poor quality, numbers and morale of the teaching staff

The media contained many comments implying that their teaching staff were of an inferior quality to those in other parts of the secondary system. Another much-repeated accusation, which was never supported by facts, was that schools had difficulty recruiting and retaining quality staff.

The schools' low expectations of their pupils' employment prospects

Many of the photos that accompanied the articles showed secondary modern pupils doing practical activities. For girls, this was some form of 'domestic science' and for boys it was wood- or metal-work. The words 'factory fodder' were often associated with any discussion about what type of jobs pupils could expect.

Comments about the pupils' limited employment horizons were sometimes conditioned by statements explaining that the schools existed during a period of buoyant demand for 'blue collar' and basic administrative jobs. The implication was that in spite of their limited education the pupils had little difficulty in finding work.

The limitations and low expectations of the exams their pupils could achieve

A common criticism was that only small numbers of pupils took and passed exams and that often it was the Certificate of Secondary Education (CSE), an exam that was deemed to be inferior to the 'O' level. It was also implied that even if the pupils achieved exam success, some were barred from continuing their education at a grammar school. These four quotes detail the main arguments about the schools' lack of academic achievement.

Secondary moderns prepared students for the CSE examination, rather than the more prestigious O level, and although training for the latter was established in later years, fewer than one in ten students took advantage of it. Secondary moderns did not offer schooling for the A level, and in 1963, for instance, only 318 former secondary-modern pupils sat A-levels. None went on to university.[4]

During the 1950s and early 1960s, grammar schools would commonly not accept entry by secondary modern students who had done well in O Levels and who wished to study for A Levels.[5]

Those who had 'failed' their eleven plus were sent there to learn rudimentary skills before advancing to factory or menial jobs. Secondary moderns prepared students for the CSE examination, rather than the more prestigious O level, and although training for the latter was established in later years, fewer than one in ten students took advantage of it.[6]

At A-level, in 1964, the secondary moderns, with around 72 per cent of Britain's children, had 318 candidates. The public schools, with 5 per cent, had 9,838.[7]

The poor physical quality of the schools and teaching equipment

Secondary moderns, it was claimed, received less funding than grammar schools. A differential of 30% less for each pupil is the figure that often appears. There was a single reference that quantified the spending differential. In 1958, it was estimated that the average grammar school pupil received 170% more per annum, in terms of resources, than the average secondary modern child.[8]

The lasting negative effect on the pupils' self-esteem of failing the 11-plus

Many of the personal accounts of attending the schools talked about the lasting feelings of failure, inadequacy and shame. There was a single study, conducted in 2012, that was used to substantiate this claim. Because the company that commissioned the study has now closed its website, it is only possible to provide an indirect reference.[9]

The imprecision, unfairness and fallibility of the 11-plus selection process

The argument that it is impossible and wrong to determine a child's destiny at the age of 11, on the basis of a single exam, was common to most of the commentators. For many, probably most, this was a self-evident truth that didn't need justification.

To compound the inequity of the exam were the claims that its administration and the differing ways children were prepared to take it were grossly unfair. Accusations were made that more girls failed than boys, because of tampering with the results, rather than a genuine gender difference in intelligence. Some children were coached to pass the exam by their school, or by a private tutor; some were not. Primary school head teachers were accused of being the real arbitrator of who went to grammar school, not the 11-plus exam score.

Selective education depended on there being winners and losers

Time and time again, secondary moderns were talked about as being the losing half of the zero-sum equation. This quote from a letter to a national newspaper is a perfect illustration of this point.

The 'success' of the grammar school is only made possible by the consignment of the vast majority of pupils, especially those from working-class and under-privileged backgrounds, to a second-rate education from which it can take years to recover.[10]

To the historians and commentators who viewed everything through the prism of 'class' the calculus was simple – middle class children went to grammar schools, the rest to secondary moderns.

Opportunities varied by where you lived

Because of regional differences in the number of grammar school places, a child's chance of exam success was determined by where they lived. Today this would be called the unfairness of the 'postcode lottery'.

The 11-plus and secondary moderns were unpopular with parents

Parents' unhappiness with selective education was an important factor that resulted in the introduction of comprehensive education. Politicians who supported, or didn't obstruct, the end of grammars and secondary moderns were following, not leading, public opinion.

––––––

In addition to these specific criticisms, discussion about selective education invariably has an implicit assumption that the schools were bad. This dialogue between Peter Mandelson and Andrew Neil illustrates how this occurs:

Mandelson: Comprehensive schools have removed that appalling selection at the age of eleven in which people were relegated to a lesser type of education.

Neil: The 11+ was far too brutal, consigning those that failed to second-rate secondary moderns. Politicians shudder at the very memory of returning to the days of the secondary modern.[11]

When the then leader of the Conservative Party (2016) talked about reintroducing selective education and grammar schools she was at pains to explain that pupils would not have to attend a secondary modern.

There are those who fear this could lead to the return of a binary system, as we had in the past with secondary moderns. But this fear is unfounded: there will be no return to secondary moderns.[12]

You might well be thinking that the case against secondary moderns is so overwhelming that I might as well end the book now, with the conclusion that they were a monstrous mistake. I must be honest that the thought has gone through my mind. But my contrarian nature still makes me want to question this majority viewpoint.

An alternative explanation for this singularly negative narrative could be that a vocal and influential minority has dominated the discourse about the subject. I keep returning to the fact that there is much anger about the schools, but little hard evidence to substantiate most of the accusations. Other evidence may exist in the world of educational academia, but it hasn't permeated into the general media.

My final comments in Chapter 1 ('The truth is what we want it to be') were about the power of 'availability cascades' to distort the truth. I have no proof that this explains how secondary moderns are perceived, but it is a possibility.

So ends the 'case for the prosecution'. It is now time to look, in a dispassionate way, at how these schools came into being and what they achieved (or didn't) in the context of the economic and social conditions of their time. Let's withhold our judgement until we return to evaluate these criticisms against my account of their history.

CHAPTER 4

A CONDENSED HISTORY OF
SECONDARY MODERNS

I f you believe the dominant narrative about secondary moderns, they were part of a failed education system. Passing the 11-plus resulted in opportunities and good fortune for the few (those going to grammar school); failure meant a second-rate education and probably a second-rate life for the remainder (those going to a secondary modern). This is something of a caricature of the viewpoint, but not much of one. I discussed the arguments supporting this opinion and why I question their validity in the previous chapter.

I have spent much of my business life trying to forecast the future, but writing this chapter required me to produce an accurate account of events and their consequences that took place over a century ago. This was a new and, if I am honest, a daunting prospect. I needed to understand what secondary moderns replaced, the rationale for their creation, what they were expected to achieve and how they performed. But, the story doesn't end with their passing and the arrival of mass comprehensive education, because that raises the question: 'Did what replaced them do any better?' An even more fundamental question is: what do we mean by 'better'?

My primary objective was to understand the story of how people like me were educated. Your average kid, not exhibiting great academic gifts, not having parents who could purchase their education, not having parents with professional jobs and connections – your Joe or Jemima Average Brit child.

After a week of researching the subject I realised the scale of the task. My list of questions and the topics to investigate grew longer by the day.

The scope of the research kept expanding to include topics I had never thought about when I started. The evolution of further education is integrally linked to the educational opportunities available to school leavers. Today the university degree is the default qualification. My classmates were far more likely to continue their studies at a technical college, probably at evening classes, studying for an Ordinary National Certificate (ONC) or Higher National Certificate (HNC). On first sight the large numbers of school leavers now taking degrees seemed like an advance, but the reported number of graduates working as baristas and as restaurant waiting staff meant it needed researching.[1]

I had not initially intended to consider the role of religion in education. My only memories of RE (religious education) were of singing a hymn each morning and the Wednesday afternoon RE class. However, I soon discovered that the church's influence on schooling was far greater than I had ever imagined. The fierce competition for a place at the local Church of England primary school close to where I live now suggests this influence still remains.

Central to the selective education system was the 11-plus exam. Was it a worthless way of determining the most appropriate schooling for children, or is its bad publicity ill-deserved? Cyril Burt, the person credited with its introduction, at least by the media, was attacked as a fraud, yet nearly all of the books subsequently written about him have defended his academic findings. Another subject that I needed to consider. More and more questions.

When to start? What to include?

My first decision was when to begin and end the story. Later in the chapter I will explain my rationale for setting the dates. Secondary moderns officially came into existence in the mid-1940s but the further I delved, the further back I had to go to understand their origins. I ended up with a start date for the history at 1916, although I could easily have gone back even further (Chapter 5, 'Between the wars').

There are still schools today that act like secondary moderns, in as much as they operate in a selective education system, alongside grammar schools

– the House of Commons library reported that there were 132 such schools in 2012 compared with nearly 4,000 in 1965. I decided to end the secondary mods' story in 1974. At that time, their numbers were rapidly falling and the momentum of their demise was unstoppable. There didn't seem any point in going any further in that section of the timeline (Chapter 6, 'Birth and death').

I concluded the history with a look at the system of schooling (comprehensive education) that replaced them, to see how it fared in rectifying the secondary modern's alleged deficiencies (Chapter 7, 'The comprehensive era'). So overall I'm covering about 90 years of history, divided into 30-year periods.

My focus has been the schooling system in England and Wales, not because it is more important than the other areas of the UK but because it was the easiest to research and affected 90% of the children. Most of the time government statistics are for these two countries; sometimes just for England. There is also a more personal and selfish reason – it was the schooling that I experienced. Working in parallel with, some would say against, the different models of state education is the world of private education (i.e. where the schooling is paid for by parents, rather than the state). I haven't attempted to include these schools in my narrative or analysis. The only time I refer to private schools is when there is a direct overlap with those in the state system.

The education system doesn't exist in a vacuum. It is impossible to ignore how major global events affect national politics and policy, as has been demonstrated in 2020–2021 by the need to close schools and cancel exams because of Covid-19. Constraints on public spending were still being experienced a decade after the financial crash of 2008.

The birth of secondary moderns coincided with the end of the Second World War (WWII), an event that created far greater havoc for the UK economy, its infrastructure and the supply of labour. The war also changed people's attitudes and expectations, especially about the services delivered by the state. I needed to understand how this affected the launch and establishment of secondary moderns.

Education is also influenced by economic and social factors, such as the demand for schooling (demographics) and the state of the economy (availability of public funds and the demand for employment). It is pointless reviewing decisions made about schooling in the context of a 'perfect world'. For much of the secondary modern's history the world was anything but perfect – the war had just finished, the economy was fragile and the country was about to experience a baby boom.

Between the 1950s and today the attitudes of society, the social mix of the country, the advances in technology and individuals' expectations have changed beyond all measure. When I was a child, you waited 18 months for a telephone to be connected. Today a new smartphone is available, on demand, at the supermarket. The likelihood of a young person participating in higher education, before they are 30 years old, is now nudging towards 50%.[2] That is very different from the 6% of school leavers attending university in 1971, the year I graduated.[3]

Life was very different. Expectations were very different. This is not to say life was better or worse, but these examples illustrate the perils of judging the past from the viewpoint of our own time.

Many accounts of the education system are based on the chronology of the numerous government reports and committees that were established to decide education policy. This is sometimes referred to as the 'acts and facts' account of history.[4] Other accounts revolve around the individuals who are credited (or blamed) with defining education policy. People in the pre-war era such as Hadow, Spens and Butler and following the war Beloe, Crowther, Newsom, Crosland, Plowden, Baker and most recently Gove. Obviously, these are two important components that determine our history, but I wanted my story to be more than a long list of facts about government reports and who said and did what. Another technique that I was determined to avoid is portraying history by 'anecdotes' and stories of individuals' experience of schooling. This approach might add richness to the story but is horribly vulnerable to the writer's bias.

Deciding the rights and wrongs of an education policy is a value decision based on attitudes and beliefs. I think there is another dimension of education history that is rarely considered and that relates to how well the policy was conceived and implemented. As I discovered, the history is littered with the results of poorly implemented 'great ideas' and idealists who failed to translate their visions into a workable reality. From the child's perspective, their education depends on the quality of both these things. I have spent much of my career as a business consultant helping businesses with what are loosely called 'change management' projects. This involved ensuring that companies had clear and achievable objectives and the mechanisms that would enable them to be delivered and measured. So I decided that I would apply my business skills and experience to evaluating how well the secondary modern schooling system was conceived and implemented.

Throughout my research I have done my best to avoid becoming involved in arguments about class and the use of schools to change the culture of the UK. I am not equipped to talk about these issues; neither am I that interested in the debate. The description of the book *Education and Social Order*, by the famous educationalist Brian Simon, states:

> *Education policy usually reflects the outcome of a struggle between progressives who see reform as a first step towards social change and conservatives who prefer a stratified system which reflects existing social divisions.*

Simon is referred to as a 'highly significant Marxist historian, as well as one of the leading Marxist educators of his generation.'[5] I made much use of his accounts of education history but always tried to untangle his political views from his presentation and interpretation of the 'facts'.

If he is correct, then maybe the struggles between progressives and conservatives, two labels that seem to have many meanings, have hampered the basic task of providing children with the best possible schooling, but that is a question for another book. I have tried to keep my account of the history grounded in how well secondary moderns and their predecessors educated children and the opportunities they provided them, rather than becoming embroiled in the wrangling between political ideologies. It is difficult enough to understand how the education system worked, without pondering its success as 'a catalyst for change' and whether it 'created a fairer society'.

The remainder of this chapter explains how the research was conducted, the resources available in the book and online and how the history timeline is divided. We then plunge into the detail. Each of the timeline periods has its own chapter; these are best read in sequence, because the story of secondary moderns is long and involved. It doesn't contain the violence and sexual intrigue of *Game of Thrones,* but its plot is just as complex.

How it was researched

I have always found researching a new subject something of a voyage of discovery. I am reasonably confident that I will recognise my final destination but the details of the route and the things I am likely to encounter are hazy, at best.

I started by studying the eight books that had already been written about secondary moderns. Their authors all had first-hand experience of the schools and all wrote during the period when they were educating the majority of the country's children.

The first book to be published was in 1946: *Education in the Secondary Modern School* by J.P. Dempster and the last, to the best of my knowledge, appeared 20 years later: *Life in a Secondary Modern School* by John Partridge. Since then, no books have been written specifically about the schools. These books provide a range of views and levels of detail about the schools.

Life in a Secondary Modern School was a depressing account of the four terms the author spent teaching at a school in the Midlands. He admitted that this short period may have been unrepresentative of the schools' performance and that this school may have been unrepresentative of other secondary moderns, but the implication was that it reflected the country-wide state of the schools. The text on the book cover was singularly negative:

> *The school seemed to justify its existence only by repeatedly*
> *ramming home its pupils' inadequacies; boys in low streams often*
> *became school odd-job men, and others in no way subnormal drifted*
> *out of the school unable to read or write. If it was typical – and there*
> *is evidence that it was – this account has alarming implications for*
> *our whole education system.*

Education in the Secondary Modern School, by Dempster, was first published in 1945 as a series of articles in *The Schoolmaster*, which was then the journal of the National Union of Teachers (NUT). The content was very practical and aimed, not surprisingly, at those teaching, or thinking of teaching, in these new types of school.

The foreword to the book contained several comments that had Delphic accuracy, including the following.

Fears as well as hopes stir in the mind as one contemplates the task that is set us by those provisions of the Education Act [he is referring to the 1944 Butler Act] which inaugurate, at long last, the era of Secondary Education For All. We may fail to take the just measure of the sheer magnitude of the undertaking. Still more probably, and perhaps even more disastrously, we may underestimate its unfamiliar novelty for a people whose educational history has trained them to think of secondary education in very different terms.

John Mander, the author of *Old Bottles and New Wine*, intended his account of secondary moderns to be a practical guide that tackled the issues of running a school, as they were in 1948, not how they were hoped to be in a decade's time. He discussed the options for their organisation, what they taught and the difficulties they faced, in particular the shortages caused by the war:

In short, it is difficult to imagine a time in which material considerations were less favourable for the development of a new type of secondary school [the secondary modern].

Harold Loukes gave a very different account of the schools in his book, *Secondary Modern*. He and his team visited 100 schools and sought to answer the question: 'Is there a secondary modern child, curriculum, school, teacher and parent?' Not surprisingly, he found a range of answers to these questions but in the main his conclusions were optimistic about their future.

This raised an interesting point. We began our study of the modern school under the impression that they were the capital problem of English education. Now it seemed I should express it differently. This was a field admittedly full of problems, but in which solutions were beginning to appear, and high hopes to be justified. Administrators and teachers had found that the theories with which they were armed did not fit the facts; and in their struggle to face the facts with theo-

ries, they had greatly enriched the concept of the education of adolescents.

Mr Loukes had a fine academic and teaching record but his book was more an intellectual debate about educational theory than a factual account of what he found. It was often difficult to extract the research data from his insightful musing on the role of schools in society and what they were trying to achieve. That said, he identified many issues that I will discuss later.

William Taylor's *The Secondary Modern School* was published in 1963 and was based on his doctoral thesis. This book review[6] was far from complimentary and I think resulted from Mr Taylor's willingness to question the prevailing educational orthodoxy:

Yet it must be said that Dr Taylor has written a book that is all but unreadable. His literary style has the flavour of a diet of gravel (and concentrated diet at that: the paragraphs often run to a full two pages) [and so the criticism goes on...]

Once the critic moved on from discussing the book's stylistic deficiencies and considered its substance, the main point of criticism was that:

Dr Taylor sees the post-war history of the secondary modern school as a conflict between the generally progressive and liberal ideals expressed in the Butler act and the pressure to seek social status and measurable reward, above all by relating the work of the school to the occupational ambitions of the children.

With the luxury of hindsight, I think many of Dr Taylor's observations were both accurate and important and although the writing style was somewhat dense it is a pity more attention wasn't given to his insights. We will return to Dr Taylor's analysis.

Harold Dent was the editor of *The Times Educational Supplement* and in later years a famous educational academic. His book, *Secondary Modern Schools – an interim report*, started with a quote from the June 1956 edition of *The Times Educational Supplement*.

*The Secondary Modern School has been the target of every newfan-
gled theory, every half-digested, ill-assorted idea… if ever it has
seen a settled objective half the busybodies in the world of education
have rushed in to save it from itself. Turn out citizens. Turn out liter-
ates. Turn out technicians. Be more vocational. Prepare for leisure.
Stick to the wider view. The wonder is that with all this and with all
the difficulties of the post-war world the secondary modern schools
have got anywhere at all. But, they have.*

How I wish I could have written this opening statement. It says so much
about the muddled thinking that accompanied the birth of secondary
moderns.

It seemed to me that Dent's reason for writing the book was to counter
the adverse press comment the schools were receiving and to explain the
difficulties under which they were launched and operated. In his obituary,[7] it
was said that Dent 'more than any other individual not in government
played a central part in the battle for the 1944 Education Act'. Perhaps his
comments resulted from his feelings of responsibility for the schools? Whatever his rationale, his insights were of considerable value in writing this
chapter. It is ironic that the writer of his obituary, Brian Simon, who was
described in his own obituary[8] by *The Guardian* as the 'Communist party
educationalist who advocated the comprehensive system' should be so
complimentary about somebody responsible for the introduction of selective
education.

*Your secondary modern schools – an account of their work in the late
1950s,* by Vincent Chapman, was a strange book. The author visited 'a
number of schools' and collected information from another 2,000-plus
schools, most of it by 'correspondence' (a way of researching that is long
since forgotten).

The book oscillated between advice about the fine details of teaching, as
illustrated by his views about the optimum sill height:

*In most classrooms both formal and informal teaching takes place,
and it is now considered advisable for the child, when he is seated,
to be able to look occasionally outside the window. In the secondary
school this means that the sill height will be about 2ft 6ins…*

... and pronouncements on the strategic questions about the schools. For instance:

> *The picture of the secondary modern school then begins to emerge, a picture which may be murky in parts but with large patches of sunlit landscapes.*

This merging of discussions of detail and policy made it difficult to extract a countrywide view about how the schools were performing; however, it contained much useful information, especially about the difficulties facing teachers.

I was worried by the title of the final book, *Secondary modern discipline*, by Richard Farley, and expected to read about the gruesome details of delivering corporal punishment. I could not have been more wrong. The book was a thoughtful, practical and amusing guide to teaching in schools where the children's background is likely to mean they have behavioural 'issues'. The author went to great lengths to explain that although these children were likely to be found in secondary moderns, they would exist in any system of schooling:

> *The book is mainly concerned with the problems that arise in socially depressed industrial areas, cities and the older overcrowded suburbs, where the handling of some secondary modern pupils raises special difficulties. Thus although certain features of school life described in the following chapters impinge on the frame of reference of most schools, it would be doing an injustice to the majority of secondary moderns to draw general conclusions from one aspect of the situation.*

I gained a lot from reading this book and have made much use of the author's insights.

These books provided a wide range of views about the performance of secondary moderns and the challenges they faced. On balance, they presented an optimistic view, while not refraining from identifying the many problems that needed to be overcome.

Harold Dent's book (*Secondary Modern Schools*) was the only one that provided 'hard' data about the schools and their achievements. The others contained some data but were mainly descriptive of the situation. In today's language, we would say they provided a lot of qualitative data but not much that was quantitative. The facts and figures would have to come from other sources.

Trying to aggregate the conclusions from such different accounts of the schools was difficult, to put it mildly, but one issue kept being referenced. The authors believed the creation of secondary moderns was a massive experiment in the education of the UK's children, which was done for all the right reasons but implemented without the necessary planning, resourcing and clarity of objectives. This is a hypothesis that I will return to many times. My other abiding feeling from reading these books was one of admiration for the authors who, with a couple of exceptions, produced beautifully written and amusing accounts that are shorn of the superfluous gobbledygook that is found in so many of today's educational texts.

I needed to put these authors' first-hand accounts of the schools into the historical context of the system of education that preceded them and the comprehensive schooling that was their replacement. To do this I used a large collection of educational history books, which are also listed at https://www.thesecondarymod.com. These books range in date from 1937 to 2019 and cover both the general aspects of education and specialist areas such as the evolution of exams, teaching methods and education funding. A few of the books are detailed accounts of the history of the Education Act of 1944 (the Butler Act). The thing that was most difficult to understand was the multiple types of schooling that existed between the wars. I was glad to learn that others also found this confusing. Helen Pearson, in her book *The Life Project,* wrote:

> *In the years before the war, the country had a bewildering array of schools: public, grammar, endowed, proprietary, elementary, first, primary, secondary, preparatory and more.*

As much for my own benefit as any other reason, I have listed and briefly described these different types of schools. I feel certain I haven't captured all the variations but it is as comprehensive a list as any and it can be found in Appendix C.

In addition to the historical questions of 'what happened when and why', there were many issues I needed to understand relating to the process of educating children. For instance, what were the ethics and accuracy of the 11-plus exam and to what extent did the social class of parents determine whether a child attended a grammar or secondary modern? I could have easily spent the next year, maybe two, reading all the research available on these types of subjects. I did my best to make a selection that would give me a comprehensive and balanced view of the issues.

The final level of research required understanding the position of education in the context of all the other events taking place at the time. There was no shortage of books providing this information, but the ones I found most helpful were the trilogy by David Kynaston that covered UK history during the period 1945–1962 (*Austerity Britain, Family Britain* and *Modernity Britain*).

The multiple levels of research are shown in the following diagram. To build a complete history of the schools I started from the centre and moved outwards. As you might imagine, there was considerable duplication in the different accounts of the schools, which was not surprising since many of the books referenced each other. What was interesting, and disturbing, was the range of conclusions that authors reached from using the same base data. Some of the authors and educational pundits openly declared their educational beliefs, which were nearly always pro-comprehensive schools, anti-selective education and often anti-private schools. Others were less forthcoming about their personal educational beliefs but their political allegiances soon became clear. Invariably, they came from the left of the political spectrum, which suggested they were opposed to selective education. This is not to detract from their scholarship but it does make me warier of blithely accepting their conclusions.

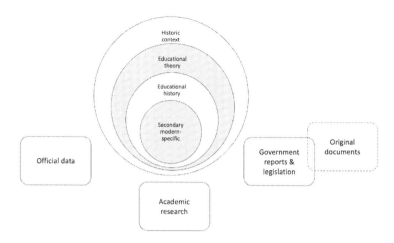

| The different sources of information used during the research

I soon decided that whenever possible I would use the original documents rather than the quoted extracts. As was shown in Chapter 1 ('The truth is what we want it to be'), there are many ways of formulating different conclusions depending on which 'facts' are selected and how they are combined. I am not going to embarrass any of the authors by 'naming names' but it was clear that their political and educational opinions did affect their objectivity.

The diagram also shows the other sources of information I consulted. The official data included the statistics that were published by the various government departments responsible for education. In an era before spreadsheets and desktop publishing it was surprising to find the volume and level of detail of the published data. An example, which is not in the least bit relevant to my studies, concerns the availability of free school milk. I doubt if many people know that in 1939 there nearly 100 million (97,667,750 to be exact) bottles of free milk distributed in schools. The mind boggles at how this type of data was collected and aggregated.

Most of these documents can still be purchased. Others can be viewed in the excellent library at the Institute of Education at University College London.

Throughout the timeline, Labour and Conservative governments had commissioned numerous reports about different aspects of education, many of which resulted in new legislation. Whenever possible I read the reports and Parliamentary Acts, rather than other commentators' summaries and interpretation. For the most important documents I tried to access, from the National Archive, the supporting Cabinet papers and memoranda, which are now available to the public under the 30-year rule. Very often these documents reveal the far from perfect circumstances in which politicians tried to reach agreement and implement educational change. They disclose the human side of things, the compromises and the conflicts, and provide a secondary benefit in explaining why today's policy makers act as they do.

Sometimes it was useful to amplify the value of these documents by looking at the Parliamentary debates that ensued. The digitised editions of the Commons and Lords copies of *Hansard*, the official record of the debates, are available online.[9]

The final source of information was academic research that is available online. Many research papers and doctoral theses have been written about the different aspects of secondary moderns. Much of it is a rehash of previous publications but sometimes I encountered some gems of information. An outstanding source of documents and commentary about English education has been created by Derek Gillard, who operates the website *Education in England*.[10] I dread to think how much time he has spent creating this repository of information.

In addition to these sources, there was the commentary appearing in the press. Most often this material was published in *The Times Educational Supplement* and was referred to in the other publications. Whenever possible, I accessed the original editions.

Throughout the research I had to keep reminding myself that the title of this chapter is 'A *condensed* history of secondary moderns'. The timeline ended up being three times longer than my original estimates – and it could have been even longer. Partly from necessity and partly because I found the history so fascinating and relevant to today, this is a long and involved story that is spread over three chapters. I hope you find reading it worthwhile.

The history timeline

Before plunging into the detail of the secondary modern's history, I will explain my rationale for dividing the timeline into three parts. When I was first thinking about writing this book I had blithely assumed that all I needed to consider was the period from the opening of the doors of the first secondary modern school through to when they were replaced by comprehensives – a period of about 30 years. That was a monumentally naïve idea.

I should have realised that the concept of selective education – with its 11-plus, grammar, technical and secondary modern schools – didn't instantaneously appear as a result of Richard Austen Butler, Baron Butler of Saffron Walden, better known as R.A. Butler, shepherding the 1944 Education Act through Parliament. The educational concepts that resulted in secondary moderns had their origins way before 1944.

When were the seeds of secondary modern education first sown, what were the factors that shaped how the schools were supposed to operate and what was the system of schooling they replaced? The Butler Act was just an administrative event; the detail I needed to understand was how an existing schooling system, with its physical and human assets and culture, became the tripartite method of secondary schooling.

Just when I thought I had found a date where I could say 'this is the starting point', I discovered the need for more historical context that drove me further back in time. Eventually, I found the period when I could say, with some confidence, 'here the story starts'. With a mix of horror and excitement, I was back at the beginning of the First World War (WWI). There is an argument that the start should be even earlier, way back in 1868, when the Taunton Commission published its findings. I thought that would be a step too far for my energy to research the subject and your patience to read. I was also influenced by the research showing that until the 1920s there was little relationship between spending on formal education and the accumulation of human knowledge. Before then 'learning by doing', not formal schooling, was more important.[11]

If the embryonic thinking about the schooling system of which secondary moderns were such an important part started with the end of one world war, their emergence as the primary type of school for educating children started at the end of the second. Since some of the preparation for their birth started during the war, I think it is reasonable to say that this first part of the history timeline, titled 'Between the wars' (Chapter 5), covers approximately 30 years.

This inter-war period was very active in the number of education acts that were passed and the committee reports about the future of education that were produced. Not all of them were involved with secondary education, but there were a dozen important reports and bills listed for this period.[12] Maybe the 13 ministers who presided over the country's education during those 30 years felt they should all leave their mark and pass a bill or commission a report? Perhaps the high level of legislative and reporting activity reflects the rapid economic and social changes that were taking place during the period?

The second part of the timeline starts after the Butler Act gained royal assent at the beginning of August 1944. By 1949 there were over a million children being educated in the 3,141 schools or departments labelled as secondary moderns.[13] Until 1972, you were more likely to attend a 'secondary mod' than any other type of school.[14]

As we will see, putting an exact date on the demise of secondary moderns is nearly as difficult as specifying when they were born, but the circular that was issued by the Department of Education and Science in 1965 signalled their end. By 1970 the number of secondary moderns was reduced to 2,691 and then the numbers plummeted to 445 by 1980.[15] A few parts of the UK decided, and were able, to retain selective education; this situation still exists today.

By 1974, less than 25% of children were in secondary modern schools and at this point I decided to conclude the second part of the timeline. There was an unstoppable momentum that was driving their decline and I thought there was little more to learn by pursuing their story beyond this time. Like the first section of the timeline, the birth-to-death story of secondary moderns extends for approximately 30 years (Chapter 6).

Understanding what happened after the secondary modern period was a necessary part of this book but very much a secondary objective. Having said that, the more I researched this period the more I realised it contained important insights, especially the time when Tony Blair was the Labour Party leader. I decided that if the first two sections of the timeline were 30 years, then I would use the same period for the final section. By then it should be clear how successful, or not, comprehensive schools had been at rectifying the numerous criticisms levelled at secondary moderns – hence the final part, titled 'The comprehensive era' (Chapter 7) ends in 2004.

The three sections cover a period of 90 years of UK history that includes a couple of world wars, seven economic depressions,[16] entry into and exit from the EU and a huge change in social attitudes. Making objective comments about events at the beginning of the timeline, immersed as I inevitably am in the conditions and values of a century later, is mighty diffi-cult. It is hard not to overlay our own assumptions and outlook onto events that occurred in very different economic and social conditions. So before I started writing, I tried to capture these changing conditions in a series of five charts that provide a context to what was happening throughout the 90-year history. I will refer to these charts throughout the book, but this seems an appropriate point to discuss their contents. An associated danger of failing to contextualise the events is evaluating the judgements from the safe stand-point of knowing their outcomes. Hopefully, I have got the balance right about putting events into their historical context while at the same time recognising that limited information was available when the decisions were made.

Before looking at what the charts tell us, I want to issue a 'health warn-ing' about how the data in the charts must be viewed and applied. It is very difficult, if not impossible, to find consistent datasets that cover these 90 years. Definitions get changed, ways of counting get modified, some data is seasonally adjusted (some not) and the available data has an infuriating habit of never exactly matching the variable being discussed. To make matters even more complicated, the variables within the charts are linked (e.g. government spending on education will be influenced by the prevailing age demographic profile). In spite of all these caveats, these charts do show the wide range of conditions that were influencing decision making in each part of the timeline. We will return to these charts throughout the next few chap-ters, so at this point I will just comment on the obvious messages that they convey.

The first chart[17] shows the numbers of children in the age ranges 5–14 and 10–14 over the period.

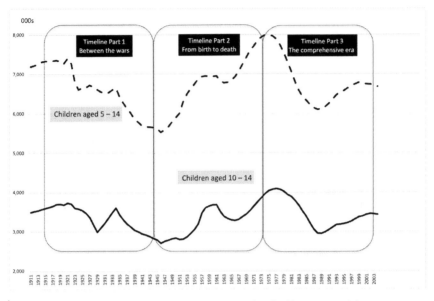

The numbers of children aged 5–14 and 10–14 during the three parts of the timeline

As can be seen, the three parts of the timeline had very different demographic profiles. During the period between the wars the number of children declined, resulting from a number of factors, including widespread access to birth control and the Spanish flu pandemic of 1918. The second period witnessed the famous baby boom. During the final period the numbers declined from the highs of the boom period and then plateaued.

Over this time, there was also a wide variation in the unemployment rate, as can be seen in the next chart.[18] The middle period, from 'birth to death', had unusually low rates of unemployment, especially compared with the period between the wars.

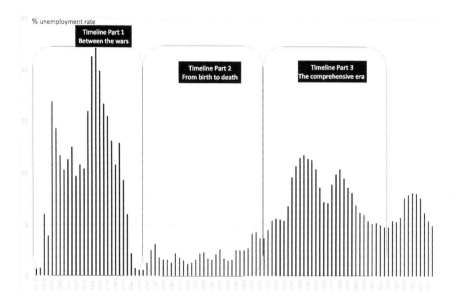

Unemployment rate (aged 16 and over) in England and Wales

The next chart[19] shows the change in average wages over the three periods. To remove the effect of inflation, the figures are all stated in 2010 sterling values. The reason for creating this chart is to see an indicator of the changing levels of prosperity.

There was a constant increase in the real value of earnings for all three periods, although this was less marked in the period between the wars. A more interesting view of the data is the changes in real earnings at the beginning and end of each period. The increases during the last two parts of the timeline were approximately the same and both were four times greater than the increase in the period between the wars. The economic effects of the wars can be seen in the perturbations in earnings at the beginning and end of the period.

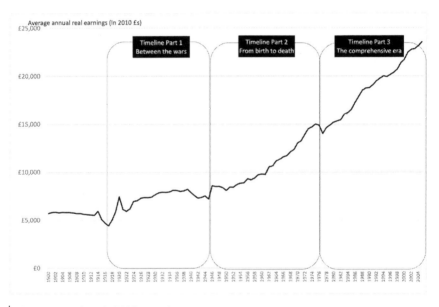

Average earnings in 2010 pounds

As the UK economy developed, so did demand for different types of labour. The interplay between the workforce's level of education, the employment profile and social mobility is complicated.

The following chart shows that between the wars there was little change in the relative numbers of people in each occupation category. This is surprising, considering the huge upheaval caused by the two wars and the resulting troubled economic conditions. Ironically, it might be because of the high levels of economic and social uncertainty that so little changed? The chart shows that in the final two periods of the timeline, there was a significant decline in demand for routine and semi-routine workers and a shift to employment in management and professional positions.

Because of the lack of consistent data, it was necessary to use two different datasets, one covering the period until 1951[20] and the other from 1951 until 2004.[21]

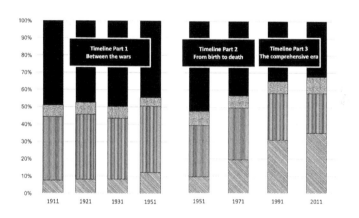

■ Routine and semi-routine

▨ Small employers & own account workers

▥ Administrative, lower supervisory and technical occupations

▧ Managerial and professional occupations

Chart showing the change in the occupation profile of the
UK for the period of the timeline

The final chart[22] shows how government spending on education changed over the three periods. It is not surprising that both wars resulted in money being diverted to other uses, as is clearly shown in the between the wars part of the timeline. It took until 1956 for the percentage of GDP spent on education to return to the high point of the first part of the timeline, a period of over 20 years. From 1956 the share of spending increased until the start of the comprehensive era, when it declined and continued to do so for over 20 years.

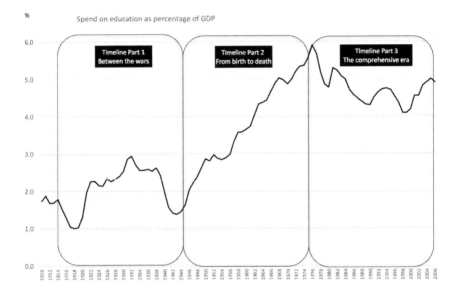

| The total government spend on education as a percentage of GDP

Let me state again my warning about the accuracy and consistency of the data. Obtaining reliable data, for the 90-year period of the timeline, is not just difficult – it is impossible. I have done my best to ensure its accuracy but have no doubt that it does contain inaccuracies. That said, the overall story that the data conveys is correct.

The next chapter tells the story of the first part of the timeline and relates how secondary education evolved between the wars.

CHAPTER 5

BETWEEN THE WARS

The date is April 1916 and WWI is under way. The great sea battle of Jutland and the nightmare of the Somme are yet to happen. How astonishing then, that the Right Honourable Arthur Henderson MP, who was then president of the Board of Education, the forerunner of the Ministry of Education, has just established a committee to consider 'what steps should be taken to make provision for the education and instruction of children and young persons *after the war*' [my italics].

I would like to think that this bold initiative resulted from his foresight and certainty of victory. More likely, it demonstrated the naïve confidence of politicians and the military that Germany would be quickly defeated. Who knows, maybe the committee was created as a symbol of defiance, a gesture to show that the government was confident of success and was making positive plans for the post-war period?

We now know the duration and awfulness of the war, something that soon became a personal tragedy for Arthur Henderson, when his eldest son was killed in the battle of the Somme, five months after the report was commissioned.

The committee published its report in 1917, nearly two years before the war ended. Its contents, sentiment and recommendations are a good place to start this first section of our timeline. Herbert Lewis MP chaired the committee and, not surprisingly, its findings are now referred to as the Lewis Report.[1]

The tone and sentiment of the report are evident from the first paragraph of the introduction, with its solemn language and the breadth of its vision.

Any inquiry into education at the present juncture is big with issues of national fate. In the great work of reconstruction which lies ahead there are aims to be set before us which will try, no less searchingly than war itself, the temper and enduring qualities of our race; and in the realisation of each and all of these education, with its stimulus and its discipline, must be our stand-by.

We have to perfect the civilisation for which our men have shed their blood and our women their tears; to establish new standards of value in our judgment of what makes life worth living, more whole-some and more restrained ideals of behaviour and recreation, finer traditions of co-operation and kindly fellowship between class and class and between man and man.

As I read these words I wondered how it would be written today? I would like to think it would be as passionate and direct, but I doubt it. Are these just fine words and sentiments or do they demonstrate the depth of feeling and sincere desire to make a better world? My guess is the latter. We will see this same commitment to changing the established order and to improving people's lives at the end of WWII, but there is much to cover before we get to that point in the timeline.

The report uses population statistics from the 1911 census and the Board of Education's school attendance data to establish the numbers of children aged 12–18 who were under 'some kind of public educational influence'. As can be seen from the table[2], formal education ceased for most children between their 14th and 15th birthdays.

Percentage of children	Age of pupil					
	12 – 13	13 – 14	14 – 15	15 – 16	16 – 17	17 – 18
In full-time courses	91%	66%	12%	4%	2%	1%
Part-time courses	4%	9%	16%	14%	13%	10%
Unenrolled in school	5%	25%	72%	82%	85%	89%

| Numbers of children in full- and part-time education

The report's authors identified that this analysis underestimated the number of children being educated, because the statistics included only data from schools that were inspected. However, the way the data was collected overstated pupil numbers, because children left school during each of the time periods, especially after the age of 13. Taking these errors into account, the committee estimated that only 13% of children were likely to get any formal education past the age of 14. What's more, most of them would be attending an elementary school, which provided a far less comprehensive and rigorous education than that given to the minority who attended a secondary school.

The size and age profiles of these two types of school were very different, as is illustrated in the next chart.[3] Using data from a decade later in 1927, the chart shows there were far more children in elementary schools – approximately 16 times more – two-thirds of them being younger than 11. Approximately half of the children in secondary schools were 14 or older. It should be remembered that a lot of data was excluded from the Board of Education's statistics, including private fee-paying schools, for younger children (preparatory schools) and schools that hadn't applied to be 'recognised as efficient' (i.e. providing a minimum of staffing and accommodation).

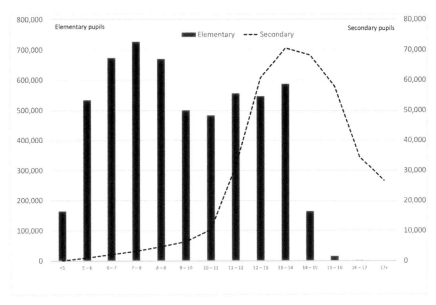

The number of pupils by age attending secondary and elementary schools in England and Wales in 1927

Children attending secondary schools were a mix of those whose parents paid their fees and expenses and those who passed an exam and were funded by the local education authority. At the time of the report there were 62,000 children with free secondary school places.[4] To put this into context, at the same time there were over a million children attending elementary schools.

At this point of studying the Lewis Report I began to see similarities between the type of education system it described and the one I experienced. Elementary schools catered for the masses and secondary schools for the fortunate few. Achieving a free place at secondary school must have been hotly contested, when you think that in the year 1911–1912, only about 5% of elementary school children transitioned to study at this type of school.[5]

Selection to move from the elementary to the secondary was done on the basis of an exam. The nature of these exams and the facets of intelligence that they measured were hotly debated. In his book *Examinations*, Robert Montgomery[6] gave a detailed description of the types of exams and how they were administered.

There was a wide national variation in the provision of secondary school places and how the demand was regulated and managed. Very often the transition between schools took place around the age of 11 years, yet more similarities with the schooling in the secondary modern era.

Montgomery's book talked about the exam system at the beginning of the war.

The majority [of the exams] used only English and arithmetic questions, although some authorities tested history, geography and elementary science. English composition was present in all written examinations. In general, the scholarship questions were sensibly centred on the elementary school syllabus, partly to eliminate the effects of excessive coaching.

I had to smile, to find that so long ago there was an awareness and concern about the distortion and unfairness that coaching children had on exam results – a subject that is much debated today.

At the time of the report, the first serious attempts were being made to examine children on both their capacity to learn and the body of knowledge they had already absorbed. This desire to be able to measure latent intelligence, which is independent of social background, was an issue that increased in importance and eventually resulted in the much-reviled 11-plus exam.

After analysing the number of children in education the report considered the opportunities for children to learn when they were employed, either by attending school part-time or by learning in the workplace. It came to the conclusion that much of the training provided by employers, including apprenticeships, was little more than a way of obtaining cheap labour. To compound these depressing conclusions was the detrimental effect that the disruption of the war was having on children's education.

Upon this educational and industrial chaos has come the war, to aggravate conditions that could hardly be made graver, and to emphasise a problem that needed no emphasis. Many children have been withdrawn at an even earlier age than usual from day schools, and the attendances at those evening schools which have not been closed show a lamentable shrinkage.

Something must be done

Having established the gravity of the problem the report stated there was only one remedy – *porro unum est necessarium* [but one thing is necessary]. Wow, can you conceive of any official document today either using Latin or being so direct?

> *[The remedy is] nothing less than a complete change of temper and outlook on the part of the people of this country as to what they mean, through the forces of industry and society, to make of their boys and girls.*

> *Can the age of adolescence be brought out of the purview of economic exploitation and into that of the social conscience? Can the conception of the juvenile as primarily a little wage-earner be replaced by the conception of the juvenile as primarily the workman and the citizen in training? Can it be established that the educational purpose is to be the dominating one, without as well as within the school doors, during those formative years between 12 and 18?*

> *If not, clearly no remedies at all are possible in the absence of the will by which alone they could be rendered effective.*

Like all committee reports, the high ideals and grand vision of the future had to be distilled and translated into concrete proposals. The Lewis Report made many recommendations and suggestions, but only one requiring new legislation. This was to ensure there was a uniform elementary school-leaving age of 14, with the abolition of all exemptions. In addition, children between the ages of 14 and 18 would have to attend, for not less than eight hours a week, or 320 hours a year, day continuation classes. What would be taught in these classes was left to be resolved by each local education authority.

You might wonder why I have spent nearly 2,000 words talking about the work of this committee, even though its impact on the history of education was, to put it nicely, limited. I think its value is in highlighting the issues that will keep reappearing throughout this chapter.

There was no shortage of desire to improve the educational lot of the mass of children, something that was heightened by the suffering endured during the war. That it was unfair and a waste of talent for only a few children to get a premium quality education was a widely held view, as was the need to liberate children's educational opportunities from the constraints of their parents' economic and social position.

But, bringing change means overcoming the hurdles of spending more money, balancing the demands of time spent working and being educated and launching new initiatives on the rocky foundations of the existing education infrastructure. This wasn't easy at the end of WWI and it didn't get any easier at the end of WWII.

The war suppressed – 'delayed' is probably is a better word – the desire for change and social tensions that were present beforehand. There was concern that the overly classics-based curriculum in schools was not equipping the UK to match the scientific prowess of Germany, Japan and the US. There were tensions about who was responsible for determining, implementing and paying for educational change. Was it at a local level (i.e. local education authorities) or controlled by central government (i.e. the Board of Education)? Indeed, the intervention of the state in the upbringing of children was not welcomed by all. Employers, religious authorities and some parents were concerned that the state was assuming too much power. As I know from bitter experience, implementing change invariably creates friction between those gaining and those losing power. Sadly, the same types of arguments are as alive today as when Lewis was trying to change the system.

With the work of Lewis complete, the responsibility to turn his grand vision into a reorganised education system was left to H.A.L. Fisher, who became the new president of the Board of Education just before the end of 1916.

The most detailed research about what happened next was done by Lawrence Andrews in his book *The Education Act 1918*.[7] Reading his account of the tortuous battle that Fisher had to get Lewis's proposals accepted and implemented provides an insight into the clash between good intentions, vested interests and economic reality.

Local authorities were concerned they were losing power to the Board of Education; employers were worried about the costs and the disruption; some parts of the educational establishment and the TUC didn't think the changes were radical enough – they wanted the leaving age raised to 16. And, if this was not bad enough, the Treasury needed to reduce public expenditure.

Lewis's vision and Fisher's struggles to make their changes a reality are now a footnote in education history. It wasn't until 1921 that the school-leaving age was raised to 14 years and continuation schools never got off the ground. In 1921 they had enrolled 95,000[8] students but by 1924 that number had fallen to 23,000 and would keep falling.[9]

Lawrence Andrews believed that Fisher's involvement resulted in long-term improvement in the system of schooling. Maybe that is so, but having studied what he and Lewis achieved I am left with the feeling that their aims, although laudable, were doomed to fail. Other than raising the school-leaving age, their proposals were vaguely defined, especially in the case of the continuation school classes, and required a significant amount of change to occur and public funds to succeed, at a time when the country's finances were in a dire state.

Change and austerity are not good bedfellows

My guess is that Fisher hoped that the thirst for change, resulting from the war, was going to be enough to demolish the many obstacles that had to be overcome. Maybe if he had succeeded in getting the education act passed in 1917 he would have gained sufficient momentum to succeed? As it was, the bill was introduced in August and withdrawn in December of 1917. The bill reappeared early in the new year, with a few amendments, mainly about better defining the role of local and central government. But the magic of 'something must be done' had dissolved and other vested interests, mainly employers, wanted further changes to the legislation. And then came the harsh reality of the financial repercussions of the war and the need to slash public spending. This period of austerity should have been predicted – maybe not the scale of the financial trauma, but the notion of increasing the spend on education was always going to be a high-risk strategy. A cursory look at the economic conditions of the time, as shown in the following chart,[10] illustrates the magnitude of the financial and social problems facing the country.

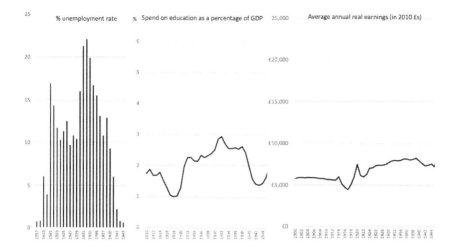

The number of pupils by age attending secondary and elementary schools in England and Wales in 1927

In business, there is an argument that changing the status quo is best done at a time of crisis. The corollary to this is that the memories of a crisis have a short shelf life, as Fisher discovered.

Although Fisher's continuation schools were never widely adopted, the desire and the need for better schooling did not disappear; rather, the ideas of what better schooling was and how it should be achieved became politicised.

Secondary schools did not have the capacity to satisfy the numbers of children from elementary schools wanting to transfer. As an alternative and as a way of satisfying local demand, a number of other types of schools appeared. These included the higher elementary school, central schools, day trade schools and junior technical schools.

At this point you are most likely becoming confused, wondering how these schools related to each other and how parents decided what was best for their children. I know the feeling!

We could spend a long time unravelling these complexities but I don't think it would be relevant to the history of the secondary modern. It seems clear that in the absence of any centrally defined policy, the local education authorities and employers were trying to find their own solutions to the need for more and better education. For readers wanting the details of these schools they are explained in Appendix C.

Schooling in England and Wales was disjointed and lacked any coherent strategy. Fisher had failed to achieve his promised transformation and, to make matters worse, the country's economic crisis resulted in a significant reduction in expenditure on education and, most importantly, a cut in teachers' earnings. It was at this time that the Labour Party, the TUC and the teaching unions sought to define their vision of how children should be educated.

The emergence of the Labour Party's education policy

Any reader of *The Guardian* newspaper would feel at home reading Brian Simon's account of the period[11] – quotes about cuts to the education budget at a time 'when hundreds of millions of pounds are being squandered on stupid imperialist military adventures' and the country's 280 millionaires having a collective wealth of £590 million (£31 billion in 2017 pounds). There are even accusations by school teachers of 'sustained attacks by the Conservative press – particularly the *Daily Mail*'.

For me, the most important outcome, resulting from this time, was the publication, in 1922–1923, of *Secondary Education for all* by the Education Advisory Committee of the Labour Party and edited by R.H. Tawney.[12] As Simon says in his book:

In all the circumstances, the Labour policy formulated in 1922 was to figure prominently on the education scene, in one way or another, during the whole of the period up to the second world war and beyond.

These few sentences from the committee's report make the Labour Party's vision of how education should be organised crystal clear.

The Labour Party is convinced that the only policy which is at once educationally sound and suited to a democratic community is one under which primary education and secondary education are organised as two stages in a single and continuous process; secondary

*education being the education of the adolescent and primary educa-
tion being education preparatory thereto.*

*Its objective, therefore, is both the improvement of primary education
and the development of public secondary education to such a point
that all normal children, irrespective of the income, class, or occupation of their parents, may be transferred at the age of eleven + from
the primary or preparatory school to one type or another of
secondary school, and remain in the latter till sixteen.*

If only today's politicians and civil servants could express their ideas
with such clarity!

I don't want to write a summary of this 149-page document, but instead
to highlight those recommendations that had a lasting influence on the
policy of the Labour Party and hence the UK's education policy. The
opening statement proposed that children should move between primary and
secondary education at the age of 11, to 'one type or another of secondary
school'. These seven words were hugely important because they positioned
the Labour Party, at this point in time, in favour of multiple types of
secondary school and a school-leaving age of 16 – that's two years older
than was then required.

The document expanded this point and said:

*Central Schools and Junior Technical Schools are important, as
representing a type of higher education designed to meet the needs of
those children who progress most easily by means of a curriculum
containing a considerable infusion of practical work appealing to
their creative instincts.*

It then explained that these schools, including the continuation schools
that Fisher tried to implement, should become part of the secondary school
system. The document didn't explicitly say that all the schools should have
the same status but I am certain that is what was implied.

Exams were seen as being necessary, but as only *part* of the selection
process.

*As long as the number of school places is inadequate, competition
for admission to the secondary school is inevitable. But examinations should be supplementary and subsidiary to the use of school
records and of reports by teachers.*

At the end of the document was a discussion of the financial impact of
its policies. This started by observing that the changes should be carried out
in gradual stages.

*What we anticipate, in fact, is not any sudden large addition to the
expenditure on secondary education, but a steady advance.*

In the final section of the document, 'Can the nation afford education?',
the tone of the writing changed. There was such an abrupt injection of
emotional rhetoric that I find it hard to believe it was written by the same
person who wrote the rest of the document. This example illustrates the
point.

The comment of the reader who turns from his Daily Mail *to glance
for the first time at these figures will be simple: 'Very nice, but the
nation cannot afford it.' At a meeting of the Federation of British
Industries a little more than a year ago, held (for the sake of economy) in the Victoria Room of the Hotel Cecil, a certain Mr. Lincoln
Chandler apparently a waggon-builder is reported, as became one of
his profession, to have driven straight to the point, and like Jehu, the
son of Nimshi, to have driven furiously. 'It was time,' he is stated to
have said in a series of striking aphorisms quoted by* The Times *of
December 1920, 'they came to plain speaking... we had embarked on
schemes without which we had got on very well...'*

And so this final section went on, in its angry way, with personal attacks
on opposing politicians and finger-waving at employers and the media
(especially the *Daily Mail*).

Whoever wrote this section was desperate to make the point that the
question of the affordability of education depended on its value to citizens
and the state, relative to other things. To support the argument, it quoted two

facts that might surprise the reader. The first concerned the consumption of alcohol: 'the nation spent in 1920–21 more than five times as much on drink as it spent on education'. The second was that in 1913–1914 the spending on defence was twice that spent on education. You might be wondering how things have changed in the past hundred years? In 2016 spending on education was four and a half times the amount spent on booze[13] and twice the defence budget,[14] almost a complete reversal of the position when Tawney's document was published.

Secondary Education for all was a clear and comprehensive statement of the Labour Party's proposed education policy and almost certainly contributed to the decision to conduct the next major study into schooling in England and Wales. This was undertaken by the Board of Education's Consultative Committee, an influential group of experts that acted as an advisory body to the government. During its time in existence, it was a major part of the education policy-making apparatus, producing 17 major reports.[15]

The other pressure for the study was the need of employers for more and better-educated school leavers and the concern that teachers' political allegiances would change, fuelled by the anger about their salaries being cut.

According to Simon, the committee's initial terms of reference were proposed by a headmaster of a London school who was a committee member.

The different types of curriculum suitable to children between the ages of 11 and 16 and the means by which these can be provided.

This 'open-ended' brief would enable the committee to consider just about anything it wanted to – most importantly, the future of secondary schools, and the possibility of increasing the leaving age to 16. You cannot help but see the similarities between this scope of vision and Tawney's publication. Perhaps this is not surprising, since Tawney was a member of the committee. There is some controversy about Tawney's influence on the committee. The paper *R H Tawney and the Hadow report*[16] stated that 'he played no direct part in the research', a conclusion the relied on there being no evidence to support that he did, rather than any proof that he didn't. It matters little, since it is obvious that Tawney's ideas permeate Hadow's conclusions.

The government didn't want the subject of secondary education opened up for discussion and it most certainly didn't want to consider raising the leaving age by two years. You can interpret this sentiment as resulting from the conservative views you expect from a Conservative government. An alternative view is that in the midst of an economic crisis, the last thing it wanted was wholesale change to the education system accompanied by an increase in public spending. I expect that both interpretations are correct and depending on your political beliefs you give more emphasis to one rather than the other.

After considerable toing and froing in defining the terms of reference, on 1 February 1924 the Board of Education asked the Consultative Committee, chaired by Sir W.H. Hadow, to consider this question:

> *To consider and report upon the organisation, objective and curriculum of courses of study suitable for children who will remain in full-time attendance at schools, other than Secondary Schools, up to the age of 15 [my underlining], regard being had on the one hand to the requirements of a good general education and the desirability of providing a reasonable variety of curriculum, so far as is practicable, for children of varying tastes and abilities, and on the other to the probable occupations of the pupils in commerce, industry and agriculture.*

Note that the age has been reduced to 15 and that secondary schools were excluded from the committee's remit. At the time of the report five times more people were employed in agriculture than today, which explains why it was listed as a 'probable occupation.'[17]

Fast forward to 1926, the committee had done its work and the final report was released – all 181 pages.

Sir W.H. Hadow was a man of many skills and interests. His six reports on education warrant only a short mention in his *Oxford Dictionary of National Biographies* entry. The account of his life is mainly taken up with his books about music, including the *Oxford History of Music*, and his academic positions. In another era, I think Hadow could have easily added being a management consultant to his CV. His report was logical, analytical and very readable, although he appears to have had an aversion to full-stops, as you will see from the length of his sentences.

After considering the views and data about the current system, he defines 'the nature of the problem' as follows.

At the present day, the years between 11 and 14–15 form the opening phase of secondary education for a small minority of children, and the closing phase of elementary education for the great majority. Is it possible so to organise education that the first stage may lead naturally and generally to the second; to ensure that all normal children may pursue some kind of post-primary course for a period of not less than three, and preferably four, years from the age of 11+; and to devise curricula calculated to develop more fully than is always the case at present the powers, not merely of children of exceptional capacity, but of the great mass of boys and girls, whose character and intelligence will determine the quality of national life during the coming quarter of a century?

In his analysis, he calculated that this 'small minority of children' attending secondary schools was approximately 10%. There was, however, a wide variation in this figure by geographic area (5–27%). Twenty years later this was reflected in unevenness (and unfairness) in the way grammar school places were distributed throughout the country.

The committee's first recommendation concerned the 'regrading' of education.

Primary education should be regarded as ending at about the age of 11+. At that age a second stage, which for the moment may be given the colourless name 'post-primary' should begin; and this stage which, for many pupils would end at 16+, for some at 18 or 19, but for the majority at 14+ or 15+, should be envisaged so far as possible as a single whole, within which there will be a variety in the types of education supplied, but which will be marked by the common characteristic that its aim is to provide for the needs of children who are entering and passing through the stage of adolescence.

The phrase 'colourless name', for the education of children aged 11 and over, made me smile. I can just imagine the committee debating what to call them and not reaching a conclusion and being forced to resort to the innocuous term 'post-primary'. What this recommendation also did was to sidestep the limitation of the terms of reference – the exclusion of secondary schools – by using the words 'envisaged so far as possible as a single whole' and 'marked by common characteristics'. You might be thinking that this is just a matter of semantics, but having spent hours in meetings, arguing over the exact use of words and phrases, I suspect Hadow and his fellow committee members anguished long and hard over this wording.

Tawney's influence on the committee shone through in the next recommendations. The words could have been copied and pasted straight out of *Secondary Education for all.*

> *The term 'secondary education' is at present employed in two senses; first, in the more general sense in which we hope that it may come to be used, to indicate the second or post-primary stage in education, in all schools of a secondary or post-primary type; and in the second place in a more restricted sense (in which it is ordinarily used today) as meaning the education given in schools recognised under the Board's Regulations for Secondary Schools.*

> *All normal children should go on to some form of post-primary education; and while, taking the country as a whole, many more children should pass to 'secondary' schools in the current sense of the term than pass at present, it is necessary that the post primary grade of education should include other types of post-primary schools, with curricula varying according to both the age up to which the majority of pupils will remain at school and the different interests and abilities of the pupils, to which the bias or objective of each school will naturally be related.*

Having established that the term 'secondary school' should become a generic term, rather than the name for the existing elite schools, the committee turned its attention to explaining the type of education that was required.

If it is important to insist that there is a point in the development of
all children at which they ought to begin their post-primary educa-
tion, it is not less important to remember that such education will be
successful only in so far as it is related to the actual requirements of
the children themselves. There are diversities of gifts, and for that
reason there must be diversity of educational provision.

Equality, in short, is not identity, and the larger the number of chil-
dren receiving post-primary education, the more essential is it that
that education should not attempt to press different types of char-
acter and intelligence into a single mould, however excellent in itself
it may be, but should provide a range of educational opportunity
sufficiently wide to appeal to varying interests and cultivate powers
which differ widely, both in kind and in degree.

It is pure conjecture by me, but this recommendation appears intended to
placate those committee members, and the likely critics of the report, who
were concerned about the curriculum of secondary schools being changed,
by using the phrases 'should not attempt to press different types of character
and intelligence into a single mould' and 'provide a range of educational
opportunity'.

The report then attempted to define the different types of school that
would be required and what they would teach. To my mind, the committee
was either unsure of what to say or fell into the trap of producing a typical
'committee-authored' recommendation (i.e. one that satisfies all the contributors but sacrifices clarity and objectivity).

First, it said that nothing should change for three existing categories of
school and specifically stated that secondary schools should continue to
provide an 'academic' education with a literary or scientific curriculum.
Later in the report it suggested these schools would be renamed as 'grammar
schools'.

As post-primary education develops, the schools dealing with the
post-primary or secondary stage of education should include (in
addition to Junior Technical and Trade Schools) at least the
following main types:

(i) Schools of the 'secondary' types now commonly existing which at present follow in the main a predominantly literary or scientific curriculum, and carry the education of their pupils forward to the age of at least 16+.

The committee recommended the provision of three other types of schooling. There would be two types of central school – one type selecting its pupils, the other type not. The curriculum of these schools would have a 'practical trend' – whatever that is; both types of school were to be named 'modern' schools.

The final category of school appeared to be some sort of 'catch-all' for children not attending the other types. The proposed name for this type of education was 'senior classes'.

Senior Classes, Central Departments, 'Higher Tops' and analogous arrangements, for providing advanced instruction for pupils over the age of 11+, for whom, owing to local conditions, it is impossible to make provision in one or other of the types of school mentioned above.

At this point you are probably thinking that 'I thought this committee was supposed to be simplifying and clarifying schooling post-11'. Maybe today's parents' decision about how their children are educated is not as complicated as that of their great grandparents.

The final set of recommendations was easier to understand. Children at primary school would move to their next level of education at the age of 11 plus. I think it worth quoting the exact words describing how the selection at 11-plus was to be made.

While we think all children should enter some type of post-primary school at the age of 11+, it will be necessary to discover in each case the type most suitable to a child's abilities and interests, and for this purpose a written examination should be held, and also, wherever possible, an oral examination.

A written psychological test might also be specially employed in dealing with borderline cases, or where a discrepancy between the result of the written examination and the teacher's estimate of proficiency has been observed.

It was recognised that mistakes would be made in assigning schools and to rectify this it recommended the following.

Adequate arrangements should be made for transferring children who show ability to profit by 'Secondary' Education beyond the age of 15+ from Central to 'Secondary' Schools at the age of 12 or 13. Conversely, similar arrangements should be made for transferring pupils from 'Secondary' Schools to Central Schools or to Junior Technical Schools, as need may be.

The committee left it to the last recommendation to make its statement about raising the school-leaving age.

The course of wisdom, therefore, it appears to us, would be to pass legislation fixing the age of 15 as that up to which attendance at school will become obligatory after the lapse of five years from the date of this Report – that is to say at the beginning of the school year 1932.

Let's draw breath at this point

We have reached the date of 1926 and already much of the educational framework that I was familiar with in the 1960s has been proposed. The division between primary and secondary education at 11 by means of an exam, the mix of grammar and modern schools, the chance to switch schools at 13 and a leaving age of 15. Children at grammar schools would study academic subjects, whereas those at modern schools would follow a curriculum that had 'large opportunities for practical work and related to living interests'. At this point, the Labour Party's vision of education, as voiced by Tawney, was pretty much identical to that of the Board of Education's Consultative Committee. The Hadow Report was conceived when the government was controlled by the Conservatives but it was a Labour government, the first one ever, that was responsible for implementing its findings.

So, what happened next? There is a long and convoluted answer to that question but the simple one is 'not much'. Ranged against the committee's recommendations being implemented was a myriad of practical issues that had to be overcome. Here are few of them.

The proposal to raise the school-leaving age in 1933 coincided with a temporary peak in the number of 11–15 year olds. When the Board of Education reported in 1928[18] it estimated that it would require 350,000 extra school places to be created, but by 1937 the population of children had declined – meaning that the extra teachers and classrooms needed for the peak would quickly become redundant. This demographic problem was compounded by the cost of the reorganisation and in particular how it would be funded by voluntary schools (church schools). When the Board of Education reported in 1930[19] its first comments were about the difficulty 'if not impossibility' of voluntary schools making the necessary changes to implement Hadow's organisational changes. I have probably not stressed enough the role of the church in determining education policy, but the fact that in 1930 the Church of England was responsible for more elementary schools than local councils were gives some measure of its importance.

The perilous state of the economy and the need to reduce public expenditure was the other and most important barrier. This is how the British Library's *Learning Timeline*[20] describes the state of the economy, which we now call the 'Great Depression'.

Britain's world trade fell by half (1929–33), the output of heavy industry fell by a third, employment profits plunged in nearly all sectors. At the depth in summer 1932, registered unemployed numbered 3.5 million, and many more had only part-time employment.

Unsurprisingly, the education budget was not immune to the resulting spending cuts. In 1931 teachers' salaries were reduced by 10% and the free places in secondary schools were replaced by means-tested contributions.[21]

The final event that halted all the changes to the education system was WWII and the preceding period of political and economic uncertainty.

There are many similarities to the way that Fisher's proposals floundered at the point of implementation. It is easy, from the comfortable position of knowing how the future unfolds, to say that the barriers to achieving success were predictable. But they were. All of the demographic information about the temporary rise in pupil numbers was readily available, the near impossibility of voluntary schools' financing the new system of schooling was known, the perilous state of the economy and its fragility was known. We now have two examples of major educational proposals that appeared to be 'right', but failed to materialise.

The counter to my pessimistic explanation of the inevitability of failure is the view that 'if you want something enough you can make it happen'. That the difference between success and failure is determined by your priorities and willingness to confront and overcome entrenched attitudes. Had the political establishment *really* wanted to adopt the new system of schools and raise the school-leaving age, the money would have been found and the barriers overcome.

To my mind, the evolution of the education system resulted from a recurring cycle of grand visions of what was 'right', doing battle with reality and invariably coming off second-best. Naturally, the proponents of educational reform were focused on, if not obsessed with, achieving their goals. But, they were competing for economic resources and political support with others, who were equally focused on their special area of interest. When the Labour government was in power in 1929–1931, it faced an awesome list of challenges, with many groups – all with visions of what was 'right' – demanding more public spending. It would seem, from the following quote, that education was not the government's main priority.[22]

> *Education was not top of the Prime Minister's list of priorities –*
> *unemployment and the economic situation were more urgent.*

Yet another report about education policy

The next event that is relevant to the story of secondary moderns occurred during the mid to late 1930s, well into the final third of this part of the history timeline. This time the Consultative Committee to the Board of Education was researching and making its recommendations about *Secondary education with special reference to grammar schools and technical high schools.*

The committee's terms of reference were:

To consider and report upon the organisation and interrelation of schools, other than those administered under the Elementary Code [Elementary Schools], which provide education for pupils beyond the age of 11+; regard being had in particular to the framework and content of the education of pupils who do not remain at school beyond the age of about 16.

Like the Hadow Committee, these terms of reference were deemed to be limited and depending on your interpretation were 'expanded' or 'ignored':

It will be noted that it specifically excludes Modern Schools from our consideration. We have, however, found it impossible to discuss the problems with which we are immediately concerned without some reference to post-primary schools which are at present administered under the Elementary Code.

The committee was chaired by Will Spens, a distinguished academic and master of Corpus Christi College, Cambridge, and in keeping with tradition the report has become known as the Spens Report.[23]

Containing over 200,000 words, the committee's findings and recommendations resulted in a long and not that easy to read report. Brian Simon's discussion of the report referred to its chapters being written by different committee members. I suspect this is why the contents contained so much duplication and the merging together of tactical and strategic recommendations. One moment you were reading about the recommendation to raise the school-leaving age; the next you encountered proposals about the teaching of scripture, physical exercises and the appointment of careers masters. There was even a section about the 'Welsh Problems'.

Another explanation for the report's lack of clarity is found in its opening words, which explained that it was really a draft report and its recommendations should all contain the proviso 'yet to be agreed'. This exhibits all the characteristics of a report written by a committee.

> *To defer publication until the Board have reached a decision on the many issues raised would involve a delay in its presentation to the public which would be unacceptable to the educational world, and which the Board themselves would regard as undesirable.*

> *It will be understood therefore that in publishing the report forthwith, the Board must not be regarded as committed to acceptance of its conclusions and recommendations [my underlining].*

I am restricting my comments to those parts of the report that have a direct bearing on the story of secondary moderns, which means I have omitted many of the findings.

The other reason for my selective focus is that none of the recommendations were immediately implemented. The report was published in 1938, less than a year before the start of WWII, after which politicians and the electorate had more pressing things to think about.

We are now used to official reports costing many millions of pounds. The inquiry into the events of 'Bloody Sunday' cost £195 million, which made the Chilcot Report about the Iraq War seem a bargain at £13 million. The Spens Report was five years in the making and cost a mere £150,000 in 2017 pounds. This comparison has absolutely nothing whatsoever to do with secondary modern schools, but is an interesting reflection on the astronomic rise in the costs of official reports.

This quote from the report illustrates the committee's overall unhappiness with the way children were being educated:

> *An examination of the present position leaves us with the general impression that the existing arrangements for the whole-time higher education of boys and girls above the age of 11+ in England and Wales have ceased to correspond with the actual structure of modern society and with the economic facts of the situation.*

Secondary (grammar) school education was seen as focused on the small group of children, less than 15% of their pupils, who went on to university. The 'increasing complexity of the political, economic and social background of modern life and the rapid growth of knowledge' were perceived as making demands that the system of schooling could not meet. Sadly, these seem to be perennial concerns that are never alleviated, since you would probably find a variant of them in any editorial in today's media about education.

The following are the report's recommendations that have a direct bearing on my story of secondary modern schools.

The adoption of a minimum leaving age of 16 years may not be immediately attainable, but in our judgement, must even now be envisaged as inevitable.

Independent of the Spens Committee, an education act had been passed in 1936 that increased the school-leaving age to 15, but not until 1939. The committee wanted this age increased even further.

Not surprisingly, the start of WWII resulted in all changes to the leaving age being abandoned. You can see that even back in 1936 there was a desire to significantly increase the time children spent at school, but it would take over a quarter of a century before this recommendation of the committee was achieved (1972). As we will see, this long wait did not result in a better understanding of how this extra year of schooling would be used.

The committee wanted the existing junior technical schools and technical schools to be rebranded as technical high schools. Later in our history timeline we will encounter this type of school again. I had friends who attended these schools (William Morris and McEntee) and was always mystified about how their school related to grammars and secondary moderns. Reading how the report described them, I can see why I was confused.

We are convinced that it is of great importance to establish a new type of higher school of technical character quite distinct from the traditional academic Grammar School.

*As a first step to this end, we recommend that a number of existing
Junior Technical Schools orientated towards the engineering and
building industries and any other Technical Schools which may
develop training of such a character as (a) to provide a good intellectual discipline altogether apart from its technical value, and (b) to
have a technical value in relation not to one particular occupation
but to a group of occupations, should be converted into Technical
High Schools.*

The committee believed that the type of school that children should
attend, from the age of 11 to 16, should be determined by means of an exam.
All types of school should be 'accorded in every respect equality of status
with schools of the grammar school type'. Words about ensuring all types of
schools are awarded the same status and parity appeared throughout the
report; the terms 'equality of status' and 'parity of status' appeared a dozen
times.

Hadow had gone to great lengths to try and remove the distinction
between grammar and the other types of secondary school. The Spens
committee picked up where Hadow had left off and recommended that the
new technical high schools become part of the same system of secondary
education as grammar and modern schools. You can see the phrase 'attainment of parity' appears in this recommendation – something we will
encounter a lot in the next section of the timeline.

*We recommend that the three types of school should be conducted
under a new Code of Regulations for Secondary Schools, and we
have examined certain administrative consequences of this proposal.
We recommend the adoption of similar standards for the size of
classes, and for the planning and assessment of school buildings,
save in so far as differences of curriculum justify different requirements. We recognise also the desirability of a uniform minimum
leaving age for all secondary schools. Another measure which we
consider of vital concern to the attainment of parity of schools is the
framing of Establishments of Teaching Posts, in order that a
teacher's remuneration shall not be so dependent as it is at present
upon the particular type of school in which he is working.*

The most obvious difference between grammar and modern schools was that the former charged fees and the latter didn't. If there was to be a single system of secondary schools then this divide had to end and so the committee recommended that 'the conditions [referencing the charging of fees] which apply to Modern Schools should be extended to Grammar Schools and Technical High Schools as soon as the national finances permit'.

So far, I have described only the report's recommendations that were about the mechanics of how schools were organised. If the committee's vision was to become a reality it was also necessary to define the characteristics of children attending each type of school and how the selection process should work.

It was at this point that the clarity of the recommendations deteriorated. The committee was not satisfied with the conventional definition of grammar schools as 'training children to work with their heads rather than with their hands'. It believed that there was a better definition.

The phrase may be restated more aptly by contrasting work with the hands with work with tongue and pen. The Grammar Schools afford in general (although not for every child) the best training for professions which involve work with tongue and pen; and, so far as they can be differentiated from other schools by reference to the vocational training they afford, they are differentiated by this as well as by the related fact that they prepare for the Universities.

Personally, I don't think this new distinction of using 'tongue and pen' was much of an improvement on the 'working with their heads rather than with their hands' distinction. Both are so vague as to be meaningless.

Whatever it was that distinguished grammar school children, the committee believed it was capable of being measured by an exam. Professor Cyril Burt was involved with the committee and his input formed the basis of the section about 'The mental development of children between the ages of 11+ and 16+'. We will encounter this academic in the next section of our timeline.

*We believe that the examination is capable of selecting in a high
proportion of cases those pupils who quite certainly have so much
intelligence and intelligence of such a character that without doubt
they ought to receive a secondary education of the grammar school
type, and also those pupils who quite certainly would not benefit
from such an education.*

However, it was recognised that there would be children who were in
neither category and that the final choice of school for this group, in the
words of the report:

*Depend on qualities which no written examination can test; but we
make our recommendation the more readily since, even in regard to
examinable capacities, an examination, however devised, is far less
trustworthy as a means of placing in order of merit a middle group
than in determining whether particular candidates are definitely
above or are definitely below such a group.*

So far, the committee had said that it was possible to select children to
attend grammar schools by an exam at the age of 11-plus but did not explain
how the exam would be used to differentiate those who should attend a technical high school. Then it said for those children in the 'middle group' a
more personal form of selection process was required.

The committee then explained that there needed to be further flexibility
in the system because of selection errors and 'late developers'.

*Not only is there need for some means of correcting initial errors in
the classification of the children, but some means also of providing
for those pupils whose later development makes it clear that an
alternative form of secondary education would be better for them.*

*We received convincing evidence as to the various circumstances
which may arise to render a change of school desirable at a later
age than 11+. We consider it essential that there should be a regular
review of the distribution of pupils as between different schools,
preferably at about the age of 13.*

I can imagine the discussions that must have gone on among committee members at this point in their deliberations, along the lines of 'for children to successfully transfer between schools at the age of 13 means that all the schools must be teaching at the same level and with a common syllabus'. Countering this argument would be those saying 'that defeats the whole idea of having different types of schools'.

I think the committee 'fudged' the way it resolved this conflict in this recommendation.

An educational principle which we advocate on general grounds has an important bearing on the later transfer of pupils between those types of school which have an age range starting at 11+, namely, that the courses of study in all schools between the ages of 11 and 13 should not differ to any marked extent [my underlining].

As to the percentage of children attending each type of school, the committee decided that 15% would go to grammar schools. As far as I can see, this figure was determined by the availability of places rather than any other reason. The report went to great lengths to stress that more grammar school places were required.

Before leaving the deliberations of the committee it is important to consider a section at the report's beginning that was a recommendation not to do something. Before there is any discussion of the analysis and recommendations is a section about 'multilateral schools'.

Before reaching the conclusion that these schools must remain a separate type of school, we considered carefully the possibility of multilateral schools. We use the term 'multilateral' to describe a school which, by means of separate 'streams', would provide for all types of secondary education.

A multilateral school was the forerunner of what we now know as the comprehensive. It is clear that there was disagreement among the committee members about the role of these schools. After listing their advantages, the report concluded:

> *But in spite of these advantages we have reluctantly decided that we could not advocate as a general policy the substitution of such multilateral schools for separate schools of the existing types.*

It would have been fascinating to witness the discussions about the wording of this statement. The use of the phrase 'reluctantly decided' indicates the magnitude of the divisions that must have existed within the committee.

I will now outline the four reasons the committee decided not to propose multilateral schooling. It will be interesting to see if their concerns were justified when we reach that part of the timeline when comprehensives became the dominant type of school.

It was thought that the size of schools would need to increase to accommodate multiple streams of children and it was believed that 'the majority of pupils gain more from being in smaller schools'.

It was believed that if a secondary school was to support a 'grammar school stream' it needed a sixth form and that it would be difficult for multilateral schools to retain enough children beyond the age of 16. Even if multilateral schools did have sixth forms, they were expected to be smaller and unable to provide the variety of courses found in grammar schools.

The committee expected to propose significant changes to the curriculum in both modern and grammar schools and it doubted whether there were enough head teachers capable of managing the level of change, if the three types of school were combined into one. They believed that because the curriculum of grammar schools had 'long-established prestige' it might overly influence what was taught in modern schools.

An inability to prove that the high cost of establishing multilateral schools would have 'a substantial balance of advantage' was the final reason for dismissing the option not just at that point in time but as a 'goal of long-range policy'.

In what seems like a sop to the committee's supporters of multilateral schools, the report had some crumbs of consolation. It stated that in special circumstances the schools might be established.

We are, however, of opinion that some measure of experiment with multilateral schools may be desirable, especially in new areas; and also, that there is one set of circumstances in which multilateral schools ought almost certainly to be provided. These circumstances arise in districts where the Grammar School is too small either to give an adequate school life or to combine reasonable economy with the provision of an adequate staff.

WWII and its effect on children's education

In September 1939 Britain declared war on Germany and the research and recommendations contained in the Spens Report were put onto the shelf, but most certainly not forgotten.

We now enter the part of the timeline that I can relate to from personal experience. I wasn't born for another 10 years, but memories of the war were still raw in the minds of my parents and relatives, which meant I heard lots of harrowing stories about how it affected their lives. For five years the war had dominated their existence and their lives were turned upside down and inside out. Thankfully they all survived, physically unscathed, but it was an all-consuming period of their life.

In 1939 my dad was a sign-writer in East Ham, London; two years later he was in the Royal Navy on a destroyer guarding convoys to Malta; three years after that his boat had been sunk and he was a prisoner in Italy; and the final years of the war were spent disarming sea mines on the UK and French coast. My mum lived through two houses being destroyed by bombs, long periods staying with relatives living in Sussex and for six months not knowing if my dad was alive or dead. I am sure that my parents' experiences were no different from – and I expect a lot better than – countless other families'.

Their reminiscences were not all negative and were laced with amusing and moving stories, but during the years 1939–1945, I doubt if they thought of much else than surviving. As we are about to see, there was another section of society that was less affected by the war and who spent their time battling, not with guns and bombs, but by writing reports and attending committee meetings, discussing the post-war education system.

In recounting this period, I have made much use of Peter Gosden's book

Education in the Second World War,[24] supplemented with insights from Brian Simon's book *The politics of educational reform 1920–1940*.[25] Both historians believe that even in its early phases the war changed public attitudes towards education. Gosden said that:

> *The pressures in society for the reform, improvement and extension*
> *of the education system increased considerably as the war made ever*
> *deeper inroads into the lives of individuals.*

He substantiated this claim with articles from *The Times Educational Supplement* and a few quotes from education journals. I would have been more convinced by the argument if the quotations had been taken from the mainstream papers.

It has become the dominant narrative that the war unleashed forces that resulted in 'society' wanting radical change. Dent's book *Secondary Education for All*[26] contained the same argument. I am not so sure. My guess is that 'improvement and extension of the education system' was way down the list of 'society's' priorities, compared with the daily worry of your child's school being hit by a bomb. The circulation numbers for the three top-selling Sunday papers in 1939 were just over 8 million copies.[27] No data exists (that I could find) about readership of *The Times Educational Supplement*, but it would have numbered in the tens of thousands. Undoubtedly, part of 'society' was concerned about the shape of post-war education, but I doubt it was a very large part.

Whatever the rationale, the educational establishment was busy during the war creating plans for children's education, assuming of course that the war was won. As you might have detected from my comments, I was surprised (and a little annoyed) that throughout these harrowing years, so much effort was spent on debating how things would be after the war. This view was shared by the historian Correlli Barnett.[28]

> *While in 1940–1 Winston Churchill and the nation at large were*
> *fighting for sheer survival in the face of Nazi Germany's then victo-*
> *rious power, members of the British cultural élite had begun to busy*
> *themselves with design studies for a 'New Jerusalem' to be built in*
> *Britain after the war was won.*

I was tempted to relate the detailed chronology of this period, with the toing and froing of civil servants, politicians, churchmen and educationalists, in what seemed to be a constant stream of meetings and the writing and discussing of draft reports. Reading Gosden's account of the period kept reminding me of the political satire TV programme *Yes Minister*. Civil servants, members of the Board of Education and government ministers were engaged in a continual contest to influence the final draft of the report. Civil servants attempted to control those members of the educational establishment who had access to ministers; reports were written in secret, with ministers excluded from the distribution list; and junior civil servants attempted to jettison the Spens Committee's research and start afresh in their proposals about the structure of schooling. All the time, everybody was fearful that Winston Churchill would become aware of the extent of the post-war planning since he had banned any public discussion of the topic.[29]

Churchill reserved for the dinner table any speculation on the postwar world. In public his only stated goal was victory. Any public discussion of the postwar world would have invited the distractions and divisiveness of partisan politics.

While the country fights WWII, politicians and educationalists ponder education policy

The war-time government was a coalition, but there seemed to be a constant temptation to revert to party political position-taking. Putting aside the politics and power-brokering of this period and moving to its documentary output, there were two reports that affected the foundation of secondary modern schools. The first of these was *Education After the War* ('The Green Book').[30] Much of this seemed to be a regurgitation and extension of the Spens Report's findings. It contained little about the purpose and evaluation of schools or what and how pupils were taught, and much about the administrative procedures and processes of how schools were organised.

The report started by stating the magnitude of the task it is seeking to address and then gave itself legitimacy and authority by using a quote from Winston Churchill.

*When the war is won, as it surely will be, it must be one of our aims
to work to establish a state of society where the advantages and privileges, which hitherto have been enjoyed only by the few, shall be far
more widely shared by the men and youth of the nation.*

What the report did not state was the context of Churchill's speech. He
was addressing the pupils at his old public school (Harrow). When talking
about 'one of our aims', my guess is he meant the aims of the public school
boys, and not the committee members. Perhaps I am being a tad cynical, but
I recognise the ploy of using a quote from 'the boss' to give your work
'authority by association'. I often used the technique during my consultancy
career.

Having stated the report's lofty objective, the committee immediately
stated the limits of its work.

*It [the report] represents nothing more than their [the committee
members'] personal views of the directions in which the educational
system stands in need of reform and their suggestions as to ways in
which such reform might be effected.*

As I have already said, much of the report restated the recommendations
of the Spens Report. For completeness, I will list the 'proposals' that were
relevant to secondary moderns, which were referred to, at the time, as 'modern' schools.

Schooling should be divided into three parts. Infant and junior schooling
should end at the age of 11-plus, when pupils move to either a modern
school (leaving at the age of 15-plus), a grammar school (leaving age 16–
18) or a technical school (leaving age 15 or 16).

There should be a single code of regulations governing all three types of
secondary school. At the time, modern schools were treated as elementary
schools, whereas grammar and technical schools were part of 'higher education', having different regulations for the standards of accommodation, class
sizes etc.

Schooling should be free, irrespective of what type of school attended,
until the age of 16.

Attendance at the three different types of school should be decided on the basis of the 'child's school record, supplemented by suitable intelligence tests'. The committee was undecided about selection at the age of 11 and was tempted to increase it to 13. Gosden detailed the committee's debates on the subject. Eventually, it was the practicalities of adapting the existing infrastructure that tipped the argument and 11 became the proposed age, accompanied by many caveats about making a transfer between schools as easy as possible, including this seemingly impractical proposal:

> *To facilitate this interchange the content of the education for the age group 11–13 to be generally the same in all types of Secondary School.*

Surprisingly, the committee suggested that the day continuation schools, which had failed to be built following the Fisher Report, should become part of the education system for young persons up until the age of 18. These schools should provide a day a week of training for children leaving at the age of 15. I thought that Fisher's explanation of what this training would achieve had been vague, something that was repeated in this report.

> *It [the continuation school] must be a real entity with its own corporate life, recognised as in some sense a Community Centre for Youth or a Young People's College. It should have all the facilities necessary to enable all kinds of activities, recreative and cultural, including school societies and clubs, to be developed in and around it outside the actual hours of instruction. Workshops and other rooms should be kept open in the evenings for the benefit of pupils following technical or commercial courses.*

The subject of comprehensive schools (known then as multilateral schools) was absent from the final version of the report, although we know it featured prominently in the committee's discussions, as it had in the production of the Spens Report. My guess is that the political and practical objections that would have resulted from proposing their creation persuaded, possibly frightened, the committee into silence. Alternatively, maybe none of the committee members felt strongly enough about them to ensure they were included in the final report?

I have commented on only a small part of the report. Other topics covered included the huge constraints of implementing change when so many schools were owned and part-funded by the church; the recruitment, training and payment of teachers; the rationalisation of how local government managed schools; the mechanics of financing education; and how the education system could be better aligned with the needs of industry. It is easy to dismiss these as 'administrative issues', but they were very real obstacles to radically changing the country's system of schooling.

Three types of children require three types of school?

The report's authors must have hoped the optimism and desire for change that they thought would accompany the end of the war (assuming it was a victory) would help them recast how the country's children were educated. There were many similarities between these sentiments and those of Herbert Lewis, way back in 1917. Those responsible for the Green Book believed that the same transformation forces would be needed to change the exam system and the curriculum taught in schools. So, yet another committee was formed to study this subject; it began work in 1941 and reported in June 1943. Under the chairmanship of Sir Cyril Norwood the committee studied and made recommendations about 'The curriculum and examinations in secondary schools',[31] although as with all these reports, the authors paid scant attention to the terms of reference.

I wonder if Winston Churchill was aware of this committee's existence? Somebody who did know and sanctioned its work was R.A. Butler, who had just been appointed as president of the Board of Education and who is credited with, or accused of – depending on your viewpoint – giving birth to secondary modern schools.

As with the Green Book, the report began by declaring that the 'Board is not committed to acceptance of its conclusions and recommendations' but that the report provided a:

Valuable contribution from an independent source to the solution of the educational problems now engaging public attention.

Yet again, the concerns of the 'public' were proffered as the reason for the committee's work. Using a verbose style of writing, the report meandered on to explain that a wholesale re-evaluation of secondary education was needed, but then backtracked by saying care was needed not to 'change for the sake of change'. Again, memories of the dialogue from the TV programme *Yes Minister*.

Much of what the report contained had already been discussed by Spens and in the Green Book. It added a little more clarity and emphasis to some of the arguments and in places reached conclusions that contradicted the proposals in both previous reports. The potential usefulness of multilateral schools was resurrected, as was the need for a common curriculum in all types of secondary schools until the age of 13+. There was even the proposal that 'In suitable circumstances secondary schools of different types should be combined', although there was little clarity about what these 'circumstances' might be.

A central tenet of the Norwood Report was the assumption that there were three types of children, of sufficiently different characters, that warranted being educated in three types of secondary school. In making this argument the report used the term 'child-centred education', not just once but six times. To the best of my knowledge this was the first time it had appeared in any Board of Education report. I had to smile, given that it was used to substantiate the argument for creating what would become the tripartite system of education, since in the 1970s the term took on a very different meaning, as we will see.

The grammar school pupil was described as a child who was:

interested in learning for its own sake, who can grasp an argument or follow a piece of connected reasoning, who is interested in causes, whether on the level of human volition or in the material world, who cares to know how things came to be as well as how they are, who is sensitive to language as expression of thought, to a proof as a precise demonstration, to a series of experiments justifying a principle: he is interested in the relatedness of related things, in development, in structure, in a coherent body of knowledge.

This contrasted with the interests and abilities of the technical school pupil, which:

lie markedly in the field of applied science or applied art. The boy in this group has a strong interest in this direction and often the necessary qualities of mind to carry his interest through to make it his life work at whatever level of achievement. He often has an uncanny insight into the intricacies of mechanism whereas the subtleties of language construction are too delicate for him. To justify itself to his mind, knowledge must be capable of immediate application, and the knowledge and its application which most appeal to him are concerned with the control of material things.

Finally, the secondary modern pupil:

deals more easily with concrete things than with ideas. He may have much ability, but it will be in the realm of facts. He is interested in things as they are; he finds little attraction in the past or in the slow disentanglement of causes or movements. His mind must turn its knowledge or its curiosity to immediate test; and his test is essentially practical.

He may see clearly along one line of study or interest and outstrip his generally abler fellows in that line; but he often fails to relate his knowledge or skill to other branches of activity. Because he is interested only in the moment he may be incapable of a long series of connected steps; relevance to present concerns is the only way of awakening interest, abstractions mean little to him. Thus it follows that he must have immediate returns for his effort, and for the same reason his career is often in his mind.

I assume – and hope – that referring to pupils as boys or 'he' was a figure of speech and not intended to exclude girls.

These are three long extracts from the report but they are important for our understanding of the prevailing mindset, which believed it possible to characterise children by such vague definitions and then to specify the schools they attended. No evidence was provided to substantiate these definitions. A few months after the report's publication, Cyril Burt published a paper in the *Journal of Educational Psychology*[32] that, in a gentlemanly way, ripped Norwood's proposals to shreds. Burt is most often quoted as comparing Norwood's ideas to the psychologist's equivalent of phrenology (i.e. the surface of the head reveals a person's aptitudes and tendencies). He might have said Norwood's conclusions were the astrophysicist's equivalent to astrology.

Norwood wouldn't have been familiar with the concept of schemas but he would have known the term 'stereotype'. I very much doubt if he realised that he was using these to categorise children into three huge groups and then to postulate the schooling they should receive.

The difference between Norwood's and Burt's ideas about intelligence had a profound impact on the post-war education system, something we will return to in the next part of timeline.

Norwood proposed one final change to the education system that, if it had been implemented, would have had far-reaching implications. Instead of children taking a school-leaving exam that was set externally (by university examining bodies), it would become the responsibility of each school to decide the syllabus and how it was examined. That's equivalent to abandoning 'A' levels and asking teachers at the local secondary school to set the exam papers.

In the interest of the individual child and of the increased freedom and responsibility of the teaching profession change in the School Certificate Examination should be in the direction of making the examination entirely internal, that is to say, conducted by the teachers at the school on syllabuses and papers framed by themselves.

By the time the Norwood Report was published, all the possible building blocks of a new education system had been designed and debated. Extending the leaving age and providing free education had been proposed on numerous occasions. The notion that children should be selected on the basis of their teachers' opinions and an exam, at the age of 11 or 13, had been considered (many times). Stereotypes of what distinguished the pupils of one type of secondary school from another had been defined, as had the possibility of establishing multilateral schools.

So much talking – so little achieved

All of this war-time thinking and reporting about schooling did not amount to a proposed legislative plan, but a long list of ideas, many of them contradictory. A sort of 'thinking out loud' of the political and educational establishment. A heap of educational and administrative 'Lego blocks' that was on the table, waiting for somebody to put them together and then to convince the public and the political elite that what they created was an improved and workable way of educating the country's children. The newly appointed president of the Board of Education, Richard Austen Butler, better known as R.A. Butler, or Rab, was the man who embarked on this daunting task. The story of what happened next is told in the next section of our timeline.

But, before leaving this 30-year section of education history, I want to take stock of what had been achieved, as distinct from what the numerous Board of Education reports had proposed. Butler was about to recommend an entirely new education system, so it is important to understand the actual state of the schooling infrastructure on which it would be built.

These statistics come from the Board of Education reports for 1928[33] and 1938.[34] In 1938 the great majority of children (91%) were still being educated in elementary schools, which was little changed from the figure in 1927 (93%). Schools were still in the process of being reorganised along the lines proposed way back in 1926, in the Hadow Report. Progress had been slow and less than half of children were educated in junior and senior schools, with the majority receiving their education in 'all-age' school departments. Little had changed over the past decade in the proportion of teachers who were 'uncertificated'.

There had been a small increase in the number of 'free places' in secondary schools. In 1939 the percentage was 47%, compared with 40% in 1928.

Correlli Barnett's *The Audit of War* portrayed a depressing state of things in pre-war Britain.

*Of the 19,000 pupils who did complete a full secondary education to
age eighteen in 1937 [less than 1% of the total national age-group
14–18], only 8000 emerged with the Higher School Certificate, the
potential passport to university or other higher education; and just
over half of these actually got to university [approximately 0.2% of
the 14–18 age group].*

Local councils owned and operated about as many schools as the church,
yet only 30% of children in elementary schools were in church schools, a
figure that had changed little in the past decade. This meant that the average
council school was much larger than one operated by the church, many of
which were in rural areas. Moulding church- and council-owned schools
into a single entity had not advanced much since WWI.

Not a great deal had changed in the past 30 years, despite the numerous
Board of Education reports, the countless committee meetings and the
endless heated debates of educationalists and politicians.

The educational and political establishment's attitudes and ideas about
education had changed but that was not translated into a tangible level of
improvement in the infrastructure and organisation of schools and the educational outcome of pupils. The inertia of the education system with its
1,000,000s of pupils, 100,000s of teachers and 10,000s of schools takes time
and continual effort to change. I don't think it was because of incompetence
or lack of drive, but rather a woeful ignorance about the magnitude of what
was required to change the direction of the country's educational machine.
In today's parlance, the skill of 'managing change'. Let's not forget that for
much of the period the country's economy had been in a fragile state. This is
a poignant message that wasn't understood by the pre-war educationalists. I
wonder if their post-war peers did any better?

As we will soon see, things were complicated by the war-time destruction of the country's schools and the years of upheaval in the lives of
teachers and their pupils.

CHAPTER 6

BIRTH AND DEATH

L ike a pile of Lego blocks, the components and structures of the new education system were on the table awaiting assembly. Some of the blocks would be surplus, some would need to be finessed into place, but they were all there. Research and debate about the purpose and structure of secondary education had come to an end. But, before the assembly process could begin there were two significant structural barriers to overcome. We will get to these in a short while.

Past attempts to effect radical change in the education system had shown it to be somewhere between impossible and extremely difficult. Despite thousands of pages of reports and endless hours of discussion, the day-to-day reality of schooling had not changed that much since the end of WWI. Some would explain this as a conspiracy by the ruling class; others as the result of years of economic austerity. Whatever the reason, that is how it was. Then, on 1 September 1939, WWII started.

I want to start this part of the timeline by considering how the war damaged the country's education infrastructure and interfered with children's day-to-day schooling. It is important we understand the scale and scope of this disruption because after the war the country's education system was totally reorganised, the school-leaving age was raised and the majority of children became reliant on secondary modern schools for their education. This would be a challenge in the best of the times, but it was being done when the education system was recovering from the systemic damage inflicted by the war.

Gosden's book, *Education in the Second World War*,[1] documented the fascinating and harrowing tale of this period. It contains accounts of bravery, incompetence, hopeless bureaucracy and outstanding dedication. It is impossible to fully comprehend the extent of the damage resulting from the war and its lasting effect; all I can do here is detail the important events, provide some of the facts and ponder their consequences. This can only begin to convey the extent of the resulting turmoil.

The rush to evacuate

In early 1936 the Board of Education began to consider how to respond if war was declared. It was not starting with a blank sheet of paper, because plans had been produced two years before by another government department, detailing the practicalities of evacuating 3.5 million people from London. Military planners assumed the war would start with the widespread bombing of urban areas, so the number one concern was children's safety; the maintenance of their education was a secondary consideration. I am sure it wasn't expressed so bluntly, but that was the situation.

Detailed planning for the evacuation began in 1939. Officials walked a tightrope, managing the complex logistics of moving and resettling millions of children and their mothers and teachers, without creating a panic. It was decided that when war was declared all schools would be closed. In those parts of the country being evacuated, schools would remain shut throughout the hostilities. In areas designated as 'neutral', schools would reopen once their likelihood of being bombed had been evaluated. Schools in the 'reception' areas, where the evacuees were taken, would reopen as soon as possible, swollen by the influx of children from the towns.

That was the plan.

On 1 September 1939 war was declared and the evacuation of the major cities began. Approximately 1.5 million people – mainly mothers and children, but also teachers and escorts – were moved to the reception areas. Even more parents and their children, approximately 2 million, made their own arrangements and moved to safer areas of England and Wales. It wasn't until the end of the war that the government appreciated the magnitude of this unofficial movement of the population.[2] My mother and sister were part of this latter group and moved to stay with relatives in Sussex. Throughout the war they moved backwards and forwards to London as the intensity of the bombing ebbed and flowed.

Two weeks after the start of the official evacuation, the House of Commons had its first opportunity to discuss its successes and failures.[3]

The debate lasted for five hours. Not surprisingly, the MPs were anxious to praise teachers, parents and children for how well they had reacted to such a momentous event. But very quickly praise turned to criticism, especially about the organisation in the reception areas and the condition and behaviour of some of the children. The early part of the debate was dominated by the health and physical condition of the children evacuated from urban areas of Scotland. There were numerous accounts of the 'verminous' state of the children and their behaviour, especially related to their 'personal hygiene' – I will spare you the graphic details.

It's likely that this debate led to the view, which still persists, that the evacuation of urban children to rural areas was a universal tale of woe. Throughout the debate the word 'verminous' was repeatedly used (22 times), although in subsequent debates it was rarely mentioned. No doubt some of the anger resulted from the culture shock of families living in the reception areas, many of whom would have been middle class, coming face-to-face with the urban poor. This outburst of anger was probably the reason children being evacuated were then medically inspected and treated for contagious conditions – in particular, scabies. Compared with the other problems that quickly emerged, the physical and hygienic condition of the children soon seemed only a minor irritant.

The transport of children out of the urban areas worked as well as could be expected. Most of the problems, not surprisingly, occurred when they arrived in the reception areas. Only two weeks into the evacuation, the drift of parents and children back to their homes had begun. Our abiding image of the evacuation is of happy children, labels around their necks, waving from the windows of trains – which is typically what's shown when children today learn about the evacuation.[4] What is not shown is what happened when they arrived – the muddle and the difficulty of finding accommodation and keeping schools and families together.

Despite the periods of angry exchanges and finger-waving during the

Parliamentary debate, there was a realisation that the evacuation was an amazing logistics feat. I thought these closing comments captured the mood:

We are very strongly aware of the size of the problem we are facing, and of the necessity under which we shall be to rest ourselves closely upon the advice and the support of the House in dealing with it. As has been said, we are dealing not with mere statistics, but with individuals. It is not enough to say that we have in England moved 673,000 unaccompanied school children and 406,000 mothers and young children. Each of them is an individual problem.

The first defeat of the war

All these people were moved in four days, relying on word of mouth, the postal service and the primitive telephone network to make the arrangements. I think it was an amazing achievement, but ironically it was deemed to have failed because the bombing did not materialise. Of course, the absence of bombing was a good thing, but it presented the government with a horrible decision. All the schools in the evacuation areas were shut. Many were no longer schools – they had been requisitioned and were being used for other war-time activities.

What would become of children who returned home? If the government reopened the schools, it would be seen as encouraging the drift back to the towns. But if it left them closed it would deprive the 'returnees', and those who were never evacuated, of any schooling.

Gosden wrote that only about a third of London's school children were still in the reception areas in January 1940. In Sheffield and Coventry, the figure was even less (10%).

On 1 November 1939, just two months after the evacuation began, the decision was taken to reopen schools in all areas. The president of the Board of Education gave a speech in the House of Lords, where he admitted the government's mistake in assuming that bombing would start at the beginning of the war.[5] He had no option but to try and reopen schools in all areas of the country.

We do not feel that this [decision to re-open schools] should be taken as the all-clear signal. We have been influenced simply and solely by the fact that as a nation we simply cannot afford to let three-quarters of a million children grow up without education, school discipline or medical care.

It is ironic that Germany's first victory of the war resulted from its decision not to bomb the UK. Forcing the government to flip-flop its decisions, and the angst and inconvenience it created for millions of people, were all achieved at zero military cost to the enemy. As some small compensation, we can assume – let us say, hope – that this experience exposed some of the weaknesses in the evacuation's organisation. Gosden went to great length to explain the complicated and petty bureaucracy that was involved, especially the wrangles over deciding who paid for the children. The lines of authority to make, and then enforce, decisions were vague. Most of the power resided with the individual local authorities. The Board of Education made the policy and relied on the goodwill of others for its implementation. Not surprisingly, parents became increasingly suspicious of the need for and efficiency of the evacuation operation.

It was a year after the evacuation by the time the bombing of large urban, industrial and military areas began. During the year of the evacuation there were 100 metric tons of bombs dropped on the UK; the following year the total was 35,000.

From then on, the movement of children followed the path of the war. Concerns about the major towns being bombed soon became the fear that coastal towns would be invaded. Then the threat moved back to large urban areas, mainly London, with the advent of the V1 and V2 flying bombs. Finally, the focus switched to historic towns such as Bath, Norwich, York and Canterbury, in what became known as the 'Baedeker raids' (named after the travel guides).

The education infrastructure suffers a deep and lasting trauma

There must have been a constant flow of children coming and going from their homes (and schools). It must have been a logistical nightmare trying to provide anything like a normal education for these war-time children.

There is little data about the national levels of school attendance during the war. We have the figures for schools in the London County Council area – what we now call Inner London. The following graphic shows the attendance percentage from 1942 until the end of the war. Surprisingly, it's over 80% for much of the time. It would have been useful to know the figures for the period 1939–1942, when I would guess the attendance levels would have been much lower.

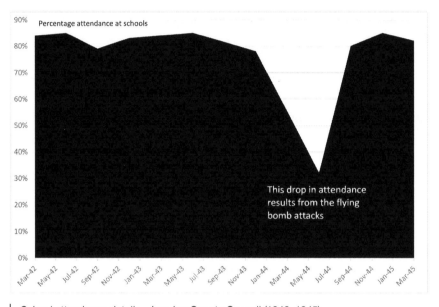

School attendance details – London County Council (1942–1945)

What these numbers don't convey is the disruption that must have accompanied the shortage of classrooms and books and the coming and going of children and teachers. This was Gosden's view about the impact:

The actual work of teaching was gravely handicapped by instability of rolls, loss of premises, changes of staff and the comings and goings from reception areas. At one typical London school with a highest roll at any one stage of 350, nearly 1,000 names were entered on the admission register in the course of two years and individual pupils had been on and off the roll as many as four or five times.

These words from Harold Dent, the editor of *The Times Educational Supplement*, expressed the enormity of problem.[6]

The evacuation of school-children which began on September 1, 1939, threw the English educational system into the worst disorder it had ever known. For weeks – months even – it was in a state of near chaos.

There has been much speculation about the social effects of the evacuation on the shape of the post-war education system. Roy Lowe suggested the evacuation brought together two sections of society that rarely met, and the resulting trauma influenced the final shape of the education system:[7]

The town children who appeared suddenly in the rural areas awoke fears that had been prevalent in the early Twentieth Century of an urban society in decay. The new middle classes turned to social welfare and a revitalized education system which kept the social classes apart. It is not too far fetched to see some linkage between the tripartite system which was introduced at secondary level after 1945 and the experience of evacuation during the early months of the War. One key effect of evacuation may have been to lessen the chances of a genuinely radical reconstruction of the education system.

I think the trials and tribulations of the evacuation might well have resulted in another enduring change in behaviour. For a moment, I am going to assume the role of the armchair sociologist. From the perspective of those being evacuated, the authorities had failed. Families had been told their children were threatened but the absence of bombing proved that to be wrong. Families in the reception areas were asked to make huge changes to their lives for a threat that didn't materialise. After the national adrenalin-rush had subsided, following the news that 'war has been declared', it must have been replaced by anger and resentment on all sides. As always, the finger of blame would have been pointed at those making the decisions – the 'authorities'.

I am sure a lasting result of this period was a lessening in trust and respect for the political and administrative establishment. Had the Germans done as expected and in September 1939 rained bombs onto London, Liverpool and Glasgow, the outcome would have been very different. The authorities would have been lauded for their astute planning and the sight of cities burning and human carnage would have generated a surge in national solidarity that would have subsumed the niggles about poor administration and dubious personal hygiene conditions – at least for a while. But that is not what happened.

There can be little doubt that there was an aggregate change in social attitudes as a result of the government's attempts and perceived failure to manage the movement of children and mothers and their rehousing and schooling. What it was, how long it lasted and what its impact was on postwar education are impossible to know (in my opinion). But there can be no doubt that the war had a detrimental effect on the cohort of children being educated between 1939 and 1945, who would soon become the first generation to experience the tripartite system of schooling.

The bombing, when it did come, was indiscriminate and so schools were damaged and destroyed. The Imperial War Museum's commentary about this period estimates that 20% of schools sustained some form of damage.[8] Gosden provided detailed data about the level of damage incurred until the end of September 1942. He didn't detail its source but I expect it was Titmuss's *Problems of Social Policy*, which is the most authoritative account of the social disruption caused by the war. By September 1943 over 4,000 school buildings had been destroyed or damaged. These statistics would have increased after the flying bomb attacks on London and Southern England in 1944.

Another way of presenting these statistics is that approximately 95% of schools suffered no serious damage during the war. I don't know why, but this number surprised me. I expected the level of damage to have been much worse, although I had no evidence to support that view. However, this doesn't mean that the damage was minor. By the end of the war, in London alone, 218 schools and other educational institutions were unusable (total loss or extensive damage). Just imagine the outcry and disruption today, if we were to remove this number of schools from London.

Two factors exacerbated the loss of schools to war damage. First, many schools had been requisitioned at the outset of the war. As we know, in the evacuation areas – London and other large cities – the plans had been to close schools for the duration of the war. Not surprisingly, they were put to other uses, such as emergency accommodation and first aid centres. So, in the areas most damaged by bombing, the inventory of available schools was also the most reduced by requisitioning.

Second, when schools were damaged, they ranked low on the priority list of buildings to be repaired. Ensuring that families had basic accommodation was the government's primary concern. Shortages of labour and building materials also forced some unpalatable decisions to be made. Gosden explained that:

> *[Following the flying bomb attacks in 1944] local education authorities within twenty-five miles of Charing Cross were told at the beginning of October that schools could only be made weatherproof and habitable; all further repairs were to be postponed.*

Winning the war didn't mark an end to the shortages. The Board of Education report *Education in 1947*[9] explained that 'little building construction of a permanent nature could be undertaken in the immediate post-war years'. It went on to say that in 1946 the amount of new school building work that had been agreed was just over £100 million, in today's pounds. To put this into context, in 2015–2016 the capital spending by the Department of Education was £5,000 million.[10]

Things did improve in 1947, when the agreed expenditure increased to just over £800 million in today's pounds. It is important to remember that there would be years of delay between the 'agreed' expenditure and the delivery of new classrooms.

We have seen how the war led to disruption in children's education and damage to buildings. To complete the story, we need to understand its effect on the teaching profession.

When children were evacuated, they were accompanied by their teachers. Parents made their own decisions about whether their children stayed or returned home. Teachers did not have the same freedom to decide. They were directed by the authorities. Not surprisingly, the link between the location of pupils and their teachers was soon broken. As Gosden commented:

These [war-time] conditions also produced a maldistribution of teachers between different parts of the country and even between different schools in the same area.

It wasn't long before accusations were being made that teachers in the reception areas were under-employed because their pupils had gone back home to the cities.

The numbers of children in local authority primary and secondary schools continued to decline throughout the war years, falling by 575,000 between 1938 and 1946. This must have helped the countrywide ratio of teachers to pupils to remain little changed, although there were wide variations throughout the country, as is shown by these numbers. In my birth place (Walthamstow), the ratio was 1:24 – the same as much of North East London. At the same time Bexhill had a ratio 1:96, Portsmouth 1:43 and Newcastle 1:42. No doubt these statistics changed rapidly, with the ebb and flow of movement of children, but they illustrate the pressure teachers must have been under in attempting to provide anything like a normal education. Optimising the use of teachers was impossible, because their pupils moved about, outside their control.

This situation was complex enough, but it was compounded by the call-up of male teachers for war-time duties. When the war started male teachers younger than 25 (known as the 'reservation age') could be drafted. By mid-1940, the deteriorating military position increased the demand for military manpower and the reservation age was raised to 30, then in July 1941 it was increased to 35, with a proposal to remove the age limit in October of that year.

It is estimated that about a quarter of teachers left the profession to join the services or did other types of war-time duties. Their replacements were either retired teachers or married women. It is hard now to believe that before the war women were expected to abandon teaching on marrying. Even though there were dire shortages of teachers, local education authorities were reluctant to use this pool of experienced women. Some authorities flatly refused the idea of employing married women even on a part-time basis.

This was Gosden's account of the situation in 1943.

There were no reserves left even to replace sick teachers. The overall composition of the teaching body and the stress of wartime combined to produce a rate of absence from duties much higher than normal. Apart from teachers, the efficient operation of the schools was threatened by the desperate shortages of the different grades of non-teaching staff whose services were essential [cleaning staff, care-takers and other ancillary staff].

As I wrote this account of the war's effect on the education system, two thoughts kept going through my head. The first was admiration for all those who attempted to deliver a resemblance of normal schooling for the country's children. The usual rules of running schools had rapidly dissolved, with decisions being made on a day-by-day basis. Any form of intermediate, let alone long-term, planning was impossible. It is so easy to criticise individual decisions and the intransigence and inflexibility of parts of the system. But, somehow, against the odds, children received an education throughout the war.

The second thought was what an awful mess the education infrastructure must have been in at the end of the war. Some children's education was probably untouched by the war; others would have lost five years of schooling. It is meaningless talking about how the 'average' level of school work changed. When peace came, this cohort of children must have presented immense difficulties for teachers. We can only guess at the trauma suffered by some children.

Before the war the supply of new schools and the adaptation of the old physical infrastructure had been constrained by long periods of austerity. German bombs then destroyed and damaged a sizeable number of schools, which would have to wait to be repaired. On top of that, the number of teachers had been depleted and the damaged and requisitioned teacher training colleges would be slow to supply their replacements.

The thought of trying to quantify these numerous problems, let alone fix them, makes me shudder.

These words from the Chief Inspector of Education, when talking about London, make a fitting end to this section:[11]

The shock of war and evacuation has been heavy on London schools that were broken up and rapidly lost their identity. Reorganisation and even merging with local schools have been continuous; changes of staff and re-evacuation have been made continuity of work and syllabuses practically impossible. There are frequent changes of head teachers and assistant staff as more teachers return and new schools are opened. It should be remembered that these children have spent the whole of their senior school years and part of their junior school years in such conditions. Nearly half of their school life, in fact, has been spent in improvised and often unsatisfactory conditions.

Butler and his Education Act

Somebody who had to confront these problems was the president of the Board of Education, R.A. Butler, who we briefly encountered in the first part of the timeline. His four years in charge of education, first as president of the Board of Education and then as minster for education, resulted in the type of school I attended. Was his vision of a better education system, what I experienced in 1961? We will soon find out.

There are numerous books dedicated to explaining, denigrating and exalting what Butler did to the education system. All books about education history will contain a meaty chapter or two dedicated to his work. In writing about this period, I used some of these sources, but mainly relied on his official biography, written by Anthony Howard, titled *RAB: The life of Butler*.[12]

Authors of books about education are bound to have their views affected by their instinctive use of mental shortcuts and attitudes/experience. This is not a criticism; it is simply a fact, as I hope I illustrated in Chapter 1 ('The truth is what we want it to be'), where I called them heuristics and personal schemas. No doubt Howard had his own biases, but he was not an educationalist, unlike most of the other authors, and was not judging Butler's actions against a preconceived set of educational rights and wrongs.

Also, Howard had direct contact with Butler and access to his papers. Butler's wife continued to support Howard's work after her husband's death, three years after he commissioned the book. The other thing that attracted me to Howard's account was that he came from a different part of the political spectrum from Butler, something that surprised him when he was asked to write the book.

> *He was under no illusion that I was a supporter of, or even a sympa-*
> *thiser with, the Conservative Party: he had, in fact, as he confirmed*
> *to* The Times, *deliberately chosen to make 'an unorthodox choice'.*
> *Elsewhere it was undoubtedly seen as an eccentric one.*

All of the quotations about Butler are taken from this biography unless a different source is stated.

In the first part of the timeline we encountered Butler after he had recently become president of the Board of Education. I think it is worth relating Howard's account of how Churchill described Butler's role, because it illustrates some of the problems he would later encounter.

Folklore has it that Churchill's vision of the job was, figuratively speaking, about 'wiping babies' bottoms'. The context of the bottom-wiping remains a mystery, but I assume it implied the job was, in consultant-speak, more 'tactical than strategic'. Anyway, Howard denied there was any truth in the phrase being used. This was his account of how Churchill explained the role.

> *'You will move poor children from here to there' – and he lifted up*
> *imaginary children from one side of his writing pad to the other –*
> *'and this will be very difficult.' Then he said, 'I am too old now to*
> *think you can improve people's natures.' He looked at me pityingly*
> *and said, 'I think everyone has to learn to defend themselves. I*
> *should not object if you could introduce a note of patriotism into the*
> *schools.'*

To my mind, this job specification is not that much better than the one involving babies' personal hygiene; however, it is clear that Churchill thought Butler would be fully occupied trying to provide war-time Britain with a semblance of normal schooling. Now that we know the raft of problems the war was causing, it is easy to understand his attitude.

I am sure Butler's preparatory reading must have included the Spens Report and the 'Green Book', and no doubt he was one of the first to read the Norwood Report when it was published. What he thought about their contents was not related. According to Howard's account, Butler didn't appear to be overly concerned with the mechanics of schooling. His main preoccupation was 'what to do about the church'.

I have already outlined the role the church played in the country's education system. Before going any further, it is worth reminding ourselves of its importance – especially its ability to thwart major change.

In 1938, half the buildings of public elementary schools were provided by councils; the other half were called 'voluntary' schools and run by various religious denominations. Despite owning the same number of schools as councils, voluntary schools educated far fewer pupils – just 30% of the total. Many of their buildings were in rural areas; they tended to be small schools and were sometimes operated by a single teacher.

The voluntary sector was dominated by the Church of England, which owned 85% of the schools and educated 73% of the children, followed by the Roman Catholic Church with 12% of the schools and educating 24% of the children.[13]

These statistics only tell part of the story. There was a stark difference in the quality of church- and council-owned schools, as was related by Howard.

In terms of modern facilities, the 1¼ million children in Church schools were getting a much worse deal than the 3 million in State schools – their buildings were older, their classrooms more antiquated, their amenities (all the way to schoolyards in place of recreational facilities) in every way inferior.

Churches didn't have the funds to modernise their schools, but they had the power to hamper radical reform of the education system. They didn't have a common voice or set of objectives, but each denomination was ultra-sensitive and ultra-competitive. Like all powerful institutions, they would fight against anything that diluted their influence. For these reasons, making changes to the dual system of education, as this split between church and state was called, was certain to result in a major battle.

Less than two months into his new job, Butler sent a note to Churchill outlining the three 'questions' he believed the Board of Education needed to address.

> *There is, first, the need for industrial and technical training and the linking up of schools closely with employment. Secondly, a settlement with the Churches about Church schools and religious instruction in schools. Both these questions are nationwide. Thirdly, there is the question of the public schools, which may easily raise widespread controversy.*

It is clear from Churchill's response that he was unhappy, to put it mildly, with Butler's suggestion.

> *It would be the greatest mistake to raise the 1902 controversy during the war [the 1902 Education Act resulted in prolonged arguments about the involvement of the church in state education]. I think it would also be a great mistake to stir up the public schools question at the present time. No one can possibly tell what the financial and economic state of the country will be when the war is over. Your main task at present is to get the schools working as well as possible under all the difficulties of air attack, evacuation etc.*

Churchill's only positive response was about the suggestion to improve technical and industrial training. He specifically ruled out the idea of a new education bill.

Butler couldn't have been surprised by Churchill's response. I am amazed that he sent the letter. The war was going badly. The bombing of Pearl Harbor had yet to happen, so America was still neutral and, in Russia, Leningrad and Kiev were under siege. The Board of Education was under pressure, because of the perceived failure of the evacuee programme as well as the host of other practical war-time difficulties. Butler's brief was to ensure that the mechanics of education kept working – not to try and resolve long-running and contentious issues.

So far, I have said nothing about 'the question of the public schools', as Butler referred to it in his letter. This was intentional. Their role, how they operated and their very existence had long been controversial (and still are).

My reason for ignoring them was that I didn't see much of a connection between their story and that of secondary moderns. It was clear from his note to Churchill that Butler perceived them as important and a 'question' to be resolved and so I now need to explain why. The existence of these schools was a bone of contention that raised issues that were interwoven with class and political prejudices – little has changed in 2021. The question of the churches was all about the practical implications of their ownership and control of so many schools. The question about public schools was all about their exclusiveness, based on the ability of parents to buy their services and their importance as the educator of the ruling elite.

The term 'public school' is confusing. I much prefer to call them 'private schools', because that is what they are. Schools where an education can be purchased. Ironically, R.H. Tawney provided an excellent source of information about the different types of private school in his pamphlet *The problem of the public schools*.[14] We first encountered Tawney in the first part of the timeline as the author of *Secondary Education for all*, which became the core of the Labour Party's education policy, and as a member of the Hadow Committee. This table, taken from his pamphlet, explains how the characteristics of these 160 schools varied by the fees they charged.

Annual school fees	Number	Not receiving grant (%)	Boarders (%)	Pupil numbers
£9,500 and over	37	92%	93%	15,191
£6,500 - £9,500	53	51%	58%	17,049
Less than £6,500	70	6%	8%	35,216

The number and characteristics of public schools in England in 1938. Fees are in today's pounds

Tawney went to great lengths to explain that there were many types of private school. Those charging the lowest fees were mainly day schools and already under some degree of control from the government because of the grants they received. They were very similar to the fee-paying secondary schools.

It was the most expensive schools that were the focus of Tawney's attention and criticism. He believed they were the enclave of the wealthy, where their children were educated in isolation from society and other parts of the education system. At the beginning of the war approximately 80% of students at Oxbridge were from private schools.[15] Above all, they were outside the control of the state, as were half of the schools charging slightly lower fees. Numerically they represented a minuscule part of the country's schools and pupils. Tawney was well aware of the criticism of 'why are you so bothered by such a small number of schools?' This was his response:

They form, it will be observed, less than half the total number of public schools in England; but their example has an influence on the social outlook and the educational methods of schools outside their own ranks.

Anybody who has experience of today's private education world might wonder if I have made a typing error with the costs in the school fees column of the table. I haven't. The most expensive private school in 1938 charged annual fees of £16,000 (in today's pounds) for a pupil who was boarding. Today, the cost would be approximately two to three times more expensive. The reasons for this cost inflation are not something I want to consider, other than to observe that these schools are even more exclusive in 2021 than they were in 1938.

The idea that money could purchase a better education was anathema to those in the Labour Party and to some members of other political parties. Interestingly, Howard wrote that the problem of church schools was of less importance to Labour politicians than private education. This was his view of Butler's attitudes to private education:

Never a worshipper at the public school, Butler was quite enough of a rationalist to see the advantages of ending 'the great divide' in British education, against which respected socialist academics like R. H. Tawney had inveighed for years.

Butler failed to win a scholarship to Eton, refused to go to Harrow and instead went to Marlborough College – all of these are private schools. We know that at least two of his sons went to Eton. Where his other son and daughter were educated is unclear. Howard suggested that Butler had an 'agnostic' attitude to private schools. Clearly, his attitude didn't influence his decision about the type of school attended by his own children.

What Butler did know, because the Board of Education had researched the subject, was that a significant number of private schools were having financial problems. Tawney was also aware of the problem and the reasons for it.

The fall in the birth-rate has hit some of them [private schools] hard. The improvement, both in quality and quantity, of public secondary education has exposed them to keener competition. War taxation has cut into family resources, which might in other circumstances, have been spent on education.

Rather than make any pronouncements about answering the 'question', Butler adopted the age-old politicians' strategy of 'kicking the can down the road' and appointing a committee to research the subject and make recommendations. Two years later the Fleming Report, named after its chairman, was published. Much had changed by this time, including the improved financial state of private schools.

The report's content didn't seem to satisfy anybody – certainly not Butler's biographer:

It has to be conceded that Butler's handling of the public school's question represented the one real failure in his general strategy for educational reconstruction. The time was ripe, the public mood was propitious, the opportunity was there. And yet he contrived to throw it all away. Why?

Howard answered his own question. He believed Butler decided that solving the 'church question' was of primary importance and would require all his energies. Maybe Butler was observing the faltering German military strategy of fighting multiple battles at once (i.e. on the fronts in Europe and Russia). One decisive victory is a much better outcome than two defeats. Three-quarters of a century later the private school 'question' is still on the table, unanswered. I think Butler made a very shrewd judgement.

Like Butler, I am going to remain 'agnostic' about private schools. I couldn't find any causal link between them and secondary moderns. I thought that gaining an understanding of why they caused such consternation was important, because many of the same arguments would also be employed against grammar schools and their fate is most certainly related to secondary moderns.

If you read the story of Butler's tortuous negotiations with the Roman Catholics and the Church of England you realise why he needed all his energies to win that battle. Perhaps I should say 'reach a settlement'. I am not going to summarise what happened. It is not relevant to my story and I doubt if I would do the saga justice.

Fast forward to early March 1943: progress had been made with the churches and Butler was invited to dinner and stay overnight with Churchill. At this stage in the war the prime minister was allowing himself to think about post-war affairs and Butler was in a position to provide him with ideas. News about the war was not all good, but in Russia the battle of Stalingrad had ended with the surrender of the German 6th army, Allied forces were advancing further into Tunisia and had retaken Libya and the bombing of the factories in the Ruhr had begun. It must have been possible to think beyond the coalition and the political truce, to the time when politics would return to 'normal'.

During the meal Churchill said that he believed that Germany would be defeated in 1944, giving plenty of time for the government to announce its post-war plans. Despite this apparent lack of urgency Butler declared his intentions:

'I am drafting an Education Bill.' To this the only response was an essentially non-committal injunction to make sure that the plans were shown to the Prime Minister when they were ready – accompanied by the slightly condescending observation that he had no doubt they would be 'very interesting'.

Not exactly a resounding statement of support, but more encouraging words than before. Ten days later, Churchill made a radio broadcast and talked about 'the question of education'.[16] Today's political commentators would criticise the address for being 'short on specifics'. Twice he mentioned 'religion', as the 'rock in the life and character of the British people' and how we had been 'pioneers of religious toleration'. His third time of mentioning must have pleased Butler:

I rejoice to learn of enormous progress that is being made among all religious bodies in freeing themselves from sectarian jealousies and feuds while preserving fervently the tenets of their own faith.

In Churchill's indomitable way he concluded his address with a warning.

I must warn every one who hears me of a certain, shall I say unseem- liness, and also of a danger of its appearing to the world that we here in Britain are diverting our attention to a peace which is still remote and to the fruits of a victory which have yet to be won.

Four months after Butler dined with Churchill, the war-time Cabinet approved Butler's white paper on *Educational Reconstruction*.[17] There was only a single modification to the text. Originally the timescale said the proposals would not be introduced 'until the end of the war in Europe'. The chancellor of the Exchequer, like all chancellors, ever conscious of public finances, requested the word 'Europe' be deleted. Three days later Butler presented his white paper to Parliament. Since the MPs had little time to read the paper, it was a short debate, but he was asked one interesting question that I thought he brilliantly avoided answering. The question regarded the various religious bodies he had consulted in preparing the paper: 'I would ask him whether he got a fair measure of agreement after meeting them.' Butler responded:

I would like to phrase it like this, that there is a wider measure of agreement than has ever been obtained before, and I think that that is so far very satisfactory.

To my mind, the white paper was a 'cut-and-paste' of the various reports we encountered in the first part of this timeline. Mention was made of increasing compulsory school attendance to 15 and then 16 'when circum- stances permit'. Schooling would be divided into three stages (primary, secondary and further education). Secondary education would be in one of three types of school (grammar, secondary or technical). No direct mention was made of multilateral schools, but:

Different types [of school] may be combined in one building or on one site as considerations of convenience and efficiency may suggest. In any case the free interchange of pupils from one type of education to another must be facilitated.

The description of how children would be selected for the appropriate secondary school was almost word-for-word what appeared in earlier reports.

Children at the age of about 11 should be classified, not on the results of a competitive test, but on an assessment of their individual aptitudes largely by such means as school records, supplemented, if necessary, by intelligence tests, due regard being had to their parents' wishes and the careers they have in mind.

At the age of 13, or even later, there will be facilities for transfer to a different type of education, if the original choice proves to have been unsuitable. The keynote of the new system will be that the child is the centre of education and that, so far as is humanly possible, all children should receive the type of education for which they are best adapted.

There was one statement in the white paper that I hadn't encountered before that made me smile. This related to the secondary school (i.e. what would become the secondary modern).

Lacking the traditions and privileged position of the older grammar school they have less temptation to be 'at ease in Zion' [I interpret this as being complacent]. Their future is their own to make, and it is a future full of promise. They offer a general education for life, closely related to the interests and environment of the pupils and of a wide range embracing the literary as well as the practical, e.g. agricultural, sides.

Another way of phrasing this statement would be that secondary moderns would not have the benefits of the long-established structure of the grammar schools and that they would have to decide their own future because nobody else was going to do it. Maybe I am being a tad cynical – we will see.

Since the war began there hadn't been any new thinking or refinement about the structure of the education system. The educational and political establishment's energy had been consumed with the difficulties caused by the war and finding a solution to the 'question' of the church and its schools.

On 29 July there was another Parliamentary debate.[18] Butler started by comparing the state of the education system with a schoolboy's jacket. Since 98% of the MPs were men,[19] it was an apt analogy that would resonate with his audience; it was also beautifully worded.

It [the education system] has done wonderful service, and much maternal care has been lavished upon it, but there are certain signs that it is becoming out of date. The sleeves are running far up the arm. The tell-tale let-down of material will barely cover the expanse of anatomy allotted to it. Stains, rents, patches and tears appear in various parts, and the shine on the nap makes one reflect on the need for change.

The debate was long (the transcript is over 40,000 words) and at times fractious. Assuming that the frequency of use of certain words is an indicator of the MPs' interests, then a word-count provides some revealing results. The words 'religion' and 'religious' appeared 70 times; 'grammar schools' 14 times and 'modern schools' just twice. Clearly, the role of the church was deemed far more important than the plans for reorganising the structure of schooling.

Following this debate, there was swift progress in transforming the white paper into the draft of the new education act and in the middle of December 1943 the Education Bill was published. It was now set for its journey through the legislative machinery of the House of Commons and the House of Lords.

All went well until the end of March 1944 when the clause concerning teachers' salaries was debated. A Conservative MP wanted this to be amended to ensure that pay would be, in modern parlance, 'gender-neutral' (i.e. men and women were to be paid the same). As I wrote these words the news was dominated by the story that the BBC pays its male broadcasters more than its female ones. And we like to think that we now live in enlightened times.

The amendment was passed by a majority of one. For the first time the national government was defeated. This event had repercussions far wider than Butler's Education Act. At the next Cabinet meeting the prime minister explained:[20]

That the Government were committed to formidable military operations in the near future. This incident [losing the vote] might well have a most damaging effect on opinion abroad, and it was essential that prompt measures should be taken to make it clear beyond any doubt that the Government had the full support of Parliament. The great majority of members were with the Government, and, if the issue was treated as a major one of confidence, he was sure that the effect would be salutary.

To the best of my knowledge this is the first and only time that a dispute over teacher salaries has been portrayed as an issue of national importance.

Clearly, neither the Labour nor Conservative hierarchy wanted the national government to fail (at this point) and for Butler's Act to be amended. Within a couple of days, the equal pay amendment was overturned. From then on, the process went without surprises and delays and on 3 August 1944 the Education Act became law.

What the Butler Act did (and did not) contain

After many thousands of words, we have reached the point that is generally thought to mark the birth of secondary modern schools. Starting way back at the end of WWI, with the publication of the Lewis Report, there has been a steady stream of events that contributed to the passing of the 1944 Education Act. Throughout this period the trajectory of the reformers' social and educational ideals has been misaligned with the practical capacity for them to be fulfilled. Before discovering if this Education Act was to suffer the same fate, we need to understand what the legislation contained and, just as important, what it didn't.

It covered numerous facets of the education system and was composed of about 50,000 words of densely written legislative text. You could argue that all parts of the document, in some way or another, relate to secondary modern schools. I know that by only commenting on the sections that I think are directly relevant to these schools I run the risk of biasing the story. For the sake of brevity, I will take the risk.

From the perspective of providing a coherent structure to educate the country's children the Act clarified the chain of command about 'who does what' and 'who is responsible for what'. A lack of structure had bedevilled previous education initiatives. Gone were the Board of Education and its president. From now on there would be a minister, presiding over a Ministry of Education, with a duty to:

Promote the education of the people of England and Wales and the progressive development of institutions devoted to that purpose, and to secure the effective execution by local authorities, under his control and direction, of the national policy for providing a varied and comprehensive educational service in every area.

Implementation of the 'statutory system of education' was the responsibility of 146 local education authorities (LEAs) in England and Wales. The 'system' was defined as being:

Organised in three progressive stages to be known as primary education, secondary education, and further education.

The LEAs were obliged to provide children with a free education that would:

Contribute towards the spiritual, moral, mental, and physical development of the community by securing that efficient education throughout those stages shall be available to meet the needs of the population of their area.

[The education they provided would be] Sufficient in number, character, and equipment to afford for all pupils opportunities for educa-

tion offering such variety of instruction and training as may be
desirable in view of their different ages, abilities, and aptitudes.

Every LEA would appoint a chief education officer, who would produce, within a year (by 1 April 1946), a development plan for the schools in its area. This would be evaluated by the Ministry of Education and, once it was approved, a 'local education order' would be issued that specified those schools the LEA was required to maintain. Proposals for opening or closing schools, or for changing their status, would need to be submitted to the minister, who was also responsible for defining the standards of the school premises. Control of appointing teachers was under the LEA's responsibility, as was the school's curriculum.

The Act defined the 'compulsory school age' as between five and 15 years, 'with the hope that, as soon as it became practicable, the upper limit would be raised to sixteen'. Within weeks of the Act becoming law, the date for implementing the extension of the leaving age was delayed by two years until 1 April 1947. As we will see, the problems of insufficient accommodation and teachers made the achievement of this new date extremely difficult. It seems certain that the words in the Act about extending the age to 16 were there for political purposes with no intent, or hope, that they would become a reality. It would be another 28 years before the leaving age was increased to 16, in 1972.

There was a section of the Act devoted to providing 'further education' for children once they left school. LEAs were supposed to establish 'county colleges' that would provide one day a month 'cultural' and 'recreative' activities for under-18s. This idea was never implemented when it was first proposed in the Lewis Report, way back in 1917, and it fared no better this time around.

That concludes, in my opinion, those parts of the Act that related directly to the formation of secondary modern schools. You are probably surprised (I was) and thinking, 'Is that it? What about all the stuff to do with the tripartite system, the 11-plus and the different types of schools?'

I haven't intentionally avoided mentioning grammar schools, modern schools (the original name of secondary modern schools), technical schools and multilateral schools (the original name for comprehensives). There was not a single word in the Act about any of these types of school. It didn't contain any guidance, legislation or any other directive about how schools should be organised.

Not one word in the Act talked about the 11-plus or any other form of academic exam. There were plenty of new rules related to 'medical examinations' and 'clothing examinations' and 'examinations for infestations of vermin'. But, no mention of the process for determining which type of school a child should attend.

There were no directions in the Act about the teaching pedagogy that should be used, nothing about the curriculum that children should be taught, other than when it related to the teaching of religion. There was no detail about the relationship between schools and the LEAs, with regard to what and how the children should be taught.

So, if the Act didn't refer to these issues, what did it do? This word cloud gives some insight into the topics it covered.

Word cloud of the 1944 Education Act. Those words that are not related to the contents of the Act have been omitted

The most frequent words and terms were 'local education authority' (329 times) and 'minister' (325 times). Words associated with church schools were popular, with 'religious' appearing 88 times and the term 'voluntary schools' 117 times.

I guess we shouldn't be surprised at the Act's content. When Butler first declared his objectives to Churchill, way back in 1941, he identified the role of the churches and private schooling as the most important issues to be resolved. He also mentioned the need to better align schooling with the needs of industry, but I am sure that was a sop to please the prime minister. We know that most of his time was spent trying to negotiate a way for church schools to coexist with the schools owned by local councils. Less time was spent on the question of private schools because he had co-opted Lord Fleming and his committee to consider that subject. By the time Fleming's report was published, Butler had been able to distance himself from the recommendations and much of the hostile reception it received.

There are as many views about the 1944 Education Act as people who have studied and written on the subject. Many times, Butler is accused of 'missing the opportunity' to fully incorporate the church and private schools into the state system. Even his critics have to admit that he was successful, unlike those before him, in achieving a significant change to the structure of schooling.

Michael Barber believed the Act defined an enduring framework for administering education.[21]

It [the Education Act] created a framework within which the education system both expanded and, incrementally developed. The act provided a basic administrative framework. It was the idea of 'a national system locally administered'.

Gosden's views about the Act, most of which were positive, included the following.

The Act did remove the religious and administrative obstacles which had prevented these reforms from coming into effect before the war and it may well be that its greatest achievement was indeed to ensure that all children came in due course to have a reasonable period of study in a secondary school.

Simon and Rubinstein had mixed opinions about what the Act achieved. Their observation of what it didn't do, but what resulted from it, is important for the next part of the secondary modern story:[22]

*The Act had laid down no rules governing the pattern of the provi-
sion [of education] to be made. Local authorities, whose plans for
educational reconstruction were often linked to plans for urban
reconstruction — as was the intention — now began to work out
their development plans. Some LEAs proposed the multilateral
school; the majority, followed the advice of the Spens and Norwood
Committees and proposed the tripartite solution.*

As the author of the current book, I get to have the last word (for now,
anyway!) about Butler's Education Act.

My first conclusion is that the Act should be renamed the
Butler/Chuter-Ede Act.

James Chuter-Ede was Parliamentary secretary to the Board of Education for the period when Butler was the president. Having read his diary,[23]
his contributions to Parliamentary debates and Butler's own comments
about him – 'I was very lucky to have this consistently loyal and wise friend
as my chief lieutenant'[24] – it is clear that he was central in formulating and
getting the Act onto the statute book.

Unlike Butler, Chuter-Ede understood the state education system. He
was educated at an elementary school and then became an apprentice pupil-
teacher. From there he went to Christ's College, Cambridge, to study natural
sciences. Clearly, a very intelligent man. Lack of money forced him to
abandon his studies and he returned to teaching, as an assistant master in a
London elementary school. His political career started as a member of the
NUT; he progressed through local politics and then on to becoming an MP.
After his time assisting Butler he became the longest serving home secretary
in the 20th century.

The reason for giving this abbreviated biography is to demonstrate
Chuter-Ede's experience and knowledge of state education – something that
was an alien world to Butler. It appears that the two worked well together.
Butler had the social contacts and high-level negotiating experience. Chuter-
Ede understood the practicalities of state education, had a very sharp mind
and was a highly competent Parliamentarian. Their complementary skills
combined to change the UK's education system far more than had been done
since before WWI. Sadly, in my view, Butler gets all the credit and Chuter-
Ede is probably remembered, if he is remembered at all, as the politician

with the strange surname. During his political life, Butler was often referred to as 'the best prime minister we never had'. Something similar could be said about Chuter-Ede, who I think would have been the best minister of education we didn't have.

As to my views about the Act. I agree with the authors previously quoted that it provided a way of organising and delivering state education, with most of the anomalies and points of friction removed. It removed the muddle of having secondary and elementary education systems running in parallel and went a long way to dismantling the dual system of church and state education. Children would receive an additional year's schooling, although it was unclear what this would entail and how it would be delivered. Finally, Butler had successfully 'kicked the can' of private schooling into the far distance.

The Act did nothing, absolutely zilch, to determine the purpose, structure and operations of secondary modern schools, how their pupils would be selected and what they would be taught. Asa Briggs, who was the first notable academic I ever met (he was chancellor of Sussex University when I was an undergraduate), said the Act:[25]

> *Provided nothing more than an outline, a statutory warrant for a more comprehensive set of measures than any educational authority would be likely to be able to carry out for a long time to come. Continued educational progress and the implementation of the ideals of the Act depended to a large extent on its interpretation on the spot [he was referring to the LEAs].*

As I wrote about this period, I kept thinking how little was done to refine the model of schooling that would work best in post-war Britain. After the burst of activity that resulted in the 'Green Book', all the intellectual and political effort was expended in specifying the processes and reporting structures of the new system and, of course, dealing with the churches and private schools.

But, what type of education, in what types of schools, would this education framework deliver? As far as I could see, that had not progressed beyond a sketchy outline. The UK Parliament's website says: 'Comprehensive schools were not actually created by the 1944 Butler Act as is often thought.'[26] What it should add is: 'neither were secondary moderns or, indeed, the 11-plus'.

The Education Act delegated to the LEAs the responsibility for creating their own plans for filling in the details.

Soon we will discover the magnitude of the task they had inherited.

The Labour Party takes control

After the Act had been passed and the celebrations and back-slapping had subsided there was a lull when very little happened. It had been agreed that the Act would not be implemented until after the war and, in any case, the first thing to do was for the LEAs to create their development plans.

On 8 May 1945, the war ended in Europe. Two weeks later Churchill resigned. He immediately returned to head the caretaker government that was in power until the general election.

Neither the Labour nor Conservative manifestos made many concrete promises about the type of schooling they would deliver.

If the Labour Party was elected it promised to build on the:

Important step forward that has been taken by the passing of the recent Education Act. Labour will put that Act not merely into legal force but into practical effect, including the raising of the school leaving age to 16 at the earliest possible moment, 'further' or adult education, and free secondary education for all.

The Conservative Party manifesto was just as vague, probably more so, with its intention:

To remodel our educational system according to the new law [the 1944 Education Act] and a vigorous drive will be needed to supply the teachers and the buildings necessary.

Secondary Education for all will have no meaning unless variety, practical training and, above all, quality of standards convince parents that the extra schooling [referring to the school-leaving age

*rising to 15] for their children is worthwhile. Technical education, at
all levels, must be greatly extended and improved.*

Reading their two manifestos, I was struck by how little importance was
given to education. In the Conservative Party manifesto, less than 4% of the
words referred to education policy. Policies about housing and food and
agriculture were the most important sections, each twice as long as the one
about education.

The Labour Party devoted even less space to education (less than 3%).
The focus of its document was 'jobs for all', which was five times longer
than the 133 words it had to say about education.

The general election took place on 26 July 1945. The Conservatives lost
– and lost badly. The Labour Party won by a majority of 146 and inherited
the responsibility for implementing Butler's Education Act.

So begins a sad part of my story, with the appointment of 'Red' Ellen
Cicely Wilkinson as the first Labour minister of education – indeed, the first
female minister of education, of any political party. The sub-titles of her
biographies give a clue to the fiery nature of the woman: *From Red
Suffragist to Government Minister*[27] and *Socialist, Feminist,
Internationalist.*[28]

It is not relevant to the story, but a woman has been responsible for
education more times than in any other part of government. It is often
forgotten that Margaret Thatcher was education minister for just under four
years. Since WWII, about 25% of education ministers have been women,
about twice the percentage responsible for either the Ministry of Health or
the Home Office. I guess this is because the majority of teachers are women.
In 1947, they accounted for 65% of the teaching workforce[29] and today the
figure is 75%.[30] Maybe the reason has something to do with the gender
stereotype that 'women are good with children'.

It is not at all clear to me why Wilkinson was given the role. She had not
spoken during any of the Parliamentary sessions when the 1944 Education
Act was debated. John Bew, who wrote a biography of Attlee,[31] was also
puzzled by the decision.

Some of the choices seemed odd, such as moving Chuter Ede from education, where he was an expert, to the Home Office, and swapping him with Wilkinson, who had spent the war in the Home Office.

Her appointment might have been a surprise, but it appears to have been popular. Even *The Spectator* magazine,[32] not known for its left-wing views, thought Wilkinson was a good choice for the 'immense job of getting the provisions of the agreed 1944 Act translated into terms of schools, teachers, scholars'.

As I have already commented, Chuter-Ede was demonstrably an able administrator and politician and destined for one of the key positions in the Cabinet. On the other hand, Wilkinson's background was, as the 'Red' prefix to her name suggests, a woman driven by political and social causes. Paula Bartley described her as being committed to the women's trade union movement, a founder of the Communist Party and a campaigner for peace and the rights of women.

During the war, Wilkinson had been Parliamentary private secretary to Herbert Morrison, the home secretary. She had special responsibility for air raid shelters and the care of the homeless. She was also in poor health, suffering from bouts of pneumonia and asthma. Wilkinson was minister of education for a year and a half before her death, aged 56. Some commentators say that she committed suicide – others that she died from an accidental overdose of barbiturates.

Like the circumstances surrounding her death, we will never know the details of her private life because her brother destroyed her personal papers. But what interests me are the events of the 552 days she was in office.

I think there is only one good thing to be said about Wilkinson's role as minister of education – her job was well defined. Today we would say that her job description contained crystal clear key performance indicators, which is not surprising given that the only thing the Labour manifesto had said about education was that it 'would put the 1944 Act not merely into legal force but into practical effect, including the raising of the school leaving age to 16 at the earliest possible moment'. It was as simple as that – no caveats and no alternative interpretations. And why should there be – senior Labour Party members were integrally involved in the formulation of the Act.

Secondary modern schools were a direct result of the Act and Wilkinson was the education minister who made them a reality, so can we – must we? – deduce that she was the person responsible for their existence? This conclusion causes those who have written and talked about her life a mixture of embarrassment, denial and obfuscation. Could it be true that the first female minister of education – a revolutionary socialist, member of the British Communist Party and then a staunch Labour Party supporter – was responsible for the 11-plus and secondary modern schools?

In 2017, her life was reviewed in the BBC radio programme *Great Lives*.[33] During the 30-minute programme, just 20 seconds were spent talking about her role as minister of education. There was much talk about her involvement with the Jarrow March, which aimed to raise awareness of mass unemployment and poverty in the north east, but her war-time ministerial experience was glossed over. For many, what Wilkinson did during her time in office spoils the story of her life's achievements and the Labour Party's role in the history of the country's education. I think this is a simplistic and sad interpretation of the facts.

As we have seen, there had been decades of reports and papers about how the country's education system should change. The 1944 Education Act provided the mechanism enabling that change to occur but it didn't prescribe *what* that change would be.

How were the children of the Great British Public going to benefit from the Act's promise to provide an 'education offering such variety of instruction and training as may be desirable in view of their different ages, abilities, and aptitudes, and of the different periods for which they may be expected to remain at school, including practical instruction and training appropriate to their respective needs'? What the hell did these words mean?

Wilkinson was the person who had to transform this fine narrative and good intentions into a reality. She was the person at the point 'where the rubber hits the road'. It was an uncomfortable place to be.

Let's put ourselves in her position when, on 3 August 1945, she became the minister of education. For the first couple of weeks she must have been immersed in understanding the Act and the preparations for its implementation. Two weeks later she attended her first Cabinet meeting and confirmed that the school-leaving age would be raised on 1 April 1947. But, this had consequences, which she listed: there would be 200,000 more pupils, requiring 13,000 additional teachers, leading to some overcrowding of classes and the use of temporary huts and prefabricated buildings. She had under two years to make the necessary arrangements – at a time when everything, especially skilled workers, was in short supply.

If achieving the 1947 date was difficult, at least it was a problem that was bounded and understood. Knowing what the children would be taught, in their extra year at school, and how their schools would be organised were issues of far greater uncertainty, complexity and controversy.

The 146 LEAs were tasked with creating development plans, to be submitted by 1 April 1946. They would then negotiate with the Ministry until they reached agreement. I expect the idea was that this would give a year to finalise the plans before the leaving age was raised. This timescale was wildly unrealistic. I very much doubt if the Ministry had the resources to process the plans had they been completed by the required date. As it was, just 16 plans were submitted by the deadline. Five years later, 15% of the plans had yet to be approved. Wilkinson must quickly have become aware that this key part of the Act's implementation was impossible. The concept that 'the devil is in the detail' was something the Ministry's officials didn't seem to have grasped.

On 7 May 1945, three months before Wilkinson's appointment and before the general election, the Ministry had published Pamphlet No. 1, *The Nation's Schools – Their plan and purpose*.[34] The content was an aggregation of the ideas that had already been expressed in Butler's white paper and other reports from the Board of Education. The stated objective was to:

> *Set out some reflections relating planning to purpose in terms, not of the legal 'child', but of living children. No attempt is made to discuss in detail the content of the education to be given, or the handling of the several subjects and activities of school curricula. All that is offered is some consideration of the objectives of different types of education and the conditions necessary to their attainment.*

At about the same time, Wilkinson was focused on achieving Labour's election victory. While the Commons was debating this document, she was recording a party political radio broadcast extolling the need for controls and central planning. The debate was dominated by W.G. Cove, the Labour MP for Aberavon, past president of the NUT and a member of the left-wing National Association of Labour Teachers. He attacked the pamphlet's content, criticising the education minister (Richard Law) as well as his fellow Labour MP Chuter-Ede.

On first reading the transcript of the debate, my reaction was one of amusement. Using a fiery style of language, Cove was clearly an unhappy man. He kept up a constant stream of questions and barbed observations. I then realised that this debate (more a monologue) rehearsed many of the arguments that would run throughout the life of secondary modern schools.

First, if the pamphlet contained the vision for secondary education, who was responsible for it? Did it result from the cooperation of Conservatives and Labour during the coalition government or was it 'a representation of the context, meaning and purpose of the Tory approach' (I have paraphrased Cove's comments)?

Was the new education system going to be 'progressive' or nothing more, quoting Cove, than a 'recapitulation of the more conventional ideas current about educational reform'? My interpretation of this question is: 'Will the new system be totally different from what had gone before or be an extension of the current system?'

I think the most important of Cove's comments was:

I thought I was helping to put on the Statute Book [by passing the Act] – and we did help – an Act which would give an extended secondary education, commonly called a grammar school education. I thought that I was helping to provide greater educational equality of opportunity for the common child of this country.

I am sure that Cove was well aware that there had never been any suggestion that the Act would deliver a grammar school education for all children, but it made a good debating point and one that was later adopted by Harold Wilson. This idea keeps resurfacing well into the third part of our timeline, when secondary moderns had been replaced by comprehensives.

Cove's final line of attack revolved around the issue of 'class' and the role of education as an instrument for achieving social equality.

This pamphlet still maintains class privileges in the educational world. This pamphlet, I say quite definitely, is educationally profoundly reactionary. There is no unity of a nation under this pamphlet. It is equally true that the real implementation of that Act – that is, giving it substance and reality, making it a progressive instrument, an instrument of social equality – will depend on Labour coming into power on the Government Front Bench.

This issue of education's role as a mechanism for 'social equality', as well as providing children with the best possible education, is as relevant today as when Cove first raised it over 70 years ago.

Soon after taking office, Wilkinson was embroiled in the arguments about Pamphlet No. 1, with the attack coming from her fellow Labour MPs. By the time of the Labour Party Conference in June 1946, the arguments against the idea of selecting children at 11 and sending them to different schools were in full flow. Simon documented the details of the Labour Party's internal politics and conference resolutions that he believed demonstrated their support for multilateral schools.[35]

Whichever way you want to interpret the events of this period, there is one fact that cannot be disputed and that trumps the impassioned speeches and conference resolutions. The Labour Party was the government of the day, with a majority of 146 votes, with the power to change educational policy, however it wanted. It chose not to do so and showed little interest in the subject. There is no record of Wilkinson's decision to 'support' the tripartite system ever being debated within the Cabinet. One can only assume that her fellow ministers either approved of her policy or didn't care enough to try and change it. Maybe the lack of desire to challenge the concept of tripartite schools was the cognitive dissonance in Labour's arguments for providing 'a grammar education for all children' with a desire to do away with the schools and replace them by multilaterals.

As we will soon see, Wilkinson was fully aware of the arguments for and against the different types of school system. But, there was a far more immediate and tangible problem that she had to solve if the government was to fulfil its promise of raising the school-leaving age.

The Ministry's report for 1947[36] detailed the scale of the difficulties. Additional school accommodation was required for the extra children who would be at school by the autumn term of 1948. The school population was expected to increase by a million within the next five years, because of the rising birth rate. To accommodate these children, there was an emergency building programme to provide 6,000 prefabricated classrooms. These went by the memorable name of HORSA (Hutting Operation for Raising the School Leaving Age). An emergency teacher training scheme had been initiated in 1944 to provide 13,000 new teachers by training suitably educated people who had been involved in war service. By the time the scheme was closed, in August 1951, it had produced 30,000 qualified teachers – well above the initial target. In subsequent years, the quality of these 'qualified' teachers was to become a controversial issue.[37]

If Wilkinson's 'problem list' wasn't long enough, another item was added at the beginning of 1947. The government was surveying the economy for 1947 and the numbers didn't add up. Key industries were short of personnel. As today, the distribution of employment varied throughout the country. There was a scarcity of workers in London and too many in Wales. The respective unemployment rates were 1% and 7.5%. To alleviate this problem the Committee on Economic Planning recommended, among other things, delaying raising the school-leaving age. Wilkinson's response was a superbly crafted memorandum[38] that combined a set of well-reasoned and facts-based arguments with an emotional plea that would have been hard to resist.

Even a limited postponement of the first effective step to implement the 1944 Act would inevitably call in question the Government's intentions with regard to social reform. Even more unfortunate would be the effect on education and progressive opinion in general, conscious as it is of the fate of the Fisher Act of 1918 [as discussed in Chapter 5, 'Between the wars'].

Under other Governments, education has too often been the first casualty of an economic blizzard. A Labour Government should be the last to seek protection – and very meagre protection at that – from a fallible forecast of economic trouble by the enlistment of child labour.

The last sentence is beautifully constructed. What government of any political complexion was going to ignore these arguments?

At the Cabinet meeting on 16 January 1947[39] it was decided that there would be no change to the schedule for raising the school-leaving age. It was noted in the minutes of the meeting that 'it was felt that the *political disadvantage* [my italics] of breaking the definite pledges which had been given in Parliament out-balanced the economic benefits which would be derived from this proposal [delaying the date]'. It is clear that the 1947 equivalent of 'spin doctors' worked on this wording, because when the plan was published it had a very different emphasis.[40]

The Government has decided that the long-term loss to the nation would outweigh the immediate gain from this step; the education of children of this age suffered severely in the war and their interests – and the long-term interest of the nation – cannot be sacrificed.

Wilkinson's arguments were about what was the 'right thing to do' – the Cabinet's decision was made on the balance of political advantage and it was presented to the public as being in the nation's interest. Why do I think this wasn't the first or the last government decision that was rephrased in this way?

Three weeks later, Wilkinson was dead.

The final insights that we get from Wilkinson's short spell as minister of education come from studying documents in the National Archive about the period when she and her political and civil service advisers were redrafting the replacement for *The Nation's Schools.*[41]

To say Wilkinson was annoyed after reading the first draft would be an understatement. She used the words 'I felt so deep-down angry' and called the document 'phoney'. I sympathise with the official who drafted the document because all he was doing (I am assuming it was a 'he' because all the officials appeared to be men) was restating the existing ideas about secondary education and secondary modern schools. Wilkinson concluded her list of objections by saying that 'as a new Minister I should never criticise without offering some alternative suggestions'.

She began by asking: 'Are we committed to the three types [I assume she was referring to grammar, technical and secondary modern]?' After discussing what this involved she concluded that, 'One grand thing about this scheme is that it won't work. At least, not peacefully.' That was a surprising statement and the first time I had seen her doubts about the tripartite system being voiced.

To illustrate the problems that would ensue, Wilkinson referred to events that were going on in an area I know well – it was where I went to school. She said, 'The quite terrific struggle in Walthamstow is the kind of storm that will arise everywhere once we try and work this scheme'. She was correct that in 1945 there had been demonstrations about schooling in Walthamstow. An account of what happened is told in the publication *We Want Winns!*[42] ('Winns' being a school called Winns Avenue). However, the event had nothing to do with tripartite schooling but was instead about a school being commandeered to be used for technical school students because their buildings were to be used as an emergency teacher training college.

Wilkinson went on to make suggestions about how the transition between secondary moderns and grammar and technical schools should be made easier. She believed that pupils in secondary moderns should be able to take external exams and the 'cultural subjects must be stressed, especially art and music both practice and appreciation, and I would like to add French'.

I have learnt so much from studying Wilkinson's short period as minister of education. I have learnt about a woman who I believe did her very best to launch the country's schooling on a new path. She faced immense practical problems and hostile reactions, nearly all from members of her own party.

Above all, by studying this period I learnt that virtually no thinking had been done about what the extra year at school was intended to achieve. The curriculum of grammar schools and to a lesser extent of technical schools was already established but virtually no work had been done about what my predecessors at secondary moderns were expected to learn and for what reasons.

So much energy was taken up with arguing about the mechanics of schooling, which seems to have become a displacement activity to avoid thinking about what would be taught. It was assumed that teachers would work out the details.

The new secondary education

The document that Wilkinson so disliked went through many iterations and was published in 1947, after her death. George Tomlinson succeeded her as minister of education and wrote this tribute at the beginning of document: 'the main credit for this pamphlet should go to Ellen Wilkinson. It was under her direction and stimulus that it was written.' We know from documents in the National Archive that her criticisms of it were 'few and not specifically important'. The main question she raised was, 'For whom is the pamphlet written?' This is an excellent question and one that I am sure was not addressed by the document's authors.

Pamphlet No. 9 *The New Secondary Education*[43] was long (63 pages containing 27,000 words). Wilkinson assumed it was not written for the LEA directors of education and teachers, because they would have been informed about its content by circulars and memoranda, and that the true audience must be:

The members of Education Committees most of whom have only a general rather hazy and often prejudiced idea of what is the Ministry's aim. [She didn't hold LEA education officials in high regard.] The second group were parents with children of school age.

Her comments about the draft report went on to make it clear that the document's primary objective should be to convince parents about the worth of the new schooling system and that it 'will be the authoritative pamphlet on the Modern School as such of my administration'.

I very much doubt if many parents will have read the document in its entirety. Its readability was much improved from its earlier drafts, but it was still a ponderous document. The first 22 pages were taken up with an abbreviated history of secondary education and details of the common features of secondary education. By the time the parent got to the part describing secondary modern schools, I am sure their attention would have waned or vanished altogether.

If the document was aimed at parents, then it was those with children about to attend a secondary modern or technical school. Well over half the document was taken up in describing – more like 'selling' – their virtues. It must have been assumed that the readership would be familiar with grammar schools, albeit by their previous name of 'secondary schools', because they were discussed in far less detail.

I have attempted to sieve through the nice reassuring words – and there are a lot of these in the pamphlet – to extract the messages it was intending to convey. My guess is that education officials in the LEAs went through a very similar process.

Message 1. We will 'work it out' as we go along

The document is littered with caveats and commentary about the scope for change and development.

Here is no blue-print of Utopia. It is a description of work in progress.

It is important not to make plans that are too rigid; it will take a generation to implement fully this great scheme.

It should be recognised at once that the modern school is a growing tree with strong roots, but so far rather a limited number of branches.

There are very few schools of this type in this country that represent, in conditions, buildings and general curriculum, the standard which all must reach as soon as possible.

Message 2. All types of school will have common standards

There were numerous comments providing reassurance that grammar, technical and modern schools would have the same quality of facilities and physical infrastructure, but with a similar number of reservations about the time it would take for this equality to be achieved.

They will have a common code of building regulations.

They will enjoy the same holidays and play the same games.

The maximum size of classes will be the same for all.

Maximum of 30 children to a class for all schools.

The definition of a qualified teacher applies to all secondary schools.

Common scale of teacher salaries.

Common facilities (gyms, libraries, arts and craft rooms etc).

Message 3. Secondary modern child learn best by dealing with 'concrete things' related to their day-to-day experiences

The definition of secondary modern children, as well as those attending technical and grammar schools, was based on the conclusions of the Norwood Report.

Experience has shown that the majority of children [those attending secondary moderns] learn most easily by dealing with concrete things and following a course rooted in their own day-to-day experience.

At the age of 11 few of them will have disclosed particular interests and aptitudes well enough marked for them to require any other course. The majority will do best in a school which provides a good all-round education in an atmosphere which enables them to develop freely along their own lines.

Such a school will give them a chance to sample a variety of 'subjects' and skills and to pursue those which attract them most.

Message 4. The technical school child will benefit from a more focused education

Some children will have decided at quite an early stage to make their careers in branches of industry or agriculture requiring a special kind of aptitude in science or mathematics. Others may need a course, longer and more specialised than that provided in the modern school, with a particular emphasis on commercial subjects or art. All these boys and girls will find their best outlet in the secondary technical school.

Message 5. The grammar school child has the ability to master 'abstract' learning and the potential to stay until the sixth form

A proportion [of children] whose ability and aptitude require the kind of course with the emphasis on books and ideas that is provided at a secondary grammar school. They are attracted by the abstract approach to learning and should normally be prepared to stay at school long enough to benefit from the 'sixth form' work which is the most characteristic feature of the grammar school.

Message 6. Comprehensive schools will need to be big – 1,500+ pupils

The document contained guidance about the conditions for using multi-lateral (comprehensive) schools.

The Minister desires to lay down no set guides for organisation but to encourage local authorities to plan as best suits their local needs. In some places where conditions are favourable the best way of carrying out the new plan may be to combine two, or three, types of secondary education in one school.

In order to ensure that a school providing secondary education for all the senior children in a given area offers proper scope and opportunity for all its pupils, it will have to be a very large school. It is doubtful whether a school with less than a ten-form or eleven-form entry (that is a total of 1,500 to 1,700 pupils) is capable of offering the necessary variety of suitable courses.

The Spens Report had stated that multilateral schools required a minimum of 800 pupils. It is unclear what research was used to reach the conclusion that the size had to be double to 1,500–1,700 pupils.

Message 7. Deciding the right type of school for a child should be done for positive not negative reasons

The document did not directly address the mechanism for deciding the type of school a child should attend. The only reference to 'selection' was when describing technical schools.

The essential consideration is not so much their 'intelligence quotient', though this must count, as the natural bent of their minds and their outlook, and that of their parents, on their own future. To ensure that the right opportunities are open to the right pupils, proper selection is essential, and selection on positive, not on negative grounds.

There was some commentary about the likelihood of 'misfits' (i.e. children who were allocated to the 'wrong' type of school).

For a few pupils it may turn out that a wrong choice of secondary course was made at 11. A few others may develop aptitudes in the first year or two at a secondary school that were dormant and unsuspected earlier. To meet the needs of such pupils all local education authorities must have arrangements which make it possible without difficulty to transfer them at any stage in their secondary school career from one type of secondary education to another.

The way must be clear for boys and girls in any type of secondary school to continue their education in such ways as will give them the opportunity to go on to higher studies at a university, college of further education, or elsewhere.

Message 8. Secondary modern schools can decide their own syllabuses and methods of teaching

Responsibility for establishing the school syllabus lay with the school's head and the teachers.

The headmaster or head-mistress is responsible for framing the curriculum and drawing up the syllabus of his or her own school. He may get advice and guidance – possibly criticism – from His Majesty's Inspectors, but never direction.

The secondary modern school must be free to work out its own syllabuses and methods.

They [the teachers] will be free to plan the curriculum of the school on purely educational lines, to provide their pupils with the best possible conditions for growing up, and to ensure that they leave school with interests thoroughly aroused and a determination to continue their education throughout their lives.

The document contained pages of ideas about what could be taught in the schools. It read like a 'brain dump' of the author's personal opinions. No references are provided to substantiate the comments.

I had to smile in particular at the suggestion that the recorder was an ideal musical instrument to be used in the schools – many parents, my own included, have had to listen to the discordant noise made while attempting to master this inexpensive woodwind instrument. Now I know who is to blame.

Message 9. All types of children will attend secondary moderns, ranging from the 'intelligent' to 'backward children' with special problems

For reasons that were not explained, secondary moderns were expected to cater for a wider range of children than grammar and technical schools. I suspect that the unwritten logic was that they were a 'catch-all' for all of the children who didn't go to a grammar or technical school.

> *Perhaps the main difference between a modern school and other types of secondary schools is its very broad outlook and objective. It has to provide a series of courses for children of widely differing ability, aptitude and social background. It has to cater for the needs of intelligent boys and girls, for those with a marked practical bent, as well as for the special problem of the backward children.*

Message 10. It is impractical for secondary modern pupils to take external exams

The document was clear that secondary modern pupils were not expected to take external exams.

> *In schools that have to cope with the wide ranges of ability and aptitude that are found in all modern schools, it is impracticable to combine a system of external examinations, which presupposes a measure of uniformity, with the fundamental conception of modern school education, which insists on variety. Internal tests, based on the syllabus of work actually covered by the individual pupils, rather than on any preconceived notion of the standards appropriate to a particular age, will alone adequately meet the case.*

In an earlier draft of the pamphlet the rationale was expressed differently: '*The secondary modern school is fortunate in being free from external examinations and any testing required must be internal.*'

I cannot believe that Wilkinson had agreed this part of the text, given that she had stated in her notes 'it [the secondary modern] must NOT be the only one of the three which does not take external examinations'.[44]

Message 11. Teaching specialist subjects is only appropriate for older secondary modern pupils

The document advised that for younger pupils there was no need for subject specialisation.

Hard and fast lines between subjects are generally inappropriate in the modern school, and for this reason it is doubtful if, in the lower forms at any rate, any very extensive measure of 'specialisation' is desirable.

Having made this statement the pamphlet then said that streaming children for English and arithmetic was thought desirable.

It is obviously sensible to group the abler children together so that the teaching may be specially suited to their needs, and the pace of their work need not be slowed down to give a chance to less able children who require a different approach and a simpler presentation of their subject-matter.

The document talked about putting children into 'sets' for certain subjects but retaining the 'form' master and mistress. This didn't seem to be a directive, but rather a suggestion for how the school could be organised.

Message 12. When the school-leaving age is raised each school can decide what to teach its secondary modern pupils

This question had scant coverage.

The lengthening of the modern school course will not mean the introduction of new subjects or any spectacular change in the approach to the old, but rather the planning of a longer course as a coherent whole.

All the same, it will demand greater elasticity in the curriculum and the time-table to suit individual needs than has up to now been either

necessary or possible. Existing schemes of work will have to be
reconsidered in this light and perhaps superseded by wholly new
ones. Particularly in the later years, it will be desirable to make
provision for a certain amount of specialisation, and so to arrange
the time-table that pupils may have the opportunity of spending
considerable periods of time on subjects of their own choice, prob-
ably things that they do well, thereby acquiring habits of work
comparable with those of adult life.

My interpretation of these directions was that nobody had given the
subject very much thought.

As you can see, few of the pamphlet's 27,000 words were used in
providing definitive guidance about the nature of secondary modern schools.
It was composed of hints and observations but few 'rules' – and even these
felt as if they could be negated by the heavy emphasis on the fact that the
new education system was a 'work in process'.

There were a couple of themes that kept appearing that must have
reflected the concerns of the Ministry's officials and the politicians. I have
previously criticised the argument that the Act was intended to provide
'grammar schools for all' as political mischief-making. Having read this
document I wondered if some, maybe many, parents genuinely believed this
was what their children would receive.

Twenty years before, the Hadow Report had used the ungainly words
'post-primary' to describe secondary education. You can understand the
committee's predicament, because the word 'secondary' had already been
claimed by 'grammar' schools. Was the rebranding of 'secondary' as a phase
of education, rather than a particular type of school, really causing confusion? The pamphlet's author certainly thought so.

There has been some confusion about the meaning of the phrase
'secondary education for all'. Until 1944 a 'Secondary School'
meant a particular sort of school to which only a small proportion of
the population could aspire, one which had better qualified and
better paid staff, smaller classes, and more attractive premises and
amenities than most of the other schools in its neighbourhood. It was
attended by some of the ablest pupils selected by a highly competi-

tive examination, and by a certain number of other pupils of varying abilities whose parents could afford to pay fees. This sort of secondary school will still remain, doing its own special job.

Just before WWII, 1.7 million children over the age of 11 were in elementary schools and approximately half a million in secondary schools.[45] Now, with the war over and the new education system in place, as if by magic the same number of children were attending grammar schools and 760,000 had become pupils at a *secondary* [my italics] modern.[46] Just to confuse the situation, about a million children went to 'all-age' schools. Perhaps the re-definition of the word 'secondary' was causing parents genuine confusion? The failure of *The New Secondary Education* to make mention of the 'all-age' schools cannot have helped. From the politician's perspective, omitting mentioning these schools was not surprising. It had been government policy to phase them out for the past 20 years, yet they still educated 20% of children. Not a fact that inspired confidence in government's ability to implement educational change.

'Parity of esteem' is a term we now use to campaign for the way society views mental and physical health conditions. It was first used to explain the equal status of grammar, technical and secondary modern schools. In this context, the word 'parity' first appeared in the Spens Report and became 'parity of esteem' in the Norwood Report. By the mid-1940s it was the 'go-to' term for elevating the status of secondary moderns and technical schools to that of a grammar school. Not surprisingly, it was used multiple times in Pamphlet 9. You can see that politicians and Ministry officials were doing their damnedest to sell parents on the idea that it didn't matter if you went to a secondary modern, technical or grammar school – they were equally good at educating children and of equal importance to society.

It looks as if these concerns persisted, because in 1950 the booklet *Our Changing Schools – a picture for parents* was published by the Central Office of Information. I had to smile at the document's construction. Gone were the long lists of facts and figures and reassuring words. Instead the approach was to use a series of short stories to make the points. There was an account of a 'Mr Jones, the retired postmaster' who wandered through different types of schools reminiscing and observing how things had changed. There were accounts of a parent–teacher association meeting and of a teachers' staff meeting. Much of the 100-page document was taken up with photos of happy and industrious children engaged in all manner of pursuits. The issues about the confusion of secondary education and grammar schools and the secondary modern's lack of prestige were raised as 'genuine concerns', given due credence and answered. Whoever wrote the document was doing their best to think and talk like a parent – unsuccessfully, in my view.

Parliament showed little interest in either of these documents. MPs mentioned *The New Secondary Education* a couple of times during the 1940s, in debates about multilateral schools, and twice more in 1950. *Our Changing Schools* achieved an even lower profile. These were the last of the publications from central government trying to sell the benefits of the new education system. The effort to win public acceptance now relied on the LEAs convincing parents that their children would flourish in the new types of schools they were planning.

––––––

We have reached an important point in the timeline. Secondary modern schools had arrived; well, let's say they were beginning to emerge. Before going further, I thought I should ensure I wasn't repeating the behaviours I discussed in Chapter 1 ('The truth is what we want it to be') and biasing my account of their history. Was I painting too bleak a picture, implying that educational developments were insufficiently planned and conducted in a haphazard way? That raising the school-leaving age and extending secondary education was driven by high ideals but lacking substance in how it would work in practice. That during a time of shortages and disruption, decisions were made without sufficient thought for the practicalities of their implementation. Quite simply, that educational reforms relied on everybody muddling through and hoping it would be 'all right on the night'.

Reading Harold Dent's book, *Secondary education for all,* came as something of a surprise.[47] It made me think that I might have been too understanding and made too many allowances and excuses for the political and educational establishment. Dent was the editor of *The Times Educational Supplement* and had a grandstand view of the educational landscape. He was scathing about what he witnessed.

Secondary education was about to be extended by a year. Dent analysed the Act and the Ministry's publications, looking to answer the question, 'Why and what is it expected to achieve?' He believed that the US's definition of secondary education was the most exact and comprehensive answer. Compared with this definition, he concluded, 'No such detailed or thorough analysis has yet been made in the country. One is urgently needed.' He went on to comment:

> *When one considers the vast amount of expenditure, in money and human ability, that is being devoted to secondary education in this country (I do not suggest that it is nearly enough), one is surely entitled to a more precise and detailed statement of what that education is expected to do.*

Rightly, in my view, Dent concluded that if you are unsure of what you are trying to achieve then building the structures to achieve it is mighty difficult. He was fearful that because grammar schools were the gold-standard of state-provided secondary education, their ethos, structures and curriculum would unduly influence the other types (e.g. technical and secondary moderns).

> *What hardly anyone appears to be prepared to face is the hard fact that to provide suitable secondary education for all children is so utterly different a problem from providing a special kind of secondary education for a few selected children [those from grammar schools].*

If this was not bad enough, Dent then observed that those making decisions about secondary education would have 'with the rarest exceptions been nurtured in the grammar school tradition'. He could have gone on to say that those who hadn't attended a grammar school would, almost certainly, have been educated at a private school.

He believed that although the discussion of secondary education might have been 'continuous and earnest', it had 'not yet produced any very satisfying conclusions'. In his view the argument that examining children at the age of 11, to decide their future schooling, was dictated by administrative convenience, not psychological evidence. Interestingly, he quoted Cyril Burt as the originator of this opinion. You might remember Burt as the man who was credited with or blamed for, depending on your viewpoint, creating the 11-plus exam.

It is all the stranger that Dent's quote about the Act ('the greatest measure of advance since 1870 and probably the greatest ever known') is often used to label him as one of its leading supporters. He is said to have made this comment in 1944. Either his opinions changed in the intervening five years, before *Secondary education for all* was published, or he was referring to the Act's scope, not the practicalities of its implementation.

As we have seen, the evolution of secondary modern schools to become the country's primary form of secondary education was influenced by a series of developments. Some of these were organisational and political pressures. Some were social and economic trends. Perhaps the most important was a rapid change in the country's demographics.

The 'baby boom' and its repercussions

In his book *Pinch*, David Willetts postulated the theory 'How the Baby Boomers took their children's future and why they should give it back'. It is an interesting argument, wrong in my opinion, but it has helped him launch a new career as head of a think tank. The irony is that previously, he was a Conservative Cabinet minister and probably most remembered for tripling the fees of university students, many of whom are the grandchildren of the despised baby boomers.

After WWII the number of children did 'boom' but for reasons that are far more complicated than is normally thought. Where I do agree with Willetts is that this age cohort had a major impact on the UK, starting back when they first went to school.

The following chart[48] shows how, after the war, the two main determinants of population growth changed. It is normally supposed that the heady cocktail of winning the war, the armed forces returning home after years separated from their families and the optimistic mood of the country resulted in a surge in babies being conceived. That is indeed true, although it was short-lived. Come 1949 this trend reversed and the number of births (per 1,000 women aged 15–44) declined and then plateaued until 1956. Maybe the drab reality of post-War Britain dimmed the desire for larger families? Most likely, the birth rate returned to a 'normal', sustainable level.

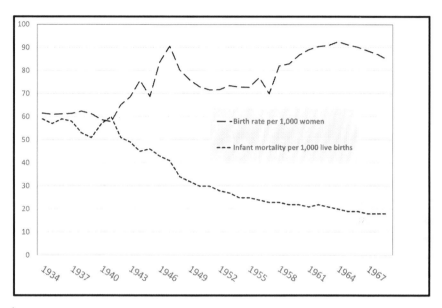

Birth rate per 1,000 women aged 15–44 and infant mortality per 1,000 live births

At the end of WWI the birth rate had also risen rapidly and then fallen rapidly, in a pattern that was remarkably similar to what happened at the end of WWII.[49] I wonder why politicians and the educational establishment didn't consider this eventuality when deciding the post-WWII education policy? Everybody agreed that implementing the Act and raising the school-leaving age (ROSLA), in a war-stressed Britain, would put the education system under considerable pressure. Why didn't they account for the likelihood of a post-war baby boom? Either they didn't consider it or they dismissed the idea. Whatever the reason, it was a mistake.

Perhaps politicians should have foreseen the change in the other factor that determined the population size: infant mortality per 1,000 live births. Since before the war, with the exception of 1940, this ratio had fallen rapidly and it kept falling. The combination of more babies being born and more remaining healthy resulted in a surge in the number of children under the age of four years, which is shown in the next chart.[50]

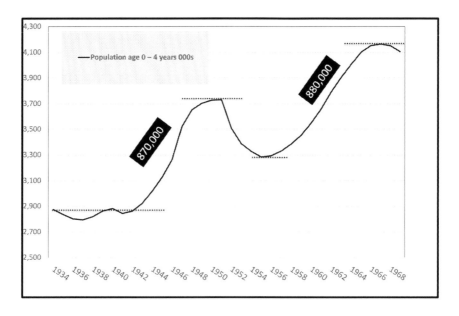

By historical standards the birth rate before the war had been low, but stable. In 1941 the number of live births declined to the lowest for over 10 years. Over the next decade there was an explosion in the number of young children (under the age of four), increasing by 870,000.

Each child would require a place in an infant and primary school and within a decade would enter the newly re-organised secondary school system. It is not surprising that responding to this wave of children, with its demands for new school accommodation and more teachers, was of equal, if not greater, importance than implementing the 1944 Education Act.

Understandably, the government was anxious to know if this surge in births was a 'one-off' event or if it marked a permanent change in the country's demographics. A Royal Commission on Population was formed to study the likely future trajectory of the population. It reported in 1949 and came to the conclusion that after the birth rate had peaked in 1949:[51]

We can forecast with a good deal of confidence, namely, a substantial decline in the annual number of births over the next 15 years.

The report made passing reference to what had happened at the end of WWI and concluded that the 'short lived boom in births which followed the

WWI period provides little parallel'. With the benefit of understanding what happened to the UK's demographics, we know that was a wrong call.

I assume that the Commission's findings became the basis of planning for government departments, including the Ministry of Education. As we can see from the previous chart, the Commission was partly right – the birth rate did decline. But it very quickly plateaued and increased again. Not only were schools having to cope with rapidly rising numbers of children, but their predications were incorrect about just how many there would be.

The next boom in the child population started in 1956. By some strange coincidence, the number of under fours increased by almost exactly the same number as the previous boom. It wasn't until the last part of our time-line (Chapter 7, 'The comprehensive era') that this second population surge affected the secondary school system.

These charts convey, at a macro level, the result of the baby boom. What is more interesting is how this surge in the numbers of school children affected the educational priorities.

The next chart[52] shows the number of children, in England and Wales, attending school. The source of the data is *Education in 1952*, so the numbers for the period 1952–1954 are forecast. You will see that the name of the school types had changed. For some reason the Ministry of Education used the terms infants, juniors and seniors when providing statistics about pupil numbers over a period of time. They thoughtfully provided an exact definition of the age range of children in each type of school.

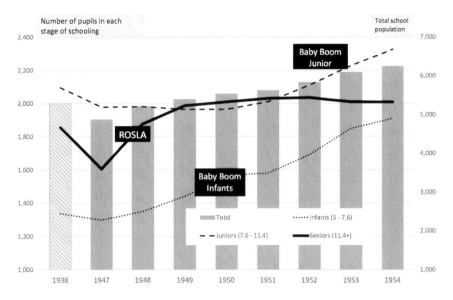

Number of children in England and Wales attending infant, junior and senior schools

If I were a sales or manufacturing manager and the lines on the chart represented the sales of products or the units of goods manufactured, I would be a happy man. But if I were responsible for educating the country's children, then my reaction would be one of concern, more likely panic. The chart's message is simple. The country was going to need a lot more teachers and schools to educate the rapidly rising school population.

We have already seen that before the war the country's birth rate was unusually low. The results of this can be seen in the fall in 1947 in the numbers of children attending all types of school, represented by the bars on the chart. There were 500,000 fewer children in school at the beginning of 1947 than in 1938. This didn't last for long and the result of the baby boom was soon felt, resulting in a rapid rise in children in infant schools. Between 1947 and 1954, the number of infants shot up by over 600,000.

You can see the increase in the pupil numbers attending junior schools as the baby-boom cohort of children moved on from their infant stage of education. Senior (secondary) schools had to cope with the demands of the baby boom *and* the step-change in numbers resulting from ROSLA. Between 1947 and 1949 there was a 400,000 increase in the number of seniors.

David Kynaston titled his history of this period *Austerity Britain*,[53] and for good reason. There were shortages of everything from labour to bricks, from asbestos sheeting to public finance. In those days asbestos was widely used when constructing schools! Yet, during the period 1947–1954 the school population increased by nearly 1.4 million children. To put this into a contemporary perspective, the numbers attending schools in England over the same number of years in 2009–2016 increased by just 0.4 million.[54]

In each of the years 1949–1954 the Ministry published an annual review of its activities. These documents provide the primary source of information about its activities, priorities, concerns and achievements. With so many demands on the Ministry's limited resources, I was interested to understand what was happening to secondary modern schools, knowing that by the end of the period they would celebrate their 10th birthday.

I have tried to summarise the main points from each of these Ministry reports and to present them as a mini-timeline over the next few pages.[55] Detailing the facts is important but I also wanted to understand the sentiment being expressed, which ranged from pessimism and concern to optimism and hope, by the end of the period.

1947

The Ministry's main activity was organising for ROSLA. Little new construction work was undertaken and what did occur provided schooling for the 'new towns';[56] places that are perhaps not best known for their architectural excellence – Stevenage, Crawley, Hemel Hempstead and Harlow. All required new schools.

1948

The first sentence of the report set the tone for its contents.

The Ministry and LEAs continued to face many difficult problems. The legacy of old buildings, unreorganised schools [all-age schools], over-large classes and wartime dislocations persisted. At the same time the rate and scope of development were limited, as in all other

departments of national life, by the exigencies of manpower and
materials.

Again, ROSLA dominated the educational agenda. The report provided a commentary about how schools were using this additional year to educate children. There was no pattern or plan to what was happening. Some 'experiments' were seen as successful; some were not. Children who were still attending 'all-age' schools (about 20% of seniors) seem to have fared the worst.

The supply of teachers was 'reasonably adequate'. I suspect that phrase covered a lot of deficiencies. Teacher supply was uneven and there were shortages of specialist teachers (e.g. 'the lack of housecraft teachers was a severe handicap').

It was the physical environment that had the most reported problems. Conditions must have been dire when providing each pupil with a desk and chair was deemed an achievement.

It must be regarded as a satisfactory achievement that during this
year a desk and chair were found for every one of the children who
remained at school until 15 and in many places considerably more
than this was done.

During the year, just 10 secondary and 15 primary schools were completed. Many more school developments were approved, most of them for primary schools.

At best it appeared that in 1948 the education system coped, just about, with the children staying on because of ROSLA. What value children gained from the additional 12 months at school seemed to depend totally on the competence of the teachers and the physical constraints of the school. I guess we would call this an 'ultra-postcode lottery'.

1949

Yet again, the report started with a warning. Yet again I expect this was intended to prepare the reader for the bad news that followed.

An increase of more than 170,000 in the school population brought
with it the year's instalment of those problems of staffing and accom-
modation that are likely to confront local education authorities for
many years to come.

Accommodating the rising school numbers was the overriding priority.
And, as before, this was being complicated by the need to provide schools
for the new towns. As the country's economic situation deteriorated, LEAs
were instructed to reduce the costs of their school building programme – in
the region of 10%.

I expect the report's author was searching for something positive to say
and resorted to the safe option of providing teachers with words of encouragement.

The disabilities under which many schools are labouring are more
than matched by the vitality and devotion of the teachers.

Teacher numbers increased, but less than expected, and there was a
slight improvement in the percentage of men employed; a shortage of male
teachers had been a problem since the end of WWII. Seventy years later the
same problem persists.

The number of new schools increased, with 68 new primary and 18
secondary schools being completed. It was now five years since the Education Act had been passed, yet the number of new secondary schools
remained low. Accommodating the baby boom-induced surge in the school
population remained the Ministry's main priority as confirmed in the
Economic Survey for 1949,[57] which stated that the 'main task for the next
few years is to provide new school places in primary school'.

1950

Rising pupil numbers remained the driving force determining the school
building programme.

The steady and substantial increase in the school population

continued to dominate the building programme and to provide
staffing problems in the schools.

The report described the 'economy of school construction' in reference to the cost-cutting exercise announced during the previous year. As you might expect, this was done 'without detriment to educational standards'. The constraints on capital spending continued, and the Ministry issued further guidance on how to reduce costs to get 'more bang for your buck' (my interpretation of what was being implied).

In fact, the planned reduction in the cost of building was far more than stated in the Ministry's report. During a Parliamentary debate the minister of education said that the cost of building schools in 1951 was planned to be 25% lower than the 1949 costs. I don't know if this reduction in costs was achieved but it must have resulted in a material reduction in the quality of new school infrastructure.[58]

During the year a further 190 primary and 34 secondary schools opened.

1951

Once more the report conditioned the reader for bad news.

Early in 1951 there seemed to be good grounds for hoping that we
would be able to deal successfully, though with slender margin of
resources, with the immense tasks confronting us.

[A few sentences later] But the year was not far spent before there
were signs that these hopes for the future were in jeopardy.

Concern had been expressed, in a government report, about the recruitment and training of teachers. The report had concluded that 'to maintain the by no means satisfactory staffing standards of 1950' would require 20,000 new teachers to be in place by 1954. Even if teacher training colleges operated at maximum capacity it would be impossible to maintain 1950's pupil-to-teacher ratio.

The news about the number of schools being built was somewhat better. At the end of the year 854 primary schools and 276 secondary schools were under construction. However, shortage of building materials resulted in a three-month ban (starting in December) on starting new school projects.

1952

This was the first of the Ministry reports that didn't start with a warning; things must have been looking up. Like the previous five reports it restated that the first priority had been to provide for the enlarged pupil registers. During the year classrooms and teachers had to be found for another 250,000 children, which must have been helped by the 432 primary and 57 secondary schools that were completed. Yet again, the number of new primary schools was far larger than secondary.

The number of teachers had increased by 6,000 – as had happened every year since 1948.

1953

At last a report starting with a sentence containing a positive word ('rejoicing'). This had nothing to do with education, however, but was about the Queen's coronation and the extra holiday that had been awarded, enabling children to join the celebrations.

Once more, there was the re-statement that the Ministry's primary task for the year was providing facilities and teachers for the extra 236,000 children attending schools.

Many more schools entered service – 425 primary and 117 secondary.

This was the first time that a yearly Ministry report addressed the topic of the forthcoming increase in the secondary school population.

There was much evidence that authorities were already starting to deal vigorously with the problems that will confront them when what has come to be known, infelicitously, as 'the bulge' [baby boom] reaches the secondary schools.

For the four years before 1953, LEAs had made available over 200,000 new secondary school places. Most of these were new schools built to provide places for children living in the new towns. Worryingly, no mention was made of preparations for increased secondary school numbers in existing towns.

1954

This year seems to have been a watershed for the Ministry. The language remained guarded but there was a note of optimism.

During the year a stage was reached when it became possible to contemplate not merely keeping pace with these demands but some additional improvement of the educational service.

The number of children in infant schools was beginning to decline as the baby boom moved to junior schools, the increase in teacher numbers was more than the previous year and the provision of secondary school places was 'well in hand'.

During the year, the number of primary schools increased by 409 and there were 158 new secondary schools. However, for the second year the priority for commissioning new schools was focused on the secondary stage of education. Well over twice the funds were committed to building more secondary schools than primary.

WWII had finished 10 years ago, and only now did the Ministry appear to be in some kind of control of the situation and to be moving out of reactive mode. During this time, teacher numbers had increased by 38,000 and the pupils they taught by 1.3 million. The numbers of children taught in 'all-age' schools had fallen, yet 700,000 were still attending these schools. Remember, it was now 28 years since the decision had been taken to phase out these schools.

If I were to name this period, the 10 years since the 1944 Education Act, it would be 'the decade of survival'. Working in the education system, from the humblest school teacher to the minister of education, must have been stressful and frustrating. Everything was in short supply except the number of children walking through the school gates.

So now, having reviewed the decade, I still think the decision to raise the school-leaving age was made with inadequate planning for how the extra year of education would be used, where the children would be accommodated and who would teach them.

What we now call the baby boom was at the time called the 'bulge'. It required scarce resources to be devoted, initially, to building and equipping new primary schools and then, as the children aged, secondary schools. From the end of the war until mid-1953, there were five times as many primary as secondary schools completed.[59] Adapting and renewing existing schools took a second place to the demand for schooling from the new towns.

If these pressures were not bad enough, they coincided with the first generation of children attending the new types of secondary schools. Most of them going to secondary moderns.

This account of what happened at the Ministry is one part of the story; the day-to-day shaping of the country's new secondary education system was being determined by the LEAs and documented in the development plans that they were busy producing. We have already discovered that few of the plans were submitted by the deadline of 1 April 1946. In the next section we will learn when they were delivered and what they said.

The LEA development plans

Part of the 1944 Education Act detailed the role and requirements of the 'development plan' that all 146 LEAs were required to produce. These covered all aspects of primary, secondary and further education. For the sake of brevity (and my sanity) I have only considered the content related to the story of secondary moderns. This summary version has no doubt sacrificed some of the Act's legal precision – for that I apologise.

The plans' production and approval process were mammoth undertakings. It was equivalent to creating a Domesday Book register of the educational resources of England and Wales and then forecasting how they would evolve, for the next couple of decades. And the Ministry wanted the work completed within 12 months.

LEAs had to detail all of their existing schools, their regulatory status (i.e. directly controlled or operated in conjunction with the church) and the age range and gender of the pupils they taught. The same level of information was required for all new schools that were to be built and those that were to be adapted. In addition, the plan had to show the timetable for closing schools that would not feature in the plan.

If existing schools were to be modernised, the proposed changes and costs had to be detailed. The same applied to the construction costs and plans for new schools. This was not a 'finger in the air' level of cost fore-cast. The plans had to be at a level of detail that showed that they conformed with building regulations. Finally, the building plans had to be prioritised and scheduled on an annual basis.

Before submitting its plan, the LEA had to 'consult' the managers or governors of the voluntary schools in its area. Objections that couldn't be resolved formed part of the Ministry's approval process. It is easy to forget that at this time 65% of the schools and departments in England and Wales were church-owned (voluntary schools) and were having to decide how they wanted to integrate with the state system. To make this decision the managers and governors needed to know how their schools would be used by the LEA and what monies would be spent on improving their facilities. In its own right this was a major task.

These requirements, although daunting (perhaps 'terrifying' is a better word), are at least reasonably easy to understand. Specifying a system of schooling that would be accepted by the Ministry was a far more vague and contentious task.

As we have seen, the Act didn't provide any blueprint for the type of schools that LEAs should use to fulfil their primary objective to:

Afford for all pupils opportunities for education offering such variety of instruction and training as may be desirable in view of their different ages, abilities, and aptitudes, and of the different periods for which they may be expected to remain at school, including prac-tical instruction and training appropriate to their respective needs.

The LEAs had the 'freedom' to decide this themselves, assisted (or confused) by the reports, circulars and pamphlets issued by the Ministry. This documentary advice was supplemented by discussions with the HM Inspectors who were associated with their schools. We have already seen the conclusions of the Spens Report and the pamphlet *The New Secondary Education*. I had assumed that *The Nation's Schools* – the document that caused so much fuss – had been quietly forgotten but I was wrong, as it appeared in the Ministry's internal document for school inspectors[60] about how they should evaluate the plans.

Reasons should be given fully when supporting any proposals which conflict with the 'Nation's Schools' or other relevant circulars and administrative memoranda.

This document had made clear that the 'most urgent reform to which the development plan must be addressed is the completion of the Hadow reorganisation' – abolishing the remaining 'all-age' schools.

There is no doubt that the Ministry's preference was the tripartite model. All of the reports and pamphlets had concluded that this was the best way of schooling – it wasn't a secret. We know, however, that there had been educationalists and politicians, nearly all of them in the Labour Party, promoting the use of multilateral schools.

When producing their reports, the LEAs had to address both the preferences of the Ministry and the demands of local economic conditions and the views of their governing political party. Those LEAs in the new town regions weren't constrained by having an existing school infrastructure and could adopt a 'blank sheet of paper' approach. But most LEAs had to contend with migrating to a new education system, while maintaining the education of children who were increasing in numbers and staying an extra year at school. All of this in the post-war period of shortages of funding and just about everything else. It must have been a nightmare for the LEAs and their counterparts in the Ministry.

Considering that the planning process must have been one of the most important, if not the most important, tasks being conducted by the Ministry, there was little mention of it in the annual education reports. Each year there were a few lines detailing how many plans had been received and how many approved. The only exception was in 1949, when the Ministry provided some commentary about how the process was progressing. We learnt that there had been many different types of schools proposed. Some schools were single-sex, some mixed. Some were secondary moderns, grammar and technical schools; some were multilateral or comprehensive. New variants of schools were mentioned, including campus and bilateral schools (see Appendix C, 'Definitions of educational institutions' for explanations).

What we know for certain is that most LEAs had no chance of adhering to the Ministry's timetable. I am at a loss to explain how the Ministry's civil servants could ever have thought it was achievable. To my mind it reveals that they were unaware of the workload involved and the practicalities of creating the plans. It wasn't long, however, before they were made aware of the LEAs' disquiet. This letter from the secretary of the County Councils Association makes the point.[61]

> *We are of the opinion that, having regard to the present shortage of staff, both administrative and architectural, and to the urgency of other problems, it is quite impractical for development plans to be submitted by county education authorities to the Minister by the 1st April next. They therefore consider that an extension of at least twelve months should be given for this purpose, and they hope to learn that the Minister concurs.*

Was this a classic case of 'ivory tower' syndrome or were the civil servants unquestioningly attempting to deliver what the politicians had promised? It is impossible to say for certain, but reading the archived files of this period it seems that the Ministry's officials soon appreciated the difficulty of the task and were not surprised when the LEAs failed to deliver.

At the same time as asking the LEAs to plan for the coming decades the Ministry, in mid-1948, was explaining its building priorities to the War Damage Commission as follows.[62]

> *Limited to what is immediately essential to cope with the raising of the school leaving age, the rise in the birth-rate and the provision of school accommodation for the population of new housing estates.*

But, delivering the Act's 'letter of the law' was their overriding priority. When an education authority pointed out that the post-war problem of shortages made it impossible to forecast with any accuracy when they could build and repair their schools the response of the Ministry was to amend the wording of its memo. I had to smile at this civil servant's suggested response to this objection.[63]

The rate at which it will be possible for the Authority to carry out their proposals will necessarily depend on the general situation existing from time to time as regards the available supply of labour and materials. ['We know the problem.']

It is necessary, however, in the view of the provisions of Section 11 (1) of the Education Act 1944, to ask the Authority to indicate in the plan its financial years... ['But you still have to give us the information.']

A perfect example of bureaucratic mentality: 'The law is the law and even though the information you provide will be inaccurate, we want you to provide it all the same.'

When the blunder became obvious, in early 1946, the Ministry informed the LEAs[64] that they could submit their plans in stages, without the detailed cost estimates (there were some exceptions) and in outline form for the later years of the plan's timetable. After reading a draft of the circular, the general secretary of the Association of Education Committees suggested that, if requested, the deadline for the plans could be extended by three months. This was incorporated into the circular and, not surprisingly, 119 of the 146 LEAs applied for the extra time. Even so, by the original deadline (1 April 1946), the Ministry had received only 16 completed plans. I am amazed they received that many.

As I was researching this section I kept asking myself this question: 'What was the relative power of the Ministry and the LEA in determining the local model of education?' Let's put it another way: 'How likely was it for an LEA to have its plan accepted if it didn't abide by the tripartite model?' Where was the balance of power between local and national politicians and the Ministry's civil servants?

We have reached a pivotal point in our timeline. Discussion and report-writing had to stop and the painting of new school signs saying 'secondary modern' or 'technical school' or 'comprehensive' had to begin. This is when the education authorities of England and Wales had to commit to a model of schooling. Way back in Chapter 3 ('A consistently negative image'), we saw that their decision to make secondary moderns the principal type of school is now perceived as being wrong. We have some way to go before I will reveal whether I agree. So, who was to blame for this situation?

Any author who has written about the country's educational history has proffered an answer. It has also become a popular dissertation subject for PhD students.

This is what Rubinstein and Simon said about the process in their book *The Evolution of the Comprehensive School: 1926–1972.*[65]

Throughout this period [1944–1950] the influence of the Ministry was continuously brought to bear on local authorities engaged on drawing up their plans. The Ministry informed local authorities [in late 1945] that it was 'inevitable... at the outset to think in terms of the three types [grammar, technical and secondary modern] and to include information of the amount of accommodation allocated to each type in the development plan'.

No doubt who these authors blame – the Ministry and, by implication, the minister in charge.

Dent said, in *Secondary Education for All,* that:

Very few local education authorities so completely disregarded the Ministry's advice as to go in wholeheartedly for 'multilateralism' or 'comprehensiveness.'

In a later book, he struck a more positive tone in his appraisal of the planning process.[66]

It is perhaps more correct to say that the plans offered a signally successful example of the virtue of co-operation between centre and locality, resulting in that 'variety within uniformity' which rightly ranks so high among the ideals of British democracy.

Maybe the blame is more equally spread between central and local government?

Denis Lawton, in his book *Politics of the school curriculum*, was in no doubt about the culprits – the 'Ministry officials'.[67] In the chapter titled 'The growing power of the mandarins' (something of a giveaway as to his conclusions) he wrote:

It is difficult to believe that the highly intelligent Ministry officials at that time could really have believed that the policy of parity of esteem would ever work out in practice, but it was a convenient political slogan and Labour Ministers were persuaded to adopt this as the official Labour Party policy.

I guess we could call this the *Yes Minister* theory whereby the cunning and conservative (with a small 'c') civil servants run intellectual rings around the malleable politicians. Another interpretation is that if you don't agree with the policies it is always easy to blame the civil servants.

Perhaps the most depressing opinions about the plans appeared in the book *Central Departments and Local Authorities*, by Professor John Griffith.[68] He pointed out that, once they were approved, the plans didn't need to be re-submitted as circumstances changed. Not surprisingly, circumstances kept changing and so the plans were soon overtaken by events. He wrote that:

Today a school development plan reads like the marching orders of some remote campaign in a long-forgotten war.

How the children of England and Wales were to be educated resulted from the aggregation of the decisions of 146 LEA education committees, all with their unique educational requirements and constraints and all governed by a range of political and educational opinions.

As I have stated before, there was no secret about the Ministry's position. Above all, it wanted to see the end of all-age schools, as soon as possible, and for the relationship between the voluntary and state schools to be regularised. Circular 90, the document that was sent to LEAs to tell them about the relaxation of the deadline for submitting plans, also contained a section titled 'Considerations on some points of policy'. What this had to say, in my view, explained the Ministry's 'red lines'; it explained the core of their thinking about the types of schools.

> *No hard and fast line can be drawn between Grammar, Technical and Modern education provision and, however these general terms are interpreted, some overlap is both proper and desirable.*

> *This should not, however, be allowed to obscure the necessity for clearly defined and adequately developed courses of the different kinds required to meet the special interests and abilities of different groups of pupils.*

It seems to me that the Ministry's primary concern was that the plans demonstrated that they were adequately catering for the three different types of child described in the Spens Report. How this was done was a secondary consideration and the Ministry was prepared to sanction 'experimentation'. The quotation marks are not intended to express my scepticism about their sincerity. I genuinely believe they were open to proposals that experimented with school models, within their clearly stated constraints.

All three types of child could be educated in a single large facility (multilateral); two types could be educated in a single school (bilateral); each type could have a separate school in close proximity (campus); or, and this was the most likely, and preferred, each type could have their own dedicated school (tripartite).

Up until now there seemed to be little or no difference between a multilateral school and a comprehensive school. I have used the words interchangeably. The distinction between the two was made clear in a Ministry circular issued in mid-1947.[69]

> *A multilateral school is one organised in three clearly defined sides, a comprehensive school one not so organised.*

The litmus test that identified a multilateral school was the presence of separate education streams delivering a grammar, technical and modern education. A comprehensive school didn't classify children into these groups and educated them as a whole. No doubt there are many other ways of defining the differences, but this one works for me and is the one I will use from now on.

The Ministry had also made its position clear about the age at which children were classified as being grammar, technical or modern 'types'. There had long been debate about whether 13 was better than 11 for this.

Proposals which seek partly to evade this difficulty [of selecting the appropriate school] by deferring decisions for all children until the age of 13 must be supported by satisfactory evidence that the interests of all the children will be safeguarded.

I don't think there is much doubt that the Ministry was signalling that it would take a lot of convincing to approve any education model using 13 as the age of selection.

It is impossible to state, with any confidence, the relative importance of the many factors that determined the dominant model of education that eventually emerged. In today's language we would talk about the relative importance of the different stakeholders. Without doubt the Ministry and successive ministers favoured the tripartite model.

There was another influencing factor that is rarely mentioned but that I think was mighty important. This was the pressure on LEAs to select the easiest and safest model on offer. In each LEA, the final decision makers were probably a handful of people who were faced with solving a catalogue of difficulties. They had to make the Education Act work, they had to raise the school-leaving age, they had to provide more school places because of the soaring birth rate and they had to do all this at a time of shortages.

Rubinstein and Simon expressed the same sentiment.

Under these circumstances [the Act, ROSLA etc] it is, perhaps, not surprising that many local authorities tended to concentrate on immediate necessities, accepting the structure that had developed and abjuring any idea of radical change.

Roy Lowe believed that extending the school-leaving age adversely affected the establishment of the new education system – especially secondary moderns.[70]

The timing meant that the raising of the school leaving age was achieved in economic circumstances which guaranteed the inferiority of the secondary modern schools in terms of staffing and accommodation thus pre-empting at the outset that 'parity of esteem' and 'unity of purpose' which were the other main planks in party policy [the Labour Party].

I think this argument can be taken one step further, to question if it would have been possible for most LEAs to select any other model than the tripartite system. They were all faced with a long list of immediate challenges and by abandoning the one type of schooling that was universally accepted as working well, albeit for a few (grammar schools), they would have been compounding their problems. There is a point at which taking a brave decision becomes irresponsible.

Those LEAs that instinctively favoured comprehensive education were faced with trading an uncertain up-side against a certain down-side of managing the additional stresses they would be placing on an already fragile education system.

So, in summary, if I was forced to name a culprit for the tripartite system it would be the unrealistic demands that politicians placed on LEAs to restructure their schools, having to simultaneously solve the problems of soaring pupil numbers and teacher shortages. All this combined with the strictures resulting from five years of war.

LEAs, when faced by so many demands and uncertainties, had to keep as close as possible to the existing education system and to minimise structural changes. They chose the least risky option. A reluctance to challenge the views of the Ministry was a secondary factor.

We know why the plans were late being delivered. The following chart[71] shows the extent of that lateness.

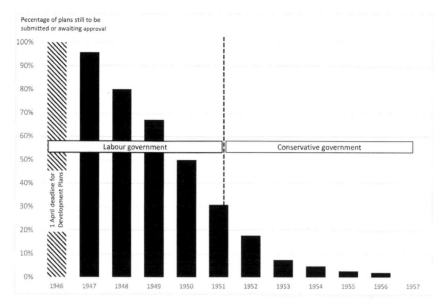

The percentage of plans that had not been submitted or were awaiting approval

The figures speak for themselves. It took much, much longer than expected to submit and approve the development plans. Not just a few months of delay, but a few years. I have no idea what repercussions this delay had for the implementation phase. Whatever it was, it wasn't good.

I have overlaid on the chart's timeline details of the political party that was in office. It is important to understand that the Labour Party was in power during the period when 70% of the plans were approved. This same point is made in the book *Education and Policy in England in the Twentieth Century*.[72]

> *The Labour government, during its terms in office from 1945 to 1951, was hesitant to push ahead with any radical departure from tripartitism. Only six Labour MPs voiced their support for comprehensive schools during this period. The 1945 Labour party election manifesto was silent on the issue.*

One example of this ambivalence was the refusal in 1949 of George
Tomlinson [minister of education] to accept the Labour-controlled
Middlesex Authority's plans for comprehensive schools.

The Labour Party's continuing support for the Education Act, which it
had helped create during its membership of the coalition government, was
soon to end. But, for the moment, political arguments about education policy
were limited to low-level skirmishes. Any doubts that the Labour Party was
responsible for the tripartite system must by now have disappeared.

In Parliament there was a small number of proponents of comprehensive
schools anxious to know why the government wasn't actively promoting this
form of education. This was mirrored by the advocates of grammar schools,
who worried that the quality of their teaching was under threat and sought
'assurances from the Minister' that this would not happen. Constituency
MPs wanted to know why XYZ school was being closed and 'will the
Minister please investigate'. There were questions about why more money
was being spent on new schools rather than repairs to existing ones. There
were questions about why LEAs were being asked to produce detailed
costed plans, when the lack of public funds meant they wouldn't be built for
five years (at least).

And endless questions about 'How many development plans have been
approved and why is the planning process taking so long?' The funding and
closure of individual church schools was also a popular subject of debate.

But, there were only a few, very few, debates about secondary moderns,
even though their number was rapidly rising. The handful of multilateral and
comprehensive schools was a far more popular subject for discussion.

So, when all of the LEA plans had been analysed, what did they reveal
about the future shape of education in England and Wales? Considering the
Ministry's penchant for publishing reports and pamphlets I had expected to
find numerous documents analysing in minute detail every element of the
plans. The Ministry and the LEAs had devoted an immense effort to this
venture but, to the best of my knowledge, they never published any analysis
of the results. Why this should be, I have no idea. Maybe the debacle of
these plans was something that the politicians and civil servants preferred to
forget.

By far the most comprehensive analysis of the plans was undertaken by

Joan Thompson in a pamphlet published by the Fabian Society.[73] Thompson must be praised for her diligence and thoroughness in analysing the contents of 111 plans, which represented 75% of the total. Most important, the plans she analysed accounted for over 90% of all school places.

Thompson's analysis made no distinction between the plans that had been approved and those still being negotiated. If her analysis was done in the year the pamphlet was published, then between 70% and 80% of the plans had received the Ministry's approval. She highlighted the approximate nature of her analysis, which was caused by the difficulty in extracting comparable data from the plans, which was in turn caused by the lack of common definitions. Even though the figures must be interpreted with a degree of caution, I am sure the overall conclusions that can be drawn are correct.

The LEAs estimated that the capital cost of the plans to repair and supply new secondary schools, in England and Wales, was £14 billion in today's pounds. To put this in context, this is approximately three times the capital investment during 2015–2016 on all types of schools in England.[74] Thompson calculated that if LEAs didn't increase the rate at which they were spending money on building works, it would take 80 years for the building plans to be completed (i.e. somewhere around 2030).

We are about to see the model of schooling that the LEAs were planning to deliver, but before doing that it is important to realise how little had changed since before the war. When the Fabian Society report was published there were 45 comprehensive and bilateral schools, educating 24,000 children. Otherwise, the secondary education structure remained pretty much as it was in 1939.

Thompson made some pointed observations about the mismatch between the official policy of the Labour Party, which supported comprehensive education, and the little influence this had on the Labour-controlled LEAs. She commented that the official policy 'has been to a considerable extent ignored'.

Most Labour-controlled LEAs are not whole heartedly supporting a policy of comprehensive schools. Of the 9 LEAs favouring comprehensive schools, 5 were Labour controlled and 4 were not.

The following chart[75] shows how the number of school places was expected to be distributed between the different types of schools, assuming the LEA development plans were implemented.

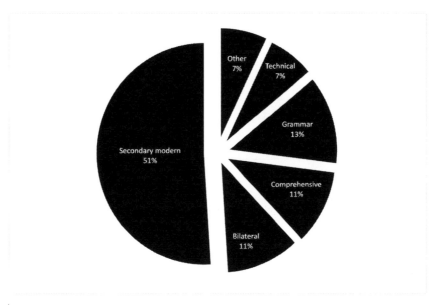

| Pupil places by type of school, including the London County Council

The London County Council (LCC) accounted for about 10% of the school population in England and Wales and planned to provide 103 'comprehensive high school units', each with between 1,250 and 2,000 pupils.[76]

Because it educated such a large number of children and planned for an education system that was very different from most other LEAs, a more representative picture is seen if London's numbers are excluded from the analysis, as is shown in the next chart.

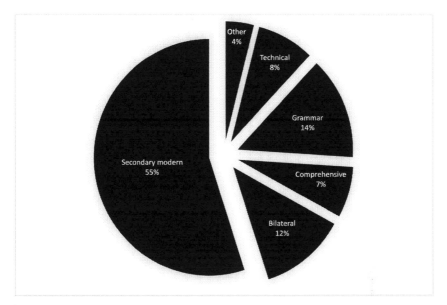

| Pupil places by type of school, excluding the LCC

I think these charts speak for themselves. Even if the London data is included, over half of children would be educated in secondary moderns.

In fact, the importance of secondary moderns was even greater than is suggested by the charts. The median percentage of pupils that secondary moderns were expected to educate, in each of the LEAs, was 62% – much higher than the mean.

Most of the schools categorised as bilaterals were establishments educating both secondary modern and technical school-type pupils. If these numbers are combined with those in secondary moderns, then nearly 67% of school children would be educated in secondary modern-type schools.

Whichever way you analyse the numbers you keep coming back to the same conclusion. Secondary modern schools were destined to become the backbone of the education system in England and Wales.

My final comments about the development plans relates to their diversity. We invariably talk about the 'average' number of school places, but this hides the huge difference between the plans. For instance, 20% of LEAs planned for comprehensive schools to educate more than 10% of their pupils. The average proportion of children expected to attend grammar schools was 14%. Many LEAs planned to provide far fewer places – 20% intended that less than 10% of children would attend these schools.

Because county councils (e.g. East Sussex and Lancashire) were more sparsely populated than county boroughs (e.g. Bolton and Southampton), they had more options and incentives to modify their education systems. The boroughs were more likely to use their existing school infrastructure and, not surprisingly, 63% of them planned a 100% tripartite system. The equivalent figure for county councils was 45%.

Secondary modern schools had a long gestation period, but by the mid-1950s they were the schools where most children were educated. There was not a uniform pattern across the country, as LEAs adopted the education model that best fitted their existing education infrastructure, and in a few places that was driven by their educational and social ideals.

Our brief glimpse at the diversity of the LEA plans shows there was no such thing as a national model of education and, most certainly, no such thing as a 'secondary modern education'. Using a term much favoured by the Ministry, education in England and Wales was about to enter a period of 'experimentation'.

Tough times. Tough decisions

One of the many unexpected benefits of writing this book has been the discovery that however dire the UK's economic and political conditions appear to be, the situation has been a lot worse in the past. Compared with what happened during WWII and the subsequent decade, the 2008 banking crash and its repercussions seem little more than a financial hiccup. That statement needs to be qualified with the caveat, 'up until now'. What might happen as central banks attempt to reinstate normal rates of interest is unknown. As for the Covid-19 pandemic, its long-term economic effects are anybody's guess but maybe the post-war experience might be a guide.

In their book *A century of fiscal squeeze politics,* Hood and Himaz analysed the causes, responses and repercussions of all the economic down-turns that occurred during the period of our timeline. The authors provide a fascinating account of the challenges that faced the two Labour and one Conservative governments that were in power between 1944 and 1955. It is the tale of a constant battle to fund politicians' spending commitments without inflicting a crippling tax burden on businesses and the public. Unless otherwise stated, I have used this book as the primary source of data for this section.

We have already learnt that funding for new schools was restricted and that what new construction took place was hampered by the shortages of materials and labour. There was, however, one commodity in bountiful supply – the stream of directives issued by the Ministry. As the LEAs wrestled with producing their development plans, they had to contend with directives about reducing the cost of construction and rescheduling (mostly to delay) their building works.

Politicians had promised to create the welfare state, build new towns, repair factories, renew bomb-damaged inner-city areas and provide the schools to accommodate the population 'bulge', to say nothing about funding the commitments enshrined in the 1944 Education Act. No doubt the science of economics has a term that describes this situation, but, in everyday language, there were too many promises and too little funding.

These economic challenges and the way that governments responded had a long-term effect on the country's economy, its politics and social attitudes. This section of the book provides an ultra-condensed account of what happened during the decade after the war – the period when most parents gained first-hand experience of secondary modern schools.

Funding the cost of fighting WWII came mainly from increasing the 'tax take' from individuals and companies. Between 1939 and 1945, the standard rate of income tax increased from 29% to 50%. Those fortunate enough to earn more than £20,000 a year (£850,000 in today's pounds) paid 98% tax. Companies that made more profit than they did before the war paid tax on the difference at 100%. The tax paid when purchasing products, the precursor to VAT, varied between zero and 100%.

Throughout the war, party politics was suspended, but the hostilities began as soon as the war in Europe ended. It was difficult for political parties to blame each other for the origins and conduct of the war, so they competed on the rewards that the electorate could expect for the years of high taxation and stagnant improvements in their living conditions.

We have looked in detail at the way the coalition government had worked together to pass the 1944 Education Act. At the same time, they were working together on another aspect of post-war policy – a committee to recommend a new system of healthcare and social support. The white paper that resulted from its deliberations soon became known by its chairman's surname – the Beveridge Report. It made recommendations about providing universal healthcare (what was to become the NHS) and how the state should support the unemployed, disabled, pregnant women and the retired. In exchange for paying a social insurance tax, citizens would be helped and protected by the state 'from cradle to grave'.

Churchill eventually accepted most of the report's recommendations, but was worried about its cost. He had told the war Cabinet that he did not wish to deceive the people 'by false hopes and airy visions of Utopia and El Dorado'.[77] His concerns were justified, when Treasury data showed that by 1944 the 'visible exports were only sufficient to buy one-seventh of the food and raw materials and other goods that were needed from abroad'.[78]

In 1945 the coalition government was dissolved, and the first election for 10 years took place. There are numerous accounts of how the election was fought and the reasons for the resounding Labour victory. And what a victory it was. In the post-war period, only Tony Blair has achieved a larger Parliamentary majority. How did the Labour Party achieve such an electoral advantage with policies that were so similar to those of the Conservatives (i.e. implementing the 1944 Education Act and the Beveridge Report)? What was it about the Labour Party's approach that chimed with the voters? Alternatively, what was it about the Conservative Party's approach that caused it to lose?

The Conservative manifesto was presented in the style of a formal speech by Winston Churchill. It seems that the party believed that the 'Churchill brand' was its biggest competitive weapon – not an unreasonable assumption, considering his role in governing war-time Britain.

The manifesto's language and style were formal and shorn of emotion, even to the extent of making only a few negative comments about the Labour Party. These were the words of a world statesman who had to balance the promises of improving people's lives with the need to ensure the country's safety, all the time being realistic about the post-war challenges.

Churchill's campaigning was very different in style from the manifesto. This is what he said, a month before the election, in a party political speech on the radio.[79]

A socialist state could not afford to suffer opposition; no socialist system can be established without a political police. They would have to fall back on some form of Gestapo.

Most commentators believed this radio performance went badly and struck the wrong note with the voters. Maybe the style of the manifesto was a reaction to this?

At the beginning of the manifesto there were commitments about the UK working with the United Nations to establish a 'World Organisation' to prevent future wars; making plans for India to achieve 'Dominion Status'; making it easier for people to move throughout the Empire; and creating a military 'national service' to train young men. Somehow, I doubt if these were promises that would inspire a war-weary populace.

There were plenty of firm pledges. New accommodation would be built – 220,000 permanent and 200,000 temporary homes. On retirement a single person would receive a pension of £43 per week (in today's pounds). Not a fortune, when you consider that in 2020 it was four times higher. There was an explanation about the new health service and its provision of a 'whole range of medical treatment from the general practitioner to the specialist, and from the hospital to convalescence and rehabilitation'.

Then came the warnings and the caveats.[80]

Our war budget has been rendered possible only by the severest taxation pressing heavily on everybody, by borrowing on a vast scale to meet the passing crisis, by huge Lend-Lease supplies from the United States and by generous gifts from Canada and elsewhere. All this cannot go on.

The State has no resources of its own. It can only spend what it takes from the people in taxes or borrowing. Britain is now a nation of taxpayers. Its record of providing more than half of the national expenditure during the last years of the war from taxation is unsur-passed. The willingness of this generation to bear their fair share of sacrifices must, though we hope for relief, be continued.

Little was said about education other than that the 1944 Act would be implemented with the objective of 'not producing a standardised or utility child, useful only as a cog in a nationalised and bureaucratic machine'. I think this referred to the Labour Party's plans for mass nationalisation, a subject we will soon discuss.

The manifesto positioned Churchill as the person who could manage the difficult transition from a war-time economy – the trusted pair of hands. What the document lacked was emotion. To my mind, it lacked the words that would convince voters that Britain really would change, as would (more importantly to them) the quality of their lives.

Those who created the Labour Party manifesto did a superb job of winning them the election. Maybe too good a job of selling to the electorate policies that it would be difficult to deliver. Most commentators believe Michael Young, later to become Lord Young, was the person responsible for its creation.[81] It was a beautifully crafted document. The central theme was that you cannot trust the ruling establishment, especially the business establishment, to ensure 'Victory in war was followed by a prosperous peace' – the manifesto's title. Voters would still have the memories of what happened following WWI with its economic hardship and unkept promises. The manifesto exploited these fears when it talked about:[82]

The 'hard-faced men who had done well out of the war' [WWI] who were able to get the kind of peace that suited themselves. The people lost that peace.

Great economic blizzards swept the world in those years. The great inter-war slumps were not acts of God or of blind forces. They were the sure and certain result of the concentration of too much economic power in the hands of too few men.

The basic proposition, which was continually hammered home, was that unless the selfish forces of the few were controlled then the voter's war-time physical and economic hardships would have been for nothing. Labour's solution was for the state to make the decisions, either by nationalising or by controlling the private sector. Targets for 'public ownership' were the Bank of England, inland transport, fuel and power and iron and steel. Then came a long list of items for which the state would control prices and supply; these included building materials, rents, the location of new factories and the 'necessities of life'. Any obstruction by the House of Lords 'would not be tolerated'. In summary, if elected:

> *The Labour Party stands for order as against the chaos which would follow the end of all public control. We stand for order, for positive constructive progress as against the chaos of economic do-as-they-please anarchy.*

Labour promised to implement the 1944 Education Act with the added commitment to 'raise the school leaving age to 16 at the earliest possible moment'. Little thought could have gone into the implications of those 12 words since that 'moment' didn't occur for 28 years. I fear that the same could be said about Labour's other promises of 'Utopia and El Dorado'.

During the war the government had controlled all aspects of people's lives, and the country had won the war. Why not continue these controls into the post-war period, to ensure that the policies of Butler and Beveridge were made a reality? An appealing and a winning storyline, which made the Right Honourable Clement Attlee prime minister in July 1945.

It is ironic that Churchill was so successful in managing a 'command economy' where the state had pretty much absolute control. In essence, the Labour Party proposed that this state of affairs should continue. The man who had made it work so well wanted the controls relaxed. Maybe the voters were more conservative in their outlook than the Conservatives?

State control of key industries didn't prevent shortages of consumer goods, food, fuel and building materials. If anything, the shortages got worse. By 1951, sterling was devalued by 30% as the country imported more than it could fund by exports or borrowing. Spending on defence plummeted but then rose again due to the Korean War. Personal taxation remained high. Rationing continued and was expanded to include potatoes and bread. Even the weather caused problems with the harsh winter of 1946–1947, resulting in energy shortages and then flooding. By 1947 the Conservative Party was ahead of Labour in the opinion polls. There was no let-up in the country's financial problems. In 1949 the government was forced to reduce expenditure by 5%. This level of cost-cutting could only be achieved by reneging on election promises. Apparently, the Ministry of Education even considered introducing fees for primary and secondary schools (an idea that was rejected).

By 1950 there was a need to reduce civil spending (e.g. schools) by 5%. In the same year purchase tax was raised from 33% to 66% for cars, TVs and domestic appliances. The policy that caused the most problems within the Labour Party was the introduction of fees for spectacles and dentures. The free NHS, the touchstone of the post-war contract with the voters, was free no more. This was too much for three senior Labour government ministers, who resigned.

In late 1951 the government called an election and lost. Attlee departed, and Winston Churchill returned as prime minister. Labour Party supporters could console themselves with the knowledge that they had polled more votes than the Conservatives, but that was little comfort since the vagaries of the electoral system would deny them power for the next 13 years.

R.A. Butler was given the unenviable task of managing the nation's finances, a job he held for the next four years. Throughout his period as chancellor of the Exchequer he was attempting, with mixed success, to cut government expenditure and minimise the pain of high taxation, all the time balancing the UK's trade balance with the rest of the world. It's ironic (and surprising) that the man credited with the 1944 Education Act put so much pressure on his successors at the Ministry of Education to reduce expenditure and even to consider charging parents fees. However, having read the deliberations of a Cabinet meeting about Butler's proposals to counter the country's dire economic problems, I can see why none of the Ministries was immune to spending reductions.[83]

In those days, the emblem of economic success, for the public as much as economists, was achieving a current account surplus. In 1951, when Labour left office, it was minus £10 billion (in today's pounds). Today, this economic indicator has lost its political relevance. I doubt if most people know, or care, that the 2017 figure was minus £83 billion. In the world of 1950s economics, devaluation of the currency was the inevitable outcome, unless action was taken. Sterling had already declined by 30% during the last two Labour governments – the last thing Butler wanted was for it to happen again on his watch. He would have been astonished to know that the exchange rate, against the dollar, would fall from 2.8 (1951) to just about 1.3 (2020).

In theory the solutions to the economic problems were simple – reduce the consumption of imported goods and services and export more; constrain government expenditure to match the money raised by taxation. Converting the theory into actionable and tolerable policies was not so simple.

Two of his decisions would have a direct effect on the public. Interest rates were raised and the amount of money a person could take out of the country was halved to £1,400 (in today's pounds). In 1952 it was halved again.

Over the period until the next election (1955) food subsidies were reduced and national insurance tax was increased. Charges were introduced for medical prescriptions, something first proposed by the previous Labour government. All the time there was much talk about 'protecting the NHS' – perhaps the most popular and longest-enduring political slogan and one that was dusted-off and used again during the Covid-19 crisis. Even the education budget was not immune to cuts, when in 1952 LEAs were asked to reduce their education spend by 5%.

This is a much-simplified account of the 10-year period after the war. As I listed the financial ups and downs (mainly downs) of the period I kept thinking about the teams of staff in the LEAs who were attempting to devise their education plans in this environment of uncertainty. Likewise, the 50,000 teachers who were trying to make secondary moderns work.

I wonder what the voters thought about the situation? They had been promised so much, but the new world of education and social support was late in arriving, unlike the bad news about the economy and its implications for their personal finances. With the benefit of hindsight, it is obvious that the horrendous financial wounds of WWII would take far longer to heal than politicians had led voters to expect. Creating a new education, health and social care system, difficult at the best of times, would be painfully slow in these dire economic conditions. I guess the one conclusion is that politicians and their advisers are lousy at planning and implementing change. An alternative interpretation is that politicians and their advisers understand the problems and risks but are unrealistic about their ability to solve them.

Reading about this era, it is easy conclude that there is no overlap with our own times, although Covid-19 might change that perception. Current forecasts suggest that the pandemic will push government borrowing to the highest level seen outside world wars in the past 320 years.[84]

We might feel that the work and financial conditions of the 1950s were totally different from those we experience. That Labour and Conservative politicians were offering a very different set of promises from their contemporary counterparts. However, the 2017 manifesto from the Labour Party promised to:[85]

> *Bring private rail companies back into public ownership... regain control of energy supply networks... replace our dysfunctional water system with a network of regional publicly-owned water companies... reverse the privatisation of Royal Mail.*

Forced by the economic upheaval of Covid-19 the Conservative government finds itself mirroring many of the policies that a year before it had criticised as being socialist day dreams. Maybe politicians' solutions are not so different?

In the early 1950s the rate of unemployment was around 1%. For all intents and purposes there was full employment. Yet consumer expenditure was limited by the levels of taxation and the availability of goods and services. The economics consultancy Oxford Economics[86] believes that the UK is in a similar position now, but for very different reasons. In 2018 the unemployment rate was at a 40-year low and seemed likely to keep falling. For reasons that I expect are not fully understood, the purchasing power of wages had stayed static and for many it had declined. Blaming the amorphous combination of 'globalisation and technology' was the most popular culprit but I am sure it is a lot more complex than that.

Maybe we have more in common with our parents and grandparents than we realise?

On the 10th anniversary of the war in Europe ending, the UK was still grappling with its physical and financial effects, but was experiencing near to full employment. LEAs had planned the future of their education policy and the landscape of schooling in England and Wales was taking shape.

A long and painful birth followed by an early death

So far, I have narrated the timeline, analysing and discussing the events that affected the history of secondary moderns in a sequential order. The drivers for educational change came, primarily, from the numerous Board of Education committees and their reports. Party political differences were always present, but they had not been the dominant factor in determining education policy. From now on, however, the political parties became deeply divided in their views about secondary schooling and their ideological differences became the dominant factor in determining the fate of secondary moderns.

Reflecting this importance of politics, I will conclude this part of our timeline by considering first how the Conservative Party and the LEAs implemented the development plans. This period ends in 1964, when the Labour Party came to office and reshaped the model of secondary education.

Even though we have only reached the part of the timeline when secondary moderns are being born, I think it will help our understanding of the final two sections to see what happened, through to the point when the schools were in terminal decline.

The following chart[87] shows the numbers of children attending the different types of secondary schools between the end of the war and 1975. It reveals the huge change that occurred to the structure of secondary education, in a matter of a few years. The danger in representing a major upheaval as a simple graphic is that it reduces the huge cost of human effort and the disruption of children's education to a series of points on an X–Y axis. Hopefully, the final two sections of the timeline will explain the story and detail the implications behind the numbers.

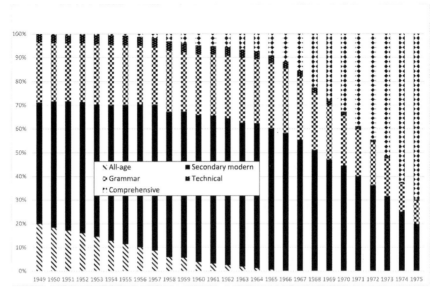

| Pupil numbers in the different types of secondary schools (1949–1975)

Of course, the reason for the demise of the secondary moderns was the switch to comprehensive education. Until 1965 the percentage of children attending these schools was in single digits. Ten years later it was 70%. It is worth dwelling on that last point for a moment. Try and imagine the decade of work, by LEAs and teachers, that went into creating the thousands of secondary moderns and how quickly they were abandoned. During this time nearly 60% of grammar schools switched to become comprehensives. Putting aside questions of the rights or wrongs of the 'comprehensivisation' of the schooling system, it is hard to grasp the upheaval and uncertainty this must have caused for a generation of children and their teachers.

The chart also describes what happened to other types of school. Ironically, the objective had been to phase out all-age schools as soon as possible, yet they were still educating 10% of pupils in the mid-1950s. As hard as it was to remove these schools, it was even harder to launch the new technical schools. They never educated more than 5% of children and failed to become an established part of the country's secondary education system. The circumstances leading to their demise have many similarities to those awaiting secondary moderns and are well documented in the book *The Secondary Technical School*.[88]

Having visited two-thirds of the country's 300 technical schools, the book's author identified multiple reasons for their probable failure. I think the primary problem, and one that could just as easily be diagnosed for secondary moderns, was this one, described by the principal of a technical college: 'Too little thought had been put into the question of exactly what these schools are to do.'

As it was the technical schools struggled to achieve the much-desired 'parity of esteem' with grammar schools; they were always the second-best option. This is not surprising if parents didn't understand what the schools were seeking to achieve and how they would benefit their children.

Many of the schools didn't have the necessary facilities to develop a distinctive excellence in technical subjects.

It must be remembered that a considerable proportion of them have not the necessary physical conditions – buildings, workshops, laboratories etc – to permit their full development.

It appeared that many of the LEAs used the schools as an 'administrative convenience' and required them to accept pupils who were 'late developers' at almost any age. This chimes with my experience where a few of my classmates moved, age 13 years, to the local technical school. Rather than building new schools, many LEAs adopted a model whereby a grammar school or secondary modern had a technical stream.

The author was right to be pessimistic about the schools and by 1985 they had almost disappeared. He was also correct in his analysis of the difficulties facing the whole secondary education system.

Today, many experiments in education organisation are being carried out without the necessary conditions that would enable them to be given a reasonable trial and allow their merits to be assessed properly and reasonably.

All forms of secondary education are now the subject of close scrutiny from the standpoint of their political significance. The schools are not in this case regarded as instruments for the education of the pupils so much as instruments for the furtherance of some political creed or philosophy.

It is very difficult for any school head teacher or for any school staff to maintain to the full an interest in the work they are undertaking knowing that their school organisation is being reviewed and that it might in the very near future disappear.

So it was that grammar schools remained the most stable part of the secondary school system. For the 20 years after 1949 they educated around a quarter of secondary pupils. Eventually, their numbers declined rapidly, so that in 1975 they taught just 10% of children. Today (2021) they educate 5% of state-funded pupils but still generate more deep feelings, in both their detractors and their supporters, than any other type of school.

We now know how the story of secondary moderns ended. But, let's return to the time when the schools were still going through their 'experimentation' phase. The time when the majority of parents would receive a letter telling them that their beloved son or daughter had not been successful in achieving a grammar school place but would be attending XYZ secondary modern.

The end of the bipartisan education policy

We re-join the timeline after the election of a Conservative government and the appointment of a new minister of education, the Rt. Hon. Sir David Eccles, KCVO, MP. It is approximately a decade since secondary moderns were born and much has happened. A detailed look at the events of 1955 reveals the hurdles they would face and some of the reasons for their demise. First, secondary education was becoming an arena for political hostilities between Labour and the Conservatives. In today's language, it had become 'weaponised', in the same way as the NHS is today. Second, the role and type of exams taken by secondary school children were in flux. GCE 'O' and 'A' level exams had been launched. I am sure these bring back fond memories for many people reading this book. Finally, the dialogue between Eccles and his advisers suggested he was increasingly unsure that the model of secondary education was on the right trajectory.

The story started with a note that arrived on the minister's desk from the prime minister, Anthony Eden.[89]

Dear David, Have you any problems to which we shall have to give our early attention? If so I would be glad to have a short note from you upon them since I am trying to review the position generally.

When it arrived, Eccles had been minister of education for six months –
enough time to understand the challenges and complexity of the job, but not
long enough to do anything to change educational policy.

He didn't believe he had any urgent educational problems but told the
prime minister about a pressing 'political problem'.[90]

> *The most political problem in education is the 11+ examination and*
> *the Socialist proposal to abolish it by rolling up all secondary*
> *schools into comprehensive schools.*

A week later he circulated a memorandum to the Cabinet, detailing the
problem and his proposed solution. His observations and proposals provide
a good starting point for this element of the timeline.[91]

> *It was hoped that modern [secondary modern] schools would attain*
> *'parity of esteem' with the grammar schools, and that as a result the*
> *disappointment and jealousy felt by parents when their children*
> *failed to qualify for a grammar school would disappear. But this has*
> *not happened, and the resentment appears to be growing.*
>
> *Although the comprehensive school is certainly not the right answer,*
> *we cannot leave the 11+ examination where it is. The anxieties and*
> *jealousies are too easy to play on. If we copied the USA we should*
> *treble our Universities, and send to them, via much enlarged*
> *grammar schools, a far higher proportion of the population than*
> *goes to them today. But the standards [of the universities and*
> *grammar schools] could not be diluted in this way without changing*
> *their whole character.*

It was interesting that Eccles raised the implications for the demand for
university places if grammar school places were expanded. The number of
young people attending university did increase, but it would take over 20
years before the UK mirrored the US and trebled the numbers. We will
cover the issue of diluting standards in later chapters.

Many of the ways that education has evolved would have surprised
Eccles. He would have been astonished to know that his counterpart in

today's government has the 'problem' that girls are a third more likely to go to university than boys. In 1955, women comprised less than a quarter of university students. Other educational issues have remained immune to change, such as the ongoing arguments about private and grammar schools.

He believed that the '11-plus problem' could be resolved by exploiting the public's awareness of the shortage of technicians and skilled workers and positioning secondary modern schools as the solution. He envisaged pupils taking vocational courses and acquiring the skills that were required of the rapidly growing and evolving workforce.

How this transformation of secondary modern schools would be achieved was not detailed in the memorandum, but it was defined in earlier drafts of the document.[92]

> *In order to build up the secondary modern schools as the feeders of the technical colleges and institutions, I am suggesting to LEAs that they should distribute secondary technical courses over as many secondary modern schools as possible, rather than concentrate them in new secondary technical schools. This has the great advantage that each secondary modern school will be able to offer some special course that no other school in the area can offer.*

> *It is, of course, a corollary of this policy that further education in technical colleges and evening institutes must be pushed forward as vigorously as possible, and its links with the secondary schools strengthened.*

I expect that Eccles was reticent about providing his Cabinet colleagues too much detail, fearing the questions it might raise. For instance, if the curriculum of secondary modern schools included the same technical content as that of the secondary technical schools, what would differentiate the two types of schools? Eccles couldn't answer this question – and six months later asked his civil servants for an explanation.

But before we get to that point we need to understand what had caused the '11-plus problem' and comprehensive schools to become a political issue.

The paragraphs below contain the comments about education appearing in the Labour and Conservative manifestos for the 1951 and 1955 general elections.[93]

In 1951, education was a minor issue for both political parties. The Conservative Party didn't mention it at all and the Labour Party offered only a few vague words about 'equal opportunities' and 'encouraging a spirit of home and adventure'.[94]

Labour will press forward towards greater social equality and the establishment of equal opportunities for all. We shall extend our policy of giving all young people equal opportunities in education. We shall encourage a spirit of hope and adventure in the young.

Things had changed radically by the time of the 1955 election. Labour and the Conservatives now had very different visions of how secondary education should be organised.

Labour manifesto promised:

- LEAs will be asked to submit schemes for abolishing the exam (11+).
- To encourage comprehensive secondary schooling.
- 'To remove from primary schools the strain of the 11-plus examination.'
- Begin to provide part-time education for children leaving school at 15 (as specified by the 1944 Education Act).

Conservative manifesto promised to:

- Reduce class sizes.
- Extend facilities for scientific and technical training.
- Complete the reorganisation of all-age classes in rural areas and 'make good progress' in the towns.
- Give parents the chance, before their children take the 11+, to discuss with teachers and the LEA the school that best suits their child.

- Make day courses at technical colleges more successful.
- 'Tackle the problem of slum schools.'

Also contained in the manifesto were these statements of policy.

To prepare for the increasing opportunities of the modern world we need all three kinds of secondary school and we must see that each provides a full and distinctive education.

Will not permit the grammar schools to be swallowed up in comprehensive schools.

It is vital to build up secondary modern schools, and to develop in them special vocational courses.

As its manifesto makes clear, Labour was intent on abolishing the 11-plus and moving to a model of comprehensive schools.

I wonder how the LEAs' heads of education reacted to the Labour Party's proposal? They had just spent a decade planning and implementing their education policy and were now being told that if Labour won the election they would need to think again about their model of secondary education. In the space of four years the Labour Party had moved from accepting the idea of secondary moderns to proposing policies that would lead to their destruction. It would be wrong to say that Labour had ever actively supported these schools but its senior politicians had done nothing to halt their creation. By 1955 this bipartisan approach to education had ended.

By comparison, the Conservatives' election promises, of giving parents the opportunity to discuss their child's future schooling before the 11-plus and of developing vocational courses in secondary moderns, appeared to be minor changes to the status quo. The most adversarial words in their manifesto were reserved for defending grammar schools against the threat of 'comprehensivisation'.

Most educational historians seem to believe that comprehensivisation was the best system of schooling and unsurprisingly interpret it as a failure that it took until 1955 for the Labour Party to adopt a national policy to end selective education. Many commentaries are critical of the educational policy and achievements of the entire Attlee era of government (1945–1951). This quote from *Education and Labour Party Ideologies* by Denis Lawton[95] is typical of the criticisms.

> *Attlee was not the only one to blame for this neglect of educational issues, however: nearly all his senior colleagues were guilty of placing education at a lower level of priority than other pressing problems. For example, Hugh Dalton, although regarded as left-wing, and as Chancellor of the Exchequer supported education spending, had almost nothing to say about education policy.*

As I have already commented, I don't agree with this conclusion because the 'pressing problems' were more akin to an economic nightmare. After a resolution at Labour's annual conference in late 1950 the party made it clear that it favoured comprehensive schools and abandoning the 11-plus; however, it believed that education policy should be left to the LEAs.[96]

> *At present local education authorities have power to select the type of school to be developed within their area, subject to approval by the Ministry of Education. This local autonomy should be preserved. It would be wrong to impose a pattern of education upon local authorities.*

Not all parts of the Labour Party favoured this policy, as is clear from the editorial section of the October 1951 edition of *The Political Quarterly*.[97]

> *No attempt is made to examine the scholastic aspects of the question, or to consider the problems involved in attempting to educate a mass of children of widely differing abilities, aptitudes, and taste, who are destined for widely different careers. The matter is argued and decided almost entirely on social grounds, in terms of a doctrinaire egalitarianism quite unrelated to genuine equality of educational opportunity.*

A policy for secondary education is, we regret to say, a shallow and superficial document which can only injure the Labour Party among persons who take a serious interest in education.

Brian Simon described this as a 'broadside from the Fabian element within the Labour Party', a group that he believed was 'determinedly meritocratic'.[98] I am left wondering if he intended this to be a compliment or a term of abuse? Whether comprehensive education was fair but fallible – excuse the alliteration – was a question that was never properly answered.

Making decisions on instinct rather than research

If we now fast forward to the 1955 election, the Labour Party's sentiment towards comprehensive schools and the 11-plus was extended by the new policy to 'ask LEAs to submit schemes for abolishing the exam [the 11-plus]'. Was the Labour Party responding to a groundswell in public anger about the perceived unfairness of secondary schooling or was it driven by political expediency or a hardening of the doctrinal beliefs referenced in *The Political Quarterly*? Perhaps the policy change was motivated by a desire to strengthen the control of central government over local authorities?

Eccles' fears and the Labour Party's policy shift were justified on the basis of his perception that the public (voters) were concerned about secondary schooling. It is impossible to quantify the negative public feelings about the 11-plus and secondary moderns and the enthusiasm for comprehensive schools. Focus groups and market research were yet to be used to guide policy decisions. Judging the public's mood relied on the instincts of a handful of politicians and civil servants, a technique that was, and still is, vulnerable to multiple types of behavioural bias.

Was Eccles correct or was he reflecting his own and his advisers' perceptions? As a proxy for measuring the strength of 'public feeling', we can analyse the newspapers' coverage of the time and gauge their interest in commenting on the subject.[99]

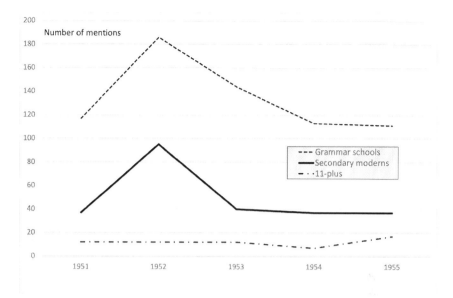

Number of times the terms are mentioned in newspapers indexed by ukpressonline

In 1955 the *Daily Mirror* and the *Daily and Sunday Express* were the highest-circulation newspapers, with a combined annual circulation of over 9 million – approximately 40 times the readership of *The Times*.[100] The annual frequency of the terms 'secondary modern', 'grammar school' and '11-plus' is shown in the above chart. This is not the frequency for each publication but their combined use of the terms. Also included in these numbers are mentions from eight other disparate publications (e.g. *The Church Times* and the *Daily Worker*. I couldn't help but wonder how many subscribers took both these publications!)

It is difficult to reconcile this analysis with the idea that there was a tide of dissatisfaction with the 11-plus and secondary moderns when, in 1955, the two highest-circulation papers in the UK only mentioned the subjects 60 times. I looked at all of these references and only two were hostile; the remainder were mentions of the schools that people in the news had attended. It's interesting to note that the papers were about three times more interested in talking about grammar schools than secondary moderns. Comprehensive schools were only mentioned twice in 1955.

Another source of newspaper content is the British Library's *The British*

Newspaper Archive.[101] In 1955, the 60 publications that referenced secondary modern schools contained, on average, about one mention every two weeks. Most of these were regional publications (e.g. *Portsmouth Evening News, Coventry Evening Telegraph*) and very few of the comments referenced the educational performance of the schools.

Another measure of the intensity of the argument about the 11-plus and secondary moderns is the number of times the terms appeared in the records of the House of Commons and House of Lords. Undoubtedly there was an increase in the references over the period 1951–1955 but the absolute number of times the terms were mentioned is tiny, as were references to 'comprehensive education' (67 references in 1955).[102]

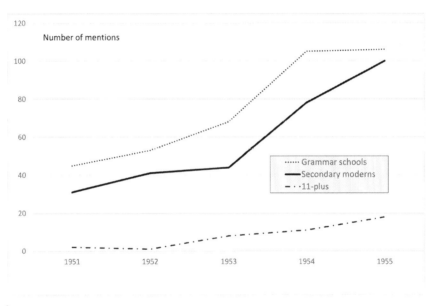

Number of times the terms are mentioned in *Hansard* (House of Commons and House of Lords)

If the national mood about selective education had changed, it was not being reflected in the political discourse or the commentary of the mass readership national and regional newspapers. Of course, this doesn't 'prove' that concerns about the tripartite system didn't exist, but politicians of the time had no way of knowing their magnitude.

The hardening in the Labour Party's policy appears to have resulted from the skill and determination of the National Association of Labour Teachers in driving the party's annual conference policy-making process to approve its vision of 'comprehensivisation'. Gary McCulloch provided a detailed, blow-by-blow account of the machinations of the Labour Party's education policy decision making.[103] His account described the party being deeply divided about its vision of secondary education and the process for its implementation. As far as the Labour Party was concerned, the sooner grammar schools were replaced by comprehensives, the better. I think this was the primary motivation, rather than ending secondary moderns.

Let's consider for a moment the implications of these developments. From its annual conference in 1950 the Labour Party, at a national level, had refined and hardened its secondary education policy to abandon the 11-plus and replace grammar, technical and secondary moderns with comprehensive schools. By 1955 the national policy had moved from 'encouraging' to 'asking' LEAs to create new versions of their development plans based on a single model of schooling. This implied that the national Labour Party had abandoned trying to improve the performance of secondary moderns and was intent on their destruction. It is important to take note of my prefix 'national', because many Labour-controlled LEAs were working as hard as they could to make their secondary moderns succeed.

It seems that Labour's reversal in policy, engineered by a minority of the party, was so successful that not only did it commit the party to abandoning secondary moderns but it seeded the same ideas within the Conservative Party.

In my judgement, those in the Labour Party driving forward the comprehensivisation model were primarily motivated by notions of social engineering; those in the Conservative Party were responding (reluctantly) to a fear of the electoral damage they might suffer. Arguments about education and the practicality of changing the system were a secondary issue.

The muddle of examining secondary school children begins

At the same time as Sir David Eccles was explaining to his colleagues his plans for countering the Labour Party's education policies, his civil servants were working on a document[104] detailing the type of external exams to be taken by secondary school children.

Before considering these proposals, it is worth a few words about the troubled and confusing story of external secondary school exams (i.e. those exams set and marked by an independent body, as opposed to internal exams administered by schools).

Much was said in the 1944 Education Act about 'examinations', but these were all related to medical examinations of children. The Act said nothing about academic exams and how they should evolve. In the previous section of the timeline (Chapter 5, 'Between the Wars') I explained the importance of the Spens (1938) and the Norwood (1943) Reports in the story of secondary moderns and their recommendations on exams. As a reminder – Norwood proposed that the School Certificate Examination, the one that children took at the age of 16 and that required a pass mark in a group of subjects, should become 'an internal examination, conducted by the teachers on syllabuses and papers framed by themselves'. If it had been implemented, this would have marked a major change in education policy.

It remained just a recommendation, but Norwood's proposal to abandon the School Certificate Examination resulted from the belief that schools, in particular secondary moderns, should be 'freed' from the constraints of having to study a syllabus that was defined by exams. You will remember that it was hoped that secondary modern schools would 'experiment' with their curriculum, making them more relevant to the lives and jobs of their pupils. Such freedom would be stifled if the curriculum were dominated by studying to pass external exams. I feel sure that this wish to free teachers from having to 'teach for the exam' would resonate with today's teaching profession. The current head of Ofsted concurs with this sentiment and modified the 2019 school inspection framework accordingly.[105]

We know that focusing too narrowly on test and exam results can often leave little time or energy for hard thinking about the curriculum, and in fact can sometimes end up making a casualty of it.

Another, more sinister, interpretation of Norwood's ideas was an intention to differentiate secondary moderns (places you didn't take external exams) from grammar schools (where you did). I find this idea hard to believe. At the time of Norwood and into the early post-war years, there was a desire to delay the age at which all children took external exams until their

17th or 18th birthday to avoid the early subject specialisation that resulted when they were taken two years earlier – an educational concept that would now be considered 'progressive'.

The story of how secondary school exams evolved was told by Peter Fisher in his book *External examinations in secondary schools in England and Wales*.[106] He provided a detailed explanation of the involved and fractious story. Unlike so many historical accounts of education events, Fisher's is unbiased and not a selective presentation of the facts to make a political point.

Much of the story involved the power struggle between the numerous organisations with an interest, both financial and educational, in the way children should be examined. Among the protagonists were central government, LEAs, universities, teachers, headmasters and school inspectors. To complicate matters, before discussing exams, these factions first had to reach agreement about the basic question: 'What was the purpose of external exams?' Were they primarily a gateway into university and the professions? Were they a measure of children's academic achievement that could be used for gaining employment? Were they a way of establishing the school's curriculum?

Or, to define their conundrum another way... The School Certificate Examination came from the era of grammar and elementary schools. How should the exam system evolve now that the leaving age had been raised and secondary schools were fragmented into grammar, technical, secondary moderns and a few comprehensives? How relevant was the pre-war exam curriculum to the challenges of the world in the 1950s?

After much debate and negotiating, a compromise solution was found that seemed to satisfy, in varying degrees, all of the parties. In 1951 the ordinary, advanced and scholarship-level General Certificates of Education (GCE) were born. It was initially intended that children would be 16+ before they could take these exams, which was something of a problem because most children left school before this age. Subsequently this rule was relaxed – perhaps I should say 'fudged'.

If you are thinking that this all seems something of mess, then you are right. The GCE was not designed to be taken by secondary modern pupils, either in its difficulty or the age at which it could be taken. By 1955, the situation had become even more complicated as other organisations (e.g.

The Royal Society of Arts and the College of Preceptors) began proposing alternative types of exam.

The issuing of Circular 289 was an attempt to clarify the Ministry's thinking about exams. It gave a cautious welcome to the increasing numbers of secondary modern pupils who were taking GCEs but was firmly against the idea of any new exam being developed for these schools. Rather than closing down the discussion, the circular heightened the disagreements about how best to examine secondary modern children.

I will explain how this story ends but I now want to consider two other issues that would soon be taxing the minister.

The decline and fall of technical schools

I have already referenced Eccles' uncertainty about the role of technical secondary schools. At the end of 1954 he wrote a note to his officials asking them to provide answers to a long list of questions, including the following.[107, 108]

> *What part can Technical Schools play in meeting these needs [to fill the shortage of trained craftspeople, engineers and scientists]. Do their number and vigour have any effect on the entry to technical and technological colleges? [Just under 5% of children went to these schools.] What are the technical schools trying to do?*
>
> *Is it a great advantage to give a technical school a separate existence or can equally good results be obtained when it is combined with Modern secondary school? Or with a Grammar school?*
>
> *What part do we expect them to play in 1975?*

By the end of January 1955, Eccles had read his officials' response and sent his reply. I think it would be safe to say that he was disappointed by their answers.[109]

> *The conclusions remind me of a stroke at billiards, when to pocket the red one must first make a cannon off the white: to get to grips*

with technical schools it seems we must first have a go at the
grammar schools. It may be so.

His officials' advice favoured the status quo, both in the ways schools
were organised and changing demand for new skills. The statistics he was
given showed that the proportion of LEAs' building programmes devoted to
places in technical schools or courses had fallen from 12% in 1951–1952 to
6.9% in 1955–1956. These numbers were followed by a sentence claiming
'present trends suggest that the present percentage of technical school places
will certainly be maintained and probably increased'. That's not the conclusion I would have drawn from the data. We now know that the number of
schools and the percentage of pupils they educated fell steadily. By 1975,
the year Eccles mentioned, they had all but disappeared, teaching just 0.3%
of pupils.

The main document produced by his officials attempted to explain the
roles of the different schools in providing the next generation of workers. I
expect I had more time to study it than did Eccles, but my eyes glazed over
after a couple of hours, not much more enlightened than before I began.
Towards the beginning of the document was a paragraph that set the tone for
the rest of the arguments – it was titled 'Presuppositions'.

If this country is to survive as a great nation into the 21st century,
society needs to develop in the direction suggested by the Minister
and this requires that a higher proportion of our young people
should be trained to understand the technical basis of our civilisa-
tion and, more specifically, to become craftsmen, engineers, scien-
tists, etc.; but that such a development will be too costly if it's bought
at the price of a loss of the values summed in the phrase 'the
humanities'.

Eccles was disappointed that his officials didn't share his vision that the
UK would need a 'revolutionary increase' in the number of highly paid technically orientated jobs and hence suitably trained people to fill them. The
note that he appended to his memo summed up his frustration.

I have in mind to ask the writers of these papers if any of them would care to visit some of the Atomic Energy production plants.

I interpreted this jibe to suggest his officials needed to open their minds to the high-tech world of the mid-1950s. As we have seen, a few months after this was written he was suggesting that 'technical courses should be distributed to as many secondary modern schools as possible, rather than concentrated in the new secondary technical schools'. Had Eccles given up on technical schools? My guess is the answer is yes. Having waded through his officials' briefing papers, it is difficult to come to any other conclusion.

What were secondary moderns supposed to be doing?

A month after asking his officials about secondary technical schools, Eccles fired off another note asking questions about secondary moderns.[110] As I read these papers I could visualise the situation as he attempted to get to grips with the reality, rather than the theory, of what was happening in the country's schools. With hindsight we know that he was asking all of the right questions, although I am not so sure he was getting the answers he expected, wanted or – most importantly – needed.

He started by asking whether the document *The New Secondary Education*[111] was still in circulation or had been superseded. He then quoted a passage of its text, followed by a list of questions.

'The aim of the modern [secondary modern] school is to provide a good all-round secondary education, not focussed primarily on the traditional subjects of the school curriculum etc.'

I don't not know what this has come to mean i.e. what HMIs [school inspectors] have told teachers it should mean. Unsystematic education? the children doing what they like best? or find easiest? [sic]

How has this doctrine stood the test of experience?

I have previously discussed *The New Secondary Education* document. I found it ponderous and unclear of its target audience. The minister of education at the time came to the same conclusion. It provided some guidance about the role of secondary modern schools but only in the vaguest terms.

Eccles asked another question.

If I am to say useful things about the desirable number of grammar school places I must know what is being taught in the modern secondaries [secondary moderns]. What alternative in academic education has the child who just fails to get into a grammar school? and this is relevant to the practical possibilities of transfer, which, if few academic studies have been taken in secondary moderns from 11 to 13, must be restricted thereby.

His sense of frustration and annoyance was evident in the document's final sentence.

I should have to think very severely if you told me that The New Secondary Education *still holds the field. And if it does not, what does?*

His civil servants were quick to respond. Yes, *The New Secondary Education* was still in circulation and was one of the Ministry's 'best sellers'. No, it contained nothing they would want to withdraw. No, they didn't think there was any need for an updated publication. The same civil servant then told the minister:

Increasingly the course of work for the ablest pupils in Modern schools resembles that of the least able in the Grammar schools. But often as yet the ablest are not adequately or properly stretched in the Modern school.

The next sentence attracted the minister's attention, because he underlined the phrase 'curricula do not prevent this' and wrote in the margin, 'This is the point'.

Transfer from Modern to Grammar is becoming more and more
common (and curricula do not prevent this) and so is retention with
adequate opportunity and stimulus in some Modern schools.

It's only a guess, but I expect he was thinking, 'What's the rationale for
having two types of school, Modern and Grammar, teaching a similar
curriculum?'

Eccles could not have been satisfied with his officials' response. How
could his civil servants believe that this document from 1947 reflected the
reality in 1954, when, on their own admission, some pupils were tackling
the same academic subjects as their grammar school counterparts? This
seemed like a 'fact-free' response that lacked insight into what was really
happening in the country's 3,550 secondary modern schools.

A weighty report was prepared for the minister by HMI school inspectors providing their observations about the state of the country's secondary
moderns.[112] The 'conclusions' section of the document was a balanced
mixture of good and bad news. There were concerns about inadequate
staffing and the poor physical state of the schools.

In the coming years, while the number of pupils entering the schools
is climbing to its peak, and before the supply of suitably qualified
teachers becomes more plentiful, are bound to be testing years.

Inadequate staffing, crowded premises and large classes are likely to
curb progress and delay the development of a large scale of those
features through which a number of schools have already established
themselves and won distinction. In some areas, even to maintain the
pattern of organisation that has been established may call for
considerable determination as well as good fortune.

Then came some hopeful comments to provide balance.

But the story is one of achievements as well as difficulties. Those
who visit secondary modern schools regularly and intensively find in
them many sources of encouragement and inspiration. From the very
nature of things, the pattern of secondary modern provision can

never be rigid or uniform, but there is already an orderliness about
it: its variety corresponds to the logic of the situation and is not
shapeless or chaotic.

And so the report went; some things were good, others bad or needed
attention. What was missing was tangible conclusions and there was very
little advice.

To my mind, this statement encapsulated the challenge that the schools
were facing.

Its many species [secondary moderns] have not yet been identified
and described in terms that the layman can recognise. It has not yet
acquired the respectability of age [compared with grammar
schools]. The individual secondary modern school, therefore, often,
starts with no traditions to support it. Sometimes it starts with tradi-
tions inherited from other types of schools, whose whole approach to
their task was different in spirit from its own. The school's own
building may be an ever-present reminder of a past which it is trying
to shed. [I assume this refers to the old Elementary schools.]

Eccles couldn't have been reassured, or greatly informed, by this and the
other documents he received. Hopefully he had a lot more dialogue with his
officials during 1955 that I didn't have access to, which may have been
more insightful and hopeful – somehow I doubt it.

It was clear to me that a decade after secondary moderns were launched
neither the minister nor his officials had much grasp of what they were
supposed to be doing. We need to remind ourselves that we are not talking
about a small number of specialist schools but the type that were educating
the majority of the country's children.

The 'second chance' that technical colleges provided

Maybe it was his frustration with the answers to his questions about technical and secondary modern schools, but in December 1955 Eccles started
work on a project concerned with post-school education. In late December
1955 he finished his outline draft of a white paper on technical education,

which was published a couple of months later (February 1956).[113] Often, a minister's original draft document – rather than the sanitised, 'civil service' version – provides the most clarity about his beliefs and intentions. So it was with Eccles' *Sketch for White Paper on Technical Education*.[114]

We know that Eccles was convinced that the latest developments in scientific research would have a profound effect on society. In 1955, the scientific revolution was all about atomic energy and space travel. The same sentiments exist today, except the technologies are now AI, quantum computing, robotics and genetic engineering. Then the fear was losing the technological race to Russia, which was thought to be educating 325,000 scientists of university standard compared with 17,000 in the UK. Today, the threat is seen as coming from companies and universities in China. Then, as now, the panacea to ensuring national competitiveness was to have a techno-logically educated workforce.

Against this backdrop it is not surprising that Eccles' *Sketch* started with a section about 'The world we live in':

The scientific revolution is world-wide. In this advance nation will overhaul nations, but so great is the gap between the new knowledge and man's present capacity to apply this knowledge to the creation of wealth that for many years the prizes will not go to sheer numbers but to the best system of education.

A month before the white paper's publication the prime minister used a more succinct version of these words in a speech: 'The prizes will not go to the countries with the largest population. Those with the best systems of education will win.' As if to demonstrate government unity, these words were quoted at the beginning of the white paper. Who knows if the prime minister really believed the necessity for improving technical education or whether it was a PR ploy.

Eccles' concern about the state of primary and secondary education appeared in a section of the draft that was scribbled out. In it, he talked about primary school teachers being hampered by oversized classes and secondary schools soon to be challenged by the surge in demand resulting from the baby boom. He also wrote about the wastage of talent due to chil-dren leaving school early and how schools and parents could do more to extend children's education. My guess is that he decided that these negative comments served no useful purpose. Maybe it was because he was very soon going to launch an enquiry to improve the education of children aged 15–18 (the Crowther Report).[115] Whatever the reason, these ideas never made it in to the final version.

The white paper's primary purpose was to announce the government's plan to increase the technical colleges' output of students from 10,000 to 15,000 over a five-year period. The intention was to achieve this by increasing by 50% the number of students studying for the colleges' advanced courses, and doubling the number of students released by their employers to study part-time day courses (day release). The bill for this expansion was £70 million (£1.7 billion in today's pounds).

Most of the white paper and the supporting archived documents explained the needs for additional funds and how they would be spent. My interest was the new insights into the Ministry's thoughts on secondary modern schools.

Much of the white paper's data and new thinking came from the book *Technical Education* by Peter Venables.[116] Eccles must have read all 600 pages of the book. He produced seven sheets of detailed notes referencing page numbers and quotes. Having used so many of the book's ideas, he might have made some reference to the book's author in the white paper, but Peter Venables' contribution to the UK's model of technical education went unreferenced.

Eccles commented about Venables' description of technical colleges as:

A retrieving mechanism for those who failed at school. He shows how many secondary modern boys get ONC and HNC. We might say 'The Technical College can give a second chance to those who slept or slipped at school'.

By the time the wording had been translated into 'government speak' it appeared as:

Too often in the past, the colleges have been thought of as mainly concerned with giving a second chance to those who missed or were deprived of opportunities at school. The stronger the schools become, the more confidently will the technical colleges be able to set their standards high.

This table shows the types of schools attended by those achieving passes in mechanical engineering exams (1952–53).

Previous education of successful candidates	Ordinary National Certificate (ONC)	Higher National Certificate (HNC)
Grammar school	47%	45%
Technical school	29%	32%
Secondary modern school	24%	23%

Students passing ordinary and Higher National Certificates in mechanical engineering

In the white paper the achievement of secondary modern pupils was described as:

Though the grammar and technical schools take, broadly speaking, the most able quarter of the boys and girls from primary schools there is substantial talent in the secondary modern schools. [It then quoted the figure of 23% of HNC students coming from these schools.]

Also quoted was the success of secondary modern children in achieving GCE 'O' levels and extending their education in the sixth forms of grammar schools.

In the original draft of the paper, Eccles wrote about 'spreading technical courses across secondary moderns'. We know that he was unsure about the role of technical schools and questioned whether they should be combined with secondary moderns that had a greater emphasis on technical subjects. Clearly, he had not abandoned this idea but in the white paper the concept had been diluted and expressed as:

*Secondary modern schools are being encouraged to develop courses
for their older pupils, which stir their interest in the careers ahead of
them, and act, as it were, as bridges between school and further
education.*

Eccles highlighted another, more controversial, of Venables' comments:
'We might paraphrase one of his remarks: "many English visitors to German
technical schools wonder who won the war".' The Ministry's officials must
have thought better of including this quote, or been unable to find a more
acceptable form of words – all reference to it was dropped from the
published white paper. The superiority of German technical and craft education is a sentiment that has been much repeated and is still heard today.

No more mention was made of secondary moderns in the white paper.
Maybe Eccles missed the section of Venables' book that investigated the
link between the test scores of those studying for the ONC, the type of
school they attended and their success at passing the first-year exam. Maybe
he ignored it because the data pointed to a conclusion that ran counter to the
government's secondary school education policy, although it probably reinforced Eccles' personal worries.

	Grammar school	Technical school	Secondary modern
Test score	Pass	Pass	Pass
165–184	1	0	0
145–164	8	0	0
125–144	20	4	7
105–124	13	11	13
25–104	5	18	23
Pass rate	72%	52%	49%

First-year exam results for students studying for the ONC at technical college

Venables used somewhat ornate and convoluted language to explain
these results.

*This limited sample shows selection of ability undoubtedly to have
taken place but by no means so clearly or definitely as some would*

suppose. It also shows that ability alone cannot guarantee success, in confirmation of everyday experience that people of less intellectual ability may do better in life because of other factors such as having, not least because of the upbringing, a stronger will and firmer resolve to succeed.

I interpret the data and his comments to mean that there was little difference in the success rates of students from technical and secondary modern schools. Students from grammar schools had the highest test score results and were more likely to pass the ONC exam, yet over a quarter of them failed. The test scores and the type of school attended were indictive of the chances of succeeding at technical college exams, but by no means a guarantee. The 'resolve to succeed' helped overcome deficiencies in academic ability.

Education policy determined by politics

Following the publication of the white paper, Eccles' attention returned to secondary education. He had finished asking questions and moved on to proposing policy changes.

Before considering his proposals, it's necessary to understand that the Labour Party was reordering its own policy agenda and propelling the subject of education towards the top spot. In July 1956 the party published a pamphlet, to be debated at its forthcoming annual conference: *Towards Equality – Labour's policy for social justice.*[117]

The document surveyed the main causes of inequalities and outlined what Labour would do 'to advance further towards a socialist society'. First on the list of inequalities was education and the first target was the 11-plus. The second target was private schools and the unfair benefits they conferred. Surprisingly, no proposals were detailed, the explanation being that a new education policy statement was in the process of being formulated.

Eccles' own paper was titled *Secondary Education*[118] and sent to the senior officials at the Ministry of Education on 18 September 1956. I couldn't find any evidence that he discussed it with other government ministers. The report's sub-title conveyed its purpose – '*The purpose of this paper is to save public schools'*. I would wager that Eccles wished he had used an alternative title. The opening statement explained that the Labour Party's pamphlet, *Towards Equality*, had reinforced his views about the threat they presented to the educational policy being pursued by the government and most of the LEAs.

> *In* Towards Equality *the first shots are fired against the Public Schools. All sections of the Labour Movement are pledged to replace the tripartite system with Comprehensive schools.*

His seven-page document was too long to analyse on a point-by-point basis. Instead I have summarised the main arguments and their implications.

Argument	Implication/solution
The 1944 Education Act has narrowed the gap between the private and state education sectors but not fast enough.	A shortcut is required.
The government claims that when secondary modern schools have 'found their feet' parents will accept the 11-plus. This might happen if politicians would 'leave the schools alone for 10 years'. But they will not.	Changes to policy are needed to neutralise the arguments about the 11-plus.
The 'bulge' (baby boom) is hitting the secondary schools and this is likely to negatively affect standards in state schools.	The rationing of secondary school teachers is likely, and this will 'make it plain to everybody the inadequacy of the state system'.
Parents with lower incomes whose children attend private schools are under pressure.	A possible solution would be to extend the number of direct grant schools (those schools that have private and state pupils).
The trouble with the 11-plus is not that it is unfair, but that parents have to accept the result.	'Postpone the examination to 15 when the parents and the child can refuse to take, preferring that the child should leave school altogether.'

I was amazed to read this last point, as must have been his officials. If he had the power to implement such a change (which he didn't) he proposed that all secondary schools would be turned into comprehensives. At the age of 15, children could leave school or move to a sixth-form college. These would be the sixth forms of the grammar school. Eccles' paper was vague about the selection process for these colleges, but he did make the point that changing the names from 'schools' to 'colleges' would encourage more children to stay at school.

In a stroke, the 11-plus would disappear and in the same stroke Eccles would align the policy of the Conservatives to that of the Labour Party.

I believe this statement encapsulated Eccles' fears and the primary motivator for the paper.

What we now have to ask is whether it is already clear that the tripartite system cannot get near enough to the independent schools [private schools] to prevent the gap being so wide that these schools come under the threat of destruction. And whether selection at 11+ does not raise more problems than it solves.

As the Ministry of Education annual reports make clear, the forthcoming influx of baby boom children into secondary schools was a major topic of concern. Eccles would have known that the secondary school population was expected to expand by approximately 850,000 pupils in the period 1954–1961. All types of secondary schools were going to be under immense stress. Grammar schools and, to a lesser extent, technical schools had some protection because of their established structures and models of working. Secondary moderns were still in various stages of 'experimentation' and would be stress-tested like never before. We now know that the secondary school pupil numbers increased even more than expected, as the baby boom moved from junior to secondary school. The minister of education must have been daunted by the problems that were likely to arise and he was expected to solve.[119]

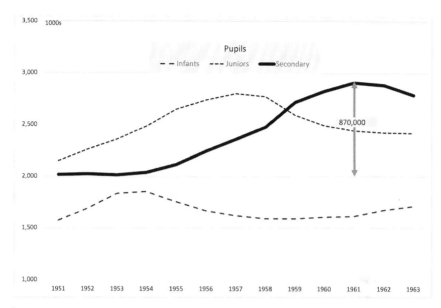

Pupil numbers in infant, junior and secondary schools (1954–1961)

In 1956 there were 59,000 teachers working in the secondary modern schools. They would have been well aware of the Labour Party's educational intentions and had some idea about the forthcoming rise in pupil numbers. What few, if any, of them could have appreciated was that the Conservative minister of education had grave doubts about the future of their schools.

His officials didn't like the paper. Some said so in the best quality 'civil servants' language'. Some were far blunter. These were a couple of the comments.

> *It is a somewhat drastic saving plan [for the public schools] to change direction in the maintained sector [state schools] – after only ten years.*

> *We really can't condemn the tripartite system or judge the comprehensives as early as 1956.*

Many of the comments flagged the similarity of Eccles' plan to the ideas of Robin Pedley, who had recently published a book titled *Comprehensive*

Education – a new approach.[120] I don't think it could have been a coincidence that a month after issuing his paper, Eccles arranged a meeting with Pedley. A record of the encounter was published in October 1956.[121]

Pedley had outlined his ideas, most of which were in his book, but there were differences. He now proposed that selection should be delayed until 14+. Children would attend the 'local secondary schools' (these would be re-christened secondary moderns), where the majority would remain until they were 15 or 16 and take some form of leaving certificate. Those whose parents expressed their intention to keep their child at school until at least 16 would transfer at 14 (not 15, as it appeared in Pedley's book) to a new form of grammar/technical school to take GCE exams.

I sensed from the account of the meeting that Eccles was not convinced by Pedley's arguments, although they were similar to his own. My guess – and it is only a guess – is that the process of probing the consequences of Pedley's plans highlighted the many practical difficulties of implementing such a scheme. Perhaps he was being polite but Eccles concluded the meeting by supporting a test of 'Pedleyism', as it was titled, if an LEA was prepared to support the experiment and had the right profile of schools.

This is not the time to judge the educational worth of Eccles' proposals. What I can do is take a peek at the next part of the timeline to see if he was right about the threats posed to government policy. Namely, the immediate political dangers of the Labour Party's education policy, the discontent of parents with the tripartite system and the attractiveness of comprehensive education. He was wrong on all three counts. He was right about the problems resulting from the baby boom. More of these issues, a little later in the book.

It would seem that political considerations, rather than systematic research about what was happening in the country's schools, were determining policy decisions. The Labour Party was clear about what it wanted abolished – the 11-plus and private schools – but vague about their replacements. The Conservative minister was wracked with doubts about the existing system and how it would respond to the forthcoming surge in pupil numbers. Missing from this conflict was dependable data about how the 3,550 secondary modern schools were actually performing. To understand this we must rely on the findings of Harold Dent, who had been the editor of

The Times Educational Supplement before becoming one of the most respected educational academics of his era.

Facts (not suppositions) about secondary moderns

Between 1945 and 1957, Dent visited 'some hundreds' of secondary moderns. What he discovered during these visits, combined with the insights gained from editing the country's leading education paper, was used to write the book *Secondary Modern Schools – an interim report.*[122]

How were secondary moderns performing? To what extent did the reality of their conditions tally with the views of the politicians? Unless I quote a different reference, the following are the findings from Harold Dent's investigations.

You may remember this passage from Dent's book, which I quoted in Chapter 4 ('A condensed history of secondary moderns'). I am repeating it because he so eloquently and amusingly described the early life of secondary moderns.

> *The Secondary Modern School has been the target of every newfangled theory, every half-digested, ill-assorted idea… if ever it has seen a settled objective half the busybodies in the world of education have rushed in to save it from itself. Turn out citizens. Turn out literates. Turn out technicians. Be more vocational. Prepare for leisure. Stick to the wider view. The wonder is that with all this and with all the difficulties of the post-war world the secondary modern schools have got anywhere at all. But, they have.*

What an evocative description of the difficulties faced by those working in these schools.

Of all the people I have quoted, Harold Dent is the person I would most have liked to meet. I sense that he was genuinely concerned about the education of children. This marks him out from many educationalists who appear vague (uninterested, perhaps) about the day-to-day matters of schooling and focused on (maybe obsessed with) the sociological aspects of education. Rather than hypothesise about the state of the country's schooling he went to see it for himself.

Dent painted a picture of secondary moderns as being in something of a chaotic and volatile state. As we have seen, educationalists and politicians rationalised the absence of structure and direction by portraying it as the 'experimentation' phase of the school's evolution – and as a strength, not a weakness. My explanation would be 'this is what happens when politicians have only the haziest notions about the schools' goals and how they should work and rely on the 146 LEAs and their 62,000 secondary modern teachers to work it out'.[123]

Harold Loukes published his book *Secondary Modern*[124] at about the same time as Dent and concluded that the schools came in all shapes and sizes, as did their pupils, teachers and parents. Dent agreed, but went further and categorised the different types of school and assessed how they would evolve. He was insistent that his findings didn't have any statistical significance and that his conclusions would soon be out of date. I think he was overly modest about the accuracy and durability of his findings. Sadly they are the only dependable insights we have.

When his research concluded in 1957 he had identified multiple types of secondary modern school, as follows.

Type 1. Schools that had changed little from those they replaced (the elementary school)

- Pupils often badly behaved and frequently found in 'rough neighbourhoods'.
- A small sub-category and decreasing in size.

Type 2. Schools providing 'highly effective senior elementary school work'

Their main purpose was teaching the '3 Rs' with the pupils' education not extended far beyond basic numeracy and literacy. They suffered from two types of constraints.

- A high proportion of children with learning difficulties and unsupportive parents.
- The lack of vision of the teaching staff. Ofsted would probably have labelled them 'coasting schools'.

Type 3. Pupils were taught subjects similar to those in grammar schools

The curriculum was not as academic and did have the same variety. They also learnt practical subjects (wood-work, metal-work and gardening for boys; cookery and needlework for girls).

Type 4. Schools where the curriculum was based on 'projects' and 'centres of interest'

When done well these schools delivered good academic results and a broadening of the pupils' education. Most failed to achieve either of these results. These schools were diminishing in number.

Type 5. Schools providing pupils with vocationally orientated courses

Pupils often followed a common first two years and then selected a vocational course. Rural and urban schools provided very different courses. Some courses assumed the pupils left school at the statutory age. Others, often called 'extended' or 'special', required the pupil to stay for an additional year (until the age of 16).

Type 6. 'GCE schools'

Taking external exams was a fundamental part of what these schools provided. Often having well-established links to technical colleges and grammar schools for pupils to take GCE 'A' levels. These schools often performed as well as the 'C' form of grammar schools (the least academic group of grammar school pupils).

As I was writing these definitions I recognised my own school (George Gascoigne Secondary Modern). It was a mix between Type 3 and Type 6 and very much like these descriptions of two schools Dent visited.

> *In the fifth year the G.C.E. was taken, and the school regularly transferred a number of boys who had secured good passes to Grammar school sixth forms and full-time courses at colleges of Further Education. In another town, a school was similarly transfer-*

ring each year to a Grammar school, pupils who had done well in the G.C.E. Boys normally took six subjects, and the school averaged 60 per cent of passes. In science and craft subjects the percentage of passes was well above the national average.

When I started writing this book, I wondered if my experience of secondary modern education was unique. At least I can now answer that question. It wasn't. I have also learnt how lucky I was to have teachers with the belief that their pupils could achieve much more than basic literacy skills.

Going back to Dent's categorisations, the first and most obvious question is why was there so much variety in the characteristics of schools labelled 'secondary modern'? Dent spent much of his book considering this question and came up with six reasons.

1. Wide variation in grammar school availability. In 1957, grammar schools educated 22% of secondary pupils in England and 39% in Wales.[125] Some English LEAs provided 40% of secondary school children with grammar school places. In others it was as little as 10%. In some parts of Wales, the figure reached 60%. I think it is fair to say that the likelihood of attending a secondary modern was the 'postcode lottery' of all postcode lotteries. This variation in grammar school provision resulted in some secondary moderns containing a significant number of pupils who, in another LEA, would have attended grammar schools. These schools had far more scope to provide an 'academic' curriculum. Clearly, the reverse situation also applied, with some schools having a high density of children with a low academic potential (as measured by the 11-plus).

It was not only the distribution of grammar school places that differed by LEA – the same applied to specialist schools (sometimes referred to as special schools) for children deemed to be ESN (educationally sub-normal). Thankfully, this term has now been replaced by 'special needs' or children with 'educational difficulties'. In the absence of an ESN school place the child was likely to attend a secondary modern. I can remember a girl in my class at school suffering from what I now know was hydrocephalus. There were a few other classmates who might well have been classed as ESN, too.

Today they would probably be diagnosed as suffering from attention deficit disorder.

2. *Some LEAs yet to abandon all-age schools*. There was a wide variation in the speed with which LEAs had implemented the 1926 Hadow Report's recommendation to abandon 'all-age' schools and create separate primary and secondary schools. The Ministry of Education believed this was a fundamental requirement for modernising the secondary education system and it was one of the statistics reported in the Ministry's annual reviews. Some LEAs had completed the transition before the passing of the 1944 Education Act. Others still operated 'all-age' schools into the mid-1960s. In 1957, 8% of children over the age of 11 were attending these schools. No doubt there were many reasons why this changeover took so long, but the most important one was the scale of the new building programme that was required. Dent calculated that to complete Hadow's recommendation would require 400 new schools to be built.

3. *Wide variation in building quality*. Dent observed 'striking disparities in the quality of the accommodation in which the new secondary schools had to grow up'. Earlier in this chapter we learnt how much of the post-war building work was focused on the 'new towns', at the expense of repairing and extending schools in urban areas. This is what Dent said about the relationship between the quality of school buildings and what was taught.

> *In my experience it was almost the rule rather than the exception for a school to blossom out on very different lines upon entering its new building; and many a school whose work would previously have been characterized as 'sound but unremarkable' graduated into the 'original' class within a few months of taking over a properly designed and well equipped new building.*

If the physical structure of the school was unaltered, a decade after changing the name sign from Elementary to Secondary Modern, it was not surprising that some schools had made little progress in escaping from their earlier roots. Dent was insistent that it was the excellence of the teaching, not the buildings, that made the biggest difference to the quality of education. However, he was also adamant that teaching in a fully equipped new school made the job much easier.

How big was the task facing LEAs, to replace their old elementary schools? According to Dent it was huge.

There still remained 2,450 schools [secondary moderns] in buildings which could not be called adequate. Some of these, admittedly, were only slightly sub-standard, but the rest ranged down from that to deplorably bad.

Remember, these estimates do not include the 400 buildings needed to replace the 'all-age' schools.

4. Too few teachers. Dent found some parts of the country suffering from a shortage of teaching staff and others with waiting lists of teachers wanting positions. In 1957 the Ministry reported that in secondary schools, 62% of pupils were in oversized classes – an increase on the previous year.[126] 'Oversized' was defined as more than 30 children. To exacerbate the problem, the baby boom cohort of children was about to move from primary to secondary schools. In the Ministry's annual review, it gloomily concluded that the irregular distribution of teachers meant that in 1958 there would be 'acute shortages'.

If Dent were still the editor of *The Times Educational Supplement* (now Tes), he would be saddened to be frequently reporting news stories about teacher shortages and their effects on the quality of children's education. Over the past half a century, politicians of all persuasions have failed to match the demand for teachers with the supply.

Most secondary moderns inherited the buildings and teaching equipment from their elementary school predecessors. Perhaps most importantly, they also inherited the teachers, who had only experienced life in elementary schools. Dent emphasised that many of these were highly competent and motivated people. What he questioned was the feasibility of expecting them to switch overnight to teaching in the 'experimental' world of the secondary modern.

For many teachers [ex-elementary school] there were no landmarks
in this new territory. There were no precise aims or objectives laid
down for Secondary Modern education, no recognized standards of
attainment, no established 'yardsticks' by which to measure the value
of anything they might attempt. No wonder they felt lost.

To make matters worse, the 'guidance' they received from the political and educational establishment was about what they should not be doing, rather than positive advice.

That the secondary modern school was not to be the old senior
elementary school under a new name, and that at all costs it was not
to become 'a pale imitation of the grammar school'.

The uneven geographic distribution of teachers was one problem; another was secondary moderns' high ratio of pupils to teachers – something else inherited from the elementary school era.

According to the 1957 Ministry annual report, the ratio of pupils to teachers in secondary moderns was 23, compared with 19 in grammar schools. In secondary technical schools the ratio was 18. Because these statistics include non-teaching staff, they should not be confused with measures of average class size. Even so, the lower the ratio, the better it was for pupils and teachers.

5. Class differences and urban v rural schools. The differing demands of urban and rural economies were the most obvious way in which local conditions influenced a school's culture and curriculum. Those attending a rural secondary modern tended to travel from a wide catchment area and left school for a job that was dependent on the countryside economy. Pupils attending an urban or semi-urban secondary modern would have very different work opportunities.

Dent commented that the class of parents also influenced the performance of schools, but was reticent to explain the details of the relationship. He used the excuse that he had 'a most superficial and sketchy analysis of the more obvious sociological factors'. I think the point he wanted to make was that a school where the pupils had parents employed in the professions would have different pressures and types of pupils from one where the parents were unskilled manual workers. He also implied that the sons and daughters of professional parents would be easier to teach than those from 'rough neighbourhoods'.

I expect that the situation is much the same today, except that the term 'professional parents' has now become the 'pushy' or 'sharp-elbowed' middle class and 'rough neighbourhood' is renamed as an 'area of social stress'.

Dent returned to the importance of the type of parents when he discussed how they influenced opinions about secondary modern schools. We have seen how agitated David Eccles, the minister of education, was about the public reaction to secondary moderns. I wonder how he would have reacted to Dent's statement that:

Contrary to popular belief, from the start, and all the way through [1945–1957] many (perhaps most) of the parents whose children were allocated to the Secondary Modern School were more or less content that they should be.

Dent's explanation for this reaction was that most parents of secondary modern children didn't care or understand, or lacked ambition for their children. There were also working class parents who believed that the local secondary modern was the best choice of school for their child. When reading these words, I couldn't help but ponder how my own parents reacted to the news that I had failed the 11-plus and was going to the local secondary modern. My guess is that their reaction is explained by this statement.

It is, indeed, quite wrong to think of the Secondary Modern School as the school to which 'failures' are sent; it is much more accurate to think of it as the school to which all but a small minority of intellectually very able children go.

At the age of 11 there was not a jot of evidence that I was 'intellectually very able' – something that hasn't changed much now, aged over 70. Looked at from this perspective, why would they have been disappointed about me attending George Gascoigne Secondary Modern? They would have been surprised (more likely astonished) had the result been anything different.

Dent identified another group of parents whom he titled 'grammar-school-conscious' parents.

These were vocal out of all proportion to their strength, and, with the aid of other sections of the public hostile to the secondary modern school, who were if anything even more vocal, succeeded in attracting a great deal of notice and much sympathy in Parliament and in the Press, and consequently among the public at large.

He didn't mention the increasingly hostile attitude of the Labour Party, but my guess is he had them in mind when writing the 'other sections of the public'.

As we have seen from analysing the popular press and *Hansard*, the actual evidence of 'public hostility' didn't support Dent's argument. The pages of *The Times Educational Supplement* may have contained letters and articles about the 11-plus and secondary moderns but we know they were very rare in the media read by the parents of secondary modern children (e.g. the *Daily Express* and *Daily Mirror*).

6. Wide variations in LEAs' plans. Each LEA's educational policy was determined by a raft of different factors. We saw this earlier, when reviewing the tortuous process they went through in creating and winning approval for their educational development plans. It is not surprising that the diverse policies of the LEAs resulted in an equally diverse range of secondary moderns. Rather than summarising Dent's comments on this subject it is best to use his words to explain the situation.

Some authorities held firmly to the tripartite organization of secondary education, keeping all their schools strictly Grammar, Technical or Modern. Some of them set out to blur the lines of the

tripartite division, by establishing Comprehensive, Multilateral,
Bilateral or other kinds of joint or amalgamated schools. Some
authorities laid down a policy for development, others deliberately
waited on events, that is to say, waited to see what their schools
would do. Some authorities encouraged schools more actively than
others and – inevitably – some authorities were more generous in
aiding with staff.

We owe a great debt of gratitude to Dent. His research demonstrated (forcibly) the error of referring to secondary modern schools as a homogenous group. For all the reasons he identified, there was no such thing as a 'typical secondary modern'. The school types were on a spectrum. At one extreme they resembled a less academically challenging grammar school. At the other, they had barely progressed beyond the old, pre-1944 Education Act, elementary school. The next time you hear somebody opining that 'secondary moderns were all XYZ' and making generalised comments (likely to be negative), remember what we have just learnt.

As Dent tried to make sense of these multiple types of schools he also pondered the issues that would influence their future development. What he couldn't have known was that many of these 'issues' are still not resolved in 2021.

He believed the secondary moderns faced a dilemma about the extent to which they should mirror grammar schools and prepare their pupils to take external exams. Specifically, to what extent should their curriculum be determined by the needs of those pupils taking GCE 'O' levels? An even more fundamental question was (and still is) the influence of external exams in shaping children's education.

The LEAs and their secondary modern teachers had to make an unpalatable decision. If they adopted the grammar school model and pursued the goal of academic achievement, as measured by GCE results, they heightened the risk that the less academic pupils would be disadvantaged. The arguments about this approach can still be heard today by those criticising grammar schools. For example, that having an academic stream 'creams off the best children', heightens the sense of failure for those not taking the exams and consumes a disproportionate amount of teaching resource. I am repeating these arguments – not necessarily agreeing with them.

Pitted against these worries was the need to convince parents and pupils that their schooling was equipping children with the knowledge and skills they needed to succeed in life. Rightly or wrongly, when a child gains a fistful of GCE passes it represents a universal symbol of achievement. Secondary moderns were seeking a raison d'être that provided the much-sought-after 'parity of esteem'. They needed to develop a model of schooling that was understandable and valued by their pupils, parents and employers. Again, achieving a fistful of GCE passes would do this.

Presenting the arguments in this way highlights the 'devil's alternative' facing the schools. It seemed that whichever route they followed, they would annoy sections of the political and educational establishment. With the benefit of hindsight, I suspect this was a false dilemma that was not supported by hard evidence. Whatever, it was the way the situation was perceived at the time. For policy makers it seemed a very real decision they believed needed to be made.

Dent voiced similar concerns about secondary moderns becoming too focused on 'special' vocational courses. He feared this would distort the curriculum and could lead to schools becoming little more than 'trade training schools'. He admitted to finding only a couple of instances of where this was happening and concluded that it might be more a theoretical than a real problem.

At the heart of Dent's worries about the future of secondary moderns was his uncertainty about the type of education that was best for the 'ordinary child'. He knew that the schools had children who were on the 11-plus borderline and who would have attended a grammar school had they been born under another LEA. For them, taking GCEs was the obvious way forward. He didn't know how big this group was but referred to it as a 'small minority'. When he was writing, one in six secondary modern pupils were taking GCEs, a figure he predicted would increase. He could also see another group who, for whatever reason, would always struggle with formal schooling and could not wait to leave school.

What perplexed him the most, and where he had his greatest uncertainties, was the large group of children between these extremes. How far and fast should these children be pushed along the academic path of taking GCEs? What mix of vocational training and academic studies should they be given? Were the more progressive teaching styles appropriate for this group or did they respond better to formal teaching techniques?

I am not going to cover Dent's views about these subjects other than to say that today's secondary school teachers would find the discourse well worth reading and horribly familiar.

Much of Dent's thinking was echoed in the letters and editorial appearing in *The Times Educational Supplement*. These two quotes are about the issues of the brighter pupils taking GCE exams, and the large group who were below this academic level, but above those struggling to achieve basic literacy and numeracy skills.[127, 128]

The trouble with the secondary modern school is that no one has bothered about the 'B' forms. So far the talk has largely been about the two extremes among the pupils – about the able and the weak. The middle batch have hardly come into the picture.

Incentives are in the air. The secondary modern schools look enviously at the grammar schools with their tempting carrot of the GCE, often the only means available of convincing the adolescent (boy especially) that the pursuit of knowledge can also lead to a good job.

Research reports reveal flaws in the tripartite system

Around the same time as Dent's book was published, a very different type of document appeared, about secondary moderns.[129] Produced by an independent think tank (Political and Economic Planning; PEP), it claimed to provide an assessment of how secondary moderns were performing, a decade after their creation.

The correspondence and minutes of meetings between the Ministry and PEP are in the National Archive and make amusing reading.[130] It was clear that the Ministry wanted the report to be accurate and reflect well on them and their political masters. My guess is that they thought, wrongly as it happened, that it would receive wide coverage in the media and within Parliament.

After receiving a draft of the report, they discovered that its author, who was a freelance journalist, had not set foot inside a single school and had relied on secondary information sources. Not surprisingly, they thought the author would benefit from gaining some first-hand experience of the subject. The words actually used were a tad more forceful than mine. The chief education officers of London, Surrey, Kent and Hertfordshire agreed that the author could visit a selection of their secondary modern schools. These offers were never taken up and the report was published without a single school being visited.

The published version of the report provided a summary of the history of secondary moderns and a distillation of the data contained in the Ministry of Education's annual reports. All of the other research sources were also used by Dent. What the document lacked, not surprisingly, was any quantitative or qualitative evidence about what was actually happening in the schools. As an ex-consultant, I recognise the style of writing – a well-crafted document that doesn't say anything new, but what it does say is said in an author-itative tone. For instance, the following profound and often-repeated statement.

> *The one characteristic which all secondary modern school pupils*
> *have in common is that they have not reached the standard required*
> *for entry into grammar schools in the area in which they live.*

Some passages of the report were very similar to sections in Dent's book. This is not surprising given that Dent was a past editor of *The Times Educational Supplement*, so his thoughts about secondary moderns were in the public domain. His work would have been a logical source of information.

In June 1956 the report featured prominently in a Parliamentary debate – the one and only time it was mentioned in Parliament.[131] It was described as being of necessity 'sketchy' and 'at times it fails to see the wood of achieve-ment because of the trees of difficulty remaining, and the forests ahead' – a description that I thought was most apt.

When the Parliamentary secretary to the Ministry of Education spoke in the debate, he seemed determined to make three points clear about the future of secondary moderns. These might have been the Ministry's views but, as we know, the minister (Sir David Eccles) was contemplating a very different future for the schools.

1. Secondary moderns would not conform to any set pattern

There is no such thing as 'the secondary modern school'. There are secondary modern schools—more than 3,500 of them, and they differ in innumerable ways.

It is much easier to define the purpose of a secondary grammar or technical school than it is of a secondary modern school, which creates and develops its individuality by adapting itself to its environment.

In the best modern schools, the education is, rightly, related to the conditions in which many of the children live, with which most of them will be familiar, and in which many of them will expect to work when they grow up.

2. It would be dangerous to focus on GCE exams

These exams would only be taken by a 'small minority' of pupils and should not interfere with the teaching of the majority.

Some pupils may want to take the General Certificate of Education. They ought to do so if they are suitable for it, but it would be a great mistake for the interest of the rest of the children to be subordinated to what is always likely to be a small minority.

The job of the modern school is to develop its own personality and not to ape the grammar school.

3. Selection (the 11-plus) was inevitable and would continue

As far as selection is concerned, my opinion is that each month sees further progress as L.E.As. improve their arrangements as a result of experience and experiment. I believe that, whatever form of secondary education we follow, some form of selection is inevitable. Our aim, I think, must be to improve it.

During the debate the Parliamentary secretary revealed two new statistics to support his argument that the government was doing its best to ensure the schools succeeded. To counter the criticism about the size of their classes, he said that they were around 30 to 31 pupils. I think he was 'bending the numbers' given that, as we have already seen, the Ministry's own data showed that over 60% of children were in classes of more than 30 children. In case you were wondering, the average size of today's secondary school class is 21 pupils, although I am sure many teachers would contest this number.[132]

Recognising the need for new schools, he declared that 536 had been built since the war. This claim needs to be put into context, because it represents new classrooms for just 15% of pupils. If the figure includes all schools under construction, then it increases to a quarter of pupils. It is impossible to know if this was a good performance or one that could have been improved. For certain, there was a long list of problems that slowed down the post-war secondary school building programme.

In addition to Dent's book and the PEP report, three other documents were published in 1956–57 that provided new insights into the workings and performance of the education system and, in particular, secondary moderns. The first of these was a Ministry pamphlet about the changes in reading ability of junior and secondary school children over the period 1948 to 1956.[133] This was a significant piece of research, based on reading skills tests taken by 6,000 children in 1948 and repeated in 1956 on a smaller sample of 3,000 children. These were the headline conclusions.

In the interval from 1948 to 1956 there was on the whole an improvement in ability of school children to read with understanding.

The improvement was particularly marked in the primary schools, where the age group born in 1945 were in 1956 on average 9 months more advanced than their predecessors born in 1937 were in 1948. The corresponding increase at the secondary stage [this included secondary modern children] was about 5 months.

It was estimated in Reading Ability that during the war standards had fallen by 12 months and 22 months for pupils of eleven and of fifteen respectively.

Having documented the disruption caused by the war, I have little doubt that it negatively affected children's education standards. This is the first and, as far as I know, only time that it was quantified. However, I think these numbers should be taken as 'estimates', because the sampling models were different before and after the war. My admiration for school teachers immediately after the war continues to grow. Not only did they have to contend with bomb-damaged buildings, the raising of the school-leaving age, the baby boom and the reorganisation of secondary education... they also had to teach pupils with significantly worse reading skills than their pre-war counterparts.

The research also provided interesting insights into how pupils' reading skills differed by the type of secondary school they attended, as shown in the following table.

Secondary school	Scores					
	Superior	Average +	Combined	Average -	Backward	Semi-literate
Grammar (boys)	37%	59%	96%	4%	0%	0%
Grammar (girls)	28%	66%	94%	6%	0%	0%
Technical (boys)	7%	83%	90%	10%	0%	0%
Technical (girls)	10%	70%	80%	20%	0%	0%
Modern (boys)	3%	40%	43%	28%	23%	6%
Modern (girls)	1%	27%	28%	32%	35%	5%
All-age (boys)	5%	32%	37%	17%	31%	15%
All-age (girls)	0%	22%	22%	37%	35%	6%

Reading test score results of children aged 15 years in different types of secondary school. The 'combined score' is the percentage of pupils who scored 'average+' or 'superior'

The first thing I noticed was that boys performed better than girls in all types of school. Today, this gender difference has been reversed in all OECD countries, with girls performing 'significantly' better than boys.[134]

Boys and girls with the worst reading skills attended all-age schools, closely followed by those in secondary moderns. Not surprisingly, the best test scores came from boys and girls at grammar schools, with over a quarter having a 'superior' reading ability.

A small percentage of those in grammar schools (more in technical schools) had a below-average score – most noticeably, 20% of girls in technical schools. This means that some 15 year olds in secondary moderns performed better (as measured by reading ability) than their primary school classmates who had passed the 11-plus. Further evidence of the fallibility of the 11-plus as a predictor of children's secondary school performance came in two other documents that were published in 1957.

The most comprehensive research was published in a 250-page report titled *Admission to Grammar Schools*.[135] In the few paragraphs that I will use to summarise its findings I cannot hope to do justice to what was an extensive research study that was based on data provided by over 80% of the LEAs in England and Wales. In addition to this countrywide analysis of selection processes, one LEA (Twickenham) provided detailed information about the academic results of children, starting in primary school and throughout their secondary schooling.

Two of the research results reinforced the conclusions reached in Dent's book. The first concerned the wide variation of grammar school places throughout the country – especially in Wales. Although the magnitude of the variation was not as large as identified by Dent, it was substantial and meant that your chances of attending a secondary modern were significantly affected by where you lived. Second, Dent claimed that over a quarter of LEAs had secondary moderns that were taking GCE exams, a result that was confirmed by the study.

Much of the research was about the variation in the procedures that LEAs used in the selection process – what we now call the '11-plus'. I wonder if the researchers were surprised by the magnitude of the variation? I was.

There was no consistency over the age at which children were evaluated and transferred from primary to secondary school. Indeed, not all children were entered for the selection process. In 13% of LEAs only children who were recommended by teachers took the evaluation tests.

There was also no single type of 11-plus exam. Some LEAs favoured what the researchers called 'traditional' tests. These were normally locally administered and employed a small number of questions (e.g. writing a short essay or composition). Other LEAs favoured standardised objective tests of ability (the IQ test) and of attainment in English and arithmetic. These exams were administered by examining authorities and contained a large number of questions that mostly had a right or wrong answer. Approximately 90% of LEAs used some form standardised objective test.

As part of the evaluation process, nearly three-quarters of LEAs required teachers to consider personal information about the pupil, such as their home background and qualities of character. A third of LEAs used the children's record cards, which provided details of their performance throughout their school life.

It seemed clear (to me) that primary schools did their very best to ensure that children went to the best school for their secondary education, although they had many different ways of achieving this goal. However, despite their best endeavours they didn't achieve a 100% success rate, or even close to that number. The study concluded:

Even the use of the best methods of allocation that, on the basis of our present knowledge, can be devised is likely to involve errors in the allocation of approximately 10% of candidates.

This conclusion was reached using a mix of statistical modelling and actual data. I cannot comment on its accuracy, other than to say that it was the most comprehensive research that had been conducted on the subject. Even assuming a confidence level of a few percentage points, it means that a significant number of children were allocated to the 'wrong' school.

Most of the LEAs appeared to recognise this problem and 75% of them employed a process to further test children who were in the 'border zone' (i.e. those whose test scores did not adequately define the type of school they should attend). The rest of the LEAs employed a simple procedure of setting an absolute 'pass/fail' score, above which you went to a grammar school and, below, the secondary modern.

Once a child had been allocated a school, aged 11, there was only a small chance of their being moved at a later stage. About 60% of the LEAs claimed to have a process to re-allocate children when they were 12 or 13 – the other LEAs had no specified policy. Whatever the procedure, few transfers actually took place. Only 3% of children left their secondary modern to attend either a grammar or a technical school. These figures did not include those transferring after passing GCE exams. Even fewer children went in the opposite direction. If you passed the 11-plus and went to a grammar school, you had a 99.5% chance of remaining at one throughout your secondary school life.

More detail on the same theme came in *Secondary School Selection*, a research study conducted by the British Psychological Society with the following objective.[136]

The aim is to provide a review of the relevant information, so that interested persons may be able to distinguish actual research findings from statements associated with supposition, prejudice and self-interest, and avoid some of the confusions which arise when questions which are fundamentally economic or administrative are addressed to psychologists.

As with the previous study, I cannot vouch for the accuracy of the forecasts but the research methodology appeared sound. Rather than repeat the many observations and conclusions that were common between the two studies, I will only mention what was new in this report. These were two of its most striking conclusions.

It will be no surprise to grammar school teachers to be told that at least one quarter of those selected, on present standards, do not deserve their places.

About 6% [of secondary modern pupils] would have surpassed the one quarter of those admitted to grammar school.

Associated with the 6% estimate is this important caveat.

Had it been possible to identify these children at 11 years of age and given them grammar-school places, it is certain that a considerable proportion would have tagged along in the grammar-school C-Streams or near the bottom of the B-streams; the number reaching 'A' Level would be far smaller than 6%. It is probable that many of

those who shine intellectually in the modern school, and who are
regarded as errors of selection because they gain numerous GCE
passes, actually do well largely because they are in modern schools.

As I wrote these words I couldn't help but think back to my own schooling. In Chapter 2 ('George Gascoigne Secondary Modern – a personal view') I related how my mum was annoyed at being told by the secretary at my primary school that in going to a secondary modern I would be a 'big fish in a small pond'. Unlike my mum, I think she was trying to be kind. More importantly, maybe she was right.

The study considered the emotional effects of the selection process on children and their parents. It found there was much speculation about the psychological damage caused by the 11-plus but little hard evidence that enabled it to be quantified. The overall conclusion was that the 'emotional effects on children are probably less severe than the ill-feeling caused among parents' and that 'there is considerably more anxiety and worry among pupils who get into grammar schools than among those who do not'. If children did suffer from strain, they were more likely to have parents in the professional classes, just as they were much more likely to be coached by private tutors to pass the 11-plus.

The researchers tried to answer the question: 'How far down in the scale of ability (as measured by standard tests) should we go in order to catch all those capable of advanced secondary schooling?' They could not provide an answer, because there were so many variables, such as the differences between schools and the 'types of pupils' – I think this was another way of saying the class of the pupils' parents. However, they did hazard a guess that 'some successes in GCE may well occur among pupils who are not even in the top 30% at 11 years of age'. Previous reports had always stated that GCEs were only relevant to 'a small minority' of secondary school children. This was the first research that questioned this assumption.

There was one final report from this period that evaluated the effectiveness of the 11-plus in determining the type of secondary school that a child attended. It preceded the three I have just detailed and was published a month before David Eccles became minister of education. The Gurney-Dixon Report was commissioned in 1952, by his predecessor, The Rt. Hon. Florence Horsbrugh.[137] Eccles didn't appear to pay it much attention –

something he has in common with educational historians, who have glossed over its findings. With the benefit of hindsight, I think it deserved more attention.

Although the report focused on explaining the variation in grammar school pupils' achievement, it also revealed how their performance compared with their peers' in secondary moderns and technical schools. However, the usefulness of its findings was not immediately obvious from the report's terms of reference.

To consider what factors influence the age at which boys and girls leave secondary schools which provide courses beyond the minimum school-leaving age; to what extent it is desirable to increase the proportion of those who remain at school, in particular the proportion of those who remain at school roughly to the age of 18; and what steps should be taken to secure such an increase.

Eccles wrote a brief summary at the beginning of the report containing the usual words of thanks and clichés about the report 'breaking fresh ground' and 'arousing great interest' and his hope that it would help address the country's shortage of trained technical workers. He then dispensed with the guarded political language and dismissed the report's two main recommendations about providing more grammar school places and increasing the maintenance allowance paid to parents. The report was mentioned in Parliament three times, briefly, but there's no evidence that it had any impact on education policy. I doubt whether Eccles and educational historians ever bothered reading much beyond the recommendations section, and fewer still seem to have studied the details of the research. That was a mistake.

The sample of children studied was 10% of the pupils in England who began attending a maintained and direct grant grammar school in September 1946. Teachers in 120 schools completed questionnaires for these 8,700 children, which included 27 questions about their social background and academic record over their seven years of schooling. Civil servants and management consultants reading these words might like to estimate how much this research and report would cost today. Excluding printing costs, the Gurney-Dixon Report cost £16,000 in today's pounds. Astonishingly good value for money when you think that the research generated 235,000 data points that had to be manually analysed and reported.

Like me, you might be wondering why the research was limited to grammar schools? The terms of reference specified studying children who attended schools beyond the minimum school-leaving age (15). In 1946, most of these children were to be found in grammar schools (95%). There was little value in studying other types of schools when they only accounted for 5% of the target group.

The research generated lots of interesting insights about the background of the pupils and their reasons for leaving school. I will focus on the research that is relevant to secondary moderns.

My first observation relates to the achievement of those secondary modern pupils who transferred to grammar schools. In 1953 these accounted for just over 3% of grammar school pupils – a very small number. Understandably, the report's authors stressed the need for caution in generalising from such a small data sample.

The following table shows the academic achievement of the ex-secondary modern pupils compared with those attending grammar school from the age of 11. On entering grammar school, the pupils were ranked into three categories of academic ability.

Academic achievement	Academic ability group age 11			Transfer from secondary modern
	Top	Middle	Bottom	
2 passes at GCE 'A' level and those still studying	32%	19%	12%	22%
Left school with 5 or more GCE 'O' levels or equivalent	28%	24%	19%	23%
Left with 3 or 4 GCE 'O' levels	14%	15%	16%	15%
Completed the 5-year course but left without 3 GCE 'O' levels	12%	21%	27%	13%
Did not complete 5-year course	14%	21%	26%	27%

The academic achievement of pupils selected at the age of 11 to attend a grammar school compared with children transferring from a secondary modern

You don't need any statistical knowledge to spot that children's ability, aged 11, does indicate their academic achievement five to seven years later. But, and it is a big 'but', the relationship is far from perfect. Pupils from the secondary moderns performed as well as the middle group of grammar school pupils and a sizeable number of pupils in the bottom group, aged 11, outperformed those in the top group. I can think of lots of explanations for these anomalies. Those transferring from secondary moderns were few in number and not representative of their peers. Judgement about the grammar school pupil's academic potential at 11 was not a precise science and probably resulted from exams taken during their first year at school. Despite these explanations, it is impossible to ignore the conclusion that testing children aged 11 was far from being a perfect predictor of later academic success.

Today's portrayal of the grammar school is that it caters for the high academic achievers with parents from the professional classes. I doubt if that is necessarily correct – it certainly wasn't in the early 1950s, as is shown in the following table.[138,139]

	Professional & managerial	Clerical	Skilled	Semi-skilled	Unskilled
Pupil's socio-economic group	22%	9%	39%	14%	5%
National analysis of social economic class	17%	11%	28%	32%	13%
Pupils passing 2 'A' levels	44%	29%	21%	10%	7%
Pupils passing 5 'O' levels or equivalent	25%	25%	25%	22%	17%
Pupils leaving schools without qualifications	7%	12%	20%	29%	40%

The social composition of children attending grammar schools and their academic attainment. National socio-economic analysis

The first two rows of the table are concerned with the socio-economic group of the pupils, as determined by their father's job. If you are wondering why the first row does not total to 100%, it is because some jobs could not be classified.

Children with fathers designated as 'professional and managerial' over-indexed, but not to the same extent as those categorised as 'skilled' (i.e. more children attended grammar school from these groups than their share of the population). It is important to know which job types were classed as 'skilled', because today they might be thought of as semi-skilled or unskilled:

Market gardeners, fitters, electricians, instrument makers, foremen, weavers, curriers, saddlers, boot and shoe makers, tailors, uphol-sterers, carpenters, joiners, engine-drivers, compositors, book-binders, postmen, shop assistants, police constables, hewers, and machinemen (in mining), bus drivers.

Only 19% of grammar school pupils had fathers working in the two lowest skilled groups, even though these groups accounted for 45% of all jobs. A note of warning about the accuracy of this analysis: the only coun-try-level source of socio-economic data was for Great Britain, not just for England.

The children transferring from secondary moderns had a surprisingly similar class profile to that of those who entered grammar schools aged 11. This surprised me, because I would have guessed they came from more working class origins. Another reminder to always question your assumptions and biases.

Not only were the children from the two lowest socio-economic groups less likely to get into a grammar school, but when they did they were less likely pass 'A' and 'O' levels and so were more likely to leave school without qualifications.

It is clear that a pupil's socio-economic group significantly influenced their chances of achieving academic success, affecting both the type of school they attended and how well they performed once there. This was obvious to the report's authors and something that has been confirmed by numerous subsequent research studies. Before the end of the book we will repeatedly return to this relationship between children's academic achievement and their parents.

One subject where the pupil's socio-economic status made little difference was the reason for leaving school before the completion of their academic studies. For boys, the chance to be 'earning and independent' was the primary reason, closely followed by the ready availability of a suitable job. For girls, a commonly cited reason was that 'the family could not afford to keep them at school any longer' – for those with unskilled fathers, it was the most important reason. As we have seen, this was an era of high employment with a ready supply of jobs for school leavers. For many, there must have been a (considerable) temptation to leave school at the earliest opportunity.

The Gurney-Dixon Report provided unrivalled insights into the social composition of grammar schools and added further evidence to question the accuracy of determining a child's academic future based on their exam performance at age 11.

Other research was published in 1956 that confirmed the report's findings and added further insights into how the figures varied throughout the country. *Social class and educational opportunity*[140] analysed the background of children attending grammar schools in Hertfordshire and Middlesbrough. In both areas, most pupils had parents who were classed as skilled workers. In the Middlesbrough schools, the children of unskilled manual workers comprised a larger proportion of pupils than those from the professional and managerial classes. I am not sure how much can be read into this data from just two areas, other than to illustrate the countrywide variations in the backgrounds of grammar school pupils.

What this section of the book has revealed is the extent of knowledge about secondary moderns that existed at the close of 1957. I believe that Dent provided the most authoritative view of how they were faring. He painted a hopeful picture of schools that, having come through a period of challenges, were now beginning to achieve success.

> *It seems reasonably safe to assume that by 1956 a large minority—and it may well have been a majority—of Secondary Modern schools was attacking the problems of the new secondary education with imagination and energy, and that many were achieving considerable success in overcoming them. In view of the formidable difficulties—material, social and psychological—with which they were faced during their first dozen years, that represents a very remarkable feat.*

Contrasted with this optimistic view of the schools themselves was the conclusion, from the four research reports, that despite the best efforts of the LEAs, the selection process determining a child's secondary school was flawed. You could argue that this was just stating the obvious, because no evaluation process can be 100% accurate. What these studies did was to quantify the extent of the flaw. Just as some children in secondary moderns should have been in grammar schools, the reverse was also true.

It was a little over a decade since Norwood's belief that children could be divided into three groups – the 'academic', 'commercial and technical' and 'practical' – had formed the basis for defining the secondary education system. Much had been learnt since then and there was now enough evidence to demonstrate that although it worked, after a fashion, it had serious defects. The rights and wrongs of selecting children's schooling at age 11 could no longer be framed in ideological terms. Put bluntly, many children were being educated in the wrong schools. This doesn't automatically mean the schooling system had to be immediately changed – it might have been the best of the possible 'flawed' models. It might have been greatly improved if more grammar schools had been built. We will have to wait until the next chapter before confronting these questions.

The Suez Crisis dominates the political agenda

I now want to return to look at the political forces that were influencing education policy. We learnt that David Eccles, the minister of education, was (very) worried about the existing model of secondary education and in September 1956 had produced a radically new plan that would have abandoned the 11-plus and secondary moderns, much to the consternation of his officials. I never discovered whether his plan was shared with other ministers but I very much doubt that it was, because an event was unfolding that was to dominate government business and resulted in the resignation of the prime minister. In the same way that Brexit dominated politics in 2018, and then vied for headlines until the 'deal' in December 2020, with its repercussions likely to be felt for some time to come, so it was with the Suez Crisis in late 1956 and early 1957. Even today, mention of the term still conjures up a period of national crisis.

Eccles' final attempt to raise the profile of education came in the form of a Cabinet paper, *A further advance in education*,[141] which started with the sentence: 'Suez has revealed our weakness.' As with Brexit, even arguments about education were framed in the context of the Suez Crisis. Eccles then returned to the theme that appeared in his white paper about technical education.

Size of population was never decisive; still less so in an age of science and technology. Education is the soil and the other social services, including council housing, are the fruit of an expanding economy.

His fear about the effect of the baby boom on secondary schools was his first concern, closely followed by the number and quality of teachers and the slowness of the new schools building programme.

Eccles must have been really worried about the future to produce this document and take it to Cabinet. He was not asking for any definite sum of money but for the commitment of the government to raise the importance of education as a national priority.

There is no evidence that his impassioned plea had any effect and one month later Eccles had departed the Ministry of Education to become president of the Board of Trade.

From the insights I got from studying his actions as minister, it was clear (to me) that he was genuinely committed to improving the country's education system, aware of its deficiencies but frustrated by the timidity of his officials and their lack of vision. Had it not been for the distraction of Suez, he may well have pursued his ideas to abandon the 11-plus and with it rewritten the history of secondary moderns. We will never know how that strand of history might have unfolded. What we do know is that he was given another opportunity to change the country's schooling when in 1959 he was reappointed as minister of education.

Meanwhile, his replacement was the Viscount Hailsham. He too was minister of education on two occasions – neither of them for very long (eight and seven months) and neither of them associated with instigating any significant changes in policy. In cricket parlance his role seemed to be as a 'nightwatchman'.

One of Hailsham's first actions was to resurrect Eccles' proposal.[142] He attempted to build on his predecessor's plea that government raise the importance it attached to education. For all the reasons that Eccles had identified, he requested an increased level of education spending. It comes as no surprise that this was not welcomed by the chancellor of the Exchequer and the proposal, although it was not rejected, was put into limbo, awaiting further refinement.

Increasing focus and spending on education

Eccles and Hailsham had to wait a couple of years before the government heeded their advice and increased its focus (and spending) on education. That change in policy occurred with the publication of the white paper *Secondary education for all – a new drive*.[143] One wonders why the delay? The need for more spending was all too obvious. Unpublished documents, associated with the white paper, reveal the extent of the infrastructure problems facing many – probably most – secondary modern schools.

Many thousands of words ago I discussed another document also called *Secondary Education for all*. That one was authored by R.H. Tawney and published in 1922 by the Education Advisory Committee of the Labour Party. It seems unlikely the choice of title was an accident; maybe it was a ploy to annoy the Labour Party.

Like many government education documents, *Secondary education for all* contained claims of what had been achieved and lists of things that remained to be remedied. Secondary moderns were mentioned in the context of their large class sizes and buildings of varying quality, ranging from the brand new, purpose-built schools to those constructed before 1900. There were a couple of references to the 11-plus, mainly in recognition of the anxiety it caused parents.

There are still too many areas in which it has not yet been possible to give the secondary schools, and in particular the secondary modern schools, the resources that they need. And this is why many parents still believe that, if their children go to a secondary modern school, they will not have a fair start in life.

The fact is that there are, to-day, too many children of approximately equal ability who are receiving their secondary education in schools

that differ widely both in quality, and in the range of courses they are
able to provide.

Despite acknowledging these issues there were no proposals to change
the secondary school system, other than statements about encouraging
secondary moderns to develop a wide range of courses (e.g. technical
apprenticeships, careers in commerce, nursing and 'so on') and to improve
the mechanism for transferring pupils to grammar and technical schools. To
my mind, these are 'just words'. Both the school curriculum and their
transfer policies were controlled by the LEAs and the individual schools –
not the Ministry.

Spending more money on schools was the white paper's proposed solution to these inequities. In today's pounds, the government, LEAs and the
churches committed to spending £6.5 billion on new school buildings, over
a five-year period ending 1964–1965. To put this into context, in 2015–2016
the spending on school buildings in England was £4.5 billion – that's for a
single year.

Increasing the number and quality of teachers was referenced in the
paper but no details were provided of how this would be achieved and
funded.

Geoffrey Lloyd had become minister of education in September 1957
and was responsible for the white paper's creation. Like other education
initiatives, it started with a request from the prime minister's office for
'ideas as to what the line of our advance should be – in particular for
proposals for definite action'. This note was sent from R.A. Butler, the
person who had masterminded the 1944 Education Act and who was
deputising for Harold Macmillan, who was absent on sickness leave.

Compared with the 'government speak' of the white paper, the Ministry
of Education's archived files provide a far more comprehensive and truthful
insight into the reality of secondary modern schools and the policies the
Ministry hoped would rectify their problems.

Lloyd wrote to the editor of *The Sunday Times*, Denis Hamilton, with an
advance copy of the white paper and detailed five points 'which you may
like to have in mind'.[144] No doubt this was another way of saying 'these are
the points we would like you to highlight when you report about the paper'.

Two of the points were about secondary modern schools and selective education.

> *The 11+ bogey can be smashed (and smashed honestly, rather than by double talk about a 'grammar school education for all') [this is a jibe at the wording of the Labour Party's education policy] by improving the modern schools to the point where they are seen by the parents to provide just as good opportunities for the average child as the grammar schools provide for the most able.*

> *By good secondary modern schools we mean not simply good buildings and enough good teachers (though the plan will provide both of these), but first-class courses leading to 'O' levels in the GCE examination, and courses of similar standing in technical subjects, which will persuade boys and girls, and their parents – that the way to a good career is to stay longer at school. I hope by the end of the five-year period nearly all the secondary modern schools will be offering extended courses of this kind.*

It is clear from the archives that the minister and his officials believed the 11-plus was causing significant political damage to the Conservative Party. But abandoning selective education would mean the end of the grammar schools and that was not an option. In the late 1950s the numbers and excellence of the country's scientists and technologists were a measure of the nation's global standing. Most of these people were the product of grammar schools. If this wasn't reason enough, there was the fear of the political repercussions of closing the schools that parents most wanted their children to attend. I believe there was also another reason for the attachment to grammar schools – one that couldn't be spoken. Secondary moderns were only just emerging from their 'experimental' era and although a sustainable model of how they would work was beginning to emerge, it was early days. Technical and comprehensive schools were few in number, meaning that the 1,241 grammar schools represented the only established and proven model of secondary education. Jeopardising the success of these schools would be more than a high-risk gamble – it would be bound to fail.

The prime minister wanted the white paper to be seen as symbolic of the importance the government placed on education and requested that it be promoted by all members of Cabinet. In a memorandum he talked about their support being necessary if the education policy was to have the 'desired impact'. I expect the 'desired impact' was to help the Conservative Party promote its credentials as being committed to the country's education system. It cannot be a coincidence that its PR launch plan extended to October 1959, the date of the next general election.[145] I am not suggesting that the white paper was purely for party political purposes, but its value in bolstering the party's popularity must have been a factor.

One of the nice things about researching old archives is encountering something that reveals the personal side of the people involved. The minister sent a note thanking his officials for their hard work in producing the white paper and referencing the prime minister's comments about his delight with its reception. One of officials noted that his 'smallest daughter insists on referring to it [the white paper] as the "white sheet"' – what a sweet comment, which reminds us that these 60-year-old documents were produced by real people with families and fallibilities.

Problems facing secondary schools – especially secondary moderns

The following were the darker messages that emerged from the Ministry's internal documents, which were only hinted at in the white paper.[146] Grammar schools and technical schools were not immune to these troubles, but it was secondary moderns, where most children were educated, that would inevitably be the worst affected.

Teacher shortages caused by the baby boom

We know that Eccles was extremely worried about the effect on secondary moderns of accommodating the surge in pupil numbers resulting from the baby boom and swollen by more children remaining at school beyond the statutory leaving age. The resulting teacher shortage was summarised by this statement.

For practical purposes we are back to the standards of the 1950s, with the important difference that whereas then the rise of junior classes was about to get worse and that of senior classes better, the position is now reversed. A slight improvement in the size of junior classes is to be expected, but the secondary schools, and in particular the secondary modern schools, will find it more and more difficult to obtain the teachers they need.

The most disturbing statement about teacher shortages appeared in another briefing document titled *The supply of teachers in the 1960s.*[147]

The crucial fact that emerges is that whereas on earlier calculations the supply of teachers was expected approximately to equal the number of teachers to eliminate oversize classes by 1968, on the new calculation THERE IS NO prospect, even on the more optimistic assumptions, of the supply meeting demand at any time in the 1960s.

I have reproduced this statement as it appeared, including the capitals and underlining. The official who created this document was trying to make a point! It must have sent a shiver down the spine of the minster (assuming he read it) and his officials.

Irrespective of the system of schooling, be it comprehensive or tripartite, the key to success was an adequate supply of quality teachers and that was not going to happen. Sadly, the same statement could be made today.

Inconsistent quality of buildings

The white paper mentioned the difference in quality of accommodation in the newly built secondary moderns and those still housed in old elementary schools. The Ministry's documents stated the problem in more expressive language.

The good news about the post-war secondary moderns:

Since the war the majority of the 900,000 places provided in secondary schools have been in secondary moderns and the standard of buildings provided has been a great improvement on anything which comparable pupils have yet enjoyed.

The bad news about those secondary moderns still housed in pre-war schools:

> *Facilities for practical and other subjects have had to be contrived in makeshift fashion and the conditions are wholly unsuitable for anything that can properly be described as secondary education.*

Just over 20% of secondary school pupils were taught in schools built since the war; double this number were studying in buildings constructed in the 1800s.[148]

Overcrowding in classrooms

The combination of a rising school population, too few quality school buildings and the lack of teachers was resulting in overcrowded classrooms – and worse was expected in the future.

> *It has been necessary to enforce a measure of deliberate over-crowding; for example, secondary modern schools designed to accommodate 450 children have regularly had to take 600 and when the pressure is at its worst may well have to take 700.*

> *New buildings will not fully keep pace with the increase in numbers and in many places conditions will be worse than today. It will not be possible to close even the worst housed schools and very little improvement to old school premises will be possible.*

What a depressing outlook for the children who would spend their final days of education in these old and unrefurbished secondary moderns. As I wrote these words, I thought that maybe the statement was a little too gloomy. When thinking back to my school, built in 1900, I remember it being a little cold in winter, but other than that I have no memories of my education being affected by the age of the building. Perhaps our laboratories resembled something from the films of *Harry Potter,* but that didn't stop us getting a good grounding in science and being able to take GCE 'O' levels in physics and biology.

GCE 'O' levels have a role in secondary moderns

Accompanying the white paper was a 32-page internal briefing document for the minister containing statistics to help with his speeches and answering questions.[149]

The desirability of secondary modern pupils remaining at school beyond the age of 15 and taking GCE 'O' level exams was referenced multiple times. Clearly, the Ministry's reservations about secondary modern pupils taking GCE 'O' levels had evaporated, but it still left unanswered a lot of other questions.

If the ablest pupils in secondary modern schools are to have the opportunities which children of similar ability in grammar schools have it must be possible to offer them courses leading to the GCE.

The main modifications which we now emphasise are the need to provide on both sides of the borderline (that is to say, normally in grammar schools and secondary modern schools) courses of approximately equal standard, mainly by encouraging substantial number of pupils to stay on beyond 15 in modern schools for suitable courses of all kinds, including GCE courses amongst others.

This is the first time I have seen the admission that there was an overlap in the academic abilities of children in grammar and secondary modern schools. To my mind this marks a turning point in the government's understanding – but not its actions. What the chief education officers in the LEAs made of the statement about 'courses of approximately equal standard', I have no idea.

In the same section of the document there were two statements about the likelihood of secondary modern pupils taking GCEs. First, the numbers 'for which this is appropriate may be relatively small'. Second, the motivator for staying at school until 15+ should not be solely for taking exams. Later in the document were the numbers of secondary modern schools and pupils taking GCEs in 1958 – 10,624 pupils from 792 schools. These numbers weren't expressed as a percentage of the total secondary school population. I can rectify that omission – 27% of pupils aged 15+, from 21% of secondary modern schools. I am not sure I would refer to over a quarter of pupils as 'relatively small'.

There were few details about the alternative to taking GCE exams. When this was referenced, it was just to say that secondary moderns could or should be encouraged to provide 'specialist courses'. This type of statement, which was supposed to clarify government policy, reminded me of the 1944 Education Act and its vagueness about the purpose of secondary moderns. Fourteen years later there was a little more clarity – but not much. The need for some pupils to have the opportunity of taking the same external exams as their grammar and technical school counterparts had now been established. But what of the others who were not in the 'relatively small' group?

Exams for those not taking GCE 'O' levels

The documents referenced the 'growing number of secondary modern schools developing their own examinations' as an alternative to their pupils taking GCE 'O' levels. What was not mentioned was the possibility of creating another external exam, below the academic level of the 'O' level. More about this subject appeared in another document, prepared by the minister.[150]

> *I am being urged from various quarters to encourage or permit a new form of external examination below the level of the GCE 'Ordinary', which would be specially designed to give school leavers from secondary modern schools a certificate of achievement of national standing. I share the serious doubts which my predecessors had about any such proposal.*

He went on to explain his worry about the curriculum of exams being set by 'persons unconnected with the school' and that such exams would 'put a premium on the memorisation of facts, as opposed to the development of intelligence and personal values'. This reflects the attitude that secondary modern schools should not conform to any set pattern and should have the freedom to adapt their curriculum to local needs.

I am at a loss to understand why officials were so concerned that secondary modern pupils would be constrained by the exam curriculum, something that applied equally to grammar and technical schools.

In July 1958, a committee was established (chaired by Robert Beloe, chief education officer for Surrey), against the advice of the Ministry of Education, to consider secondary school exams other than GCEs. The saga of the Ministry's attempts to stop the committee being formed and what it eventually recommended had a significant effect on school children for the next 25 years. We will soon return to this story.

Objections to comprehensive schools

The role of comprehensive schools had become the dividing line between the Labour and Conservative Parties' education policies and so it was not surprising that there was much advice about the government's reaction and attitude to these schools. At the press conference to launch the white paper, the minister's briefing notes contained a section called 'What about comprehensive plans?'[151] Here is a summary of the government's position.

The phrase about a word's meaning 'just what I choose it to mean – neither more nor less', attributed to Humpty Dumpty, was used to describe the way the word 'comprehensive' had lost any widely accepted meaning. Applying good debating tactics, the notes urged the minister to take control of the language and clarify the four most common ways it was applied to secondary schools – which were as follows.

- Organising secondary education like the American high schools, where pupils were not graded. The government rejected this model because it believed that selection was essential 'to do justice to different needs of individual children'.
- Abolishing selection at 11-plus so that all children attended their local non-selective comprehensive. The government rejected this model because it would involve the destruction of well-established grammar, technical *and secondary modern schools* (my italics). It argued that comprehensive schools would result in a waste of school premises because smaller schools would need to be closed or amalgamated into large comprehensives. It also

implied that LEAs would have less power to organise the schools to reflect local educational needs.

- Using the word to describe the 'comprehensive system' of providing a wide range of courses. The Labour Party was accused of using this term and attaching to the definition the condition that the 11-plus would be abandoned. I think the argument was that 'comprehensive' was being used to mean 'wide-ranging' when in fact it was a cypher for 'non-selective'.
- The government's preferred definition was that comprehensive schools – along with the other types of secondary schools – had merits, but only in the 'right' circumstances. They may have been appropriate in rural areas, where there was a low population, and in new housing developments, where there were no existing schools with 'well-established traditions' – I think this was code for grammar schools. To prove the government's open-mindedness, it detailed the 100 comprehensive schools that were operating.

Let's step back a moment and consider the Conservative government's policy options. It hinted at, but dared not explain in detail, the dreadful state of the secondary school infrastructure and the pressures it was facing from the rising pupil population and insufficient numbers of teachers. Budgetary and practical constraints limited the number of new schools that it could build and teachers that it could train. For the next decade there would not be enough of either to avoid many children being taught in old schools and overcrowded conditions. By now, the minister and Ministry officials could have no doubt that many children were educated in the 'wrong type' of schools. There was incontestable evidence showing that dividing children into three intelligence groups, at the age of 11, was an inexact science. Mistakes were made – lots of them.

It was never expressed in these words, but the government's policy (in my opinion) was to hope that parents (and voters) would be satisfied knowing that more schools were being built and that secondary moderns were evolving to look more like grammar schools. Their pupils could remain beyond the statutory leaving age and have the opportunity to take GCE 'O' levels. What would happen to the pupils who were thought incapable of taking these exams (the large majority) was glossed over and it was left to the LEAs and schools to find a solution.

Grammar schools were the 'crown jewels' of the secondary education system. They had a long history of academic success and were held in high regard by parents; this was not contested by the political parties. Where Labour and Conservative policy differed was their future role in the secondary education system. The Conservatives believed they should continue into the 1960s as they had since the 1944 Education Act – the best schools for the brightest children. The Labour Party believed it had a policy to make those schools' benefits available to all children. At the same time as the white paper, the Labour Party was promoting the concept of 'a grammar school education for all',[152] which would be achieved by combining secondary moderns and grammar schools into single institutions – comprehensive schools.

I very much doubt if any of the Conservative Party's policy makers would have called themselves marketers or looked at their predicament in marketing terms. Had they done so they would have been mighty worried. The Labour Party seems to have formulated a powerful selling proposition. Parents wanted (so it seemed) to have a grammar school education for their children but not the trauma of the 11-plus exam. With a pinch of magic dust the comprehensive school gave them both. We will come back to the Labour Party's policies in more detail soon; what matters now is the challenge they presented the Conservative government.

Within a year of the white paper's publication, the political parties had to distil their education policies into manifestos to fight the October 1959 general election. This was the essence of their commitments.[153]

Labour Party	Conservative Party
• Reduce class sizes to 30 in primary and secondary schools. • Expand facilities for technical education. • 'Get rid of the 11-plus examination'. • 'Grammar school education will be open to all who can benefit by it' and 'comprehensive education will not impose one uniform pattern of schooling'. • Give 'LEAs the right to decide how best to apply the comprehensive principle'.	• Improve the quality of school buildings and train and recruit more teachers. • 'Defend grammar schools against doctrinaire socialist attack' and 'bring modern schools up to the same high standard'. Belief that 'this is the way to deal with the problem of the eleven-plus.' • Plan by 1965 that at least 40% of children will remain at school after the age of 15.

1959 general election party election manifestos

As you can see, the role of the grammar school was central to both parties.

It is easy to forget that the political parties' popularity was determined by many factors other than their education policies, something that is graphically demonstrated by analysing the education policy as part of the overall content of the manifestos. Neither party devoted more than 5% of its manifesto to the subject – something that has remained remarkably constant over time. In 2017 the figure was 7%.

The Conservatives won the October 1959 election, nearly doubling their Parliamentary majority, and began another five years in government. David Eccles returned to the Ministry of Education and started his second period as minister. Since the publication of the white paper, his predecessor hadn't initiated any significant policy initiatives. In the months before the election the prime minister had asked for his agenda for the coming five years, which contained nothing new and was essentially more of the same. More money to be spent doing minor repairs to school buildings and recruiting more teachers.[154] There is no doubt that this was necessary, but perhaps his lack of imagination was why he lost his ministerial position?

Secondary modern pupils and exams – the battle continues

Before talking about the pressing items in Eccles' in-tray it is necessary to remind ourselves of the Ministry's views about secondary modern children taking exams. We have touched on the subject before and will return to it many more times. With hindsight we can see that the topic acted as a proxy for the competing visions of secondary modern schools. The collective view of the Ministry's officials was that only a small minority of secondary modern pupils were capable of taking GCE exams. External exams were beyond the ability of the remainder; indeed, they were potentially dangerous to their schooling.

An official in the schools branch of the Ministry, Toby Weaver (later to become Sir Toby Weaver), produced a document, for internal use, providing a comprehensive summary of the Ministry's views.[155] Exams were a contentious subject:

The current debate bears out the testimony of history that on the subject of examinations people of comparable intelligence and good-will are capable of reaching diametrically opposite conclusions on the same evidence.

I have little doubt that historians will write similar statements about Brexit. Mr Weaver's personal views were revealed in the document's opening sentence, which referred to the 'examination virus working vigorously on the education body'.

Here is the crux of Weaver's arguments.

It is taken here as axiomatic that the Minister wishes to encourage the heads and staffs of secondary modern schools themselves to establish whatever objectives, curricula, syllabuses, methods and quality of life they find by experience and experiment will most fruit-fully meet the widely differing needs and circumstances of their pupils and neighbourhoods.

The corollary is that, if they are to have freedom to do so they must be protected with reasonable limits from outside forces which are

*prima facie damaging, whether these take the form of an instrument,
such as an external examination, or an idea, such as that secondary
modern schools should be conditioned to a pre-established pattern of
what 'the secondary modern school' should be.*

Clearly, he retained the mindset that secondary modern schools were of an infinite variety and needed the freedom to adapt what and how they taught to local conditions – teachers should be able to determine what was taught, rather than adopting a standardised syllabus set by external examiners.

Weaver finished the document with some tactical advice for the minister.

*I suggest that if the Minister is to take and keep the initiative, he
must aim at putting the question of external examinations firmly in
the context of a positive policy – the development of the secondary
modern schools and their relationship with the technical colleges.*

There was general agreement from other officials with the fundamentals of Weaver's arguments. Most of the comments were about the tactics of how the minister should present the conclusions – especially the one about fostering the relationship between secondary modern schools and technical colleges. As I read these remarks, I kept asking myself, 'Do these people truly believe these ideas or are they just formulating debating arguments?' Many times during my consulting career, I had to concoct proposals that were little more than 'word games', with little chance of ever being implemented. This tactic, about technical colleges becoming the route to exams for secondary modern pupils, has all of these hallmarks. That's not to say it is a bad idea – it might have been a brilliant idea – but other than helping the minister sell his proposals, I doubt if the policy would have been implemented. It reminded me of the pre-WWI proposals to create continuation schools.

This controversy over external exams had resulted in an unusual and difficult situation for the minister. Eccles' first significant action was to understand and formulate a response to a report he had commissioned in March 1956, during his first time as minister. Containing over 700 pages of research and recommendations, the Crowther Report[156] provided interesting insights into the culture and attitudes of children in their mid-teens. Eccles then received the Beloe Report[157] (which I have also previously mentioned). Not requested by any minister, indeed in spite of the Ministry's best efforts to stop its creation, it landed on his desk.

The histories and outcomes of the Crowther and Beloe Reports were closely intertwined. It is a tale of the clash between different organisations and personalities, with very differing views about secondary education. I will do my best to relate an ultra-summarised version of the saga. Peter Fisher's book[158] provided an excellent, blow-by-blow, account of the story and its consequences.

Contained in the detail of the 1944 Education Act was the provision to establish the Central Advisory Council for Education (CACE) to 'advise the Minister upon such matters connected with educational theory and practice as they think fit, and upon any questions referred to them by him'. What is important for this story is that the members and chairman of the council were appointed by the minister. A separate council was established to advise on educational maters in Wales.

A much older advisory council, the Secondary Schools Examinations Council (SSEC) had been established in 1917 to provide the minister with advice about external exams for secondary schools with 'the duty of co-ordinating examinations and of negotiating with professional bodies for the acceptance of certificates'. The minister and Ministry had far less control over how this was constituted and operated. I guess it is like the Bank of England being independent from the Treasury. It can do and say what it wants (within reason).

All was well as long as the two organisations shared a common outlook about secondary school exams and, by definition, the role of secondary modern schools. There had been skirmishes between the organisations in the past, but on the subject of creating another exam to complement GCE 'O' levels they had diametrically opposite views.

Crowther's committee was managed by the CACE and tasked to:

Consider, in relation to the changing social and industrial needs of our society, and the needs of its individual citizens, the education of boys and girls between 15 and 18, and in particular to consider the balance at various levels of general and specialised studies between

*these ages and to examine the inter-relationship of the various stages
of education.*

After the committee had started work it was asked to consider an additional question:

*To provide views on the place of examinations below the level of that
for the General Certificate of Education in the education of boys and
girls between 15 and 18.*

It is not surprising that the SSEC believed it was its role to advise on all issues connected with exams. Against the advice and then the instruction of the Ministry, it set up its own committee to consider:

*The question of examinations other than the GCE in secondary
schools.*

To my mind, it made a lot of sense for Crowther's committee to take the lead in considering the issue of exams. If it was researching the education of children aged 15–18, then its conclusions should have covered the types of exams they would take. That's the logical conclusion, but not (in my view) the reason it was given the task. A more likely explanation was that the Ministry expected it would reach the 'right' conclusion – one that chimed with its views.

Beloe's committee was not without its perceived weaknesses. In 1958 a question was asked in Parliament about the composition of the SSEC, pointing out that it contained only one person representing secondary modern schools and that the majority of its members' 'experience is quite remote from present-day living conditions and problems in secondary schools'. In defence of the accusation, it was claimed that two of its members had first-hand experience of secondary moderns. That might represent a doubling of the experience, but was a paltry reflection of the importance being given to the schools that were then educating the majority of the country's children.[159]

As expected, the two committees came to different conclusions, which resulted in a public battle of ideas, with the minister, a far from impartial referee, stuck in the middle. All children in the UK, especially those in secondary moderns, experienced the outcome of the conflict for the next two decades.

Beloe's report had many conclusions and recommendations but it was the following points that most affected secondary moderns.

The number of pupils for whom the GCE 'O' level taken in the range of four or more subjects is a suitable examination must be regarded as very strictly limited, amounting at most to 20% of the age group at 16. Below this group [the top 20%] there may be a band of pupils who may, not without some benefit, attempt 'O' levels in two or three subjects.

Below the top 20% there are candidates in the next 20% of the age group that might take the examinations [the newly proposed exam] in a fair spread of subjects, say four or five.

Candidates with a range of the next 20% of the age group, who are around about average ability, might attempt, and often secure passes in, fewer subjects.

The examination should not attempt merely to provide a replica at a somewhat lower level of the GCE 'O' level examination, but that they should seek to achieve aims and a character of their own. We think it important that wherever the subject allows, the examination should provide for practical work.

As an aid to my understanding of these recommendations (and hopefully yours, the reader) I have translated them into a table format.

Ability group	Possible exams	Report's comments
Top 20%	Four or more subjects at 'O' level	This group (mostly pupils attending grammar schools) 'must be regarded as very strictly limited, amounting at most to 20% of the age group at 16'.
Small number of students at the top of the next 20%	Two or three at 'O' level	These pupils 'may, not without some benefit, attempt 'O' levels'.
The next 20% (i.e. 60–80% range)	Four or five subjects in the new exam	'The examination should not attempt merely to provide a replica at a somewhat lower level of the GCE 'O' level examination, but that they should seek to achieve aims and a character of their own. We think it important that wherever the subject allows, the examination should provide for practical work.'
The next 20% (i.e. 40–60% range)	Fewer subjects	Pupils who 'are around about average ability might attempt, and often secure passes in, fewer subjects'.
The bottom 40%		No recommendation/not mentioned.

Crowther's committee rejected the proposal for establishing another external exam. While recognising that it was a popular idea and refraining from totally discarding the notion, he proposed an elegant 'sitting on the fence' solution that involved conducting experiments for the next five years. Today we would say he was 'kicking the can down the road'.

His first statement was not so much a recommendation as a conclusion about the dangers of exams for the majority of secondary modern pupils.

Many, probably more than half, of the pupils of the modern schools would have their education deflected from its proper lines by being prepared for an external examination. It is important that attention to the needs of the minority should not be allowed to lead to neglect of the interests of these boys and girls, who are and will remain by far the largest single group in the modern schools.

He defined an 'examinable minority' of pupils as dividing into two groups.

One of these consists of those pupils who have the ability to attempt some of the subjects in the G.C.E. at Ordinary level. It is important that none of them should be denied the opportunity to do so. [This group is not quantified.]

The other group consisting of about one-third or rather more of the
pupils in modern schools – for whom external examinations below
the level of the G.C.E. may serve a useful purpose, and official
policy should be modified to recognise this.

After this admission that a sizeable group of children would benefit, he rejected the idea because of the perceived dangers and offered other solutions.

We are, however, impressed with the dangers of large-scale external
examinations, which a national system could not avoid. External
examinations should therefore develop on a regional, or preferably a
local, basis. Some of the purposes served by an external examination
can also be met by a formal assessment by the school, at the time of
leaving, of a pupil's performance and attainments during his whole
time at the school.

Secondary modern schools didn't have the luxury of time to await the pronouncements of these educational committees. They were already submitting pupils for other types of exams, including those managed by the Royal Society of Arts and the College of Preceptors. Taking Royal Society of Arts exams was a significant part of the last two years of my schooling. Perhaps I took them in preparation for my GCE 'O' levels or maybe they were a fall-back, in case I failed? Even now I remember my inability to pass the RSA English exam (twice), which didn't auger well for my future career as a part-time writer.

Eccles' public response to the Beloe Report contained the usual platitudes of 'I think this is a most valuable and stimulating report and shall be glad to publish it as your council recommend'. From a cursory reading of the Ministry's press release, announcing the report's conclusion, you could be forgiven for believing that Beloe was recommending a continuance of the status quo.[160] Much space was given to highlighting concerns about a new exam and listing the caveats and conditions for its implementation. Clearly, the Ministry was not going to give up without a fight.

I was able to study some of the feedback that followed the report's publication and much to my surprise I had sympathy with the views expressed by organisations I wouldn't normally associate as being of a like mind. A discussion statement from the Communist Party Education Advisory Committee[161] made the following points.

The figures, especially that of 20% [those who would take GCE 'O' levels], put forward in the report, are purely fictional and based on no supporting evidence whatever.

No account is taken of the possibility of achieving higher attainment in our schools given better education conditions. Not a word in the report condemns inadequate education provision as the cause of relative backwardness.

In the same vein, but in much more detail, the views from the National Association of Labour Teachers[162] condemned the report for 'drawing conclusions from the evidence as presented and treated in the report, [that are] alarmingly unscholarly'.

I thought the precision of the report's conclusions was unsubstantiated, like that of the Norwood Report. You'll remember that report as the document that divided secondary school children into three types – the grammar, technical and secondary modern child. Beloe made the same, sweeping judgements about the academic potential of children. The committee had asked Sir Cyril Burt (the retired expert on intelligence testing whom we also met earlier) for his advice, but he failed to respond. There was nothing in the report showing how the grouping of children into the 20% bands was derived and how it related to existing knowledge about the distribution of children's intelligence.

It was Eccles who best explained the problems that could result from the Beloe Committee's recommendations.[163]

I do not want a first eleven GCE [similar to a football or cricket team], a second eleven Beloe and all the rest non-players. I find it doubtful whether the staff of say a comprehensive or a large secondary modern could cope fairly and adequately with three grades of children.

The exam that Beloe and his committee recommended was to become the Certificate of Secondary Education (CSE). After being launched in 1965 it was the primary exam taken by secondary school children until 1987.

What disturbs me about this whole affair is that neither Beloe, Crowther nor the Ministry seemed to base their decisions on anything approaching reliable evidence. Feelings ran high about what was the best approach, but they were not grounded in the research of the day about the evolution of children's intelligence. The most quantified conclusions came from extrapolating the past and not from questioning how this would have changed had circumstances been different.

Beloe and the SSEC had won the battle and secondary moderns now had to contend with two types of external exam. We have reached one of those *Sliding Doors*[164] moments. The timeline might have continued with pupils increasingly taking the GCE 'O' level, but instead they were much more likely to take CSEs or, as Gary McCulloch[165] referred to them, the sub-GCE. By 1969, half of secondary modern pupils were limited to taking CSE exams, compared with just 1% of those in grammar school. Many secondary modern pupils took a mix of both exams (40%), with just 10% focused exclusively on GCE 'O' levels.[166] Not surprisingly, the question of the equivalence between GCEs and CSEs soon became an issue – i.e. what pass grade of CSE exam should be considered the same as a GCE 'O' pass, and at what grade? By 1964 syllabuses for the two exams were being administered by the same organisation. Beloe was concerned about this development and it was agreed that the 'interests of the average child should not be allowed to suffer'.[167] My suspicion is that they did.

Crowther's report changed little, either in the policy or practice of education. If his recommendations had been accepted and if they had been implemented (two big 'ifs'), then this is how secondary moderns would have changed.

Extended courses should be made available for all modern school pupils. By 1965 we think it possible that extended courses will be needed for half the 15-year-olds, averaged over the country as a whole. This is therefore the target at which, in the absence of special circumstances, local authorities should aim.

*Authorities and governing bodies should not judge their modern
schools by public examination results.*

*The raising of the school-leaving age to 16, and the creation of
county colleges for compulsory part-time day education to 18 –
should be re-affirmed as objectives of national policy and the raising
of the school-leaving age should have priority in time over the introduction of compulsory county colleges.*

*The school leaving age should be raised in either 1966–67, 1967–68,
1968–69. The year should be chosen and announced now and a
programme of action set on foot to ensure that the necessary conditions are prepared [the actual date was 1971].*

*The proportion of young people in the three years 16–18 in full-time
education is now only a little over 1 in 8. We recommend that the
objective of policy should be to raise it to 50 per cent within twenty
years from now.*

Asking government to name the date for raising the school-leaving age
was the most important of the recommendations and the one that attracted
the most attention. It should be remembered, however, that this was one of
those 'when the time is right' policies that had been around since the 1944
Education Act. Likewise with introduction of county colleges, to provide
part-time compulsory education for all young people aged 16 and 17. The
time was never right for this idea.

Beloe's recommendation for the CSE exam would affect all secondary
moderns in a matter of months. Crowther's proposals were all about changes
far in the future. This was not the first time that teachers had heard promises
about raising the school-leaving age and I expect their attitude was 'I will
believe it when I see it'.

Three months after its publication, Sir Geoffrey Crowther gave an
address at the University of Manchester about his report and how it had been
received.[168] Over half of the talk was about raising the school-leaving age,
something he kept apologising for and explaining that it reflected the quantity of plaudits and criticism the idea had generated. He went to great ends to

explain that the 'raising the school leaving age should not be done <u>now,</u> but in seven to nine years' time'. So much of what he recommended depended on having an adequate supply of teachers and, as we have already seen, the Ministry's forecasts painted a dismal picture of this happening. Before the report was complete, Crowther wrote to the minister highlighting this problem. He must have known that without enough teachers it would be difficult to get traction for implementing his ideas.

Towards the end of Crowther's address, his language became more passionate when he talked about the findings of his research about a group of children he named 'the second quartile'. I will use his words to explain the issue.

Grammar schools contain, at 15, about a quarter of our children, and they are supposed to be in the upper quartile by intelligence.

Children who leave school as soon as they are allowed to and have, in most cases, no further contact with the educational process, are about half of the total. [These are the third and fourth quartiles.]

There remains the second quartile. And let us never forget that the way we treat them is a disgrace to our educational profession.

Crowther had discovered that many of this group left school at 15 and had no further involvement with formal education. Of those who did go to college, three-quarters were unlikely to complete their studies. These words expressed his feeling: 'How monstrously unjust! And how terribly wasteful.'

I am sure the research that caused Crowther's misgivings (he mentioned it in his address) was the analysis his committee undertook about the backgrounds and abilities of the 9,000 recruits who were completing their national service in the army and RAF.[169] During the enrolment process the recruits were tested for their academic and practical skills and awarded an ability score. Not surprisingly, those with the highest ability scores had stayed at school at least until the age of 16. What came as a surprise was the backgrounds of those with the second order of ability. Two-thirds of this group had left school at the first opportunity (i.e. when they were 15).

Almost all of them came from secondary moderns and hadn't taken GCE 'O' levels. Over half of the remainder of the group, who had attempted GCE 'O' levels, had passed with four or more subjects.

Crowther rightly concluded that there was a large pool of young adults with the ability to take GCE 'O' levels who, for whatever reason, didn't. He saw this as a terrible waste for the individuals and for the country, which desperately needed a better-educated workforce.

There was another statement in his report that he didn't quote, perhaps because it questioned the core of the government's education policy. His committee had found, through 'much careful research', that by the age of 15 approximately 14% of pupils were in the wrong type of secondary school. Put quite simply – Crowther was questioning the idea that a child's schooling could be determined when they were aged 11 – the basic assumption of the tripartite system.

His indignation was not shared by others. He quoted the results of a colleague's analysis of the media's coverage of his report, which found that only 4% of the comments related to the 'second quartile' issue.

Why were so many children with the academic potential not staying at school for an 'extended course'?[170] His committee had commissioned a research study to interview a group of 2,700 children, together with their parents, who were attending grammar, technical and secondary modern schools. The aim was to discover the differences in their backgrounds and attitudes to schooling.

As so often happens, little attention was paid to the research findings, which were soon forgotten. I have always found there is much enthusiasm about the process of commissioning and conducting research, but that it rapidly fades when it comes to deciding what to do with the conclusions. Some things don't change.

From the research, the committee found a simple explanation why so any children left school at the first opportunity.

The evidence seems to us to establish that it is insufficient opportu-
nity, at least for a very large number of children, and not lack of
desire for more education, that makes them leave school at 15.

In economic terms, they decided it was a supply, not a demand, problem. To support the conclusion they focused on three pieces of evidence. Approximately 5% of 11 year olds were still being educated in all-age schools, where they received, in the committee's words, 'little more than the minimum education provision'. There were 17% of secondary modern schools that were too small, in terms of the number of pupils, to provide extended courses. Finally, only a minority of large secondary moderns had decided to provide the courses. To substantiate this last point, they mentioned that in one of England's largest cities only a third of secondary moderns had extended courses in operation.

Crowther's argument was that if the extended courses were available then parents would be prepared for their children to attend school for the extra year. In the long term I suspect he was right but there were a couple of pieces of evidence, from his own research, that suggest the rate of up-take might have been slower than he expected.

The parents of children attending grammar and technical schools were better educated than those of children at secondary moderns. Only 2% of secondary modern children had both parents who had remained at school after the age of 14 years. The parents of most children (88%) had left before their 14th birthday. My parents were in this group.

You could argue that the parents' schooling was immaterial to how they viewed their children's education. Indeed, you could argue that parents with little education would want the very best for their children – to have the education they were denied. These arguments were not supported by Crowther's research. Secondary modern parents were far less willing than those in grammar and technical schools, by a factor of 6, for their children to stay at school until the year end (i.e. their children finished their education at the first opportunity).

There were numerous reasons determining the likelihood of children taking an extended course. I am sure Crowther was right in thinking that once the supply was there the demand would increase. It was his assumption about the speed this would happen that I think was optimistic.

We know that the Beloe Committee's report led to the introduction of the CSE exam, but what was the impact of Crowther's endeavours?

At 3.52pm, on 21 March 1960, Eccles got to his feet in the House of Commons to begin the debate by proposing that the:

House welcomes the report of the CACE [the Crowther Report] as a constructive contribution to the formation of educational policy for the next twenty years.

The first four minutes of his address were the usual words of thanks and compliments with lots of statements such as:

This well-balanced Report is a work of scholarship and art, which I believe the House will judge worthy to rank with Hadow and Spens.

He devoted half of his time to explaining why raising the school-leaving age was a good idea but wouldn't happen until the circumstances were right – i.e. when there were enough schools and teachers.

He took another 10 minutes to support Crowther's recommendation that county colleges were a second priority to keeping children at school for an extra year. Then he used his remaining few minutes to comment on the report's other recommendations and concluded by explaining how the government was spending record amounts of money on education.

His 50-minute address could have been summarised as 'no change to education policy'. The Commons spent a further six hours debating the report, including a Labour Party amendment proposing a date be confirmed when the leaving age would be raised. As expected, this was defeated. Throughout the debate not one word was spoken about the 'second quartile'.

It could be argued that the lasting result of Crowther's Report was to nudge a step closer the time when children would leave school at 16. Maybe it did – but I doubt it. His Committee's years of work provided an excellent historical snapshot of the secondary school system in the early 1960s. But, as for the headmasters, headmistresses and teachers who were working at the chalk-face of education, I doubt if it made a jot of difference.

A few days after the Commons' debate, the House of Lords had its turn to discuss the report.[171] Nothing new was added to the debate, but there was one contribution that I think worth mentioning.

Lord Silkin began his speech by talking about the 'method of separation of children between the grammar schools and the secondary modern schools'. He was unhappy about the 11-plus and what he believed was the 25% of children being sent to the wrong type of school. As a life-long

Labour Party supporter, it is not surprising that he believed comprehensive schools might partly solve the problem; however, he qualified this by saying that there might be other ways of dealing with the problem. By now I would think that few would disagree with his concluding statement.

But this problem has got to be dealt with if we are to have an effective educational system in this country.

Since the war, multiple research studies had revealed the large numbers of children who were receiving the 'wrong' type of schooling. This was not a matter of political doctrine – it was a fact, supported by a stack of evidence. As I have said before, the Conservatives believed the solution was to endow secondary moderns with the ability to mirror the educational opportunities of grammar schools, providing a route to exam and employment success. Well that was the theory!

The 'bottom half' of secondary modern pupils – the forgotten group

So far the focus had been on the effectiveness of the secondary education system, viewed from the perspective of the academically gifted children. Even though Beloe and Crowther disagreed about the policy of external exams, both concentrated on the needs of the 'examinable' child. During all this time, precious little had been said about schooling pupils in the bottom classes of secondary moderns – the ones who wanted to leave school at the first opportunity. What were the goals of their schooling and how should these be achieved?

A year after Crowther's Report, Eccles initiated yet another study from the CACE, to:

Advise him on the education of pupils aged 13 to 16 of average and less than average ability.

This committee was chaired by John Newsom, formerly the county education officer of Hertfordshire, and I wondered why he agreed to do it after seeing Crowther's endeavours summarily praised and dismissed in an afternoon. He hadn't been the first choice for the job and took over when the original chairman went to be high commissioner for Canada. Like many successful people, I expect Newsom thought he would succeed where others had failed.

Equally baffling was Eccles' rationale for requesting yet another research study. I am sure it wasn't an intentional distractionary tactic, although he could be accused of substituting 'researching something' for 'doing something'. None of the fundamentals of schooling had changed since Crowther's Report. Teachers and decent school buildings were in short supply and would stay that way. Why Eccles acted as he did remains something of a mystery and is a question that is glossed over by education historians.

The most detailed account of the workings of the Newsom Committee is Garry McCulloch's paper *Representing the 'Ordinary Child': the case of the Newsom Committee.*[172] He began the paper by emphasising the huge gulf in the social and educational backgrounds of those formulating education policy and the mass of the population who were its recipients. You have to go back to 1947 to find a minister of education (George Tomlinson) who wasn't educated at a private school and then university. All but one of the ministers had studied at Oxford, as had Beloe and Newsom. Crowther was state-educated, at a grammar school, and then went to Cambridge. I don't know for certain, but I expect most of the senior administrators at the Ministry of Education shared an equally distinguished – perhaps I should now say 'privileged' – academic pedigree.

McCulloch didn't pose the obvious question: 'What could these people possibly know about the children in the bottom forms of secondary moderns?' I think the answer was obvious. Not a lot.

The educational background of today's ministers of education is not that different. Of the last half a dozen, half attended private schools and four studied at Oxford. They had varied careers but none had spent any time as a teacher. The exception is the current minister (Gavin Williamson), who has no teaching experience but attended a comprehensive school and then Bradford University. Perhaps their understanding of the 'ordinary child' is not that much better than their predecessors'?

During Eccles' first period as minister, he had been prepared to question the status quo and ask awkward questions. So he did again, as I expect he felt ill-equipped to formulate education policies for pupils and their parents who were so different from his peer group and hoped that Newsom would provide him with some answers. Another explanation is that Beloe's Report had formalised the academic hierarchy in secondary moderns. At the top was the GCE stream; below them, those studying for CSEs. Then came those of 'average and less than average ability'. Were they to be taught a simplified version of the curriculum studied by their more academic peers or were their educational needs fundamentally different?

You would think that 17 years after the 1944 Education Act the politicians and administrators of the country's schooling would have known the answer to this question. Remember, the original concept of the secondary modern was to educate the non-academic children – the ones who wouldn't take exams. Here we are, all those years later, pondering how to educate the sub-set of pupils thought to be beyond studying an exam curriculum. These were the very same children whom secondary moderns were originally created to educate.

Nothing I read in the archived documents of the period led me to believe that the Ministry officials or members of the Newsom Committee appreciated the irony of this situation. There was no hint that they experienced déjà vu.

The notes prepared for the Committee's first meeting contained a long list of the questions it needed to address.[173] All of these were good questions, but I had, rather naïvely, assumed they would have long since been answered.

Are the following among the common attitudes which need to be examined, modified or rejected?

That the C. and D. pupils required a watered-down version of what is given to the A.s and B.s [the streams in secondary moderns], the latter itself deriving largely from the grammar school's approach to acquiring knowledge.

That essentially all that can be attempted with C.s and D.s is to reinforce the elementary work of the primary school.

*That the degree of success with the least able can, or should, be
measured by the amount of knowledge acquired.*

*That success must be measured in terms of personal development
and of the pupil's improvement on their own performance during
their time in school.*

*The problem of defining the education aim in terms which can be
understood and accepted by the pupils themselves, when measurement by external examination is largely or wholly inappropriate.*

*Do we assume too uncritically that there must be 'differentiation' for
the C.s and D.s, or is the conflict of principles over this more
apparent than real?*

One question stood out, for me, as crystallising the fundamental issue
the Committee wanted to resolve.

*Is the kernel of the problem to think out and organize a plan for a
progressive 4/5 year course for the 'less able' pupils in terms of their
nature and present and future needs, not borrowing or adapting from
courses designed for pupils aiming at examinations?*

I need to reiterate the point that surely these were questions that should
have been asked, and answered, when secondary moderns were first
established?

Much could be said about the workings of the Committee and the people
and organisations it interviewed. As interesting as these details were, it was
the half a dozen conclusions and recommendations of the report that had a
lasting impact on secondary moderns and the schools that replaced them. In
August 1963 the Newsom Committee's Report was published[174] and it was
the responsibility of a new minister of education, Sir Edward Boyle, to deal
with its proposals.

The Report's first 300 words contained a recommendation that was
profound but had few immediate political consequences, another that would

have delighted the minister and one that gave him a political problem – although not an unexpected one.

The scope of the first recommendation was so wide in ambition that it was impossible to translate into specific demands on the government. For certain it was a grand-sounding statement (and probably correct) but unlikely to result in any discernible outcomes.

> *We are concerned that the young people whose education we have*
> *been considering should receive a greater share of the national*
> *resources devoted to education than they have done in the past. We*
> *are concerned that there should be a change of attitude towards*
> *these young people not only among many of those who control their*
> *education but among the public at large and this cannot be achieved*
> *solely, if at all, by administrative action. It involves a change of*
> *thinking and even more a change of heart.*

Recommendation number two was a confirmation of the government's education policy. It was a 'negative recommendation' in that it explicitly didn't question the existing model of secondary education. However, it was a statement that should have caused the Labour Party to question its belief that educational nirvana would result from changing the structure of schools.

> *We cannot stress too strongly that the solution to these problems is*
> *not necessarily to be found by a reorganisation of the present pattern*
> *of secondary education. However large or small the school, whether*
> *it is one-sex or co-educational, however wide its range of intellectual*
> *ability, the problems peculiar to the pupils we have been considering*
> *still remain to be solved.*

The third recommendation echoed the Crowther Committee's main proposal that a date should be set for raising the school-leaving age. Yet again, the government's unwillingness to name a date for this event was challenged.

> *We fully endorse and reaffirm the conclusion reached in the Coun-*
> *cil's last report [the Crowther Report] that there is an urgent need to*

raise the school-leaving age to sixteen and that a specific date
should be announced for the implementation of this decision.

It took only another 100 words to state the next two recommendations. The first of these put an end to the idea that colleges of further education could provide an alternative path for a child's secondary education, once the school-leaving age was raised.

We maintain that during the whole secondary period the full-time
education of pupils should be either in school or based on a school,
despite the fact that we consider it important that the older pupils
should have experience outside its confines.

I have already said that I didn't think this was ever a serious proposal, but the idea was now well and truly dead.

Then came Newsom's recommendation of a distinction between the curriculum and teaching methods for the examinable and non-examinable secondary modern pupil. Of all his recommendations, this was the one to have the most impact.

We consider that much fuller use should be made of the natural inter-
ests of older boys and girls in the work they will eventually under-
take and that this fact should be reflected not only in the content of
the curriculum but in the method of teaching and, above all, in the
attitude of the teacher to the pupil when the pupil is, in effect, a
young adult.

Notes from the Committee's meetings, summarising the evidence it had received, provided deeper insights into what this recommendation meant.[175]

A fairly frequently recurrent suggestion in the evidence is that for
'our' pupils [the majority of pupils in secondary modern schools], as
they get older, work should have an increasingly 'realistic' and
'practical' character.

There appears to be a recommendation that the school ought consciously to be looking to develop interesting and future needs of the young adult. Work in this sense is 'realistic' and 'practical' when the pupil can see a relevance to adult life.

Learning is said to be 'realistic' or 'practical' when it is applied rather than theoretical and derives from an actual situation or activity. It is said that many of 'our pupils', and particularly the 'below-average', find this a more helpful and comprehensible way of learning.

This recommendation led to the recognition of a new category of secondary modern pupils, who needed a different type of education that was 'realistic and practical' – and became known as the 'Newsom child'. Deciding whether this was a terrible blunder or a milestone in education history will have to wait for a later chapter.

In reaching its conclusions, the Committee took evidence from numerous groups and individuals. It also conducted a research project involving 6,000 fourth-year pupils in 75 secondary modern schools. Teachers provided details about the pupils, including their weight, height, behaviour, social class, type of housing, parents' employment type and the likelihood of them staying at school into the fifth form. Added to this descriptive information was the result of a reading and vocabulary test that was used as a proxy for the children's 'ability'.

Attempts were made throughout the Newsom Report to humanise its findings by combining its quantitative analysis with individual children's stories. In a similar vein, the Report's authors avoided labelling children by their academic performance. Instead of dividing the pupils' ability into a hierarchy labelled top, middle and bottom, they were given abstract titles (Brown, Jones and Robinson). To reiterate that there was no status associated with these titles, the other options were listed: Athos, Porthos and Aramis (the names of the *Three Musketeers*) and Tom, Dick and Harry. No doubt this non-judgemental naming policy bolstered the Report's authors' progressive credentials, but it did nothing to help its readers.

Those children in the Brown group scored an average of 27+ in the reading test, which was very close to the score on the ninetieth percentile.

They were in the top quarter of secondary modern school pupils, a score that was the same as many in the lower forms of grammar schools.

Children in the Jones group scored between 18 and 26 in the test, placing them in the middle two quarters of pupils, and the Robinsons scored 17 or less: the bottom quarter of secondary modern children.

For some reason, slightly more details were collected about the boys in the research sample. I am sure there were interesting insights to be found in the differences between the boys and girls but for the sake of simplicity I only studied the findings for the boys. The following table represents a tiny extract of the research findings, but I think it clearly shows the significant differences between children in the top and bottom groups of the test scores – the Browns and Robinsons.

	Brown Top 25%	Jones Middle 50%	Robinson Bottom 25%
Social class			
Professional or managerial	7%	4%	2%
Unskilled	9%	16%	20%
Clerical	11%	9%	7%
Skilled	59%	55%	53%
Semi-skilled	14%	16%	18%
Housing			
Mining	6%	11%	12%
Problem areas	13%	17%	24%
Mixed areas	40%	31%	23%
Rural	11%	12%	10%
Council housing	30%	29%	31%
Schooling and discipline			
Leave school asap	46%	74%	93%
Likely to complete 4th year but not 5th	12%	10%	4%
Likely to stay on for 5th year	42%	16%	3%
Discipline – especially difficult	2%	2%	10%
Discipline – thoroughly cooperative	72%	64%	55%

Research findings based on approximately 3,000 male secondary modern fourth-year pupils

Robinson children were more likely to come from households in 'problem areas'. These were neighbourhoods of bad housing and social deprivation. A fifth of secondary modern schools and 18% of secondary modern pupils were located in these areas. These children were more likely than the other groups to live in mining areas.

The parents of Robinson children were less likely to be in professional, clerical, skilled or semi-skilled professions. Robinsons left school at the earliest opportunity and were the most likely to have discipline issues. Only

3% of them stayed to complete a fifth form, compared with 42% of Browns.

Although children in the Brown group were more likely to have parents in professional and skilled professions and to live in more prosperous areas, their backgrounds weren't significantly different. Nearly a third of Browns lived in council housing and 13% in problem areas. Only 7% of their parents were in professional or managerial jobs. Most of these children left school without taking GCE 'O' levels (i.e. they didn't stay for a fifth form). The biggest difference was in how teachers rated the discipline problems of the Robinsons, who were the clear winner of the title the 'naughty' boys.

I was surprised at the numbers of school children who are eligible for free school meals today compared with those in Newsom's research. Just over 5% of secondary modern pupils received free meals; today the figure is 16.2% of all pupils in English secondary schools. Either the levels of deprivation have increased greatly, or the entitlement rules have been relaxed – I suspect the latter is the explanation.[176]

Just think for a moment of the challenge of trying to teach pupils with such a range of backgrounds, abilities and ambitions as those in the Brown, Jones and Robinson groups. A quarter of the children wanted to leave school ASAP and quarter wanted to achieve success at GCE 'O' levels.

Grammar and technical schools had to cater for a range of abilities but nothing like that of secondary moderns. Now imagine the additional difficulties when you combine all these children into a single school – the comprehensive.

Still little clarity about teaching the non-academic child

We have reached a point where the Crowther, Beloe and Newsom Reports have all researched the nature and needs of secondary modern pupils. You might ask, 'How did all of this research fit together to produce a unified vision of these children?' A very good question and one that I don't think has been adequately answered. Although Newsom's report referenced the findings of Beloe and Crowther, they weren't used as a foundation for its conclusions. To rectify this omission, I have combined the three Committees' views into a chart. Beware – the chart provides only an approximate view of how their findings compared, because the Committees analysed and reported on the academic capabilities of the pupils in different ways.

Academic level	Crowther	Beloe	Newsom
Top 25%	Capability to pass GCE 'O' levels	Some of this group could take GCE 'O' levels – others, CSE exams	Likely to pass exams – the best pupils GCE 'O' levels; CSEs for the remainder
Upper-middle 25%	Capability to pass exams	Some could take CSE exams	Some will pass CSE exams
Lower-middle 25%	Exams would be a distraction	Might pass a few CSE exams	Some might pass exams but for most they are 'entirely inappropriate'
Bottom 25%	Exams would be a distraction	Unlikely to pass exams	Exams are 'entirely inappropriate'. Pupils require education that is practical

A comparison of how the Crowther, Beloe and Newsom Reports viewed the academic potential of secondary modern pupils

Where the three Committees were in most agreement was about the academic potential of the top and bottom quartiles of pupils. All three believed the top 20–25% of secondary modern pupils had the potential to pass CSE exams or their equivalents, with the most academic candidates for GCE 'O' levels. None of the Reports proffered a percentage estimate of how many could take the more advanced exam. There was full agreement that exams were inappropriate for children in the bottom group.

There was less agreement about the middle two quartiles of pupils. Exams, probably CSEs, might be taken by the upper-middle 25%. It was thought unlikely that children in the lower-middle quartiles had exam potential.

Where the three reports were in full agreement was that pupils' chances of achieving their full academic potential depended on there being enough suitable school buildings, staffed with enough teachers of the right types. None of these were likely to be available in the foreseeable future.

Way back in 1943 the Norwood Report had defined the characteristics of the children who were destined to become the pupils of secondary moderns. It was thought that they would: 'learn most easily by dealing with concrete things and following a course rooted in their own day-to-day experience'.

Here we are, 20 years later, with a slightly different, though not more refined, definition recognising the same thing.

What did the politicians make of Newsom's recommendations? The timing of the Report's publication was unfortunate because it coincided with the release of another study that had considered the UK's requirement for higher education. The Robbins Report, as the study was named, was packed with 170 recommendations, the most eye-catching being the need to increase the number of full-time students from 216,000 in 1962–1963 to 390,000 in 1973–1974, reaching 560,000 in 1980–1981. Achieving this goal would require the creation of six new universities, awarding university status to some existing colleges of education and the expansion of existing universities.

There was no contest in terms of which report received the media and political attention, as was illustrated by this statement in the House of Lords by the Earl of Longford in an exchange with Lord Eccles[177] – the same David Eccles who had initiated the Newsom Report when he was minister of education.

The Government have accepted much of the Robbins Report.

Towards the Newsom Report they have exhibited an unpleasant reserve, reminiscent, I am afraid, of their attitude to the ill-fated Crowther Report.

It was clear yesterday that the Government spokesman would not have mentioned the Newsom Report had not the Leader of the Labour Party asked him to say something about it. Today, I do not know whether I missed something – I did not hear the noble Lord say anything favourable about the Newsom Report. Was I wrong? Did he praise the Newsom Report? Did his remark escape me? I thought perhaps it may have slipped out at the corner of his mouth. I remember hearing no mention, and certainly no praise, of it.

In response to this criticism, Eccles quoted a couple of passages from Newsom's report that supported the government's education policy and made one reference to its recommendation about raising the leaving age.

I think the Government could and should name a date before the end
of this decade when the school-leaving age can be raised by law
to 16.

As if to support Longford, rather than refute his indifference to
Newsom's work, he used most of his 4,000-word speech to praise the
Robbins Report. It looked as if Newsom's endeavours would have as little
impact as those of Crowther.

At last the school-leaving age is raised

Ironically, it seems to have been the gushingly enthusiastic acceptance of
Robbins' recommendations that led the government (reluctantly) to name
the date for the school-leaving age to be raised. This was the view proposed
in the book *Secondary Education and the Raising of the School-Leaving
Age*[178] by Woodin, McCulloch and Cowan, and I agree. The book's authors
quoted a memo from a senior official at the Ministry of Education that
neatly summed up the rationale.[179]

There is a considerable section of thoughtful and articulate opinion
which will be very critical of any suggestion that we believe, as a
Government, in increasing opportunities for the ablest boys and girls
[by accepting the Robbins Report] while neglecting the average and
below average [the Newsom Report].

There seems little doubt that the Conservative government believed in
the principle of raising the school-leaving age. Its reluctance was to name
the date it would happen. The cumulative effect of the Newsom and
Crowther Reports, both recommending a date be fixed, combined with the
political advantages that naming a date would have in the coming general
election, was enough to convince the government to change its mind.

As Woodin, McCulloch and Cowan explained, the costs of the extra year
at school were relatively easy to quantify, unlike the benefits it would
deliver and the risks of failure because of the poor secondary school
infrastructure. The Treasury objected to the costs involved and many MPs

questioned what benefits it would deliver to those children intent on leaving school at the earliest opportunity.

It seems that the unquantifiable 'feel-good' arguments were the ones that tipped the balance and changed the government's mind. It was known that more secondary modern children stayed at school for a fifth form in the south of England than in the north. Ministry figures showed that 30% of secondary modern children in Surrey stayed for the additional year, compared with 13% in Durham. Forcing all children to stay for an additional year, it was argued, would counter this lack of 'social fairness'.

So it was that on 7 January 1964, Sir Edward Boyle, minister of education, announced to the House of Commons that:

> *It is the Government's intention that the school-leaving age should be raised to 16 in the educational year 1970–71, and future planning will be on that basis. This means that the school-leaving age will be raised to 16 for all children entering the secondary schools from September 1967 onwards.*

During the debate, Boyle talked about the 'great deal of constructive thought going on already about the best kind of five-year course for the non-academic child', referred to as 'Newsom children'. As we have seen, this was thought to apply to at least half of secondary modern pupils. It is ironic that Newsom went to great lengths to avoid labelling children and to ensure they were represented as individuals, not statistics, yet here we are, with his name used as a label for children thought to be of low academic potential.

Meanwhile, according to a Fabian Society publication,[180] the top 25% of secondary modern pupils had become 'grammar school boys manqués' – 'manqués' meaning 'a person who has failed to live up to a specific expectation or ambition.'

By 1964 it appears that politicians and their advisers had become convinced that a substantial number of secondary modern pupils were capable of taking the same type of exams as those in grammar schools. Another group of children, probably the majority, needed another type of schooling – one that wasn't orientated around an exam syllabus.

How this realisation would translate into what happened in the classroom was far from clear. Even less opaque was how the Newsom children would benefit from 12 months longer at school.

The times they are a-changin

For the remainder of 1964, the government was left to digest three major education reports and to prepare for a general election, in October. This marked the end of any new Conservative Party policies affecting the workings of secondary moderns. Although these schools were educating over half of all secondary school children, their dominance had begun to decline. In 1962 they taught 62% of the children in England and Wales. In two years, it had fallen to 60% and would keep on falling.

No single event triggered this decline. Attitudes of the political and educational establishments were evolving, as were those of parents. Together they combined to alter the structure of secondary education, a trend that accelerated after the general election. Maybe it was prophetic that 1964 was the year when Bob Dylan released his iconic album *The Times They Are a-Changin'*?

The times were definitely 'changin' for secondary moderns and this would be a good place to consider why. Let's start by looking at how the policies of the political parties had evolved.

We have seen that the Conservative Party had instigated multiple studies of the education system. Some resulted in change occurring; some didn't. The current minister of education, Edward Boyle, had continued his predecessor's habit of requesting new reports, when in 1963 he asked the CACE to study *Children and their Primary Schools* (the Plowden Report).[181] It was four years before it published its conclusions and much would have changed in the interim, as we will see later in the timeline.

Boyle understood the workings of the Ministry, having spent two years as the Parliamentary secretary to the minister of education (1957–1959) before becoming the minister. Much has been written about the man – much of it by Boyle himself. Some critics accused him of abandoning the Conservatives' support for selective schooling and heralding the widespread adoption of comprehensive education. Maybe this is true but, for now, I want to focus on the insights his writings provided about the state of secondary moderns and the 11-plus at the time of the election. These two quotations are taken from a paper he published in 1972, after leaving politics.[182]

> *When I returned to Curzon Street as Minister, in July 1962, it was clear to me, and indeed to my advisers within the Ministry, that support for the development of secondary education along comprehensive lines was gaining considerable momentum, and that one could no longer plausibly stand by the whole of the position set out in the White Paper of 1958 [this reiterated the government's support of the tripartite system].*
>
> *My officials estimated that by 1963, no fewer than 90 out of 163 local education authorities in England and Wales had in a few cases completed, or else were working on, reorganisation schemes which they wanted to implement for the whole or a part of their areas. Furthermore, many of these authorities were not Labour-controlled, so that their plans could not simply be written off as politically motivated.*

Boyle believed that the pressure for LEAs to embrace comprehensive education – or was it a rejection of secondary moderns and the 11-plus – came from the 'middle band of society'. He described the evolution of the country's social structure as changing from a hierarchical, pyramid shape to that of a diamond. This resulted in an increased number of parents who were relatively affluent and valued the benefits of education. He feared that this group, who today would be labelled as middle class or even the 'sharp-elbowed' middle class, were unhappy about accepting the consequences of their children failing the 11-plus and sending them to a secondary modern. For understandable reasons, he didn't state the corollary to his argument that working class parents either didn't value education or were more compliant – or both.

Another issue, which was not mentioned in the paper, was the fallibility of the 11-plus in allocating children to the correct school. Boyle would have been aware of the numerous reports that detailed this problem.

If Edward Boyle represented the liberal wing of the Conservative Party, then Angus Maude was considered the polar opposite: 'representing the voice of English history, English traditions and experiences.'[183] I am not so sure that these two people were that far apart in their views about the challenges facing secondary moderns.

Maude wrote a book about the state of the education system that was published just before the general election.[184] Not surprisingly, it portrayed the 13 years of Conservative government as having transformed its quality for the better. However, it was disarmingly forthright about the mistakes that were made and the inequities that still remained. The book echoed Boyle's comments about the changing shape of British society and the pressures this created on the model of selective education. These statements don't seem like those of somebody intent of defending the status quo.

The time has surely come to recognize frankly that the rigid assumptions on which the old 'tripartite' theory was based are simply not valid.

The myth that there are three readily distinguishable types of pupil, to be categorized and segregated with even tolerable precision at the age of 11, was little more than a rationalization designed to fit the fact that three types of school already existed.

It has already become obvious that the proportion of children capable of something like a 'grammar type' of education is considerably higher than was at one time supposed.

Where the two politicians differed was in their views about the motivations of the Labour Party. Maude believed the party was cynical in its support for the 'grammar school principle' and was motivated by 'political prejudices rather than educational needs'. Boyle was less dogmatic and appeared to rationalise their comprehensive school policy as responding to the mounting rejection of selective schooling by the LEAs – many of them being Conservative-controlled – a fact that he often repeated.

Both the progressives and traditionalists in the Conservative Party understood the fallibility of selective education but were alarmed that its abandonment would destroy the much-valued grammar schools. In hindsight, I am sure they realised that the early years of secondary modern 'experimentation' were wasted years. They hoped that providing better school facilities and encouraging secondary moderns to offer the equivalent of a grammar school stream would enable more children to achieve an academic education and, as a consequence, diminish parental concern about the 11-plus. Perhaps Boyle agreed with these sentiments, but thought the policy was unlikely to work? Maude seemed convinced that there was still time to counter the drift towards comprehensivisation.

Boyle initiated the Conservatives' final item of education legislation (the 1964 Education Act),[185] which he referred to as 'my parting gift to the Ministry'.[186] The Act increased the options for how LEAs could restructure their secondary schools – before, children had to change school at the age of 11, but this constraint was now removed.

The Labour Party rebrands its views of grammar schools

When we last looked at the policies of the Labour Party, in 1955, it had moved from 'encouraging' to 'asking' LEAs to create new versions of their development plans based on the comprehensive school model. At a national level, the Labour Party was abandoning its support for the tripartite system. Rather than seeking ways of improving the performance of secondary moderns, it was set to replace them with comprehensives. These ideas were not necessarily mirrored in Labour-controlled education authorities. When Boyle was explaining how some Conservative-controlled LEAs were moving to comprehensivisation[187] he noted that:

> It was much more often in a Labour-controlled city, or a coal-mining area, that one was most conscious of what the grammar school still meant to an able boy or girl from a modest home in a poor district.

In his account of the Labour Party's education policies, Gary McCulloch painted a fascinating picture of the party's torturous process of trying to accommodate its competing opinions about education and formulating plans for comprehensive schooling.[188]

This is a brief summary of what happened.

It must have come as something of a shock when, in 1957, Michael Stewart, the secretary of state for education (Labour's 'shadow' minister), received the results of a public opinion poll that had been commissioned to understand the electorate's attitudes to reforming education in the state and private sectors.[189] Two things emerged from the research that questioned the Party's assumptions about the electorate's attitudes to education.

> *He [the MD of the research company] had found that education for their children was of little consequence to most working class parents, who were generally content to leave matters as they were. Moreover, the idea of the comprehensive school had made practically no impact on them, and they did not appear to be interested in spending more money on education.*

Worse still, some respondents in the research sample thought the words 'comprehensive school' had distasteful connotations and that the name should be changed. The final blow was the recommendation that the party adapt its education policy to emphasise its benefits for the 'bright child', rather than as an instrument to create a more egalitarian society.

McCulloch portrayed Stewart as a realist who was well aware of the difficulties in changing both the electorate's opinions and the country's system of secondary education. Even so, it must have come as something of a surprise to read these research results and recommendations.

It seemed that the working class element of the British public, unlike Labour politicians, wasn't demanding a radical reorganisation of secondary education – quite the opposite. Parents wanted changes to their children's schools, but what they wanted was change in their performance not their organisation (i.e. a reduction in the size of classes). This was consistent with the conclusions that I drew after analysing how the newspapers of the time reported issues related to secondary education (in Chapter 3, 'A consistently negative image'). My research showed there was little coverage of comprehensive schools and little criticism of secondary moderns and the 11-plus.

Labour concluded two things from its study. First, it needed a sustained period of propaganda (the word it used) to educate and convince the general public of the benefits of comprehensive education. Second, it would need to adapt its arguments about why comprehensive schools were the best approach.

A policy argued around 'conventional educational improvements' might win popularity, it concluded, but 'one that argues on manifestly doctrinal or egalitarian grounds would prove unpopular even among our own supporters'.

The electorate's priorities were concerned with practical issues, not idealism, unlike the politicians'. I feel sure the last sentence has resonance today! Being concerned with 'practical issues' was the defining characteristic of the majority of school children – according to Norwood and Newsom – so it shouldn't have been a surprise that they retained that inclination when becoming an adult.

After much 'debate', the party published a pamphlet, *Learning to Live,* that was intended to clarify its education policy and explain its intentions to provide 'comprehensive secondary education'.[190] This was a well-written document that seemed (to me) to be targeting the people troubled by the demise of grammar schools. It contained far fewer arguments about the benefits of comprehensives over secondary modern schools. Stewart seems to have accepted and acted on the results of the research.

Much use was made of the word 'segregation', as in: 'segregation at 11 is the enemy of true selection'. A nice play on words, an ideal slogan, although I am not sure what it means.

Posing the question about what motivated the defenders of grammar schools the pamphlet stated:

Is it their learning and zest, which are admirable: or the segregation from the rest of the community, which is not?

A section of the document was devoted to 'extending the grammar school tradition' and contained answers to refute the arguments that comprehensives threatened grammar schools. For instance, to counter the claim that comprehensive schools restricted parental choice, it said that:

It is the nature of the comprehensive education that the virtues of the grammar school are not destroyed, but extended to a wider group.

To the criticism that comprehensives were larger and had more pupils than existing schools, it answered that their class sizes would be smaller. It accepted that in local areas there might be fewer schools but claimed parents would have more choice of schools that offered 'a grammar school education' (i.e. the comprehensive school). The academic results of existing comprehensive schools were said to refute the accusation that 'the gifted [were] being held back or the less gifted disadvantaged'. At that time, only 2.5% of secondary school children attended a comprehensive school, so that claim was followed by the admission that: 'we need more and longer experience before advancing dogmatic claims'. I wonder how many of today's political documents would be so measured?

To counter the wrongs of the existing education system, the Labour Party proposed the following.

The Labour Government will require local education authorities to prepare secondary education development plans designed to:

- *achieve, in five years, the reduction of classes to a maximum of 30.*
- *make possible, at a later date, the introduction of a five year secondary course [increase the leaving age].*
- *adopt the comprehensive principle [with all reasonable speed] and provide in each secondary school a wide range of courses.*

Arguments about creating a better society were replaced by those aiming to convince parents that Labour was a proponent of, not a threat to, the 'grammar school tradition'. As for how these schools would improve the lot of secondary modern children, this was not so clearly expressed. In his New Year's message to the Labour Party,[191] its leader (Hugh Gaitskell) claimed it was possible to abolish the 11-plus and secondary moderns and provide every child with a grammar or technical school education. If only it were that simple.

Are we to confine the chances of a Grammar school education to those who pass the eleven-plus examination and slam the door of opportunity in the face of other children? This is the Tory idea. Or

shall we abolish the eleven-plus examination and give every child a
continuing opportunity of the education – grammar or technical –
for which they are best suited?

Learning to Live became the basis for Labour's 1959 general election manifesto, when Labour proposed to end 'segregation' and provide a 'grammar-school education for all'. As we know, these promises weren't enough to win them the election, but they formed the basis for its education policy for the coming five years and its manifesto in 1964.

Labour appears to have 'put education on hold' in the years between the elections. Richard Crossman was Stewart's replacement as shadow secretary of state for education, for two of these years. His voluminous diaries of his time as a backbencher contained hardly any references to education,[192] but there was one amusing account of a television appearance with Edward Boyle, the minister of education. Crossman was determined not to be rude to Boyle but found it was just as difficult to give 'the impression of somebody who cared about education, not party polemics.' My guess is that during these years, Labour's focus was on convincing the LEAs it controlled to support comprehensivisation, rather than national-level politics.

It seems to me that at the time of the 1964 general election, neither of the political parties were that confident about their secondary education policies. The Conservatives understood that selective education was based on a flawed proposition. There was ample proof that at the age of 11 it was impossible to group children by ability with a high degree of confidence. The Labour Party realised that large parts of the electorate were not convinced by the idea of comprehensive schools. Certainly, their role in making a more equal society had little resonance with voters and their ability to improve educational outcomes was far from proven. Both parties knew that whatever policies the national government proposed, the LEAs were the ultimate arbiters of the type of schooling that was delivered.

Ironically, both parties agreed that damaging 'grammar schools' was a dangerous policy. Protecting the schools was a key Conservative policy and Labour was doing its best to prove its attachment to the 'grammar school tradition' and to show it was something it wanted to extend – not to destroy. Sadly, neither party seemed sure how their policies would improve the lot of the secondary modern child. Perhaps I am being too harsh? Perhaps not.

An insight into the public's attitude to secondary schools

The views and policies of the political parties were well documented, but what was the mood of the electorate in the year of the election? Politicians were engrossed in the arguments about the 11-plus and comprehensive schools, but was this reflected in the content of the high-circulation newspapers? It is a decade since we analysed how the newspapers were reporting the issues of secondary education. To gauge how their interest had changed over this period, the following chart plots the percentage increase in the frequency of the terms '11-plus', 'secondary modern' and 'grammar school'. I appreciate that measuring word frequency doesn't tell us anything about *what* was reported, but it indicates their level of interest in the subject.

There are a couple of insights to be taken from the chart.[193] First, the frequency of articles mentioning 'secondary moderns' and 'grammar schools' increased, but this was tiny compared with the surge in mentions of '11-plus'.

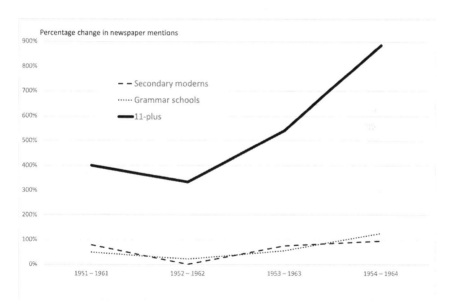

The percentage change in the number of times the terms were mentioned in selected newspapers indexed by ukpressonline and British Newspaper Archive

It is important to realise that as a percentage, the frequency of mentions had increased, but the actual number of times these terms appeared remained low. For instance, the term '11-plus' appeared 69 times during the 12 months of 1964. In the same year, less than two articles a month (on average) mentioned comprehensive schools. More interest was shown in secondary moderns, but it was articles referencing 'grammar schools' that dominated the media coverage, by a considerable margin. This is the same pattern that we saw 10 years earlier.

These newspapers were primarily read by the working and middle classes. An analysis of the reporting of *The Sunday Times*, a newspaper of the managerial and professional classes, shows exactly the same pattern of word frequency. In 1964, the term 'grammar school' appeared three times more than 'secondary modern' and 10 times more than 'comprehensive schools'.

Newspaper coverage of selective education had undoubtedly increased, especially articles about the 11-plus, but it was still a low-interest subject. Like the politicians', the newspapers' interest was mostly in grammar schools. Articles mentioning secondary moderns were far less popular and those about comprehensives a rarity.

There is another research study that enables us to understand the attitudes of the electorate in 1964. We have already learnt that CACE was preparing a report about primary schools; as part of its enquiry it had commissioned a research study that interviewed a little over 3,000 parents with children in 173 junior and infant schools.[194] This was not intended to be a representative sample of the English electorate but was chosen to understand the attitude of parents with children about to enter secondary schools. In this era, few mothers were in employment so, not surprisingly, most of those interviewed were female – the children's mother. Having children at junior school meant that the women were not representative of all age groups. Indeed, the opinions of mothers may have been very different from those of the fathers. However, the research was conducted professionally, and the sample was chosen to represent a cross-section of the country's population by geography and social class.

One of the questions was about their husbands' income. I was surprised that almost all of the women were willing to declare the figure. What the answers revealed was how income levels in society have increased for the high earners. The median annualised income of the highest social group (professional) was £26,000–31,000, in today's pounds. Those in the two lowest groups, the semi- and unskilled, were paid approximately half this amount.

Some measure of comparison with today's earnings is possible by relating them to the median salary level of English civil servants.[195] Those working in the most senior grades are paid an annual income of £65,000–83,000, with the most junior workers earning approximately 25% of these salaries.

These numbers show how those in the highest social classes have experienced a considerable increase in the real level of their income, unlike those in the lower levels, adding credence to today's concern about increasing income inequality.

In case you are wondering, this analysis has nothing at all to do with matters of education, but it illustrates the dangers of using today's assumptions about social class and applying them to the past.

Parents who knew their child's secondary school were asked how this compared with the type of school they had hoped they would attend. The table shows their responses grouped by social class.

		Social class of parent					
	Type of school	Professional	Managerial	Non-manual	Skilled manual	Semi-skilled	Unskilled
		%	%	%	%	%	%
Parent hoped child would attend	Grammar	69	66	68	48	42	30
	Secondary modern	14	15	10	25	30	45
	Comprehensive	3	3	8	4	7	3
	Had no opinion about type of school	0	9	6	15	12	19
Type of school child will attend	Grammar	52	33	39	18	18	7
	Secondary modern	21	50	42	66	68	81
	Comprehensive	10	4	9	7	6	4
Difference between the percentages of parents who hoped for a grammar school place and those who were successful		17	33	29	30	24	23

The types of secondary schools children attended and their parents' preference, grouped by social class

These findings told an interesting story. Awareness of and support for comprehensive schools was low. Grammar schools were clearly the first choice of parents in all of the social groups, although the percentage reduced among the semi-skilled and unskilled groups, who showed more of a preference for secondary moderns.

What I found most interesting was the difference in the percentages of parents wanting their children educated in a grammar school and those who were successful. The professional parents were the most anxious for their children to attend a grammar school and were the most successful in a place being awarded. The difference was most pronounced for children from the managerial, non-manual and skilled manual groups. I think these three groups represent the centre part of the 'diamond' shape, the middle class, that so concerned Boyle. Given that they accounted for well over half of married males aged 20–64, he was right to be worried.

Another insight into parents' attitudes came from the responses on 'whether any type of secondary school was particularly disliked for their child and if so what?'

	Social class					
	Professional	Managerial	Non-manual	Skilled manual	Semi-skilled	Unskilled
	%	%	%	%	%	%
Parents answering yes to the question	46	30	26	16	15	9
Secondary modern	26	14	13	6	6	3
Comprehensive	7	3	3	1	1	
Mixed-sex schools	8	7	6	3	4	3
Religious schools	2	2	2	2	1	2

Secondary schools that parents particularly disliked for their children

Secondary moderns were the schools most mentioned. That did not surprise me. What did, was the low percentage of parents who answered 'yes' to the question and their level of objection. Other than the professional social group, the percentage objecting to secondary moderns was in the low teens or single digits.

This research from the Plowden Report and the newspapers clearly shows that the electorate's awareness and concern about selective education was increasing, but this provides no measure of its intensity. The data sources I have analysed suggest it was more a low level of anxiety than an intensely felt anger. Others have labelled the public mood in more extreme terms. In his address to the Royal Historical Society, Peter Mandler claimed that:[196]

> *Even as secondary moderns improved the cap on grammar school*
> *places left more frustrated parents – there were no more working*
> *class children in grammar schools in 1961 than there had been in*
> *1950 – public opinion was at boiling point.*

I have mentioned the many caveats about the accuracy of my analysis; however, it's difficult to conclude that public opinion was at 'boiling point' – more of a low-level simmer. The 'hot spot' for this anger was among the 'middle' not the working class.

Was the LEAs' rejection of the tripartite system overstated?

Theoretically, national politicians established the overarching education policies, in response to the electorate's concerns, but it was the LEAs that had the ultimate power to shape how secondary education was delivered. Of course, the Ministry had the ability to influence and veto certain of the LEAs' decisions. The electorate's influence on their children's schools was indirect, in that their local political representatives were elected for many reasons, education being but one. It was the education administrations within each of the 163 LEAs[197] where the real power resided to change the nitty-gritty of how schools were organised.

It is difficult to summarise what the 163 LEAs in England and Wales were thinking about secondary education in 1964. This quote from a Department of Education and Science book, published six years later, confirmed that the task of reorganising it didn't become any easier.[198]

> *For many areas of the country it is not possible to describe in a few*
> *words all the complexities of reorganisation. Nor is it generally*
> *possible to give dates for implementation.*

And this is the answer the minster gave to the question, 'How many education authorities either have changed or are proposing to change their secondary education system from a substantially tripartite to a substantially comprehensive basis?'

In January 1964 there were 189 comprehensive schools in England and Wales and 39 local education authorities had some secondary school provision of a comprehensive type. A large number of authorities are considering secondary school reorganisation and several are planning to introduce comprehensive schemes in the next two years; but the situation is one of constant development and I cannot say exactly how many plans for comprehensive schools have taken definite shape.[199]

We now know that an official in the Department of Education and Science had produced a document detailing the LEAs' 'current practice and future plans for secondary education.'[200] Although information from this document appeared in a Cabinet paper issued by Stewart and his officials, I doubt whether he was aware of all of its contents, especially the caveats about the accuracy of the data.

According to this report, the LEAs were reorganising their secondary education in three ways – as shown in this table.

The status of the LEAs' plans to reorganise their system of secondary education	Number of LEAs	Percentage of secondary school population
Had implemented or were considering proposals for some form of comprehensive reorganisation.	68	63%
Contemplating changes but had not made any definite plans.	21	11%
Not contemplating reorganisation.	59	26%

The status of the LEAs' plans to reorganise their system of secondary education

Attached to the report was an appendix detailing what the Ministry knew about each of the LEAs' policies. This revealed a more complicated picture than was suggested by the headline numbers. Of the 68 LEAs that had implemented or were considering opening comprehensive schools, 70%

intended, at some stage, to do away with selection at the age of 11. Only 28 of the LEAs were already operating comprehensive schools, although most of these (20) intended to expand their numbers.

When the report was produced, London's local authorities were being reorganised, resulting in their plans being omitted from the figures. This explains why the number of LEAs appeared to have been reduced to 148, rather than the previously quoted figure of 163. The report's author explained the omission of these numbers and commented that 'there is a general impression that a number of the new boroughs [London LEAs] may veer towards a comprehensive system.'

The Sunday Times in November 1964 conducted its own research to discover the mood of the LEAs towards comprehensivisation. In the week of the article's publication all of England's LEAs were telephoned to 'discover their plans'. Each of the LEAs was listed along with a five- to 20-word description of its policies. The conclusion from the research was that:

Of the 149 authorities [none of the Welsh LEAs were contacted] 120 are considering or are introducing some reorganisation. Already 65 introduced some comprehensive schools or are considering them.

So, what are we to make of these very different snippets of research? If the minister knew about all of the report's findings, he could have made a much more positive claim about the LEAs' rejection of selective education. As it was his claim erred on the side of caution by stating that '39 local education authorities had some secondary school provision of a comprehensive type'. He could have said that 68 LEAs were considering comprehensivisation and that they were educating 63% of the country's children – a much more powerful argument.

What I find strange is Boyle's response to the question, which claimed a far higher adoption of comprehensivisation, especially since he had access to the same information and Ministry officials as Stewart. There are many possible explanations for why this happened, but my hunch is that Boyle's account of the situation, with his claim about '90 out of the 163 LEAs working on reorganisation schemes', wanted to emphasise the momentum that already existed for comprehensivisation. We can see from the Ministry's data that to claim the figure of 90 LEAs 'working on plans' assumed a very vague definition of the term. Boyle's article was written in 1972, by which time he had left politics and like many politicians wanted to write his account of history, a story that the LEAs were the driving force ending selective education. His interpretation of the data substantiated that claim.

It is the conclusions from the article in *The Sunday Times* that I question the most. I spent much of my career organising and conducting market research and know the difficulty in getting accurate answers to complex questions. Imagine telephoning your local council and receiving a succinct summary of its plans for secondary education. Even with the prestige of working for *The Sunday Times* this would be mighty difficult. Now imagine getting answers from all 149 English LEAs and completing the task in less than a week.

I don't doubt for a moment that *The Sunday Times* made the calls, asked the question and received an answer. What concerns me is the value of the responses. Many of them were precise and either detailed their change to comprehensivisation or their intention not to change, but many were vague, containing terms such as:

Considering reorganisation – looking at comprehensives – reorganisation being considered – have some comprehensives – under discussion – considering various schemes.

I have analysed the article and categorised the responses as shown below.

Plans for secondary education	Number of responses
Not considering comprehensive education	35
Considering reorganisation but not necessarily ending selective schools.	54
A mixture of terms: 'Have plans to change', 'moving towards', 'experimenting with comprehensive education', 'abandoning the 11+ but keeping grammar schools'	60

Analysis of LEA plans for comprehensivisation according to research conducted by *The Sunday Times*

There were 60 responses that indicated the LEA was either undertaking or soon to be making *some* changes that moved them away from the tripartite schools. Here are a few examples.

Where	Response
Bolton	'Modified tripartite system; considering abolishing all selection.'
Liverpool	'Full comprehensive proposed and abolition of 11-plus. Awaiting Minster's decision.'
London	'Pioneer authority of the comprehensive idea.' [Approximately half of all comprehensive schools were in London.]
Northampton	'Abolishing 11-plus in one area and will consider extension; grammar schools remain.'

Examples of the responses from LEAs that were considering abandoning the tripartite system

The responses from a second group of 54 LEAs suggested they were considering changing but gave no indication about the nature or timescale for that change. For whatever reason, *The Sunday Times* concluded that the move to comprehensivisation was much more advanced than we now know it was.

I think it is safe to assume that the Ministry's official analysis of the LEAs' plans was unbiased. I am not sure we can say the same for the others who commented on the situation. As I wrote this section I was reminded of Chapter 1 ('The truth is what we want it to be'), which showed the danger of allowing our biases to determine how we interpret the 'facts'.

There can be no doubt that the LEAs were 'on the move' towards comprehensivisation, but in my view, the magnitude of the move was overstated.

Slowly becoming more 'academic'

The Conservatives hoped that if pupils had the opportunity to stay an extra year at school and take GCE 'O' levels this would dull the opposition felt by their parents towards selective schools. I was interested to understand whether parents were convinced by this argument.

One of the topics in the Plowden Committee's research into parents' attitudes was to investigate whether they wanted their child to stay at school beyond the statutory leaving date. The majority of parents were enthusiastic about the idea, with very few indicating an outright rejection, even among the social classes with children most likely to attend a secondary modern. However, it should be remembered that these children were only just about to start their secondary schooling, so the parents had a long time before they would have to make the decision. The professional class was the most certain about its decision; the unskilled the least.

	Social class					
	Professional	Managerial	Non-manual	Skilled manual	Semi-skilled	Unskilled
	%	%	%	%	%	%
Stay on beyond 16	84	77	77	65	62	53
Stay on longer but no age given	7	8	9	10	7	11
Unsure if their child would stay on longer	9	13	12	17	20	21
Leave at statutory age	0	1	0	3	4	7

Parents' attitudes about their children remaining beyond the statutory leaving date

I couldn't find any statistics that enabled me to judge the change in percentage of secondary modern children who stayed at school for an extra year, so I estimated the figure by combining several data sources. According to *Trends in British Society*, in 1967 the figure was approximately 24%.[201]

An analysis of the Ministry's annual statistics shows that in 1964, for all types of secondary schools in England and Wales, the figure was 20%, almost double that of a decade earlier.[202, 203] This is an approximation, because the way the statistics were collected had changed over the period. The figure for secondary modern children was lower than 20% because grammar school children, most of whom stayed on at school, were included in the data. I think it is unlikely that in 1964 more than 20% of secondary modern pupils stayed until the end of the fifth form.

These numbers suggest that secondary moderns had been partly successful in getting children to extend their education, but progress had been slow. Most children left school at the first opportunity.

The trouble with deducing conclusions from 'the average' is that it tells us nothing about regional variations and the different behaviour of boys and girls. In 1964, secondary modern boys were more likely to stay at school than girls. If children lived in London or the south east they were twice as likely to extend their school life as those in the north. Where children attend school still remains a significant factor in determining their chances of academic success. Today the measure of achievement is the number and grades of secondary school exams. Top of the league table is outer London and bottom is the West Midlands.[204]

My schooling forms part of these statistics. In 1964 my parents decided I should stay for an extra year and take some GCE 'O' levels. I am confident that at least half the parents of my classmates took the same decision – it might have been as high as three-quarters. Compared with the average figures for London this represented a high percentage. Perhaps the catchment area for my school contained more parents who valued their children's education? That seems unlikely. I expect the explanation lies in the trust parents had in the school's headmaster and his teachers. Parents were confident that an extra year at school would help their child's prospects.

It is very easy to become embroiled in the intricacies of how the model of secondary education evolved and lose sight of the paramount importance of teachers and the person in charge. The inspired leadership of the headmaster or headmistress can overcome the problems of the education 'system'. I am sure that is as true today as it was in 1964.

Both the Crowther and Beloe Reports stressed that the reasons for 'staying the extra year' were not all about passing GCE 'O' levels. The document my parents received explaining the benefits of my remaining at school echoed this point, but it also – somewhat reluctantly – recognised the value of exams.[205]

Laudable as success itself is, it cannot be too strongly emphasised that examination successes are by no means the greatest achievement to be gained from a good education.

With tremendous effort the academically minded can work for qualifications and certificates which are, in the rather mad 'rat race' of the modern world, the 'Open Sesame' to better jobs.

This table[206] shows the rapid increase in the number of secondary modern pupils sitting GCE 'O' level exams.

1955	1956	1957	1958	1959	1960	1963	1966
7,300	8,600	11,300	16,787	19,407	21,670	56,000	71,562

| The number of secondary modern pupils sitting GCE 'O' level exams by year

By 1960, 40% of secondary modern pupils who were aged 15 in the previous January took the exams and approximately 9% of pupils passed in five or more subjects.[207] By 1966 the number of pupils had trebled. The momentum of this change continued after the general election and by 1969 over 100,000 pupils were taking a mix of GCE 'O' levels and the new CSE exam.[208] There was a weighty mass of evidence showing that many children in secondary moderns had academic potential. Once they were given an opportunity, the numbers demonstrated that 'potential' could be converted into exam success.

Compared with the success rates of grammar schools, those of secondary moderns were modest (extremely). In the year I sat my GCE 'O' levels, my school achieved a median pass rate of three subjects. This was better than the national average, but only half as good as that of the local grammar school. In truth, comparing the exam results of the two types schools tells us very little. For much of their 20-year life, the political and education establishment were trying to 'protect' secondary moderns from the perceived pressure of exams, unlike grammar schools where academic achievement was central to their culture. The question I am left wondering is: how much better could the national results have been if more schools were like the one I attended?

The Conservative Party must have viewed the schools' modest exam success with some satisfaction but a lot of worries. Was it 'too little too late'?

Starting the next experiment – 'going comprehensive'

We have seen the many factors determining the national mood about the rights and wrongs of how secondary schools should be organised. I expect for many parents, perhaps most, their children's schooling was just one of the many uncertainties in their lives. When they thought about schools, it would have been about those in their neighbourhood, not the rights and wrongs of the national policies. We know that England and Wales were a patchwork of different education plans, determined by the LEAs and regional differences. All of this makes concluding with a couple of pithy sentences, explaining the electorate's thinking before the election, extremely difficult – in fact, impossible.

When the policies of the political parties appeared in their manifestos there were no surprises. The Labour Party stuck with its claim of extending grammar school education by reorganising on 'comprehensive lines'. Public schools, an old enemy of the Party, had reappeared in its plans with the promise to establish an 'education trust to advise on how to integrate public schools into the state system of education'.

The Conservative Party reiterated its existing policies while positioning itself as safeguarding parents' rights against 'the socialist's plan... to impose the comprehensive principle'.

With the benefit of hindsight, over half a century later, I think the Labour Party's policies can be summarised as muddled and more form than substance. Those of the Conservatives were 'tired', defensive and uninspiring. I am glad I wasn't a parent in 1964 having to choose between the two.[209]

Labour manifesto	Conservative manifesto
Promise to:	
• Reduce size of classes to 30 in primary and secondary schools.	Promise to:
• Raise the school-leaving age to 16.	• Raise the school-leaving age, in 1967, to 16.
• Extend compulsory day and block release for the first two years after leaving school.	• Increase day release for industrial workers, under 18.
	Statements:
• Establish an education trust to advise on how to integrate public schools into the state system of education.	• 'The socialist's plan is to impose the comprehensive principle, regardless of the wishes of parents, teachers and LEAs.'
• Reorganise secondary education on comprehensive lines.	
Statements:	
• 'Grammar school education will be extended'.	

Comments about education appearing in the 1964 Conservative and Labour manifestos

The election took place on 15 October 1964 and Labour won, with a small majority. Neither party devoted more than 6% of its manifesto to issues of education, so it seems unlikely that it played much part in determining the outcome.

And so started six years of Labour government. A new prime minister (Harold Wilson), a new minister of education (Michael Stewart) and the word 'Science' added to the Ministry's title (Ministry of Education *and Science*). Most important, a new group of politicians, intent on ending selective education.

When the Conservatives next returned to power, the number of secondary modern schools had decreased by a third and five times more children were being taught in comprehensives. All thoughts of improving secondary moderns and grammar schools had gone – the only question was how (and how fast) could they be replaced by comprehensives?

I could argue that this shift in government policy meant there would be little point in continuing the story of secondary moderns. Future developments would all be about the abandonment of selective education and the evolution of comprehensive schooling. The counter to this argument is that in 1964 there were 2.3 million pupils attending secondary schools that were destined to be reorganised – 1.6 million were in secondary moderns and the remainder in grammar schools.

Their story didn't end in 1964. They were about to become part of the

'The Great Experiment', the phrase used by Gary McCulloch to describe this period.[210] I winced when I read this title because it was also the name given to the early years of secondary moderns. Then, it meant that government 'left it to the schools to work out their own future'. Now the experiment was a gamble on the government's vision of secondary education being an improvement on the current model.

The move to comprehensivisation required a major upheaval to the schools and teaching infrastructure. In this final section of the timeline I want to understand the magnitude of this disruption and its impact on the education of millions of children.

I was one of those affected. The year I left my secondary modern school it was shut. Two years later, the grammar school I attended to take my GCE 'A' levels became a comprehensive. All of the teachers at the secondary modern had to find new positions and many of those at the grammar school decided to leave. It is impossible to quantify the impact of these upheavals, but for certain there was a short-term cost to achieve the theoretical long-term benefits. I would like to think that the politicians realised the magnitude of the disruption they were causing, but I doubt they did.

My primary objective when writing this book was to understand how people like me were educated. Your average kid, not exhibiting great academic gifts – your Joe or Jemima Average Brit child. The country was 'going comprehensive' but the circumstances and educational needs of these children remained much the same.

One of the first things that Stewart did, on becoming minister, was to write a document outlining his proposals for implementing comprehensive education. This was the starting point for a series of circulars and consultations that nudged the LEAs into changing their education plans as well as diminishing their power compared with that of central government.

By following the evolution of this discussion we see how Labour's simple policy proposition, of 'reorganising secondary schools on comprehensive lines', rapidly morphed into policies that had to adapt to the realities of the real world. The person who was soon to succeed Stewart as minister (Tony Crosland) was fond of using the Latin phrase 'we did not start off *tabula rasa*' (with a 'clean slate'). I doubt that Stewart or Crosland realised how apposite this phrase would be to the task they had embarked on.

The following is a summary of Stewart's original, handwritten, draft of the paper. Most of it was based on *Learning to Live*, the Labour Party policy document that he had authored in 1958 and that we have already considered.

General policy

These were the stated reasons why Labour wanted to reorganise secondary schools on 'comprehensive lines'.

- The fallibility of assessing children at the age of 11.
- The wide local variation in the standard of attainment required to attend grammar schools.
- The inability of many secondary modern schools to cater for children who were capable of 'advanced academic work'.
- The present 'separatist' system (Labour's derogatory term for the tripartite system) that divided society by preventing 'mutual understanding' between those with different academic abilities – he probably meant 'different classes'.
- The pressure on primary schools to become 'cramming establishments' for preparing children for the 11-plus exam.

Because of the 'very many' LEAs that were experimenting with reorganising their secondary schools, it was proposed to give them a 'national lead indicating the principles to be observed.' I think this was code for saying 'this is how we want you to behave'. Stewart's political instincts were obvious in his use of the language 'separatist' and 'cramming establishments' – words that he knew had negative connotations.

Possible methods

He described different models of comprehensive education, but it was clear his preference was a single school that educated children from the age of 11 to the end of their school life. These later became known as the 'orthodox' or the 'all-through' comprehensives. It was noted that 'a good school of this type need not contain more than 1,000 or even 800 children'. This was to counter the criticism that comprehensive schools were large, impersonal and hence difficult to manage. The other variants of comprehensivisation divided the child's secondary education into multiple phases – for instance, educating children aged 11–14 in a junior comprehensive school and then providing parents with the option of schools, depending on whether their children wanted to leave as soon as possible or stay into the sixth form. All these models had one thing in common – entry to the schools was not determined by exam.

Objections of principle

This section detailed the objections to the proposals that were expected to be raised by the Conservatives, all of which I have already covered.

Particular difficulties

The provision of secondary education involved many organisations and groups of people – what we would now call stakeholders. All of these would be affected by the move to comprehensivisation and all would have their own set of issues needing to be resolved. The most important groups were the following.

- Teachers – in 1964 there were 116,000 teachers in secondary modern and grammar schools.
- Parents – in 1964 there were 6.5 million children attending primary and secondary schools.
- LEAs – although government had some influence on the policies of LEAs, it had little control over their school building programmes, which had already been authorised until 1967–1968.
- Direct grant grammar schools – 100,000 children attended these schools that were outside the direct control of central or local government.
- Voluntary schools – nearly 10% of secondary school children attended schools operated by the Church of England and Roman Catholics and a further 250 schools that were not linked to the churches.

Stewart didn't suggest that any of these groups could veto the government's plans but acknowledged that resolving their concerns would not be an easy or quick process. These were his words about the timescale for reorganisation.

> *It is the nature of these difficulties that there is no one grand answer to them. In some areas these difficulties are absent, or slight; in others we must accept that re-organisation can only proceed slowly. The complete establishment of a comprehensive secondary organisation will take **twenty years or more** [my emphasis]. I believe, however, that in five years such progress could be made that the comprehensive system would be accepted as the normal pattern, towards which all LEAs were working, though necessarily at different speeds.*

How to proceed

To my mind this was the crux of the document, with the preceding sections providing the justification for what he wanted his Cabinet colleagues to agree.

> *In the light of all these considerations I believe that my next step should be to issue a circular to local authorities **requiring** [my emphasis] them to submit plans for the reorganisation of their secondary schools on comprehensive lines.*

Stewart expected a range of reactions to his circular, with the most negative resulting in 'delaying tactics and perhaps, in a few cases, out-right refusal'. To counter these recalcitrant LEAs he proposed the circular should: 'indicate that the policy would ultimately (I hope next session of Parliament) be given a firm basis in legislation'.

It needs to be remembered that the minister's power to influence the type of schooling delivered by each of the LEAs was limited. We've seen that the 1944 Education Act didn't specify any particular model of schooling, even though it was obvious that the preference was for a tripartite system. Stewart was proposing that national government should now be given the power to dictate how the LEAs behaved – abandon secondary moderns and grammar schools and change to comprehensives.

In his autobiography,[211] Stewart recalled the positive response that his document received from his officials at the Ministry.

The paper was well received, except for the reference to legislation. The general view that I should go ahead as far as I could under the existing law… if I were questioned on the matter I should say that the government would be prepared to legislate.

Having studied the comments of his officials I think he was overly positive about their response. Maybe he was shielded from the most extreme criticism? There were many notes that 'it is perhaps worth making the point' followed by detailed suggestions of additions and rephrasing, most of which were incorporated in later versions of the document.

Most of the officials' comments were about the potential difficulties that 'going comprehensive' would create. These were more important points, some of which still have resonance with today's schools.[212]

Comprehensivisation would need to use the existing stock of school buildings. Since the end of WWII, 60% of secondary schools had been renewed or were in the process of being replaced. Once the existing building plans were complete, over two-thirds of children would be educated in new schools. Only a handful of these were designed for the comprehensive model; most were built for the 'separatist' system. Because of the constraints on public spending, there was little likelihood of constructing significant numbers of new, purpose-built comprehensives. The fact that the country had so many new schools could be interpreted as a compliment to previous Labour and Conservative governments. From this Labour administration's perspective, it presented a problem.

Comprehensive schools would inevitably reflect the social composition of their neighbourhood.

Schools in middle class areas will be and will be seen to be better than comprehensive schools in poor socially under-privileged areas.

It was noted that areas where parents were engaged in their children's education had good pupil discipline, which made it easier to attract and retain good teachers. The social mix of children attending a secondary modern school had much to do with determining its reputation. Comprehensive schools were expected to have the same problem. There was the added concern that 'bright children', who in the past could escape the constraints of their neighbourhood by going to a grammar school, would be deprived of the opportunity.

The building programmes for secondary schools were preparing for the rise in the school-leaving age, then scheduled for 1970–1971. LEAs had committed to building projects extending for the next four years (until 1967–1968). Even those authorities that were supportive of comprehensive schooling would encounter practical problems in making significant changes to their plans. Labour politicians seemed intent on making life difficult for themselves by extending the school-leaving age with an upheaval in the system of schooling. Clearly, they hadn't learnt any lessons from their previous time in government after WWII.

Most grammar schools were too small to be used as all-through comprehensives. Only 8% of grammar schools had over 800 pupils – the minimum size that was now believed to be suitable for this type of school. Over 60% of grammar schools had fewer than 600 pupils, which meant they would have to be converted to become part of a multi-tiered comprehensive model.

Schools outside state control would be difficult to integrate into the comprehensive school model. Voluntary schools, especially those operated by the Roman Catholic Church, would require funding to help them adapt to become comprehensives. Many of the non-denominational voluntary grammar schools were unlikely to accept the government's changes.

Some comments were downright critical about Stewart's conclusions and recommendations. The schools inspector, Percy Wilson,[213] was cynical and dismissive in his appraisal of Stewart's paper. I doubt if today's civil servants would dare be so forthright.

In the long run (? two generations) and after the expenditure of fantastic sums of money it is possible that a number of good and very well equipped and well-staffed comprehensive schools and/or

sixth form colleges could produce between them reasonable numbers
of boys and girls as well educated as the majority of grammar
school sixth forms are now. Till then – and it is a hypothetical 'then'
– the new policy will cause a decline in education standards at the
age of 18, in circumstances more adverse in this nation than
elsewhere.

Wilson went on to comment about the dangers of Stewart's proposed
dilution of local government control: 'I think a central directive in this
matter will bring other and undesirable centralising tendencies in its wake.' I
don't think he could have imagined how right he was about that prediction.
Stewart commented in his autobiography that, 'There was one official who
made no secret of his hostility to comprehensive secondary education and if
I had stayed longer at the Department we might have come into serious
collision'. My guess is he is referring to Percy Wilson.

The deputy under-secretary of state for education (H.F. Rossetti)
disagreed with Stewart's attempt to obfuscate about closing grammar
schools.

His line dodges the straightforward issue that the grammar schools
would go and deals with a different point regarding 'grammar
education' and it seems to me unwise to take it. [This refers to
Labour's approach about comprehensives providing a grammar
school education for all.]

To prevaricate in dealing with an assertion that grammar schools as
now known cannot exist under a national comprehensive policy will
do more harm than good.

At the bottom of this note was a handwritten comment saying that
Stewart had already considered this point and would make up his own mind.
Then it made what I think was a revealing and chilling observation: 'To me
the battle is about slogans, not realities.' It is impossible to be certain who
wrote this, but I suspect it was the Labour politician Reg Prentice, who
assisted Stewart as minister of state. Prentice was much more hawkish than
Stewart about the pace of change and the need for legislation. Who could

have guessed that 13 years later he would reject the Labour Party and became a Conservative?

There is a handwritten note in the files, from Stewart, reluctantly agreeing about two important changes being made to his document. He had originally said that a move to comprehensive education would take '20 years or more'. He decided to change this to 'a considerable time': 'in deference to Reg Prentice's view: I am not fully in agreement with him on this, but I accept that we need not put in a definite figure.'

His second change was to become the most controversial – his expression of how the LEAs should respond to his request. His original draft had said that a circular would be sent to the LEAs 'requiring' them to submit plans for the reorganisation of the schools on comprehensive lines. He was now persuaded to change the wording.

> *I agree that we must drop 'requiring'. I should like 'calling on'*
> *unless there are insuperable legal objections to this: if there are I*
> *will (regretfully) accept 'requesting'.*

For whatever reason, 'calling on' was not used and the original intention to 'require' LEAs to create plans for comprehensivisation was diluted to a 'request'.

Stewart's Cabinet colleagues required one further changed to his paper. Edward Short, who was a Cabinet member, recalled in his autobiography:[214]

> *The Cabinet rejected his plea [to announce legislation to force LEAs*
> *to end selection at 11] and decided that the case for comprehensive*
> *schools should be put to them in a carefully drafted circular which*
> *asked for their cooperation. After an appropriate period of, say a*
> *year, we would be able to judge how far we could move without*
> *legislation.*

These were the words used in the minutes of the Cabinet meeting[215]:

> *Any reference to legislation should avoid using terms which could be*
> *represented by the Opposition as a threat to the independence of the*
> *LEAs or the freedom of choice of parents. It would be better not to*

*legislate until a need to do so could be demonstrated by the response
of the LEAs to the proposed circular.*

The minutes also made clear that 'going comprehensive' wouldn't
receive additional funding.

*The adoption of the comprehensive principle need not in itself neces-
sitate additional expenditure; and, although reorganisation might
proceed faster if local authorities could be given financial help,
inability to find the extra money would not prejudice its quality.*

On 21 January 1965 Stewart took part in a Parliamentary debate to
defend the government's comprehensive schools policy. He adhered to the
wishes of the Cabinet and gave a non-committal answer about the government's intention to use legislation to force LEAs to adopt their comprehensive policies.

*I explained that I believe that there will be a very large measure,
indeed, of willing co-operation from the local authorities, and that I
would not go further than that; that I would not ask the House for
legislative powers unless that were absolutely necessary for the
continuation of policy.*

I had to smile when I read what Stewart said in the debate about the
circular to be sent to the LEAs: '*calling on* [my italics] them to submit plans
to me for the reorganisation of their secondary schools on comprehensive
lines.' As we know, he didn't like the word 'requesting' and preferred the
even less precise term 'calling on'.

The day following the debate Stewart was replaced as minister by Tony
Crosland. These two events are in no way connected, because he was
promoted to the much more prestigious role of foreign secretary.

The beginning of the Crosland era

Stewart had created the foundation of Labour's comprehensivisation policy.
I am sure he never thought it would be easy to radically change the system

of secondary education, but I expect he was surprised at both the practical difficulties and the political sensitivities that would have to be overcome. His three months as minister revealed that 'going comprehensive' relied on using existing school buildings, that voluntary schools might be difficult to integrate into the state system and that Labour's claim to be providing a 'grammar school education for all' meant fundamentally changing the role of most existing grammar schools.

As for the LEAs, they must have been confused as they witnessed the strength of the government's determination to impose its policies diluted from a statement to 'require', then to 'request' and finally to 'call on' them to create plans to end selective education.

Five months after taking office, Crosland had adapted Stewart's Cabinet paper into Circular 10/65.[216] It took 10 drafts before the final version was agreed and consumed much time in consultations and meetings with his officials and stakeholders. The final version was undoubtedly a well-crafted document but, to my mind, added little of substance over and above Stewart's Cabinet paper.

The National Archive has four folders of documents giving a blow-by-blow account of how the circular was drafted and records of the innumerable meetings that took place. In an effort to refine and to achieve approval for the document, 27 organisations were canvassed for their comments, many of them having face-to-face meetings with Crosland and his officials. I doubt whether Crosland expected to change the opinions of organisations that were firmly against Labour's policies, but I am certain that as a consultation exercise it was successful, resulting in a more user-friendly version of the circular, with the most contentious statements and words removed. For instance, Crosland had adopted Stewart's phrase of 'calling on' the LEAs to act – this was changed to 'requesting'. Most important, the many meetings gave Crosland and his officials the opportunity to explain their policies and to hone their responses to the questions that kept being asked.

1. How does 'going comprehensive' relate to the recommendations of the Plowden Report? You might remember that way back in 1963, when Boyle was minister, Baroness Plowden had been asked to consider 'the whole subject of primary education and the transition to secondary education'.

Three years later, in late 1966, she was scheduled to publish her recommendations. Lady Plowden's own words eloquently explained the problem this presented.[217]

If LEAs this year [1966] are to make plans for reorganising their secondary education on the basis of 11 as the age of transfer, and we recommend (and you accept) another age, does this not postpone for a long time any implementation of our recommendations? If also we recommend (and you accept) a reorganisation of the ages of entry to infant and junior school – which at the moment seems probable – ought this not to be considered by the LEAs at the same time as they are considering secondary education, so that the whole span of education, and in particular the buildings to contain it, can be considered as a whole?

Crosland's officials were aware of Plowden's likely recommendations and briefed him accordingly.[218] When the report was published it was as they expected and recommended that the phases of children's schooling should be radically changed to provide:[219]

A three year course in the first (at present the infant) school at a median age of five years six months followed by a four year course in a middle (at present the junior) school with a median age range from eight years six months to 12 years 6 months.

Perhaps as a sop to Plowden, the circular described a form of comprehensivisation in which children transferred from a primary school at the age of eight or nine to a comprehensive 'middle school' and from there to the main comprehensive at 12 or 13, where they could remain until they were 18. All the other models assumed the status quo, with children changing from junior to secondary school aged 11.

In summary, Crosland decided that his circular trumped (in the sense of importance) Plowden's advice to fundamentally change the structure of primary, junior and secondary education. Of course, there was a much more diplomatic way of expressing this decision. When asked about it at a meeting, with a group of local government organisations,[220] he responded that it was: 'Not practicable to delay the implementation of Government policy on comprehensive education to wait the reports of Lady Plowden.' He then suggested that it was partly the fault of Plowden's committee.

He had considered the possibility of asking for interim recommendations but decided that this would not be helpful. The Council [Plowden] was not ready to make agreed recommendations on the subject; and even when they were, there was bound to be considerable delay between making the recommendations and the formulation of Government policy.

Plowden and her committee reached their conclusions based on 'educational needs'. It took them three years, involved evaluating evidence from over 400 witnesses and producing 800 pages of report and research. Stewart and Crosland undertook no research and reached their decisions for 'ideological reasons'. Along the way they received numerous warnings about the difficulties their policies would create and either ignored them or found a 'form of words' that made them disappear. As is so often the case, ideology triumphed over rational analysis.

I have already talked about *Sliding Doors* moments, where a single decision changed the trajectory of education. Had Crosland attempted to integrate his proposals with those of Plowden, the shape of education would have been very different – not necessarily better, but different. That was not to happen – political commitments had been made and they took priority.

2. What legal powers did the minister have to impose a national policy of secondary education? Reading Crosland's response to this question convinced me that he would have been a formidable poker player. Somehow, he was able to manufacture a convincing argument by combining a set of unrelated half-truths – the equivalent of winning the pot in a game of poker having been dealt a pair of twos.

First there was statement of fact: 'He had no specific power to require authorities to prepare reorganisation plans.'[221] Then came the quasi-legal explanation that by making this request he was fulfilling his general duty under the 1944 Education Act.

To secure the effective execution by local authorities, under his control and direction, of the national policy for providing a varied and comprehensive educational service in every area.

In the Act, the word 'comprehensive' was used in the context of being 'far-reaching' – not as a system of education. To confuse things further, he then claimed that 'reorganisation on comprehensive lines was now a national policy' that had been endorsed during the debate in Parliament, just before he replaced Stewart as minister.[222] This interpretation of events is not strictly true. The relevant sentence from the Parliamentary motion was:

[That Parliament] believes that the time is now ripe for a declaration of national policy.

Parliament agreeing that the time 'was ripe for a declaration' is very different from empowering the minister to make or enforce a national policy.

He ended by saying that all he was asking for was their cooperation in fulfilling the 'national policy' that was already a 'trend' being followed by many LEAs and that he wouldn't consider the 'hypothetical questions' that would arise if it were withheld.

The 'bottom line' was that Crosland had little power to make the LEAs respond to his circular, other than the vague threat that, if they didn't, the 'hypothetical question' would become a real one.

3. Would he only approve major building projects that were part of a comprehensive organisation? I expect that most organisations understood the limitations of the minister's powers, but the LEAs and their representative bodies realised that previous ministers had exercised their influence by rejecting proposals for new school buildings. Not surprisingly, they wanted to know if Crosland intended to do the same. If they expected a 'yes or no answer' they didn't receive one.

*Government policy for reorganization on comprehensive lines would
be one factor to take into account in considering future building
proposals.*

When Stewart was preparing his document for Cabinet, his officials
attempted to clarify the legal basis for the minister to reject previously
agreed plans or new building proposals. It appeared there was a long-established understanding that once a plan had been approved it wouldn't be
rescinded.[223] As for his legal authority to force LEAs to adopt a particular
form of secondary education by withholding approval for new building
projects, that could only be determined in a court of law.

When the final version of the circular was published it talked a lot about
buildings, mainly in the context that funding new school projects would be
limited. This ungainly sentence illustrates the difficulties the Ministry had in
conveying this message and relating it to comprehensive reorganisation.

*It would not be realistic for authorities to plan on the basis that their
individual programmes will be increased solely to take account of
the need to adapt or remodel existing buildings on a scale which
would not have been necessary but for reorganisation.*

I don't think I am the only person who found this explanation vague and
confusing. Within nine months, Circular 10/66[224] was issued. This one left
no doubt that only new buildings conforming to Labour's comprehensive
plans would be approved:

*Accordingly, the Secretary of State will not approve any new
secondary projects which would be incompatible with the introduction of a non-selective system of secondary education.*

Opinion is polarised about the role played by Crosland's circulars, especially 10/65, in converting England and Wales to comprehensive education.
Stephen Pollard was particularly scathing about its impact.[225]

*On 12 July 1965 [when Circular 10/65 was published], the English
state education sector was injected with a dose of poison. The system*

was far from perfect; there was a long tail of underperforming
schools. But on that day, the British government pledged its official
commitment to the end of all that was good about state education.

Although these were damning words about the outcome of the circular,
he was, in a negative way, complimentary about its effectiveness.

Other commentators, especially educational historians and journalists on
the left of the political spectrum, were less convinced about its importance.
Clyde Chitty, an academic and life-long proponent of comprehensive education, said:[226]

Circular 10/65 did not, in fact, compel anyone to do anything, and is
somewhat reminiscent of the type of 'permissive legislation' much
favoured by Disraeli [this was not meant as a compliment].

An article in the *New Statesman* described Crosland's contribution to
education as 'lifting hopes with many small, brave gestures, but achieving
so very little.'[227]

After spending so much time studying Crosland and his circular, I think
his critics were wrong. Considering the limitations of his negotiating position, he accelerated the country's transition to comprehensive education. His
success resulted from his engagement with his officials and stakeholders,
rather than the content of the circular. A highly effective form of sales technique is the 'assumptive close', whereby you assume the person is going to
buy the product and use language and adopt a demeanour that reflects the
inevitability of that outcome. I am sure it wasn't intentional, but Circular
10/65 and Crosland's approach were textbooks examples of this technique.

Had Stewart remained minister, I am sure he would have produced just
as good a version – if not a better one – of the document, but I doubt if he
would have been as successful in getting it adopted. As a senior Ministry
official explained, Crosland's task was to:[228]

Put the suggestions in a logical order, and above all, to enter into
dialogue with various interested parties. This was to be his most
important task in connection with the Circular's publication.

The same official, when talking about the two ministers, said:

Stewart was not a revolutionary sort of chap. He was very practical, but very quiet and shy; he never spoke to us.

Crosland had a different personality, more open, he had been a university teacher, he liked sitting around the table chucking the ideas about.

According to Kevin Jeffreys, Sir Herbert Andrew, the permanent under-secretary at the Department of Education and Science, thought that Crosland was 'eminently rational' and praised him for:

Accepting that decisions could only be taken after consultation with the 'robber barons' of the education world, such as the teachers' unions and LEAs.

A skilled negotiator makes everybody believe they have 'won' or at least been listened to and achieves concessions. When commenting about Anthony Crosland's achievements, *The Times Educational Supplement* never mentioned the word 'negotiator' but that was what they meant.[229]

It would seem to be that he has been able to give his friends the impression that great reforms are afoot while lulling his enemies into a sense that nothing really is going to happen.

Almost everything that has been written about Circular 10/65 focused on the mechanics of its creation and questioned whether it should have had more legal authority and been more prescriptive in how the LEAs should adopt comprehensivisation.

Its effect on the children whose schooling was being reorganised was rarely questioned. If Crosland and his officials ever considered the issue, I suspect they assumed it was a problem for the LEAs to resolve. My guess is that the LEAs were consumed with the logistics of remodelling their secondary education system, preparing for the leaving age to be raised and the problems caused by the shortage of teachers. If that wasn't enough, they had to manage the launch of the CSE exams and implement the recommendations of the Newsom Report.

Circular 10/65 might have been successful at establishing 'going comprehensive' as a national policy, but at what cost? We will discover the answer to that question in the final part of our timeline in Chapter 7, 'The comprehensive era'.

Government is distracted by other priorities

On 31 March 1966 there was a general election. The manifestos of the two parties were almost the same as those used in 1964, with Labour confirming its commitment to abolishing the 11-plus and the Conservatives opposing the 'hasty and makeshift plans' to convert grammar and secondary moderns into comprehensives. Yet again it was a Labour victory, except this time the Parliamentary majority increased from four to 98 seats. Alongside this victory, Labour triumphed in the local elections, controlling the majority of LEAs.

Any doubts about the government's ability to impose its education policies, should it decide to do so, had disappeared.

Theoretically, the Labour Party's Parliamentary majority enabled it to change the education system in any way it wanted. Yet, during the next four years in power it did little to progress the cause of 'going comprehensive'. Indeed, it did little to change any factor of secondary education. There are many explanations why so little effort was committed to advancing its flagship education policy. Dennis Dean believed that as much as Crosland wanted to end selection and grammar schools he was equally, if not more, motivated to do away with private schools.[230]

Crosland intended to end selection in the maintained sector [state schools] promptly to proceed to mount an assault on the more deeply entrenched forces in the private sector. He was aware that this task was more difficult but by settling the debate about selection in the maintained sector and promoting widely an ethos of opportunity he hoped to weaken the position of the public [private] schools by isolation.

A few months after the release of Circular 10/65, Crosland appointed Sir John Newsom – the man responsible for the study about educating secondary school children of 'average and less than average ability' – to 'advise on the best way of integrating the public schools with the state system of education.' According to another member of the Cabinet, Barbara Castle,[231] Crosland was not optimistic about the outcome of a study. When announcing his intentions, he said: 'This is a strictly insoluble problem' – a tactic we would now call 'managing expectations'.

It wasn't until April 1968 that the first part of report was released and by then Crosland had moved jobs, becoming president of the Board of Trade. I think it is fair to say that Crosland's gloomy predictions were correct. The report's recommendations pleased nobody and were soon forgotten. Labour's annual conference voted unanimously to reject the recommendations[232] and the private schools' governing bodies accused the report's authors of 'doctrinaire rigidity' and 'woolliness of thought'.[233] Half a century later, the Labour Party is still talking about the evils of private education and theorising about how to engineer its demise.

Crosland didn't confine his attention to attacking grammar and private schools – he was also convinced that higher education needed reform and openly criticised the universities, which he believed 'pursued their own ends and had created barriers to educational and social advance'.[234]

In 1966 he issued the white paper *A Plan for Polytechnics and Other Colleges*, which recommended establishing a network of polytechnics that would be 'large and comprehensive institutions offering full-time, sandwich and part-time courses of higher education at all levels.'[235] This development is best known as the 'binary system' of higher education. Ironically, the same people who supported Crosland's comprehensive schools policy criticised him for creating a two-tier system of higher education, which they believed erected the same social barriers that 'going comprehensive' was trying to destroy.

If Crosland were alive today, I think it would be the unravelling of his vision of higher education that would pain him the most. As I will discuss in Chapter 9 ('Half a century on – what lessons can we learn?'), his critics eventually prevailed (in 1992) and a single format of higher education prevailed (universities). I am sure Crosland would look at the results and say 'I told you so'!

It seems to me that Crosland's approach to changing the education system was to 'kick-start' initiatives and shepherd them to a point where he believed they were self-sufficient. By issuing Circular 10/65, establishing the Newsom Committee and introducing the concept of polytechnics he thought he had laid the foundations for permanent change to the secondary and higher education sectors. His scope of ambition was admirable, but his critics would argue, in today's parlance, that he took his 'eye off the ball' and failed to provide the sustained attention necessary to create lasting change. There is probably some truth to this view, but I think the most important explanation for Labour's lack of attention to secondary education, and most of its other policies, lay in the economic problems it faced and the resulting tensions – maybe 'battles' is a better word – between members of the Cabinet.

There seems to be some immutable and timeless rule of government, of all political persuasions, that electoral promises fail to account for the constraints and uncertainty resulting from the financial realities of the real world. So it was throughout the second Labour government.

One of the pre-election promises was not to raise taxation. Soon after the election there was another 'balance of payments crisis', yet the government's message in the chancellor's 1967 budget remained remarkably bullish:[236]

I sum up the prospects for 1967 in three short sentences. We are back on course. The ship is picking up speed. The economy is moving. Every seaman knows the command at such a moment, 'Steady as she goes'.

Unfortunately, the 'course' led to a major economic crisis in late 1967 and in early 1968 the government announced that public spending had to be cut. Defence expenditure was reduced and so was the education budget.

Capital spending on higher education was delayed, but what must have been the most unpalatable decision was the postponement of raising the school-leaving age (ROSLA). On 5 January 1968 the Cabinet decided that it would be delayed until September 1972, rather than 1970. This was slightly better than the original proposal to delay it until 1973. The precarious and unpredictable state of the country's finances was laid bare in a study of the dealings between the UK government and the International Monetary Fund (IMF),[237] which painted a picture of a government constantly reacting to financial pressures and setting objectives that it failed to achieve. As a Cabinet minister, Crosland would have been involved in the fractious discussions about the fragility of the economy and the impossibility of delivering the government's policies.

By the time the decision to delay ROSLA was made, Crosland was no longer in charge of education – but he was a leading voice, with Michael Stewart who had earlier been minister of education, in opposing the decision. According to Crosland's wife (Susan), he was alleged to have said:[238]

> *The delay would 'only' [my quotes] affect 400,000 children. But they're not our children. It's always other people's children. None of us in this room would dream of letting our children leave school at fifteen.*

Susan Crosland's account of the Cabinet meeting described the then secretary of state for education (Patrick Gordon Walker) being confronted with the question of whether he would prefer to help the 400,000 school children who would miss an extra year's education, or university students? He (allegedly) answered: the university students.

Barbara Castle's account of the meeting said nothing about these antics but did remark that opinion was evenly split about agreeing to the delay. The *Crossman Diaries*[239] provided the only other narrative about the event and, in the main, echoed Susan Crosland's account, referring to Patrick Gordon Walker as 'feeble' and 'trembling', but added that there were parents and teachers who would welcome a postponement. Perhaps he had in mind the leading article in *The Times Educational Supplement* (January 1966) that discussed the many voices that were concerned about the readiness to implement ROSLA in 1970.

> *What is the strength of the misgiving? Put briefly it is that we cannot hope to have enough teachers to raise the school-leaving age in 1970 and that we cannot hope to have enough buildings. We are in fact facing a commitment for which we have not the material means.*

Even that stalwart of the Labour Party, *The Guardian*, was raising the same concerns. In January 1966 it wondered whether the money would be better spent increasing the number of primary schools and suggested that the plans were 'based more on faith than finance'. We will find out whether these concerns were justified when we reach the time of ROSLA's eventual implementation. What is clear to me is that the portrayal of Patrick Gordon Walker as callous and weak, for agreeing to the delay, was a cynical simplification of the situation. Maybe a more forceful character would have responded by accusing Crosland and Stewart of failing, when they were running the Ministry, to recruit enough teachers, build enough schools and create the curriculum that would have ensured ROSLA's success. Who knows what might have been? As it is, Susan Crosland's account of her husband's honourable words remains the story that is most repeated.

Maybe it was the personalities involved or perhaps it resulted from governing the country during a period of economic turmoil, but the Labour government appeared to be an unhappy and dysfunctional place. These tensions must have contributed to the lack of progress in implementing its secondary school's policies.

Social upheaval influences a new generation of teachers

Labour's two periods in government were also accompanied by upheavals in society that affected the implementation of 'going comprehensive'. Such was the magnitude of these changes that they continued to reverberate until the end of the timeline in 2004. This was the time of the 'sixties revolution', when many of the unspoken rules that had governed society were being questioned and rejected.

I expect we have all heard the phrase that 'if you can remember the 1960s you weren't really there'. In 1968 I was 18, about to go to university and very much 'there'. I am sure that many of my contemporaries' recollections of the era would be dominated by reminiscences about the culture of 'sex, drugs and rock and roll'. No doubt there were opportunities to indulge in all of these, but maybe not as many as some recall. Perhaps, being a shy and retiring boy, I should have 'got out more'!

My abiding memory of the time is the atmosphere that legitimised, indeed expected, the questioning of authority, hierarchy and the rules that governed my parents' lives. I was a student at Sussex University. In the 1960s, along with the LSE and Essex University, it was a hotbed of student unrest. Occupation of the administrative buildings and angry marches were part of student life – especially for those in the arts and humanities faculties. Students studying the sciences, myself included, seemed less intent on changing the world. Events occurring on the global stage fuelled this feeling of change and disruption. This was the time of the Woodstock concert (August 1969), the riots in Paris (May 1968) and the violent anti-Vietnam war protests in London (March 1968).

There was also some evidence of this unrest in the classroom. The minutes of a meeting of the Inspectorate of Schools contained a section on instances of 'pupil unrest'.[240] This included accounts of political demonstrations and the Revolutionary Socialist Students Federation distributing leaflets outside the school gates. Children in a few London schools marched to and demonstrated outside the Department – echoes of today's young eco-protesters. As an antidote to pupil anger, it was concluded that 'a lively classroom atmosphere with plenty of opportunity for debate was probably one of the best safety valves'.

There were also other types of anger. One of these was aimed at immigrants and the fear of how they were changing society – especially the disruption to schools. Enoch Powell's 'river of blood' speech (April 1968) represented these feelings. It is rarely mentioned that three years before, Crosland had issued a circular[241] advising schools on how to manage the rising number of immigrant children; his advice was that no more than a third of pupils in any class should be non-English speaking children. Today, English is the second language for the majority of pupils in more than 2,000 primary and secondary schools.[242]

The relationship between workers and employers was also deteriorating, resulting in strikes and industrial disruption. In 1970, over 10 million days were lost to strike action, the highest number since 1926. Trade unions were increasingly challenging government policies, creating yet another problem for the Labour government – and one that heightened when the Conservatives returned to power.

My reason for recounting these events is that my fellow undergraduates and contemporaries attending teacher training colleges would soon become teachers and educational academics. Many carried with them the desire to change 'the system', which was soon to manifest itself in the way schools were run and how children were taught. All of this was happening at the same time as thousands of secondary moderns and grammar schools were transforming into comprehensives.

Let me add one caveat to my account of the times. Researching the last century of history has taught me that each generation believes it is radically different from its predecessor. What I don't know is whether the changes that took place in the 1960s were exceptionally significant or if we (my generation) just like to think they were. The historian David Kynaston agreed with the observation and believed there was much mythologising about the era and that 'for most people it was a pretty normal decade'.[243] In a later lecture, he attempted to identify similarities between the sentiments of Brexit leavers and those that existed in the 1960s, within parts of the working class.[244] An interesting hypothesis but, in my view, a leap of historical logic, too far. What is beyond doubt is the era had a lasting impact on children's schooling.

LEAs apply the brake to Labour's 'go comprehensive' plans

The fate of the thousands of secondary modern schools was being determined, not by the intrigue occurring within government or the convulsions in society's culture, but by the decisions being made by the individual LEAs. Schools were having to organise for ROSLA, prepare children to take both GCEs and the new CSE exams and embrace the changes to the curriculum and method of teaching proposed by the Newsom Committee – all while wondering if they were going to become part of 'going comprehensive'.

Circular 10/65 'requested' the 165 LEAs to submit their plans for comprehensivisation by 12 July 1966. On this date, 69 had produced plans covering all their schools. A small number (10) had either refused or were proposing schemes that were almost certain to be rejected. The remaining 86 either were in discussion with the Ministry, had asked for a delay or expected to submit their plans by the autumn.[245]

It is probable that these [the 'others'] will also include some half-hearted schemes which merely toy with the mechanics of comprehen-

sivisation, apply to only a small part of their respective areas, or are patently evasive.

This was not an auspicious start, although it was an improvement on the LEAs' response to the requirement of Butler's Education Act that they submit development plans within a year. In 1944, the low response had resulted from administrative difficulties; in 1966 it was the LEAs' reluctance to obey the request.

A year later (1967), 23 LEAs were still to submit a plan, although only four authorities were refusing to take part in the planning process. A further 12 had their schemes rejected and the rest were either approved, in full or in part, or still under consideration.[246] In this year, the declining popularity of the Labour government spilled over into local government politics, resulting in Labour losing control of all but two of the 12 largest cities in England and Wales.[247]

The following year (1968) the Conservatives gained control of even more councils as Labour's popularity continued to plummet. By then, Edward Short was secretary of state for education and during a debate in the House of Commons he and his junior minister, Alice Bacon, gave this information about the state of the plans. Of the 163 LEAs:[248]

116 have plans implemented or approved; 89 relate to the whole or greater part of the area and 27 to a smaller part.

Of the remaining 47 authorities, 16 have a scheme under consideration.

7 have not yet submitted revised schemes.

17 have not yet submitted any formal scheme.

7 have declined to do so.

During the debate the minister detailed the current state of comprehensivisation. There were 748 comprehensive schools, within 81 LEAs, of which seven were 'wholly comprehensive'. On the basis of these numbers, he expected that by January 1971 their number would rise to 1,180 schools and the number of LEAs with comprehensives to 105, of which 30 would be 'fully comprehensive' (i.e. not a mix of selective and comprehensive). When commenting on these figures Short said:

Reasonable progress is being made, progress which shows that reorganisation is generally accepted. It also shows that the new concept of secondary education which I intend to embody in the Bill will be generally acceptable in spite of the hysteria of some of the Tory backwoodsmen.

I wonder if Crosland would have been satisfied with this 'reasonable progress'? Short's statement implied that six years after Circular 10/65 was issued only 30 LEAs (18%) would be fully comprehensive. We now know that by the end of 1973 the actual number was 42 (25%), with 19 LEAs yet to open a single comprehensive school.[249] Do these numbers substantiate the comment that 'reorganisation is generally accepted'? I think not.

The Ministry's archived files enable us to see the depth of Edward Short's frustration and annoyance at the slow progress. Much of his time seems to have been consumed with enacting the legislation, referenced in his statement, to force the recalcitrant LEAs to submit acceptable plans. More of that soon.

Secondary moderns morph into comprehensives

We know that the pupil population of comprehensive schools increased throughout the period of the two Labour governments, but due to budget cuts there was little opportunity to construct purpose-built comprehensives, so the 'new' comprehensives were repurposed secondary moderns, technical and grammar schools. The following table[250] shows how the share of the secondary school population changed over the period 1960–1975.

334 | THE SECONDARY MOD

	Secondary modern	Grammar	Technical	Comprehensive
1960	61%	25%	4%	5%
1965	60%	28%	3%	9%
1970	45%	21%	2%	33%
1975	19%	9%	1%	66%

The percentage share of the pupil population attending the different types of secondary school

During the period 1960–1965, the percentage of children attending grammar schools actually increased. Secondary moderns and technical schools experienced a slight fall in their share of pupils. During the next five years, the percentage of children at grammar schools fell a little, but nowhere near as much as in secondary moderns and technical schools.

The number of grammar and secondary modern schools peaked in 1964. By 1970, when Labour left office, 260 grammar schools had been shut or converted to comprehensives. Five times as many secondary moderns had suffered the same fate. Technical school numbers started to decline much earlier. By 1970 their numbers had fallen to 82, a third of the 251 at the start of the decade.

What these numbers tell us is that by 1970, most children attending comprehensive schools came from secondary moderns and technical schools. But were schools with the name comprehensive really 'comprehensive'? According to David Rubinstein and Brian Simon the answer was a resounding 'no'. They believed that by 1970, only 12% of pupils attended 'true' comprehensives (i.e. where the pupil intake was not 'creamed' by coexisting alongside grammar schools). The Ministry's figure claimed the number was 32%. I have no way of checking this claim, but I am sure the number was much lower than the official statistics.

The 'bottom line' conclusion from this analysis is that by 1970 there were many more schools called comprehensives but most of them were really rebranded secondary moderns and technical schools.

'Going comprehensive' – the antithesis of evidence-based policy making

Many questions remained about how fast and how well 'going comprehensive' was progressing but few doubted it was destined to become the dominant model of secondary education. Secondary modern schools were born following the research (albeit it of dubious quality) and recommendations of the Norwood Committee. There had been no equivalent 'XYZ Committee' that concluded that 'going comprehensive' was the best system of schooling and providing a long list of recommendations on how it should be implemented. Since starting the timeline, we have encountered numerous committees, studying all types of educational issues, but never one that considered comprehensivisation. I think this quote from Brian Simon, a vocal and committed supporter of comprehensivisation, summed up the situation.[251]

> *No overall planning for this change [the transition to comprehensivisation], no serious thinking through of its implications on a national basis ever took place, either now or later [the book was first published in 1991]. At no point, for instance, was any official thought, enquiry or study made as to what should comprise an appropriate curriculum for the new comprehensive schools now coming into being.*

Crosland had begun talking about researching comprehensive education in February 1965 and a month later established a working group for that purpose. The National Archive files for this endeavour weren't opened until 1996, long after Simon's book was published, so he can be forgiven for not mentioning the project.

I have accessed these archives and they reveal the interesting, and at times amusing, story of Labour's research into the type of school it was so anxious for the LEAs to adopt. This research only had a tangential impact on the story of secondary moderns, but it said a lot about the intellectual foundations, or lack of them, supporting comprehensivisation.

It all began in early February 1965, when the Ministry started a file titled 'Comprehensive schools – comparison with other schools'.[252] Among the press cuttings about the performance of comprehensive schools is the record of a meeting between a Ministry official and Lord Bowden, the Labour spokesman for education in the House of Lords. Bowden wanted to discuss an article, published in the *Observer* (17 January 1965), that featured the results of a survey conducted by Dr Robin Pedley that purportedly showed how well comprehensive schools were performing. This was the same Robin Pedley whom we first encountered in 1956 when he met the Conservative minister (David Eccles) to explain his ideas about comprehensive schools.

Bowden was anxious to use the research as ammunition to defend the government's education policy and was upset when the official suggested that the study might not be statistically sound. Other documents explained that the Ministry had previously encountered Pedley's research and found it to be 'unscholarly to put it at its mildest'.

This triggered an exchange of memos about how, if at all, the research could be used. The conclusion was that it should be ignored. In an attempt to replicate Pedley's research, the Ministry assembled its own data and concluded that it was extremely difficult to measure the respective effectiveness of comprehensives and selective schools. One of the documents explained the differences in the schools' catchment areas and the complications they created.

These figures [the percentage of pupils staying at school] show something of the drastic effect that social and other factors have on the whole situation. They also show that education systems don't overcome these factors.

This echoed the concerns that had already been expressed about creating a uniform 'neighbourhood school' when the social composition of neighbourhoods differed so greatly. It wasn't a problem – really more a fact – that would go away and is something we will return to time and time again.

The next set of papers in the file relate to the research findings from the Medical Research Council, which claimed:

The academic progress of children in areas providing a substantial proportion of secondary education in comprehensive schools does not differ substantially from the average for the whole country; and for the girls there is some evidence to suggest it is worse. There is

*also evidence that in comprehensive school areas the lower manual
working class pupils are handicapped [when judged on 'O' level
results].*

Unlike Pedley's research, this was produced by another government
department, which probably explains the volume of correspondence it
created. I thought this concern resulted from the document's findings that
questioned government policy, but the main worry was the Ministry being
associated with its suspect analysis.

The comments echoed those made about Pedley's analysis. In summary:

*Their [the government's statistics branch] conclusions were that the
statistical methods are suspect, and the paper is full of unsound
arguments and assumptions.*

These were the only two research documents in the file. One showed the
benefits of comprehensivisation; the other, its disadvantages. Neither set of
conclusions was thought to be substantiated by the data and its analysis.

In the book *Going comprehensive in England and Wales*, four academics
presented a thorough review of the research conducted in the 1960s and
1970s, attempting to compare comprehensive and selective education.[253]
Even with access to the additional datasets that were available in 1991,
when the book was written, their conclusion was as follows.

*Once we controlled for their ability and family background, there
were no differences between the average academic achievements of
students in comprehensive and selective schools, irrespective of the
specific definition of the appropriate samples to be compared. Yet,
there was a general tendency for high-ability students to perform at
somewhat lower levels and low-ability students to perform at somewhat higher levels in the comprehensive schools.*

*We have noted, however, that even the statistically significant results
reported in this chapter are only limited.*

338 | THE SECONDARY MOD

We thus appear to be faced with the difficult task of deciding on the lesser of two evils. Do we choose a system that sacrifices some of the highest performances in order to facilitate greater achievement by low-ability students, or do we sacrifice achievements by low-ability students in order to offer an enriched academic diet to 'the brightest and best'?

In light of these findings it is not surprising that the Ministry found the two research projects wanting in their methodological rigour. There had been many claims, mainly from politicians, that 'going comprehensive' was to the detriment of the 'bright child'. This was the first credible evidence supporting the accusation. Likewise, the belief that comprehensivisation helped 'low-ability' children seemed to have some substance. At the time these were no more than hunches. In truth, Labour lacked any evidence that its education policy could improve children's academic performance, let alone the much harder to quantify metrics of 'fairness' and social mobility.

It says something of Crosland's instincts that during a meeting to create the working group, to advise on the research project, he voiced doubts about what could be accomplished, saying 'plainly it is better to undertake something than do nothing'. Maybe he had an aversion to research studies; more likely he realised that whatever was achieved would have little effect on the upheaval taking place within secondary schools?[254]

Crosland 'the politician' was ever-present and he stipulated what the project would not do:

- Compare selective versus comprehensive systems.
- Hinder the LEAs in the preparation of their plans.
- Question government policy that 'must be taken as read'.
- Assume the government would await the results of research work before going ahead with particular solutions.

Despite these constraints, he recognised that little was known about the different methods of 'going comprehensive'; indeed there was 'little research in any of the questions raised by comprehensive education as a whole'. Let me paraphrase Crosland's position: 'Despite little being known about the educational outcomes of comprehensivisation I am only willing to sanction a research project as long as it doesn't question the conclusion that it is the right solution.'

Attending the meeting was a group of educational academics who raised many more questions and issues that needed to be studied. Crosland concluded the meeting by asking his officials if they had any objections to the project, other than the obvious political danger that 'the government had gone ahead with comprehensivisation without knowing enough about the implications'. I think it was more in hope than expectation that he thought the project could be conducted without attracting public attention. His officials had no objections, as long as the research refrained from 'going into the comparative merits of comprehensives and selective schools'. If any subject was 'off limits', it was this one.

A working group was formed to decide the objectives of the research, and it had its first meeting on 5 March 1965. The minutes showed that the overall objective was to 'investigate the possibilities of research within the field of comprehensive education within the framework of socialist policy' – a statement that surprised me and the civil servant who had read the document, since they had handwritten, alongside 'socialist', the word 'government?'

During my consultancy career I attended many meetings with clients who believed that research was a 'good thing' but had little idea of what should be investigated. They invariably had created a vaguely worded statement of purpose, containing few details about what they intended to do with the results of the research study. Reading these minutes reminded me of this type of meeting, as it meandered around different topics of things that 'could be researched'. There was no driving sense of purpose about why it was necessary and how the research would be used to improve the effectiveness of 'going comprehensive'– or indeed any other facet of education. A meeting with the portents of disaster written loud and clear.

After a couple more meetings the working group produced its report, which covered four areas.[255]

- *The topics to be covered.*
- *The nature of the enquiries which might be made.*
- *The agencies which might be employed.*
- *The probable organisation and cost of the research proposed.*

It was the following recommendations that interested me, because they revealed the primary motivations driving Labour's education policy. The research programme was intended to test the effectiveness of comprehensive schools over the following objectives.

- Gathering pupils across the whole ability range in one school so that by association they benefit each other.
- Concentrating teachers, accommodation and equipment so that pupils of all ability groups may be offered a wide variety of educational opportunity and that scarce resources may be used economically.
- Collecting pupils from a cross-section of society in one school:

So that academic and social standards, an integrated school society and a gradual contribution to an integrated community beyond the school may be developed out of this amalgam of varying abilities and social environments.

I have paraphrased the first two of these objectives. The last one is a direct quote from the report. The ungainly wording suggests to me that the authors were anxious about its true meaning and resorted to vagueness. I think they meant that 'mixing children from all social classes together will result in a better society'.

Unlike its objectives, the mechanics of conducting the research were more precisely stated. Most of the work would be done by the National Foundation for Educational Research, in conjunction with the University of Manchester. The total budget for the exercise, over a four-year period, was £135,000 (£2.5 million in today's pounds). Managing the project was a committee of Ministry officials and representatives of the universities, LEAs and the social sciences. Not surprisingly, Robin Pedley was a member. In what appeared to be an afterthought, 'the teaching profession' was added to the list.

Five months later the Consultative Committee on Research into Comprehensive Education met (10 September 1965) and work began.

The project was not without its operational hiccups. As expected, trying to hide its existence from the media was impractical and a press release was issued explaining its purpose. Most of the press commentary was neutral-to-favourable, as illustrated by *The Times'* article (5 October 1965), which began on a somewhat negative note: 'up to now nobody has put much faith in educational research' and then warmed to the idea that evaluating the different types of comprehensive schools was a good idea.

It was the friction between the university academics that made me laugh. Having been an associate lecturer at a couple of universities, I have witnessed first-hand the tetchiness that they often exhibit towards each other, especially when it comes to the allocation of research funding. So it was with the academics on this committee. There were some amusing notes from Ministry officials about trying to manage the 'confrontation' between the warring factions – especially the challenge of getting the 'psychometricians and the sociologists to work together'.[256]

Another challenge was to agree a 'statement of objectives' about the purpose of education. A group of 'educational theorists' (e.g. philosophers, sociologists, psychologists and research workers) formulated one version; another was created by a group of 'educational practitioners' (e.g. school heads, teachers and inspectors). They then came together to 'agree' a combined statement. I would have loved to be a fly on the wall at that meeting!

Progress was slow and the 'long-delayed' initial report was issued in November 1968. This provided a 'fact-finding' exercise about the functioning of the 331 comprehensive schools that existed in 1966.[257] The second report, published in 1970, was a more detailed qualitative investigation of 59 schools. Perhaps its most important conclusion, which supported an earlier observation, was that 'the more able pupils are under-represented in the schools studied'. Instead of 20% of pupils being from this group, the schools contained 12% – a finding the researchers attributed to the grammar schools taking the brightest children.[258]

In 1972 the final report, *A critical appraisal of comprehensive education,* was published.[259]

The one thing this report was not, was a 'critical appraisal' of comprehensive education, or any other type of education. On its own admission, it had become a collection of case studies of 12 comprehensive schools, educating 11,300 children. It must have been a difficult report to write, being so far removed from the one that was originally promised.

You know a research project has gone horribly wrong when the chapter about the 'the study in perspective' starts:

In some respects it [the six-year study] falls short of what was originally intended when the project was launched, but in others the research team feels it succeeded.

A long list of reasons was given for its failure to deliver, most notably the difficulty of reaching conclusions about comprehensive education from such a small sample of schools, which differed in their location, organisation and size – the smallest contained 240 pupils (rural Wales), the largest 1,800 (urban northern England).

Significant problems were encountered in measuring the schools' achievements against the defined objectives, as this sentence showed: 'there is inevitably a steep descent from the lofty ideals to scores on questionnaires... highly generalised objectives have to be re-cast into lists of mundane attributes'. Imagine how difficult it must have been for the researchers to write simple questions to measure children's 'wholeness', 'self-realisation of the individual' and 'feelings and emotions'.

The 240-page report contained some interesting observations about individual schools but was adamant that its contents shouldn't be used to compare selective and comprehensive education or to draw any generalised conclusions about the effectiveness of 'going comprehensive'. Certainly, there was nothing 'critical' about its contents, in any meaning of the word! Another failing, because it questioned its objectivity, was the authors' reliance on the research conducted by Caroline Benn and Brian Simon,[260] two of the most vocal supporters of comprehensive education. As we will soon see, this project and the work of the Consultative Committee was abandoned, following the accusation that it was little more than a propaganda exercise for comprehensive education.

The cost of the project rose to £200,000 (£3.5 million in today's pounds) and it produced few worthwhile insights.

Not surprisingly, the study and its findings are rarely referenced by historians. My reason for recounting the project's unhappy story is that it seems emblematic of Labour's 'going comprehensive' policy. A concept based on high ideals but with little thought about the practicalities of what was required and how it would be achieved – the antithesis of 'evidence-based policy making'.

The Plowden Report – mixed messages about comprehensives

For the remainder of Crosland's time as secretary of state for education, his involvement with secondary schools appears to have been one of reacting to events rather than guiding and implementing policy.

In November 1966 the Plowden Report was published.[261] I have already discussed Crosland's refusal to delay 'going comprehensive' to incorporate Baroness Plowden's recommendations. We know of her annoyance with his decision, but I am certain it didn't influence her committee's findings. However, I am not so sure that it didn't have a bearing on the manner in which its conclusions were expressed in the report. There were plenty of statements that couldn't have pleased Crosland or the current secretary of state for education.

On the subject of 'streaming' in comprehensives, a subject that became hotly debated in the following years:

Our evidence from witnesses goes to show that transfer between streams in comprehensive schools is uncommon just as transfers between modern and grammar schools are. The strictly educational, as opposed to social, argument against a selective system starting at 11 does not lose its force because the selection is between streams instead of between schools. This rigidity inside comprehensive schools may be unnecessary and may be temporary; but it has to be taken into account.

The report took a neutral-to-sceptical position about the allegation that the selection procedure (i.e. the 11-plus) had a negative effect on children and their primary schools.

The number of complaints from parents to the Department about errors in selection has declined recently. The growing opportunities offered by GCE courses in secondary modern schools probably explain why parents are complaining less often about selection.

*An assessment by HM Inspectors of the ill effects of selection in
schools in the National Survey suggested that these effects [nar-
rowing of the curriculum and focus on the 11-plus exam] were lessening, perhaps because teachers' estimates were tending to replace
externally imposed attainment tests.*

Although it recognised that selection procedures were misplacing 10–
20% of children into the wrong school, the committee believed that:

*In the past 50 years persistent efforts have been made to refine
methods of selection. As a result, the World Survey of Education in
1962 commented that 'Great Britain has made the greatest
advance... in developing reliable and valued methods of testing and
examining scholastic aptitude and ability.*

The report concluded that abandoning selective education did not negate
the need for some form of testing, although the widespread procedure of
testing children as soon as they arrived in their new school was thought to
be 'deplorable'. A head teacher was quoted as saying: 'I found I was testing
what children had forgotten in the holidays.' Although intelligence tests had
their problems, they overcame the difficulty teachers had in forming objective judgements of pupils who came from a spectrum of social classes. It
was also pointed out that most teachers came from middle class backgrounds, unlike many of their pupils.

*No test with predictive value can be 'culture free' but a non-verbal
intelligence test is a sensible check to use on impressions gained
from attainments in class work or verbal tests.*

Plowden did not object to the policy of 'going comprehensive' but questioned some of the justifications for its adoption, as well as highlighting the
unresolved issues about how and when children should be tested and how
the results affected their schooling.

The rise of parent power

Another irritant for Crosland and his successors was the growing power of parents. The Labour Party had used parents' perceived disquiet about the 11-plus and secondary moderns as a political weapon to pressure the Conservatives. How representative these parents were is unknown but they were the ones who knew how to organise and get their voices heard.

Times had changed and these parents were now questioning the authority of LEAs and the Labour government to change the 'character' of schools – which was code for 'closing grammars and opening comprehensives'. It's ironic, and a little amusing, that it was probably the same middle class parents who were fearful of secondary moderns and the 11-plus who were the most vocal in their actions to protect existing grammar schools and to thwart the Labour Party's policy.

Labour couldn't have been surprised that closing grammar schools would antagonise some parents. When they first came to power in 1964, the then minister (Michael Stewart) had been warned by his official H.F. Rossetti about the party's misleading policy about grammar schools.

To prevaricate in dealing with an assertion that grammar schools as now known cannot exist under a national comprehensive policy will do more harm than good.

Rossetti was right and parents soon realised that 'a grammar school education for all', Labour's election slogan, involved radically changing the 'character' of existing grammar schools. Unlike the post-war invention of secondary moderns, many grammar schools had a long and prestigious history and their closure enraged parents of past, present and future pupils. How widespread this parental anger was is impossible to say.

Maurice Kogan[262] provided an excellent account of the rise of parent power and the most notable confrontation, which occurred when the law was used to delay the conversion of a grammar school in Enfield (Middlesex) into a comprehensive.

The details of the legal arguments the parents and their supporters deployed are not relevant to our story. But, as a result of their action, the parents delayed the LEA in converting the school and forced the government to enact new legislation[263] to stop others from using the same arguments.

What interested me was the authorities' arrogance in the way events were handled. The secretary of state gave the parents only five days to object to the new admissions procedure at the school, something the courts thought was unreasonable. And rightly so. Reading the Ministry's files about the conflict,[264] I was struck that at no time did anyone ask: 'Do the parents have a point – are we (the government) and the LEA being unfair?' The only consideration was how to protect the minister and to ensure the case did not delay 'going comprehensive'. This attitude was illustrated in the draft of a memorandum that was sent to the prime minister about what was to become the 1968 Education Act.[265] It proposed extending to parents the right to make representations to the minister when schools intended to change their range of ability. On first reading, this appeared to give parents more power. But this was not its primary motivation, as was explained.

> *Its chief attraction [the proposed new power], and the reason the change is needed urgently, is that it would work both ways. Parents and others would be able to protest to me against an attempt by LEAs reversing a previous decision to establish a comprehensive school. I would thus have a general power, which I do not at present possess, to prevent such a reversal [underlined in the original document].*

The memorandum then explained that giving parents this power would not delay the progress of comprehensive reorganisation, because the LEAs already had to give two months' notice when they intended to convert a school to a comprehensive. The minister would receive the parents' representations at the same time and, by implication, they would be ignored.

This cynical manoeuvring must have been made all the more urgent by the losses that Labour was suffering in local council elections and the fear that LEAs under Conservative control would start reversing their predecessors' comprehensivisation plans.

Kogan concluded that the incident showed that:

> *Parent power was now able to move from talking and pamphle-*

teering about general issues of standards and participation, towards taking expensive, technically sophisticated and politically tough actions against elected councils and the Department of Education.

'Window dressing' rather than progress

For the final two years of the Labour government, Edward Short was the minister of education and, unlike most of his predecessors, had been a teacher and a headmaster. Having witnessed the difficulties affecting the 'going comprehensive' policy, he came to office determined to accelerate its implementation.

- It took a year before he proposed his plan to the Cabinet (8 May 1969). He started by explaining that the policy was inching forwards but slowly. Of the 163 LEAs, some were ignoring the policy, others had fully committed – and all points in between.[266]
- 97 had plans approved covering the whole or the greater part of their areas, but over half of them (52) did not include all of the maintained voluntary schools. These were often state-aided grammar schools that refused to become comprehensives.
- 24 had plans approved for a small part of their areas and some of these had no intention of making further progress.
- 26 had not submitted a plan. Of these, eight had formally declined, eight had their plans rejected and 10 had not indicated their intentions.

There was no record about the status of the other 16 LEAs.

The Ministry believed that 23 LEAs (14%) were refusing to cooperate with national policy and some of those with approved plans weren't pushing ahead with any urgency. Short admitted that the progress was not always due to the rejection of comprehensivisation but sometimes resulted from the lack of suitable school buildings.

It will be some years before all selective schools can be eliminated. Both pre-war and post-war school buildings are generally too small to be turned into comprehensive schools.

Michael Stewart had identified the constraints of needing to use the existing infrastructure of schools back at the very beginning of 'going comprehensive'. The Labour-controlled Inner London Education Authority, for example, was committed to comprehensive education but was unwilling to implement it using its old and unsuitable schools.

Short believed that he required additional powers to break the impasse that existed with the recalcitrant LEAs. He asked the Cabinet to let him draft legislation that would ensure:

> *Every LEA should have regard to the need for securing that educa-*
> *tion in schools maintained by them [both state and maintained*
> *voluntary] should be provided in non-selective schools and should*
> *have the duty to submit to me proposals for the organisation of*
> *secondary education in their area and in particular have to specify a*
> *date by which selection would be eliminated.*

And so began the tortuous process of creating the legislation and getting it accepted by his colleagues – in particular the prime minister, Harold Wilson – and through the legislative procedures of the House of Commons. When reading the first draft of the bill I wondered if it was worth all the trouble.

> *It is not intended that the Bill should directly affect the substantive*
> *function of local education authorities with regard to the provision of*
> *education i.e. although the Bill <u>will require</u> [my underlining] them to*
> *submit plans for reorganisation, it will not require them to carry the*
> *reorganisation out.*

Short understood the legislation's limitations because in the concluding sentence of the document that he submitted to the Cabinet, he said:

> *This proposal does not go as far as many would wish but I believe*
> *that it is the most we can do in the context of general education law*
> *[the 1944 Education Act] as it now stands.*

A comment from an official at the Ministry (G.E. Dudman to the Office of Parliamentary Council, 29 June 1969) summed up the purpose of the bill:

I have already told you on the telephone that the Bill is regarded by the Secretary of State as a window-dressing operation. I can only add the hope that the dressing will be sufficient to cover the bareness of the stock room.

For something that was to provide no more than 'window-dressing' the Bill must have consumed a lot of Short's time, energy and what we now call 'political capital'. What seemed like a simple idea became horrendously complicated as soon as it was translated into legal language. As *The Times* explained,[267] the main problem was that the legislation was to be a 'small Bill that cannot contradict the spirit and intention of the major Act at present in force [the 1944 Education Act] in any radical manner'. Another difficulty was how, if at all, the new legislation would apply to direct grant and independent schools.

Towards the end of 1969 (26 November), the frustration with the legislative process led Harold Wilson to propose a radically new approach and that they 'start afresh, legislate positively, and then repeal the offending clauses of the 1944 Act'. He was disturbed that the bill emphasised the abolition of grammar schools rather than ending the 11-plus. He was also concerned that its phrasing, 'admission of pupils is not based on selection by reference to ability or aptitude', implied that these qualities would be ignored in the future – something he considered as being 'dynamite'.[268] In essence, the bill was negatively phrased and was about what Labour didn't want, rather than positive aspects of its education proposals. It seemed the politicians had difficulty understanding (maybe accepting) that they had little leverage over the behaviour of LEAs, which, in turn, didn't control the policies of the voluntary sector. As the legal adviser to the Department noted, when commenting on Short's legislation: 'central government acts as a snaffle not a spur' (i.e. as a restraint – the term refers to a part in a horse's bridle).

Despite all of these obstacles, and many I haven't mentioned, the bill narrowly failed to complete the Parliamentary process before the general election was announced. All those hundreds of hours of meetings, all of those carefully crafted memos – all abandoned – for the sake of producing some 'window dressing'. Needless to say, the 1,250,000 pupils still attending secondary moderns gained nothing from all of these political shenanigans.

'A scream of pain'

I doubt that many people reading *The Times* on 5 March 1969 noticed the article on page 10 titled 'Education right wing fights back'. It was the education correspondent's account of a paperback pamphlet titled *Fight for Education*, which had been published as an 'appeal to fight the spirit of anti-education that its authors claim is abroad in England'. Edited by two academics (Brian Cox and Tony Dyson), it was a collection of articles about the ills of contemporary education, especially:[269]

> *The introduction of free expression in schools; the Labour Party's plans for comprehensive education; and student demands to participate in university government.*

Because its contents were dark and gloomy, and as a ploy to gain attention, it was called a 'Black Paper' – a pun on the Parliamentary 'white paper'. The initial circulation was a couple of thousand, plus copies sent to MPs. It couldn't have been popular with Labour Party members of Parliament but one of them – Edward Short – took particular exception to its contents and it is thanks to him that it rapidly gained national visibility. Nicholas Timmins' book, *The Five Giants*,[270] told the story of the meteoric rise in the document's notoriety.

A month after its publication, Short was addressing a conference of the NUT, where he claimed that the Black Paper was 'one of the blackest days for education in the past 100 years' and that it was provoking 'the crisis of the century'. Could he really have believed these words? During his time as a minister he had encountered (and overcome) many challenges and appeared to be a man of sound judgement. Today, his comments would be dismissed as a joke, but then they attracted derision as being an ill-timed over-reaction. His audience of teachers appreciated his words but this 'blackest day' speech was to haunt him for the rest of his career, even being quoted in his obituary.[271] Thirty years later the papers still ignited strong feelings among 'progressive' educationalists. Roy Lowe talked about their immediate precursor being the 'McCarthyite rhetoric of the late forties and fifties.'[272] I am not sure if Lowe or Short wins the prize for exaggeration.

It's ironic that at the time, Mrs Thatcher was the Conservatives' shadow minister of education. Many years later she coined the phrase 'the oxygen of publicity' – in the context of denying terrorists media coverage. Had Edward Short applied this concept, the Black Paper might have remained a 'page 10' item and soon been forgotten. As it was, four more sets of papers were published – one of them titled *Goodbye Mr Short*. This edition focused on the failing of comprehensive schools and progressive teaching techniques. When the fourth edition was published in 1975 it became the sixth-best-selling paperback in the country.[273]

I think that Timmins' conclusion about the role of the Black Papers was accurate. He believed they demonstrated that:

After the heady expansionism of the 1960s, Labour's determination to achieve entirely comprehensive education had broken a form of laissez-faire post-war educational consensus.

In essence the Black Papers were a scream of pain against a growing anti-examination, pro-egalitarian culture in education, of dismay at the apparent destruction of authority in universities and secondary schools. This decline, in turn, was blamed on progressive education and comprehensives.

The Black Papers provided a focus for the grievances and fears about what was happening in schools and universities and contributed to the hardening of attitudes at both ends of the political spectrum. From now on, the system of education – comprehensivisation – was integrally linked to the changes in curriculum and teaching methods that were bundled together as being 'progressive'. I believe this was unfair. Secondary moderns – even grammar schools – would have been changed by these new ideas about education. It was also unfortunate, because it made it very difficult to differentiate the performance of the 'comprehensive system' from that of the comprehensive school. This was not helped by Labour's aversion to objectively researching the performance of their cherished comprehensivisation.

'A botch-up job from the start'?

A general election ended Short's reign at the Ministry. He wasn't happy about his or the government's performance in implementing comprehensive education and used these damning words to describe the venture:[274]

> *In spite of all the efforts of Tony Crosland and his successors, of whom I am one, the Government's refusal to legislate and the Chancellor's refusal to make funds available meant that comprehensive reorganisation was a botch-up job from the start.*

These are the words of an angry and frustrated man and help explain his outburst about the Black Paper.

Short's frustration with Labour's achievements was echoed by other commentators.

In his book *Education and Labour Party Ideologies*, Denis Lawton[275] blamed the lacklustre progress on the 'lack of interest in education by senior Labour politicians and a lack of vision by those responsible for policy'. Having studied the biographies of Short's Cabinet colleagues, I concur with the observation about the 'lack of interest' in education. Housing, employment and financial policy generated far more discussion and interest than schools and universities. I am not so sure about the policies lacking 'vision'. I would say that there was an absence of the knowledge, skills and determination to translate Labour's laudable ideas into a reality – something that is all too familiar in governments of all political persuasions.

Just before the election, the *New Statesman* magazine – normally a supporter of the Labour Party – published a long and highly critical article about the government's failure to reshape secondary education.[276] An annotated copy was widely circulated within the Ministry, which suggests that it was deemed to be important.

This is how the article concluded:

> *Is it [the Labour Party] prepared to exchange the role of a party of ultimate revolution for that as an instrument of real and speedy change? Is there a future, not so much for socialism as for socialist government? Now that Harold Wilson [prime minister] looks like*

*winning the next election the party's answer to these questions will
determine whether or not it was worth it.*

During the next part of the timeline we will learn how future socialist
governments fared in transforming secondary education, but this would have
to wait for a few years because Harold Wilson failed to win the election. So
began the reign of a new minister – Margaret Thatcher.

There is not a lot to say about the education policies that appeared in the
election manifestos. Labour's promised 'more of the same' with the reintro-
duction of legislation to force all LEAs to 'go comprehensive' and the 'aim'
to reduce class sizes.

The Conservative Party's position on secondary education remained
largely unchanged. LEAs would be free to choose their own system of
schooling, freed from central government-dictated national policy. One new
policy commitment was concerned with the age at which children moved to
their secondary school, echoing the recommendation of the Plowden Report.

Labour manifesto promised to:

- Legislate to require the minority of Tory LEAs to abandon
  selection at 11.
- Raise the school-leaving age to 16 in 1972.
- Provide extra funding in areas with the worst slum schools.

Also contained in the manifesto were these statements of policy.

- Aim of 'reducing to 30, the size of all classes in schools.'
- Claim that 'comprehensive reorganisation has been vigorously
  pursued' and that in the past six years, 129 of the 163 English
  and Welsh LEAs have agreed plans for reorganising their
  secondary schools.

Conservative manifesto promised to:

- Give priority to the primary schools [expenditure].
- Maintain the existing rights of LEAs to decide what is best [the type of secondary education] for their area.
- Raise the school-leaving age as planned.
- Give parents the freedom to send their children to independent schools.

Also contained in the manifesto were these statements of policy.

- 'LEAs will take into account the general acceptance that in most cases the age of eleven is too early to make final decisions which might affect a child's whole future.'
- 'Most imaginative new schemes abolishing the eleven-plus have been introduced by Conservative councils.'
- 'All children must have the opportunity of getting to "O" level and beyond if they are capable of doing so'.

During the six years of Labour government, there had been few policies and little drive to improve the schooling of children in secondary moderns and grammar schools. Many of these schools had been rebranded as comprehensives; many more were in a state of limbo waiting for LEAs to finalise their plans.

All the government's energy had been focused on a policy that seemed 'the right thing to do' rather than necessarily the most effective way of educating children. At that time, nobody knew if this was the right approach, because nobody had researched the subject.

I wonder how secondary moderns would have evolved if the Conservative Party had remained in power? My guess is that the situation wouldn't have been that different. Fewer grammar schools would have closed but the secondary moderns would have looked much the same as the new comprehensives. I have no doubt that the trend for secondary modern pupils to take GCEs (and CSEs) would have been encouraged, narrowing the distinction between them and grammar schools. Speculation is worthless because there had been six years of Labour cajoling the LEAs towards comprehensivisation. Its policy may have been roundly criticised, but nobody knew what its long-term effect would be on the remaining 2,690 secondary modern and 1,040 grammar schools. The new minister was soon to find out.

A new political party in power, a new minister of education – Mrs Thatcher

The Conservative manifesto had promised to reverse Labour's policy of imposing a national policy of comprehensivisation. Margaret Thatcher, the new minister, had the job of delivering on this commitment. It seems that the speed with which she acted and the mechanism that she used surprised her Ministry officials and Cabinet colleagues.

On her first day as minister (20 June 1970), I expect her Ministry officials were planning a series of 'getting to know you' meetings in which they would brief her about outstanding issues and help her to understand the scope of her ministerial brief. That's not how the day turned out. According to her biographer,[277] she instructed her officials to immediately withdraw Circulars 10/65 and 10/66 – the two documents that were supposed to hasten the end of selective education. I have already explained the over-rated importance of these circulars, something that Edward Short and his predecessors came to understand. Yet Thatcher's first priority was their removal. My guess is that this swift and decisive action was intended, in today's parlance, 'to send a message' to the LEAs, the teaching establishment and her colleagues – 'this minister intends to deliver on the manifesto commitments and fast'.

Thatcher seems to have been surprised that the process for cancelling a circular involved issuing a new one. Normally this would include much discussion and multiple drafts. Rumour has it that, frustrated by her officials' lack of urgency, she wrote the document herself. Whatever the truth, 10 days later Circular 10/70 was issued.[278] This scrapped the restrictions on the character of secondary building projects, the regulatory mechanism with which Labour had tried, with mixed success, to enforce comprehensivisation. LEAs would now be 'freer', not free, to determine the shape of their secondary education system and could amend their existing plans and submit new ones as long as they ensured:

Educational considerations in general, local needs and wishes in particular and the wise use of resources to be the main principles determining the local pattern of education.

Terms like 'educational considerations', 'local needs' and 'wise use of resources' weren't in the vocabulary normally used by education ministers. Absent from the circular was any mention of the manifesto promise that the LEAs should take into account that 11 was too early to make final decisions that 'might affect a child's whole future', something her political opponents were quick to point out.

There was another legacy from the Labour era that Thatcher also wanted scrapped. I expect that she had already read the first and maybe the second of the reports from the National Foundation for Educational Research (on admission to grammar schools, in 1957, and the ill-fated 'critical appraisal', which was still a work in progress when she took over). She was not impressed. Claiming that the research project was little more than a propaganda exercise for comprehensivisation, she cancelled its funding from December 1971 and disbanded the committee established by Crosland to research comprehensive education. As we've seen, the results from this project were far removed from the original objectives, producing few useful insights. I think the accusation of it being propaganda was a little unfair – it was more a case of being vaguely conceived and lacking purpose. Above all, it lacked the conviction of Labour politicians to objectively analyse the performance of comprehensive schools.

I found it interesting and, dare I say, amusing researching this period of Thatcher's political career. Commentators at that time were writing about a politician in her first ministerial position, not the woman who became the country's first female prime minister and who ruled for 11 years. However, the personal qualities that infuriated her opponents and thrilled her supporters were already becoming evident.

A week after her appointment *The Sunday Times* published a long article titled 'The lessons Mrs T will have to learn',[279] which made a series of observations and predictions, all of which proved to be correct.

- Belief in the unfairness of selective education and support for comprehensives was no longer confined to the political and educational 'left', but had spread to the centre stage of politics – including Conservative LEAs.

- Her laissez-faire educational policy of allowing LEAs 'to do what you wish as long as it is on educational grounds' begged the question of what constituted 'educational grounds' and how and by whom these 'grounds' would be judged.
- Arguing that comprehensive schools, as defined by Labour and as understood by parents, could coexist with grammar schools was a logically indefensible position.
- Seeking to improve secondary moderns' exam results, although a laudable objective, weakened the argument for the selective system.

The article's concluding paragraph stated that Thatcher must be aware of the limitations of her power.

Until the law is changed, they [the secretary of state for education] must rely upon their bark rather than their bite: this should be consoling for those out of office as it may be frustrating for those in power. Mrs Thatcher must already know these lessons.

I am certain that she understood the regulatory constraints of her position. Had she emotionally accepted that the LEAs would be the final arbiter of the shape of secondary education? I have my doubts.

Four months later another article appeared in *The Sunday Times*,[280] which was far more judgemental about Thatcher the person, rather than her policies. It acidly commented that she was neither a minister with experience of education nor a 'real intellectual power'. Balancing these criticisms was the observation that her detractors, mainly Labour politicians, plus a few Conservatives, seemed as much driven by snobbery as by their 'egalitarian ideals'.

The Labour-supporting *Daily Mirror* reported that her scrapping of the two circulars was turning the education system into a lottery in which the quality of a child's schooling was dependent on where the parents lived – an observation that was as valid throughout the timeline as it is today. The *Daily Express* reported Edward Short's claim to be putting Thatcher 'on trial', when the issue was discussed in Parliament. Here he accused her of 'high handed ideological arrogance', 'doctrinal reaction', 'anti-progressive', 'returning to an elitist system' – and so on and so on. It was only a year since Short had made his fateful 'blackest day' speech and he still seemed wedded to excitable language. Thatcher's response to this litany of accusations was to observe that Short hadn't got over losing the election.

Cancelling the circulars and the research exhibited her trait for decisive action. Another side of her character was revealed a year after she became minister, when she had to overcome an onslaught of political and media criticism. The event that triggered this had no relevance to secondary moderns but had (in my view) a major effect on Thatcher and greatly influenced her behaviour when she became prime minister.

On taking power, the Conservative government had undertaken a review of public expenditure. Like other heads of spending departments, Thatcher had been asked to make cuts. After much argument the Cabinet decided to stop providing free school milk to children aged seven years and older, extending a decision that Labour had made two years earlier when it ended free milk for children in secondary schools. It seems to be generally agreed – even by her detractors – that, other than this decision, she was successful in defending her education budget and ensuring that more money was spent on primary school buildings and protecting the Open University, a project that many of her colleagues wanted abandoned. But the damage was done and the massed ranks of the NUT, the Child Poverty Action Group and of course Labour politicians, especially Short, criticised the decision. Never wanting to understate an issue, this is what he said during a Parliamentary debate to pass the Education (Milk) Bill.[281]

I have been a Member of the House 20 years this year, 14 of them, unfortunately, with a Tory Government in office. This is the meanest, most unworthy Bill that I have seen in the whole of that time—taking the milk away from the nation's young children. It is mean, squalid and unworthy of a great country.

According to her biographer, the media started by criticising the policy then broadened its attacks to Thatcher's personality and motivations. *The Sun* asked 'Is Mrs Thatcher human?'[282] and other articles and TV programmes portrayed her as the archetypical aloof, Tory middle class woman, lacking in empathy and understanding.

In her opinion, sacrificing school milk to protect the more important parts of her education budget was the right decision. But, being right does not necessarily result in being popular. Of course, the press opprobrium burnt itself out, but I am certain that Thatcher emerged a wiser and much tougher politician. As we know, she and her style of politics and economics (Thatcherism) drove parts of society and the media far beyond criticism into visceral hatred. I am certain that her experience with school milk helped prepare her for the battles and vitriol she was to face as prime minister.

My primary concern is to understand what happened during Thatcher's time as minister that directly affected secondary modern schools and their pupils. But before telling that story, I will briefly mention two of the educational initiatives she undertook.

In March 1972 a government-sponsored report was published that contained worrying conclusions about children's literacy standards.[283] *The Times* newspaper commented that children's reading standards aged between 11 and 15 were no better than 10 years before, whereas between 1948 and 1964 there had been a steady improvement. Thatcher was reported to be 'studying the research and considering what action is needed.' It didn't take long before she decided that the 'action' was to establish a committee to investigate the problem. In June 1972 the membership of the committee, chaired by Sir Alan Bullock, the distinguished historian and vice-chancellor of Oxford University was announced.[284]

By the time the committee reported in September 1974 Thatcher was no longer minister. Sadly, the size of the report, over a quarter of a million words, seems to have blunted its impact. As *The Times Educational Supplement* commented: 'In common with, I suspect, most of the country's 350,000 qualified teachers, I have not read the Bullock report.'[285]

I have no memories about the report, but I do remember buying a copy of Sir Alan Bullock's most famous book – *Hitler, A Study in Tyranny*. I was daunted by its size, so this 850-page paperback still remains on my bookshelf, mostly unread. Many years later the author was quoted as saying, 'I only write enormous books'.[286] It is a great pity that Thatcher didn't make brevity one of the committee's objectives because it doesn't seem that many, if any, of the report's numerous recommendations were ever implemented.

Much of Thatcher's time was spent in formulating her 10-year strategy for education, which was published as the white paper *Education: A Framework for Expansion*.[287] I had to smile when reading it and the accompanying press release.[288] The documents were all about the increase in spending on education – not a single word about its organisation. It seemed that the words 'comprehensive', 'grammar', 'technical' and 'secondary modern school' had been banished from the documents.

Media sentiment towards Thatcher had started to change during the early part of 1972, when *The Times* wrote that 'she may well be given the sort of hindsight credit for real achievement which Lord Eccles, also belatedly, received for his in the same job.'[289] This turnaround in her reputation, accelerated after the publication of the white paper, attracted positive comment from all parts of the political spectrum. 'Considerable advance says teachers' union' was how *The Guardian* reported the launch of the paper.[290] It was not only the NUT that was impressed: similar comments came from the Association of Education Committees and Baroness Plowden. *The Times* was thoroughly convinced by the white paper and wrote:[291]

> *Mrs Thatcher has just produced a plan for education expansion and the definition of priorities which even her most doctrinally motivated critics have scarcely been able to fault. This intelligent and hard working minister is like to leave a much more positive mark on the nation's educational advance than any of her predecessors in the last decade or more – and certainly more than the chilly and trendy Mr Short.*

When Parliament discussed the white paper on 19 February 1973, there was just one passing mention of secondary moderns and comprehensives, with all of the debate focused on the financing of education for the coming decade. Thatcher appeared to be in her element, explaining the intricacies of the plans. By this time, Short had been transferred and Labour was without a shadow minister. Roy Hattersley, who in a few months would take over the post, led Labour's attack, but it seemed to be a half-hearted effort. Thatcher had survived the 'milk incident' and gone on to be praised for her management of the education brief. It was a brief period 'in the sun', as things were soon to change for her and the Conservative government.

Trade unions' power to use strikes to secure higher wages (consequently increasing the cost of living) had been a constant problem throughout the previous Labour administration. Union militancy intensified when the Conservatives were elected and by 1972 the number of days lost to industrial action had reached 23 million, double that experienced by Labour. In November 1973, following threats of disruption by the mine workers' union, the government declared a state of emergency. By the end of the year the rate of inflation was 9.2% and unemployment was rising. Worse was to come at the beginning of 1974 when, to conserve energy supplies, the government announced the 'three-day week'.

Government spending plans had to be re-evaluated, including those in Thatcher's white paper. All the good intentions to build new primary and nursery schools were abandoned as capital spending was reduced by 20%.[292] As so often happens, ministers and their officials laboured to produce plans and regulations that never got implemented because they ran out of money or time. Thatcher ran out of both.

Secondary moderns under Thatcher

During the period of Thatcher's reign as minister, comprehensives increased in number and became the country's primary form of secondary education. This was mirrored by the dramatic decline in secondary modern schools (1,200) and the children they educated (420,000). These metrics showed that Thatcher was more 'successful' in achieving the goal of comprehensivisation than her Labour predecessors – an astonishing fact. Her supporters and detractors were, and probably still are, baffled by what happened.

Not for a moment do I think she was converted to the doctrine of comprehensivisation. So what was the explanation? In January 1972, Thatcher and her officials met the prime minister to discuss issues related to education.[293] This section from the minutes of the meeting explained her position and the limits of her power.

The Prime Minister asked whether it could be argued that certain comprehensive schemes should be turned down on educational grounds. The Secretary of State [Thatcher] said that it might be possible to argue that a comprehensive scheme would involve the disappearance of uniquely good grammar schools and that the local education authority had not discharged the onus of proof.

But it is difficult to establish how a child would suffer particularly as educational opinion, rightly or wrongly, was still strongly in support of comprehensive schools. It was agreed that the essence of the present arrangements was that the re-organisation of secondary education was a matter for local government rather than at Westminster.

If the procedure for local objections was allowed to influence policy, as opposed to being simply a means of allowing the difficulties of individuals to be taken into account, the Government might get the worst of both worlds.

In other words, she was 'between a rock and hard place'. All her instincts told her that closing grammar schools was wrong, but she had few powers to prevent it happening. It's ironic that for all their political differences, Margaret Thatcher and Edward Short had one thing in common – they couldn't control the actions of the LEAs.

When Thatcher was questioned about comprehensivisation, early in her days as minister, she said: 'I think it is coming with increasing speed', but went on to say, 'I do not accept that it will stop there: non-selective education is not the last word in education.'[294] We know that Thatcher admired Friedrich Hayek and his philosophy explained in *The Road to Serfdom*.[295] Central to his beliefs was a deep distrust of the state as the arbiter and enforcer of policies. He thought competition, be it of markets or ideas, was the most effective way of selecting the best, the most effective option. In her speech to the 1973 Conservative conference, Thatcher declared her dislike – maybe 'hatred' is not too strong a word – of Labour's national policy of enforcing a single type of schooling: 'Under Socialism there would only be one kind of school and that would conform to Socialist state policies.'[296]

Perhaps this explained her resignation to the freedom of the LEAs to be their own masters and adopt comprehensivisation, even though she had deep reservations. As long as LEAs were not compelled to accept a single system (e.g. comprehensives) they would, in her mind, eventually evolve to use a mix of selective and non-selective education. Of course, this could be an argument to help rationalise her powerlessness.

According to an article appearing in the *Journal of Educational Administration and History*,[297] the comprehensive schools lobby believed Thatcher's policy of allowing the LEAs to decide their own system of schooling would result in them rushing back to selective education. The *New Statesman* said, in what must be one of its less objective observations, that the destiny of many children was being 'committed to the municipal martinets of the nation's county halls – to the butchers and bakers, without any serious interest in education policy'. I think this was its way of saying that the elected local counsellors would overturn the wishes of the educational experts – those favouring comprehensivisation. I am sure it hadn't escaped the journalist that Mrs Thatcher's father was a grocer and a local councillor.

There was no deluge of LEAs wanting to change their education policy, despite the anger of some parents about losing their local grammar school. The pace of change to comprehensives might have been slowed, but the direction of travel remained the same. Instead of approving or rejecting the LEA plans in their entirety, Thatcher began using a regulatory mechanism (Section 13) that enabled her to consider them on a school-by-school basis. Even so, this did not materially alter the flow of changes, as was confirmed by Benn and Simon's 1970 report *Half Way There*, which we encountered a few pages ago.

It was true that overall not many schools have been actually rejected under Section 13 – only about 50 in the first two years of Conservative government – but all a scheme needs is to have one or two grammar schools 'left out' to be converted from a scheme abolishing the 11+ to one which must retain it.

Of course, they were right that if an LEA retained a single grammar school this invalidated its claim to be 'totally comprehensive'; however, it seems clear that they were surprised that Thatcher intervened on so few occasions.

Between June 1970 and February 1973 Thatcher rejected less than 150 of the 2,765 comprehensivisation schemes that she was asked to consider.[298]

During her four years as minister she approved 3,286 comprehensive schemes and rejected just 326.[299]

There are two more explanations for her acquiescence to the drive for comprehensivisation. One was that political control of the LEAs was moving in Labour's favour when, in May 1972, it gained control of 30 county boroughs. The other reason returns me to the subject of secondary moderns. Thatcher appeared devoid of policies for the development of these schools. Having read many of her papers and the commentary from the times I found nothing about her vision for these schools and their pupils. It was if they had been written out of the educational script.

I can only conclude that on taking office she made the decision that secondary moderns would somehow morph into comprehensives. Maybe she didn't know, or care, how they would develop? Without doubt, retaining grammar schools was her number one priority. Whatever the explanation, the last vestiges of hope for these schools died during Thatcher's reign.

Perhaps I have overcomplicated the explanation of what happened; maybe the desire to dump secondary moderns and grammar schools and move to comprehensives was too strong – even for Mrs Margaret Thatcher to stop.

The following table[300] summarises the change in the state of secondary education during Thatcher's time as minister. I think the figures speak for themselves.

	Secondary modern	Grammar	Technical	Comprehensive
1970	44.60%	21.10%	1.50%	32.70%
1975	18.70%	9.20%	0.50%	66.00%
Change in the number of schools	-1,514	-472	-53	1,819

The percentage share of the pupil population attending the different types of secondary school and the change in the number of schools between 1970 and 1975

At long last the school-leaving age is raised – just about

For the past 30 years, Labour and Conservative politicians had promised to raise the school-leaving age to 16 – when the time was right. Providing children with 'more education' was a goal that seemed, instinctively, 'a good thing to do' and was a promise both political parties had made in their 1970 manifestos. Rather like the game of 'musical chairs', Thatcher won the prize of being the minister who had to deliver on the commitment.

On 24 August 1971, the Ministry issued Circular 8/71,[301] which committed secondary schools in England and Wales to raising the upper limit of compulsory schooling to 16, from the beginning of the school year 1972–1973. The circular detailed the preparations that were under way.

- £125 million (1.7 billion in today's pounds) had been allocated to provide the extra classroom accommodation.
- Teacher numbers were increasing faster than ever before and although there might be a small decline in the pupil-teacher ratio, it would be temporary.
- Individual schools, supported by the Schools Council, had responsibility for defining the curriculum.

The Schools Council had been created in 1964 with the wide remit of advising on matters of curriculum, teaching methods and exams. One of its first actions was to start a programme of work to: 'help the schools and others concerned to turn an act of faith [raising the school-leaving age] into an established success.'[302]

When, at the beginning of 1972, Thatcher met the prime minister (Edward Heath),[303] she reiterated her confidence that there would be enough teachers to cope with the increased number of children. She was less confident about the adequacy of the school buildings, but thought 'they would probably be satisfactory'. It seemed that Heath was most concerned that the curriculum had been 'properly worked out', referencing the problems when the leaving age was last raised (1947). If I had been the prime minister I would have been concerned by Thatcher's evasive response.

The Government had no power to dictate the curriculum. Much useful work had, however, been done by the Schools Council and it was clear there were educational benefits for those who stayed at school for a further year. At present 91% of those who left school at

15 had no GCE or CSE qualification: this was true of only 7% of
those who left school at 16.

This doesn't sound to me like a ringing endorsement of the readiness of
the schools to provide an extra 12 months of worthwhile teaching to children who were being forced to extend their schooling. In truth, at this time
Thatcher had little idea what the LEAs were doing to prepare for ROSLA.[304]

Studying the media of the period reveals a questioning of the relative
worth of ROSLA, compared with the other pressing educational needs.
These concerns came from all parts of the political spectrum. In May 1971
The Guardian talked about 'The prisoners in our schools' and questioned
what benefits the quarter of a million children forced to stay at school for
the extra year would gain. In another article, the newspaper wrote about
'The wasted years'.[305]

It seems fairly clear that most schools will be offering in the 'extra
year' the kind of curriculum which the newly trapped young people
do not particularly want.

Let's pause for a moment, and consider the magnitude of the challenge
facing the LEAs to make ROSLA a success.

Virtually all pupils in grammar schools were already staying at school
beyond their 16th birthday. The 'trapped young people' were in secondary
moderns and comprehensives. As is shown in the table below, the number of
children who were voluntarily staying at school was increasing and, by
1969, approximately half of pupils had decided to stay for the extra year. By
1972 the numbers would have been even higher. The default decision for the
others – the less academically able pupils – was to leave and get a job.
ROSLA was about to delay that freedom by 12 months. The table[306] also
shows the significant regional variation, with London and the south east
having the highest percentages of children voluntarily staying for the extra
year. The story was very different in the north and the Midlands.

Geographic region	1964	1969
South East (includes Greater London)	47%	63%
South West	40%	59%
Wales	30%	50%
West Midlands	33%	50%
North West	33%	48%
East Anglia	28%	47%
East Midlands	29%	47%
Yorkshire and Humberside	30%	47%
North	24%	45%

Percentage of pupils staying on at 15 in secondary schools

ROSLA was only one of the challenges facing the LEAs. Since the Newsom Report (1963), 'average' and less academically able children were receiving a different curriculum and style of teaching, from their contemporaries who were taking external exams. These non-academic pupils were the group most likely to leave school at the first opportunity and the most affected by ROSLA. Schools had to find ways of ensuring these young adults would benefit from another 12 months in the classroom.

To compound the problems, most LEAs were in the process of moving to some form of non-selective education and had been planning to implement ROSLA in 1970. All this had changed when the Labour government delayed the date of its implementation by a couple of years. Politicians might be able to alter dates in an instant but the repercussions for the LEAs were far-reaching, forcing them to reschedule their building and teacher recruitment plans. If you are getting the impression that ROSLA's success was far from guaranteed, then you are right. 'From HORSA huts to ROSLA blocks'[307] gives an excellent account of the difficulties the LEAs faced in providing the accommodation for this new cohort of pupils. The vision of the Ministry's Architects and Building Branch was that the 'Newsom children's extra 12 months at school needed accommodation that was more akin to a college than a secondary school.

*Here was a vision of self-directed and motivated young adults coop-
erating on various types of ongoing projects in an environment that
was more or less separate and freed from the regime of the wider
school, which catered for younger pupils. It blurred the lines
between learning and recreation in a quasi-professional setting
signified by soft furnishings, carpets and magazines.*

Ministry officials were not confident that this, rather idealistic, scheme
of accommodation was likely to materialise.

*If the matter is left to the unaided efforts of local education authori-
ties the more fortunate and the more efficient will solve their own
problems. But in many areas the result will be a makeshift assembly
of expedients which, from a building point of view, will bring about a
depreciation of standards which will be regretted for a generation.*

Minutes of the meetings of the Inspectorate of Secondary Schools give a
depressing account of the fate of the 'non examination' pupils, suggesting
that the teaching profession was essentially 'academic' and ill-equipped to
deal with these less gifted pupils, especially when they were forced to
extend their schooling.[308]

All these fears were well founded. To mark the beginning of ROSLA, in
September 1972, the NUT published a survey of the LEAs' preparedness.[309]
Its findings were damning. Over half of the authorities intended to cope with
the extra numbers of children by using temporary accommodation and
mobile classrooms and it seemed that the preparations for the new
curriculum were even less developed.

The most extensive account of this period is given in *Secondary Education and the Raising of the School-Leaving Age*.[310] This statement from the
book captures the essence of the challenge that ROSLA presented.

*The attempt to reform a diffuse education service, 'a national system
locally delivered', in which the central government, LEAs, schools
and teachers each jealously guarded their autonomy, meant that a
variety of responses emerged.*

There were many instances of schools that were well prepared, with the classroom accommodation and curriculum to engage their reluctant pupils. Unfortunately, these were matched by as many schools that had done little planning and consequently struggled.

As I read the book, I was struck by the similarities to the previous time the leaving age was raised. Then, there had been a failure to translate the theoretical benefits of an extra year's schooling into a reality. I think that ROSLA also highlighted the chasm that still existed in secondary schools, be they secondary moderns or increasingly comprehensives, between the 'academic' and 'practical' children and the different type of schooling they were provided. These arguments sounded surprisingly like those contained in the Norwood Report, nearly 30 years before.

I want to conclude this account with a personal experience of how ROSLA was implemented. Close to where I lived in East London was a comprehensive that until recently had been a technical school. A very good friend taught at the school and these are her memories of the period.

The children had been expecting to leave school at 15 and suddenly found that they had another year to complete. They were reluctant. Although it had been a long time coming, I have no recollection of my training college providing any preparation or support for ROSLA.

The school's headmaster had decided to group together the young people with 'behavioural issues' and those where English was not their first language and deposit them as far from the main school building as possible. Our teaching accommodation was two huts; managed by me – a rookie just out of college – and a teacher who was near retirement [let's call him Mr Bennett, not his real name]. The other teachers were ecstatic about not having to teach these problem children.

There were no case files, no background materials about these students, just their 'reputations'. We had no staff meetings about the students, no mentorship programmes, no work experience opportuni-

ties. It felt like the two of us were on a desert island in the far reaches of the playground.

I stayed for two school terms. I enjoyed working with the students, especially when we were out of the enclosed school environment. That was a challenge in itself as they liked to show their appreciation by thieving perfume from shops and, for their amusement, harassing tourists. Mr Bennett mentally disintegrated before my eyes. Sometimes I would look across at his classroom and in the midst of the mayhem he would have his head resting on the desk, while the boys attempted to set fire to the classroom. It was not a good way to end his career. He had compassion and empathy for his students, but no support at all from the school management.

It was exhausting providing a complete curriculum to interest and involve students with such diverse needs and most with literacy problems. Teaching became policing.

I was possibly the only teacher who established any relationship with the kids. Living near the school I might be out at the weekend and hear a wild cry of 'Miss, Miss!' On many occasions I remember them helping to push-start my old car. Individually, they were fine. Together they were a nightmare. I felt that I had failed the group, but traditional schooling was never going to be the right setting for these pupils. It was a rotten start for them and for me.

This is the story of what happened in one school. I am certain other accounts would paint a very different and more positive picture. As has been said, time and time again, secondary education's fragmented organisation resulted in an inconsistent quality, especially when implementing major change projects. ROSLA was a case study in demonstrating the system's flaws.

I have noticed that accounts of Thatcher's time as minister rarely mention her role in ROSLA. In truth I doubt if she had much. She was more an observer than a director of the process. She didn't possess the levers of control, even if she had wanted to use them, and by the time ROSLA was happening the government was enveloped in serious political and economic problems. Just as the 'milk incident' had taught Thatcher a lesson, I suspect she learnt another from watching as the ROSLA saga unfold. Faced with implementing a major change to the country's schools she had witnessed the education experts and the LEAs fail to deliver. When she became prime minister and wanted to overhaul the education system, she would do things very differently.

In early 1974 there was a general election and Labour returned to power. Thatcher became the shadow minister of the environment but before leaving the Ministry was given a farewell party by her civil servants. *The Times* reported[311] one of them saying that 'it is a unique occasion, never before had an outgoing education secretary been given a parting on this scale'. The article went on to say that 'historians will probably judge her achievements as remarkable'. What a prophetic statement.

The new Labour government removed any doubts that the selective system of secondary education was finished and brought with it the death of secondary moderns. What replaced them was not just a different system of education but schools that were struggling to adapt, in the aftermath of ROSLA, and to embrace the new progressive teaching practices. That was not all. There was a change in the old hierarchical relationship between teacher and pupil as the mentality of the 'swinging sixties' entered the classroom.

To sum up – what did actually change over the 30 years?

I tried, and failed, to end this section by writing a few pithy sentences that summarised the past 30 years. Since the start of the timeline, during WWII, there had been huge changes in attitudes towards education and in the structure of society, but the same mistakes kept being made. The time for summarising and drawing conclusions will have to wait until I have finished the final section of the timeline.

I think the best way of ending 'Birth and death' is to contrast its educational and economic metrics with those of the first 30 years of the timeline. This 'helicopter' view of the period demonstrates the magnitude of the change.

The economic importance of education

Following the economic disruption of WWII the percentage of the country's GDP spent on education rose consistently and ended at almost double
the maximum it had reached in the first part of the timeline.[312]

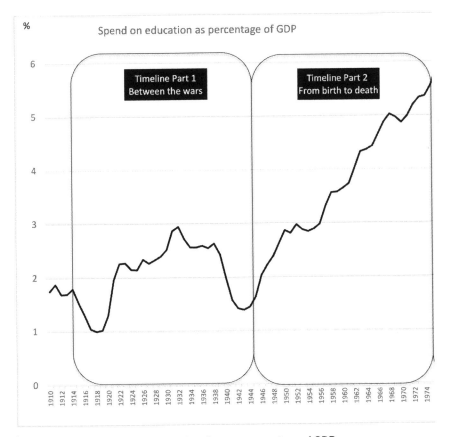

| The total government spend on education as a percentage of GDP

Increase in the numbers of secondary school children

The baby boom of the mid-1940s returned the population of children and young adults to the levels reached in the 1920s. However, the magnitude of 'boom' resulted in continual classroom and teacher shortages.[313]

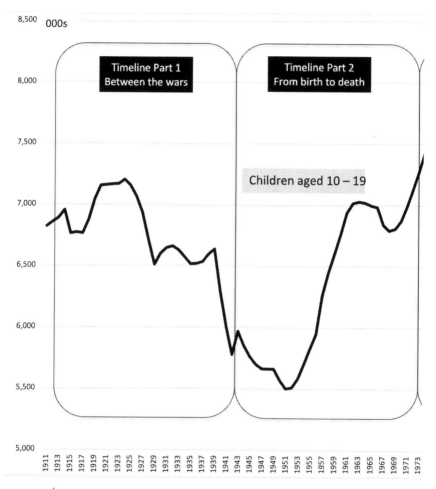

The numbers of children and young adults aged 10 –19

The economy required a higher standard of education

Demand for unskilled labour declined as jobs increasingly required higher-skilled and better-educated employees.[314]

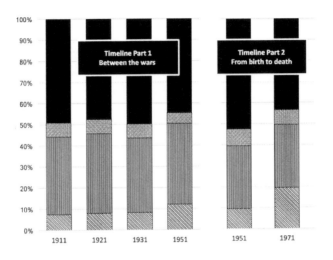

■ Routine and semi-routine

▓ Small employers & own account workers

▥ Administrative, lower supervisory and technical occupations

▨ Managerial and professional occupations

| Change in the UK's occupation profile

A time of relative national prosperity

Average earnings almost doubled during the period. Despite the fragile state of the economy, consumers experienced a significant increase in their spending power.[315]

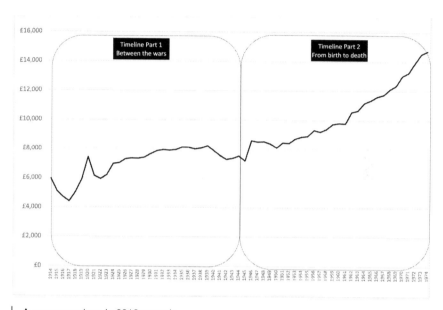

Average earnings in 2010 pounds

A period of near-full employment

The high unemployment rates of the first part of the timeline had gone. Throughout the second part there was no shortage of work, although things were beginning to change towards the end of the period.[316]

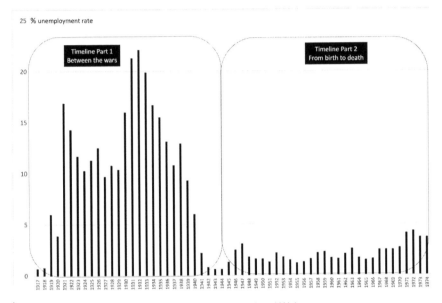

| Unemployment rate (aged 16 and over) in England and Wales

Increasing industrial unrest and disruption

The number of days lost to strikes increased towards the end of the period, causing economic and political problems for both Labour and the Conservatives.[317]

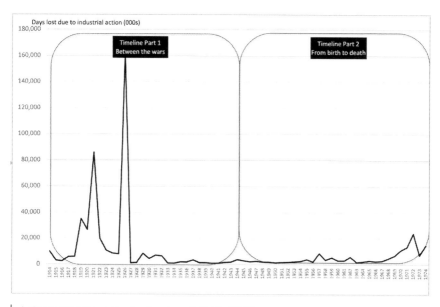

| Labour disputes, annual estimates – 1891 to 2018

CHAPTER 7

THE COMPREHENSIVE ERA

At the close of 1974, less than a quarter of pupils attended secondary moderns. A decade later the figure had shrunk to 5%. Almost all of the LEAs were moving to comprehensivisation and abandoning the tripartite system and the 11-plus. Meanwhile, educationalists and media pundits were busy writing the secondary modern's obituary. As we've already seen, it wasn't complimentary.

So began the comprehensive era.

After a gestation period of 30 years, involving the wholesale rearrangement of secondary schools, did comprehensivisation fulfil its supporters' promise to improve the quality and fairness of secondary education? This will always be a difficult question to answer, made even harder by the effects of other changes taking place. New 'progressive' teaching techniques, national and global events affecting the economy and society's changing attitudes to authority all influenced what was happening inside the classroom. Trying to isolate the success or failure of the comprehensive system from the results of these other factors is mighty difficult – maybe impossible.

Providing a succinct account of these schools' performance is complicated by the polarisation of opinions in how commentators have related their history. As much as I hate generalisations, I am going to generalise here. Much of the published material seems intent on justifying the rationale for their existence and extolling their benefits over selective schooling. A much smaller body of commentary is focused on highlighting their failures and associating them with all the ills of society. Labour Party politicians and most educationalists had staked their reputations on comprehensivisation succeeding. Equally partisan were the Conservatives and their supporters, who believed comprehensives would fail to provide the levels of excellence of the grammar schools. When a subject is discussed in ideological – rather than rational – terms, the chance of encountering inaccuracies caused by author bias increases. Echoes of the Brexit 'debate'!

Before embarking on this final part of the timeline, I therefore reminded myself about the dangers of biased behaviour that I related in Chapter 1 ('The truth is what you want it to be'). You might want to do the same.

It was never my intention to recount the story of the comprehensives in the same detail as their predecessors. The definitive critique of comprehensives is yet to be written, but somebody else can accept that challenge. My approach when writing this section of the timeline was much the same as before. I have related the chronology of events, but with less use of the original documents at the National Archive. Instead I have relied more on the biographies of the politicians who were responsible for making and delivering the policies. Wherever possible I have supplemented this with commentary from the media and the views of historians and educational academics, all the time being aware of their possible bias.

And so starts the final part of the timeline.

During a lecture, the historian David Kynaston talked about the 1960s having a zeitgeist that was more complex than unbridled individualism combined with 'sex, drugs and rock and roll'. No doubt the zeitgeist of the 1970s was equally complicated but, if the period – especially the latter half – had to be distilled into a few words they would be 'uncertain and disruptive'; perhaps 'depressing' should also be added.

Central government v the LEAs – a familiar story

On taking power the Labour Party resumed its quest to force all the recalcitrant LEAs to abandon selective education and to 'go comprehensive'. Within a month of becoming minister Reginald Prentice withdrew Thatcher's circular that enabled the LEAs to decide their secondary schooling and issued his own (Circular 4/74[1]). LEAs were expected to 'direct their efforts to planning the organisation of secondary schools in such a way as to avoid the need for selection'. Labour had criticised Thatcher for failing to consult the LEAs and teachers, but Prentice did exactly the same thing, issuing his circular within a month of taking office. Of all the Ministry circulars I have studied this was the worst written. Much of the language was vague and the logical flow was poor. Despite these failings its intent was clear – Labour wanted all of the LEAs to abandon selective education, even though local government was undergoing a major reorganisation as a result of the 1972 Local Government Act. Yet again a politician paying scant attention to the practical difficulties of satisfying their demands.

It was not only the LEA schools that Prentice wanted converted to comprehensives, but also the direct grant grammar schools that educated both fee-paying and publicly funded pupils. Way back in 1970, the Donnison Committee,[2] which owed its origins to Crosland, had recommended, 'That schools which intend to secure continuing support from public funds [direct grant grammar] must participate in the movement towards comprehensive education.'

Prentice intended to make this a reality when he declared in Parliament[3] his intention to stop LEAs using direct grant schools, starting in September 1976. He was forcing these schools to make the choice of converting to state-run comprehensives or becoming exclusively for privately funded pupils. A large majority (70%) took the latter option.[4] Those that became comprehensives were mainly Roman Catholic schools that lacked the financial means to operate independently. In what the Conservative shadow minister described as 'an unprecedented step of educational vandalism' Prentice removed over 14,000 grammar school places from the state system.[5] Some of the most prestigious schools in the country were lost to the state system, including Haberdashers' Aske's School, Latymer Upper School and Manchester Grammar. Commenting about this event, Brian Simon said:[6]

This was scarcely a satisfactory solution but at least it put an end to this anomaly which remained a contentious issue since the war.

To my mind, removing access to so many high-quality schools from children whose parents could not afford their fees was a high price to pay to end an 'anomaly'.

If implementing the Labour Party's election manifesto was a measure of success, then Prentice scored highly, especially considering how brief his period as minister was. He had wielded a stick to persuade the LEAs to implement comprehensivisation and removed the 'anomaly' of direct grant grammar schools. From the perspective of the average pupil his performance was not so good, providing nothing in the way of carrot to improve the quality of their schools and teaching.

Bernard Donoughue, the head of Harold Wilson's Policy Unit, thought Prentice 'seemed inactive' but tempered this criticism by quoting the prime minister, who thought the Ministry was powerless and little more than a 'post box' between local authorities and teachers' unions.[7]

Prentice was soon replaced by Fred Mulley. Both held office for one year and three months, just enough time to understand their brief but not enough to make much positive difference. Mulley continued the 'battle', because that is what it had become, with the LEAs that were delaying or refusing to 'go comprehensive'. A third of them claimed they couldn't make the conversion until after 1980 and a few flatly refused to abandon their grammar schools.[8] Some of the 'hold-outs' were supporters of comprehensivisation but refused to convert unless they received additional funds, something the dire economic conditions made difficult. A little 'new money' was made available in 1975 (£190 million in today's pounds) but that was more of a gesture than a serious attempt to fund the required changes to the schools' infrastructure.

In July 1975 Mulley issued yet another circular,[9] which confirmed the end of direct grant grammar schools and at the beginning of 1976 he shepherded a new education act through Parliament. After years of trying, Labour had eventually passed legislation that 'required' rather than 'requested' the LEAs to produce plans that ended selective education.[10]

He [the secretary of state] may require the authority to prepare and submit to him, within such time as he may specify, proposals for the purpose of giving effect to that principle [comprehensivisation].

It wasn't until late 1976 that the bill became law and by then he was no longer minister. If Mulley is remembered at all, it is for the change in sentiment towards education that occurred during his time in office.

Bad marks for progressive teaching

The fourth of the Black Papers[11] had been published just before he became minister and its criticism of the state of secondary education had been widely reported. In a leader article, *The Times* commented:

> *The suppressed suspicion that such doubts [about comprehensives and progressive teaching techniques] are in fact quite widespread is perhaps one reason why comprehensive enthusiasts have greeted the successive Black Papers with such dismissive fury.*[12]

In what I think was a balanced article, it went on to criticise the Black Papers for blaming all the ills afflicting schools on the 'comprehensive system'.

> *Certainly, reorganisation has made these ills [deteriorating standards of achievement and behaviour] more visible but many other factors, the growing size of schools, the changing attitude of teachers and the decline of traditional authority in the family at work, and in the state itself, have contributed to the disturbing conditions in some secondary schools.*

If the Black Papers could be scorned as the work of education traditionalists, the findings of a study by the University of Lancaster (known as 'the Bennett study') were harder to dismiss.[13] Its objective was to answer two questions: 'do differing teaching styles result in disparate pupil progress?' and 'do different types of pupils perform better under certain styles of teaching?' A large number of the primary schools in Lancashire and Cumbria (766) took part in the project. The study reached many conclusions, all with caveats explaining the limitations of the research methodology, but when they were reported in press the messages were stark and simple:

- The effect of teaching style is statistically and educationally significant in all attainment areas. In reading, pupils of formal and mixed styles of teaching progress more than those of informal teachers. The same applies to the teaching of maths.
- Teaching well using the informal style is more difficult than under the traditional formal method. It requires a special sort of teacher to use informal methods effectively. The implication was that in many cases the teachers were far from 'special'.
- Progressive teaching is likely to be less effective, particularly with brighter children and anxious ones.

'Please Sir, Don't be Trendy' was how *The Daily Mirror* reported the study.[14] The *Observer's* headline was more damning: 'How progressive schooling has failed'.[15] In more measured words the editor of *The Times Educational Supplement* said:[16]

Now for the first time there is a piece of solid research which measures the progress of pupils under different types of classroom regime and comes up with clear-cut and uncompromising findings.

The Guardian was a lone voice in attacking the research and concluded that the 'explanation for the results lies in the random difference in the quality of teachers'.[17]

Five years after the research was published its conclusions were questioned when the data was re-analysed using more sophisticated statistical techniques,[18] resulting in a critical analysis being published in 2006.[19] I am not equipped to pass judgement on the accuracy of the research; in truth, whether the results were right or wrong is now only of academic interest. What is important is that the report's conclusions resonated with the concerns being expressed about the failures of the new teaching techniques.

The 'mood music' about progressive education, and by association comprehensives, turned even darker when the press started reporting the chaotic state of a junior school in Islington, a borough in north London. In 1974, Terry Ellis became headmaster of William Tyndale Junior School, which had 220 pupils drawn from a catchment area of working and middle class families. Like many schools it was short of teachers and equipment and suffered from high staff turnover.

In the course of the next two years the education practices that Ellis and a fellow teacher (Brian Haddow) introduced created a rift among the teaching staff, with some supporting their ideals and others vehemently against them. As the conflict became more vitriolic parents withdrew their children, pupil numbers plummeted and press interest soared.

What should have been resolved in a matter of weeks escalated into a national news story that ended with the dismissal of the headmaster and six teachers, the resignation of a senior official at the Inner London Education Authority and the intervention of the prime minister.

Every detail of this saga was forensically analysed and documented during a public enquiry, conducted by Robin Auld, QC, who was tasked with understanding what had gone wrong and who was to blame. After considering a million words of evidence, his 300-page report was published in August 1976.[20] Costing over £400,000, in today's pounds, the report read like a high court judgment. The media portrayed it as a verdict against the techniques and ideals of progressive teaching and the poor management of the LEA.

Even with the benefit of 40 years of hindsight it is difficult to understand how the misfortunes of an insignificant junior school triggered a change in direction and management of the country's education policy. I will do my best to explain.

Ellis and Haddow had been at university in the 1960s and, like many, entered the teaching profession with 'progressive' ideals about how education could change society. They were very much a product of their times, full of high ideals but not so good at fulfilling them.

Their views were broadcast to an increasingly wide audience as William Tyndale went from being a local Islington issue to a national news story that questioned the effectiveness of the entire country's education system. The failings of a few staff in this tiny London school eventually embroiled the LEA, the Ministry and the minister.

Why were newspaper readers so interested in the story? I think it must have been because William Tyndale's chaotic state symbolised millions of parents' worst nightmares about how their children were being 'educated'. No doubt they had heard much about 'progressive education' but now they were seeing the reality of what that meant. Children were able to plan their own schooling day and select the subjects they wanted to study. Teachers' role was one of encouragement, rather than imparting knowledge. Theoretically, children were taught by teams of teachers but often this resulted in a disorganised muddle. Come the end of the affair Ellis, Haddow and their supporters refused to allow the school to be inspected. All of this was a world away from the schooling that parents had experienced.

Some of the media defended Ellis's teaching techniques, claiming that when they were practised by skilled practitioners they worked well. There was always the subtext that if they were poorly executed they resulted in an undisciplined muddle. That is pretty much what happened at William Tyndale. Parents became increasingly concerned that their children were not learning 'the basics' and voted with their feet. At the end of the saga the school roll had fallen below 100.

Two journalists from *The Times Literary Supplement* published a book about the William Tyndale affair[21] and concluded:

> *The powers and responsibilities of LEAs, the control of the curriculum, the criteria for assessing a school's efficiency, the aims of education, the need for testing, the role of the inspectorate, the function of school managers and the professionalism and accountability of teachers – are proper subjects for consideration by the Secretary of State for Education.*

> *After William Tyndale, he can no longer pretend, as he and his predecessors have so often tended to do, that it is all happening somewhere else.*

Comprehensive education was not an issue in this story, but it was swept up with the concerns about education standards and the competence of those running the country's schools and their motivations. That was not all, according to Simon: 'Teaching had been brought into disrepute. Teachers' control of the curriculum – their autonomy – was now very sharply called into question.'

Mulley must have watched this saga unfold with horror, but feeling powerless to intervene given that the LEA had day-to-day control. His list of misfortunes was about to get longer, as were his feelings of impotence to effect change. Tameside was an education authority in Greater Manchester and had, under the Labour-controlled council, decided to 'go comprehensive'. Following a local election, the Conservatives were returned to power and cancelled the plans. Mulley tried to over-rule the decision and a legal battle ensued, concluding with the House of Lords deciding he had acted unlawfully. On 3 August 1976 he was forced to address the House of Commons and admit defeat.[22]

It's hard to believe but there was one further humiliation awaiting Mulley. This wasn't delivered at the hands of courts or the Conservatives but by his boss – James Callaghan, the new prime minister. Harold Wilson had astonished the nation and resigned on 16 March 1976. I remember hearing the news and along with everybody else was baffled by his decision. There was no prior warning or speculation leading up to the announcement – one day he was prime minister and the next day he had gone. If the TV series *The Crown* is to be believed, he had been diagnosed as having Alzheimer's.[23] I doubt if we will ever know the reason for his abrupt departure.

Callaghan was his successor and as part of his 'getting to understand his brief' process met Mulley during May 1976. According to the diary of Callaghan's senior policy adviser, Bernard Donoughue, he was not impressed.[24]

He [Callaghan] quizzed Mulley for a solid hour, very cleverly, innocent questions, but absolutely on the ball. The weaknesses of the DES [Department of Education and Science] – and Mulley – were exposed.

According to Clyde Chitty the 'innocent' questions covered four areas.[25]

- Was he satisfied with the basic teaching of the three Rs?
- Was the curriculum sufficiently relevant and penetrating for older children in comprehensive schools, especially in the teaching of science and mathematics?
- How did the exam system shape up as a test of achievement?
- What was available for the further education of 16–19 year olds?

What happened next is vague and the story differs depending on whose account you read. We know for certain that the Ministry created a document[26] to answer Callaghan's questions. Did Mulley or the prime minister and his advisers brief the Ministry on the document's contents? I am not sure, and the answer really doesn't matter. Likewise, why the document had a yellow cover (and so was known as the 'yellow book') is another mystery. Perhaps the Ministry officials wanted to ensure it wasn't seen as a government green or white paper?

Two months after their meeting the document was completed. In the introduction it stated that the prime minister requested its creation and explained that it would address the same questions that Mulley had been asked. It made interesting reading, echoing the concerns that were circulating about the state of the country's education system.

I had to smile when I read what it said about secondary moderns:

> *The secondary modern school failed to hold its own when the tide towards comprehensive education began to flow strongly in the early '60s. Nevertheless, some became very good schools and the subsequent development of comprehensive education could not have proceeded as it did without their pioneering work in adapting secondary education to the needs of the less able.*

It's an interesting (and incorrect) narrative to portray secondary moderns as being part of an evolutionary process that resulted in comprehensivisation. As we have seen, that is a distortion of the truth. I do agree with statement about their 'pioneering work' since for most of their brief existence they were in 'experimentation mode' and responding to the latest ideas in educational theory.

Although much of the document defended the status quo and explained forthcoming Ministry initiatives, it also detailed the failings of schools in unusually frank language.

Much was said about deficiencies in the teaching workforce. I have highlighted in bold the phrases that probably made Mulley wince.

> *The teaching force contains a disproportionate number of young and inexperienced teachers. In the less definable qualities of skill and*

personality, while the best teachers are up to very high standards, **the average is probably below what used to be expected, in, for example, a good grammar school.**

One consequence of teacher inexperience (in some cases, incapacity) may have been overcompensation for their worries over disciplinary problems. Many teachers have felt these to have been **accentuated by comprehensive reorganisation and the raising of the school-leaving age.**

In an almost desperate attempt to modify styles of teaching and learning so as to capture the imagination and enlist the cooperation of their more difficult pupils, some of them have possibly been **too ready to drop their sights in setting standards of performance, and have failed to develop new styles of assessment.**

Unfortunately, these newer and freer methods could prove a trap to less able and experienced teachers who failed to recognise that they required a careful and systematic monitoring of the progress of individual children in specific skills, as well as a careful planning of the opportunities offered to them.

A further weakness, as we may now perceive it, is that some teachers and some schools may have **over-emphasised the importance of preparing boys and girls for their roles in society** *compared with the need to prepare them for their economic role [i.e. getting and doing a job].*

There were also some disturbing comments of a more general nature.

A further source of worry is the **variation in the curriculum followed by pupils in different schools or parts of the country** *or in different ability bands. The time has probably come to try to establish generally accepted principles for the composition of the secondary curriculum for all pupils, that is to say a 'core curriculum'.*

The greatest concern, however, is for the 40% of school leavers who leave school at 16 and get no further education or vocational training.

*The criticisms commonly heard of the primary schools may be imprecise and vague but they fall into a recognisable and fairly consistent pattern. They are not narrowly confined to any particular social or economic group. They **blame the schools for a lack of discipline and application, and a failure to achieve satisfactory results** in formal subjects, particularly in reading and arithmetic.*

It is difficult not to feel sorry for Mulley. These were long-standing failings and it was his misfortune that they were catapulted to national attention during his short time as minister. His authority was further diminished (if that was possible) when the prime minister decided to make the state of the country's education system an issue that, in today's language, he 'wanted to own'. Donoughue's diary claimed this was his idea, as was the decision to use Callaghan's speech at Ruskin College Oxford[27] as its launchpad.

The 'great debate' begins

Chitty confirmed that Donoughue and his policy unit, not Mulley and the Ministry, were responsible for the speech's contents and went on to recount the furore that erupted when sections of it were leaked to the press, just days before the event. Was this part of an organised government media campaign or the work of a disgruntled civil servant? What role (if any) did the yellow book play in determining the contents of the speech? All are interesting questions but there is one that I think is more important. The accepted narrative is that Callaghan's adoption of education as his personal project was a proactive decision, the decision of a statesman driven by a desire to improve the country's education system. This is a plausible story, but equally believable is that it was the reaction of a politician who was aware that the problems engulfing Mulley were damaging his government.

There is no doubt that Donoughue was a key player in this story, and we know that he was worried about the radicalisation of the teaching profession. Living in Islington, the location of William Tyndale, had just given him first-hand experience of the damage this could inflict on children's education. He must have known that the public would associate the ills of progressive education with the left of politics and that meant the Labour Party. The more I read about Donoughue the more I warmed to his character. Maybe it had something to do with our shared experience of attending a secondary modern before moving to a grammar school. It is clear from his autobiography[28] that he held a deep distrust about the motives of those in the Labour Party who were so anxious to destroy grammar schools.

The achievements of Nettleton [the name of his grammar school] were vandalised by the egalitarian experiments and politically correct claptrap of the local Labour Party.

He was equally forthright about the 'disappointing' comprehensive school his sons attended in London. There was a paradox at the heart of his views about education. His writing dripped with contempt for much of the education establishment, especially the NUT and Ministry officials, but if anybody could change things it was the elite that he was part of, his friends and colleagues. He portrayed events as if he were an 'observer' rather than part of the story.

The speech was given in Oxford on 18 October 1976, to the background noise of student militants demonstrating about cuts to the education budget. It was titled 'A rational debate based on the facts', now abbreviated to the 'great debate'. I am always wary when politicians call for a 'debate'. Invariably it means they plan to make a 'pronouncement' and have already made up their minds – and so it proved in this case.

There was enough ambiguity in the speech's language that it could be portrayed both as a major policy statement and as the musings of a reasonable man who was worried about the state of education. Much of it covered the political niceties of thanking everybody for doing a splendid job and claiming how well Labour was serving the county, but there were words of criticism – lots of them. Callaghan made 10 observations, sometimes phrased as questions, sometimes as recommendations and all but one related to schools. I have stripped out the caveats and pleasantries, to list the essence of his claims.

- Standards must improve.
- Education policy cannot be left to the experts.
- The worries of parents and employers about standards cannot be ignored.
- Informal methods of teaching need excellent teachers; not all are.
- Is there a need for a basic curriculum with universal standards? Callaghan thought there was.
- It is a laudable goal to create socially well-adjusted pupils, but they must also have basic skills and knowledge.
- Improving the education system cannot rely on more funding – budgets aren't going to increase.
- The quality of schools (and teachers) needs more rigorous inspection.
- The proposed new exam that merges CSEs and GCEs needs further refinement – an indirect criticism of the Schools Council.
- Not enough university science students are encouraged (or able) to follow a career in industry.

Towards the end of his speech he said 'my remarks are not a clarion call to Black Paper prejudices'. That claim would have been even harder to defend had he used the original version of the speech, which according to Donoughue's diary contained more explicit and critical language.

To my mind his speech and the yellow book marked the end of the Labour Party's single-minded obsession with comprehensivisation to the exclusion of all other education issues. Callaghan had admitted that there were problems with the culture and practice of teaching and verbalised topics that had long been claimed by the Black Papers and his political adversaries. The Conservative education spokesman wryly commented that Callaghan was probably asking the right questions but 'we would have expected more firm answers'.[29] Three years after returning to power, Labour was only now recognising there was more to education than 'going comprehensive'.

The newspapers gave a favourable response to the speech. *The Daily Mirror* headline read 'Big Jim's teachin-in – Premier calls for a hard look at learning';[30] *The Times* was more measured: 'Mr Callaghan calls for improved education standards'.[31]

Educational historians tend to attribute darker motives for the speech. This is what Simon said.

> *On a political level to steal the thunder of the Black Paperites and their colleagues (in the Tory Party), but, on a deeper level, to assert new forms of control over the social order – to issue a clear warning that educational developments should not get out of hand; in short to slam the lid and screw it securely down.*

Chitty believed the speech was:

> *An attempt to wrest the populist mantle from the Conservative Opposition and pander to perceived public disquiet at the alleged decline in educational standards. Sections of the popular press had played a major role in undermining public confidence in the comprehensive system; and popular reservations about 'progressive' teaching styles appeared to be justified by the William Tyndale case and the Bennett study.*

So was the Ruskin College speech given by Callaghan 'the politician', who was reacting to the 'alleged decline' in education standards, or Callaghan 'the statesman', who was genuinely concerned with the state of the country's schooling? Had he skilfully identified the 'hot buttons' that he knew would resonate with parents or did he believe the criticisms listed in his speech? I tend to believe the latter.

Kathryn Riley spoke to Callaghan and Donoughue when writing her book *Whose school is it anyway?*[32] Having read these interviews I am convinced that the speech 'came from the heart' (perhaps more of Donoughue's heart than Callaghan's) and was motivated by both men's contempt for the 'trendy left' ideas that were prevalent among educationalists. That Callaghan's daughter sent her daughter to a private, rather than state, school might also have influenced his actions. These words from Donoghue could well have been extracted from one of the Black Papers.

There was clear evidence that working-class parents and children wanted education and what they wanted was not the same as the middle-class Labour people from Islington, the trendy lecturers from higher education who wanted education at the expense of working-class kids. Whenever I heard those people talk, I got very angry... Their thinking was based on Guardian *style ideologies and prejudices.*

As I wrote this section, I kept thinking how the education of untold children had been affected by the cranky ideas that had taken hold in many of the country's secondary schools. How could the authorities, be they central or local government, let things get so bad?

Labour lays the foundations for the Conservative policies of the 80s

By this time Mulley had been moved to the Ministry of Defence and been replaced by Shirley Williams. At the time of Callaghan's speech, she had been in office for a month and now she had the dubious honour of leading the 'great debate'.

The accounts of her two and half years as minister were surprisingly consistent. She was liked but thought to be ineffective – a good 'talker', but poor at 'delivering'. These assessments may be accurate, but her performance must be judged in the context of the situation she inherited. Her agenda had been set by the prime minister and she was part of a government that was under severe strain, as we will soon see. Another common criticism was that she ceded authority to her Ministry officials, who used the opportunity to strengthen their powers.[33]

The Great Debate was a very poor substitute for a coherent policy on education. Shirley Williams had allowed the Great Debate and the ensuing Green Paper to be 'captured' by her Ministry officials.

As far as I can see, little came of the debate. Williams chaired eight regional events that I assume contributed towards a green paper published in July 1977. She spoke about the debate 'showing the strong support for comprehensive education' along with a 'strong undercurrent of worry about the mastery of basic literacy and numeracy, shared not only by parents but also by employers'.[34] Her recollections were little more than an echo of the Ruskin College speech.

Donoughue's diary provided a detailed account of the green paper's troubled history. Initially it was rejected by the Cabinet, being 'sparse in content and complacent in tone'. Following multiple redrafts (*The Guardian* reported six versions[35]) it was accepted, but with reservations. Clearly, he wasn't enamoured of the outcome: 'The paper represented Whitehall at its self-satisfied, condescending and unimaginative worst.'

Only three of its 200 paragraphs were devoted to the growing public criticisms of the current system, with only three bland paragraphs on 'standards' and 'discipline'.

In the short term, I doubt if the document made a jot of difference to the quality of children's schooling, but it did explain why parents and industry had justified concerns.

Undoubtedly higher standards have been more difficult to achieve in recent years because of the high rates of wastage and turnover among teachers in primary and secondary schools, especially in some deprived urban areas. In 1962, the proportion of teachers who left the profession – the wastage rate – was 8.4% ; by 1972, it had risen to 9.5% and in addition a further 11% changed schools. In some urban areas the percentages were much higher: as many as 25% of all teachers in some LEAs left their schools during 1973.

The pace of change has outstripped the supply of appropriately qual- ified and experienced teachers. Some did not understand sufficiently clearly the nature of the changes on which they were embarking, nor did they all have the benefit of adequate support from in-service courses. This is particularly true of teachers changing from a grammar or secondary modern school to a comprehensive one, usually faced with teaching pupils of a wider or different range of ability.

Had I been a teacher reading these words I would have been mighty annoyed. Rather than attributing these problems to those who made the radical changes (politicians and their officials) they shifted the blame to those at the chalk face. Changing a massive infrastructure system, like secondary schooling, causes disruption and that has a 'cost' in both financial and human terms. Politicians repeatedly failed to take this into account and sadly still do.

What the green paper did achieve was to question the status quo and propose changes that Labour was unwilling and probably incapable of implementing – unlike the Conservatives, who pursued them in ways that Williams could never have envisaged.

Her paper proposed the mildest of changes to the setting of the schools' curriculum. Couched in lots of vague words about 'consultations' and 'reviewing frameworks' it suggested that 'parts of the curriculum should be protected because there are aims common to all schools and pupils'. This became the national curriculum, introduced in 1988.

Another recommendation, which a Conservative government implemented, was the 'need for a coherent and soundly-based means of assessment for individual pupils and schools' – 15 years later the Office for Standards in Education (Ofsted) was established.

An initiative the paper delayed was the merging of the GCE and CSE into a single exam – the Conservatives went ahead with this idea with the first pupils taking GCSEs in 1988.

There were a few instances when the green paper made firm recommendations. One was the rejection of the 'idea that rigid and uniform national tests should be applied to all children at certain ages'. The Conservatives disagreed and introduced Standard Attainment Tests (SATs) in 1990. The other was the rejection of 'league tables' based on exams or standardised test results 'as they could be seriously misleading'. These were introduced by the Conservatives in 1992.

I had to smile when I read Williams' account of the paper's long-term intent to make the teaching profession all-graduate entry.[36] At the time, her contribution was to make 'O' level passes in English and maths a minimum entry requirement. I suppose that was a start to improving teachers' academic credentials.

What else did Williams do during her time as minister? Like her predecessors she was responsible for a couple of circulars to force LEAs to submit plans to change their secondary schools to comprehensives.[37, 38] By the time she left office there were only a handful of authorities still refusing to ditch selective education. How much her circulars influenced the LEAs' decisions is impossible to know, but I doubt it was a great deal.

In May 1978, Baroness Warnock's committee published its report about the education of handicapped children and young people. Initiated by Thatcher in November 1973, the study had had a long gestation period. Williams did little with the report's findings other than to initiate 'extensive consultation with special interest groups'. Yet again, it was left to the Conservatives to turn the recommendations into actions.[39]

During the final period of the Callaghan government, Williams attempted to give parents more rights to select their child's secondary school, an idea that was opposed and defeated by the comprehensive purists in the Labour Party, especially Tony and Caroline Benn. Another idea that initially came to nothing but that the Conservatives adopted.

This list of initiatives that Williams failed to adopt appears to confirm her reputation as a person who would rather talk than act. It's very easy to accept this account but before doing so it is necessary to understand what else was going on during her period as minister.

I have already mentioned that the Labour government was under 'severe strain', but I expect that is a common complaint for all of those wielding political power. Few would disagree that the economic and political shenanigans resulting from Brexit have created a fair amount of 'strain'. Each era of politicians faces different challenges, but during the late 1970s the financial and social instability that engulfed the Labour Cabinet was immense. Williams was minister in a very different country from today's.[40] These words were written before the Covid-19 pandemic and it is too early to know if the resulting disruption will be worse than that facing the Labour Cabinet.

- In 1979 30 million days were lost to industrial action compared with 0.3 million in 2018.
- Between 1974 and 1979 the average inflation rate was 15.7%, peaking at 24% in 1975. In July 2019 it was 2.1%.

- Between 1974 and 1979 the average interest rate was 10.5%, peaking at 17% in late 1979. The rate in 2019 was 0.75%
- In 1979 the unemployment rate was 5.4%. In July 2019 it was 3.8%.

When Williams first became minister, she and her Cabinet colleagues faced a deterioration in the country's finances that required a huge loan from the IMF. At the time it was the largest loan the IMF had made to any country (£26 billion in today's pounds) and it came with many politically sensitive conditions.[41] It has been suggested that Callaghan used the IMF's involvement to try and impose economic discipline on his Cabinet colleagues – an indicator of the political disunity he faced.[42]

Throughout Williams' time as minister the country bounced from one crisis to another. These extreme economic conditions resulted in equally extreme political tensions within the government. Attempting to govern with a tiny majority resulted in constant battles between the different factions. As well as being minister, Williams was involved in all of these events.

The final blow to Callaghan's government came at the beginning of 1979 when the UK was engulfed in deep snow and blizzards – it ranked as one of the worst winters of all time. I have clear memories of the time, not because of the low temperatures but the huge piles of rubbish that were all over London. Each day I walked past a mountain of black rubbish bags that filled Leicester Square. This was the 'Winter of Discontent' when strikes sanctioned by trade unions, mainly in the public sector, created havoc to day-to-day life. It was every bit as grim and depressing as the accounts of the time portray.

The snow eventually disappeared, as did the piles of rubbish, but the Labour government was finished and eventually lost power to a vote of no confidence at the end of March 1979. Williams lost her seat at the ensuing election and by 1981 had resigned from the Labour Party to become a founder of the Social Democratic Party (SDP).

Labour had been in power for just under 2,000 days and what had it achieved? It had given more teeth to the legislation, forcing LEAs to 'go comprehensive', but the move in that direction was already well under way. It had been forced to confront the widespread disquiet about the state of the country's schools but had done little to change them. It had been involved in a continuous tussle with the trade unions – including the teaching unions – and had lost.

Recounting these times reminds me why I associate the words 'uncertain, disruptive and depressing' with the atmosphere of the late 1970s.

The memory of these times left deep scars on the British electorate and Labour was not to return to power for 18 years, but it had achieved its primary objective of converting almost all of the secondary schools to comprehensives – just 500 secondary modern schools remained. Had this delivered an improvement in the quality of children's education? The problems that emerged during Callaghan's 'great debate' suggested that the answer was somewhere between 'unlikely but maybe' and 'no'. Donoughue was of the mind that 'little change was visible in schools' and: 'it awaited Mrs Thatcher's – and Tony Blair's – new and radical broom to make any serious practical progress.'

So begins the Thatcher era

On 3 May 1979 Mrs Thatcher established two 'firsts' in the history of UK prime ministers. She was the first woman to hold the post and the first person who had also been minister of education. She would remain prime minister for just under 12 years, the seventh longest of all time.

The Conservative manifesto echoed many of the concerns that Callaghan had raised in his 'great debate' speech and summarised its attack on Labour's education record with the statement:

> *The Labour Party is still obsessed with the structure of the schools' system and not the quality of education.*

The Conservatives' solution was to do the following.

- Repeal the legislation that 'compels LEAs to reorganise along comprehensive lines'.
- Set national standards for reading, writing and arithmetic that are monitored by tests.
- Create a parents' charter that places a duty on government and LEAs to take account of their wishes when allocating schools.

- Ensure schools publish prospectuses giving details of their exams and other results.
- Restore the direct grant principle to enable bright children from modest backgrounds to attend private schools.

Labour's manifesto said little about education other than the usual promise to convert all secondary schools to comprehensives and to re-echo its long-held aspiration to 'end fee paying independent schools'. Forty years later, Labour was still promising to abolish these schools and, in addition, to 'redistribute their endowments, investments and properties to the state sector.'[43] Six months after these extreme threats the policy was tempered to a more traditional Labour Party policy of handing the issue to a 'commission' to decide.[44]

Closing the tax loopholes enjoyed by elite private schools and use that money to improve the lives of all children, and we will ask the Social Justice Commission to advise on integrating private schools and creating a comprehensive education system.

Education was unlikely to be Thatcher's main priority on entering Downing Street. She inherited a country in economic turmoil. Trade unions had wreaked havoc on the Callaghan government and their attitude to a Conservative prime minister was likely to be even more confrontational – if that was possible. Not surprisingly, three times more space in the manifesto explained the Conservative Party's trade unions policy than its intentions about education.

We cannot go on, year after year, tearing ourselves apart in increasingly bitter and calamitous industrial disputes. Between 1974 and 1976, Labour enacted a 'militants' charter' of trade union legislation. It tilted the balance of power in bargaining throughout industry away from responsible management and towards unions.[45]

The first priority of the new minister (Mark Carlisle) was to end the disruption that the teaching unions were causing in schools. Demanding a salary increase of 36.5%, teachers were 'working to rule', resulting in schools closing early, lunchtime meals being unsupervised and children's exams being disrupted. This huge salary claim needs to be viewed in context: inflation in 1979 was 13.5% and the starting salary for teachers was £15,000, in today's pounds – half that earned by today's teachers working in London.

Carlisle's second priority was to repeal Labour's Education Act (1976) and to halt the legal proceedings against LEAs refusing to abandon selective education and 'go comprehensive'.[46] This ping-pong of passing and repealing legislation, every time a new government was elected, had been going on since 1970.

Within a year, further legislation was passed that reinstated the assisted-places scheme, whereby the state paid for some children to attend private schools. This act also enabled parents to express a preference over which school their children attended and required schools to publish their admissions policies.[47]

Conservative politicians inherited a system of schooling that at best they tolerated and at worst they hated. Now that 80% of secondary schools were comprehensives, turning back the clock to the old tripartite system was not a realistic option. Anyway, Thatcher knew from personal experience that as long as the power resided with the LEAs and the schools, central government would be little more than a spectator in determining the evolution of secondary schooling. This is pretty much how Callaghan and his predecessor had seen the situation, too.

The days when LEAs managed the tactics and much of the strategy of secondary education policy, nudged along by central government interventions, were drawing to an end. The views of teachers and parents had always played some part in determining policy, but their voices were getting louder and their influence increasing.

In common with most parts of the public sector, the teachers' unions were adopting an increasingly confrontational attitude. The NUT was twice the size of the other teaching unions and its views were well to the left of centre. Matters of education policy might have been important to the unions but 'industrial relations conflicts' were invariably about matters of teacher pay and performance.[48] Bernard Donoughue, the policy adviser to the last two Labour prime ministers, was damning about the NUT. His wife worked for the NUT president and his diary contained multiple mentions of the organisation, mostly prefaced with the word 'appalling'.[49]

This is what he said about the NUT in his memoirs.[50]

> *In all my many dealings with the NUT I never heard mention of education or children. The union's prime objective appeared to be to secure ever decreasing responsibilities and hours of work for its members and it seemed that the ideal NUT world would be one where teachers and children never entered a school at all – and the executive of the NUT would be in a permanent conference session at a comfortable seaside hotel.*

The outgoing Labour minister (Shirley Williams) recounted the 'surreal' pay claim the NUT made and the indignation she felt at being called a liar by the NUT's president, somebody she knew well and liked. She reconciled herself to this by acknowledging that it was probably because, like other 'moderate and sensible leaders he was being harried by their extremists.'[51]

These sentiments were shared by Sir Keith Joseph, who later became minister.[52]

> *The teacher unions were... perverse, perverse; except for one or two of them, they didn't concern themselves with quality, or didn't appear to. I had union leaders make half-hour speeches without mentioning children. It was a producer lobby, not a consumer lobby.*

My personal memories of the NUT came from watching televised debates from their annual conferences and wondering how representative the speakers were of the average teacher. All the teachers I knew were nothing like the young union officials who made angry impassioned speeches with long lists of demands about their pay and working conditions. I remember wondering how much damage these scenes did to the public's perception of the teaching profession. Chris Woodhead, who was Her Majesty's Chief Inspector of Schools, had the same opinion.[53]

> *We watch the teacher union conference on TV every Easter, and we see the Socialist Worker's Party [A far left political party] members*

behaving in a way that most parents would find totally unacceptable.
The whole image of the teaching profession is tarnished.

The NUT has become the National Education Union (NEU) but has lost none of its 'radical' approach. Its policy of delaying the opening of schools during the Covid-19 pandemic was roundly condemned, with past Labour education ministers (Alan Johnson, David Blunkett and Andrew Adonis) being the most vocal critics. At the end of 2020 the teaching unions attracted condemnation from parts of the media. The leading article in *The Times* – 'Obstructive unions give teachers like me a bad name' – echoed the much-repeated argument that most teachers were doing a valiant job but their union's negative, confrontational approach tarnished their reputation.[54]

Teachers exercised their power – however much they had – through their trade unions. Parents had no such organisations, but exerted influence through other channels. The same could be said about employers, who had to recruit the school leavers.

'Parent power', especially that of the middle classes, contributed to the abandonment of the 11-plus and the subsequent campaigns to retain local grammar schools. It is natural for parents to be concerned and involved in their children's education and when they are unhappy they have recourse to local and national elections to change politicians. During the early 1970s this indirect power was supplemented by direct action, with parents employing legal means to prevent grammar schools closing (Enfield in Middlesex) and removing their children from failing schools (William Tyndale). Callaghan's 'great debate' had started the process of formally recognising the wishes of parents, something the Conservatives continued with their manifesto promises.

Roy Lowe, visiting professor at the Institute of Education, eloquently summarised this change in parents' attitude.[55]

Not only were parents increasingly ready to challenge what went on
in their children's schools but they looked increasingly for an educa-
tion which would confirm their life chances by linking more closely
with the routes through higher education and into careers.

Employers' unhappiness about the skills and knowledge of their young employees was not a new issue and is a complaint still heard today. The Confederation of British Industry (CBI) *2018 Education and Skills Annual Report* concluded that '44% of its members felt young people leaving school, college or university were not work ready.'[56] In 1979, the vulnerability of the UK's economy had heightened these concerns, giving additional urgency to the employers' demands. It remained anathema to most Labour politicians and educationalists that children's education should be conditioned to meet the demands of 'the employers', but the idea resonated with the beliefs of the new prime minister, as I expect it did with most parents.

Until now, most of the political disputes about education had revolved about the arguments over selective versus comprehensive education. Just as that battle had been decided a new one was beginning, which was about the relative power and role of the education stakeholders. Who should decide the school curriculum and measure how successfully it was being delivered? How much information should parents have about their child's performance and that of individual schools? What freedoms did parents have to decide where their children were educated? What was the role of central and local government in determining the strategy and tactics of education policy? How much freedom did teachers have to determine what was taught in their classrooms? Lots and lots of questions; none were new – but now they had taken on a new importance.

Lots of 'consultation' but little direction

Politicians and 'experts' have long resented the power of the media to determine public attitudes and the resulting pressure this generates for change. Of course, when the media agrees with their viewpoint this objection evaporates. Many commentators at the time thought the media was to blame for the public's disquiet about the state of the schools. Lowe believed that:

> *At the precise moment that the British press was lost to its local proprietors and came under the influence of multinational conglomerates, it reconstructed itself in a form which was better able to peddle what I construe as a kind of political fundamentalism.*

I assume that he was referring to the acquisition of *The Sun* newspaper in 1969 by News UK, a wholly owned subsidiary of Rupert Murdoch's News Corp, and the change to a tabloid format of the *Daily Mail* (1971) and the *Daily Express* (1977). These newspapers were associated with views on the right of the political spectrum and had 'traditionalist' opinions about education. Today, little has changed, except they are now accused of supporting 'popularist' ideas.

This idea that opinions are formed through a mist of 'fake news', or at least 'biased news', makes life difficult when trying to relate a historical story. Implicit in this assumption is that the masses are gullible, unlike the few who know 'the truth'. I am fully aware of the bias of news sources, but I don't think the left or the right, the 'progressives' or the 'traditionalists', have a monopoly on the purity of their insights. So yes, I believe that education was an easy target for newspapers that were ready to think the worst and check the facts later. But there was a wealth of evidence showing there were significant problems that needed putting right.

In losing the 1979 election the Labour Party took its lowest share of the vote since WWII. It strains the bounds of credulity to think that the strength of feelings that led to this rejection and the retention of the Conservatives in power for so long resulted from public anger conjured up by a biased media.

It is easy to forget that during this period of upheaval, 4 million children were attending secondary schools in preparation for their first job or going on into further education. They were having to contend with the upheavals caused by comprehensivisation and the disruption resulting from their teachers' industrial action. Many of them were also the guinea pigs for the new progressive teaching methods.

Towards the end of 1979 Carlisle received two research reports that provided a rare glimpse into the reality of how the 105 LEAs managed their schools and the workings – warts and all – of the education 'system'.

The first report contained the results of a research project initiated by Williams back in 1977. Following Callaghan's 'great debate' there had been disquiet about the content of children's schooling, especially the teaching of basic literacy and numeracy skills. This research had been intended to reveal what the schools were actually teaching, by asking the LEAs to explain their 'policies and practices in curricular matters'. That this subject needed researching reveals a gap in the Ministry's knowledge about what was happening in the country's schools.[57] As we will see, they were not the only ones unaware about what was happening in the primary and secondary schools.

There were two parts to the report. First, the minister summarised and responded to the research findings. Then came a section containing an analysis of the LEAs' responses. I doubt whether Williams' commentary would have been markedly different from that of Carlisle, who concluded:

> *On the evidence of the replies many authorities need to increase their working knowledge of what goes on in their schools, in order to improve their capability to develop and implement more effective approaches to staffing, curriculum development, assessment and the distribution of resources, all of which should be closely related to their curricular policies and the aims of the schools.*

What the research revealed was astonishing – well, at least to me. The LEAs' oversight and direction of the schools – theoretically in their charge – was at best informal and worst non-existent. Not only that, but this state of affairs was portrayed as an intentional policy, not an oversight. These extracts from the report illustrated the LEAs' laissez-faire approach.

> *Most authorities do not have systematic arrangements for regularly collecting and monitoring curricular information from their schools, relying instead on occasional enquiries about specific topics. [Only 20% of secondary schools and 10% of primary schools had any programme for monitoring curriculum information.]*

> *Most authorities [approximately 70%] stress that they do not seek to control the detailed curriculum of each school.*

> *A quarter of the replies indicated that the authority analysed schools' external examination entries in order to gain information about the range of subjects offered. [In other words, 75% had little idea about what GCEs and CSEs were being taught.]*

*The authority's function was seen as being principally to provide
guidance and support, particularly by means of its advisory services
and in-service courses, and 'through consensus rather than
direction'.*

The report contained a liberal smattering of the words 'consensus' and
'consultation' but 'co-operation' was especially popular, appearing 30 times.
These are all nice, reassuring words, but they meant that decisions about
children's education were made (or not) by the collective wisdom of the
country's 231,000 secondary school teachers.[58] Perhaps it was not a surprise
that the word 'teacher' appeared 10 times more than 'parent'.

My years in business have taught me that 'hierarchy-free' organisations,
although they may be a nice idea, rarely work. Reading the report's conclusion gave me a fresh insight into why so many centrally initiated education
policies had failed.

*Most LEAs see these processes [making decisions about curriculum]
as stemming from a complex inter-action between the various
parties, none of whom plays a markedly dominant part in determining policy.*

The report said little about the one thing that provided consistency to the
curriculum taught in secondary schools – external exams. It is ironic that the
reputation of secondary moderns improved once their pupils' curriculum
was aligned with taking GCE 'O' levels, yet at the time many teachers
portrayed this a problem, because they were having to 'teach for the exam'.
If, as it seems, external exams were the only mechanism providing any
uniformity to the curriculum in secondary schools, who decided if the exam
syllabuses were fit for purpose? As we will soon see, others were asking the
same question.

Little attention was paid to the report. Perhaps its findings confirmed
what everybody instinctively knew but failed to verbalise. That neither the
minister nor the LEAs had much knowledge or control over the curriculum
was unlikely to be popular with parents. The Ministry could publish all the
advice and guidance it wanted, but there were no mechanisms that ensured it
was listened to and applied.

I wonder if politicians of the time appreciated the irony of the situation. The Labour Party's policy had employed draconian command and control techniques in an attempt to create a nationwide system of comprehensivisation. This was anathema to the Conservatives, who believed the state should stay out of directing how schools were organised. Yet it was the Conservatives – against objections from Labour – who would drive the quest for greater state control, right down to specifying the details of the curriculum.

The second research report was published at the end of 1979 and shed some light on what was happening in the 4,200 secondary schools, especially during pupils' 4th and 5th forms – that's Years 10 and 11 in today's language.[59] A sample of approximately 10% of all secondary schools were studied by HM Inspectors, during the period 1975–1978.

This must have been a difficult task because many of the schools were in the process of converting to comprehensives. Secondary moderns were the most affected, representing over 90% of the schools that the study classified as being 'in transition'.

The report contained lots of facts, few conclusions and no recommendations. None of the findings came as a surprise, but they helped quantify the scale of the anomalies within the system of secondary schools. Despite the limitations of the research's accuracy it was the best available. These were the main findings.

Comprehensivisation was less advanced than the official statistics suggested. The research classified 42% of schools as 'full-range comprehensives', which was just under half the number quoted by the 1979 Ministry statistics. Part of the difference can be explained by the change in the categorisation of schools that occurred during the four years of the research. The other reason was that many comprehensives operated in areas that had retained some form of selective education. These schools were labelled as 'restricted range comprehensives' but were really secondary moderns, in the various stages of becoming comprehensives.

The intake of grammar schools was very different from other schools'. Only 16% of secondary moderns' pupils came from 'prosperous suburban' areas, compared with 47% attending grammar schools. The difference was even more pronounced for pupils with 'learning difficulties'. Nearly half of secondary moderns reported 11–20% of pupils in this category, whereas grammar schools had virtually none.

It was recognised that where children lived was a major factor influencing their academic achievements – a theme that we've seen in earlier research, too. These comments wouldn't be out of place in a report about today's schools:

Many of the average and less able pupils, especially the less able, brought with them from home already low expectations of themselves as learners. These attitudes, understandably but regrettably, were only too likely to be reinforced by the low expectations of their teachers. Many of these teachers, especially the less experienced under pressure of behavioural problems, found themselves teaching for containment rather than learning.

Inspectors commented that there were many examples of schools that operated in 'difficult' areas that were deemed as being 'problem free'. Most of these were grammar schools but there were also some full-range comprehensives and secondary moderns. With the right headmaster and teachers, it was possible to compensate for the pupils' difficult backgrounds. Another sentiment that is often heard today.

Full-range comprehensives contained large numbers of children. About 60% of these schools housed over 1,000 pupils. Only 5% of grammar and secondary moderns were this large.

Grammar schools had larger average class sizes than other schools. Twice as many classes in grammar schools had 27.5 pupils per class as in secondary moderns (11%) and full-range comprehensives (17%). This result is contrary to the usual narrative that they were better staffed than other schools. These numbers refer to the teaching of 4th form core subjects. I have no doubt that in the 6th form the pupil-teacher ratio was much better.

Three-quarters of teachers in grammar schools had degrees, compared with 25% in secondary moderns and 37% in full-range comprehensives. From my personal experience, I am not sure that teachers with a degree are necessarily any better than those without. At the time, as now, possession of a degree was seen as a measure of teacher quality.

Teachers in comprehensives were younger and had less experience than those in grammar schools and secondary moderns. Half of grammar school teachers had over 10 years' experience, compared with a third of those in comprehensives. The same pattern applied to the heads of department.

HM Inspectors commented that secondary moderns and comprehensives were particularly affected by shortages of staff qualified to teach the core subjects of English, maths and science. This statement came as no surprise, given that only a couple of years earlier Williams had wanted to improve teaching standards by requiring 'O' levels in maths and English as a requirement for all teachers.

Expectations and achievement of academic success were far higher in grammar than other schools. The exam targets for 5th formers are shown in the following table.

Target exams	Secondary modern	Grammar	Full-range comprehensive
GCE 'O' level or above	9%	74%	23%
GCE 'O' level /CSE	6%	10%	8%
CSE	62%	12%	53%
All other exams	23%	4%	15%

The exam targets for 5th formers in secondary modern, grammar and full-range comprehensive schools

These numbers suggest that CSEs had become the primary external exam taken in secondary moderns and full-range comprehensives. Few pupils took the exam in grammar schools, where the GCE 'O' level reigned supreme. The fears that the CSE exam would reinforce the distinction between grammar school-educated children and 'the rest' had come true.

As had so often happened, the report was critical about the distortions that external exams had on the school timetable.

If schools believe that their work is appreciated only as far as it is reflected in examination results, they will be tempted to subordinate all else, even though this may lead paradoxically to their narrowing the work in a way that precludes them from responding to other public demands upon them.

'The public', particularly parents and employers, were blamed for this problem.

Full-range comprehensives offered far more exam options than other schools. Only 2% of grammar schools provided pupils with the chance to study more than 31 subjects, compared with 28% of secondary moderns and 84% of full-range comprehensives. This is partly explained by the fact many comprehensives were coeducational and would need to teach specialist subjects for boys and girls. In those days only boys did metal-work and girls studied domestic science.

Of course, the other reason is that full-range comprehensives had to provide courses, including both GCE 'O' level and CSE, for pupils of all levels of ability, unlike secondary moderns and grammar schools.

Having to provide so many courses came at a cost, which was detailed in the report.

The effort to provide a very wide range of options often results in a complexity of organisation which makes it more difficult for teachers to coordinate the learning of the pupils, to plan and consult together and to attain a synoptic view of the curriculum offered by the school and of their contribution within it.

Particularly at risk are those aspects of education which are not simply identified with particular specialist subjects (e.g. language development, reading skills, health education and careers education).

The report offered no solutions, but suggested that it 'may be necessary to develop a more explicit rationale of the curriculum'. I interpreted this as hinting there was a need for a national curriculum.

There was insufficient provision for more able pupils. The report said little on this subject but what it did say was clear and to the point.

There were a few schools, selective and non-selective, in which the ablest 15 and 16 year olds were found to be doing distinguished work.

There is, however, a good deal of evidence from the survey to suggest
that more able pupils need more opportunities and stimulus to
pursue their own initiatives.

I have no idea what was done with the findings of this report. Very little,
I guess. After reading the report, I concluded that secondary schools were
still straddling the old days of selective schools and the hoped-for future of
full-range comprehensives.

It seems that Carlisle channelled his energies into trying to make sense
of what the schools were teaching and why. His first action was to issue a
'consultative' document that outlined the Ministry's views on the 'framework' for deciding and managing the curriculum.[60] In a nutshell the idea was
to ensure:

Each LEA should have a clear and known policy for the curriculum
offered in its schools; be aware at any time of the extent to which
schools are able to make curriculum provision consistent with that
policy and plan future developments accordingly.

[It would do this by introducing a core curriculum] that would
ensure that all pupils get a sufficient grounding in the knowledge and
skills which by common consent should form part of the equipment of
the educated adult.

These statements contained lots of praise about how much progress the
schools had already made and the importance of consultations with teachers,
parents and school governors. I have excluded that text, however, because I
suspect its sole purpose was to make the proposals more palatable to the
LEAs and teachers.

After 15 months of 'consultations' a further document was published
that set out the Ministry's proposals in more detail.[61] It was not the details of
the proposal that interested me, rather the timid expectations for how it
would be implemented.

The guidance given in this paper reflects what many authorities and
schools already do, often as the result of sustained effort and experi-

ment over the years. Further progress will similarly be gradual and
will be affected by the availability of teachers and other resources.
The Secretaries of State believe that all concerned in the education
service will wish to maintain momentum in the improvement of the
school curriculum and to review progress regularly.

If Carlisle's intention was to avoid antagonising the LEAs and teachers, then he probably succeeded, but parts of the educational press objected to his 'interventionist stance'.[62] A sympathetic description of his approach would be 'cautious and thoughtful'. A more critical appraisal would be that it was 'limited and timid'. A circular was issued that formally informed the LEAs of his proposals. When they read this document and learnt that he would like to review their progress in 'about two years from now', my guess is they put it into the 'non-urgent' file.[63] By the time it was published Carlisle was no longer minister and had been replaced by Sir Keith Joseph.

Carlisle's obituary diplomatically described his difficulties as minister: 'his task at Education was made more difficult by Thatcher having held the post herself, and by his being identified as a political "wet".'[64] The prime minister had first-hand experience of the inertia within the education system and its resistance to change. She knew that Carlisle's tentative approach had little or no chance of working.

From the perspective of secondary school children, therefore, little happened during the first two years of Conservative government. Thatcher's choice of Joseph as the new minister suggested that was about to change. He was called a lot of things but the one word that was never used was 'wet'. As a key ally and mentor of Thatcher he is often praised or blamed – depending on your political perspective – for her policies. Neil Kinnock, the leader of the Labour Party (1983–1992), referred to Thatcher and Joseph as being the 'top Tories'.[65] Given that he was so aligned to her own thinking and wanted the education portfolio, he should have been the perfect choice. Sadly, that turned out not to be the case.

Thatcher and Joseph's understanding of the country's problems and the necessary solutions had a direct bearing on the future of secondary education. It is worth taking a moment to understand the core of their shared beliefs. When Thatcher came to power the rate of inflation was 13.4% and set to increase to 18.0% in 1980. It is easy to read these numbers without understanding their implications. Anybody living through this time knew all too well the resulting difficulties. That level of inflation meant that what cost £1 to buy in 1980 would have doubled in price by 1984. Not surprisingly this led to a constant demand to increase wages in an attempt to maintain purchasing power. As we have already seen, the teachers were striking for a 36.5% wage increase. Harold Wilson neatly summed up the resulting problem: 'one man's wage rise is another man's price increase'.[66]

Thatcher's mechanism for breaking out of the wage spiral and controlling inflation was to employ the theories of the Nobel Prize winner for economics, Professor Milton Friedman. Much has been written about the merits or fallacies of this approach (monetarism), but what is beyond dispute is that by 1983, inflation had fallen to 4.6% and remained around that level for the next five years. This was partly done by imposing rigid controls on public expenditure and that meant restraining the education budget.

At the core of Thatcher's and Joseph's belief system was that economic growth was more likely to result from a free market, where consumers (voters) made decisions, rather than the state usurping their role and making the decisions for them. This is perfectly illustrated by their distaste for Labour's imposition of a single model of schooling (comprehensives) rather than parents having the choice of their children's school. An adjunct to this argument is that when the state becomes the monopoly provider of services – such as education and healthcare – the service risks being operated for the benefit of the providers (teachers), rather than customers (parents), something that is exacerbated when the providers are unionised. A state of affairs that is best known as 'producer capture'.

This ultra-summarised version of monetarism and free market economics misses out many of the nuances of the beliefs and gives none of the counter-arguments, especially the one about 'choice' being a theoretical construct, rather than something consumers could actually exercise. It leaves us in no doubt, however, that the LEAs and teachers – more specifically teachers' unions – would no longer be viewed as powerful but neutral stakeholders. Rather they were seen as barriers to be overcome.

A+ for thinking but C- for effectiveness

Joseph was responsible for the country's education for nearly five years; that's longer than Thatcher and any subsequent minister. He and his officials produced numerous papers, circulars and bills, so if this output equated to achievement, he did well. However, as we know, administrative activity isn't necessarily an indicator of success. His time in office was about as long as most children spent at secondary school. What differences – what improvements – did he make to their education?

Peter Ribbins and Brian Sherratt published a series of interviews with Conservative education ministers including Joseph's predecessor (Mark Carlisle) and his successor (Kenneth Baker).[67] As friends and colleagues they naturally portrayed his achievements in the most positive light. Educational historians, most of whom view events from a left-of-centre perspective, are not so complimentary. Taken together, I think these contrasting views provide a balanced, but polarised, assessment of his accomplishments.

Carlisle seemed to find it difficult to recount the details of what happened during Joseph's time in office. Perhaps this was genuine, or perhaps he was being diplomatic? He painted a picture of a man who was frustrated by a lack of administrative machinery that would transform his ideas into policies and then actions. He related the story of Joseph pacing around the Ministry asking, 'Where are the levers?' I assume he meant the levers of power. His most complimentary comment referred to Joseph's renowned cerebral abilities.

By the time he had left office his radical reform agenda had been thought through and that was implemented by his successor.

Baker had more to say and in the main echoed the previous sentiments. He talked about Joseph's 'clear ideas and views of startling simplicity' but also his problems 'dealing with the actual administrative consequences' of his policies.

Much of his commentary was about the tension between Joseph and his officials. In theory, the beliefs and agenda of the Ministry officials shouldn't interfere with them implementing the policies of the politicians. Clearly it did and this wasn't just a problem for Joseph, but something that Thatcher also experienced during her time as minister of education.

> *I think he (Joseph) was intellectually seduced by a very clever department who wanted to do its own thing. They have long been one of the feudal armies in the great battle structure that passes for British government. They wanted to do things their way and tended to count ministers in and count ministers out.*

Reading these words it is difficult not to conjure up the comical scenes from the TV series *Yes Minister*, which depicted a light-hearted interplay between civil servants and politicians.[68] Baker described a darker, antagonistic relationship, with officials holding views that were the antithesis of Thatcherism and actively thwarting policies they disagreed with.[69]

> *There was clear 1960s ethos and a very clear agenda which permeated virtually all the civil servants. It was devoutly anti-excellence, anti-selection and anti-market.*

He went on to say that it was not just the Conservatives who suffered from the officials' attitude 'that they knew better than the politicians'. Following Callaghan's Ruskin College speech, the Ministry produced a green paper that was described as being 'sparse in content and complacent in tone'. As we know, these sentiments were echoed by Donoughue, who believed: 'The paper represented Whitehall at its self-satisfied, condescending and unimaginative worst.'

I wondered to what extent Baker's reaction to the Ministry's civil servants and their advisers resulted from their limited powers to affect how education was delivered? Was their reluctance to adopt new policies a result of doctrinal opposition or because they knew the 'levers' for their implementation didn't exist?

Like all large bureaucracies the Ministry must have suffered from institutional inertia that meant it changed at a slower pace than politicians would have liked. Or maybe that's too fair and unbiased and we must conclude that the Ministry was indeed an impediment to change? What has become known as the 'insolence of office affair' supports this conclusion.

In June 1983 a report was published that identified serious failings in the English secondary school system, especially with comprehensive schools.[70] How the Ministry responded to this criticism raised serious questions about its impartiality and competence.

The 1980 Education Act had required LEAs to publish school performance data. Although it was not explicitly specified, this resulted in the publication of schools' public exam results.

Up until this time the Ministry hadn't revealed any information about the relative performance of LEAs and schools. No government analysis was ever published that compared the performance of selective and comprehensive schools. Crosland forbade it and no subsequent Labour or Conservative minister had changed the decision.

The report's authors, Marks and Cox, had analysed the exam results of 350,000 children from 2,000 schools in more than half of English LEAs (74). That there were significant differences in the exam performance of LEAs couldn't have come as a surprise. That some LEAs achieved twice as many GCE 'O' level results as others with the same social class groups must have been something of a shock. Maybe these unexplained anomalies were known but ignored?

It was these conclusions that appear to have sent the Ministry into crisis mode:

Pupils at secondary modern and grammar schools obtained more GCE 'O' Level results than pupils at comprehensives both nationally and within the same social group – between 30–40% more GCE 'O' Level passes per pupil nationally. Secondary modern schools did particularly well.

Some of the analyses suggest that providing more teachers and spending more money per pupil does not necessarily lead to better exam results.

What happened next was related in the book *The Insolence of Office*.[71] The book's cover featured a cartoon by Gerald Scarfe showing the civil service characters in the TV series *Yes Minster* discussing the report. Sir Humphrey Appleby is saying to his underling, Bernard Wooley, 'I don't think we need trouble the minister with this one, Bernard.' In real life the minister was Sir Keith Joseph. The steps that the Ministry went to to discredit the report's finding were extraordinary.

To cut a very long story short, the Ministry produced its own report that was highly critical of the findings and concluded that the authors' statistical methodology was unsound. Marks and Cox were prevented from seeing this document, but its details were leaked to *The Guardian, The Times Educational Supplement* and Labour politicians. If there had been any balance in the Ministry's report it was lost in the ensuing newspaper articles, which used the words 'rubbished', 'discredited' and 'flawed' to describe the research findings.

Eventually the authors obtained a copy of the Ministry's report and found that it had made several basic errors that invalidated its conclusions. In today's language it seems that the Ministry combined with the media in an attempt to 'cancel' Marks and Cox – but failed.

Joseph and his senior advisers attended a meeting at the House of Commons where Marks and Cox explained the mistakes in the Ministry's analysis. A few days later Joseph made a statement in Parliament that vindicated the researchers and congratulated them on the pioneering nature of their work. By its actions the Ministry had diminished its reputation for objectivity and competence.

There has never been any suggestion that Joseph was involved in the Ministry's campaign to discredit the report's findings. It was the work of senior civil servants who disagreed with the report's conclusions and wanted them buried. Their bungled actions had the very opposite effect and resulted in a flood of critical media comment such as the following:[72]

> *Something much more fundamental., however, arises from this example of a commitment by civil servants to particular policies that brook no dissent. The Comprehensive system was originally brought in as an experiment, and there are growing misgivings about the quality and relevance of the secondary education which is now available to many of our children.*

The Guardian and *The Times Educational Supplement* were having none of this and continued with their original stories of discredited research. This did more harm to their reputation for accurate reporting than to Mark and Cox.

Meanwhile, Baker also believed that the most recent bout of industrial action by teachers so dominated Joseph's last two years as minister that it prevented him from instigating other policies. He was referring to the teachers' programme of strikes and 'working to rule' for a salary increase of £3,500 per year in today's pounds. This dispute dominated the policy agenda as well as affecting children's education and the lives of their working parents.

Lady Warnock, a natural supporter of teachers, believed they had greatly damaged their reputation by their strike action and put themselves on the same level as other wage earners, making them the 'enemy of parents'. These criticisms came from a respected educationalist who was an outspoken critic of Conservative education policy and all things associated with Thatcherism.[73, 74] Even the NUT's account of this period was critical of their own actions.[75]

> *The 1980s pay dispute was characterised by inter-union rivalry and division, and division within unions themselves. Some in the NUT felt the final settlement was too modest yet it was a fact that the Union lost nearly a third of its membership during these years.*

The longer the strike action continued, the worse became the teachers' negotiating position and public image. If they were a barrier to Joseph's implementation of policies, then Baker was the beneficiary of the dilution of their reputation and power.

Joseph's grand design for improving schools

It was clear that Joseph's fellow Conservatives respected his intellect and contribution to formulating education policies but believed it was left to his successors, primarily Baker, to implement them. So what were the policies that Joseph bequeathed to his successors? The contents of the Conservative manifestos for 1983 and 1987 provided the best guide to what he was seeking to achieve.

By 1983 the policies divided into two groups. Many were focused on giving parents more power and information about the schools and their children's performance. Making HM Inspectors' school reports available to parents sounds like a small thing to do but it required a huge change in a culture that was rooted in the belief that these things were best left to experts. Schools were to be encouraged to keep records of pupils' achievement. It should be noted that schools were not to be 'instructed' or 'required' to keep records, but only 'encouraged' – an indicator of Joseph's lack of 'levers' to make things happen.

The other group of policies involved improving the quality of teachers and their training by remodelling the training colleges and teacher selection. In 1981 HM Inspectors visited 294 schools in England and Wales to study the quality of newly trained teachers and how well their training had prepared them for 'doing the job'. In 1982 the findings were published, and concluded that: 'a quarter of the teachers in the present sample considered poorly or very poorly equipped for the task they are given to do.'[76]

Not surprisingly, the teacher training institutions were blamed for this high level of failure. When questioned about their difficulties the newly qualified teachers often remarked that their training:

seemed to be preoccupied with the theory of education without any attempt to consider the practical problems that would be faced in the classroom.

Some thought that 'work in education studies became increasingly theoretical and distanced from the school as the course progressed through the four years.'

At about this time I knew half a dozen recently graduated teachers, and I remember they were also critical of their college tutors' focus on the theoretical aspects of education and its social implications rather than the practicalities of classroom teaching.

A year later a white paper, titled *Teacher Quality*, was published.[77] Considering the magnitude of the problems exposed by HM Inspectors, it contained few detailed recommendations. It was, however, especially critical about the lack of experience of training college lecturers, saying that 'too few have sufficient regular contact with classroom teaching'. One of its few proposals about what teachers should be taught said:

Touchstones for the professional recognition of courses [in teacher training colleges] should be their ability to provide basic and appropriate curriculum knowledge, professional competence, and classroom skills.

I assume that the word 'touchstones' means 'requirements' but the paper's authors seemed reticent about being too assertive. It is astonishing to me that these most basic of course contents were not necessarily being taught. How could anybody believe this proposal would begin to rectify the problems of how teachers were trained?

In the 1987 manifesto the education policies were described in more detail and used far more positive language. They were presented as four innovative reforms, suggesting that they were new ideas. Most were not, but now they had some substance and sounded as if they might become a reality.

Establishment of a national core curriculum for pupils aged five to 16, including maths, English and science. These subjects were to have a syllabus and defined attainment levels, enabling parents and teachers to measure pupils' performance at the ages of seven, 11 and 14.

All secondary schools to be given control of their budgets. Headteachers and governing bodies, rather than the LEAs, would decide how their money was spent. Clearly, this policy was aimed at weakening the LEAs' control over the day-to-day running of schools, but its educational benefits were opaque.

Parents to be given more choice about the schools their children would attend. LEAs were to lose the power to control the numbers of children attending each school. If a school was especially popular with parents, it would no longer be able to limit pupil numbers below its maximum capacity. Of course, its budget would increase accordingly.

Popular schools, which have earned parental support by offering good education, will then be able to expand beyond present pupil numbers.

The outcome of this policy – which wasn't spelt out in the manifesto – was that schools that didn't earn parents' approval would be closed or forced to take measures to improve their performance.

As part of the promise to 'give parents more choice' the number of assisted places in private schools was to be increased from 25,000 to 35,000 and a new type of school introduced. These city technology colleges would be funded by national (not local) government and, as their name suggested, specialised in technical subjects. However, only 15 were ever built and so their immediate impact on the secondary school system was minimal. In the longer term, the model of funding and management that they established had a significant effect on secondary education – more about this later.

State schools could 'opt out' of LEA control if the parents and governing body agreed. This would result in the school's funding and direction coming from central government, not the LEA. In London, this change from local to central control could apply to all schools in a borough.

It's plain that these policies were intended to dilute the power of the LEAs, shifting control to central government, schools and parents. These were ideologically driven educational policies in the same mould as Labour's intent to abolish selection and force all children to attend a single type of secondary school – the comprehensive. My use of the term 'ideologically driven' is shorthand for saying that the policies resulted from fundamental beliefs rather than systematic research.

How these upheavals would benefit the lives of secondary school children and in what timeframe was not defined.

The new GCSE is launched despite widespread criticism

During Joseph's time in office he was responsible for one development that definitely did change the lives of secondary school children. In 1984 the decision was made to merge the dual system of CSEs and GCEs into a single exam – the GCSE. When CSEs were first introduced (1965) their critics had warned that they would perpetuate the divisions in secondary schools between the 'academic' child and the 'rest'. To a large extent they had been proved right. Arguments about why they should be replaced began almost as soon as the exams were launched.

In July 1976 the Schools Council had recommended adopting a single exam that children would take before leaving school or studying for 'A' levels, a suggestion that had been supported by a white paper in 1978.[78] Most of the preparation work had been done before Joseph became minister but he was the person who pressed the button to launch the new exam.

As with so many major changes to the education system, the introduction of GCSEs was a long and painful process ending with an outcome that pleased nobody. It is a story that I don't intend to recount, except to view the events from the perspective of the 700,000 children taking the new exam.

Few pupils would have read the white paper (*Better Schools*) and discovered that their new exam would be a 'single system with differentiated assessment'.[79] In practice this meant that some exam questions and papers would only be answered by the brightest pupils. After the battle to end selective education, the new GCSE exam seemed to be reintroducing it in the guise of 'differentiation'. This is how Clyde Chitty interpreted what happened.[80]

> *Differentiation means that the system will still be divisive: that there will be separate routes to the examination; that some candidates will not be eligible for higher grades (if they take the less difficult route); that teachers will still have to decide which students are suited for which route/course/range of grades; that in some cases these decisions will still have to be made as early as 14.*

For many of those involved in education it was (and still is) anathema for a child's perceived intelligence to determine how they were taught and examined. They believed that children shouldn't be segregated by academic aptitude, despite the difficulties of teaching a diverse range of abilities. It must have been extremely difficult to devise a single type of exam that could test the abilities of the brightest yet be suitable for low achievers. This deficiency soon became clear and in 1994 a new grade was introduced (A*) that supposedly signified an exceptionally high achievement.

Those taking the new GCSE would have become well acquainted with the demands of preparing 'coursework'. GCE 'O' levels had been criticised for testing children's ability to remember and present knowledge, as much as their understanding of it. Timed exams still formed part of the GCSE assessment, but so did the marks awarded by teachers for the pupils' project coursework. That some parents helped their children prepare their coursework couldn't have been a surprise, in the same way as parents helped their children with their homework and exam preparation. It had been a long-standing objective to measure a child's inherent intelligence, rather than that conferred by their parents' social class and education. It's ironic that the much-reviled IQ test, especially in the form of the 11-plus, attempted to do just this – to provide an exam that minimised the influence of the child's parents and teachers.

In an attempt to test more than a child's ability to recall facts and to reveal the depth of their knowledge, the GCSE asked 'empathy questions'. The knowledge these were supposedly testing was illustrated by this question in the first GCSE history exam: 'An Irish peasant farmer and his wife in the early 1850s decided to emigrate to America – what were their hopes and fears as they boarded the emigrant ship?'[81] An interesting question but one that it is hard to answer without using generalisations and stereotypes, and one that appears to test the child's power of expression rather than their knowledge of Irish history. Needless to say, these questions attracted much criticism and were cited as proof that the exams were being 'dumbed down'.

Teachers were vocal about having too little time to prepare for teaching and marking the new exam. Conservative politicians and much of the media accused teachers of creating the problem themselves because of their lengthy industrial action and refusal to participate in the exam's launch programme. Even *The Guardian* newspaper, which was normally supportive of the teaching profession, was critical of their actions. In an editorial it commented:[82]

> *The way some teachers talk, you would think that they had no clue*
> *how to teach their subjects to 15 and 16 year-olds unless someone in*
> *authority has spelled the whole thing out to them in advance...*
> *Teachers should not make a meal of their objections.*

These were the views of the teachers' trade union (NUT) and did not necessarily reflect those of teachers themselves. But yet again it reflected badly on the teaching profession. In the same article, *The Guardian* expressed its belief that preparations for the exams were insufficient and should be delayed – one of the few times when the newspaper's view coincided with that of Mrs Thatcher. At the time, she didn't comment publicly about the readiness to launch GCSEs but 30 years later her concerns were revealed when the National Archive documents were released. This story was widely reported in the media, with *The Times* providing the most detailed account.[83]

She believed that the exam 'lacked rigour, offered more scope for teachers' "bias" and would create a "can't-fail mentality"'. Despite her long list of objections she allowed the exam to go ahead. Nobody knows the reason, but overruling Joseph would have come at huge personal and political cost. My guess is the principal reason she didn't intervene was that delaying their launch would have been portrayed as bowing to pressure from the teaching unions. At this time the battle between the Conservative government and the trade unions was in full flight, culminating in the prolonged and violent miners' strike in 1984. Isn't it strange to think that the fate of children today, who are still taking a variant of GCSEs, is linked to events that took place nearly 40 years ago?

When *The Times* article about the archive documents was published, Michael Gove was the minister. His special adviser (Dominic Cummings) was quoted as believing that GCSEs had been a catastrophic mistake: 'It was a big mistake for the Conservative party to introduce GCSEs and put politicians in charge of exams and the curriculum'. Cummings has become well known for masterminding the campaign to leave the EU, his central role in making Boris Johnson prime minister in the 2019 general election and the year he spent at the centre of government. It is often forgotten that he was responsible for much of the research that influenced the recent Conservative governments' education policy.

In the years following the publication of the first GCSE results, children of the UK appeared to undergo an astonishing improvement in their academic achievements. In 1988 only 8.4% of children achieved an A grade but by 2011 this had risen to 23%. During the same period there was a significant fall in pupils with the lowest grades (D–U) from 58% to 30%. Year in year out the newspapers announced a rise in GCSE passes, followed by howls of derision that children weren't getting smarter, but the exams were getting easier. The following chart shows the pattern of GCSE results until 2018. Those gaining the top grades has continued to climb. In 2019 it was 22% and in 2020 an astonishing 28% – a threefold increase from when the exams were introduced. Now only a handful of pupils fail.

Later in the book I will consider the role of 'grade inflation', rather than improvements in children's intelligence, as an explanation for these results.[84]

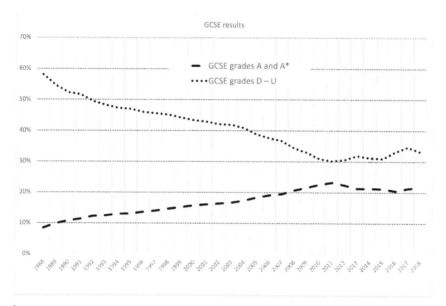

GCSE results

Analysis of GCSE results from 1988 until 2018. Grade A and A* are the highest grades. Grades D–U are the lowest grades and generally considered a failure

Without doubt, the class of 1988's exam experience was very different from, although not necessarily better than, that of their older brothers and sisters. Flaws in the format and content of GCSEs were visible long before the exams were introduced. Rectifying these problems has resulted in a constant tinkering with their structure, which continues to this day. While I was writing this section of the book, a leader article in *The Times* titled 'GCSEs: tested to destruction'[85] listed the exam's faults and concluded they should be abandoned.

The story of these exams has parallels with the introduction of ROSLA (1972) – another event that had long been anticipated, yet was badly implemented. Thatcher was minister at that time, and I described her role as 'more an observer than a director of the process'. I think the same words apply to

Joseph and GCSEs. Both major projects were poorly handled, revealing (in my view) fundamental flaws in the machinery of government.

Yet another attempt to provide technical and vocational training

During Joseph's reign as minister there was another development that affected secondary school children. In late 1982, Thatcher announced a new scheme for the technical and vocational education of 14–18 year olds.[86] Since the beginning of the timeline (1914) these two aspects of education had been constantly criticised as being deficient – and they still are, now! The Technical and Vocational Education Initiative (TVEI) was the latest in a long list of initiatives attempting to solve the problem.

The ground-breaking thing about the TVEI was that it was devised and managed by the Manpower Services Commission (MSC), a non-depart-mental public body of the Department of Employment – not Joseph's Ministry of Education and Science. Joseph seems to have been fully supportive of the initiative, something that couldn't be said for his Ministry officials.

When Thatcher launched the scheme, she explained that it would be funded 'within existing financial resources'; the MSC was in charge, 'sup-ported by the ministry' and 'where possible assisted by the LEAs'.[87] Responding to her announcement the leader of the Labour Party (Kinnock) was dismissive, stating that the educational establishment and the LEAs hadn't been consulted and the scheme lacked new funding. He also attacked its limited scope, involving only 10,000 children during the pilot phase.

Kinnock's knee-jerk anti-Thatcher criticism was to be expected, but perhaps he had a point? There is little doubt that other government educa-tion policies were aimed at weakening the influence of both the LEAs and the 'educational establishment'. Ill-defined objectives and lack of govern-ment commitment, when both political parties were in power, had contributed to the demise of technical secondary schools.

The doom-mongers were proved right, but not for the reasons they predicted. In 1991 the National Audit Office published a review of the TVEI's effectiveness, showing that after its successful pilots (in 1983) the scheme was extended nationally in 1987.[88] LEAs received government funding and assistance from specialist advisers to help them adapt their school and college curricula to:

- Relate what children learnt to the world of work.
- Provide young people with direct experience of work.
- Improve pupils' skills and qualifications, particularly in science, technology and modern languages.
- Provide better guidance and counselling on employment and further education.

Unlike previous schemes, the TVEI was intended for all 14–18 year olds 'irrespective of their ability, gender or background'. It was not aimed at children who were 'low achievers' – the Ministry had launched another programme aimed specifically at this group. The 'Lower Attaining Pupils Programme (LAPP)' had begun in July 1982 and was targeted at helping the 'bottom 40%' of children who were thought (by the Ministry) not to be suitable to take GCSEs.

The national take-up of the TVEI was impressive. By 1988 all of the LEAs in Great Britain had adopted the scheme and three years later its influence extended to 80% of schools and colleges. Kinnock's accusations about its limited scope were wide of the mark.

Approximately £2 billion, in today's pounds, was spent on the TVEI, making it among the most ambitious, and longest-running, curriculum development scheme ever undertaken.[89] Kinnock's criticism of its lack of funding had also been wrong.

When the National Audit Office (NAO) reviewed the TVEI's progress it was a mature scheme that had been running for eight academic years. It reached its conclusions after visiting a small sample of schools and colleges (46) and interviewing an even smaller number of employers (14). This is the most authoritative research available, but I have my doubts about its accuracy. Understanding variations by region and type of institution is impossible using a research sample of 1% of the schools and colleges taking part in the scheme.

The report was critical of the LEAs' delay in putting in place key components of the scheme, especially the mechanisms for sharing experiences, engaging with industry and changing classroom practices. It was thought that these glitches had been overcome and it was optimistic that the changes to technical and vocational education would continue once the government funding ceased. The scheme was always conceived as a 'pump-priming' exercise – it was never intended to be a permanent source of financial support.

So why has the TVEI joined the ranks of other failed government initiatives?

The accounts of those people directly involved with TVEI projects were, in most cases, positive about its accomplishments.[90] There is no evidence that the money and time spent on improving children's technical skills and their transition into the workforce succeeded, but then there is no evidence to say that it failed. The criticisms of the scheme, which have established the accepted narrative of the TVEI's 'failure', are primarily ideological in nature.

Baker recounted that Labour councils were stubbornly against the initiative and perceived it as a 'cuckoo in the nest', something that was confirmed by Brian Simon, who stated that initially 'the scheme was boycotted by most Labour Councils'.[91] Simon was deeply suspicious of both the TVEI and LAPP schemes, believing they were part of the Conservatives' grand scheme to force selection into comprehensive schools with 'an academic track via GCE, a technical–vocational track via TVEI and a "bottom 40%" track via LAPP'. It has to be remembered that Simon was a committed Marxist and tended to view politicians' actions through the prism of class conflict.

Many commentators, most with left-wing views, feared – more likely expected – that the TVEI was intended to create 'worker pupils' who would be segregated and directed to study a technical and vocational curriculum enabling them to become fodder for the capitalist system. Perhaps I am overstating this sentiment but that was the gist of their arguments.

Undoubtedly, there was some confusion about which children the TVEI was intended to benefit and that is not altogether surprising. When Thatcher launched the scheme, she made it clear that it was intended for pupils 'irrespective of their ability, gender or background'. I would guess, and it is no more than a guess, that in practice its activity was focused on the less academic. These were the children about to start work – they had the most immediate need. The TVEI must have resulted in a multiplicity of projects with numerous objectives. Central government provided the funds, but not the day-to-day management. That was in the hands of the 106 LEAs.

I think the following factors explain why the TVEI 'failed' to become a lasting part of the education system rather than 'failed' to help many thousands of children.

Towards the end of the scheme's life the policy focus on defining what children were taught moved from the TVEI to establishing a national curriculum. I'm not sure this signified that the TVEI hadn't worked; more likely it was an example of government changing its priorities and rebranding its policies. It would be nice to think that the national curriculum evolved from, rather than replaced, the TVEI. I will soon return to this question.

Like all pump-priming activities, when the stimulus is removed – in this case, money – there is the risk that progress stalls or, worse still, old behaviours return. Maybe this is what happened with the TVEI.

Finally, I expect the 'not invented here' syndrome was partly responsible for the TVEI's reputation of failure. All the main education stakeholders were excluded from its formulation – the Ministry, LEAs and the education establishment. The interloper that devised and funded the scheme was the government department responsible for employment. No doubt the demise of the TVEI helped speed the recovery of many bruised egos that felt their power and influence had been diluted.

So much needs changing, so little achieved

At the 1987 general election, Joseph left Parliament, having been replaced as minister the year before by Kenneth Baker. I wonder how Joseph would have described his achievements and failures as minister? He died in 1994, before Ribbins and Sherratt published their book of interviews with Conservative secretaries of state. The authors were anxious to include Joseph's views and recollections and so constructed an 'as if' interview, based on a collection of his comments from other sources. Clyde Chitty compiled that collection and I'm sure he did his best to represent Joseph's views. However, his version must be viewed as opinions, not facts. Chitty was once called the 'patron saint of comprehensive education',[92] so I think we can assume he probably wasn't a natural supporter of Joseph's policies.

So much of what Joseph did, or attempted to do, was driven by the belief that:

- Secondary education attempted to 'impose a diluted grammar school curriculum on everybody and it hadn't worked'. First it failed secondary modern pupils and the same mistake was being made in comprehensive schools.
- His role was to take the side of consumers (parents) and fight to improve the quality of their children's education. This involved confronting the education establishment – something he called a 'producer lobby' that through its representatives, the trade unions, was primarily focused on improving the welfare of teachers.
- Much could be learnt from other European countries (especially Germany) but the Ministry's culture was unwilling (maybe incapable) to adapt to radical new ideas. Ministry officials didn't seem to care that the state education system, the one they were responsible for, failed 50% of pupils. Joseph is quoted as saying that his officials believed 'this seems an awful lot, let's say 40%', giving birth to the term the 'bottom 40%'. Thirty years before, David Eccles had expressed similar feelings.

He is portrayed as a man who felt constrained and let down by his own officials and the education establishment, as somebody who understood the enormity of the problem but was frustrated, angry and eventually disillusioned because he lacked the tools and the support to make any real difference.

With such a depressing view about the education system it is not surprising that he struggled to identify any lasting achievements from his time as minister. He conceded that he had forced his officials to value the quality as well as the quantity of education they delivered – a task he started but was far from complete. He was baffled that his officials, school inspectors and even parents were so complacent about the low standards of education that many children received.

He believed children could achieve much higher standards and by implication teachers expected too little. The exam standard of the then 'average pupil' was, in his view, achievable by 80–90% of pupils.[93]

Identifying what he had got wrong was far easier. He was dissatisfied with the format of the GCSE exams, believing that the role and importance of teacher assessment was far greater than he had been led to believe. Exam grades should, in his view, indicate that 'pupils obtaining a particular grade will know certain things and possess certain skills or have achieved a certain competence'. That's not how it worked because much of the grading system used 'norm referencing', whereby grades were awarded relative to other exam-takers' scores.

He was also fearful that his principle that the school curriculum and exams should be 'differentiated', to take account of pupils' different aptitudes, would be abandoned.

Chitty concluded his 'as if' interview with Joseph's poignant and disturbing words:

I reckon that we've all made a right old mess of it. We've all got it wrong. And it's most hurt all those who are most vulnerable.

I guess that he was referring to the children who in the past would have been attending secondary moderns.

Thatcher appeared to share Joseph's sentiments and was self-critical about the limited achievements, related to education, of her first two terms as prime minister. That's not surprising since they shared the same beliefs and he was a good friend and mentor. Also, she had first-hand experience of the problems he encountered. After being in power for over eight years she concluded:[94]

I wish we had begun to tackle education earlier. We have been content to continue the policies of our predecessors. But now we have much worse left-wing Labour authorities than we have ever had before – so something simply has to be done.

A little later, in another newspaper interview, she sounded more like the combative Mrs Thatcher that most people remember: 'There is going to be a revolution in the running of the schools.'[95]

If the government didn't think they had done enough, many historical commenters believed they had done too much and most of it wrong. Brian Simon thought it was a 'disastrous period for education, culminating in a crisis almost reaching the proportions of a Greek tragedy'. Sally Tomlinson interpreted Joseph's desire for 'differentiation' as a 'preparation for a class-divided hierarchical society'.[96]

The driving forces that were moulding education policy differed depending on your political affiliations. Those on the left of the political spectrum believed the Tories were intent on reducing spending and perpetuating a class-based education system that divided children into winners and losers. Viewed through the eyes of Conservatives, the Labour Party – in collusion with the LEAs, teachers' unions and the Ministry – was more concerned with preserving the existing education system than improving the quality of children's schooling.

If secondary school children thought about these ideological differences at all they would have paled into insignificance compared with their biggest concern – getting a job. In the early 1980s, the rate of youth unemployment had reached levels last experienced 50 years before.

Despite the economic difficulties and the pressure to reduce government expenditure the average annual spend on education was more during Thatcher's first two periods as prime minister than that of Labour, during its time in office.[97] Her critics might argue that the money was spent in the wrong way, but they cannot accuse the Conservatives of not valuing children's education.

Any traces of a bipartisan approach to education had now disappeared. Secure in her political position, having won a 102-seat majority, Thatcher was intent on making up for lost time and her government immediately started producing legislation to embed lasting changes to the schools system.

The 'landmark' Education Reform Bill

The Education Reform Act 1988[98] was passed a year after Thatcher's election victory and I think deserves the prefix 'landmark' because it has determined the foundations of primary and secondary schooling to the present day. The previous 'landmark' act (1944) had been known by the name of its architect – 'The Butler Act'. I don't know why Baker's legislation is rarely associated with his name but is instead known by its full title or as ERA, the Education Reform Act. During its passage through Parliament it had a more memorable nickname, 'the GERBIL' (the great educational reform bill).

Butler's 1944 Act had enshrined in law the authority for delivering children's education with the LEAs and individual schools. ERA re-wrote the rules and shifted the centre of power towards central government and parents. What might seem like a relatively small change required 300 pages of legislation, three times the size of Butler's Act.

Most of the policies contained in the 1988 Act had been outlined in the Conservative Party manifesto (1987) and have already been discussed. Because they have determined so much of today's system of schooling, however, I think it worth reiterating the Act's objectives and how they were to be achieved. To help us understand the changes, I have mapped objectives to specific policies, but the reality was more complicated, with many policies helping to achieve multiple objectives.

Objectives	Policies to achieve objective
To give parents more control and choice over their children's education	Establish city technology colleges that were funded by central government and industry.
	Provide central government funding for children to attend private schools (Assisted Places Scheme).
	Enable parents to nominate the school they wanted their children to attend – known as 'open enrolment'.
Diminish LEAs' power over the running of schools	Allow secondary and primary schools to 'opt out' of LEA control and become grant-maintained. Funding would then be provided by central government, not the LEA, and schools would have far more autonomy over how they operated.
	Local management of schools, which would allow head teachers and school governors to manage their own finances, rather than being controlled by the LEA.
	Abolish the Inner London Education Authority.
Achieve greater consistency in what children were taught and the educational standards they should achieve	Divide the pupil's school lifetime into four 'key stages'. At the end of each stage, the pupil's achievements would be measured against an absolute set of learning standards.

The 1988 Education Act – objectives and how they were to be achieved

For instance, the use of testing at the end of each key stage also provided parents with more information (and control) over their child's schooling. City technology colleges gave parents a greater choice of schools and weakened the power of the LEAs. Grant-maintained schools not only circumvented control by the LEA but also increased the variety of schools that parents could choose for their children. For instance, if the governors received sufficient support from parents, schools could implement a selective admissions policy.

There were many things the Act didn't do. Like its predecessor, it made no mention of the type of secondary school that children should attend. It didn't directly challenge the supremacy of the comprehensive model that was the dominant system throughout England and Wales.

What it did, above everything else, was to alter the balance of power of those determining the day-to-day working within schools. Teachers and the LEAs no longer controlled the education agenda. Some parts they shared with central government and parents; over other elements they relinquished control.

For the great majority of children, the arguments about grammar versus comprehensive schools and selective versus non-selective education now seemed like ancient history. If the 11-plus and secondary moderns were mentioned at all, it was as a warning from the left about the 'bad old days'. With 90% of secondary children attending comprehensives in 1987, any debate about the 'system' of education was over. What was taught in the comprehensives and how they and their pupils were evaluated were the new battle grounds of education politics.

Since I began relating the history of secondary education it has been littered with examples of central government's education policies failing or taking an excruciatingly long time to implement. Ministers such as Joseph looked in vain for the 'levers' of the command and control system to translate their policies into actions. Central government used to do little more than provide the mood music, with the LEAs and teachers doing pretty much what they wanted. That era had ended.

Many parts of the education world were distraught. Nobody likes having their authority weakened, especially if it is done by a government that they perceive as being the evil enemy. Clive Chitty mustered together a barrage of quotes from educationalists and the media about Baker's Act – none of them complimentary.[99] A 'Gothic monstrosity of legislation' was perhaps the most expressive description; most expressed fears of the legislation's consequences.

> *Children's futures were now threatened by a scheme casually destructive of the best in the maintained system, dangerously divisive, and administratively unworkable.*

> *If market forces were allowed to prevail, planning would, in future, be retrospective: a matter of picking up the bits and presiding over the bankruptcies after the consumers have made their educational purchases.*

Likewise, Brian Simon listed educationalists, LEA officials and even senior clerics who disagreed with Baker's policies.[100]

The quote that I think best expressed the anger was contained in the book *The Education Reform Act 1988*.[101] It wasn't just that some people disagreed with the details of the policies, but they felt belittled and slighted.

> *If we might now be witnessing the demise of liberal education, it is because, after decades of exhortation, Thatcherism has attacked directly, and with scant regard of the opinions and feelings of professional educationalists, its institutional base.*

When James Callaghan made his Ruskin College speech (1976) his policy adviser Bernard Donoughue commented that his boss had trespassed into the education establishment's 'secret garden'. Up until then politicians had left the details of the curriculum to the 'experts'. Since then the gate to the garden had been gradually opened – Thatcher tore it down.

Using selective quotes to substantiate an argument can be misleading. It is too easy to select the opinions that support your argument and ignore those that don't. For instance, in *The Times Educational Supplement*, which contained many of the criticisms, was an article lambasting teachers for ignoring parents – a quote that rarely appears.[102]

Too many in education, teachers and administrators alike, treat
parents as an alien force, at best to be humoured at worst kept at
bay. Yet services exist for their customers, not for professionals – a
statement of the blindingly obvious as true for education as for the
health service.

At the time of the 1988 Act the school population was in rapid decline. Between 1980 and the early 1990s, secondary school pupil numbers fell by 1 million.[103] Over the next decade numbers gradually increased again, but not back to the earlier level. Fewer pupils required fewer secondary schools and fewer teachers. This must have created fear among the educational establishment, which may have been expressed as anger and criticism. Handling this contraction would have been difficult at the best of times but it was being done during a period when the rules governing the education system were being rewritten.

The Conservatives were in power for almost another decade, during which time they produced numerous circulars, white papers and education acts. These refined the individual policies of the 1988 Act but did not radically change its framework. Their details don't affect the overall story of secondary moderns and their influence, so I want jump to the point when Labour regained power and to consider the model of secondary education they inherited.

But before doing that, let's pause to consider a couple of questions I want to address. First, why was so much effort directed at diminishing the LEAs' powers? Second, were the fundamental changes in the Conservatives' education policy mirrored in those of the other political parties?

Labour's central and local government politicians shift to the left

I have explained on many occasions how LEAs hampered central government's attempts to implement its policies. Labour ministers had complained about Conservative-controlled LEAs thwarting the drive to 'go comprehensive' and when in power the Conservatives complained about Labour LEAs destroying grammar schools. So, it comes as no surprise that a government had decided to curb the LEAs' powers. I'm surprised that it took so long. However, this doesn't explain the intensity of Thatcher's distrust and dislike.

The battle to wrench away control of schools from the LEAs was but one flashpoint in a bitter war the Conservatives were waging for 'who controlled' the country and some of the LEAs were seen as the enemies.

How long a government remains in power is often inversely related to the number of LEAs that its local politicians control. I don't fully under-stand why this happens, but this rule applied during Thatcher's reign and exactly the same thing occurred during the 13 years when the Labour Party returned to power. In 1976 the Conservatives controlled 50% of councils and Labour 15%. By the time the Conservatives left office in 1997 they controlled less than 5% of LEAs and Labour's share had risen to just under 50%. When Labour left office in 2010 the situation had reversed, and the Conservatives' share of LEAs had recovered to over 50%.[104]

Having different political parties in control of central and local govern-ment was not new; nor were the tensions that resulted. But during Thatch-er's premiership the antagonism reached extreme levels. The left would probably rationalise the problem and blame it on Thatcher's combative personality. That may have been a contributory factor, but the primary reason resulted from the convulsions taking place within the Labour Party.

Michael Foot led the Labour Party at the time of the 1983 general elec-tion. He came from the left, some would say far left, of the party and was better known for the quality of his oratory than his leadership skills. He based Labour's campaign on a manifesto to nationalise large parts of British industry, give greater powers to the trade unions and increase public spend-ing. It is now better known as the 'longest suicide note in history'.[105]

Following its electoral defeat, the worst result since 1918, the Labour Party underwent a period of internal battles between its left-wing and centralist supporters. Although the voters resoundingly rejected Foot and his policies, elements of the left retained his ideology and continued their battle for control. Much of their power was exerted through local politics, especially in urban areas. London's Greater London Council (GLC) was the largest and most influential centre of left-wing power. It believed that the 'whole point of our administration is that we are a challenge to the central capitalist state' and that the restriction of its right to increase spending by raising the rates would have been 'accepting subservience to Tory class rule'.[106] These class-based, anti-capitalist sentiments had been common in the universities during the 1960s and 1970s and had now –

unsurprisingly – found their way into 'grown-up' politics. Some might say, 'grown-up politics' had regressed to the level of ideologically driven student activists.

The conflict that ensued was not the usual Conservative government versus Labour LEAs. It was a battle between a government and a left-wing sect of the Labour Party. After many skirmishes the Conservatives eventually took draconian action and 'capped the rates', something that made the LEAs' loss of influence over education appear inconsequential.[107]

In recounting these events of 36 years ago it is difficult not to see the parallels with the state of the Labour Party before the 2019 general election. Not only were the circumstances similar, but so were some of the protagonists. The deputy leader of the GLC and one of its most ardent advocates of fighting the Conservatives was John McDonnell. He became Labour's shadow chancellor and an architect of Labour's 2019 manifesto, which resulted in a defeat that was greater than that of 1983.

These words from Thatcher captured the seriousness of the threat she believed faced the country.[108]

> *At one end of the spectrum are the terrorist gangs within our*
> *borders, and the terrorist states which finance and arm them [the*
> *Irish Republican Army bombed the Conservative annual conference*
> *in 1984]. At the other are the hard-left operating inside our system,*
> *conspiring to use union power and the apparatus of local govern-*
> *ment to break, defy and subvert the law.*

This might be an extreme statement of the situation, but my memories of the time support the sentiments. No doubt many LEAs were governed by reasonable people, but many were not. All of local government was affected by the Conservative government's determination to neuter its power, none more so than the LEAs.

It comes as little surprise that the new leader of the Labour Party (Neil Kinnock) had more important things on his mind than refining education policies. The Party's 1987 manifesto seemed like a 'cut-and-paste exercise' using much of the content from past documents. There was one new commitment to implementing a national curriculum and testing pupils' achievements throughout their school life. Where the policy differed from the Conservatives' was Labour's intention to work with the LEAs in achieving it.

Despite Labour's inward-looking focus it took every opportunity to score political points against the Conservatives. This is what its shadow education minister (Jack Straw) said about the Act:[109]

> *Under the guise of arguments for an agreed core curriculum, the Bill*
> *will seek to impose a centralised state syllabus. Under the guise of*
> *higher standards, the Bill will label children as failures at the ages of*
> *seven, 11, 14 and 16, impose selection and segregate children by*
> *class and by race.*

I think this sounded like political bluster rather than a reasoned criticism of the Act. Talk of failure at 11 was no doubt supposed to resurrect memories of the 11-plus. Talk of 'selection' and 'segregat[ing] children' was supposed to do the same thing about selective schools. As we will see, once Labour emerged from fighting its internal battles it embraced most of the Act's provisions.

Another result of Labour's internal strife was the creation of a new political party, formed by four former Cabinet members. One of these was Shirley Williams, the person responsible for managing Callaghan's 'great debate' about education. The 'gang of four', as they became known, formed the Social Democratic Party (SDP).[110] By the time of the 1987 election, it had formed an alliance with the Liberal Party. This new combined party may have won only 22 seats, but its share of the vote was not far behind that of the Labour Party.[111] The SDP's views about education – and there were a lot of them – were interesting because they revealed the beliefs of the centrist side of the Labour Party and the Liberal Party. These extracts are taken from their manifesto and have many similarities to those of the Conservatives.

The teachers' ongoing disruption of the schools

> *The action by the teachers' unions should cease. It does nothing to*
> *achieve their aims. It is damaging pupils' education, is alienating*
> *public opinion and undermining the standing of teachers in the*
> *community. It is in no-one's interest that it continues.*

Requirements to publish records of school performance and targets

Both maintained and independent schools should publish indicators showing progress in academic results related to intake and social factors such as community involvement, truancy, and delinquency. Each school to set targets for improvement.

Schools that aren't adequately performing would be subject to 'special inspections'.

LEAs to be set rules ensuring that they:

- Give parents a voice on the education committees.
- Publish their policies on home/school links.
- Appoint an advisory officer with special responsibility for developing a closer partnership with parents.
- Train parent governors.

Schools to have full charge of their own budgets, ensuring that a fully representative governing body is accountable for making the most effective use of the available money.

Commitment to a national curriculum: A 'broad and balanced curriculum' would be 'established by consensus' and would provide a 'core range of subjects to be studied by all pupils' but allowing for 'local needs to be reflected and innovation to be tried'. This half-hearted proposal had all of the hallmarks of Shirley Williams, somebody who put great value on achieving 'consensus' and not being constrained by hard and fast statements of policy. But behind all the caveats and vagueness was the acceptance that all children should be taught a core curriculum.

Much of the historical commentary about the 1988 Education Act suggested that there was a gulf between the Conservatives' education policies and those of everybody else. I don't think this is validated by this summary of the other parties' policies. No party was questioning the need for a national curriculum, pupil testing or greater power for parents and school governors. The demarcation line was the role of the LEAs in controlling education – as little as possible being the Conservatives' line, with the other parties wanting to retain some involvement. Because supporters of the LEAs rarely explained what 'value add' they provided made them an easy target to attack.

Conservative education policies span the political divide

Tony Blair became prime minister on 2 May 1997, ending nearly two decades of Conservative government. The centrepiece of Labour's manifesto was a 10-point 'contract with the people' and improving education was its number one task.[112]

> *Education will be our number one priority, and we will increase the share of national income spent on education as we decrease it on the bills of economic and social failure.*

'Education' is always ranked as a high priority by incoming governments but in his 1997 manifesto launch speech, Blair awarded it the top three priorities: 'education, education, education we said would be the top three priorities'.[113] How Blair's declared passion for education translated into delivering a better education for secondary school children will be our topic for the final part of the timeline.

Although the secondary education system he inherited was built on the framework established by Baker's 1988 Education Act, it had been refined and extended in the intervening nine years. During that time there had been a further three education acts and numerous reports and white papers. Don't worry, I am not about to relate the many details contained in these documents. My interest is how they materially affected the primary policies of the original Act.

City technology colleges (CTCs). Baker had viewed these as a 'proof of concept' venture that enabled him to demonstrate how private industry and government could work together to create a new type of learning institution. Only 15 CTCs were opened, which is not a resounding proof of their popularity. No doubt there were a host of factors that explained why so few were built. Most 'new ideas' don't succeed in their first iteration, the funding model required a significant contribution from the industrial partner and the focus was on a single discipline (technology). Although the CTCs operated outside LEA control, they still required their cooperation – something that was often not forthcoming.

But in the long term Baker's instincts proved right, because a modified version of the CTCs was adopted by the Blair government. Initially these were called 'specialist' schools and then they were re-christened as 'academies'. By 2008 all but three of the CTCs had converted to this new structure. The remaining CTCs still operate, all with outstanding records of academic success.

Perhaps it was a case of Baker having the right idea but at the wrong time.

Assisted-places scheme. Strictly speaking, this scheme preceded the 1988 Act but I have included it in my analysis because its aims were congruent with the Act's other policies.

By 1997 the scheme was funding the education of 34,000 children in 355 private schools. Over 40% of the pupils who benefited from the scheme came from low-income families and they achieved a higher pass rate at GCSE than their peer group in state and private schools.[114]

Despite the scheme's apparent success, it was not expanded by the Conservatives and was finally abandoned by the Blair government on the basis that its funding could be better spent reducing class sizes in state schools.

Grant-maintained schools. These schools had considerable autonomy over their operations and received funding from central government, not the LEAs. Their effectiveness was not just measured in how well they taught children but also their competency in financial management.

In 1994 the NAO studied the 'value for money' performance of 70 grant-maintained schools (GMSs) and concluded they had:[115]

Responded well to the challenge of managing their own finances and that there were numerous examples of schools implementing good practice as regards ensuring propriety and achieving value for money.

By January 1998 there were 1,261 GMSs. Just over half of these were secondary schools. The remainder were primary and 'special' schools – for pupils with particular educational needs.

Considering that the scheme had been running for 10 years, few schools had decided to manage their own affairs. Less than a quarter of secondary and only 3% of primary schools completed the process and voted to change to maintained status.[116]

Just before the 1997 general election, the government published a white paper[117] proposing new measures to extend the number of schools. Clearly, it had not given up on the idea, although this document might have been a response to the declining numbers of schools transferring to maintained status. Since September 1994 only 250 schools had become GMSs.

Rather like the CTCs, the scheme cannot be described as a success, at least in achieving its initial objectives. It was abolished by the Labour government, but some elements of self-governance were retained. Ironically, Blair sent his two sons to a school that had previously been grant-maintained.

Local management of schools. Unlike the previous policies, the local management of schools (LMS) didn't result in new types of schools but instead changed the way school finances were managed. Maybe it was the technical nature of the policy, but it didn't seem to generate much public interest, despite its weakening of the LEAs' day-to-day management of schools.

Each year LEAs decided the value of their education budget. Part of this was spent on centrally provided services that included building projects and children's school transport. The balance was a school's potential budget and at least 85% of this was controlled by the school's governing bodies. In 1997, schools in England managed approximately 90% of this budget. How much money was allocated to each school was calculated using measures of need that were mainly determined by the size of the school's roll.

The 1997 white paper proposed to increase the percentage of budget that schools controlled to 95%, further reducing the influence of LEAs.

A research paper published in 1998 quoted a survey of 160 schools and found that over 90% of head teachers 'welcomed the responsibility and flexibility' of LMS. The paper concluded that:[118]

The Local Management of Schools is generally regarded as a successful policy which is set to continue under the Labour Government. Despite initial reservations most head teachers approve of it, apart from particular details, and would not wish to return to the status quo ante.

The national curriculum. The 1988 Act defined the broad structure and objectives of the national curriculum. Its aims were to be 'balanced and broadly based' and promote the 'spiritual, moral, cultural, mental and physical development of pupils', while preparing them for the 'opportunities, responsibilities and experiences of adult life'.

These worthy (but vague) objectives were to be achieved by teaching pupils 10 foundation subjects. Three of these – English, maths and science – were designated as 'core' subjects; the others were art, geography, history, music, physical education and technology, with a modern foreign language taught from the age of 11 onwards. Over time, the distinction between the 'core' and the other 'foundation' subjects became clear, but in the original Act it was difficult to see how they differed. An interesting explanation for this vagueness came in a 2015 blog post by Dominic Cummings, written a year after he left the role of chief of staff to the then minister (Michael Gove). He quoted Baker's permanent secretary (David Hancock) as saying:[119]

We devised the notion of the core and the foundation subjects but if you examine the Act you will see that there is no difference between the two.

Cummings believed this was a 'totally cynical and deliberate manoeuvre on Kenneth Baker's part to con Thatcher into agreeing his scheme'. He believed she wanted a limited core curriculum based on English, maths and science, but that Baker and his officials wanted it to be broadly based. It's a frightening thought that for the past 30 years, part of the framework for children's secondary education may have been based on a political 'con'.

Of all the provisions of the 1988 Act it was the complexities of the national curriculum that most perplexed the seven ministers who served throughout the Conservatives' time in power.

The responsibility for converting the outline curriculum into detailed materials that could be used in schools was the responsibility of a newly formed organisation – the National Curriculum Council (NCC). It has been blamed for creating the resulting 'complexities' and Baker was accused of not taking greater care with how it was constituted. A detailed account of the NCC's failings was given in the pamphlet *Progressively Worse*.[120] Cumming's blog post provided a more succinct explanation:

> *Like many ministers, he [Baker] did not understand the importance of the policy detail and the intricate issues of implementation. One of Baker's spads [special advisers] said he was conned into appointing [to the NCC] 'the very ones responsible for the failures we have been trying to put right'... 'he never envisaged it would be as complex as it turned out to be'.*

In this account of what happened, Baker is either guilty of making the wrong appointments to the NCC or not paying enough attention to how it operated. Certainly, the interviews with subsequent ministers conducted by Peter Ribbins and Brian Sherratt[121] echoed these problems, but diplomatically they didn't point the finger of blame at Baker.

MacGregor (minister 1989–1990):

> *I did worry about the extent to which – and perhaps I am being rather unkind in putting it in this way – some educational experts saw the National Curriculum as the opportunity to put into practice their own pet views and pet theories. I had to put a brake on the over prescriptive educational establishment.*

Clarke (minister 1990–1992):

> *We had created debating societies [referring to the NCC subject committees] with a curious mixture of people who didn't seem altogether agreed on their purpose and certainly didn't seem altogether to be agreed on the purpose which I'd expected – so I had trouble with them from the start.*

His concern that these committees kept extending the scope of the curriculum forced Clarke to personally intervene when he over-ruled, and modified, their recommendations on the sport, music, geography and history curricula.

Patten (minister 1992–1994):

> It was a gold-plated kitchen sink into which everything went and I think we found out all too painfully, and I got some of the sharper end of it, that the national curriculum was over-crowed, over-elaborate and over-prescriptive.

The practical and political pressure resulting from the unwieldy state of the curriculum forced Patten to ask Sir Ron Dearing to consider 'slimming down the National Curriculum'.[122] Dearing's report was published at the end of 1993, but it was left to the next minister (Gillian Shephard) to implement its recommendations. In 1995 an updated national curriculum was published that reduced the amount of prescribed content and restricted testing to the core subjects – an outcome very close to Thatcher's original vision.

It seems the national curriculum project followed the wrong path from the start, and it took eight years for the resulting problems to be rectified. Weaknesses in the workings of the NCC were visible from an early stage but the political and administrative machine was slow to respond. Sadly, the national curriculum is another item on the lengthening list of poorly managed education policies.

The cost of this mistake was not just financial. Between 1987 and 1991 the national measure of reading age declined by an equivalent of six months. There are two explanations: the national curriculum was introduced, resulting in less time spent teaching literacy, and during this period the rate at which primary teachers changed jobs was abnormally high. Nobody knows the relative importance of these events, or indeed if they were connected, but the damage caused by the decline in the literacy rate affected the cohort of children throughout the remainder of their school lives.[123]

Measuring pupils' understanding of the national curriculum. In parallel to devising the national curriculum was the need to devise the testing procedures that would report how well it was being understood. The School Examinations and Assessment Council (SEAC) was responsible for this task.

In the same way as the NCC created an overly complicated curriculum, SEAC repeated the mistakes with the testing procedures. All the sources I have quoted for their accounts of the national curriculum are equally damning about SEAC's failings – in some cases more so.

In addition to considering the curriculum, Dearing was asked 'how the testing arrangements might be simplified'. Most of his recommendations were implemented and the level of testing reduced.

There are arguments in defence of the NCC and SEAC, namely that they were badly constituted and briefed. Whoever is to blame, there is little doubt that testing and the national curriculum were badly implemented. In 1993 the School's Examinations and Assessment Authority was created, replacing both organisations.

I will give Cummings the final word on these two aspects of the 1988 Education Act.

Thatcher never wanted a big national curriculum and a complicated testing system, but she got one. As some of her ideological opponents in the bureaucracy tried to simplify things, when it was clear Baker's original structure was a disaster, ministers were often fighting with them to preserve a complex system that could not work. This sums up the basic problem – a very disruptive process was embarked upon without the main players agreeing what the goal was.

If Thatcher is associated with 1988 Education Act then her successor (John Major) is remembered for its successor, the Act passed in 1992 – and in particular its creation of the Office for Standards in Education (Ofsted). Inspecting the performance of schools had been the responsibility of Her Majesty's Chief Inspector. Its brief was not to regularly study the performance of individual schools but rather to report to the minister about particular aspects of education and in extreme circumstances report on a school. The staffing levels of the Inspector meant that a secondary school could expect an inspection about once every 40 years and a primary every 200 years. According to Patten, some LEAs inspected their schools, but few did so on a systematic basis and if reports were produced, they were for the benefit of the LEA not parents.

The creation of Ofsted considerably increased the number of inspectors, many of them employed by companies, not the government. The regularity of inspections was increased, with the target of each school being visited every four years. Most importantly, the inspection reports were released into the public domain and designed to be read by the general public, not just education specialists. Well, that was (and still is) the theory of how it should work.

The process and results of an Ofsted inspection caused considerable concern and anxiety among teachers. This is not surprising given that, in little over a decade, the workings and performance of individual schools and their pupils had gone from being opaque and unmeasured to being regularly quantified and reported. It's not unusual for employees of companies to have their work appraised and graded but it was a totally new experience for teachers.

Most elements of today's system of schooling were created during the 18 years of Conservative government. That it still remains largely intact, 24 years later, is a testimony to its creators. That said, the post-1988 Education Act undoubtedly resulted in considerable upheaval and its implementation was poorly managed.

It's impossible to know to what extent it benefited the generation of children who were at school during this time. My guess, and it is a guess, is that it made little difference to the quality of their schooling. Most of the changes were aimed at improving how schools were managed and providing parents with meaningful information about their children's achievements. If that improved what happened in the classroom, it would be accrued by future generations of children. Certainly, the botched implementation of the national curriculum and pupil testing had an initial negative rather than positive outcome.

Critics of the Conservatives' education policies continued to claim that they were politically rather than educationally motivated and were all about centralising control and bypassing the influence of the LEAs and teachers. Defenders would counter that they provided a nationwide consistency to what was taught and gave power to the ultimate 'customer' – the parents. Like the battle of ideas between selective and comprehensive education, these arguments were really about political doctrine not education. Until now it was impossible to know the effects (if any) of these opposing theories on the quality of children's education. That had changed with the new regime of school and pupil testing. It was now becoming possible to measure politicians' effectiveness at translating their educational promises into tangible benefits.

The Conservatives lost the 1997 election and the Labour Party returned to government with the largest majority in post-WWII history (179). As we've already seen, Labour promised that improving education was its primary objective. Its Parliamentary majority and the public goodwill that accompanied its election meant it could do pretty much what it wanted. In the past, the first actions of an incoming government had been to undo much of what its predecessor had created. Which of Thatcher's policies did it want to replace or merely adapt and extend? Had we returned to a bipartisan approach to secondary education or did fundamental differences still remain?

'New Labour' jettisons Labour's education policies

The answers to these questions would have been very different but for one major event. On 12 May 1994, John Smith, the leader of the Labour Party, had suffered a heart attack and died. His beliefs about education and the policies he would have enacted, had he become prime minister, had been documented in a green paper by his shadow education minister (Ann Taylor).[124]

Smith's introduction to the document set the tone:

> *We reject the approach of a Conservative Government which is driven by consumerist dogma, by oppressive dictation by the central state, and by a false and inadequate theory of choice.*

Without abandoning all of the Conservatives' policies it reinterpreted them through the lens of socialist ideology. It contained some hard and fast policies but much of it was concerned with 'visions', 'principles' and establishing 'frameworks', a word that appeared 25 times in the document. Depending on your political affinity it was little more than a collection of 'buzz words' and platitudes that would delight the educational establishment. Alternatively, it was the 'framework' for building a fairer and more inclusive system of education. What jumped out of the document was Smith's distrust of the 'market' and his confidence in the LEAs.

There is little doubt what Blair and his supporters thought about the document. Within a week of taking office, at the press conference to launch Taylor's paper, Blair made his views crystal clear. What happened was recounted by Blair's biographer.[125]

> *That day he commandeered his shadow Education Secretary's news conference. Where Taylor was opposed to league tables of school exam results, he said he was in favour of publishing information. In case journalists did not spot the difference, they had been briefed beforehand by Blair's staff that his words would contradict those of Taylor.*
>
> *On the lunchtime television news Blair was asked what the main points of the document were, and his first point was that unfit teachers should be sacked – another 'tough' message, designed to distract attention from the document itself.*

The Guardian's reporting of the press conference was surprising.[126] It made much of how the document had been 'born and bred under John Smith' and how he had 'openly boasted about not allowing consumers too much say on education'. After welcoming some of its recommendations *The Guardian* concluded with the damning words: 'It is time for Mr Blair to apply his stamp and demonstrate the radicalism that John Smith had left out.' It would seem that Blair had listened to the advice.

Three months later, Taylor had the policy document endorsed by Labour's annual conference.[127] This was a totemic victory: two weeks later she was replaced by David Blunkett, whose views about education were more aligned with those of Blair.

We cannot be sure to what extent Blunkett's biographer reflected his own or Blunkett's views about Taylor, but this is what he said.[128]

> *Taylor was, in effect, the National Union of Teachers' Westminster spokeswoman, representative of a tradition in which Labour's education policy was in thrall to the teaching unions and the education*

*establishment of which the NUT was by far the most antediluvian
example.*

For the next four years, Blunkett played a key role in formulating and
delivering Labour's education strategy, during which time he made no secret
of his views, often negative (very), about the educational establishment.

One of Blair's most trusted advisers, Peter Mandelson, also held forthright views about the competency of those working in education.[129]

*The teacher unions have tried to focus the public debate about
education on pay and resources, rather than outputs. The education
egalitarians regard the structure of schools as far more important
than the quality of what is learned and have sometimes seemed to
show a far greater concern for the social balance of a school's
admissions than for the destination of a school's graduates.*

During late 1994 and 1995, the Labour Party was re-christened 'New
Labour'. Along with the new name came new ideas and discarding long-
held ideals. If there had been any doubt that Blair was leading a new-style
political party, it dissolved when he removed the socialist 'Clause IV' from
the Party's constitution. This was not just a cosmetic change in wording but
a message that the party was abandoning its adherence to socialism. Gone
was the Party's commitment to securing for workers the most equitable
distribution by the 'the common ownership of the means of production,
distribution and exchange'.

In the space of under a year the Labour Party had experienced a very
public *Sliding Doors* moment. Smith would have taken the Party in a totally
different direction from Blair, whose policies were surprisingly similar to
those of the Conservative Party. As it was, Blair was less concerned with
Labour's long-held ideals and more concerned with what would get it (and
him) elected to power – even if this meant mirroring Thatcher's policies. His
recognition (and admiration) of her perception of public sentiment was
made clear in his autobiography.[130]

*Where Mrs Thatcher was absolutely on the side of history was in
recognising that as people became more prosperous, they wanted the*

freedom to spend their money as they chose; and they didn't want a
big state getting in the way of that liberation by suffocating people in
uniformity, in the drabness and dullness of the state monopoly. It was
plain that competition drove up standards, and that high taxes were
a disincentive. Anything else ignored human nature.

If Labour was capable of renouncing the key tenets of its constitution, then creating a radically different education policy was a simple task. In 1995 it published *Diversity and Excellence – a new partnership for schools*.[131] This bore little resemblance to its predecessor. Gone were the ideals about 'opening doors to a learning society'; now the focus was 'diversity' and 'excellence', two words that rarely appeared in the 'Old Labour' lexicon.

The most vicious critics of this document were not Conservatives but Labour politicians. On the day of its publication, Roy Hattersley, a distinguished Labour MP, who had been the Party's deputy leader, vented his disapproval in an article published by the *Independent*.[132]

Diversity and Excellence is the sort of soft-sell slogan that possesses
all the meaningless charm of a detergent commercial... It is so
preoccupied with emollience that it accepts – perhaps even extends –
the divisions which disfigure secondary education.

Hattersley's reaction was surprising because he was considered to be on the right of Labour's political spectrum and Blunkett on the left. Not only were Labour's policies changing, but so were the political allegiances of its senior politicians.

The Guardian was not happy with Blair's education policy.[133] Its headline read 'Labour completes U-turn on schools' and the article went on to accuse Blair of reversing Smith's pledge to ditch Tory reforms and instead aiming to 'woo uncommitted voters'. One of those 'ploys' was 'instead of returning control to local authorities having the aim to build up parent power'.

Comprehensives become an embarrassment

To my mind, the *Diversity and Excellence* paper marked the beginning of the end of comprehensive schooling as the cornerstone of Labour's education strategy. Even though the document contained one mention of the schools ('Labour's commitment to lifelong learning and comprehensive education') it seemed to be included because it should be rather than as a policy commitment.

By the time the 1997 Labour election manifesto was published, the schools were portrayed as being part of the problem, rather than the solution.

We reject both the idea of a return to the 11-plus and the monolithic comprehensive schools that take no account of children's differing abilities. Instead we favour all-in schooling which identifies the distinct abilities of individual pupils and organises them in classes to maximise their progress in individual subjects. In this way we modernise the comprehensive principle.

I have highlighted those parts of the text I think reveal New Labour's beliefs and intentions. This statement was a superb example of 'the third way', a phrase (or was it a philosophy?) that defined so many of its policies. It positioned New Labour as being against the bad old days of the 11-plus but also as rejecting the uniformity and inflexibility of comprehensivisation. It recognised that schools needed a better way of catering for the wide range of children's abilities and that this would be achieved by modernising the comprehensive 'principle' – not the 'school'. It was a blatant attempt to appeal to parents (voters) with concerns about the effectiveness of comprehensives but fearful of a return to selective education. It echoed Harold Wilson's promise to provide 'a grammar school education for all children' at the same time as closing grammar schools.

By the time of the 1997 general election the Conservatives were a spent political force. Their manifesto handed Blair an easy target to attack when it promised to increase the number of grammar schools by having 'a grammar school in every town where parents want that choice'.

Blair took this commitment, having omitted the condition about 'where parents want the choice', and claimed:[134]

John Major's promise of a grammar school in every town means four or five secondary moderns in every town.

This was a perfect example of a politician weaponising the words 'secondary modern'. It was unfair but it worked, and still does. When Blair entered Downing Street, as prime minister, just 91 secondary moderns and 158 grammar schools remained. If he was to deliver on his electoral promise of raising educational standards, then he had to improve the performance of the 2,900 comprehensives.

Why did New Labour fall out of love with comprehensives? I am not sure I know the answer. I am not sure anybody knows the answer. There hadn't been any acrimonious campaigns by educationalists or politicians demanding a change in strategy. If anything, the loudest voices came from those defending the schools. No report was published that provided irrefutable evidence of their failures. The Conservatives were so weak that if they had attacked the schools it would have been futile. But there were no attacks. During the Conservatives' time in power they permitted (rather than encouraged) comprehensives to become the dominant system of schooling.

The strange death of the comprehensive school in England and Wales was published in 2004 and identified multiple reasons for their demise.[135] The author made no attempt to prioritise the causes but implied that taken together they sealed the schools' fate. It is not a very satisfactory answer, but I think it is the right explanation, although some of his points sound more like excuses than convincing arguments. These are his reasons for their 'strange death', in a mixture of the author's and my words.

The work of dark forces. There had always been powerful groups of people who were against the 'comprehensive ideal' and who, even if they were not actively working to bring about their failure, would capitalise on their weaknesses. These included the 'usual suspects' of Conservative politicians, right-wing think tanks, senior civil servants and employers. All the while the national press was quick to publish negative news about the schools. This created a feedback loop with politicians and policy makers reacting to the adverse commentary and promising to rectify the schools' deficiencies – actual and perceived.

Marginalising of the educational establishment. Callaghan was credited with – or blamed for, depending on your viewpoint – breaching the walls of the 'secret garden', where questions about curriculum and teaching methods were decided. Up until then, the LEAs, teachers and educational academics policed this discourse and were, in the main, supportive of comprehensive schools and their political ideology. The intervention of politicians and their advisers meant that policy decisions now had to account for the views of parents (voters).

Comprehensives were never given a chance to succeed. Successive Labour governments had failed to honour their promises to incorporate grammar and private schools into the comprehensive system. As a result, comprehensives never had a truly balanced intake of children because the brightest children went elsewhere.

A hierarchy of comprehensive schools existed from the beginning. Those that were converted secondary moderns had to battle against their school's historical reputation. Brand new comprehensives and those that were converted grammar schools were at a distinct advantage. These differences were exacerbated once parents were permitted access to schools' performance results. Good schools were oversubscribed, whereas poorly performing schools were shunned and became the dumping ground for disruptive pupils. These 'sink schools' further tarnished the reputation of all comprehensives.

The polarisation was further increased by the ability of the much-criticised 'sharp-elbowed' middle classes to 'work the system' and get their children into the best-performing schools.

In short, the community comprehensive never really existed and was never given a chance to prove its worth.

Support for comprehensives was built on weak foundations. Central to this argument is that parents (and many politicians) supported comprehensive schools because of their antipathy towards selection and the 11-plus, rather than their commitment to the comprehensive ideal.

There always had been, and still are, those who believed that educating children of differing abilities together results in a net benefit to them and society. There were many others who rejected selection at 11 because of its perceived unfairness or (more likely) because they feared their children would be on the wrong side of the exam result.

Comprehensives never established a widespread reputation as good and effective schools for delivering academic success. When their detractors offered alternatives that didn't involve the 11-plus, they didn't galvanise the intensity of support that helped protect grammar schools.

What the paper's author failed to mention was that on the instructions of Crosland (when the Labour Party and most educationalists were committed to promoting the 'go comprehensive' policy), no research was to be done into the effectiveness of comprehensive schools. There was no credible evidence that the comprehensive principle had been successful in raising standards.

Do what I say, not what I do. The Conservatives had always believed in the freedom of parents to choose the type of school their children attended. That many Conservative politicians had attended private or selective schools was consistent with their beliefs. This raised questions about how much they knew about state schooling, but that is a different argument.

But when senior Labour politicians, who professed their beliefs in the principle of comprehensive schooling, sent their own children to private or selective schools it reeked of hypocrisy. As we have seen, Blair sent his sons to a school that had been grant-maintained. This was followed in 1996 by Harriet Harman, the shadow health secretary, sending her son to a grammar school. This presented Blair with a major problem, with calls for Harman's resignation and criticism of him for defending her. In his autobiography, Blair recalled the event and why he decided to support Harman's decision. I think his words revealed his uneasiness about the core belief of many Labour members.

> *Labour people would understand why Harriet might have to resign*
> *over this – no ordinary person would. Some woman politician*
> *decides to send her kid to a grammar school. She thinks it gives him*
> *the best chance of a good education. Her party forces her to resign.*
> *What do you think? You think that's a bit extreme; and not very nice;*
> *and a bit worrying; and is that what still makes me a bit anxious*
> *about those Labour people? [This was before the 1997 election.]*

Little has changed with today's generation of Labour politicians and supporters, who are vehemently against private schools. Yet, many of them choose private or selective schools for their own children. Witness the decisions made by Shami Chakrabarti, Emily Thornberry, Diane Abbott, Seumas Milne and many others.

New Labour had different values from the 'old' version. When asked about her greatest achievement, Margaret Thatcher is said to have replied: 'Tony Blair and New Labour'. Maybe it was true, maybe not. That Blair and his supporters had little in common with their predecessors is beyond doubt. Just as Clause IV had become a superfluous anachronism so the rallying cry of 'go comprehensive' now sounded like an echo from a bygone era. In his autobiography, Blair made this revealing statement about his battle to change the Labour Party's ideas about schooling:

Schools were a constant object of controversy in those early days as I tried to wean the party off its old prejudices (though I think they may have called them beliefs).

In 1996, Blair and his deputy (John Prescott) gave speeches to commemorate the 20th anniversary of Callaghan's Ruskin College speech. How they portrayed comprehensive education could not have been more different. Blair's speech didn't mention the schools but instead focused on 'raising standards' and holding education providers 'accountable for their performance'.[136]

Prescott's speech was splattered with references to comprehensive schools (23) and with words about how he 'passionately supports comprehensive education'.[137] Much of the speech attacked the Conservatives and most of the remainder was a parable about how he had achieved success despite attending a secondary modern.

New Labour still contained supporters of comprehensives – or was it a visceral hatred of selective schooling? – but their influence was waning.

The world had changed since the times of Attlee, Wilson and Smith. The Soviet Union was collapsing, along with faith in the effectiveness of centralised state planning. This was a time when the approach of 'do what works' was gaining ascendancy over 'do what our ideology demands'.

Damned by association. The heyday of comprehensives coincided with the rise of progressive teaching techniques and the influx of teachers who had been educated during the social upheaval of the 1960s. When the press reported stories of 'teachers doing little more than crowd control' and pupils' unruly behaviour undermining those children who were anxious to learn, it was comprehensivisation as much as 'progressive teaching' that was blamed.

Engulfed as they were by so many negative forces it's not surprising that by the mid-1990s articles critical of comprehensives were regularly appearing in the press.

The state-school system is failing our children. Ofsted called for the dismissal of bad teachers and demanded improvements in 4 out of 10 secondary schools. [138]

He [David Blunkett] accused comprehensive schools of 'enforcing drab uniformity in the name of fairness.' At the same time, they had failed to reduce education inequality, the supposed reason for their introduction. [139]

The comprehensive schools in inner-city areas of London are very bad indeed and are failing our children. Thus, said Bernie Grant, the left-wing Labour MP for Tottenham, north London, speaking from bitter experience. [140]

It was against this backdrop that the first phase of New Labour's schools-related legislation was enacted. By the end of 1999, two education acts had been passed plus a flurry of education initiatives. The rhetoric of the 1997 election campaign had now been converted into tangible policies. What follows is an ultra-summarised account of this frenetic period of political activity.

New Labour's first action, as promised in the election manifesto, was to phase out the assisted-places scheme, which was funding 34,000 pupils to attend fee-paying schools. [141] The saving of £180 million was theoretically diverted to reducing class sizes for five-, six- and seven year olds. The actual savings would have been much lower than the headline figure because it didn't account for the costs of absorbing those being privately educated back into the secondary school system. However, these accounting details would have spoilt the story – New Labour had fulfilled its election promise.

One year later the School Standards and Framework Act was passed.[142] This was long and complex legislation (120,000 words). Grammar schools were mentioned 26 times but the country's most common secondary school – the comprehensive – didn't get a mention. It's as if those drafting the legislation were instructed to avoid the word. Maybe that's the explanation?

In January 1995, Blair and Blunkett attended an education seminar at which Professor Michael Barber introduced the concept that in education 'standards matter more than structures'.[143]

Barber's ideas chimed with Blair's and by the time the Act was passed this phrase had been abbreviated to 'standards not structures'. From now on this mantra would be central to determining the government's education strategy. The Act's name might have contained the word 'standards' but much of its content was about 'structures'. Professor Barber is somebody who became key to delivering New Labour's education policy, as we will see later.

This is how the BBC's website explained the Act's effect on the structure of schools.[144] If parents hadn't already been confused by the nomenclature of their children's schools, they probably were now.

Three new categories of schools: community, foundation and voluntary, to replace the existing school structures. County schools will become community schools, and voluntary controlled and voluntary aided schools will retain their existing characteristics within the new voluntary category.

Grant-maintained schools are expected to become foundation schools, although they will be able to choose which category of school they want to come under when the structures change. Eventually all schools will be able to choose which school category they wish to belong to.

LEAs had to create a 'school organisation plan' that explained how they would restructure, a demand that echoed the 1944 Education Act's requirement for the production of 'development plans' and the 'request' made in 1966 for them to submit plans for comprehensivisation. In half a century secondary schools had been restructured three times and more reorganisation was on its way.

These three new types of school had first been mentioned in New Labour's *Diversity and Excellence* paper in 1995 and that is the best source for a detailed explanation of their characteristics. Most of the existing comprehensives, which were originally secondary moderns, were re-christened as community schools. In most other respects, nothing changed. To my mind it seemed little more than a rebranding exercise. Instead of the admissions policy being dictated by the LEA it became 'based on parental preference agreed by the LEA'. I doubt if many parents were aware of, or cared about, the renaming exercise.

One group of parents who would have known about the Act were those with children attending the country's 1,200 grant-maintained schools – including, of course, Mr and Mrs Blair. The Act transferred the financial responsibility for these schools from central government to the LEAs, resulting in them losing an estimated £174 million in funding (in today's pounds). To help bridge this financial shortfall some schools asked parents to pay a voluntary 'levy'. The BBC reported that the Blairs received a letter asking for £80 a month, in today's pounds, to help with the education of their two sons.[145] No doubt this was an unwanted additional claim on their finances but was nothing compared with the political embarrassment it caused.

Parts of the Act did address New Labour's stated goal of raising standards and awarded LEAs a greater role in achieving this objective. The Act gave them greater powers to intervene where schools or teachers were deemed to be 'failing'. In line with the Conservatives' policies, schools were given more control of their budgets. Parental involvement was taken one step further with the introduction of 'home–school agreements' that specified the responsibilities of parents as well as their rights.

No education act enacted by Labour, new or old, was complete without mention of the few remaining grammar schools and how their demise could be engineered. In this case the Act gave the school's parents the right to initiate a ballot to decide whether the school should retain selective admission procedures. Only one ballot was ever held (in March 2000), when the parents of Ripon Grammar School voted 2:1 to reject any change. Labour's 'anti-grammar' stance was not abandoned but had become more a gesture to satisfy members on the left in the party. Since then the number of grammar schools in England has remained constant (162).

The final component of the Act that was relevant to secondary schools was the introduction of 'education action zones' (EAZs). These were partnerships between schools, LEAs and local businesses and were intended to tackle problems of under-achievement and social exclusion in poor areas. Each zone was intended to include around 20 schools – two or three secondaries and the remainder primary and nursery schools.

The zones were initially unpopular with the NUT, who believed they were a step to privatising the education service. In a memorandum they sent to the Select Committee on Education and Employment they sounded a more supportive tone because they had ensured all of the zone's project directors 'have education or public sector experience rather than purely commercial backgrounds'.[146]

Diminishing the involvement of business was something of a Pyrrhic victory: in 2003 Ofsted concluded, after studying the effectiveness of the action zones:[147]

Most of the EAZs in the first round of inspections had a limited initial effect on school improvement. Their effect has been stronger in tackling disaffection and promoting inclusion than in raising standards of achievement, especially in secondary schools.

In general, they have not accorded sufficient priority to the improvement of standards.

In November 2001 the government announced the zones would not be extended beyond their initial five-year term.

I have few detailed memories of this time but do recall that New Labour seemed to be for ever announcing new 'initiatives' – some were new, others were re-packaged schemes started by the Conservatives. Perhaps I am being a tad cynical, but my guess is this was a clever way of controlling the narrative appearing in the news media. They didn't require legislation and could be timed and packaged to maximise their political advantage. By the end of

462 | THE SECONDARY MOD

1999, most schools were likely to be part of one or more of the following schemes.

Fresh Start. The 'Fresh Start' scheme began in 1998 as a solution for England's failing schools. As the name suggests, the idea was to close the school, replace the headmaster and some or all of the teachers and re-launch it as a new school. In March 2000, Blunkett formalised the criteria for 'failing' when he announced a 'three strikes and you're out' policy. If 15% of a secondary school's pupils failed, for three consecutive years, to achieved five or more A–C grades at GCSE, it was automatically considered to be reborn.

An article published by the *British Educational Research Journal*[148] provided a good account of the scheme and the problems it suffered. It appears that the time and effort required to reverse a school's performance were underestimated. By the end of 2000 the new minster (Estelle Morris) said that the 'scheme should be reserved for the hardest cases'.[149] Ofsted classified poorly performing schools – those that were failing to provide an acceptable standard of teaching – as being on 'special measures'. Of these about 2–4% were thought bad enough to be considered for Fresh Start. By 2004 the scheme had all but disappeared from the government's education agenda.

Beacon schools. The Beacon school initiative, launched in 1998, combined two of the incentives that New Labour was keen to employ in its policies – collaboration and competition.

Through a competitive process, schools could apply for 'Beacon Status', an accolade that implied they were 'among the best in the system'. Their reward was additional funding that could be spent on teaching resources, equipment and administrative support. The 'collaborative' element of the deal was that they would work closely with partner schools and disseminate their good practice. In other words, good schools got more money to help improve the not-so-good.

The number of Beacon schools reached a peak of 1,145 in September 2002 but the scheme was discontinued in 2004. In 2004 the National Foundation for Educational Research tried to measure the effectiveness of the programme.[150] In common with many of these evaluations it concluded that there were unquantifiable benefits but in terms of its impact on raising school standards it concluded:

There is some limited statistical data that addresses the question of whether there were any improvements in student outcomes as a result of the sharing of good practice via the Beacon initiative. A simple value-added analysis revealed no evidence of statistically-significant improvements (or declines) in partner schools over Key Stage 3 from 2000 to 2001.

Ironically, the research found some evidence of improvements in pupil outcomes in the Beacon schools themselves, not those they were supposed to be helping.

Excellence in Cities. In March 1999 Blunkett announced 'Excellence in Cities' as 'a major new framework for our inner-city schools' that would fund projects in six major urban areas. This was intended to provide:[151]

A substantial expansion of specialist and beacon schools promoting diversity and excellence. Every youngster who would benefit will have access to a learning mentor, with extra help available for those who need it most. This strategy will give every pupil an entitlement to new and more challenging opportunities.

By the end of 2001 the scheme had been extended to include about a third of England's secondary schools.

When, in 2003, the Ministry reviewed the effectiveness of this scheme it reached mixed conclusions.[152] The report was littered with caveats that indicated (to me) the difficulty in evaluating its performance. Despite identifying many unquantifiable benefits, the 'bottom line' was that the scheme provided little improvement in academic standards.

There was no substantial evidence to show that EiC [Education in Cities] had an impact on levels of attainment in English or Science at the end of Key Stage 3 [14 years old]. In 2003, there was little evidence to suggest that the pupils in EiC areas were making more progress during Key Stage 4 [16 years old] than similar pupils in non-EiC areas.

Specialist schools. The origin of the term 'specialist school' goes back to the city technology colleges that were launched in 1988 by Kenneth Baker, the Conservative minister. As the name suggests they specialised in teaching technology and were part-funded by central government and private sponsorship. Before the Conservatives left government, the scheme was broadened to include schools that specialised in the languages, arts and sports.

The 1998 Education Act permitted existing specialist schools to continue and enabled new schools to select 10% of their pupils by 'aptitude'. When Labour came to power there had been 225 of these schools and over the next couple of years a further 160 were opened.[153]

Before the 1997 general election, Blair had seemed intent on ending all selection in schools. In 1995, Blunkett had said these much-quoted words to the Labour conference: 'Watch my lips. No selection.' This promise morphed into a commitment that no new schools would be allowed to select students by exam. Specialist schools took this one step further and permitted selection as long as it was done on the 'aptitude' of the child.

Maybe it was because the number of schools involved was small, but this tweaking of the policy didn't cause much reaction from the supporters of the 'comprehensive principle'. As we will soon see, this would change when these schools became a major part of New Labour's education policy.

Blair has his 'Thatcher moment'

At the start of Thatcher's third period as prime minister she had looked back with regret at her limited achievements in improving the country's schools and looked forward with a new resolve to do better. We've already seen the actual words she used: 'There is going to be a revolution in the running of the schools.'[154]

Blair's autobiography suggested that by contrast his doubts and renewed determination started midway through his first period as prime minister:

> *Literacy and numeracy hours were a step forward for primary schools, but what about failing comprehensives, particularly in the cities, which were the real Achilles heel of the state school system? And failing local education authorities? And the teaching profession?*

In my heart of hearts I knew I wouldn't send my own children to most inner-city secondary schools. Discipline was variable, sometimes awful.

If you repeat a statement enough times it gains legitimacy but New Labour's claim to have invented 'literacy and numeracy hours' was incorrect. The initiative had been the brainchild of the Conservatives and had launched in autumn 1996 as part of the National Literacy Project.[155] Blair's belief that primary schools' standards were permanently improved might have been premature, however, as we will soon see.

All persuasions of politicians have the habit of laying claim to other people's good ideas and forgetting their own failures. It's like the notion that the Labour Party invented the NHS rather than its being the brainchild of William Beveridge (in his report *Social Insurance and Allied Services*). The Conservatives' 'big idea' for improving schools had become a policy, to be launched by New Labour.

It seems that Blair had reached the conclusion that although New Labour's numerous education initiatives might raise standards their potential was limited by the culture and infrastructure, and the teachers, in the state education system. We know about Thatcher's distrust and contempt for much of the education establishment. It looks like Blair was beginning to share a milder version of her sentiments. These comments describe his solution to these limitations and explain much of what he did during his second term as prime minister.

For public services to be equitable, and free at the point of use, they did not all need to be provided on a monopoly basis within the public sector, controlled in a rigid way by national and local bureaucracies often deeply resistant to innovation and genuine local autonomy.

Maybe it was the start of the new millennium that infused New Labour with the resolve to radically change its education policy or maybe it was in preparation for the next general election. Whatever the motivation, the evolution of secondary schools was about to experience another change in direction.

During an interview with David Frost, in January 2000, Blair said:[156]

*We are going to be announcing a whole new wave of specialist
schools, which specialise in particular subjects. By the end of 2003 I
want one in four of comprehensive schools to be specialist schools.*

To achieve specialist status a school had to raise £85,000 in business
sponsorship, set improvement targets and involve the local community –
whatever that meant. In return it would receive a £170,000 capital grant and
£200 extra per pupil per year for at least four years (all the amounts are in
today's pounds). Revamping and expanding specialist schools was one part
of New Labour's grand plan. The other component came to light in March
2000 during a speech given by Blunkett:[157]

*City Academies, to replace seriously failing schools, will be estab-
lished by partnerships involving the Government, and voluntary
sector, church and business sponsors. They will offer a real change.
The aim will be to raise standards by breaking the cycle of underper-
formance and low expectations.*

A week later it emerged that the legal arrangements for establishing city
academies were to be the same as those used by the Conservatives when
launching their city technology college programme. The exact details were
defined in legislation passed in July.[158]

Blair's recollection of the launch of the academies differed slightly from
what actually happened but the reasons they were introduced seemed clear.

*To give schools independence, to set them free from the local
authority system of hands-on control; and to let them innovate,
including in how they employed staff.*

By this time it seems that Blair had aligned with Thatcher's belief that
the LEAs were part of the problem and not the solution.

The document *City Academies – schools to make a difference* detailed
what they were expected to achieve and how they were intended to
work.[159] What follows is my summary of Blunkett's introduction to the
document.

We need a dramatic increase in the number of successful schools in our cities because far too many schools are under-performing.

Deprivation and high pupil mobility are reasons for bad schools but so are the failure of management and leadership and poor support from the education authority.

City academies provide a radically new type of school. Situated in major urban areas, they will replace schools that have poor track records.

They will be publicly funded independent schools with private and voluntary sector sponsorship and management, and will have greater freedom than is currently available to other schools.

Business, the churches, individuals and voluntary organisations could be potential sponsors and partners (called 'promoters') for the academies.

Business has much to contribute to both the basic curriculum and curriculum enrichment activity, and to providing effective work experience programmes.

City academies will take account of the best lessons of city technology colleges and charter schools in the United States.

Academies and specialist schools had much in common but differed in two important respects. Specialist schools were partly funded by third parties, but they remained embedded in the state school system.

Academies required a much higher level of investment from their 'promoters', amounting to 20% of the initial and ongoing capital costs. For this investment the promoters were outside the state system, owning and running the schools and receiving grants from central government that were equivalent to the cost of educating pupils in specialist schools.

But that wasn't all. As well as launching new initiatives during the first quarter of 2000, New Labour also ended its lasting opposition to its long-time enemies, the grammar and public schools. News of the cessation of hostilities with grammar schools came during an interview Blunkett gave to *The Sunday Telegraph* newspaper.[160]

> *I'm not interested in hunting the remaining grammar schools... I'm desperately trying to avoid the whole debate in education once again, as it was in the 1960s and 1970s, concentrating on the issue of selection, when it should have been concentrating on the raising of standards.*

Removing Clause IV from its constitution is often seen as a defining moment for the Labour Party. For me it was the decision to stop hounding the remaining grammar schools. Clyde Chitty believed this decision might have marked a genuine change in ideology – or it may have been an admission of defeat. Remember the parents of children at Ripon Grammar School had voted, decisively, to retain selection?[161] That had happened just two days earlier.

It's difficult to know if 'Old Labour' disliked grammar more than private schools. Perhaps since the former were no longer the enemy it had decided to embrace the latter? The schools minister, Estelle Morris, announced in 2000 that there had been a 'huge cultural change' in the party's perception of public schools: it had come to 'like the independent sector in the same way that we like the other sectors.'[162] Grammar and private schools were now perceived as being part of the Party's goal of enriching the diversity of school types.

Within the first three months of 2000, therefore, the foundation for New Labour's secondary school policy was in place. The Party's emphasis on standards and diversity, on the involvement of business and the churches in running schools and the declaration of peace with 'elitist' schools was nothing short of astonishing.

Needless to say, there were howls of anguish and claims of betrayal from the educational establishment and reactionary members of the Labour Party. Their distress wasn't helped by the derisory comments made by Alistair Campbell, the prime minister's press spokesperson. During a briefing in early February 2001, Campbell added the prefix of 'bog-standard' when talking about comprehensives. This couldn't have improved the atmosphere in the Campbell household given that his partner, Fiona Millar, was (and still is) an ardent proponent of comprehensive education.

Some of Campbell's political colleagues, including Blunkett, were extremely upset by this aside.[163]

> *Blunkett was very pissed off, wrote me a pained letter saying his job was difficult enough and this didn't help. I apologised to him when he came over for a meeting with Tony Blair.*

Blair himself was far more relaxed and reassured Campbell that he had used the term before and that 'nobody had batted an eyelid'.[164]

The comprehensive era – RIP

I suspect that the term 'bog-standard comprehensive' will forever be part of Campbell's political legacy. However, had the term not resonated with other commentary in the media, I expect it would soon have been forgotten. Within days of the furore, Blair was launching an education green paper (*Schools – building on success*[165]) that was a political sales pitch for the forthcoming election laced with more veiled criticisms of comprehensives. *The Daily Telegraph* reported his speech under the headline 'Blair: comprehensives have failed'.[166]

> *Introducing a Green Paper outlining the plans, Mr Blair said comprehensive education had been allowed to become an end in itself. Despite all the idealism that had surrounded it, only a minority of pupils had gained good qualifications and levels of failure remained stubbornly high. The time had come to move on to a 'post comprehensive' era.*

What did we learn from the green paper? Little was said about comprehensive schools – just five mentions, none of them complimentary. They were criticised because 'inclusion too readily became an end in itself' rather than satisfying the needs of individual pupils. And because they were established by reorganising an existing model – I assumed this meant secondary moderns – they had little scope to develop a distinctive character. It was

New Labour's strategy to move beyond the old purpose of comprehensives to satisfy the full range of individual talents.

Of course, the green paper didn't include the term 'bog-standard'; however, that's what it implied and that's what New Labour intended to change. Michael Barber, who was soon to become a key figure in Blair's Cabinet office, was involved in drafting the paper. He recounted the difficulties in reconciling Blair's desire to 'state clearly that for secondary education we were now moving to a 'post-comprehensive era'' with Blunkett's jitters about offending the teachers and parts of the Labour Party.[167]

The policies that would deliver this reform were all prefixed with the word 'more'. Spend more money, establish more specialist schools (1,000 to be operational by September 2003), allow more 'specialisms' (adding engineering, science and business), create more Beacon schools (1,000 by September 2001), allow more faith-based schools and finally – encourage more academies.

This shopping list of education policies and promises was what appeared in New Labour's manifesto. The general election took place in early June 2001 and as expected New Labour retained power with a majority (167) that was nearly as big as in 1997.

Blair's victory speech, outside Downing Street, talked of how the voters' support had given him a mandate to invest in and reform the public services – especially the NHS, transport and education.[168] He believed his electoral support came with an implied instruction from the voters 'to deliver'. I think this put a positive spin on his need to move from being a prime minister with lots of new ideas and fine words to one who delivered demonstrable success.

The BBC reported details of the new government organisation and priorities and it was clear that the civil service was an important part of Blair's agenda for radical reform.[169]

Prime Minister Tony Blair is to further tighten Downing Street's grip on all areas of government with a shake-up of Whitehall and Number Ten.

A newly created group called the 'delivery unit' – based in the Cabinet office – was to be the driving force that would ensure the civil service 'delivered'. Clearly, Blair had fears about Whitehall's ability to translate his policies into actions. Not all civil servants welcomed politicians meddling in their territory and it wasn't long before their concerns appeared in the media: 'Top mandarin: Blair circle acts like the Third Reich'.[170] Twenty years later, the current prime minister (Boris Johnson) has the same worries and is attracting the same push-back from the civil service.

The details of the green paper were further extended, but not materially changed, when they appeared in an education white paper.[171] In July 2002 the policies were passed into law.[172]

I am fast approaching the end of the timeline in 2004, a date that was chosen for arithmetical symmetry rather than any educational reasons. If each of the first two sections of the timeline lasted 30 years, it seemed sensible to use the same period for the final one. I thought this would be long enough to demonstrate how successful, or not, comprehensive schools had been at rectifying the numerous criticisms levelled at secondary moderns. This is a question I will attempt to answer in Chapter 8 ('Much maligned or monstrous mistake?').

Isn't it ironic that comprehensivisation disappeared on the watch of a Labour prime minister and the destruction of selective schools peaked when Thatcher was in power? Yet another issue, more a paradox, that I need to address.

During the next two years there was an avalanche of initiatives, consultations and studies. These didn't materially affect the secondary education strategy, which remained focused on increasing the diversity of schools, improving their effectiveness and focusing on standards. By the end of 2004, New Labour's overhaul of the secondary school system was nearly complete.

This period witnessed a further fracturing of views between New and Old Labour. The government had now been in power for five years and had a 'track record' that its critics (mostly Labour Party supporters) could attack. There were some conciliatory noises from the government, but it continued to promote the message that comprehensives must 'modernise' – code for 'be replaced'.

It was the minister's (Morris) task to placate the supporters of traditional comprehensives and at the same time make the case why change was necessary and inevitable. An article she authored in the *Observer* illustrated what a difficult task this was.[173] It started with lots of complimentary comments about comprehensives and how they replaced the iniquities of the 11-plus – the obligatory boilerplate text. Then came the criticisms. More children were going into higher education – but not from the working classes. Thirteen percent of children were leaving school without basic literacy skills. There was a huge difference between the best and worst-performing schools. She went to great lengths to claim her beliefs in the 'comprehensive ideal' but admitted that 'it has not solved the problems that it was hoped it would solve'.

The article continued with praise for schoolteachers and workers and her appreciation of their hard work in difficult circumstances. Then came the most interesting part, where she attempted to solve the paradox of how the much-lauded teaching profession and the 'comprehensive principle' failed a sizeable proportion of children. She believed there were two explanations. Decades of under-investment in schools by the Conservatives had taken their toll on performance. (Attacks on the Conservatives were guaranteed to satisfy all parts of the Labour Party.) The second explanation was far more contentious:

> In the pursuit of opportunity for all, comprehensive schools have concentrated on their sameness. In the fight for equal opportunity we may have emphasised the equality too much and the opportunity too little. This is characterised in our attitude to excellence. Too often it was confused with elitism and our failure to understand that celebrating those who achieve doesn't hold back others.

These are powerful words and an indictment of previous Labour Party educationalists. Concentrating on the 'sameness' of schools, allowing the ideal of 'equality' to harm the provision of 'opportunities' and confusing excellence with 'elitism'. These arguments sounded surprisingly like those promoted by the Black Papers.

Morris concluded by neatly presenting the multiplicity of schools that were being created (specialist schools, training schools, Beacon schools and city academies) as being part of the 'comprehensive family'.

This was a well-crafted article that made a valiant attempt to 'square the circle' by separating comprehensive schools (which were bad and had failed) from the 'comprehensive principle' and the 'comprehensive family' of schools (which were good and would succeed).

Within days of this article, Morris repeated the same messages when she addressed the Social Market Foundation. To add authority and colour to the speech she reflected on her experiences as a comprehensive school-teacher. Unfortunately, she said something that enraged the easily enraged NUT.[174]

> *I know that all secondary schools are not identical. As a teacher, I go into some schools and think 'I would like to work here' but there are some I wouldn't touch with a bargepole.*

Alistair Campbell had his 'bog-standard comprehensive' moment and now Estelle Morris had uttered the words that would forever haunt her.

The 'bargepole' incident was one of the many problems facing her. Earlier in the year she had had to contend with striking London teachers who wanted a substantial increase in their salary. Her warning that they were returning to the 'dark ages of dispute and conflict' had, yet again, annoyed the NUT. She must have known that the hyper-sensitive teacher's union bridled at the slightest criticism of its members – irrespective of how deserved these might be.

Morris was facing other problems. By July 2002 the Department knew it would fail to achieve its target for the percentage of 11 year olds achieving the required reading level. After rapidly improving in 1998 and 1999, the results plateaued between 2000 and 2004, something that undermined Blair's claim to have 'fixed' the literacy and numeracy problems in primary schools. Michael Barber, who was now in charge of the delivery unit, believed the lack of improvement was his fault and he should take the blame, which Morris and Blair rejected.

Then there was the 'problem' of the abnormally high pass rate at GCE 'A' level. You would have thought this was something to celebrate. It had become something of a summer ritual that when the GCE exam results were published they were better than the year before. This was followed by a mix of congratulations for the diligence of the pupils and teachers and accusations that it resulted from exam grade inflation. In the summer of 2002, the 'A' level pass rate jumped by a record-breaking 4.5% on the previous year.

Pupils gaining the top grade increased by 2.1%. This ignited an acrimonious battle between the Ministry and the exam boards.

The objection by parts of the Labour Party to the role of state-funded faith schools was another distraction that Morris had to battle. I am not sure if the concerns raised were genuine or a proxy for attacking Blair's policy of increasing the diversity of schools. In early February 2002, a Labour member of Parliament (Frank Dobson) attempted to force all new religious schools to admit a minimum of 25% of children who didn't share the school's faith. It was defeated with support from the Conservatives.[175]

What caused the issue to become a national news story was the report that a city technology college had included 'creationism' in the teaching of biology and the indignation this caused. A letter was sent to Blair, signed by six bishops, Richard Dawkins, the astronomer royal and even David Attenborough.[176] The accusation was investigated and it was found that the school's hall had been rented by a group with creationist beliefs. When Ofsted next inspected the school, it was awarded an 'outstanding' grade.[177]

Morris was not directly involved in any of these issues, with the exception of the 'bargepole' comment, but because she was the minister they were her responsibility. At the end of October 2002 she resigned, stating she lacked the skills to do the job, especially those of strategic management and media relations. Blair commented that politics is extremely rough, and she just felt overwhelmed. At the time, I remember feeling sorry for her since she seemed a thoroughly decent person but without the toughness, and probably the inclination, to play political games and to duel with the media. Her replacement, Charles Clarke, couldn't have been more different. He had no experience in teaching and education but had a reputation for being a political 'bruiser'.

Before creating his own education polices, he had to continue implementing those of his predecessor, while resolving the immediate problems – of which there were many. It is not surprising that it was the summer of 2004 by the time Clarke launched Labour's new five-year education strategy.[178]

I am surprised its title didn't contain the word 'personalised', because it appeared 64 times throughout the document. Clarke's three-page introduction talked about 'personalised education', 'personalised opportunities', 'personalised systems' and 'personalised services'. As much as to explain

Labour's vision for the country's schools, I expect its purpose was to convince the electorate of Labour's achievement at the forthcoming general election (2005). Not surprisingly, the title of the manifesto's section about education was 'Forward to **personalised learning**, not back to mass failure'.

Specialist schools were to be given more autonomy and would be the key to delivering this 'personalised' education.

At the heart of our reforms is the development of independent specialist schools in place of the traditional comprehensive – a decisive system-wide advance. We are not creating a new category of schools – rather, giving more independence to all schools within a specialist system.

In addition was the plan to create 200 independently managed academies, to become operational by 2010. Some of these would replace underperforming schools. However, the scheme had been widened to create new academies, particularly in London, to help satisfy the demand for school places.

Achieving 'foundation status' was to be an option for all types of schools, giving them the freedom to: 'own their land and buildings, manage their assets, employ their staff, improve their governing bodies, and forge partnerships with outside sponsors and educational foundations'. This policy marked a significant dilution of the LEAs' powers – and one they weren't happy about. Instead of being the supplier and manager of local schools they were to become the 'commissioner and quality assurer of educational services'.

I expect the following condition was a token concession to Labour MPs (including the deputy prime minister) who still favoured comprehensive education.

A strict national requirement for fair admissions will remain; and we will not allow any extension of selection by ability, which denies parents the right to choose.

All secondary schools were to be refurbished or rebuilt over the next 15 years. A policy that I am sure was welcomed but discounted because of its long delivery timescale. Many of the new schools were built using private finance initiative (PFI) contracts. The implications of this financial engineering technique is a story in itself and one I will skip over.

The strategy also contained the surprising pledge to 'slim down' the headcount at the Department of Education Skills by a third. I have no idea what prompted this commitment, but it had disappeared from the agenda come the time of the general election.

Clarke's interview with *The Guardian* revealed some of the rationale behind his plans.[179] It emerged that although only 7% of the country's children were educated in the private sector the figure was much higher in parts of central London (20%). The minister thought middle class parents were opting out of the state system out of 'despair', rather than because they wanted to send their children to private schools. I expect that the decision to create 60 academy schools in London was intended to placate these parents (voters).

In the era of grammar, secondary modern and technical schools, parents understood what they could expect from each type of school. Now the nomenclature of school types had become so complicated that Clarke admitted parents were confused. About the city academy idea, he believed, 'Some people have got their knickers in a twist because they don't understand it.' I don't suppose the clarity of the schooling system was improved when during another interview he talked about his expectation that all secondaries would become 'independent specialist schools' with foundation status.[180]

In the same interview he went on to extol the characteristics of fee-paying schools: the uniforms, the house system and competitive sport – all things that I had experienced in a secondary modern, 40 years before. The introduction of the word 'independent', when describing specialist schools, was aimed at aligning their ethos with those of public schools. Clarke even said that the 'term "independent" should not be reserved for fee-paying schools'.

What was the legacy of the comprehensive schools?

I think this is a fitting and improbable point at which to conclude my account of the 'comprehensive era' – with a Labour minister wanting state schools to be more like public schools, which they had for so long despised. What would Tony Crosland, Reg Prentice and Shirley Williams have thought of their cherished plan to 'go comprehensive' having floundered in such a way?

This just leaves one final question to answer – what was the legacy of this period? Since the era started in 1974, comprehensive schools had gone from being the solution to providing a consistent and equitable system of secondary education to a concept that New Labour was doing its best to forget. In 1974 Labour's election promise had been to 'speed the development of a universal system of fully comprehensive secondary schools'. By 2005 it wanted 'the development of independent specialist schools in place of the traditional comprehensives'.

The demise of comprehensivisation, as we have seen, was not a constant trend throughout this 30-year period of the timeline, but started with the election of Blair as leader of the Labour Party in 1994. So, to be strictly accurate, I should talk about two legacies – one before and the other after Blair. For a host of reasons, primarily its difficulty, I will just comment on the state of secondary education as it existed in 2004.

Types of secondary schools. At the beginning of the era there were 43 specialist schools.[181] By 2004 the number had increased to 2,000, two-thirds of all secondaries. Most of them (28%) specialised in technology, a generic term that included maths, science and design technology. The other schools focused on a range of other subjects that is shown in the following table.[182]

Technology	28%
Arts	16%
Sports	14%
Science	11%
Languages	10%
Maths/computing	8%
Business and enterprise	7%
Other	5%

Specialism of specialist schools in the UK 2004

This was a strange, and I expect unplanned, distribution of specialisms with more schools declaring an excellence in sports than those in either science, languages or maths/computing. I cannot believe this reflected the country's priorities for its children's schooling.

For all the importance that Blair's government placed on academy schools, only 17 were open at the end of 2004. By the time the Conservatives regained power in 2010 the number had increased to 203, just 6% of all secondary schools.[183]

There were still 164 grammar schools in England, the same number as today, and 130 secondary moderns.

The most surprising thing about the analysis is that the official statistics record 83% of schools in England and Wales as just plain vanilla 'comprehensives'.[184]

Conflict between parental choice and equality. During the 'after Blair' section of the era the shift of power from the LEAs to schools and parents went far beyond anything that the Conservatives had proposed. Not all of the Labour Party and educational establishment understood or accepted the local council's new role as the 'commissioner and quality assurer of educational services'. The Audit Commission report on *School place planning* stated that the 'promotion of social inclusion is a central task for the council as a whole'.[185] This was wishful thinking and if councils ever could achieve this goal, they certainly couldn't in 2004. That some parents, more than others, would exercise their rights to select their child's school was bound to result in a fragmentation of the school system, as the report concluded.

> *The increasing polarisation between popular and unpopular schools demands more immediate and decisive action. The weakest and least popular schools frequently serve the poorest, most vulnerable and most disaffected groups.*

Similar concerns were expressed in a report from the Select Committee on Education and Skills.[186] This group of mostly Labour MPs (66%) had studied the practicalities and performance of the schools admission process and concluded:

*The Labour Party approached the 1997 election with two key priori-
ties in relation to school admissions: to limit selection and to
promote parental preference. It is our conclusion that the Government has been less successful than they intended in both respects.
The facility for secondary schools to select their intake has increased
under the present Government through the expansion of the
specialist schools initiative.*

It believed the rush to expand parental choice and increase the diversity
of schools resulted in more pupils being selected on 'aptitude', a nicer way
of saying 'ability' but something that had the same result. The chairman of
the committee (Barry Sherman) made no secret of his contempt for Blair's
education policies. He was quoted by the BBC as calling the idea of giving
parents more choice as 'naïve' and 'bloody awful'. His solution to allocating
children to schools was a computerised lottery.[187]

The committee's criticisms were somewhat undermined by research,
conducted by the Ministry, showing that a large majority of parents were
happy with how the system worked. Over 90% of parents were offered a
place in their first preference school. Since 1994 the number of parents
appealing against their children's secondary school had doubled, but it was
still only 10%.

Government spending on education. Charting the share of national
expenditure devoted to education tells us something about the importance
that politicians attributed to it. At the beginning of the era the percentage of
GDP spent declined, initially under the Labour government and continuing
during the Conservatives' reign of power. However, Blair's 'education,
education, education' mantra was, after a three to four-year delay, translated
into a steady increase in education spending. These details are shown in the
following chart.[188]

Public expenditure on education and training increased, in real terms, by
19% during the last two terms of the Conservative government (1987–
1997). During the first two terms of the Labour government (1997–2004) it
increased by twice this amount.[189]

These variations in spending resulted from a combination of changing
political priorities, the state of the economy and population demographics.
However, the lowest point during this time, in 1990, when the spending was

4.3%, was higher than for the first 20 years of when secondary moderns were evolving. When the first secondary moderns were opening their school gates the percentage spend was 1.5%.

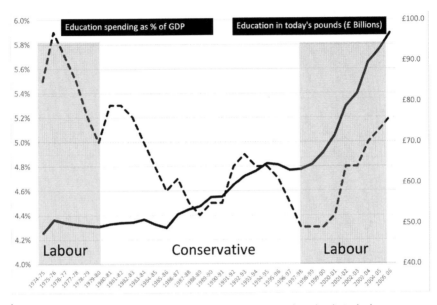

Spending as a percentage of GDP (%) and spending on education in today's pounds (£ billions)

During this period, as now, there was only a tenuous link between how much was spent on education and the results it generated. For instance, throughout the spending ups and downs of this era the class size in primary and secondary schools stayed constant at 27 and 22 pupils per teacher respectively.[190]

A feature of the Blair policies was an explosion in the number of new schemes and initiatives that were targeted at schools. We have already seen that some of these were of dubious value. The cost–benefit of most of them was never evaluated. In 2004 the secretary of state for education and skills (David Miliband) was asked to provide details of all the funds and grants that were in operation. It was a long list of 70 schemes, totalling £8.5 billion in today's pounds.[191] Each of these required teachers' time to implement and staff at the Ministry to administer. My experience has been that organisations with a scatter-gun approach to solving problems are the least effective. I wonder if during the latter period of the comprehensive era this approach to using funds and teachers' time caused problems. In 2010, Blunkett and Clarke were interviewed and asked if they were responsible for too many initiatives. I think their comments speak for themselves.[192]

*[**Blunkett:**] I plead guilty to initiative overload because there seemed to be so much that needed tackling all at once. We were demanding the most enormous amount of change from teachers, but frankly it was needed. We had a crap teaching profession.*

*[**Clarke:**] I think there is an absolutely core problem in education certainly over the recent period, of too many initiatives, too much change, lack of consistency and change of personnel both in terms of Ministers and senior officials. The biggest kind of structural failure has been failure to be able to build a serious partnership with the teaching procession on change.*

Improvements in GCSE exam results*. I doubt if many parents knew or cared about the percentage of GDP that the government spent on education. What mattered to them, as for today's parents, was the value their children got from their time at school. At primary school, a key measure was their children's numerical literacy and how well they could read and write. As we have seen, after an initial improvement between 1998 and 2000, reading ability at age 11 remained static. At secondary school, the measure was, and still is, GCSE exam results. Lack of success erects a barrier for taking GCE 'A' levels and going on to university.

The following chart[193] shows the benchmark measurement of secondary schools' achievement[194] – the proportion of pupils achieving five passes at GCSE, with a C-grade or above. In 1988, two things happened. The GCE 'O' level and CSE exams were replaced by the GCSE and there was an apparent significant improvement in performance.

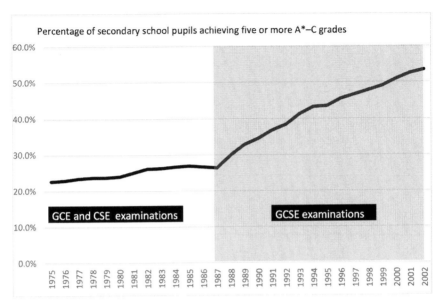

Percentage of children at secondary school achieving five or more A*–C
grades at GCE/GCSE during the comprehensive era

For the first 13 years of the comprehensive era, the GCE 'O' level exam
was the benchmark for performance. The percentage of pupils achieving
five good grades did increase, but only by 3.8%. During the next 15 years
this measure jumped by 23.6%.

I've already commented on the rapid improvement in GCSE exam
results. Pupils achieving A-grades increased from 8.4% to 23% (2011).
During the same period those failing the exam, with grades (D–U), fell from
58% to 30%. Pupils' achievement, or grade inflation, depending on your
viewpoint, has continued to rise with 28% being awarded the highest grade
pass and only a handful of pupils failing in 2020.

Much has been written to explain this remarkable improvement.
Dominic Cummings, who was for four years the minister's (Michael Gove)
chief of staff, was adamant that 'the sharp rise in GCSE results reflects
easier exams rather than real educational improvements' and provided
numerous references to substantiate his claim.[195]

A less analytical but more passionate view came from Chris Woodhead,
the outspoken head of Ofsted (2000).[196] He described as 'fanciful' the
explanation that children had become more intelligent or worked harder,

though he did begrudgingly concede that teachers might have improved. That exams had become easier was the primary explanation, which he felt 'raised the terrifying prospect that we are living in an education cloud cuckoo land'.

He blamed multiple culprits for the problem. Exams had been divided into multiple modules that pupils could keep taking until they passed. It was impossible to ensure that coursework was done by the child, not the parent. The academic rigour of exams had been diluted. And if all this wasn't bad enough, the pass scores had been lowered. Woodhead's forthright views brought very different responses from the media. *The Guardian* hated it and commented: 'like all demagogues, he was telling people what he thought they wanted to hear, and built a whole reputation on stating the obvious.'[197] *The Daily Telegraph* thought it should be required reading for all politicians and educationalists.[198]

What neither of the reviewers said was why, with so many obvious failings, wasn't action taken? Woodhead believed there were too many vested interests that benefited from the ever-improving grades. The government, the exam boards, the Qualifications and Curriculum Authority, the teachers' unions, the teachers and the pupils – all gained from the improved results.

I instinctively feel that there is truth in Woodhead's comments. However, when Steven Timms, the minister of state who was responsible for school standards, defended the accusation of 'grade inflation' he was unequivocal in his response.[199]

We have careful, thorough quality control procedures in place to ensure that standards are maintained. Teachers, schools and pupils have worked very hard, and that is the reason that we have hit the target of at least 50 per cent. of our young people getting five good GCSEs a year ahead of our deadline. That is down to the hard work and success of schools.

Steve Timms was one of the few MPs whom I knew and worked with. I always found him to be highly competent and honest. He was a man of firm principles who must have believed these comments to be correct.

I am in two minds whether there was a real or imaginary improvement in the exam results of secondary pupils. Their meteoric rise once GCSEs were launched seemed too good to be true. However, the cumulative improvement in education spending might have been responsible. I just don't know.

What I do know is that in 1955 only 10% of school pupils achieved the benchmark 'O' level grades and very few, if any, would have attended a secondary modern. By 2004, lots of pupils who would have failed the 11-plus were gaining good grades and access to higher education. For whatever reason, that has to be a good thing, although it creates its own problems as we will see in Chapter 9 ('Half a century on – what lessons can we learn?). Yet major problems remained and as late as 2007, the then prime minister (Gordon Brown) was threatening to close 670 schools where less than 30% of pupils achieved the benchmark targets.

The sacrifice of fairness? At the end of the comprehensive era, virtually all of the criticism about schooling came from within the Labour Party and its notional 'supporters'. The Conservatives had adopted a position of passive observers as New Labour's policies were attacked by Old Labour members and many in academia and the teaching profession.

Their discontent – perhaps 'obsession' is a better word – was that the fairness that comprehensivisation had brought to secondary education was being sacrificed to provide parents with a greater choice of schools and the relentless quest to raise standards. All of the assumptions in this argument were questionable – however, that is what many people passionately believed.

These arguments formed the basis for a TV documentary (*The Best for My Child*) that described the consequences when parents chose the 'best' rather than the local schools for their children. Fiona Millar, who made the programme, said:[200]

I am well prepared for the brickbats coming my way for suggesting that choice is just an illusion and that we should be looking at ways of encouraging people to use local schools.

Brickbats were what she received from Chris Woodhead, who reviewed the programme in *The Times*.[201]

Her argument is as simple as it is terrifying. The problem with state education has nothing to do with weak leadership and incompetent

teachers. It is that parents are, in theory, at least, encouraged to
choose the school they wish their children to attend. The ambitious
middle class play the system. They pretend to be religious to secure a
place in the local church school. And they condemn children from
less affluent homes to the misery of sink schools.

Similar sentiments were expressed by the commentator Polly Toynbee, who decried the policy of specialist schools and parental choice.[202]

Much double-speak surrounds the whole subject where schools can
select on 'aptitude', a nice distinction from grammar schools
selecting by 'ability'. Another fiction is 'parental choice' in a system
with no overcapacity, where schools with falling numbers are rightly
closed. Under these mendacious banners – diversity, aptitude and
choice – government policy has been marching backwards into a
pre-comprehensive school era.

Many academics were making similar arguments. This is what Sally Tomlinson, now an emeritus professor, said.[203]

But education in England, under New Labour, had by 2000 been
reduced to economic ends and a competitive scramble for creden-
tials, in which the higher social classes were emerging, as always, as
the victors. Notions of education as a humanising, liberalising, egal-
itarian, democratic force had been put on hold.

I have quoted the views of Millar, Toynbee and Tomlinson because they are still making these very same arguments. Arguments that reveal the conflict at the core of comprehensivisation – the rights and motivations of the individual and what is perceived to be best for society.

As we neared the end of the timeline the opposition to Blair's policies intensified. One of his own MPs, David Chaytor, attempted to repeal the provisions of the 1988 Education Act that enabled specialist schools to select pupils on the basis of aptitude.[204] He failed.

Official reports containing any hint of criticism were used to discredit the government's schools policy. In this example, *The Guardian* attacked the introduction of academies by quoting a consultant's report (by PWC) that was purported to say: 'The growth of academies and the introduction of a "quasi-market" in education could create a two-tier system'.[205]

As so often happens, the longer a conflict goes on the more entrenched become the views of the opposing sides. That's what happened at the end of the comprehensive era.

My final words about this era come from a government report about education that was published in 2004. Mike Tomlinson, a former chief inspector of schools at Ofsted, was asked if the exam system satisfied the needs of children and industry.[206] He concluded it didn't and proposed a radical change. Nobody disagreed with his analysis, but politicians and industry rejected his solutions.

In a letter to the minister, accompanying the report, he said:

Too many young people leave education lacking basic and personal skills; our vocational provision is too fragmented; the burden of external assessment on learners, teachers and lecturers is too great; and our system is not providing the stretch and challenge needed, particularly for high attainers. The results are a low staying-on rate post-16; employers having to spend large sums of money to teach the 'basics'; Higher Education struggling to differentiate between top performers; and young people's motivation and engagement with education reducing as they move through the system.

These are not the comments of somebody trying to promote or rubbish a particular type of education system or set of ideological beliefs. It is a blunt set of observations about education in 2004, after 30 years of the comprehensive era.

We know the dominant narrative about secondary moderns is uniformly negative. Strangely, no equivalent exists for comprehensives; it's as if they were best forgotten.

CHAPTER 8

MUCH MALIGNED OR
MONSTROUS MISTAKE?

T he name of this chapter captures the essence of the question I have been trying to answer. The extra punch given by the alliteration is a happy bonus.

Relating why so many people believed secondary moderns were a monstrous mistake was easy. Writing that story took a couple of days and only 3,000 words – see Chapter 3 ('A consistently negative image'). Understanding whether the schools were 'much maligned' was an order of magnitude more difficult, requiring four chapters, 140,000 words and many months of research.

The first part of this chapter contains a summary of material that has already been discussed. My primary reason for doing this was to amass the arguments in a systematic way. I also thought you might appreciate a reminder about events that were discussed several hundred pages ago.

The imbalance in the evidence for the prosecution – and that for the defence – revealed much more than the pros and cons of secondary moderns. It resulted from a weakness in human behaviour that impels us to distil complex issues into neatly packaged sets of black-and-white arguments. What was atypical about secondary moderns was that all the arguments were 'black'. The unwavering certainty of commentators, when describing the schools and their pupils, was illustrated by this account in the *Telegraph*.[1]

They were housed in decaying buildings, taught by often unqualified teachers, given only a third of the funding per head of their contemporaries at grammar schools and barred from public exams. The middle classes feared the system, lest their children should fail the 11-plus; the working classes saw it as a way to keep them in their place. Many emerged with no qualifications – only the top stream took CSEs – to become factory fodder.

Cassandra Jardine, the journalist, deserved an A+ for relating so many failures in so few words. She detailed nine 'facts' about the plight of the 11 million children who attended secondary moderns in the space of a paragraph. If only life was that simple; no nuances, no context and not a hint of uncertainty.

Another, and more disturbing, example of this behaviour was the reporting and public dialogue about the Covid-19 pandemic. Much of this chapter was written when the media reported little else than virus-related stories. Never in my lifetime has a single subject been reported and discussed by so many people for so long in so much detail with so little reliable data. Each day the media reported 'shock' new research findings, revelations of 'blunders' by politicians and officials, adulation for the 'heroes' and distain – and often much worse – for the 'villains'.

I was involved, in a very small way – analysing research about the apparent variances in the virus's effects on different ethnic groups. This was a complicated issue, requiring multiple factors to be correlated using incomplete datasets of varying quality. Yet the media and politicians wanted to simplify the findings, seeking certainty when all the research screamed 'there are no simple answers'. Worse still, often – too often – the 'facts' were used to substantiate a commentator's personal views about society's imperfections.

What I found scary was that this rush to simplify and discard the uncertainties and complexity was happening in 2020, in plain sight, at a time when accessing information has never been easier. Most of the secondary modern's story occurred half a century ago in far less data-rich times. Ever since their launch, the dominant narrative has been condensed and repeated until it became little more than a collection of derogatory comments.

The 'simplification problem' was succinctly expressed by the historian

Mary Beard: 'We don't disseminate a complicated view of the past; we disseminate a simple view.'[2]

Even though the dominant narrative is invariably established by a small group of people, often motivated by ideology rather than historical accuracy, it can soon become widely accepted as a truth.

Trying to resurrect the 'truth' from this simplified account of the past has been difficult, but was made possible by the wonders of 'historical perspective'. I never understood what these words really meant until I started journeying along the timeline starting in 1916. Like a time traveller, I was able to 'watch' politicians and educationalists, who were certain of their rightness (and righteousness), come and go, sometimes changing things for the better, often not changing things at all. New ideas about education replaced those of the past, themselves to be rejected by the next generation of 'enlightened' educationalists. Time and time again new education strategies were abandoned as they were swamped by economic events.

My purpose in writing the four chapters of the schools' history was to reconstruct the layers of complexity and context that time has eroded. To replace the facts and arguments that have been omitted and to provide perspective, so the schools can be judged against what they replaced. Later in this chapter I consider whether their successors fared any better.

Judging their achievements and failures requires an understanding of their origins and the existing level of educational achievement that they were expected to improve. So, let's start by reviewing the foundations on which secondary moderns were built and in particular the role that WWII played in determining their future.

An era of good intentions and then there was WWII

The period between WWI and WWII is related in Chapter 5, which is called, not surprisingly, 'Between the wars'. A more descriptive title would have been 'the era of unfulfilled good intentions.' Even before the end of WWI there was a desire to improve the fairness of society, a desire that was accelerated by the awfulness of the war. Providing working class children with a better education was part of this movement.

Despite impassioned speeches and many government enquiries, little of substance changed. The school-leaving age was raised to 14 in 1921 but plans to provide post-school training never got off the ground.

The culprits for this failure, which reappeared throughout the timeline, were the constraints on public spending, the unwillingness of vested interests to relinquish power and the inability of government to turn policies into reality. We need to remember why events of this era are prefaced with the word 'Great'. The immensity of the Great War and the Great Depression wrought havoc on the economy. I think the Spanish flu epidemic of 1918 also deserves the title of 'Great', given that it affected a quarter of the British population and killed 230,000 people. To put that into perspective, it is the equivalent of five times as many people who died of Covid-19 in 2020.

These were testing times in which to implement social change as illustrated by the following facts about education just before WWII.

In 1938 the great majority of children (91%) were educated in elementary schools; that was little changed from the situation in 1927 (93%).[3] Here they received a basic education, which finished for most of them when they left school at 14. Secondary schools were for children with parents able to pay their fees and those in receipt of a state scholarship, having passed an entrance exam. The ratio of state to privately funded pupils in these schools had barely changed since 1928, rising from 40% to 47% in 1939.

At the onset of WWII, schools were still being reorganised along the lines proposed by the Hadow Report, way back in 1926. Change had progressed at a snail's pace. Less than half of children were educated in separate junior and senior schools, with the majority receiving their education in 'all-age' school departments.

Most children left state-funded schools at the first opportunity. In 1937 less than 1% of them remained in school until they were 18 years old and just 0.2% attended university.[4] At the beginning of WWII approximately 80% of Oxbridge students had attended private schools.[5]

The church retained a major role in determining education policy, operating and owning as many schools as local councils. This parity in school ownership was not reflected in the pupil numbers. Elementary schools, owned by local councils, educated 70% of pupils; the remainder were in smaller, church-owned schools, often in rural areas. These tended to be older and had less amenities than those operated by the state. Despite a desire to mould church- and council-owned schools into a single entity little progress had been made since WWI.

It shouldn't be concluded from this sorry tale of inaction that there wasn't a desire for change. Much thought had been given to how the system of schooling should be improved. The difficulty in converting desire into action was the problem – and a portent for what would happen when WWII ended.

Although no clear-cut decisions had been made, certain concepts about the organisation of schools had become generally accepted, most with the support of both political parties.

For instance, there was general agreement that the:

- School-leaving age should be raised to 15 years and then again to 16 years when circumstances allowed.
- Transition from junior to the next phase of schooling should take place when children were 11 years old.
- Separate structures of elementary and secondary schools should be combined, requiring both types of school to be free for all pupils.
- Name 'secondary school' should become a generic term for all schools educating 11 year olds, rather than the label of the existing elite schools.
- Type of school children attended, aged 11 years, would be determined by some form of exam and reference to their junior school performance and teacher's recommendations.
- Division of children at 11 years would inevitably misplace pupils who were 'late developers', requiring procedures to rectify this mistake.
- Old secondary schools would continue for academically gifted children, with the remainder attending a new 'modern' school. A third, vaguely defined, 'technical' school was also proposed.

I had assumed that WWII would have halted all thoughts of reorganising education. Much to my surprise this was not the case and the outline framework described above began to coalesce into firm proposals. Much of this was the responsibility of Sir Cyril Norwood who, between 1941 and

June 1943, conducted yet another official enquiry into the future of schools.

Norwood's recommendations were based on the assumption that there were three types of sufficiently different children that warranted them being educated in separate secondary schools. It is difficult to know whether to laugh, cry or get annoyed when reading the characteristics ascribed to 'modern' school pupils. Remember that these children would constitute the majority of the country's future adults. It was thought that they 'deal more easily with concrete things than ideas'. They were practical, not conceptual. 'Abstractions mean little them' – they were 'interested in things as they are'. They must have 'immediate returns for their effort' and so the stream of platitudes continued.

It is easy to mock the words written in another era, but Norwood's ideas were ridiculed at the time. A few months after the report's publication, Cyril Burt published a paper in the *Journal of Educational Psychology*[6] that, in a gentlemanly way, ripped Norwood's proposals to shreds. Burt is most often quoted for his suggestion that Norwood's ideas were the psychologist's equivalent to phrenology. He might have said Norwood's conclusions were the astrophysicist's equivalent to astrology.

Why did Norwood's investigation come to these simplistic and naïve conclusions? It is too easy to dismiss the proposals as the prejudiced and uninformed views of the upper class gentry about working class children who were a world away from their experience. Yet many of the committee members had a distinguished teaching background.

I concluded that the proposals were little more than putting some fine words and rationale around the status quo and presenting it as a new idea. The pre-war school system was built on the assumption that about 15% of children would benefit from an academic education and the remainder needed basic literacy skills that would enable them to live a productive life. The infrastructure of schools and teachers was organised to fulfil that objective and that's how it seemed destined to continue.

Secondary moderns would have had an inauspicious start if this had been their heritage, but the effects of WWII made things worse – much worse.

The physical destruction of school buildings was the war's most visible legacy. It is thought that about 20% of schools sustained some form of damage.[7] By September 1943 over 4,000 school buildings had been destroyed or damaged. More would suffer the same fate during the flying bomb attacks on London and Southern England in 1944.

Two factors exacerbated the shortage of classrooms caused by this destruction. First, many schools had been requisitioned at the outset of the war to provide emergency accommodation and first aid centres. Second, when schools were damaged, they ranked low on the priority list of buildings to be repaired, a rule that extended into the immediate post-war years. In 1946 the amount of new school building work was 2% of that in 2016.

The disruption and loss of life caused by destroyed buildings were terrible. Worse still was the upheaval experienced by children as they were moved around to avoid the bombing. During 1939, 3.5 million mothers, children and teachers left their homes in urban areas and moved to the countryside. After a few months many returned home when the aerial bombardment didn't materialise. So started five years of stop-start education for a generation of children.

There must have been a constant flow of children coming and going from their homes (and schools). It must have been a logistical nightmare trying to provide anything like a normal education for these war-time children. This situation was complex enough, but it was compounded by the call-up of male teachers for war-time duties. It is thought that about a quarter of teachers left to join the services or did other types of war work. Their replacements were retired teachers and married women.

No systematic research has been done to quantify the effects of all of this disruption on children's academic and emotional development, let alone the trauma caused by living with uncertainty about the safety of their mothers and fathers. We can get some measure of how children's education suffered by comparing the entrance test results of the cohort of young men joining the army immediately after war, with those who joined beforehand. Some 72,000 men, with an average age of 19 years, enrolled in the army at the end of 1946. Their results showed a serious drop in the level of scholastic attainment and an increase in those graded educationally backward and retarded.[8]

It was estimated in Reading Ability that during the war standards had fallen by 12 months and 22 months for pupils of eleven and of fifteen respectively.[9]

Having documented the disruption caused by the war, I have little doubt that it negatively affected children's education standards. This was the first and, as far as I know, only time that it was quantified. However, I think these numbers should be taken as 'estimates', because the sampling models were different, before and after the war.

As I am writing these words the media is full of stories about the dreadful effects of the closure of schools due to Covid-19 on children's education and mental health. Most schools shut their doors at the end of March and reopened in September 2020 – a period of six months. At the beginning of 2021 the school gates were closed again. I don't wish to diminish the severity of the problems this disruption caused, but it is small compared with that experienced by the first generation of children entering secondary moderns. Their education had been disrupted for 10 times longer.

Let's remind ourselves why I'm recounting the very unstable foundations on which secondary modern schools were built. These schools didn't instantaneously appear in 1944. They emerged from the combination of the old elementary and secondary schools. The bricks and mortar were the same, as were the teachers – all that had changed was the sign at the school gate. And let's remember that their first cohort of pupils had just emerged from five years of war.

Judgements about what secondary moderns did or didn't achieve cannot be made in a vacuum. Consideration must be given to how these schools began, what they replaced and the conditions their pupils had endured.

Secondary modern's birth and parentage

The myths and misunderstandings about the origins of secondary moderns remind me of what happens with a recalcitrant child who grows into an unruly adult. Nobody wants to take responsibility for their parentage and upbringing. As time goes by their heritage is forgotten; worse still, it becomes a lie.

I want to consider the most frequent misunderstandings about how the schools came into being and who was responsible for ensuring their success.

They didn't begin with the 1944 Education Act

For some reason the 1944 Education Act, or the Butler Act as it is often called, is often thought to mark the point when secondary moderns burst into life, along with the 11-plus.

For certain the Act contained lots of words, about 50,000, but not a single one of them referred to secondary moderns or any other type of school. In no place was the 11-plus discussed. No directives or guidance appeared about what the schools should teach and how they were to be judged.

Much was said about the teaching of religion and examinations, but this related to 'medical examinations' and 'clothing examinations' and 'examinations for infestations of vermin'.

Nothing was said about the process for determining the type of school a child should attend, what they should learn and how they should be examined. Other than specifying that the leaving age was to be raised, no rules or guidance were given about how the extra 12 months of schooling should be used.

If the Act didn't specify these fundamentals of schooling, what did it cover? It removed (clarified) two major organisational roadblocks. The muddle of secondary and elementary education systems running in parallel was abandoned and it went a long way to dismantling the dual system of church and state education. This might not sound much, but overcoming these hurdles meant that material change could be made to the country's system of schooling.

You could argue that the Act's overriding purpose and success was in reducing the power of the church to influence education policy. Some proof of this is the regularity with which words associated with church schools appeared – over 200 times.

Local councils – not the government – were in charge

The Act gave responsibility to the local politicians, via their LEAs, to decide on the organisation of primary and secondary schools, requiring them to:

afford for all pupils opportunities for education offering such variety
of instruction and training as may be desirable in view of their
different ages, abilities, and aptitudes, and of the different periods
for which they may be expected to remain at school, including prac-
tical instruction and training appropriate to their respective needs.

As time evolved it was clear that the Ministry wanted (let's say encouraged) the LEAs to adopt the tripartite system; however, the final choice about all matters schooling resided with local politicians, their officials and the schools themselves.

Asa Briggs, the esteemed historian, said the Act:[10]

Provided nothing more than an outline, a statutory warrant for a
more comprehensive set of measures than any educational authority
would be likely to be able to carry out for a long time to come.

To my mind, Butler replaced one set of conflicts, that between state and church, with another, between central and local government. Both political parties suffered the frustration of seeing their grand education policies reliant on the whims of the LEAs and their schools.

Part of the Act mandated that the LEAs should produce a comprehensive 'development plan' detailing the nuts and bolts of how their schools would be organised. This huge task was supposed to be done within 12 months – a naïvely optimistic objective. As it was, just 16 out of 146 councils submitted plans in this time. Five years later, 15% of the plans had yet to be approved.

There was no alternative system of schooling

The dominant narrative suggests that the LEAs had a choice, when creating their development plans, between providing a mix of secondary moderns, grammar and technical schools and a single system of comprehensive education. We know they chose the tripartite system, now seen as the wrong decision, igniting the battle to convince and cajole them to adopt comprehensives. As with all theories of education this failed to produce the hoped-for results and was replaced.

Portraying the LEAs as having a binary decision is, in my view, nonsense. They were faced with a long list of immediate challenges and abandoning the one type of schooling that was universally accepted as working well, albeit for a few (grammar schools), would have compounded their difficulties. I suppose there is the 'equal pain' argument that unless high-quality education is available to all then none should have it, but I don't think anybody was seriously suggesting that was an option.

Not only were LEAs contending with the consequences of the war, they had an impossible timescale in which to explain how they would make the Education Act work. And that's not all. Solutions to two other problems had to be found – and fast. The school-leaving age was set to rise, requiring more teachers and classrooms, and the baby boom, resulting from the fall in infant mortality combined with the rising birth rate, meant that more primary and secondary schools would soon be needed to accommodate a bulge in pupil numbers. More about these two issues in the next section.

The LEAs' only guidance about the 'right' type of schooling was the contents of the Spens and Norwood Reports and the 'Green Book', all favouring tripartite schooling.

The final reason to adopt this solution – if one was necessary – was that it matched their existing schools' infrastructure.

Some might have dreamt that comprehensivisation was not only the right but a viable option. Those at the sharp end of making decisions disagreed, and rightly so. There was only one solution and that was a system of schooling that could use the existing infrastructure of schools and teachers. Only one model was on offer that could do that – secondary moderns, grammar and technical schools and the 11-plus.

My conclusion that 'there wasn't an alternative' is a controversial point and one you will not find repeated by educational historians. That said, it isn't a question many have specifically addressed. If you aren't convinced by my reasons for reaching this conclusion then you may want to revisit the account of this period in Chapter 6 ('Birth and death').

The Labour Party was responsible for the conception and birth

The Beveridge Report was published in 1942 and proposed, among other things, the institution that evolved into the NHS. Both Conservative and Labour Parties were committed to implementing this recommendation. At the 1945 election the Labour Party was victorious, becoming the first party to gain power after the war. It claimed the prize of launching the health service, something that it proclaims to this day.

My reason for recounting this fact is that Labour MP Chute Ede was a partner with Butler in the formulation of the 1944 Education Act and, as with the health service, both political parties were committed to its implementation. On forming the government, Labour began the process of implementing the Act. Perhaps a more accurate way of describing events is that the Labour government, assisted by local councils, which were predominantly Labour Party-controlled, adopted the tripartite system, lock, stock and barrel.

With a majority of 146 MPs, the Labour Party had complete control of central government; likewise with local government, where it was the controlling party. This report from *The Guardian* summed up its electoral success.[11]

Councils go the way of Parliament. Nearly everywhere the story is the same. The councils of England and Wales are on the way to becoming as Socialist as Parliament.

It is strange that subsequent generations of Labour politicians have been keen to claim ownership of one part of the war-time coalition policy (health) but determined to forget the other part (education).

If any names are to be associated with the birth of secondary moderns it is the prime minister, Clement Attlee, and his education minister, Ellen Wilkinson.

Let's be clear, I am not blaming the party or its leaders for secondary moderns. Far from it; as I have explained, they had no alternative. My objective has been to clarify who were the custodians in the early years of the school's life.

An impossible job

Wilkinson had the unenviable task of working with the LEAs to approve their development plans, while finding solutions to the perfect storm of events that were enveloping her Ministry. Summarising these challenges concludes my account of the troubled origins of secondary moderns.

A surge in pupil numbers

The minister's reputation was as a campaigner, not an administrator. Famed for her involvement with the Jarrow March, Wilkinson was a revolutionary socialist and originally a member of the British Communist Party.

For many, her time as minister spoilt the story of her life's achievements and the Labour Party's role in the history of the country's education. I think this is a simplistic and sad interpretation of the facts. She was the person at the point 'where the rubber hits the road'. It was an uncomfortable place to be.

At the top of her 'to-do list' must have been to solve the problem of surging pupil numbers. The commitment to raising the school-leaving age, in April 1947, could not have come at a worse time. It was accompanied by an increase in the birth rate and the continuing fall in infant mortality, which had begun five years earlier. These events combined to create a surge in pupil numbers.

Additional space was required for the high numbers of children who would be at school by the autumn term of 1948. During the period 1947–1954 the school population increased by nearly 1.4 million children. To put this into a contemporary perspective, the numbers attending schools in England over the same number of years in 2009–2016 increased by just 0.4 million.[12]

To accommodate these children, an emergency building programme was initiated to provide 6,000 prefabricated classrooms. These went by the memorable name of HORSA (Hutting Operation for Raising the School Leaving Age). Suitably educated people, who had been involved in war service, were recruited into an emergency training scheme to equip them to be teachers. Initiated in 1944, this scheme created 30,000 new teachers.

Uncontrollable demographic change was responsible for the baby boom, but extending the school-leaving age – something that could have been delayed – must have adversely affected the establishment of the new education system, especially secondary moderns. This is a view shared by Roy Lowe.[13]

> *The timing meant that the raising of the school leaving age was achieved in economic circumstances which guaranteed the inferiority of the secondary modern schools in terms of staffing and accommodation.*

The unfinished business of 'all-age' schools

Elementary schools originally educated children from the starting age of five until they left to find work, hence the name 'all-age school'. As I have already explained, in 1926 the Hadow Report had recommended, and the government accepted, that schooling should be divided into three stages – infant, junior and senior. So started the slow conversion of schools to a three-tier model that was suspended during WWII.

As local councils wrestled with implementing the Education Act, over 20% of pupils were still taught in all-age schools. The numbers fell gradually. By 1955 over 10% of pupils remained in these schools. How could it be that 30 years after deciding to abandon these schools so many remained? After the war the LEAs' school building priorities were limited to coping with the rise in pupil numbers and providing schools for the new housing estates. No mention was made of all-age schools.[14]

At least secondary modern schools have claimed some place in history but all-age schools and the children who attended them are forgotten. Dismantling the remaining schools continued as secondary moderns were launched. Yet another difficulty that had to be overcome.

It is necessary to read Chapter 6 to fully understand the troubled conditions existing when secondary moderns were launched. They were the main component of secondary schooling that replaced an education system that was little changed since WWI. Fuelled by the hopes and energy that resulted from the victorious ending of WWII, they had to contend with the consequences of those five years of disruption. If this wasn't difficult enough, they had to accommodate a surge in pupil numbers.

It is against this backdrop that I will be judging their successes and failures.

What was the purpose of secondary moderns?

An account of secondary moderns needs to establish a clear statement of what they were expected achieve and when, during their lifetime, it is reasonable to judge their performance. Neither of these is easy to do – and the former is nigh on impossible. It feels rather like a combination of two much-repeated sayings: 'if you don't know where you are going, then all roads lead there' and 'one place is as good as another'. Sometimes mixing metaphors does work!

It's hard to believe that no blueprint, no set of rules, no instructions were ever created to explain what was expected of the schools and how they should operate – but that is how it was. Just before the 1944 Education Act, a government white paper *(Educational Reconstruction)* talked about the forthcoming secondary schools that would become secondary moderns.

> *Lacking the traditions and privileged position of the older grammar school they have less temptation to be 'at ease in Zion' [I interpret this as being complacent]. Their future is their own to make, and it is a future full of promise. They offer a general education for life, closely related to the interests and environment of the pupils and of a wide range embracing the literary as well as the practical, e.g. agricultural, sides.*

Politicians and their officials were making a virtue out of their vagueness and lack of direction. According to a Ministry pamphlet *(The Nation's Schools)*, issued in 1945: 'free from the pressures of any external examination, these schools can work out the best and liveliest forms of secondary education suited to their pupils'.

As I have already explained, the 1944 Education Act made the LEAs responsible for deciding the system of schooling and providing adequate teaching capacity. Teachers were left to decide what happened in the classroom.

If this constituted a strategy then it was one of encouraging maximum flexibility, allowing each school to adapt to its local conditions, free from central government diktats and the constraints of preparing pupils for external exams. The exact opposite of today's system of schooling.

In 1947 the Ministry issued another pamphlet (*The New Secondary Education*) that explained the unique challenges faced by the schools.

> *Perhaps the main difference between a modern school and other*
> *types of secondary schools is its very broad outlook and objective. It*
> *has to provide a series of courses for children of widely differing*
> *ability, aptitude and social background. It has to cater for the needs*
> *of intelligent boys and girls, for those with a marked practical bent,*
> *as well as for the special problem of the backward children.*

Remember that all that had been 'officially' specified about secondary modern pupils were the vague abstractions contained in the Norwood Report. They were thought to be better at dealing with concrete things than ideas – practical, not conceptual matters; interested in things as they are. Only one factor united all of these pupils – they failed to get admitted to a grammar or technical school.

Having such a range of pupils, with such ill-defined characteristics, was seen as another reason why it was impossible to prescribe any model for the schools to follow.

> *With such a wide variety of ability the modern school must be free to*
> *work out its own syllabuses and methods. Teachers must constantly*
> *be ready to ask themselves 'Why?', 'When?', 'Where?', 'How?' and*
> *'What?', and be free to act on the answers.*

If there was an 'official' prescribed approach to teaching this majority of the country's children, it was to 'experiment', a word that was peppered throughout the document. Perhaps it was assumed (hoped) that the most effective mode of teaching would naturally emerge, through some sort of Darwinian process? Maybe in the immediate post-war period of shortages and disruption it was a rational decision to let those at the chalk face make the decisions?

However, I don't believe this 'policy' was based on any such logic;

rather, I get the impression this 'hands-off approach' resulted from an absence of understanding how secondary moderns were to achieve their daunting task. Transferring responsibility to the schools to make the decisions was not a policy – it was the result of not having one.

If we fast forward a decade to 1958, Harold Dent, the editor of *The Times Educational Supplement,* said of the policy that 'no brief could have been more formidably vague.' His observations about the early years of secondary moderns were far more evocative and eloquent than I could hope to achieve:

> *The Secondary Modern School has been the target of every newfangled theory, every half-digested, ill-assorted idea... if ever it has seen a settled objective half the busybodies in the world of education have rushed in to save it from itself. Turn out citizens. Turn out literates. Turn out technicians. Be more vocational. Prepare for leisure. Stick to the wider view. The wonder is that with all this and with all the difficulties of the post-war world the secondary modern schools have got anywhere at all. But, they have.*

My instinctive feeling about this period is one of anger. How could they – the Labour and Conservative politicians and their advisers – believe an efficient system of schooling would result, having delegated the responsibility for its creation to tens of thousands of teachers? And remember, most of these teachers' experience and mindset came from working in the pre-war elementary schools.

A more sympathetic view says that this was 'the decade of survival' when working in the education system, from the humblest schoolteacher to the minister of education, was agonisingly stressful and frustrating. They were coping with the aftermath of the war and everything was in short supply except the number of children walking through the school gates.

I have the luxury of viewing these events with the benefit of hindsight and to my mind it was a grave mistake to concurrently increase the school-leaving age and implement a new system of education. An error that was compounded by doing it during a period of maximum post-war stress, when most of the meagre spending on education was directed at building primary schools for the baby boom. But that is how it was, and I must focus on the implications for secondary moderns.

Between 1945 and 1957, Dent visited 'some hundreds' of secondary moderns and used his findings to write *Secondary Modern Schools – an interim report*. His record provided the only reliable research on how the schools had developed. Chapter 6 contains details of his findings.

His first conclusion was that there was no such thing as 'the' secondary modern school. For all the reasons I have related, he discovered numerous types with different objectives and methods of teaching. He categorised them into five groups.

- Schools that had changed little from the elementary schools they replaced.
- Those providing 'highly effective senior elementary school work'. The main purpose was teaching the '3 Rs', with the pupils' education not extended far beyond basic numeracy and literacy.
- Teaching practical subjects alongside either a simplified and restricted version of the grammar school curriculum or one based on projects and centres of interest.
- Providing vocationally orientated courses that were relevant to the school's location.
- 'GCE schools' that had well-established links to technical colleges and grammar schools for pupils to take GCE 'A' levels.

We owe a great debt of gratitude to Dent. His research demonstrated (forcibly) the error of referring to secondary modern schools as a homogeneous group. The schools were on a spectrum. At one extreme was the less academically challenging grammar school and at the other, the old, pre-1944 Education Act elementary school.

Not that it was needed, but Dent's view of the schools was confirmed by the Parliamentary secretary to the Ministry of Education, when he spoke in a Commons debate in 1956:

There is no such thing as 'the secondary modern school'. There are secondary modern schools—more than 3,500 of them, and they differ in innumerable ways.

It is clear that by the mid-1950s there were no parameters or measures to judge the success or failure of the schools. Indeed, in the mid-50s the story of secondary moderns could have come to an abrupt end. Had it not been for the distraction of Suez, the Conservative minister (Eccles) may well have abandoned the 11-plus and with it rewritten history. We will never know how that possibility might have unfolded.

If we fast forward another decade to 1964, had anything changed materially?

During the intervening years much consideration had been given to the suitability and desirability of secondary modern pupils taking external exams. Remember that the great benefit these schools were claimed to have was their freedom from being constrained by the exam syllabus.

Three official reports came to differing conclusions but there was some measure of agreement. When ranked by academic ability, secondary modern pupils could be expected to achieve the following levels of exam success:

- The top 25%: the ability to pass GCE 'O' levels.
- Upper–middle 25%: the ability to pass some types of external exam, unlikely to be GCE 'O' levels.
- Lower–middle 25%: some might pass exams but for most they were inappropriate.
- Bottom 25%: exams would be a distraction.

All these years later it was still unclear how to educate the sub-set of pupils thought to be beyond studying an exam curriculum. Teaching these children was the reason the schools were originally created. All that had changed during this time was the realisation that they only constituted the bottom 50% of secondary modern pupils, ranked by intelligence.

If the 20-year period since Butler's Act had taught us anything, it was the difficulty a single school has teaching children with such a wide range of academic abilities– pupils capable of studying GCE 'O' level syllabuses sitting alongside those who would struggle to pass a single external exam.

What happened next would be comical if it were not so tragic. Having made little progress in finding ways to engage this 'bottom 50%' of pupils, the government decided to increase the leaving age – meaning that teachers had to fill another year, even though the formula for teaching non-academic children still hadn't been found.

It seems that unquantifiable 'feel-good' arguments prompted the government to make this long-awaited decision. Secondary modern pupils in the south of England were increasingly staying at school voluntarily – unlike those in the north. Forcing all children to stay for an additional year, it was argued, would counter this lack of 'social fairness'. Here we have another example of government making what was probably the right decision for the wrong reasons and in the process compounding its problems.

As to the question of knowing how to judge the performance of secondary moderns, I think it had become harder than ever. By 1964 over 50% of LEAs were planning some form of comprehensive education and the percentage of pupils educated in secondary moderns and all-age schools combined had been falling for four years.

The Conservative Party's commitment to the tripartite system was beginning to crumble. That it lost the 1964 general election and was out of power for the next six years meant this was something of an irrelevance. The incoming Labour Party was committed to 'going comprehensive'. A secondary-aged child, irrespective of their intelligence, would go to the local community comprehensive schools, which would satisfy the needs of all levels of intelligence. Well, that was the theory, if not what happened in practice.

In just 20 years, secondary moderns had gone from birth to – if not death, a state of irrevocable decline. Under the best of conditions, 20 years would have been a short time to judge the success or failure of a new education system. The period after WWII was far from the 'best of conditions'. With only the vaguest guidance about how the schools should work and what they should achieve, judging their performance was impossible.

The most useful thing we can do is establish what insights emerged from this gigantic, 20-year-long, experiment in teaching 'non-academic' children?

- Given the right teaching environment, many more of this group were capable of passing external exams than originally thought.

Between 1955 and 1966 the number of secondary modern pupils taking GCE 'O' levels increased tenfold, raising the question of how many more children could achieve exam success.

- There might be educational arguments that 'teaching for the exam' is wrong but they are the one universally accepted symbol of educational success. Preparing children for exams was beginning to provide secondary moderns with the structure and purpose they sorely lacked in their early days.
- Teaching a wide range of abilities in a single school was difficult. After 20 years, educational experts were still grasping for a solution. Despite this experience, Labour politicians wanted to increase the spectrum of academic abilities attending a single school.

If only politicians and the educational establishment had 'learnt the lessons' from the secondary modern's short life. If only the next phase of secondary education had evolved from this period rather than being a root and branch upheaval. If only...

The secondary modern's supposed failures

So far I have recounted how and why the schools came to exist and their troubled history. I now want to address the arguments (criticisms) that invariably appear whenever secondary moderns are discussed. For more details and how I deduced these points, see Chapter 3 ('A consistently negative image').

In the previous section I explained how in the space of 20 years political opinion went from believing that external exams were a constraint on the development of secondary moderns to becoming an important part of their raison d'être. I want to start by considering the accusation that banning secondary modern pupils from taking exams was discriminatory and done for negative reasons.

Disadvantaged by not taking GCE 'O' levels

It is often claimed that secondary modern pupils weren't permitted to take GCE 'O' levels. A variant of this criticism is that only small numbers took and passed this exam and that instead they were forced to take CSEs, exams that were thought to be inferior. It was also implied that even if the pupils achieved exam success, they were barred from continuing their education at grammar schools.

An article in the *TES* in 2016 reported that the Institute of Directors had accused schools of becoming 'exam factories' that fail to prepare pupils for the workplace. Two years before, the same accusation had been made by the CBI. These sentiments were echoed by the NUT's report *Exam factories?* In May 2020 the BBC reported a warning from the head of Ofsted about the constraints that exams place on the schools: 'Exam results are important but have to reflect real achievement'. In late 2020 an organisation was launched (Rethinking Assessment) that as the name suggests believes the present system of exams is not fit for purpose.

The Ministry had expressed these same concerns over 60 years ago in a report warning of the dangers exams posed for secondary modern pupils.

> *It is taken here as axiomatic that the Minister wishes to encourage the heads and staffs of secondary modern schools themselves to establish whatever objectives, curricula, syllabuses, methods and quality of life they find by experience and experiment will most fruitfully meet the widely differing needs and circumstances of their pupils and neighbourhoods.*

> *The corollary is that, if they are to have freedom to do so they must be protected with reasonable limits from outside forces which are prima facie damaging, whether these take the form of an instrument, such as an external examination, or an idea, such as that secondary modern schools should be conditioned to a pre-established pattern of what 'the secondary modern school' should be.*

I don't want to discuss the 'rights and wrongs' of exams but rather to illustrate the long-standing view that external exams could be limiting to a child's education. I expect today's progressive educationalists would have few arguments with the Ministry's statement – a view that would be shared, to varying degrees, by the teaching unions, business leaders and the authority responsible for measuring the performance of schools. School exams seem to be considered a 'necessary evil' but they come with a cost to the breadth of children's education. Maybe this is true? Maybe not?

What this account demonstrates is that there are two interpretations of the fact that when they were launched, secondary moderns were discouraged from preparing pupils for external exams. There was the view that this was done for discriminatory reasons, to in some way disadvantage the pupils compared with their contemporaries attending grammar schools. Alternatively, it could be presented as permitting pupils to pursue a broader education, released from the constraints of studying for an exam curriculum. Allied to this argument was the concern that the less academic pupils would suffer as teaching resources focused on the small minority taking exams.

I believe there were genuine concerns about the detrimental effect of exams. However, the prevailing mindset within the Ministry was that external exams were beyond the abilities of most secondary school pupils.

Any discussion about decisions taken in the past invariably raises the question of whether they should be judged using today's knowledge and morality or those of the time. I am a supporter of the latter view. However, when applied to the establishment views about exams it only explains their decision to a limited extent. As we will soon see, it didn't take long before the fallibility of evaluating pupils at 11 became obvious. Likewise, the unfairness caused by the geographic variation in the opportunities for bright children to attend a grammar school. It was blindingly obvious that some secondary modern children who were capable of taking external exams were denied the opportunity.

There is no doubt that it was a conscious, but not formally recognised, decision to ignore the resulting inequities. Thankfully many schools ignored this official anti-exams view and prepared pupils for GCE 'O' levels; however, many pupils were not fortunate enough to attend schools with this enlightened attitude.

Allied to the question of discouraging external exams were a number of other specific allegations.

Blocked from progressing to grammar school

Having achieved GCE 'O' level success, it is claimed that pupils were discouraged from extending their studies at a grammar school. There were a few anecdotal accounts of this happening but no evidence that it was a widespread policy. An explanation for this accusation is the Ministry's view that technical colleges were the best route for pupils to extend their education. We know the minister (Eccles) agreed with the view that, 'The Technical College can give a second chance to those who slept or slipped at school.'

My headmaster was firmly of the opinion that moving to a grammar school was the right decision; I took his advice. My sister also attended a secondary modern and continued her education at a technical college. There is no data showing one route was better than another and none suggesting pupils were constrained from continuing their studies other than by their parents.

Pupils didn't have the opportunity to take GCE 'A' levels

Ministry records showed secondary moderns having low numbers of pupils taking GCE 'A' levels. This wasn't surprising since few schools had sixth forms. As I have explained, the pathway for pupils to extend their education was via a grammar school or technical college. There was no systematic way of capturing how many pupils followed this route and their level of success.

Thinking that GCE 'A' levels were the natural and preferable next step for secondary modern pupils reflects our current obsession with academic qualifications. Approximately a quarter of those taking ONC and HNC certificates – vocational exams – came from secondary moderns.

Forced to take the inferior CSE exam

I believe the introduction of the CSE exam was a mistake. It was not the choice of the government but resulted from a battle between two parts of the educational establishment. Chapter 6 contains a detailed account of how they came into existence. It might have been grossly unfair, but the CSE soon gained a reputation for being an easy version of the GCE 'O' level and the 'exam for thickies'. The minister at the time when the exam was proposed (Eccles) said of it:

> *I do not want a first eleven GCE [similar to a football or cricket team], a second eleven [the CSE] and all the rest non-players. I find it doubtful whether the staff of say a comprehensive or a large secondary modern could cope fairly and adequately with three grades of children.*

I think he was right. Despite his opposition it was launched in 1965 and until 1987 was the primary exam taken by secondary modern and comprehensive school pupils. In grammar schools the GCE 'O' level ruled supreme. By 1979 the CSE was the primary exam taken by fifth formers in comprehensive schools (53%). In grammar schools it was the main exam for 12% of pupils.

There is little doubt that the CSE reinforced the view that the grammar school provided the Premier League-quality education while children in comprehensive and secondary moderns laboured in the lower leagues.

The imprecision, unfairness and fallibility of the 11-plus selection process

Determining a child's destiny at the age of 11, on the basis of a single exam, is wrong and a self-evident truth that doesn't need justification. Few people would question that statement, including me.

Compounding the inequity were claims that the way the exam was administered was unfair. For instance, it was believed that a child's date of birth influenced their chances of passing the exam and more girls failed than boys because of the way the results were adjusted to maintain a gender balance (see the next sections for more on these claims). Some children were coached to pass the exam by their school, or by private tutors; some were not. All in all, the 11-plus seemed to have been a nightmare with no redeeming features.

It is easy to see the faults of the exam and, in a moment, I will provide details that confirm its fallibility. However, if the 11-plus hadn't existed how would secondary education have worked? That's easy: don't examine children and send them all to the same type of school – but that wasn't a feasible alternative. They should have built more schools and recruited more 'good' teachers – an equally attractive but impractical idea.

I have already explained that it wasn't feasible to instantaneously transform secondary education to a comprehensive system. The tripartite system had to be built on the remnants of pre-war schools, with all of their imperfections. As unpalatable as it might be, there had to be some mechanism to make an unfair system as fair as possible. If the 11-plus seemed inequitable, then consider that when it was introduced only 3% of state school leavers went to university.

Moving on from 'was the 11-plus fair' – it wasn't – then the issue becomes, how effective was it at matching children to the most appropriate type of schooling? A secondary question is: how effective was the political establishment in responding to the inadequacies of the selection process?

In 1956 a set of literacy tests (*Standards of Reading 1948–1956)* were taken by children in all types of secondary schools. Overall, secondary modern children didn't do well, with 40% of girls and 30% of boys judged as backward or semi-literate. Children in all-age schools fared even worse, with over 50% of boys in this category.

In addition to revealing these children's poor reading skills the research also showed that an appreciable percentage of pupils who had passed the 11-plus scored lower than their ex-classmates who were now in secondary moderns. Grammar schools contained 4% of boys and 6% of girls in this category, with higher percentages among pupils attending technical schools. This was the first evidence I discovered that gave quantifiable evidence about the inaccuracy of the exam.

The results of another research project (*Admission to Grammar Schools)* were published in 1957 and provided a wealth of details about the workings and accuracy of the exam. I had wrongly assumed that there was a single type of 11-plus exam. That was not true – each LEA adopted its own procedure. Some favoured 'traditional' tests (e.g. writing a short essay or composition), others used standardised objective tests of ability (the IQ test). Let's remember the reason for using the IQ test was to measure a child's innate intelligence rather than the 'intelligence' resulting from their background.

There was no consistency in the age when children were evaluated and transferred from primary to secondary school. Indeed, not all children were entered for the selection process. In 13% of LEAs only children who were recommended by teachers took the evaluation tests.

Nearly three-quarters of LEAs required teachers to consider personal information about the pupil, such as their home background and qualities of character. A third of LEAs used the children's record cards, which provided details of their performance throughout their school life.

It seemed clear to me that primary schools did their very best to ensure that children went to the best school for their secondary education and used many techniques to achieve this goal. However, despite their best endeavours they didn't achieve a 100% success rate, or even close to that number. The study concluded:

> *Even the use of the best methods of allocation that, on the basis of our present knowledge, can be devised is likely **to involve errors in the allocation of approximately 10% of candidates.***

I have emphasised the wording about the magnitude of the allocation error. Later research suggested this number was 14% (Crowther), or even 25% (Silkin). Nobody knows the true level of allocation error, but it was significant.

Most of the LEAs appeared to recognise this problem and 75% of them employed a process to further test children who were in the 'border zone' (i.e. those whose test scores did not adequately define the type of school they should attend). The rest of the LEAs employed a simple procedure of setting an absolute 'pass/fail' score, above which you went to a grammar school and, below, the secondary modern.

The majority of LEAs claimed to have a process that would re-allocate children between the different types of school when they were 12 or 13. In practice few transfers actually took place. Only 3% of children left their secondary modern to attend either a grammar or a technical school. Even fewer children went in the opposite direction. If you passed the 11-plus and went to a grammar school, you had a 99.5% chance of remaining at one throughout your secondary school life.

Chapter 6 contains details about the mounting evidence that demonstrated that although the tripartite system had worked, after a fashion, it had serious defects. The rights and wrongs of selecting children's schooling at age 11 could no longer be framed in ideological terms. Put bluntly, many children were being educated in the wrong schools.

Before we become too smug and judgemental, we should remember that today over 10% of students fail to finish their degree courses, with all of the resulting financial costs and damage to their self-esteem. Maybe our ability to predict individuals' academic potential has not improved by as much as we might think.

Now let's get back to those two claims about the administration of the 11-plus that relate to the pupil's date of birth and gender.

A pupil's birthdate influenced their 11-plus performance

A child's birthdate affected when they started school and therefore the amount of schooling received.

The Plowden Report (1967) found evidence that children born in the summer, who are younger and have a shorter time at school, tend to be placed in the less academic stream in their junior schools.

In 2007 a report from the Institute of Fiscal Studies (*When you are born matters*) concluded that there was a 'significant penalty associated with date of birth, such that the youngest children in a particular year perform significantly worse in academic tests'. Worse still, the younger child was more likely to be diagnosed as requiring special educational assistance. This 'age penalty' continued to affect their academic performance, even potentially affecting their further education choices.

Most recently, in 2018, the Office of the Schools Adjudicator ruled that the 11-plus arrangements of Colchester County High School for Girls were 'unfair to summer-born girls' with birth dates between the first of April and the end of August.

Today, the examining boards that administer the 11-plus exam that is taken for admission for the few remaining grammar schools adjust the results to account for the age of pupils. Until the adjudicator's ruling this was not done by the one involved with the Colchester school; it is now.

I haven't discovered any evidence that confirms or denies whether the authorities that administered the exam took account of children's age when processing the results. I am sure that there were no 'official' rules explaining how this was to be done. My guess is that it was left to each LEA and the examining authorities. It is possible that schools were also involved in the decision.

The inherent weakness of the 11-plus was made even weaker by its penalising children born during the summer. Being a December-born child doesn't provide me with an excuse for failing the exam.

Girls had their 11-plus scores reduced

Many commentators believed the 11-plus exam process discriminated against girls to maintain a gender balance within grammar schools. The justification for this claim was based on anecdotal evidence and the claims that girls scored higher marks because they 'matured' before boys.

We know from the 1956 reading tests that in all types of school, boys performed better than girls. In the same year three-quarters of new entrants to university were men. Until 1987 there was very little difference in the GCE and CSE results between boys and girls.

Any measurement of intelligence is affected by 'nature' and 'nurture' factors. To what extent did the balance of these change over time and influence girls' exam performance? Nobody can answer that question. For instance, I am sure that parental expectations and demands influenced why so few girls went to university; that certainly happened in my school. There might well have been external factors that influenced the reading and external exam scores. Whatever the reasons, for much of the secondary modern era it is wrong to say that 'girls scored better than boys'. Today things are very different. With the introduction of the GCSE exam girls started (and continue) to outperform boys. Girls achieve significantly better scores at reading, writing and general English in tests at Key Stages 1, 2 and 3. Since 1996 there has been an increasing imbalance in the number of girls going to university. Today, over half of girls embark on higher education (57%), compared with 44% of boys.

I couldn't find any conclusive evidence that the 11-plus scores were manipulated to the detriment of girls. Between 1947 and 1969 there was less than one percentage point difference in the numbers of boys and girls attending grammar schools. By 1979 girls were the majority of grammar school pupils, but only by 1.3%. This consistency of scores, over such a long time period, suggested to me that the scores were manipulated, but not necessarily always to favour boys.

I am sure that 11-plus scores must have been standardised to maintain a gender balance; however, compared with the many failings of the selection process, this was one of its lesser faults.

As much as it seems unfair, in the immediate post-war period a mechanism was needed to direct children to the most appropriate type of schooling. It was done by the 11-plus, which was not a single exam but multiple types of selection tools. I believe that in the main the LEAs did their best to make the process as fair as possible but, however it was organised, errors would be made and children sent to the wrong type of school. All examining procedures have their weaknesses but relying on the unregulated judgement of teachers is not without its risks. The debacle that resulted when Covid-19 caused the cancellation of GCSE and 'A' level exams illustrated how hard it is to be fair and consistent without using them.

Was the 11-plus's error rate, be it somewhere between 10 and 25%, a superb achievement or a dismal failure? I have no idea. What I do know is that neither political party formulated policies to improve its accuracy.

The Conservatives' primary objective was to save the grammar school. Belatedly they discovered that this could best be done by enabling secondary moderns to provide a watered-down academic syllabus. The Labour Party became obsessed, a word I use advisedly, with a wholesale change of the system to comprehensive education, irrespective of the disruption costs. Their preoccupation was to outlaw the 11-plus, not to try and improve it.

Both parties, but especially the Labour Party, gave up trying to make the existing system work better. The selection process and with it the secondary moderns were abandoned when they were still a 'work in progress'. Early in this chapter I asked the question, 'When was the right time to judge how secondary moderns had performed?' It wasn't now, but that's what happened. In a while we will learn whether the system of schooling that replaced the 11-plus removed its unfairness or just created another type.

Educational opportunities varied by where you lived

If I was writing about today's schools the title of this section would be 'Children's education is a postcode lottery'. Since postcodes are a relatively modern invention – first used in 1959 and not associated with the term 'lottery' until the late 1990s – I decided to stick with a descriptive rather than the contemporary phrase.

Another reason for not using the term 'lottery' is that it would imply the type and quality of schooling was randomly dispersed. As I will explain, there was nothing haphazard about the evolution of the education infrastructure. Where the 'lottery' analogy is useful is that the 'prize' of attending the best schools depended on a child's parents being able to purchase so many tickets that they were certain to win.

One of the greatest inequities, if not the greatest, of the tripartite system was the wide variation in the availability of grammar schools. Children of equal intelligence ended up in different types of schools depending on how many grammar school places their LEA decided to provide.

In 1957, grammar schools educated 22% of secondary pupils in England and 39% in Wales. Some English LEAs provided 40% of secondary school children with grammar school places; in others it was as little as 10%. In some parts of Wales, the figure reached 60%.

If children in England were to have the same chance of attending a grammar school as those in Wales, the English LEAs would have needed 620 extra schools – that is an increase of 60%. Another way of looking at this unfairness is that if in 1957, the provision of grammar schools in England and Wales had been the same, 325,000 children would have attended grammar rather than secondary moderns. I am playing with 'averages' in making these calculations so treat these figures as illustrative, not actual.

The obvious question resulting from this analysis is: why was there such a huge discrepancy?

An ultra-summarised answer begins with the Schools Inquiry Commission Report (1868), which had found a lamentable supply of endowments for secondary education in Welsh schools. The commissioners estimated that only two boys – note it was boys, not children – for every thousand of the population attended secondary schools. That was eight times less than the required number.

In 1889 the Welsh Intermediate Education Act was passed and initiated a building programme of 'intermediate' schools, which soon became known as 'county schools'. It also unified the way Welsh LEAs provided secondary education. By the time the 1944 Education Act was passed, Wales had far more academic secondary schools than England, per head of the population, and their LEAs worked in a more integrated manner.

Many of the pupils who benefited from Wales' high-quality education system went on to further education, explaining why Welsh teachers were so common in English schools. In my secondary modern at least five of the teachers, including the headmaster, were Welsh.

Two important messages can be taken from this story. First, there was nothing random about Wales having so many grammar schools. Second, its high-quality education infrastructure resulted from events that took place 76 years before the 1944 Education Act was passed. Central and local politicians make decisions about education and expect results in a few years. Changing the infrastructure, building schools and educating teachers take many decades. It is as extreme as the difference between biological and geological timescales.

My intention is not to castigate Wales for having too many grammar schools but to criticise the deficient and haphazard provision of the schools in England. But, as I have said before, and no doubt will say again, the tripartite system had to use the network of schools as they were before the onset of war. Unfortunately, Wales' excellent education system is no more. What had taken many decades to create has been badly damaged by the policies of the devolved Welsh government. Terry Mackie's book, *The slow learning country*, related in detail this sorry story.[15]

The extent of the variation in the educational opportunities went beyond the irregular provision of grammar schools. Post-war school building work was focused on the 'new towns', at the expense of repairing and extending schools in urban areas. When the physical structure of a school remained unaltered, decades after changing the name sign from elementary to secondary modern, it is not surprising that it would struggle to escape from its earlier roots. The same principle applied when secondary moderns were converted to comprehensives. More of that later in this chapter.

Dent's book estimated that approximately 70% of secondary moderns were in buildings that at best were not adequate and at worst 'deplorably bad'. He also found that some parts of the country suffered from a shortage of staff and others had waiting lists of teachers wanting positions. In 1957 the Ministry reported that in secondary schools, 62% of pupils were in over-sized classes – an increase on the previous year.

Historical structural issues accounted for much of the disparity in the provision of schooling, but so did the variation in LEAs' plans to organise their secondary schools. As usual, Dent's comments perfectly explained this point.

> *Some authorities held firmly to the tripartite organization of secondary education, keeping all their schools strictly Grammar, Technical or Modern. Some of them set out to blur the lines of the tripartite division, by establishing Comprehensive, Multilateral, Bilateral or other kinds of joint or amalgamated schools. Some authorities laid down a policy for development, others deliberately waited on events, that is to say, waited to see what their schools would do.*

If more reasons were needed to explain the variable quality of secondary education then remember that during the first decade of their existence, secondary moderns were encouraged to 'experiment' with their curriculum and teaching style. Alternatively, you could argue that because the infrastructure was so variable, they needed the freedom to adapt.

I don't know which of these explanations was most important and it really doesn't matter – the result was the same. This comment from a 1958 white paper said it all.

> *The fact is that there are, to-day, too many children of approximately equal ability who are receiving their secondary education in schools that differ widely both in quality, and in the range of courses they are able to provide.*

I am switching to the present tense, for the final few paragraphs of this section, since what I have to say is as pertinent today as at any point during the timeline. This is more of an observation than a proven conclusion. There appear to be three things that determine how well parents navigate the hotch-potch of schools – their wealth, their education and the value they place on their children's schooling. That these things are inter-related is obvious; the extent and logic of the inter-relationship is hard to know.

Having enough money enables parents to opt out of the state system and send their children to the private school of their choice. Alternatively, their wealth can be used to purchase property close to a high-performing school, thus ensuring their child is within its catchment area.

Rightmove is the UK's largest property website and in 2017 calculated that there was an 18% price premium to live in a property close to a top-performing primary school. Provided on its website is a tool (School Checker) that displays the Ofsted ranking of nearby schools for each property. Another property website (PrimeLocation) estimates the premium is a little less, 12% for secondary and 8% for primary schools. I live close to a 'good' primary school, but more than that, many of its pupils graduate to the local grammar school. What premium this adds to the property price is difficult to know – my guess is somewhere around 10%.

The importance of parents' attitudes to education in determining the school attended by their child is hard to 'prove' but the ethnic breakdown of pupils attending the remaining grammar schools suggests it is true. There is much anecdotal evidence that certain ethnic groups place greater emphasis on their children's educational attainment than others. The term 'tiger mother' is now widely used for somebody who pushes her children to high levels of achievement. Originally, this was associated with parents originating from China and other parts of East Asia and it is now widely used in the West.

It comes as no surprise that grammar schools have a higher than average proportion of non-white pupils (36%) compared with the expected (26%). The prize for attending one of these schools was highlighted in a report from HEPI, a higher education think tank, which showed that in 2019, these 163 schools sent 30% more non-white students to Cambridge than all 1,849 non-selective schools combined. As you might expect, this research generated an avalanche of condemnation from the 'anti-grammar school' lobby. More about this in Chapter 9 ('Half a century on – what lessons can we learn?').

The influence of ethnicity on educational performance doesn't just apply to children of high academic achievement. Chinese children who are eligible for free school meals - the most often used measure of economic disadvantage – are four times more likely to go on to higher education than their white contemporaries.

The 'unfair' distribution of high-achieving schools linked to the 'unfair' ability of parents to determine the school their child attends leads to an 'unfair' educational outcome for many pupils. This applies to elementary and secondary schools, the tripartite system, comprehensives and the current model of schooling. An enduring constant throughout the timeline.

More money was spent on grammar school pupils

One of the alleged faults of the tripartite system was that pupils in secondary moderns received less funding than those in grammar schools. The justification for this claim originated from research, published in two books, by the educational economist John Vaizey. The first of these (*The Costs of Education,* published in 1958) detailed the expenditure on secondary education from the pre-war era until 1955 and concluded that the average grammar school pupil received 170% more per annum, in terms of resources, than the average secondary modern child.

Whether you present this uplift in educational expenditure as a bonus for one type of child or a penalty for another, it seems unquestionably wrong. However, when you understand how this number was derived it diminishes the iniquity of the funding difference. Another good example of how over time the context, details and analysis supporting a 'fact' evaporate, leaving behind a misleading conclusion.

The following is a summary of Vaizey's rationale for his much-quoted '170%' grammar school pupil bonus.

In principle the allowances of each child, whatever its school, were the same, so there was not differentiation.

But:

The inheritance of grammar schools in buildings, staff and equipment was much richer than that of other schools.

And:

The average length of a school life in a grammar school was a third greater than that of a child at a secondary modern.

Because:

The staffing of schools was based on a unit total, according to which children over the age of 15 were counted as several children meaning that the staff ratios and the qualification of the staff in grammar schools are therefore above average.

Combining these factors meant:

Allowing for this [the longer time grammar school pupils remained at school] and for the difference in the inheritance (both of which raised maintenance costs) it is likely that the average grammar school child received 170% more per year, in terms of resources than the average secondary modern child.

What is the context for this number? Vaizey estimated that before the war this figure was between 190% and 200% and that the 1944 Education Act 'may have halved the benefit of a grammar school award.'

In his second book (*Resources for Education,* published in 1965) he studied how this 'grammar school bonus' had changed during the decade ending in 1965. Maybe it is because I have an uncorrected proof copy of his book but the clarity of his explanation of 'what happened next' was unclear and somewhat ambiguous.

Because of the massive increase in recent buildings in use in the secondary sections, ... the difference between grammar and non-grammar school pupils had been eroded to a small extent.

Also:

*School life was still notably different, and so was the staff ratio
generally prevailing, so that the relative figures given above [refer-
ring to the 170% figure] could be significantly but not wholly
amended, since the massive increase in staying on was chiefly in the
academic streams and schools.*

As a result:

*Perhaps the difference in expenditure per school year was by 1965 of
the order of 14% or more, in terms of returns, for the grammar
school pupil, as opposed to the secondary modern pupil.*

For unexplained reasons, Vaizey stopped comparing secondary modern
and grammar school pupils and instead contrasted the difference in spending
on the 'academic' and 'non-academic' child.

*The greater part of the increase [spending on secondary education]
had gone to non-academic secondary children... [And there] was
little significant difference, at ages below 16, in terms of expenditure
per school year.*

I expect his change in terminology resulted from the increasing numbers
of secondary modern pupils successfully taking GCE 'O' levels, who would
need to be reclassified as 'academic children'.

If we use all of Vaizey's conclusions, then the message about spending
on grammar and secondary modern pupils looks somewhat different. The
headline number of a '170% grammar school bonus' now has some competition for the reader's eye. I have highlighted these 'facts' below.

The tripartite system **halved the spending differential** between children
attending elementary and secondary schools. During the first decade after
WWII grammar schools still benefited from their inheritance of better buildings and more teaching staff. This combined with the way that spending per
pupil was calculated resulted in children who extended their school life –
mainly those in grammar schools – attracting a disproportionate level of

funding. These factors meant that by 1955 the **differential was 170%.** A decade later there was **little difference** in the spending per child for those classified as 'academic' or 'non-academic'.

It is amazing how the message changes the more information is added.

There is no doubt that secondary modern pupils received significantly less funding than those attending grammar schools. We know from the 1957 Ministry annual report that the ratio of pupils to teachers in secondary moderns was 23, compared with 19 in grammar schools. In secondary technical schools the ratio was 18. But, and it is an important 'but' – this was not done for malicious or preferential reasons. It resulted from the hangover of the old system of schooling and the fact that the average length of a pupil's school life in a grammar school was a third more than those in a secondary modern. The longer the tripartite system had to become established, the more equitable the pupil funding.

The problems of secondary modern teachers

This is what Wikipedia had to say about secondary modern teachers (September 2020).

> Secondary moderns were generally deprived of both resources and good teachers. Staff turnover was high and continuity in teaching minimal.

The briefing paper about secondary moderns produced by the Cambridge University's SESC project talked about them 'employing teachers not as well paid or as academically qualified as grammar school counterparts'. Reference was made to the 'condensed teacher training' received by the ex-military staff who qualified through the war-time national emergency scheme. Perhaps this implied they were in some way second-best to teachers who qualified in the normal way? Perhaps I am being over-sensitive?

All these observations I understand and will address. Where I metaphorically 'lost the plot' was SESC's comments that:

> Progressive ideas were poorly understood and implemented in the

secondary modern school, so that the intended focus on the individual child became a limiting conception of pupil capability.

And that:

This mixture of staffing provision in the secondary modern, combined with teachers' poor understanding of popular sociology and child-centred teaching methods, made secondary moderns a key site of gendered anxiety about age and class in postwar Britain.

Progressive education was gendered feminine, thus it was more likely to be resisted by male secondary modern teachers, leading to a negative othering of the male secondary modern pupil.

As I wrote the words and pondered how the 'negative othering' might have affected my life I couldn't help wondering what Mr Dixon, my headmaster, or Mrs Wright, my form teacher, would have made of the comments? I am pretty sure I know but it's probably best not to put them into words.

In this section I will restrict myself to commenting on the material criticisms that secondary modern teachers, when compared with those in grammar schools, were:

- Not as academically qualified.
- Of lower quality.
- Not as well paid.
- Difficult to recruit and retain.

Teachers in the pre-war elementary schools were far less likely to have a degree than those in secondary schools. When the school names changed to secondary moderns and grammar schools that situation continued. There is no record of what percentage of the 30,000 teachers who qualified through the post-war emergency training scheme were graduates but my guess is it was low.

In 1955 about 16% of secondary modern teachers had degrees compared with 80% of those in grammar schools. By 1978 the number had increased to a quarter but throughout their life the figure never approached those found in grammar and technical schools.

It needs to be remembered that during the post-war period recruiting graduates into the teaching profession was not a priority. Getting teachers, any type of teachers, to cope with the growing school population was the number one priority. In 1977, the education minister (Shirley Williams) might have talked about her long-term intent to make the teaching profession an all-graduate entry but at the time her aspirations were somewhat lower – ensuring trainee teachers had GCE 'O' level passes in English and maths.

That I have been talking about the percentage of graduates implies possessing a degree equates to being a better teacher. When teaching pupils for Oxbridge entrance, possessing a degree in the subject being taught must be an advantage. The relevance of a degree is not so clear for those teaching in secondary moderns when so many pupils didn't take external exams. Even by the end of the timeline a significant percentage of children didn't follow an academic curriculum – a third of children left school without five GCSEs. Dent suggested that the academic background of teachers came with disadvantages.

Because of their intellectual ability and the nature of their education, a great many teachers in secondary modern schools have the utmost difficulty in comprehending the ways in which the minds of less intelligent children work.

The pros and cons of teachers having degrees is not a subject I want to cover. That secondary moderns had far fewer graduate teachers than other types of school is a fact. What difference that made to the quality of the education provided is not so certain.

Were those teaching in secondary moderns paid less than those in other types of school? In April 1945 the Burnham Committee – the organisation responsible for setting teachers' pay – announced national pay scales for all types of teacher. Theoretically, teachers of similar experience, in grammar and secondary moderns, were paid the same. I expect that the average salary level of grammar school teachers was higher than that in secondary moderns because they were older and better qualified. That's my guess for the enduring idea that 'teachers in secondary moderns were paid less'.

I found it impossible to confirm or refute the view that the 'quality' of secondary modern teachers, all 77,000 (1962) of them, was lower than those in grammar and technical schools. My guess is that all types of school had a similar distribution of teaching excellence from the dire to the inspiring. This is certainly true of the schools I attended, both secondary modern and grammar.

Since WWII trying to recruit and retain enough teachers, especially those with maths and science qualifications, has been a perennial challenge. As changes in demography and education policy increased the school population, teacher numbers were always struggling to catch up. This is still a familiar story today. In the period 2004–2018 there were only five years when the target number of new teachers was achieved.

During the 1960s the situation was particularly bad as the children of the baby boom entered secondary schools – mainly secondary moderns. An internal Ministry document (*The supply of teachers in the 1960s*) used capitals, a rarity in civil service documents, to emphasise the magnitude of the difficulty.

The crucial fact that emerges is that whereas on earlier calculations the supply of teachers was expected approximately to equal the number of teachers to eliminate oversize classes by 1968, on the new calculation THERE IS NO prospect, even on the more optimistic assumptions, of the supply meeting demand at any time in the 1960s.

A comprehensive analysis of how this problem affected secondary moderns is found in the Newsom Report (1963). A detailed account of the report's findings and implications can be found in Chapter 6.

Newsom's research covered the period September 1958–September 1961. When he studied the turnover of teachers, he assumed it was reasonable that 10–15% of new appointments would move schools within three years of their appointment. He found the numbers to be much higher, with 35% of the women and 42% of their male colleagues moving school or leaving the profession. These numbers varied greatly depending on where the school was situated. In rural areas it was 24%, socially mixed neighbourhoods 30% but in 'problem areas' the number increased to 45% and in the worst 'slum schools' it was an astonishing 66%.

To provide balance and context to these numbers Newsom said:

To some extent this is clearly a national problem – one consequence of the general shortage and wastage of teachers and the greater opportunity of promotion to graded posts since 1956.

The highly regarded study *Born to Fail* studied the lives of over 10,000 children born in March 1958 and concluded that at the age of 11 'disadvantaged children were not more likely to be affected by higher teacher turnover than the "ordinary child".' These results would be nearly a decade later than Newsom's research – it would seem that the turnover rate had improved greatly.

There are some other factors that I think help put these statistics into perspective.

In today's schools (2017) over 15% of new teachers leave the profession within the first 12 months. A third of all new teachers in 2013 had departed within five years. These numbers reveal a terrible waste of effort and distress to those involved. However, they show that 60 years after Newsom's research, retaining teachers is still a huge problem, something that is not specific to secondary moderns.

For much of their short life, secondary moderns were under threat of being reorganised. According to Anthony Sampson (*Anatomy of Britain*) in 1965 over half the 148 LEAs had produced plans to implement some form of comprehensive education and a further third were considering the option. All teachers had to live with this uncertainty, including those in grammar and technical schools. Many teachers must have responded to the forthcoming upheaval by changing schools. To some extent this must be reflected in Newsom's analysis.

Whatever the excuses and explanations they don't mitigate for the disruption that so many secondary modern pupils suffered, especially those in the poorest areas. I am not sure that this problem was the fault of the system of schooling so much as the lack of focus given to these 'problem areas'. In later years it was recognised that to change deeply entrenched social and educational problems required extra levels of resources. Even then it is not clear how successful we have been in solving the deeply entrenched problem.

Selective education favoured the middle class

Many commentators about education viewed it through the prism of 'class' and concluded that the upper class went to private schools, the working class to secondary moderns and the middle class to grammar schools. Sampson's description was more graphic: 'at eleven all British school children were divided into two classes, "eggheads and serfs".'

Wealthy parents – those able to spend £40,000 per year on their child's education – can afford one of the top-charging private schools. It is difficult to know if the ire of those condemning selective education is more directed at this class of parent or the next echelon down, those who seek out the best state schools, the 'middle class'.

I have never understood the hierarchy of class, especially the point where working class ends and middle class begins; to be honest I have never cared. John Prescott, a former deputy leader of the Labour Party, was forever proclaiming his working class credentials –especially his failure of the 11-plus – yet famously said 'we are all middle class now'. This was just before the 1997 election and no doubt was intended to extend the Labour Party's multi-class, electoral appeal. You can understand why I find the subject confusing.

Rather than considering the beneficiaries of selective education posed in terms of 'class' I prefer using more tangible factors about parents such as their wealth and attitude to education, a topic I have already considered in this chapter. It doesn't do any harm to repeat my conclusion that both factors are hugely important in assisting a child's education. However, these metrics are rarely used by educationalists, probably because the data is difficult to collect. They prefer to categorise parents by their type of employment and for much of the timeline just the profession of the father.

There were three reports, commissioned by the government, that added context and detail to the simple conclusion that secondary moderns were a ghetto for the working class; Chapter 6 contains a detailed review of the research.

Before considering these insights, I want to dispel a common myth about class and education that is illustrated by a letter in *The Daily Telegraph* (2014).

> *The 'success' of the grammar school is only made possible by the consignment of the vast majority of pupils, especially those from working-class and under-privileged backgrounds, to a second-rate education from which it can take years to recover.*

This sentiment assumes that secondary moderns were the losing half of the zero-sum game equation. It is the same argument that claims that 'the advantages of the rich result from the deprivation of the poor.' When phrased in terms of class, it blames the 'privileges', a much-loved word of the 2020s, of the middle class for the 'deprivations' of the working class. I believe that the explanation for the relative advantages of people, call them 'classes' if you will, is far more complex than this notion that somebody winning means others must lose. When I have the time I will write a full justification for this belief – but not now.

The first of the reports (Gurney-Dixon) was published in 1954, but the research began in 1946, when a sample of 10% of the pupils in England attending maintained and direct grant grammar schools were studied for the duration of their school days. One of the many factors researched was the relationship between their academic performance and their fathers' employment.

It came as no surprise that many parents (22%) were classified as being in 'professional and managerial' employment. However, most (39%) had 'skilled' jobs. What surprised me was the types of work included in this category.

> *Market gardeners, fitters, electricians, instrument makers, foremen, weavers, curriers, saddlers, boot and shoe makers, tailors, upholsterers, carpenters, joiners, engine-drivers, compositors, bookbinders, postmen, shop assistants, police constables, hewers, and machinemen (in mining), bus drivers.*

I am not disputing that this employment is 'skilled' but I wonder if today these job types, where they still exist, would be associated with the 'middle class'. This highlights the danger of using terms that change in character over time.

Children of the 'unskilled' were the least likely to attend grammar schools. Their parents were navvies, porters, dock labourers, lift attendants, hawkers, newspaper sellers, watchmen, bottle sorters and kitchen hands. With the exception of 'kitchen hands' all of these other job types have disappeared. An interesting and sad conclusion was that when these children passed the 11-plus, many of them performed badly at grammar school. The report concluded that only a third of them 'obtained the benefit that the grammar school is specifically designed to give' – another illustration of how a child's home life determines their success.

A decade later Newsom's report considered a very different group of children – those aged 13 to 16 of average and of less-than-average ability. A substantial sample of 6,000 fourth-year pupils in 75 secondary modern schools were researched.

What leapt out from the findings was the extent to which the academic achievement of secondary modern school pupils was stratified by the employment of their parents. The brightest pupils, based on their reading proficiency, were three times more likely than the bottom group to have parents classified as professional and managerial. They were half as likely to have 'unskilled' parents. The most extreme difference related to the decision to stay at school and complete a 5th form – with the potential to take GCE 'O' levels. Just 3% of those with the lowest literacy scores made this choice compared with 42% of the top performers.

It was undoubtedly true that class, as defined by parents' employment, was important in determining whether a child passed the 11-plus. However, it remained equally important, if not more so, in determining how well pupils performed once they got to their grammar or secondary modern school.

The final report, a survey by HM Inspectors of schools, was published in 1979 and drew its conclusions from researching 10% of pupils in the country's 4,200 secondary schools. Pupils in their 4th and 5th forms (Years 10 and 11) were studied and, among many other things, their performance analysed by where they lived – a proxy for the parents' wealth and profession.

Only 16% of pupils in secondary moderns came from 'prosperous suburban' areas, compared with 47% attending grammar schools. Pupils with 'learning difficulties' were educated in secondary moderns, with nearly half of the schools reporting 11–20% of pupils in this category. Grammar schools had virtually none.

The school inspectors concluded that where children lived was a major factor influencing their academic achievements but, with the right headmaster and teachers, it was possible to compensate for these difficult backgrounds. Neither comment would be out of place in a report about today's schools.

Few would disagree with the view that parents want the best education for their children; however, some parents want it more than others and some parents have the financial resources to ensure they get it. If you agree with this statement then the real question to answer is did selective education, *more than other systems of education*, favour the middle class? I am not sure that it did, but I will return to the question later in the chapter, when I have more to say about comprehensives.

The lasting effect of failing the 11-plus

We know from an inquiry conducted by the British Psychological Society (1957) that there was scant evidence supporting the accusation that the 11-plus resulted in children suffering psychological problems.

> 'The emotional effects on children are probably less severe than the ill-feeling caused among parents' and that 'there is considerably more anxiety and worry among pupils who get into grammar schools than among those who do not'.

But, did the trauma of failing the 11-plus and the consequences of attending a secondary modern have a long-term effect on their pupils' self-worth and life chances? Did these schools' (alleged) low expectations of their pupils condemn those pupils to a future of 'blue collar' and basic administrative employment?

It is easy to trivialise these claims by stating what their consequences would have been if they were true. An ageing generation of workers would have spent their lives in the most basic form of employment with feelings of intellectual inferiority compared with their children and grandchildren educated in post-tripartite times. Of course, that is not how things worked out.

To the best of my knowledge there hasn't been a national malaise known as 'secondary modern syndrome'. According to an OECD report *(Building skills for all),* England is the only country in the developed world where adults aged 55–65, many educated in secondary moderns, perform better in literacy and numeracy than their grandchildren's generation aged 16–24.

In a different study, the OECD ranked the UK as joint bottom for adult financial literacy in a league table of 17 nations and it was the only country where the numeracy skills of 16–24 year olds were lower than the over-55s.[16] Most recently the ONS concluded that older people are far more likely to understand day-to-day economic statistics than the young, with the over-65s twice as likely to be able to define the meaning of GDP than 18–24 year olds.[17] Andy Haldane, the Bank of England's chief economist, said:[18]

Every other country is becoming more numerate over time, yet our young people have fewer skills, and that's super relevant right now as younger people are bearing the brunt of the Covid-19 crisis.

So much for the proposition about stunted educational attainment.

I looked to find where these claims originated. There was one, much-quoted, report that purported to have measured the lasting psychological harm of the tripartite system. In 2012 *The Daily Telegraph* contained an article titled: 'Adults put off education for life after failing 11-plus' based on a press release from a company called Love to Learn. This organisation, part of the Pearson Group, sold online courses to adults wanting to continue their education. Unfortunately, the following year the company was closed and all details of its research – a sample of 1,000 over-50s – were lost.

Without access to the research methodology it is impossible to comment on its veracity; however, I am always suspicious of company-sponsored market research reaching conclusions that support the organisation's marketing objectives. An academic paper published in 1998 *(The two components of a new learning society)* came to a very different conclusion. It found that an older person's chances of restarting their education were dependent on the motivation they had at the time, rather than what happened during their time at school. In short, there are no quantitative studies that consistently support or disprove the accusation.

Several research projects have attempted to provide qualitative insights by collecting the stories of pupils who failed the 11-plus and recording their school-day recollections. Most of these are not only critical, some intensely so, but also intensely bitter about how they were failed by the education system. Researchers collecting these reminiscences, mostly in the form of blog postings and interviews, are invariably advocates of comprehensivisation, believing secondary moderns were a terrible mistake.

Passive research, especially when conducted by biased researchers, is fraught with problems, starting with the difficulty in sourcing a balanced sample of contributors. When respondents are self-selecting they frequently have extreme views. These are the people who feel sufficiently incensed about a topic to commit the time and energy to have their voices heard. For evidence of these factors watch the BBC's *Question Time* programme, which is theoretically a representative group of the UK's population but whose audience is drawn only from those who apply to participate.

Another problem is collecting a sufficiently large respondent sample. The most prominent of the research websites had 32 contributions over a period of six years. I feel sure these people were relating their 'felt' experiences as accurately as they could, but the views of a handful of people cannot be extrapolated to represent millions of past pupils.

The claim that secondary moderns' expectations of their pupils were so low as to restrict them to 'blue collar' and basic administrative employment isn't supported by any evidence. For sure there are lots of references linking the schools to the term 'factory fodder' – at last count over 600 matches using Google search. Photographs of the schools often reinforce the 'practical' nature of the education (and gender stereotypes), with girls doing domestic science and boys metal-work. In contrast, grammar schools are illustrated with studious-looking pupils gazing at science experiments. So the contextual evidence suggests there might be some truth to the proposition.

I rephrased the claim to make it more tangible and to provide a metric that could be measured: 'during the tripartite era social mobility was reduced compared with subsequent education systems'. I assumed that even its most ardent critics would concede it was an improvement on pre-war schooling.

A research study published in 2014 (*The mobility problem in Britain: new findings from the analysis of birth cohort data*) compared the changes in social mobility from the end of WWII until the conclusion of my time-line. It was a longitudinal study using four cohorts of people born in Britain in 1946, 1958, 1970 and 1980, and studied both intergenerational and birth cohort class mobility. The purpose of the research was to test the hypothesis that social mobility in the UK was in *decline*. An interesting starting point that is the opposite of what you would expect – it should be *improving* if the claims about the tripartite system were correct.

The researchers found that men's social mobility remained remarkably stable across the cohorts, although the upward mobility component tended to fall and the downward to increase. For women there was a slight increase in social mobility.

I was surprised by these results. Over the research period the education spend per pupil had greatly increased, yet it doesn't appear to have delivered a matching improvement in social mobility. On the basis of this one study, a dangerously small research sample, it would seem that neither the system of secondary education nor the level of education funding are determinants of social mobility. I will return to this topic in the final chapter, 'Half a century on what lessons have we learnt?'

Secondary moderns were unpopular with 'the public'

To what extent did the public's rejection of selective education result in the demise of secondary moderns? Were the tripartite system abandoned and comprehensive education introduced to please voters or Labour politicians?

In 1957 the Labour Party wanted to understand the electorate's views about the country's provision of secondary education. This was decades before policy was formulated using focus groups, an era when politicians rarely asked the public for their opinions. It must have been something of a novelty when Labour's shadow education minister (Michael Stewart) commissioned a market research company to interview 400 parents to seek their views about secondary schools.

The results came as a shock. Most working class parents were generally content to leave the education system as it was. Few had heard about comprehensive schooling and when they had their opinions weren't favourable. Using today's marketing jargon, the researchers' advice was to rebrand the concept of comprehensive schools to emphasise their benefits for the 'bright child', rather than as an instrument to create a more egalitarian society.

Another view about parents' attitudes was provided by Dent's report:

Contrary to popular belief, from the start, and all the way through [1945–1957] many (perhaps most) of the parents whose children were allocated to the Secondary Modern School were more or less content that they should be.

At least in 1957, most sections of public opinion seemed content with the education system, which makes it hard to understand how the Crowther Enquiry (1959) reached the view that there was a 'public clamour against a competitive element in grammar school selection, which seems to parents to be contrary to the promise of secondary education according only to "age, aptitude and ability"'.

As I have already stated, the first rule of market research is to choose a representative sample of respondents, something that I suspect Crowther ignored. He was reacting to what Dent called 'grammar-school-conscious' parents who he thought to be 'vocal out of all proportion to their strength, and, with the aid of other sections of the public hostile to the secondary modern school'.

To understand how public sentiment changed I searched the UK's high-circulation newspapers for instances of the words 'secondary modern', '11-plus', 'comprehensive school' and 'grammar school'. Measuring word frequency doesn't tell us anything about what was reported, of course, but it indicates how the public's level of interest changed over time.

During the period 1951–1964 the frequency of articles including these words climbed, with references to the '11-plus' rising the most. However, the actual number of times the terms appeared remained low. For instance, '11-plus' appeared 69 times during the 12 months of 1964. In the same year, less than two articles a month (on average) mentioned comprehensive schools. More interest was shown in secondary moderns, but it was articles referencing 'grammar schools' that dominated the media coverage – by a considerable margin. All the details of my research are in Chapter 6.

The pages of *The Times Educational Supplement* regularly contained letters and articles about the 11-plus and secondary moderns, but in the media read by parents with children at the schools (e.g. the *Daily Express* and *Daily Mirror*) they were a rarity.

Labour politicians were quick to proffer the justification of having public opinion on their side to vindicate the abandonment of the tripartite system. Undoubtedly, the reaction of some sectors of society justified this claim, but they were in the minority. The influence of committed and vocal parents was again seen when they campaigned to retain grammar schools when the battle moved to the courts.

Was comprehensive education introduced to please voters or Labour politicians? I couldn't find any convincing evidence of the working class demanding the education system be changed. It seems that politicians' ideology greatly outweighed public discontent in deciding to dump the schools.

I have now completed the first two parts of this chapter. I started by discussing the factors associated with the schools' birth – what they replaced, their goals and the difficulties of educating the growing post-war school population. The second section considered the validity of the criticisms that are most often levelled at the schools and their teachers.

Finally, I want to discuss the topics that are rarely, if ever, mentioned when the schools are discussed. I don't think these omissions occur for malicious reasons – well, not most of the time. Rather, they are issues and events that complicate the dominant narrative and remove some of its certainty. The black-and-white arguments about secondary moderns, which are mainly black, become a light shade of grey. It is much easier to omit the topics. I have already quoted Mary Beard's view about this problem and it is one she reiterated in a recent debate at the RSA: 'we don't disseminate a complex view of the past; it is always a simple view'.

Judging the effectiveness of policy decisions before they have been fully implemented is a mistake made by businesses and governments alike. Secondary moderns were a victim of this problem, something that I have referenced throughout this chapter. By 1962 the Conservative minister (Boyle) was resigned to accepting the tripartite system being replaced by comprehensive schools. From the late 1950s onwards the Labour Party was committed to, and actively seeking to, abandon the 11-plus, secondary moderns and especially grammar schools.

My reason for reiterating this point is that it is unfair and wrong to talk about the schools failing when they were never given the time, let alone the resources, to succeed. It's like building a new type of diesel car but not having the time and money to properly assemble the engine and then, when it underperforms, saying it 'failed'. It's valid to oppose the decision to build the car in the first place and to argue it should have been a hybrid or electric-powered. But it's inaccurate to say it 'failed'; it was 'abandoned'.

Another, related factor, is the difficulties caused by inheriting the infrastructure and reputation of the schools they replaced. When secondary moderns were launched, they were the same schools with the same teachers that many of the pupils' parents experienced. Twelve years after the end of the war only 10% of secondary moderns were 'new builds' and most of these were in the 'new towns'. When the bricks and mortar stayed the same, is it any surprise that they struggled to cast off the reputation of being rebranded elementary schools – because that's what most of them were.

Comprehensive schools encountered exactly the same problem. Most of them were secondary moderns with new name signs at the school gate. Often this is proffered as an excuse for their patchy performance but when applied to secondary moderns it becomes another explanation for their failure. The difference is that comprehensives had and still have a loyal band of supporters, something that secondary moderns never acquired. Comprehensives were the progeny of the Labour Party. Grammar schools were the adopted child of the Conservatives. Secondary moderns were orphans.

There two more issues that should be part of any discussion about secondary moderns but are rarely discussed. Did the system of education that replaced them do any better and are today's schools an effective way of educating pupils who struggle to achieve academic success?

Comprehensives an unattainable ideal or a practical solution?

The story of comprehensive schools is told in Chapter 7 ('The comprehensive era'). Using a motoring analogy, it is a tale of 'stops and starts', with an unexpected 'handbrake turn' when Tony Blair took control of the

Labour Party. It was a time when the building blocks of secondary education were being rearranged. What children were taught, how they were evaluated and the role and attitude of teachers – all were in flux. I will be referencing these changes but for the detail you should consult the chapter.

When the Labour Party's education minister (Ellen Wilkinson) implemented the 1944 Education Act she was trying to provide the best quality of education for the maximum number of children, using the resources available. I am sure she didn't think of it that way but that was effectively her role. Rightly or wrongly – in my view rightly – the best way of doing it, *at the time*, was the tripartite system.

There was a small number of Labour Party politicians who thought she was mistaken and that there was a better way. They believed it was impossible and wrong to decide a child's secondary school when they were 11 years old. On that point they were correct. Instead they wanted a system where all the children from a local area (we would now call it a 'community') attended the same school – a comprehensive. There they would receive the most appropriate education to match their talents. These were terrific aspirations but immediately following the war this was a dream, not an achievable policy.

These early proponents of comprehensivisation must have thought it was as effective as the tripartite system and no doubt a lot better. There isn't any evidence that they had considered the practicalities of making it work, let alone formulated policies for overcoming the horrendous consequences of reorganising schools in the shadow of the war. For these people, optimising the use of the scarce educational resources was of secondary importance. Creating a system of schooling to serve a social (and socialist) purpose was their primary goal.

In 1969, Robin Pedley, a well-known advocate of comprehensivisation, wrote:

Comprehensive education does more than open the doors of opportunity to all children. It represents a different, a larger and more generous attitude of mind... the forging of a communal culture by the pursuit of quality with equality, by the education of their pupils in and for democracy, and by the creation of happy and vigorous local communities in which the school is the focus of social and educational life.

It was this quote that Melissa Benn, Fiona Millar and Andy Burnham, recent advocates of the schools, used in their writings to capture the essence of the comprehensive 'ideal'.

Part of me wants to mock the words as a pretentious collection of soundbites. After all, phrases such as 'forging of communal culture', 'pursuit of quality with equality', 'happy and vigorous communities' and 'focus of social and educational life' are easy to write, but they describe objectives that are both vague and horrendously difficult to achieve. Yet how can I criticise the ideals – they are all laudable.

My reason for acknowledging this is that the battle (a word I have chosen with care) between the supporters of the tripartite and comprehensive system was only partly about providing the best system of schooling. The supporters of comprehensives were trying to achieve much more. They wanted schools to be a tool for remoulding society. Unfortunately, they never asked 'society' if it wanted to be remoulded and into what shape.

I dread to think how many thousands of hours have been spent comparing the performance of the tripartite model with that of comprehensivisation. The more of these comparisons I have read, the more worthless they seem. From its conception onwards, the faults of the tripartite system were there for all to see. That it should have been improved or replaced was a 'no brainer'. The worthwhile questions were 'what with' and 'when'?

Did comprehensivisation learn from the tripartite system's mistakes and provide a more effective system of education and did it capitalise on the improvements in the country's economic and demographic conditions? You might have guessed from my account of its wider, social objectives that there is another question to answer: 'did its social engineering aims interfere with its educational effectiveness?' The scope of these questions is worthy of another book and one I don't intend to write. Instead I want to explain why the comprehensive 'ideal' failed to fulfil its proponents' dreams. And yes, I am aware that this selective use of facts makes me vulnerable to bias – something I will do my best to avoid.

A policy driven by the heart, not the head. Academics working in the disciplines of medicine and education are fond of using the term 'evidence-based'. Lately academics have incorporated it into their writing and their titles as a kitemark of quality. To my mind it is an unnecessary term and a tad pretentious.

Its use suggests that marshalling 'evidence' to aid decision making is a new invention – obviously it is not. However, it was conspicuously missing when politicians formulated their education policies. There was the pretence of using research to justify the tripartite policy but that was little more than a smokescreen for repackaging the preceding system of schooling.

It isn't an exaggeration to say that the policy of comprehensivisation was an 'evidence-free zone'. That the schools that replaced secondary moderns were conceived without a scrap of research prompted me to devote a section of Chapter 6 to the subject ('Going comprehensive – the antithesis of evidence-based policy making').

A vocal and committed supporter of comprehensivisation (Brian Simon) summed up the situation this way:

> *No overall planning for this change [the transition to comprehensivisation], no serious thinking through of its implications on a national basis ever took place, either now or later [the book was first published in 1991]. At no point, for instance, was any official thought, enquiry or study made as to what should comprise an appropriate curriculum for the new comprehensive schools now coming into being.*

As far back as 1951, parts of the Labour Party were concerned with the lack of 'scholastic' rigour supporting the party's education ideas. The editorial section of *The Political Quarterly,* a publication that was sympathetic to the party, criticised the policies for making no attempt to 'consider the problems involved in attempting to educate a mass of children of widely differing abilities, aptitudes, and taste'.

Anthony Crosland, Labour's minister of education and the person most often credited with disassembling the tripartite system, not only avoided researching the relative strengths of comprehensivisation and the tripartite model – he explicitly instructed his officials not to do it.

During a meeting in 1965 Crosland told his officials that whatever research was conducted about comprehensives, it would not include comparing them with selective schools and that government policy 'must be taken as read' and not to be questioned.

To my mind the most damaging result of Crosland's aversion to using 'evidence' occurred in 1966 when the Plowden Committee was about to report its findings. Over the previous three years it had interviewed 400 witnesses, conducted primary research studies and created 800 pages of report. Rather than using Plowden's findings to mould his policies, he very publicly ignored them.

There was so much that could have been learnt from the growing pains of secondary moderns, from Plowden's research and the knowledge residing within the Ministry, but Labour politicians resolutely ignored it all. Far too much of their time was consumed trying to change the structure of schools rather than addressing the huge challenge of providing children of differing abilities with an effective education. Resolutely rejecting research to inform their decisions didn't help.

A school's pupils reflect the class of their parents. It has long been understood that a school's catchment area often contains a high concentration of a particular class of parent. In urban areas, pupils from the unskilled classes were likely to be found in 'slum schools', which were later referred to as 'inner-city' schools and which we now politely call 'areas of educational deprivation'. At the other end of the class spectrum are schools with a high intake of pupils from professional and managerial parents.

When Pedley talked about creating 'happy and vigorous local communities' I expect he imaged a mixing together of children from different backgrounds. He believed (hoped) that breaking down the class barriers at an early age would lead to a more understanding and fairer society.

It was a nice theory and no doubt it did occur. Unfortunately, the rationale that determined where schools were built took no account of balancing their mix of pupils. If schools were to educate pupils from different social strata, they would have required a level of intervention that few LEAs were prepared to consider. Social mixing could be achieved by 'bussing' children outside their home area, for example. Allocating school places using a lottery, known as 'random allocation', was tried by some LEAs, most notably Brighton. These were extreme and controversial measures that few local politicians were prepared to take.

As I have already commented, parents differ in their ability to 'game' the school system using their wealth and intelligence. Some were much better at it than others. Ensuring comprehensive schools had children of all classes was the touchpoint where the power of the state conflicted with the rights of parents to seek the best school for their children. Since the rights of parents invariably 'won', there was a fundamental flaw in the comprehensive ideal.

Tainted by association with 'progressive' teaching. Perhaps it's too simplistic to say that the students of the 'swinging 60s' became the 'progressive' teachers of the mid-1970s – but it does contain a grain of truth. Two such teachers applied their progressive theories to a school in north London (William Tyndale) with disastrous results. This landmark incident and its repercussions are explained in Chapter 7 ('The comprehensive era').

A school suffering 'staff problems' might be expected to arouse local interest, but the troubles of this small junior school captured the attention of the national press. Much of the reporting was about the failures of 'progressive' teaching techniques. Stories and arguments about these new ideas were rife at the time. The media stories about William Tyndale Junior School must have encapsulated public concerns and confirmed the view that there was something very wrong with children's schooling. How true this was and what general lessons could be learnt from this one school is impossible to say. What's certain is that children's education had become a political issue and was portrayed as a problem needing to be solved.

I believe that comprehensivisation was swept up in the widespread feeling that schools weren't working properly and that something should be done to put them right. This is unfair since the model of secondary schooling is only loosely connected with how and what teachers teach. But when has fairness been important in determining how the story of education is told?

By the mid-1970s two-thirds of secondary school pupils attended comprehensives. When the political repercussions of the Tyndale affair translated into new education policies it was these schools and pupils who experienced the changes.

Similarities with secondary moderns. Comprehensives and secondary moderns faced many of the same challenges. I am sure that wasn't how it was seen at the time, with the former heralded as the bright new future of secondary schooling and the latter, something best forgotten. Perhaps if politicians had been more understanding of the challenges that secondary moderns had faced, it would have helped the introduction of comprehen-sives. But that was not to be.

Probably the most important similarity was both were founded without a scrap of research, something I have already explained. In addition, both types of school had to contend with the following problems:

- It took time for secondary moderns to establish a different identity from the schools they replaced (elementary schools). Likewise, comprehensives inherited the reputations – good and bad – of the secondary moderns.
- At the time they were introduced there were tight limits on education funding. Both new models of schooling had to forge a new identity using the existing infrastructure of schools and teachers.
- Responsibility for implementing both types of schools was shared between central and local government and the schools. As I have explained, many times, this resulted in a host of problems.
- Judgements were made about the performance of the schools before either system had time to become properly established. It didn't take long for the post-war agreement about schools to disappear and for it to become a partisan issue. Once this happened there was always one political party anxious to highlight the failings of the other's educational policies. And don't forget the media, which has never been renowned for its balanced reporting of issues.
- Secondary moderns and comprehensives were badly affected by the shortage of teachers, especially those able to teach the core subjects of English, maths and science. Teachers in these schools, on average, were younger and had less experience than those in grammar schools.
- Try as they may to avoid it, both models of schooling provided a diluted version of a grammar school education. Even when the number of grammar schools had been culled, they still represented the benchmark of excellence against which other schools were measured. Secondary moderns couldn't hope to compete; neither could comprehensives.

- Secondary modern pupils included those who narrowly missed a grammar school place and children with learning problems. Of all the difficulties faced by the schools it was teaching this huge range of academic abilities that posed the greatest challenge. Comprehensivisation exacerbated the problem by adding the academically brightest children to the school registers. Both models of schooling struggled to stretch their finite (and often inadequate) teaching resources over such a wide range of pupil needs.

'The Government's refusal to legislate and the Chancellor's refusal to make funds available meant that comprehensive reorganisation was a botch-up job from the start.' These are the words of the Labour minister Edward Short (1989), but they eloquently express the conclusion that I reached, too.

'The Labour Party rejected both the idea of a return to the 11-plus and the monolithic comprehensive schools that take no account of children's differing abilities.' Again, these are not my words but taken from the Labour Party's 1997 manifesto.

In the pursuit of opportunity for all, comprehensive schools had concentrated on their sameness. In the fight for equal opportunity they may have emphasised equality too much and the opportunity too little. Too often Labour's attitude to excellence was confused with elitism and the failure to understand that celebrating those who achieve doesn't hold back others. You guessed it, not my words, other than a couple of minor changes of tense, but those of Estelle Morris, the Labour Party education minister (2002).

I could go on with quoting Labour politicians expressing their concerns and frustration about the way the comprehensive 'ideal' had soured. A diminishing band of their colleagues kept doing their best to defend the policy but they didn't control the levers of power.

There is no agreement about why Labour's 1974 election promise to 'speed the development of a universal system of fully comprehensive secondary schools' had, 30 years later, become 'the development of independent specialist schools in place of the traditional comprehensives'.

No single issue resulted in the demise of the schools. I believe the basic premise of comprehensivisation had serious fault lines that were exacerbated by the way the policy was implemented. Taking a helicopter view of the post-war era there is no doubt that during the comprehensive era the overall academic achievement of children improved. We could ponder forever whether this resulted from the upward trend in spending on education, exam grade inflation or the improved effectiveness of the comprehensive system.

Driven by the notions of fairness and equality, comprehensivisation had lost sight of the differing needs of individual pupils. This was the essence of Tony Blair's message when he talked about Labour's education policies in February 2001. His actual words were:

Inclusion, a good principle, became an end in itself, rather than a means to identify and to provide better for the talents of each individual pupil.

The words of his combative spokesman (Alistair Campbell) are probably the ones most remembered: 'The day of the "bog-standard" comprehensive is over.'

Educating the non-academic child

Secondary moderns were created to educate the non-academic child. The words used at the time gave a more positive 'spin' to their purpose, labelling these children as being 'practical, not conceptual' and 'interested in things as they are rather than abstractions'. The phrase 'non-academic' had no quantifiable definition, but rather labelled the child as unsuitable to study the grammar school curriculum.

Today we rely on an absolute measure of GCSE exam failure to mark out the less academically gifted. Indeed, we don't refer to pupils by their lack of academic achievement but as those 'failed by the education system'. During the final part of the timeline the percentage of children falling into the non-academic category fell (a lot), something I discussed when reviewing the comprehensive school era. In this section I wanted to see if the trend continued and if so why.

When secondary moderns were created around 70% of children were pigeonholed as non-academic. This was a notional number representing the children failing to get a place at one of the existing grammar or technical schools. As I have already shown, if England had mirrored Wales' provision of grammar schools the figure would have been less than 60%.

By the time of the Newsom Report (1963) the size of this group had fallen to 50%, a number resulting from research rather than the practical reality of how many grammar schools had been built. Over time the measure that separated the academic from non-academic was passing five GCSEs with grades A*–C, including maths and English. Each year more pupils achieved the target grades so that by 2016 only 40% of children were deemed to be non-academic. Recent research puts today's figure at 33%, a number I will return to in a moment.

Being unable to achieve the right number, grades and combination of GCSE passes marks a child out as being unlikely to extend their education. It probably also means that they will have difficulty coping with day-to-day literacy and numeracy tasks.

Thinking of explanations for the shrinking percentage of non-academic children is easy; proving them is near to impossible. Maybe politicians and the education establishment have become smarter at devising policies? Maybe teachers have become better at teaching? Maybe secondary moderns just weren't very good at doing the job and later systems of schooling were more effective? A lot of 'maybes' but no definitive answer. In fact, the more I looked the more unsure I became about the legitimacy of these measures of academic improvements. As for unpicking the factors responsible, real or imaginary, I concluded that it was impossible.

Fundamental to this issue is deciding if the rise in academic achievement was real or the result of changing the arithmetic for identifying the 'academic child'. Between 1975 and 2016 the percentage of children receiving five A*–C grades at GCE/GCSE increased from 23% to 58%. Those gaining the top grades increased even more, from 8% in 1988 to an astonishing 28% in 2020, by which time GCSEs were graded 1–9, with 9 equivalent to A*. One can only marvel at these achievements and their effect on driving up the numbers of young people going into higher education (50% in 2018).

The story seems one of continuous improvement until you encounter the following commentary in *The Daily Telegraph* (2019):

More than half of pupils are failing to achieve a 'strong pass' in their English and maths GCSEs. At state schools in England, 57% of

pupils were not able to get a grade 5 or above in the two core
subjects, according to provisional data published by the Department
for Education.

I am a fan of science fiction and one of the phrases that often appears is 'this does not compute'. My guess is many parents have used variants of this phrase trying to make sense of these numbers.

Why this (apparent) relentless improvement in academic success has gone into an (apparent) reverse is explained by my liberal use of the word 'apparent'. The exam score that marks out a child as being non-academic is not an absolute measure, but something controlled by examiners at the direction of politicians.

A few more words are needed to explain the comments from *The Daily Telegraph*. In 2017 59% of children achieved 'good' grades in English and maths but by changing the content of the exams and defining a new datum of success – a 'strong pass' – the number fell to 39%. This was the official explanation for the changes:

The qualifications have been designed to ensure that young people
have the knowledge and skills required to better prepare them for
employment or further study. They cover more challenging content
and are designed to match standards in high performing education
systems elsewhere in the world.

Things improved in 2018, but not by much, with 43% getting a strong pass in both subjects.

It is not my intention to critique the intricacies of the GCSE exam system, but rather to use this example to illustrate the impossibility of comparing academic achievement over a long time period. Soon after the birth of secondary moderns the GCE 'O' level became the dominant external exam, replacing the School Certificate. It was then joined by the CSE, which operated in parallel until they were both replaced by the GCSE. Since then this exam has undergone continuous tinkering with its curriculum and grading. No wonder comparing educational attainment, or the lack of it, is such a nightmare.

It is difficult to know how many children would now be classed as non-academic. David Laws was the minister of state for schools in 2015 and in the book *The Forgotten Third* (2020) he says:

About a third of pupils complete their education without securing the basic minimum suite of qualifications which will allow them to compete successfully for good, better paid jobs and prepare them for success in life. It's not that they don't master the more complex subjects such as a foreign language or physics – they don't even leave school with the basic levels of literacy and numeracy which are needed.

I have no idea if the figure of a third is correct. Instinctively I feel that the percentage of non-academic children has diminished but it is mighty difficult to say by how much. Whichever way you manipulate the numbers you have to conclude that a sizeable group of children finish their 12 years of schooling with the most basic education.

There is no shortage of explanations of why this is or what to do about it; however, I find myself agreeing with Estelle Morris (secretary of state in Blair's government) and her comments in *The Forgotten Third*:

There is no widespread agreement of why – or evidence – as to what works. This issue can't be just an interesting academic debate. It is one of the biggest challenges for this generation of educationalist.

Undoubtedly there is a link between the socio-economic standing of the parents and their children's academic achievement. But, a little probing of the analysis reveals a far more complicated inter-relationship between the different factors. Children with the same levels of deprivations achieve very different academic outcomes, something that is invariably explained by the variable quality of schools and especially the style of teaching imposed by the head.

I cannot add any value in unravelling the whys and wherefores of this question other than to highlight that secondary moderns had to cope with exactly the same challenge as today's schools. For some reason the third of pupils today who are deemed non-academic are the victims of their parents' economic plight, an explanation that is rarely (never) mentioned when discussing secondary moderns.

For completeness I wanted to look at the performance of the UK's schools on the international stage. I will make this account short because the results are depressing. Launched in 2000, the Programme for International Student Assessment (PISA) ranks the attainment of 15 year olds in maths, reading and science. Every three years this assessment is repeated to provide comparable data, enabling countries to improve their education policies and outcomes.

The results for 2018 showed the UK as 'improving' but not from a very high base. In reading skills the country was ranked 14th, up from 22nd in 2015. The performance in maths was worse, ranked at 18th up from 27th. Politicians are fond of saying that 'education is the key to a country's competitive success'. If these results are true – there are lots of people who question their validity – then they don't bode well for the future.

What disturbed me the most about the PISA assessments was the poor performance of Wales, a nation I have repeatedly referenced for its success. Earlier in the chapter I explained why the prevalence of Welsh teachers in English schools resulted from the country's high-quality education system.

Times have changed and now Wales languishes behind England, Scotland and Northern Ireland in its ability to educate its children in reading, maths and science. It is a salutatory lesson that the 'right' political decisions created a highly effective education system but it can crumble fast when later decisions are 'wrong'.

Three-quarters of a century after the end of WWII we still have a significant number of children who struggle at school. Less than there were during the secondary modern era but then we now spend far more money on education and have had nearly 50 years to make improvements. Countless initiatives and numerous models of schooling have only dented the problem. You have to conclude that the reasons and the solutions are beyond schools' ability to solve.

Yes, but what's the answer?

Since I began writing this book my friends have been asking me about its conclusions. My answers have depended on which part of the timeline I was researching and the most recent nugget of history I had unearthed. Hopefully, in this chapter I have woven together this patchwork of insights and provided a comprehensive answer to the question 'Were secondary moderns much maligned or a monstrous mistake?' As a rule of thumb, books' concluding chapters are short – but not in this case. Mine spans numerous topics and required 23,000 words. Its length is not a mistake. I have said before that time erodes the accuracy of our recall of historical events, making it vulnerable to bias and inaccuracies. The tale of secondary moderns is a case study in how these distortions can destroy the truth.

However, I know there is an expectation for a concise and punchy answer. Certainly, Stella, my wife, and my closest friends (Malcolm and Brian) have repeatedly, and patiently, asked variants of the question, 'So what will be your conclusions?' This is my ultra-summarised answer.

Let's start with the easy question – were secondary moderns much-maligned? Most definitely *Yes* is the answer. More importantly, the intensity and accuracy of the criticisms have been, and continue to be, undeserved. When in a tolerant mood I rationalise this as a natural consequence of time distorting the truth. In my less forgiving moments, of which there are many, I believe their history has been wilfully misrepresented. I sense their maligned reputation is the collateral damage in the battle waged by the disciples of comprehensivisation against selection and grammar schools. A 'battle' that I suspect had little to do with matters of education but was a proxy for competing visions of how society should be organised

Answering the question, 'Were they a monstrous mistake?' is not so simple and needs a more nuanced reply. It was nonsense to believe that children could be evaluated for their academic potential at age 11, and then consigned to one of three types of school. Calling it a monstrous mistake assumes there was a feasible alternative and I don't believe there was.

Immediately following the war, the only way of providing secondary education was to repackage pre-war elementary schools and their teaching staff, both of which were damaged and disrupted by five years of war. Rationing was widespread during the early part of the post-war era and education was no exception. Schools capable of providing an academic education were in short supply and entry by exam was the best, the only, mechanism available. Sometimes there are no right solutions, just the best of a bad lot. This was such a time.

From the 1944 Education Act onwards mistakes were made – and many of them. The absence of any meaningful vision for how the schools should work and what they should achieve was a mistake. Central government's inability and desire to deliver a consistent countrywide standard for schools was a mistake. Repeated failures of central and local government to manage changes affecting secondary schools, such as raising the leaving age and devising external exams, were a mistake. When considered together these probably deserve the collective term of being a 'monstrous' mistake.

Let's play a mind game and imagine how secondary schooling could have evolved if these mistakes hadn't been made. From the outset it was clear that a much higher percentage of children could benefit from an academic education – Welsh schools proved that beyond doubt. Rather than telling secondary moderns to 'experiment', they could have been directed to cater for an 'academic stream' of children – something they eventually did.

Rather than defending the rationing scheme of the 11-plus its inherent faults could have been recognised from the beginning and a process of continual improvements made. Errors would always have occurred but then no exam system is perfect – including the existing GCE 'A' levels and GCSEs.

For all of this to be possible LEAs would have had to become the channel to deliver education policy rather its originator, another change that was eventually made. If this mistake had been avoided it would have reduced the difficulties that always accompanied the implementation of major policy initiatives.

The system of schooling that would have resulted from this 'mistake-free' world would probably have looked much more like a comprehensive than a tripartite model. This model of schools would have evolved and not been imposed. Comprehensives suffered from many of the structural problems that plagued secondary moderns.

As it was, secondary moderns spent their first decade of life groping for a workable model that addressed the iniquities caused by the patchy provision of grammar schools. The LEAs were the final arbiters on how the schools were run, something that they delegated to their teachers. What resulted was more of a monstrous mess than a monstrous mistake.

Let's return to the mind game. We have had half a century to work out solutions to the long list of criticisms that are always levelled at secondary moderns. Much more money is now spent on secondary schools, but has all this been able to break the link between the social class of parents and their children's educational performance? Do all children receive an adequate level of academic education that equips them with basic literacy and numeracy skills? Sadly the answers are 'No' and 'No', with little chance that the answers are approaching being 'Yes'.

Schools and teachers, however they are organised, cannot reverse the deep-seated social issues that result in a sizeable percentage of children who don't achieve their academic potential. No doubt they make valiant efforts, but they are failing.

The narrative about secondary moderns ignores this truth and they are blamed for the problems that we now explain away as resulting from inequality, disadvantage and the multiple failures of 'society'. Secondary moderns were not a monstrous mistake. They had an impossible job to do and were given abysmal guidance and support on how to do it. No doubt many of their pupils received a rotten education, but many pupils did well, far more than the schools' critics admit. I was one of the lucky ones, for which I will always be immensely grateful.

CHAPTER 9

HALF A CENTURY ON – WHAT LESSONS CAN WE LEARN?

I have been fortunate – dare I use the word 'privileged'? – to have the time and resources to study one subject in considerable depth. Making sense of the evolution of secondary education, since the end of WWI, might be an odd topic to research, but it was essential in creating a balanced account about the life and times of secondary modern schools. That was my primary objective and I believe I have achieved my goal. Hopefully, others think the same.

Concluding the previous chapter was the logical place for me to stop, but I decided to keep writing, so think of this as a 'bonus chapter'. As I journeyed along the timeline a pattern emerged of similar problems occurring that seemed beyond the power of the establishment to solve. Each new generation of politicians was certain they could resolve the difficulties that had eluded their predecessors. Sometimes they did; more often their dreams ended in failure. Of course, the story was not all negative and the quality of children's education has undoubtedly improved – though maybe not by as much as the exam results suggest.

Perhaps I have taken an overly pessimistic view about the subject? Perhaps these repeated difficulties resulted from unrealistic expectations about education's ability to right the ills of society. There were too many unanswered questions so I decided to try and make sense of what I witnessed.

I don't think for a moment that I possess the solutions to the problems that have challenged the best brains of the political and educational establishment; however, my immersion in the history of secondary education provided me a ringside seat to watch intelligent and well-meaning people make blunder after blunder. One thing is for certain – repeating the same flawed solutions and expecting the results to be different doesn't work.

My hope is that by understanding the structural causes of these repeated failures we could adapt and improve our chances of success. But where to begin? A subject of this complexity deserves its own book, and I am covering it in a single chapter. I know I am running the risk of overly simplifying the subject and, worse still, my account could easily become a biased attack on the ideas that have most irritated me. I will do my very best to avoid both pitfalls.

Faced with these difficulties I decided to return to the tried and tested basics I learnt during my 50 years in business. Long, long ago I was taught to follow four steps when tackling projects involving creating new policies and their implementation. At the time I thought they were obvious, simplistic and hardly worth consideration. On too many occasions I ignored or rushed one or more of the steps and paid the price. Now I realise they are the essential building blocks for achieving successful and lasting change.

Making significant changes to secondary education is a highly complex task and so it's reasonable (essential) to expect the educational establishment to follow these steps. Of course, the process would have been expressed using 'education speak', but the fundamental logic should have been the same.

The four steps are as follows.

Step 1. Avoid rushing to begin and to be seen being decisive until you are crystal clear about your goals and what 'success looks like'.

Step 2. Detail how this objective will be achieved by formulating the policies, setting the timescales and gaining the agreement of those responsible for ensuring the project's success.

Step 3. This is the most difficult and undervalued activity: implement the delivery plan.

Step 4. As soon as it is possible to evaluate the performance of the project:

- Learn from the mismatch between theory and reality.
- Review the goals, policies and plans.
- Adapt objectives, modify policies and improve plans, then repeat the process.

Don't worry, I am not going to descend into a morass of 'management speak' and abstract theories. There will no PowerPoint slides and fancy-looking diagrams.

In very simple terms, I wanted to know if such a systematic process was followed in the evolution of the education system and, if not, why not?

Let's start with my conclusions in a single sentence. During most of the timeline, Steps 1 and 2 were often done badly, or not at all, Step 3 was never given the attention and resources it required and the three activities in Step 4 rarely took place.

Perhaps by understanding the fundamental reasons for these failures we can adapt and improve our chances of success? I fear that is a faint hope – but it is the purpose of this final chapter.

Step 1. What do we want from our schools?

Children spend over 25,000 hours in school and doing school-associated activities. I stopped trying to calculate how much this costs, but it's a lot. Add to this the time and money devoted by parents and the numbers skyrocket. What do we – children, parents, taxpayers, politicians and future employers – expect from this massive investment?

This is not a question I could hope, or want, to answer. It is a subject that has been pondered and argued over by countless academics, politicians, businesspeople and media pundits. It is no surprise that the most-watched TED Talk of all time (69 million views) is about the purpose of education.[1]

Despite the question's importance and the aeons of time consumed seeking an answer, the lack of agreement today is wider than when I began the timeline, way back during WWI. These are my observations and thoughts about why reaching a lasting and durable answer is so difficult.

It's not about education – it's about ideology

The purpose of the NHS is 'to provide a comprehensive range of health services free at the point of use'. What is meant by a 'comprehensive range' of services and how they are delivered might be hotly debated but the essence of the NHS's role is clear and rarely questioned. If only things were that simple when defining the role of state education.

There is agreement that schools should ensure children can read and write, but step beyond these most basic of functional skills and the consensus evaporates. Some politicians and most academics contend that schools must do more than provide the knowledge and skills enabling young people to join and contribute to society. Even the words in that statement are contested – what do you mean by 'contribute' and 'society'? Many of the problems resulted from the inability to define and then explain the very basics of what schools were expected to achieve.

The disruption caused by two world wars and repeated waves of economic upheavals resulted in huge challenges. There were never enough teachers with the right skills or enough decent classrooms. Despite these practical difficulties, politicians spent an inordinate amount of time arguing about the rights and wrongs of competing models of schooling – the tripartite and comprehensive systems.

I soon realised that this conflict wasn't about operational effectiveness, but was about opposing visions of how society should be organised. Once I had the 'light bulb moment' all became clear; arguments about education weren't about education – they were about ideology.

These conflicts played out in many different ways. Various attempts by the Conservatives, and later by New Labour, to use schooling to improve the employment prospects of children were opposed for not being about 'education' but 'training'. For example, the Department of Employment spent £2 billion funding a technical and vocational skills initiative[2] that was opposed by the leader of the Labour Party and initially boycotted by Labour LEAs. The details of this episode are discussed in Chapter 7 ('The comprehensive era').

In Chapter 8 ('Much maligned or monstrous mistake?'), I explained that today's promoters of comprehensivisation still adhere to Robin Pedley's vision of how it represents 'a larger more generous attitude of mind' and the 'forging of a communal culture by the pursuit of quality with equality'.[3] These are admirable ideals but have little to do with providing the skills and knowledge needed to join adult society.

The critics of comprehensive schools argue that the practical difficulties caused by mixing together children of widely different talents penalise those at the top and bottom of the academic spectrum. Proponents of the schools believe that this mixing helps socialise children and improve their understanding about their peers from different social classes.

It seems to me that those with beliefs on the 'left' frame the purpose of education as being about creating a fairer, more equal society. Those on the 'right' believe it is primarily about ensuring children receive the necessary skills and knowledge. I appreciate this is a caricature of the ideological differences, but it illustrates why it has been so difficult to achieve a consensus about the core objectives of state education.

Rather than there being one single vision of what schools are supposed to achieve, there are many, often coupled with the words 'progressive', 'traditionalist', 'elitist', 'egalitarian'. This lack of a consistent and enduring vision explains why it is so difficult to even begin answering the question 'What do we want from our schools?'

Academics add complexity but not clarity

I have spent a little time working in academia and a very long time reading its output in the form of doctoral theses and journal papers. How can I put this without sounding condescending and being too critical? Academics adopt a model of thinking and writing that often diminishes the clarity of their expression – for the uninitiated, anyway. They seek new insights by drilling deeper into a single subject rather than understanding how multiple subjects interrelate. There is often a mismatch between the type of knowledge they pursue and its practical application. My observations are primarily based on the contribution of academia to the field of education and to a lesser extent to that of business theory. I appreciate that these are huge generalisations and that many academics are lucid polymaths. And yes, I know that huge advances have been made by the highly focused pursuit of abstract knowledge.

Let me justify my observations with some examples, starting with the type of language that is often used by academics when discussing education. I think the following sentence makes sense, yet after multiple readings I am still not certain. As to the value it adds to our understanding of the secondary modern era – I leave it for you to decide.

> *'Secondary moderns were a key site of gendered anxiety about age*
> *and class' and that their male teachers were more likely to resist*
> *progressive education because it was 'gendered feminine' leading to*
> *a 'negative othering of the male secondary modern pupil.'*[4]

This use of overly complex and specialised language is the least of the problems. During the timeline there were a couple of instances where academics were at the forefront of advising government about 'the purpose of education' and what children were taught. On neither occasion was it a resounding success.

In 1965 Anthony Crosland, the Labour minister of education, somewhat reluctantly initiated a research project to study various aspects of comprehensivisation.[5] A full account of what happened is provided in Chapter 6 ('Birth and death').

Problems started from the outset when trying to agree a 'statement of objectives' about the purpose of education. There are some amusing notes from Ministry officials about trying to manage the 'confrontation' between the warring academic factions – especially the challenge of getting the 'psychometricians and the sociologists to work together'.[6]

A group of 'educational theorists' (e.g. philosophers, sociologists, psychologists and research workers) formulated one version; another was created by a group of 'educational practitioners' (e.g. school heads, teachers and inspectors). These were combined into a set of attributes that were to be researched. Well, that was the theory.

Researchers struggled to measure the abstract objectives of education formulated by the academics. It was a struggle trying to quantify attributes about a child's 'sense of wholeness', their 'self-realisation of the individual' and 'feelings and emotions'. A footnote in one of the reports summed up their difficulty: 'there is inevitably a steep descent from the lofty ideals to scores on questionnaires'. The project was not a success and it was cancelled by Mrs Thatcher on becoming minister. Having read the reports, I concur with her decision.

It was under Thatcher's reign as prime minister that academics again played a significant role in defining education objectives. The search for the ethereal 'purpose of education' must at some stage translate into the day-to-day mechanics of what children are taught. Throughout the timeline there have been bitter disputes about the detailed contents of the school curriculum.

In 1988 the minister (Kenneth Baker) set in train a process to define a national curriculum and the regime for testing children's performance. The ensuing difficulties are discussed in Chapter 7. A more emotive account of events can be found in Robert Peal's paper *Progressively Worse.*[7]

Educational academics, with the involvement of teachers, created an overly complex and functionally unworkable solution. Peal argued that this resulted from the intentional sabotage of the project by academics who disagreed with the whole concept of set curricula and testing. Others believe it was the natural tendency of academics to overly complicate things and pay little attention to how their recommendations would be implemented. I expect both factors played a part in its failure. The project was a disaster and had to be reworked by subsequent ministers of education.

In more recent times academia has been responsible for the theoretical concepts that changed much of how and what teachers teach. The 'traditional' assumptions about the value of factual knowledge and the directive role of the teacher have been challenged by their new 'progressive' ideas. I am not equipped to comment about the rights and wrongs of these changes but Daisy Christodoulou's book *Seven Myths About Education*[8] presents a disturbing account of their consequences.

What seems certain is that no consensus exists about the value of academia's contribution to the understanding and practise of education. In many disciplines, especially the sciences, it is easy to identify the evolution of knowledge and understanding as successive generations of academics build upon the achievements of their predecessors – progress by 'standing on the shoulders of giants'. Perhaps the 'giants' of education have yet to emerge?

The purpose of education depends on who you ask

Part of the problem with trying to answer the question of what we want from our schools is that it is easy to assume we all think the same about the identity of 'we'. This is clearly not the case. Throughout the timeline there has been a constant tension between the different groups that influence what schools deliver and those who judge the value of their output. The constituents of the group 'we' are constantly changing. As much as I question the value of personal anecdotes, I will start by illustrating this issue with a personal experience.

Many years ago, I was asked by a friend to help him and his fellow governors (many were also parents) to decide if their school should join one of the then government's education initiatives. To help reach a decision I was asked to run a meeting attended by the governors and the teachers. I started by asking a question along the lines of 'what factors should we use to judge the success of the school?' I was amazed by the response. The teachers' main spokesman replied that 'we can tell by the faces of the mothers at the school gate'. There was much nodding from other teachers so it appeared they concurred with the response. This seemed a rather vague measure, so I attempted to find other criteria that could be quantified and measured. The harder I questioned, the more the teachers became defensive and annoyed.

Perhaps the fault was mine and I was lousy at conducting the meeting. Most likely I was experiencing the instinctive reaction when people feel their position in the power hierarchy being threatened. I was trying to deconstruct their role (and in their eyes diminish it) into a series of targets – they were defending an idealistic concept about producing the rounded happy child.

Another example of this mismatch of expectations is the disappointment of employers and higher education institutions in the skills and knowledge of school leavers. I have lost count of how many times I have read reports detailing the unhappiness of employers about young people's readiness to enter the workplace. Enter into Google the words 'employers unhappy about school leavers' and you see a mass of commentary detailing the failings. This is not a new phenomenon. I first encountered it 1917 in the contribution of employers to the Lewis Report.[9]

More recently, employers expressed their unhappiness with young employees in a report from the CBI that concluded '44% of its members felt young people leaving school, college or university were not work ready.'[10]

About half of all school leavers now go on to higher education and most of them to university. These institutions are only marginally happier about the preparedness of school leavers than employers. A report published in 2017 showed that university admissions officers believed that too many schools were not equipping children with the fundamentals of independent learning, time management and thinking skills.[11]

Another dimension of disagreement is between the educational establishment and the wishes of parents. An extreme example of this conflict is illustrated by a *Guardian* columnist in her article '"Choice" is code for inequality'.[12] The 'choice' she refers to is when parents use their wealth and intelligence to seek out the best education for their children. She concludes it is 'polluting the education system'. Her unwritten, but strongly implied, solution is to reduce the power (choice) of parents.

There has always been a small group of parents who are wealthy enough to opt out of the state system and send their children to private schools. Starting in the decade after WWII, parents of children within the state system have increasingly exercised their rights to choose the best schools for their own children. That some parents are better equipped to do this than others rankles with parts of the teaching profession, much of academia and politicians – in particular those on the left of the political spectrum.

Over time the influence of the 'stakeholders' responsible for providing and consuming the product of schools (educated children) has changed. Before WWII the religious institutions were pivotal to the provision of secondary and primary education. The influence of the church has drained away while other religions have become more influential. Local authorities were once the gatekeepers of deciding and implementing education policy. Their role has diminished, as has that of teachers.

This short account of the ebbs and flows of influence of those deciding what schools deliver and those who judge their performance illustrates why there are multiple answers to the question 'what do we want from our schools?' What they are depends on who and when you ask the question.

The default decision is 'academic' education

Following their birth, secondary moderns were told to go forth and 'experiment'. Those weren't the words used, but that was the intention. My account of the evolution of secondary moderns, in Chapter 6, describes what happens when politicians initiate an education policy with only the haziest notions about its goals. After the inevitable confusion it was left to the 62,000 secondary modern teachers to decide how the schools should operate. Not surprisingly, no single model of schooling was established. Some secondary moderns were little changed from the elementary schools they replaced; others emulated the academic goals of grammar schools. Between these extremes were at least half a dozen variants.

This mishmash of schools needed to convince pupils, parents and employers that they were capable of equipping children to succeed as adults. Seeking a raison d'être that conferred the much-sought-after 'parity of esteem', secondary moderns increasingly enabled their pupils to take external exams. Rightly or wrongly, when a child gained a fistful of GCE 'O' level passes it provided a universally recognised symbol of achievement. By default, rather than intention, the various models of secondary moderns converged to provide, for the minority, a watered-down grammar school education. That is, they could leave brandishing external exam certificates.

When the Labour Party was selling the concept of comprehensivisation to the electorate it used the slogan 'providing a grammar school education for all children'. Perhaps it wasn't surprising that once comprehensives became the established format of secondary education their performance was compared with the schools they were supposed to have replaced. Being judged by the same standards, it was inevitable they would teach a cut-down version of the grammar school syllabus.

All of this is of course an ultra-simplification of secondary education history, shorn of all complexity. In writing it I wanted to highlight that achieving success in external exams – the ones taken by grammar schools – has been the primary driver of schools, spanning the tripartite and comprehensive era. This wasn't the plan of politicians and educationalists, many of whom did their best to stop it happening. For all the evils of external exams there was never a consistent and enduring alternative, as I hope I have explained. Nature abhors a vacuum and since the end of WWII schools have focused, in varying degrees, on an academic syllabus determined by the demands of external exams.

My contention is that this behaviour has become hardwired into the state education system, extending from the primary to the higher education sector. Things are the same with private schools. Arguably they are responsible for the focus on exam success, because achieving as many top grades as possible helps justify the fees they charge.

Fuelled by increasing numbers achieving GCE 'O' levels – now replaced by GCSEs and the baccalaureate – and 'A' levels, university education supply has expanded to accommodate the demand. This has come at the expense of all other forms of higher education, especially colleges of further education. Again, I want to flag that I have grossly simplified the sequence of events. Other factors also contributed to the expansion of mass university education.

When the colleges of advanced technology were awarded university status in 1966 and the polytechnics became the 'new universities' in 1992, this changed the nature of the institutions providing much of the vocational training. Politicians used the size of the university population as the yard-stick of success for their education policies. The most notable example of this was Tony Blair's promise to ensure 50% of 18 year olds went on to higher education. This policy was so successful, I would argue, because it was pushing at an open door. Schools were already encouraging pupils to reach for the top rungs of academic success. Getting a BSc or BA degree was the inevitable final step on that ladder.

Mary Curnock Cook, the past head of the University and Colleges Admissions Service (UCAS), used a different analogy when describing the education system.[13]

There is a super-highway from GCSE to A levels and then to univer-sity with a poorly signposted slipway to various vocational options.

In 2018–2019, of those pupils going onto higher education, 95%[14] studied for a degree. I don't think it's an exaggeration to say that achieving this symbol of academic success is now the only game in town.

Throughout the timeline there have been voices arguing this is wrong and dangerous. In 1958 the Belcoe Report said:[15]

Pupils and teachers had become unduly concerned with examina-
tions; concentration on examination syllabuses and the requirement
that pupils must pass in a group of subjects has restricted the initia-
tive of the teachers.

Sixty years later the Covid-19 pandemic resulted in the cancellation of
GCSE and GCE 'A' level exams in 2020. At the time of writing, it would
seem the same thing will happen in 2021. These decisions have once again
raised the question of abandoning the GCSE exams altogether and radically
changing 'A' levels.[16] Even the minister responsible for the birth of GCSEs
(Kenneth Baker) now believes they should be scrapped because of the
distortions they cause to children's schooling.[17] For reasons I will explain in
a moment, I very much doubt if these voices will have much effect.

The 'superhighway' analogy is a good way of describing the default
pathway followed by half of young people. It is well signposted and difficult
to get lost. What it lacks is a slow lane or alternative route for the 'non-academic' child. Repeated attempts have been made to reduce the size of this
group and with some success. However, how much of this is a real improvement, or an illusion resulting from reducing the height of the academic
hurdles, is unclear. Repeated schemes to provide these children with alternative types of schooling have been tried (and failed). Newsom's efforts in
1963 and the university technical colleges in 2020[18] are good examples.
These initiatives failed to achieve a critical mass to succeed and dissolved
back into the mainstream academic model.

This could be a good point to end this section with 'glass half full'
conclusions. Despite the education policy 'emerging' rather than being ratio-
nally formulated, it has produced spectacular exam results. The numbers
going to university and the classes of degree they achieve are orders of
magnitude higher than when their grandparents studied. Despite the continuing problems of catering for non-academic children, the system is working
for the majority. Our economy requires a highly educated workforce and that
is what schools and universities are providing.

Before writing the book, I would have shared this optimistic view,
perhaps with a few caveats about the exaggerated claims of exam success.
Now I am not so sure. The 'glass half empty' conclusions have a compelling
logic. They predict a future of disappointment for many of the young people

pursuing the superhighway from school to university, with the plight of their non-academic classmates not improving but deteriorating.

Worse still, the consequences of dividing people into two classes – those with the rewards of academic achievement and 'others' – are badly distorting the cohesion of society.

David Goodhart's book *Head Hand Heart*[19] describes these concerns and their implications far better than I could hope to do. He argues that:

In recent decades in the interests of efficiency, fairness and progress western democracies have established systems of competition in which the most able succeed and too many of the rest feel like failures. And who are the most able? People with higher levels of cognitive ability, or at least those certified as such by the education system.

It is important to note the emphasis Goodhart places on the 'most able' being determined by the certification of the education system. Of historical interest is that the distinction between 'head and hand' is at least a century old and aligns with the distinction between children attending grammar and elementary schools. Goodhart readily acknowledges this is not a new idea and has been proposed by those from all parts of the political spectrum. First by Michael Young (the socialist)[20] and then by Daniel Bell (centrist)[21] and Charles Murray (conservative).[22] Goodhart also acknowledges that their warnings have had little effect.

I think there are three strands to their arguments, which I will now briefly explain, adding my own observations. Apologies to the authors if I have over-simplified or misrepresented their views.

The disconnect between the workplace and the education system. Putting the words 'workplace' and 'education' in the same sentence doesn't imply that the only purpose of attending school and university is about 'getting a job'. There are the immeasurable but very real benefits of 'studying for its own sake' and socialising with your peers. Students, however, cannot help but have expectations about the tangible benefits their studies confer. Their experience of the education system has been all about methodically climbing the ladder of academic achievement, claiming the prizes and moving onto the next step. For most people the BSc or BA is their final reward. Understanding the value of this final academic accolade is mighty important because it comes with a hefty bill attached that somebody has to pay.

Throughout the timeline politicians have told the same story: that the world is becoming more complex and technological and that increasing national prosperity depends on having a workforce equipped for the challenges this creates. Way back in 1956, David Eccles was trying to change the education system to equip the country for the 'age of science and technology'. Soon afterwards Harold Wilson (1963) made his famous 'white heat of technology' speech, which he later said was about 'replacing the cloth cap with the white laboratory coat as the symbol of British labour'. From Tony Blair onwards, the rallying call has been about equipping children with the skills to thrive in the 'knowledge economy'. Most recently, Boris Johnson expanded the objectives to the technologies and skills associated with the 'green economy'.

It is easy to dismiss these as empty phrases that sound good in speeches. My guess is that they were genuinely meant but they are misleading and were misunderstood by those making them. Worse still, they have all failed to divert the education machine to equip enough young people with the necessary type of knowledge and skills.

These statistics are taken from recent research and are deeply concerning. Unless otherwise stated the Institute of Fiscal Studies (IFS) is the source of the data.

- The lifetime earnings of a sizeable group of graduates (20%) will be less than those of their contemporaries without a degree.
- Gaining a degree, on average, increases lifetime earnings by £70,000. A sizeable amount of money, but not a fortune. However, this measure is misleading because for some the benefits are well over £500,000 and for others it is a negative amount.
- Only a quarter of students will fully repay their loans; the balance is funded from general taxation. By the middle of this century the value of outstanding loans, which are funded by taxation, will be in excess of half a trillion pounds.[23]
- Over a quarter (28%) of graduates in England work in jobs that

do not require a degree, double the average for OECD
countries.[24] Research from the ONS puts the figure for the UK
considerably higher (37%). Inner London is the only region
where the number dips below 30%.[25]

- Since 2010, the annual rate of young people failing to complete
their degree studies has been over 10%.[26]

It is difficult to piece together the size and shape of the problem that
these numbers represent. If I was a young person, the sizeable risk of failing
to achieve a 'graduate job' would be my major concern. If I was a politician,
I would shudder reading this statement from Paul Johnson (head of the
IFS):[27]

*There are twice as many creative arts students at English universities
as there are engineering students. On average, each student of the
creative arts ends up earning rather little and costs the taxpayer a
considerable sum. On average, each student of engineering earns
rather more and benefits the taxpayer.*

I could explain that over 90% of companies[28] struggle to find workers
with the right skills at a time when new graduates struggle to find jobs.
However, I think I have said enough to illustrate that the headlong rush from
school to university has significant problems.

The situation I describe has been slowly growing worse. It most definitely is not a temporary state of affairs and is one that will be exacerbated
by the economic results of the Covid pandemic.

What's the purpose of a degree? According to Goodhart, the majority of
the UK's under-30s are graduates. I rank this as a grade-A 'wow, I didn't
know that' statement. Assuming he is correct, and the school-to-university
machine keeps working at its current rate, the majority of the UK's population are destined to have degrees.

Surely that's something to celebrate and something that can only benefit
the country? I am not so sure. Even to question this outcome seems wrong,
since it implies begrudging people the opportunity to achieve their academic
potential. I am prepared to face that criticism because the potential unintended consequences could be mighty dangerous.

The crux of my concern relates to the supply of and demand for 'graduate jobs', something that I partly covered in the previous section. A deeper dive into the subject starts with understanding what constitutes a graduate job. I expect for most people it is an instinctive feeling along the lines of 'Did I need three years' university study to do this job?' The trouble with this definition is that it depends on why the person is doing the job. For instance, somebody working as a barista might answer 'yes' if it was part of the company's management training scheme and 'no' if it was the only job available or one they chose for its flexible terms of employment.

Policy makers use the 'official' definition that is based on the ONS's standard occupational codes – all 369 of them. Each has been categorised as being 'graduate' or 'non-graduate' by researchers at the universities of Warwick and the West of England. They applied the criteria that 'a non-graduate role is one which is associated with tasks that do not normally require knowledge and skills developed through higher education to enable them to perform these tasks in a competent manner'. How on earth this was done is beyond me.

A cursory look at this data raises questions about its accuracy and usefulness. For instance, why is a 'hotel and accommodation manager and proprietor' a graduate job when a 'restaurant and catering establishment manager and proprietor' is judged as 'non-graduate'? Despite my concerns, it's the best data available and is what I have analysed.

Forty percent of UK jobs are classified as requiring a degree level of education. However, this number falls to 32% if you remove those that are vocations (e.g. teachers, nurses, doctors and dentists). There is no useful definition of what constitutes a 'vocation'. Perhaps the best determinant is that these jobs are most closely related to their holders' degree studies, something that is confirmed by research conducted by HESA.[29] Graduates in the vocation professions are twice as likely to see the relevance of their degree to their job as those who studied English, history, philosophy, social studies and many of the generic science degrees.

When the knowledge and skills amassed at university have little or no relevance to preforming the job, what is their value? At this point matters become highly subjective because the award of a degree becomes little more than a 'signal' of the person's cognitive potential. The degree isn't about what you learnt but what it signals to employers.

A cursory look at the definitions and the data reveals the weakness of labelling jobs as graduate or non-graduate based on something as flimsy as the signal conveyed by possessing a BA or BSc. It is an arbitrary decision and one that can rapidly change. This is best illustrated by how in 2010 the nursing profession was decreed to be a graduate profession and at a stroke nearly 700,000 jobs suddenly become graduate only.

The deeper you delve the clearer it becomes why so many graduates have difficulty finding jobs that demand their level of education. None of the remaining non-graduate job categories look likely candidates to start demanding three years at university.

But this is the situation today and those championing the ever-rising number of graduates contend that the nature of employment is changing. That technology is replacing low-skilled jobs and the remaining ones are becoming more complex and demand higher levels of education. Again, I am not so sure. I think this is an outdated and overly simplistic view of the relationship between work and education.

There is no doubt that in the past, many low-skilled jobs have been automated or exported to countries with lower costs. Arguably, this trend is slowing, although the consequences of the Covid-19 pandemic are visibly accelerating unemployment in some job types. Nearly a million people are employed as 'sales and retail assistants' and their jobs are threatened by the meteoric rise in online shopping. Of course, there are winners from this change, notably the non-graduate jobs of van drivers and warehouse staff.

Goodhart believes, and I agree, that we have reached the point where it is extremely difficult to automate or move abroad the non-graduate job types that employ large numbers of staff. For example, care workers, nursing auxiliaries, cleaners and catering assistants. Even if it were possible to do this there are few financial incentives since these tend to be minimum wage jobs, which explains why they are difficult to fulfil and are often undertaken by non-British workers (e.g. 15% of care workers are from overseas).[30]

Graduate-graded employment has been more immune to replacement by technology and offshoring, although IT jobs first began moving abroad at least 40 years ago. Goodhart believes this situation is changing and jobs requiring a significant application of cognitive skill and judgement will at least plateau and probably decline. He recognises there will always be a demand for students from top universities, with the intelligence and personality attributes that mark them as high-flyers. It is the middle-ranking employment categories that he thinks are under threat – those undertaking the more routine aspects of professional work in the law, accountancy, medicine and public administration. The widespread use of cloud computing and the emergent use of AI-driven algorithms will undoubtedly change the demand for middle-level cognitive skilled jobs.

It is very difficult to prove his contention, but I instinctively feel he is correct. During the later part of my career, I witnessed the trend for large companies to reduce the numbers of staff with 'permission to think'. The CIPD researched the level of discretion a worker has in their job, believing it to be a good proxy for the role's skill requirement. It found that over half of graduate job types showed no evidence of increasing the freedom to make decisions.[31] By systematising work tasks, be they for graduates or non-graduates, companies were able to reduce costs and achieve consistency of quality.

Smaller organisations were increasingly outsourcing work to low-cost suppliers using online marketplaces for freelance services, like Upwork, Fiverr and LinkedIn. The website associated with this book was created in Thailand, the one before that in Canada and my last smartphone app was developed in India.

Nobody knows for certain how the dynamics of the employment market will develop but this evidence convinces me there is something horribly wrong with the assumptions upon which the school–university model of education depends. Not only does this question the demand for graduate jobs but it also reveals distortion in the funding and demand for other channels of education. When the signal conveyed by gaining a university degree trumps the value of qualifications gained at other institutions, especially further education (FE) colleges, it is little wonder that they suffer.

The magnitude of the effect is illustrated with these two facts taken from the Augar Review into post-18 education. In 2017–2018 the level of government funding for university students was 6.5 times more than for those in FE colleges. Between 2005 and 2016, the numbers of people training in FE colleges halved.[32]

There is one final distortion to the education system that has worrying consequences. Subjects that were once taught with an emphasis on their practical application have become academicised, primarily to justify their degree status. It is a problem I recognise but is not a recent development, as my own university education illustrates.

Electronics was the primary subject of my degree in applied physics. I had an excellent grasp of the maths and theoretical physics of the subject and did very well in passing the exams. Where I struggled was in the practical use of electronics to build circuitry that actually worked. A couple of years after graduating I had a part-time job teaching maths at an FE college, to HND students studying electronics. Their practical knowledge and skills were amazing and yet my degree had so much more perceived value than their qualification. My guess is that many of my FE students would today be going to university, which probably explains the shortage of skilled technicians.

As I relied heavily on Goodhart's thinking it is only fair to use his words to summarise this section. He believes that the UK and the US are guiding too many school leavers into academic higher education that provides little more than a signal of their cognitive ability. We have become dangerously focused on the 'head' aspect of intelligence. At the same time, we have been neglecting – worse still, damaging – the supply of other types of skills.

> Employment that had traditionally been seen as being about the 'hand' or the 'heart' have either become deemed as basic employment requiring no qualification (e.g. Care work and the trades) or needing a degree that is gated by having the right exam results.

The misplaced superiority of the cognitive class

Achievement of academic success depends on a host of factors that are outside our personal control. The wealth, education and background of our parents, the genes we inherit, where we were born, the availability of good schools and 'luck' – all influence how far up the school–university ladder we ascend. My favourite way of expressing these advantages of birth is as 'a following wind or a gust of privilege'.[33]

For much of the timeline, politicians have endeavoured to 'level the playing field', to compensate for inherited advantages. They are to be applauded for their efforts, but their success has been limited. Very rarely does hard work alone determine our academic achievements without the following wind's helping hand.

There is nothing profound or new in these statements. You might say, 'that's the way it has always been' – and you would be right. What I think has changed, perhaps I should say 'become more pronounced', is that an individual's academic awards increasingly signal the 'rightness' of their views and their position and value to society. This hypothesis is impossible to prove but, if it's true, it explains some of the tensions that trouble our society.

When I started my secondary education just 4% of school leavers went to university. By the time I had graduated the figure was 6%. Graduates comprised a tiny percentage of the population, far too few to constitute a homogenous group with any common beliefs. Nobody was interested how our views varied from the rest of the population. How different the situation is today, with the majority of the UK's under-30s holding a degree.

Commentators discussing the opposing views about major issues invariably refer to the education level of their supporters. Be it about Brexit, the national elections in the UK and the US, views about the environment, opinions on sexuality – the measures of support or disapproval are regularly linked to level of education. Here are a few examples:

Once again, less-educated whites spurned America's Democratic nominee (Joe Biden).[34]

The MP for Huddersfield claims most of those who voted Remain in June's EU referendum 'were the better educated people in our country'.[35]

Trump still king of the 'poorly educated'.[36]

Education has also been an increasingly prominent predictor of voting behaviour, having been a divide in the 2019 General Election and the EU Referendum.[37]

People with more education tend not only to be more concerned about the environment, but also to engage in actions that promote and support political decisions that protect the environment.[38]

57% of those with university degrees voted to remain [in the EU], 65% of those with higher degrees and 81% of those in full time education.[39]

It is totally valid and relevant to analyse what people think based on where they live, their age, gender, ethnicity and their level of education. What is unprofessional (in my view) is to omit highlighting the high correlation between these factors, especially between age and education level. What is downright wrong (in my view) is to go further and imply the rightness or wrongness of the views as being associated with level of education.

Most likely you will agree with these statements but might dispute that this is actually happening. Perhaps when you look at the previous quotes you see the references to education as point of fact. When I look, I see them as a point of condemnation.

Let me try and justify my position. The socio-economic groups that comprise the 'establishment' (professional, managerial and technical occupations) are nearly all 'graduate only' jobs. Based on data from the CIPD report, I estimate that today the graduate share of these groups is approximately 75%. In 1990 the figure was less than 25%.[40]

This rapid rise in academic level is most striking in the transformation of the Labour Party. As recently as 1960 about 40% of its MPs hailed from working class backgrounds. By 2010 it had fallen to 10% and has kept falling. In 2017, there was a higher percentage of Labour MPs with degrees than their Conservative adversaries. Following the 2019 general election, 85% of MPs had been to university. Possessing a degree is not a formal qualification for becoming an MP but it most certainly helps.[41, 42]

In recent times the 'establishment' has become an 'all-graduate' group – what Goodhart called the 'head class'. This is not a conspiracy, but the inevitable outcome of an education system focused exclusively on achieving exam success. Along with this homogeneity of educational background has come a convergence of views about major issues – voting to leave the EU was wrong – voting for Trump was wrong (insane) – support for draconian interventions to save the environment is right – condemnation of the country's colonial past is right.

When these views are questioned (rejected) our old friend cognitive dissonance jumps to the rescue and the outcome is rationalised as resulting from the opposing believer's lack of education. Something that heightens the discord is that the opposing views often mirror the differing beliefs of the old and the young, further irritating the latter's anger about intergenerational unfairness in the allocation of wealth and opportunity.

At this point you might think these arguments are unfounded and pure conjecture – I hope you are right. If you think they have substance, then there are two more factors that will exacerbate the situation.

Peter Turchin, an American academic, coined the term 'elite overproduction' to describe the outcome when society's ruling classes outgrow the supply of jobs that members of those classes normally occupy, a prediction based on US data.[43] As we have seen, the UK seems to be following a parallel path. Turchin foresees this supply and demand imbalance resulting in a catastrophic outcome. Hopefully he is wrong.

The other factor aggravating the situation is the short- and long-term economic repercussions of Covid-19. Many commentators believe the pandemic accelerates the outcome of existing trends. If this is true, then it will speed up the rebalancing of the demand for jobs requiring the 'head' and the other two intelligences of the 'hand' and the 'heart'.

My worries about the divisions in society are a long way from how the chapter began with the question of 'What do we want from our schools?' I feel confident in my analysis of the beginning (an academic education is the default) and the end (the tensions between the educated class and the rest). I leave it to you to judge if I have justified the causal chain that links the two.

Trends go on until they stop

My account of the unstable state of the education system leaves an unanswered question hanging in the air. If am correct, then surely it will change and soon? The truthful answer is I don't know but, somehow, I doubt it. This response invites the retort 'well things cannot be that bad'.

I think things are 'that bad' but the huge inertia of the school–university machine isn't going to be diverted by official enquiries, policy tweaks and new initiatives. Already I have described how these invariably fail to reach a critical mass and dissolve back into the mainstream academic model. Only a significant change to the variables of the education model will alter its trajectory. This will not come from the supply side (schools and universities) but the demand part of the equation (the students and parents).

We are awash with numbers quantifying the extent of the problem. Many influential and powerful voices have been repeating the same message that the education machine is unstable and not working. Alison Wolf's book, *Does Education Matter*, described the problems with forensic detail.[44] In 2011 the government commissioned her to review the state of the UK's vocational education (the Wolf Report).[45] She was damning in her condemnation of the failures of an education system that each year sees 'at least 350,000 students getting little to no benefit from the post-16 education system'. Politicians seemed genuinely shocked by her findings and new policies were implemented.

Four years later Wolf authored another report in which she concluded:[46]

In post-19 education, we are producing vanishingly small numbers of higher technician level qualifications, while massively increasing the output of generalist bachelor degrees and low-level vocational qualifications.

The situation seems little changed because today Wolf is still pressing the same message that there is a mismatch between the labour market and the output of higher education.[47]

In 2019 Philip Augar chaired a panel that reviewed post-18 education and funding, reaching conclusions that were similar to those of the Wolf Report – unsurprisingly since Wolf was a member of the advisory panel.[48]

Our core message is that the disparity between the 50% of young people attending higher education and the other 50% who do not has to be addressed. Doing so is a matter of fairness and equity and is likely to bring considerable social and economic benefits to individuals and the country at large.

Reading the Augur Report made me think it might have been easier to have used his words, rather than my own analysis. These words seemed very familiar.

> *Many graduates are working in non-graduate jobs and some employers report dissatisfaction with graduate skills. Both higher technical and craft skills are in short supply with long-standing skills gaps in strategic sectors such as engineering, IT and digital. Migrant labour is required in many sectors and at different levels.*

A *Guardian* journalist, commenting on the report, said: 'instead of abolishing the grammar school system, we've merely delayed it to the age of 18. And the resources go, largely, to those who continue to swim in the upper stream.'[49] That pretty much sums up the situation and neatly links back to my tale of the 11-plus and secondary moderns.

From what I have written, do you think Augar will be more successful than Wolf in changing the education model? I would put the probability in the low single digits.

Pitted against the mountain of impeccable research and sensible recommendations are the implacable forces that lock schools and universities into this failing model.

- Every new employment category that is labelled 'graduate only' reinforces the value of pursuing the school-to-university pathway. This fuels a feedback loop resulting in more job types elevating their status by requiring a degree-level qualification.
- Any politician advocating reducing the numbers attending university would be ridiculed. It would be like saying we need to reduce the number of doctors in the NHS. Political prestige comes from cranking up the existing education model, not changing it.
- The timescale needed to create meaningful change is far longer than the political five-year cycle. What politician is going to suffer the inevitable pain of uprooting the current system with zero chance of receiving the plaudits for its replacement?
- Children have experienced only one route to achieving respect

among their peers and parents. Get as many GCSE A*s as possible (now grade 9) – get as many A*s at 'A' level as possible – get to Oxbridge or at least a Russell Group university – whatever, get to 'uni'.

- School teachers and university academics may intellectualise the rationale for changing the system, but they will inevitably (maybe unconsciously) block it happening because it would threaten their status and livelihood.

There are no signs that the school–university machine is slowing – if anything it is about to move into a higher gear. Now that 28% of graduates gain a first-class degree, even more academic awards are needed to reach the very top rung of the escalator.[50]

Over 355,000 students enrolled to study for a taught master's degree in the academic year 2018–2019, up over 21% on four years before. Writing about this rise in post-graduate study, *The Times* quoted the head of admissions at a Russell Group university.[51]

A master's used to be reserved for those seeking a career in academia. Now it is much more democratic. Many more young people have degrees, and most of those are good degrees, so it is seen as something that will set them apart when they start their careers.

And so it goes on – students need higher status signals of their cognitive achievements and the universities get a new stream of income to repair their battered finances.

What possible reasons are there for the status quo to change? If anything, might it become even more entrenched? The following ideas might sound like I am 'grasping at straws'. And you might well be right.

The percentage of graduates in non-graduate jobs is somewhere between 28% and 37%. What happens when that number reaches 50%? I have no way of knowing if and when this will occur, but a point will be reached when children and parents seriously consider jumping off the academic escalator. Younger brothers and sisters will see what happens when their older siblings return home, the years at uni behind them, frustrated and looking for jobs they could have done when they were 18. More and more stories will appear about the premium wages being earned by those with in-demand skills that were gained outside university. As the population ages the job opportunities for young workers are likely to increase.

If the ONS survey of graduate wellbeing is to be believed, their time at university doesn't seem to be the 'best years of their life'. Graduates rated their life satisfaction and happiness less highly than the general population and they were more anxious. The younger the graduate the less happy they were – especially men. Of course these results could reflect the anxieties of youth – or maybe something more fundamental is occurring?[52]

In short, if change occurs, it will be driven by the mass realisation that the school–university model is associated with a high chance of ending in personal failure rather than success. And yet, I wonder if even this will change how young people behave. In the US the proportion of graduates in non-graduate jobs has been steady at 30% for the past 30 years. Youthful optimism is a mighty powerful motivator.[53]

Excuse the mixed metaphors but there are a couple of 'elephants in the room' that might 'go nuclear' at any time.

The first elephant wears a sign titled 'student loans disaster'. When the achievement of a degree doesn't lead to the hoped-for financial returns the taxpayer picks up the bill. As we have seen, this debt is ballooning as only 25% of students fully pay back their loans. The scheme is a horrendous mess. It doesn't work as a control mechanism to regulate the subjects that students study and instead becomes a disincentive for them to earn more money, all the time increasing the enormous government debt that will eventually have to be written off. The same is happening in the US. It is the closest thing I have seen to the sub-prime mortgage disaster that caused financial mayhem in 2007.

The second elephant goes by the name of 'university funding crisis'. Many universities have got themselves into dire financial straits by increasing debt levels to expand their facilities and becoming over-reliant on overseas students paying premium fees. On top of this is the huge deficit growing in the Universities Superannuation Scheme – their pension fund. Between 2017 and 2019 this averaged a deficit of £5 billion. In 2020 the figures reached £20 billion.[54] The most discussed and most likely outcome of these woes will be a forced reduction in university numbers.

Labour politicians believed that education policies were mechanisms for shaping society. I was always sceptical about these high ideals but now know they were right. Where they got it hopelessly wrong was believing the political and educational establishment would be the originator of these policies.

Instead, we have a policy of 'academic by default' that emerged when politicians and the educational establishment failed to implement anything better and has resulted in the long list of problems I have outlined.

Step 2. More reasons for poor policy making

Without having an agreed and consistent vision of what education should achieve, devising policies is nigh on impossible. That alone explains why the timeline is littered with policies that have been tried, floundered and been forgotten. To make matters worse, the machinery of the educational establishment contains structural weaknesses that contribute to its repeated failures.

I think it is worthwhile briefly describing these flaws. Because I have already covered some of these arguments and there is a minimal chance of the failings being addressed, I will make this section short.

We are constantly reminded that the best decisions result from listening to a diverse range of ideas and opinions, from people of varied backgrounds. For this reason, the first fault is all the harder to understand. The educational establishment – by which I mean academics, the civil service, educational charities and NGOs involved in education – has a disturbing uniformity to its culture and views.

Iain Mansfield, a former senior civil servant at the Department for Education, said, when commenting on the establishment's universal condemnation of grammar schools: 'It appears likely that this homogeneity of opinion may have resulted in a degree of unconscious bias driving its agenda.'[55] That was something of an understatement, judging from the torrent of condemnation he received after challenging its orthodoxy with his research paper.

I appreciate that I am making some huge generalisations about a large group of people and there are always going to be exceptions. However, or should I say 'but', having spent so much time observing its behaviour, these are my conclusions. Compared with those who label the education establishment the 'blob', a term of ridicule, my observations are mild.[56]

Uniformity of views

The first chapter of this book ('The truth is what you want it to be') discussed the dangers of behavioural bias. Some might have thought it a strange topic to include in a book about secondary modern schools, but I suspected it was an important factor in determining how the education system evolved. That hunch proved to be correct. My mistake was underestimating its importance. Since I completed that chapter several new books have appeared on the subject, most notably *Factfulness* by Hans Rosling. He described the 'mega misconceptions' that determine how we view the world, starting with the 'gap instinct'.[57]

The irresistible temptation we have to divide all kinds of things into two distinct and often conflicting groups, with an imagined gap—a huge chasm of injustice—in between. It is about how the gap instinct creates a picture in people's heads of a world split into two kinds of countries or two kinds of people: rich versus poor.

The behaviour of those formulating education policy is a case study demonstrating the dangers resulting from this instinct. For much of the timeline, children's education was viewed through the prism of class – those who made the rules for their own advantage, the masses who obeyed them and those best placed to manipulate them. Better known as the ruling, working and middle classes.

In recent times this perspective has been supplemented by divisions based on the 'identity' of a group's race, gender, sexuality and religion. Francis Fukuyama describes the forces driving this new vision of society as the perception that:[58]

The group's dignity had been affronted, disparaged, or otherwise disregarded. This resentment engenders demands for public recognition of the dignity of the group in question. A humiliated group seeking restitution of its dignity carries far more emotional weight than people simply pursuing their economic advantage.

The business world long ago realised the futility of grouping large numbers of people together and assuming they will think and behave in similar ways. Marketers now use a mix of segmentation based on consumer characteristics and their attitudes.

I fear that the education establishment hasn't learnt these lessons and still divides parents and children into groups that are too large to provide insights into educational needs. A little later I will illustrate this point with the example of using a child's receipt of free school meals – a measure of 'disadvantage' – as signalling a host of needs and behaviours. Another example is to devise policies based on the idea that there is a single homogenous 'BAME community' (Black, Asian and Minority Ethnic). How can such a large group of people, representing 14% of the UK's population, containing children from the highest and lowest levels of school performance, be treated as having the same needs?

By viewing children and parents using these crude groupings the establishment risks creating policy based on caricatures. A child attending private school becomes the 'Eton toff', a child at a grammar school is there because of their 'sharp-elbowed' middle class parents and a child receiving free school meals is a victim of the 'system'.

This simplistic way of ordering the education world is exacerbated by the way that policies are created in an environment of political conflict, not cooperation. Perhaps this is inevitable when the country is governed by two political parties. Immediately after WWII the ideological gap between them was small, as it was during Blair's period leading the Labour Party. During other times the differences widened, and the rhetoric intensified. Today the situation is further complicated by the emotions of nationalism as Wales, Scotland and Northern Ireland adopt their own education policies.

Like many things I have said in this chapter it is very difficult to substantiate the next statement – it is impression, not a deduced fact. It seems to me that legitimate differences of opinion over how children are educated have been replaced by impugning the motivations of the opposing side. Journalists have always seen politicians as fair game for attack. Accusing Conservatives of believing working class children 'are generally less bright than middle class children' and of hating 'classrooms that cross the lines of social class', and viewing the prime minister as somebody with a 'gold-plated Eton education', are all part of the media rough and tumble.[59, 60] However, these are not just any journalists making these comments; they are leading media pundits about education.

What is deeply disturbing is when politicians, who are respected members of the establishment, say – and presumably believe – 'It is a cardinal principle of right-wing Tories that other children – not their own – need to fail in order to demonstrate the success of theirs.'[61]

Of course, this polarisation doesn't just apply to matters of education. Even well-respected journalists like Martin Wolf (chief economics commentator at the *Financial Times*) sometimes say things that startle the reader: 'Indeed, making government fail is the core of right wing politics.'[62]

Discussions about the NHS invariably degenerate into accusations that Tory politicians want to privatise it and Labour wants to throw open the 'spending taps'. Perhaps the intensity of these divisions has always existed, and social media has made it more visible? Whatever the truth, it doesn't bode well for the stability of an education system that must function whichever political party is in power.

Earlier in the book I wrote that much of the discourse about education was really about social policy. A famous doyen of the Labour Party's education philosophy said, way back in 1939, that:[63]

Educational policy, in short, is always social policy. Educational history, therefore, is true to life only when it is treated as a chapter of social history.

I now think the establishment is far more interested in the 'social' than the 'education' aspects of policy making. The importance of applying education as a balm to cure the irritants of society now overshadows the nuts and bolts of devising ways of improving how children are educated.

The establishment's obsession with how the disruption caused by the Covid-19 pandemic has widened the 'inequality gap' is a good example of this distorted thinking. Research studies abound demonstrating how privileged private school pupils were receiving X% of their lessons online and the poorest receiving none or a tiny fraction of X. Of course, this is an important issue and one needing attention, but it was only part of the much larger subject of how half a million teachers provided 9 million pupils with online teaching.

You might say that what I have described are minor niggles about the establishment. On their own, they don't make much difference, but added together they are a concern. What makes them a problem – we can argue about its magnitude – is the consistency of the establishment's response to all these issues. If the nickname of the 'blob' refers to how it behaves, as a single entity, then it might be an apt description.

Places that are 'off limits' for discussion

As you travel along the timeline, especially in the last few decades, you realise that certain subjects are not discussed or, if they are, it is done using some sort of code. It's as if a rule book of education etiquette exists that excludes certain subjects from being questioned.

The first taboo is to avoid blaming parents and teachers for educational problems. This was graphically illustrated during the deliberations of the Education Committee of the House of Commons during its meetings to understand why poor white pupils performed so poorly at school compared with other ethnic groups.[64] What was unusual about this investigation was that the normal culprits of poor school performance – poverty, bad housing and 'austerity' – were no longer excuses because they applied to all disadvantaged children, yet white children still occupied the bottom rank.

One of the witnesses was unusually forthright in her explanation. She said the fault was: 'the engrained attitude by many of the families (white) over generations. They have a disregard for education.' This sparked defensive comments from the other attendees: 'I think that kind of language is very damaging in building relationships between home and school'… 'making assumptions that people have negative attitudes is quite short sighted and will only build up the barriers' etc.

This instinctive reaction to the accusation of blame results in a barrier that prevents people from understanding the root cause of problems. If only educationalists used one of the simple techniques that expose the difference between cause and effect. For example, the iterative interrogative technique of the 'five whys' would have saved much time in explaining white children's poor performance.

For example, this is how the technique might start: *Poorly performing white children often come from families eligible for free school meals (FSM). **Why** are they eligible for FSM? – because of the low level of family income. **Why** is the income low? – because the family members are likely to be unemployed. **Why** aren't the parents working? – because the families are likely to be single mothers. **Why** the high incidence of single mothers? – because of the high numbers of broken marriages and partnerships.* And so the process could continue.

To be fair, once the accusation had been made, evidence started to emerge that substantiated the claim. Approximately 80% of a child's life is spent at home, making it key to their early educational development. The home background of children from wealthy communities is three times more likely to be stable than those from poor backgrounds. The following show the kinds of comments that were made.

> *'The stability of the home in our poorest communities is collapsing and we are expecting teachers to solve what is not within their power'… 'In different ethnic groups you have completely different rates of stability. Indian and Chinese families, very high rates of family stability and marriage'… 'In the poorest communities, half of children starting primary school have already seen their parents separate'…*

I know this reticence to ask difficult questions angers Trevor Phillips, the former chairman of the Equality and Human Rights Commission. When writing about why some ethnic groups perform so well, he said:[65]

> *There could hardly be a more important research task than finding out what these communities are doing that others are not. Yet in my years at the commission I found it impossible to persuade research groups to undertake such work; they feared being denounced by activists who object to any investigation of ethnic disparity that does not conclude the answer is 'structural racism', preferably without recourse to data or analysis.*

Philips went beyond my explanation of the behaviour resulting from 'reticence' – he believed it's driven by fear and he is in a much better position to know than me.

This avoidance of confronting uncomfortable truths might seem like a small matter, but I think it is not just inefficient but leads to poor decisions being made. Another variant of this behaviour is to talk about issues using terms that are vague and open to multiple interpretations. For instance, these words and phrases are regularly sprinkled throughout education literature – disadvantaged, privileged, underperforming, diversity, austerity, social mobility, inclusion, cooperative learning, child-centred, support mechanisms, communities, parental priorities, enrichment programmes, cultural capital...

All fields of study have their own language and jargon, but education seems to have more than its fair share. What is disturbing is that my writing has started adopting some of the phraseology – it must be contagious. When I toss the word 'disadvantaged' into a sentence I assume, wrongly, that the reader shares my understanding of a term that has multiple interpretations. I have tried to catch myself and I apologise if any instances slip through.

The term 'nature or nurture' occasionally finds its way into the discussions of the establishment but very rarely are the full implications of the 'nature' component explored. Only a handful of times did I encounter mentions of the strong link between genetic inheritance and intelligence. On each occasion, after recognising that the two might be linked the discussion ended abruptly.

The first instance appeared in a report from an all-party Parliamentary committee that was studying social mobility, or the lack of it. A couple of oblique references were made to children's 'innate ability'.[66] The subject was given more attention in the first Parliamentary study about the poor school performance of white working class children.[67]

Professor Robert Plomin was called as a witness and had related the results of his research showing that 50% of the variation in children's individual educational achievement was the result of genetic factors. He made a comment, which he has since repeated on numerous occasions, that: 'genetics is the "elephant in the classroom"'.

I had to laugh at how the committee rationalised Plomin's statements. First, they pointed out that no policy conclusions followed from the result.

Then they used his comments to support their defence of teachers' and parents' role in education.

> *One thing that would seem to follow from recognising and respecting genetic differences between children is that you do not just blame teachers, and you do not just blame parents. Kids are different; they are different from birth.*

The committee accepted that genetics, like social disadvantage, had a role to play in educational outcomes but it wasn't clear to what extent. And that was that. A factor that could explain the dogged persistence of educational inequalities was dismissed as 'having a role to play'. Less than 0.5% of the report was spent discussing the matter.

Five years later the politicians are still seeking solutions to the problems of white working class children. This time they haven't even bothered to consider the role of genetics.

I don't have the knowledge to contribute anything to the discussion about the relationship between our DNA and cognitive performance. What I do know is there is mounting evidence that it plays an important role and that the establishment appears petrified of recognising that possibility. At best the issue is dismissed as being unproven. At worst it results in accusations of it being a smokescreen for some form of eugenics.[68]

Surprisingly, an article in the *New Statesman*, a magazine on the left of the political spectrum, summed up the position very well.

> *Scientists who are researching the role of genes are already labouring under a cloud of suspicion, if not outright contempt, from some educationalists. Such polarisation and conflict should trouble us all, though. Because, like it or not, genetics is going to enter the educational arena, and we need to have a sober, informed discussion about it.*

My final example of how policy making becomes distorted by the unwritten rules of the establishment concerns the importance of a child's entitlement to receive free school meals. Each of the nations of the UK has slightly different rules governing the eligibility for this benefit, ranging from

England, where 17% of children claim the benefit, to Scotland (38%). These numbers about bound to rise as a result of the Covid-19 pandemic.

When schools perform very well or very badly, the percentage of children receiving FSM invariably forms part of the explanation. The opponents of grammar schools accuse them of not having enough FSM children; the defenders of a failing school use their high percentage as a defence. Just because the FSM percentage is an easy figure to calculate doesn't mean it is a useful education metric. It says nothing about pupils from households that are just below the median income level and treats all of those in the top 85% as a single group. To the best of my knowledge there is no research proving its usefulness as metric for judging schools and pupils.

Strangely, there is a characteristic of FSM children that is rarely mentioned. So rarely that I wonder if it is part of the etiquette rule book?

Pupils known to be eligible for and claiming FSM accounted for 40% of all permanent exclusions and 37% of all fixed period exclusions.[69]

Just think what might be discovered if this statement was expanded using the 'five whys' technique? I will leave that for somebody else to do.

The inappropriateness of the FSM measure is one issue, but another is the distortion it creates by overly focusing on children from households with the lowest income, those who perform badly at school. Of course, this is an important group and one requiring special attention but where are the measures indicating a school's ability to take the 'average' child and make them exceptional? Where are the measures showing how effective schools are in using their funding?

I am going to conclude this section with one of those statements that you might think deserves the condemnation, 'You cannot say that – how can you prove it?' The establishment lacks sufficient diversity in its views, especially about the role of education in moulding society. As a result, it constrains its policy making options by avoiding facts that it finds unpalatable and by viewing its options through the narrow prism of class and identity.

Step 3. Implementing educational policies: one step forward, one step back

If you agree with my thesis about the flaws in executing the first two steps you are probably wondering why I am bothering to discuss Step 3? It is a good question and one that needs a convincing answer. My rationale is similar to why we spend so much time anguishing over the workings of secondary schools when we know that children's first 11 years of life – their home environment and their time at junior school – determine so much of their educational destiny. We retain the hope that the next step, secondary school, can compensate for any deficiencies. That same optimism applies to the idea that poorly formulated policies, if well implemented, can evolve to rectify their initial flaws.

That is part of my reason for considering the implementation phase; however, there is another more personal reason. My career in consultancy provided many opportunities to observe the machinery of government in action. Putting it politely, I was underwhelmed. These feelings have nothing to do with the political ideology of the governing party, since the problems were as bad for Labour and Conservative administrations.

My encounters with the agencies of the public sector were of short duration and never provided me the opportunity to fully understand why things so often went wrong. However, after spending a prolonged period studying the workings of state education, I now have a pretty good idea of the reasons. I suspect, but cannot prove, that the faults are also mirrored in other parts of the public sector. These are what we might call systemic flaws in the machinery of government.

Perhaps you think I am taking an overly gloomy view of the situation? Maybe I am. However, the following is a list of the education policies that floundered during their implementation. It is a long list. Each mistake can be explained away because of specific circumstances but my hunch is there was a common, underlying fault leading to their failure.

There are many other policies that I could have added to this list that were plainly daft and bound to fail however well they were implemented. The events and characters responsible for these policies can be found in Chapters 5, 6 and 7.

The story starts at the end of WWI with Fisher's proposals for tertiary education (continuation schools), which never reached a critical mass and were soon forgotten.

Hadow's (1926) plans to close all-age schools were painfully slow in their implementation. The last of these schools were shut in the 1960s.

Butler's plans (1944) for the country's system of secondary education relied on central government providing the overall framework; LEAs delivering the infrastructure and choosing the secondary education system; and the schools being responsible for everything else. At best you could say it had its 'checks and balances'; at worst it was a recipe for conflict, something that Conservative and Labour ministers discovered.

The timescale demanded by Butler's Act for LEAs to produce plans detailing how their schools were to be organised (development plans) was ridiculously short and bound to fail. Only 10% of the plans were submitted on time.

The Labour government's decision to raise the school-leaving age in 1947 exacerbated the problems caused by WWII and the baby boom. That it was done without clarity about what the children would be taught, and concurrently with launching a new secondary education system, was at best risky, at worst plain crazy.

Launching secondary moderns, the schools that would educate the majority of children, with little guidance other than to 'experiment' was a mistake. I am tempted to use the word irresponsible. Harold Dent used slightly more measured words.

When one considers the vast amount of expenditure, in money and human ability that is being devoted to secondary education in this country one is surely entitled to a more precise and detailed statement of what that education is expected to do.

Creating technical schools with only the sketchiest of plans about how they related to secondary moderns and grammar schools and how they could be afforded had little chance of success. They never educated more than 5% of secondary school pupils.

In 1951 the ordinary, advanced and scholarship-level General Certificates of Education (GCE) were launched. The exams' high standards and the age they could be taken at were a barrier for secondary modern pupils. Only by a combination of 'fudging' the rules and forcing schools to raise their expectations of what their pupils could achieve were they made to work.

During the early 1960s two parts of government battled over a proposal to create a new exam for secondary school children. Against the wishes of the minister the CSE exams were launched in 1965. They were immediately labelled inferior to the GCE 'O' level and reinforced the distinction between grammar and secondary modern pupils. Commonly known as 'the exam for the thickies' they were ignored by grammar schools but taken by the majority of secondary modern pupils (1969). Throughout their life they were always seen as second-class qualifications.

In 1964 it was announced that the school-leaving age would rise to 16 (1970–1971). From the beginning there were arguments about the rationale for doing this, since secondary modern pupils were increasingly staying at school for the additional year and studying for external exams. *The Times Educational Supplement* (January 1966) expressed what many were saying:

> *We cannot hope to have enough teachers to raise the school-leaving age in 1970 and that we cannot hope to have enough buildings. We are in fact facing a commitment for which we have not the material means.*

Even though the date was delayed until September 1972 the concerns of the critics proved correct. This was the second time that raising the school-leaving age was poorly planned and executed.

The comprehensive reorganisation was a 'botch-up job' from the start. These are not my words but those of Edward Short, the Labour minister in charge of education during the introduction of comprehensivisation. No overall planning for the transition to comprehensivisation took place, no serious thinking through of its implications on a national basis, no thought, enquiry or study of what should comprise an appropriate curriculum for the schools. Again, not my words, but a paraphrasing of one of the schools' most vocal supporters (Brian Simon). In 1965 the Labour minister (Stewart) was warned (in detail) by his officials about the pitfalls that comprehensivisation would face. He ignored the advice, as did his successors. By 2001, Blair had done his best to obliterate all memories of comprehensivisation.

Two of the problems that have existed throughout the timeline and still persist today are the academic performance of children in the bottom 40% of the intelligence spectrum and deficiencies in the provision of vocational and technical education. In 1982 the Lower Attaining Pupils Programme (LAPP) was launched to tackle the former and the Technical and Vocational Education Initiative (TVEI) to address the later. The problems they were aiming to solve were real enough and the fundamentals of the schemes were sound but, like so many initiatives, they were unsuccessful in changing the trajectory of the underlying education system. They worked for a while and then vanished.

In 1988 pupils took the first GCSE exams, which replaced the CSE and GCE 'O' level. From the outset the exam's format, especially the contribution of coursework, was seen as being unfair and incapable of differentiating the average from the most intelligent children. Since its launch, the percentage of pupils achieving the top-grade passes has tripled, resulting in constant accusations of grade inflation. Despite numerous tweaks, the calls for GCSEs to be abandoned are louder today than ever.

The 1988 Education Act began the process of creating a national curriculum for schools. In parallel to deciding its contents it was necessary to devise the testing procedures that would report how well it was being understood. The minister who initiated the project soon departed (Baker) and it was left to his successors to make it work. This is what a couple of them said about the venture: 'some educational experts saw the National Curriculum as the opportunity to put into practice their own pet views and pet theories' (MacGregor), 'the national curriculum was over-crowed, over-elaborate and over-prescriptive' (Patten). It took until 1995 to create a workable, 'slimmed-down' curriculum that reduced the amount of prescribed content and restricted testing to the core subjects.

During the Blair era there was a plethora of new education 'initiatives' that are now long since forgotten. How many people remember education action zones, Fresh Start, Beacon schools, Excellence in the Cities and specialist schools? In 2004 there were 70 schemes in operation, costing £8.5 billion in today's pounds. David Blunkett, who was minster during this period, 'pleaded guilty' to 'initiative overload' but justified it because he thought 'we had a crap teaching profession'. Another minister, Charles Clarke, said 'certainly over the recent period, there were too many initiatives, too much change, lack of consistency and change of personnel both in terms of ministers and senior officials'. The one policy of Blair's era that is remembered today is the target for 50% of pupils to move on to higher education. We have already seen the unintended consequences of this idea.

My list stops at the end of the timeline in 2004 but unfortunately this doesn't mark the end of troubled education policies. Today (2021) the controversy is over the sustainability of student fees, the usefulness of the UK Apprenticeships Scheme and the closures and poor performance of the university technical colleges.

Each of these policies has a unique story about what went wrong. The media, if it bothers to comment, apportions blame on the politicians or the 'education system'. Only when you have slowly walked through the past 90 years of education history and have the time to look beyond the obvious blunders do you recognise the real culprits responsible for so many of the failures.

The levers of control don't control

Not only was Butler responsible for the 1944 Education Act, he also said the famous quote that 'The Civil Service is a bit like a Rolls-Royce.' Rarely do you see the remainder of the quotation – 'I think it's a bit too smooth: it needs rubbing up a bit'.[70] You are even less likely to read the adjunct to the analogy that 'Rolls-Royce Cars failed and had to be rescued by the Germans' (BMW).

That politicians criticise the administration that is supposed to implement their policies is nothing new. What has changed is the willingness of civil servants to defend themselves and highlight the failings of politicians. An article in *The Economist,* 'From Rolls Royce to old banger', beautifully described the fractious relationship that so often exists.[71] Politicians blame the civil service for incompetence in implementing their policies. Civil servants respond that failure occurs because politicians wouldn't listen and take their advice.

At the time of *The Economist*'s article, the prime minister (Blair) had just received a report from the New Labour-supporting think tank, the Public Policy Research, that said:

Whitehall is poor at reflecting on its purpose, strategic thinking, dealing with inadequate performance, managing change effectively, learning from mistakes or working across departments.

I recognise these failings, but it was this conclusion that most echoed my feelings.

The anachronistic and severely inadequate constitutional conventions governing relations between the civil service, ministers, Parliament and the public have become a recipe for ambiguity, confusion, weak leadership and buck passing.[72]

The politicians and their officials I have encountered (with a few exceptions) were well-meaning and motivated people. Unfortunately, in my view, their cultures, priorities, timescales and expectations are hopelessly misaligned. I am reminded of the book *Men are from Mars, Women are from Venus,* which relates the very different mindsets of men and women.[73] Politicians want the seamless conversion of their ideas into actions; civil servants want to maintain order and retain the status quo. Politicians exist in electoral time, civil servants in career time. Politicians are rewarded by 'quick wins', civil servants by not being associated with mistakes and playing by the rules. Yes, yes, I know these are crude generalisations, but they illustrate the massive difference between the two groups.

Having started to make generalisations I am going to make one that I think goes to the heart of the problem. The civil service culture values its ability to advise far more than it does its ability to implement. Politicians, and their political advisers, increasingly know (or think they know) what they want to happen. They expect the civil service to make it a reality. And there you have one mega-mismatch of expectations.

This problem is not new and is typified by the story of Sir Keith Joseph's bafflement at the difficulty in getting things done and asking his officials 'where are the levers' – the levers that would turn his policies into actions. The archived papers of a previous minister (Eccles) showed his frustration with his officials' lack of urgency and unwillingness to question the status quo.

Blair suffered from the same frustrations, which turned to anger when in 1999 he said:

The public sector are more rooted in the concept that 'if it's always been done this way, it must always be done this way' than any group of people that I've ever come across.

This speech is best known for the moment he grasped his arm to signify an imagined injury and said, 'You try getting change in the public sector and public services – I bear the scars on my back.'[74] Soon after being elected for his second term as prime minister he set up the Prime Minister's Delivery Unit (PMDU) to take control of the implementation and delivery of the government's domestic policy priorities. This was headed by Michael Barber, somebody who had been involved with Blair's education policies. A very public statement had been made about Blair's lack of faith in the civil service and his intention to exert far more control over how his policies were implemented.

Talking about why the PMDU was created, Barber said:[75]

In trying to effect change, however, the prime minister discovered that the levers he controlled were weak, the leaders of the public service workforce were prepared to defend a manifestly inadequate status quo, and there were no systems in place to drive and monitor delivery.

Those missing levers of control, again.

David Cameron replaced Blair and soon had his own issues with the public sector. At the Conservative conference in 2011 he spoke about 'the enemy within' and how it was stifling private enterprise: 'the bureaucrats in government departments who concoct those ridiculous rules and regulations that make life impossible for small firms'.

The primary reason Boris Johnson, as prime minister, appointed Dominic Cummings as his adviser was to improve the implementation of government policies. Commenting on this move, the director of the Strand Group, based at Kings College London, said:[76]

What you need is a Number 10 where you push a button or pull a lever and things actually happen. There's nothing more frustrating for a prime minister than the idea that you have the power but nothing actually happens.

Following Cumming's departure, Johnson has followed in Blair's footsteps and appointed Barber, now Sir Michael Barber' to:

Conduct a rapid review of the arrangements for driving and monitoring delivery both at the centre of government and in departments, and to suggest to us how they could be strengthened.[77]

I doubt if Barber will find much has changed in the past 15 years since he last tried to improve the effectiveness of the government machine.

As I am writing these words the media has polarised into those that blame the delays and mistakes that have been made in the response to Covid-19 on 'the government' and those that see them as further proof of the broken 'machinery of government'. These words from *The Daily Telegraph* sum up this position: 'One can hardly berate a Secretary of State for pulling the wrong lever if none of the levers in front of him are connected to anything meaningful.'[78]

What's to be done? I don't have any solutions. It seems to me that those making policies and those making them happen are locked in a failing relationship. The inertia of the state machine is so huge that politicians never have the time in office or the power to change it. Maybe the enormity of the mistakes made during the Covid-19 pandemic will be the catalyst for things to change? However, I expect as life returns to 'normal' we will want to banish memories of the pandemic rather than anguishing over its gory details.

Change has a cost

Built into the fabric of our democracy is change – change of the political party in power – change of ministers running their departments – change in policies that deliver public services. In the main, the word 'change' has positive connotations, unlike its antonym 'stagnation'. Google has 10 times more references to 'change for the better' than 'change for the worse'.

Of course, the reason things change is the implicit assumption that the outcome will be better than what's being replaced. The thing that we tend to ignore is that along with the expected benefits, change has a cost. If this is considered at all, it is limited to the monetary costs – the disruption and the loss of the benefits that would have been delivered by what is being replaced are rarely considered.

You might well be thinking, 'What does this have to do with education policies?' Consider these few facts and their implications.

During the 90 years of the timeline the average time ministers were in charge of the education portfolio was a little over 24 months. In a few instances the individuals had prior knowledge of education, but most had only had their personal experiences of being at school and university to guide them. During that short period they had to understand the complexities of their brief, deal with the inbox of their predecessor, attend to their Cabinet responsibilities and then – if there was time – think about education issues.

Since the early 1980s there have been 28 major pieces of legislation related to vocational, further education and skills training, and six different ministerial departments with overall responsibility for the brief, involving 48 secretaries of state.[79] For the past 40 years the further education sector has been in a state of constant change.

By the time the tripartite system was stabilising and learning from its early mistakes it was completely reorganised to implement comprehensivisation. Nobody attempted to calculate the benefits of this change, let alone the costs. Within 20 years the political party that forced through this change uprooted the system again and changed its electoral rallying cry from 'go comprehensive' to 'standards not structures'.

I have no idea how many government reports and archived educational documents I have studied but I do know that none of them attempted to quantify the total costs involved in changing the education system.

Who knows – maybe all this change was worthwhile? Since nobody ever calculated the benefits, let alone the costs, we will never know.

I am sure the reader must have spotted the ironic connection between the last two sections. Rebuilding the public sector as an efficient delivering mechanism is a change that is crying out to be made but it seems beyond the powers of politicians to make it happen.

The same mistakes – the same problems

I should be concluding this chapter by discussing how education policies are improved by regularly evaluating their performance, learning from the analysis and adapting them accordingly. There is very little to discuss. There are no systematic review processes. The successes and failures of one policy aren't used to improve the performance of its successor.

If a policy goes terribly wrong, a commission or inquiry might be held to investigate the reasons. By the time it has been established and reported the educational world will have moved on. The report will be warmly welcomed by the minister, who is unlikely to be the one responsible for the policy being investigated. There might be a short period of media attention and then it will disappear from sight. Something very similar happens when an ad hoc enquiry is established to investigate a particular topic in education. Once completed the minister warmly thanks the committee for its fascinating new insights and promises to thoroughly study their recommendations. Sometimes real change results; mostly it doesn't.

The National Audit Office (NAO) is the UK's independent public spending watchdog, employing over 800 people and tasked with 'holding government to account and helping to improve public services through high-quality audits'. Throughout the timeline I have referenced many NAO enquiries into matters related to education. The quality of the work is first class, but I cannot think of any instances where their findings have made much difference.

Individual schools are regularly investigated by Ofsted. Most teachers would say too regularly. Ofsted's purpose is to 'make sure that organisations providing education do so to a high standard'. Their energies are focused on the individual school, not national policy.

And finally, there is the contribution of academia. I have read at least a hundred PhD thesis submissions that have analysed, in immense detail, some aspect of education policy. No doubt they served their purpose of gaining the author the coveted title of Dr but they contributed not a jot to improving the lot of the country's children. Much the same can be said for the papers appearing in academic journals. Their authors' careers benefit from the publication, but they don't help improve education.

This chapter has highlighted the many reasons why, when government tries to change education policies, things go wrong. It is truly baffling why this keeps happening. You would think such a distinctive pattern of failure must eventually be recognised and stopped. The easy explanation is to blame the people involved for not caring or not being very bright. But that's not the case.

No, the explanation is that the machinery of government doesn't learn from its mistakes. It is not part of its culture to evolve by continuous improvement. And, the primary reason for this is its lack of institutional memory. This is how the Institute of Government describes this fault (taken from its investigation of further education policies):

> *The evaluation or evidence about which policies and reforms have worked, and which have not, is in short supply. It is difficult to access information about the initiatives and policies that have been tried before. In fact, consistent churn in the system has created what has been described as a 'collective amnesia'.*

Researching for this book provided a rich collection of 'lessons that can be learnt'. The final one I will add is that the government machine is incapable of remembering and hence incapable of learning.

By now you are probably thinking that my account is overly gloomy, overly pessimistic and overly critical. Believe me, I would dearly like that to be true. But how else do you explain the perennial problems that bedevil the education system and the numerous policy mistakes that have been made?

How else can we explain the fact that try as we may, we seem unable to deliver high-volume, high-quality technical and vocational training? As much as we rejoice – wrongly, I believe – in the ever upward rise in children going to university, the bottom third of pupils depart school with few qualifications and life skills. Every time school performance statistics are reported we know that there will be a huge gap between the best and worst. Since WWII there has been a shortage of teachers, especially in science subjects and partly caused by high rates of attrition.

Finishing a chapter is difficult. Finishing a book is mighty difficult. The previous chapter was the logical place for me to stop. All my questions about secondary modern schools had been answered and I had produced what I hope is a balanced and unbiased account of their history. By continuing, it was never my intention to provide a 'Dick Stroud vision' of the way forward. I offer no solutions. I do think, however, that I now understand why we are where we are. That might not sound like a great achievement, but I am satisfied.

Although the examples I have used are all related to education I think the same top-line conclusions would have been reached if I had studied any area of public services. This is not a condemnation of those who work for the state, although some of them deserve condemnation. It is about the engine of government – the mechanism that translates the fine aspirations of politicians and voters into workable solutions. At best this is adequate but most of the time it is flawed – and badly flawed. The lessons of failures and successes, if they are learnt, are soon forgotten and so the cycle repeats itself time and time again.

APPENDIX A

GEORGE GASCOIGNE EXTENDED COURSE

GASCOIGNE 1964

Extended Course

The advantages of Education and the benefits of the 'Extended Course'

For some considerable time the members of the third forms, together with their parents, will have been considering the whole question of whether to remain on for an extended course or to leave school at the earliest opportunity after reaching the statutory leaving age. Slowly the national picture in education opens up. More and more young people are choosing to remain on, and more and more are now proceeding to heights not thought possible before. The 'Extended Courses' conceived in the past few years have opened up not only academic possibilities. Indeed, greater numbers than ever, who are by no means academic are remaining, either to make up gaps in their general education or indeed to reach maturity in reasonable surroundings.

Some ten years ago the teachers at Gascoigne grasped the opportunities presented of founding extended courses. These teachers have gained considerable experience, and our thoughts on this matter are set out in the following lines as a guide to parents facing this difficult decision. These thoughts are given in sketchy form, in some parts even as 'notes'.

The advantages of continued education:

a. Greater maturity – a widening of horizons – a touching of life at more points and an introduction to more interests in preparation for intelligent use of leisure.

b. The making up of gaps in our education and the provision of greater opportunity to use one's abilities to the full.

c. With tremendous effort the academically minded can work for qualifications and certificates which are, in the rather mad 'rat race' of the modern world, the 'open Sesame' to better jobs.

Note: Very few grammar school or public school boys and girls leave school before sixteen. Why then should secondary modern people be expected to 'complete their education' before these others? It really does not make sense. The government, and education circles generally, have already recognised the necessity for further education. In 1970 the leaving age will be raised compulsorily (by Act of Parliament) to sixteen.

In most countries the leaving age is higher than ours. In America, for instance, the leaving age is round about 18.

In an age of increasing mechanisation and automation unskilled labour is becoming more and more redundant.

What can Gascoigne offer in its extended courses?

The first requirement of any school trying to serve the needs of its pupils is an adequate supply of competent teachers. In recent years secondary schools have been passing through very difficult times, and excellent schemes have suffered. At Gascoigne our children would have suffered by this failure of the nation to provide the necessary teachers had it not been for the tireless efforts of so many of our staff who have sacrificed so much for our children. Until very recently we felt that Gascoigne's numbers and staffing might mean a severe readjustment in our schemes, because of administrative difficulties.

The picture is now clearing and it now is clear that we shall be able to provide for the many needs of our pupils. One thing is most certain. The loyalty of those who form the backbone of the Gascoigne team can be relied upon in the interests of its pupils. Given reasonable Ministry support therefore, it should be possible for Gascoigne to offer benefits as here recorded:

What does Gascoigne offer?

1) Most important of all, individual opportunity to develop to the fullest one's abilities and aptitudes – the less academic making good gaps and gaining confidence and poise, the academic, by hard personal studies, to gain examination successes

2) We enter boys and girls for 'O' level at GCE (at London University Exams or the Associated Board's) in the following: English Language, Literature, Mathematics, Economic History, British Constitution, Geography, Art, Science and in Technical Drawing.

In this respect a good boy or girl (good academically) <u>with really hard personal work</u>, could gain 5 passes, which is considered by most professional boards a good GCE result. (Over the past few years, passes in 6, 7 and 8 subjects have not been uncommon – thanks to the VERY hard work by the students and the heavy sacrifices of many teachers).

3) We enter other examinations also. While it is not possible to meet all demands there is no reason why work in the extended courses should not take on a vocational trend and enable particular students to follow particular courses aimed generally at their future. Within

our capacity it will certainly be the aim of Gascoigne to SERVE the needs of the children who elect to WORK in their interests.

4) On the completion of our two-year extended courses we can transfer children who have gained at least 4 'O' levels to appropriate grammar schools and technical schools or colleges. We have excellent relationships with the Sir George Monoux Grammar School, The Leyton County High School, the Walthamstow County High for Girls, the Woodford County High for Girls and the William Morris Technical School.

All these schools have rendered Gascoigne great service: scores of our children have been SERVED well by them, and we are grateful. Moreover, these schools have been most ready to acknowledge the good quality of some of the young people thus 'handed on'.

5) At these 'selective' schools boys and girls can enter for advanced-level GCE work. Recent history amply proves the success these transfers have gained. (There is a growing tendency for secondary schools to provide their own sixth form 'A' level courses. At Gascoigne we do not feel this to be in the general interest. Staffing and administrative difficulties are likely to be with the nation for some years yet, and we shall continue the policy of 'planning' for our students in their best interests. (It is true we have a sixth form where many have gained in confidence by consolidating their gains before passing on for further education. This policy we shall continue.)

6) Many such boys and girls who have gained their 'A' levels have gone on to universities, colleges of advanced technology and teacher training colleges. Our last prize day programme listed twelve boys and girls now doing exactly this. Last year two of our students who had been out at Industry and who have continued their studies in private before entering university gained for themselves honours degrees in science. Yet the Extended Courses started only ten years ago.

Only last week we were thrilled to have the news of one of our extended students, completing his university studies after a further two years at the Sir George Monoux School, who gained the high distinction of becoming a B.Sc with a FIRST class honours in Maths and Physics – an unusually high distinction.

When it is remembered that most of our pupils have 'failed' the 11-plus, it should make clear to all the stupidity of believing that it is possible to segregate children on education grounds at all. Some of these boys and girls who have gained distinction left us with no more that 3 or 4 'O' levels – but they had TREMENDOUS DETERMINA-TION and had learned the art of personal study and application to WORK.

Some features of the Gascoigne scheme:

1) We still do not 'stream' our fifth year extend form. This fact alone is evidence that the course is not only for the 'brighter' ones. Several wonderful students (among them some of the VERY BEST Gascoigne has produced), fully mature, socially conscious, loyal and hardworking, have left our extended courses, deriving therefrom great benefit of the first order – although, measured academically in terms of examinations, the gains were indeed meagre.

Laudable as success itself is, it cannot be too strongly emphasised that examination successes are by no means the greatest achieve-ments to be gained from a good education.

2) We believe in an <u>active</u> school for active youngsters. Our extended fifth year students are an active busy lot. They have addi-tional lessons after school hours on a few days of each week. They are encouraged, however, to join in social activities and to 'extend' themselves. Thanks to the very hard work of some of our teachers the following clubs are now thriving for them.

Woodwork Club
Social Club and Dancing
Chess Club
Drama
Visiting Club
Badminton Club
Table Tennis Club
The School Choir
The Arts Festival

A Youth Hostels Association group is now being set up and the present Fifths and the incoming Extended people can look forward to much organised hostel life.

Moreover, Gascoigne plays a not unimportant part in the youth club life of our borough and our students are encouraged to join themselves to worthwhile youth clubs. If they are selective in their looking they can find very much of value in Walthamstow and Waltham Forest.

In a world of increasing leisure, it is important that ALL should develop worthwhile and satisfying leisure activities.

The NEWSOM REPORT states: 'The school programme in the final year should be deliberately outgoing – an initiation into the adult world of work and leisure.'

We believe that, as far as staffing and conditions allow, our school extended course does just this.

(The Newsom Report is one of the enlightened documents of this age. Its study is a MUST for anyone who wishes to be up to date in education matters).

3) Gascoigne has an EVER OPEN DOOR to parents who wish to talk to us or to seek our aid on any matters which are in the interest

of the child. There are no particular 'Office Hours' because we know how difficult it is for you sometimes to arrange to come. You are, however, most welcome to come along at any time. I will be ever ready to meet you, and I shall endeavour to make it possible for the teachers to join our talks wherever appropriate. In some cases an evening appointment might be the only one possible. Well, that can be arranged if you let us know.

So much good, academically and socially, has come from the extended courses that we feel every child should be given the opportunity to benefit. One thing only is asked – and this an ESSENTIAL – that he should promise to work up to his capacity – no one can do more that, of course.

It cannot be too strongly stressed however, that if a person has not this strong WILL TO WORK he should be advised against the extended course.

Pressure of work has made it impossible for us to meet the parents of our thirds this year. During the FIRST week of the coming session, however, such a meeting will be held when a firm decision about the extended courses must be taken. Meantime, please complete and return the accompanying slip to enable us to take preliminary steps in planning our efforts.

Thanks.
J Dixon, Head

APPENDIX B

ANALYSIS OF PUBLICATIONS

This appendix contains the word cloud and summary comments from the analysis of six publications that were used to understand the attitudes and arguments about secondary modern schools.

Publication	Publication frequency	Reason for selecting
The Guardian	Daily	Views to the left
The New Statesman	Weekly	Views to the left
The Daily Telegraph	Daily	Views to the right
The Spectator	Weekly	Views to the right
The Economist	Weekly	Global and centrist
Tes	Weekly	Specialist publication for teachers

I have purposely ignored comments about expanding the number of grammar schools and, by implication, secondary moderns.

The Guardian

The attitude of *The Guardian* is reflected in this heading from a recent article[1] that appeared in the 'Long Read' section of the newspaper.

Secondary modern pupil remembers the inept teachers, classroom riots and useless qualifications of the two-tier education system

The author of the article, like many of the people who comment about the schools, failed the 11-plus but subsequently went to university and has achieved success in their working life – in this case, as a journalist and author.

The articles appearing in this publication were very long on their anger about the selective education system that created secondary moderns, but short on factual data. These were the only data and the arguments that appeared in the articles:

- Between 1944 and 1976 around 30 million people took the 11-plus, with over 20 million failing the exam.
- Working in a secondary modern school during the late 1960s

must have amounted to 'professional suicide for any schoolteacher'. The implication being that they were only able to attract second-rate teachers.

- Children who attended these schools until the age of 14 or 15 were then expected get a job as an apprentice or continue to receive some sort of on-the-job training from their employer.
- The 11-plus test came to be widely feared and disliked as a crude rationing mechanism that the well-informed could manipulate.
- Many pupils were not allowed to either take 'O' or 'A' levels, but were expected to take CSE exams that were perceived as an inferior qualification.

The Daily Telegraph

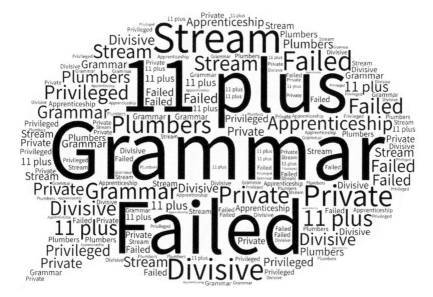

The Daily Telegraph's views about secondary moderns were as negative as any publication's, perhaps with the exception of *The Guardian*. As with the other publications, the schools were defined by 'not being grammars' and by being the home to 11-plus 'failures'.

These were the main criticisms made about the schools:

- They were housed in poor-quality buildings and given only a third of the funding per head of their contemporaries at grammar schools and barred from public exams.
- The quality of teachers in the schools was inferior to those in grammar and technical schools.
- Many pupils left school with no qualifications and only the top stream took the CSE exams. They were the first to take this type of exam.
- Those failing the exam felt ashamed.

This section of text[2] summarises the sentiment of *The Telegraph*.

> *Grammar schools were great news for the mainly middle-class chil-*
> *dren lucky enough to be selected, but extraordinarily divisive for the*
> *roughly 75pc of the population who were not. Most of the secondary*
> *moderns to which they were sent instead were rough old places*
> *where many kids sunk.*

There was another quote, in the same article, that at first sight seemed contradictory.

> *Upward mobility in this period was experienced almost equally by*
> *people at all levels of educational attainment. Grammar school or*
> *secondary modern – it made little difference.*

The explanation for this apparent contradiction was that the author believed the economic conditions in the 1960s and 1970s resulted in a high demand for labour that improved the material wellbeing of people irrespective of the type of school they attended.

The Spectator

The articles in *The Spectator* repeated many of the negative sentiments and research references found in other publications. For instance, it included a research report about the long-term effects of failing the 11-plus that also appeared in the *New Statesman*. There were a few positive comments that didn't appear in any other publication. For instance, in defence of the argument that grammar schools deprived other schools of their brightest children, the point was made that their rights had to be respected.

> *What have bright kids done to deserve being treated as teaching aids for the less able, rather than children who have their own educational needs?*

Like the other publications, secondary moderns were only referenced in the context of grammar schools and the 11-plus. There was little discussion about the schools themselves and what they achieved.

The text that best summarises the sentiment of the publication:[3]

Highly qualified teachers flock to schools with the smartest children. Poorer children, meanwhile, congregate in secondary moderns, and come with a higher likelihood of other issues: poor behaviour, malnutrition, and troubled families. (A stereotype, but borne out by data.) With equal funding, grammars flew: their results brilliant, their pupils off to university. Secondary moderns, meanwhile, became a byword for 'sink school'.

The Economist

During the past few years *The Economist* contained few mentions of secondary moderns. If the schools were referenced, it was as the inevitable results of selective education and grammar schools. The articles contained little factual data about the schools. The most frequent claims were that 80% of children went to secondary modern schools, and left school at 15 or 16, some with CSE exams, and that grammar schools received a much larger share of the funding than secondary moderns.

These two extracts capture the sentiment of *The Economist* towards the schools.

> *The 11-plus, a British school examination that divided children between a gifted elite destined for academic grammar schools and those consigned to run-of-the-mill secondary modern schools.*[4]

> *The 'secondary modern' schools which took the children who did not get into grammars failed their brightest pupils in part by not teaching courses that prepared them for university.*[5]

The New Statesman

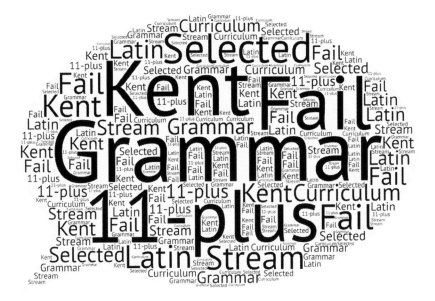

Many of the articles in the *New Statesman* were based on personal reminiscences of the perceived inequities of the selective education system.

When articles contained factual data, it was to illustrate the failure of grammar schools to improve social mobility and their negative impact on other local schools. The high number of times the word 'Kent' appears in the word cloud reflects the commentary about this county's retention of selective education.

A single research report, produced for a defunct website in 2012, was used to prove the long-term effect of attending a secondary modern. This research claimed that failing the 11-plus resulted in a third of their pupils, in later life, lacking the confidence to undertake further education and training. This quote from the research study appeared in this publication and on another dozen websites.[6]

Some adults claimed that low scores in entrance tests acted as an 'albatross around their neck' for more than 40 years because of the shame of being branded a failure at the end of primary education.
The disclosure – in a survey of more than 1,000 adults aged 50.

The *New Statesman*'s view about selective education was negative, without exception.

Selective education was seen as being unfair because some primary schools coached their pupils for the 11-plus exam and some didn't. It was claimed that the policy of selective education was disliked by three in four voters. This quote represents the sentiment of the publication.[7]

'Schools for thick working class kids, destined to be at the bottom of the heap' was not the way to sell them. Ministers had the brilliant idea of calling them 'secondary modern'. Then as now, the word 'modern' was thought to make anything attractive. It was not an accurate description; it was a feel-good description.

Tes

Considering *The Times Educational Supplement* (also known for a while as the *TES* and now as Tes) is the primary publication for the UK's teaching profession, its articles contained few facts about secondary modern schools. There was a comment that: 'the topic is neglected by educational researchers, partly because so little information is available.'

The words 'recruitment' and 'vacancy' appear in the word cloud. This results from the articles that talked about the perceived difficulty in recruiting teachers to schools where selective education still exists. Like the other publications, the word cloud shows how the commentary was dominated by arguments against grammar schools and selective education.

One of the articles noted that: 'Until 1966 more than 85 per cent of pupils left at 15. A small proportion stayed on to take the CSE exam, which was always a poor relation of the traditional O-level, a palliative to a system that did not work.'

The following text[8] is indicative of the *TES*'s attitude towards secondary moderns.

> *Ask anyone who grew up in the 1960s and they will probably know someone whose aspirations were damaged by secondary moderns. While the 'brightest' 20% went to well-resourced grammars, the rest were consigned to secondary modern or technical schools. As 11-plus 'failures', they typically were taught by less qualified staff, in inferior buildings and with fewer resources. Unsurprisingly, most left school with no qualifications.*

I found only one article[9] that provided a counter-argument to all the negative sentiments. This was titled: 'It's time for an end to the lazy assumptions about secondary moderns; we are not an anomaly that can be ignored' and was written by a head teacher and founder of the National Association of Secondary Moderns.

Like *The Guardian*, the TES was long on anger and short on facts about the schools. It should be noted that its online search feature only accessed recent editions of the publications. Older editions of the magazine, which are only available on microfilm and CD, had a much more balanced and informative approach to the issue of selective education.

APPENDIX C
DEFINITIONS OF EDUCATIONAL INSTITUTIONS

A s I researched the 90-year period of education in England and Wales I encountered many types of schools and educational institutions. I endeavoured to define their purpose when I first mentioned each name, but for easy reference this appendix provides a short description of all the institutions referenced in the book.

Because so many sources were used in creating these definitions, I decided it was too complicated citing them all in the footnotes. Whenever possible I used the definition appearing in a document issued by the Ministry or other government department. This is not a definitive directory of educational institutions and does not cover the most recent developments. Many of the schools existed for a short period of the timeline; some began as the names of specific types of school and then became generic terms for a period of children's schooling; some changed their purpose over time.

Rather than listing the definitions in alphabetical order I have grouped them into the sections of the timeline when they first appeared. Some of the institutions appear more than once, signifying they underwent a major change of purpose.

Between the wars

All-age schools

Elementary schools originally educated children from the starting age of five until they left to find work, hence the name 'all-age school'. In 1926 the Hadow Report recommended, and the government accepted, that schooling should be divided into three stages – infant, junior and senior. The move away from all-age schools was slow to occur and by 1955 they were still educating over 10% of pupils. It wasn't until the early 1960s that the last of these schools was replaced.

Central schools

Central schools were an intermediate stage between the secondary school and the junior technical school and trade school. They provided a general education of a practical character, sometimes with an industrial or commercial bias, for pupils between the ages of 11 and 15. Many of these schools were established in London, Manchester and other large cities from 1911 onwards.

Continuation schools/classes

The Lewis Report (1917) recommended that 'children between the ages of 14 and 18 had to attend, for not less than eight hours a week, or 320 hours a year, day continuation classes'. What would be taught in these classes was left to be resolved by each local education authority (LEA).

Continuation schools never got off the ground. In 1921 they had enrolled 95,000 students but by 1924 that number had fallen to 23,000 and would keep falling.

Day trade schools

The following paraphrases the Hadow Report's description of these schools. They were first established in London in 1901 to provide a three-year training in furniture and cabinet making. Designed to take boys on or near the completion of their elementary school career, for a period of one to three years, they provided specialised training that would equip the children for employment. The first of these schools for girls was opened in 1903.

Elementary schools

Before the 1944 Education Act these schools educated the majority of children aged five to 14. Most of them were maintained by the local education authority (LEA). A small minority were attached to 'boarding institutions' that received their grants directly from the Board of Education. If the buildings were also provided by the LEA (not the church) they were called a 'council school'.

Grammar school

Grammar schools, in one form or another, had existed since the 16th century. The modern-day grammar school dates from the Hadow Report, which recommended the secondary schools that existed at the time, providing an academic education for the minority of children, be renamed as 'grammar schools'.

Junior technical schools

These schools resulted from regulations issued by the Board of Education in 1913 and provided two to three years of post-elementary school training. In addition to providing a general education, they prepared children for industrial employment at the age of 15 or 16.

Like the technical schools that appeared after the 1944 Education Act, they failed to achieve their expected success. By the early 1930s there were 100 junior technical schools with approximately 30,000 students.

Modern schools

The modern school was the name suggested by the Hadow Report (1926) to replace the term 'central school'. When the tripartite system of education was introduced, secondary moderns were often referred to as 'modern schools'.

Secondary school (pre-Hadow)

These were a specific type of school that was recognised under the Board's Regulations for Secondary Schools.

Pupils left school later and received a more thorough education than those attending elementary schools. Pupils were a mix of those whose parents paid their fees and expenses and those who, after a period at an elementary school, passed an exam and were funded by the local education authority. In 1917 there were 62,000 children with free secondary school places. To put this into context, at the same time there were over a million children attending elementary schools.

Secondary school (post-Hadow)

Hadow recommended that the term 'secondary school' refer to schools providing the 'post-primary' stage of education. This meant that grammar, technical and secondary moderns were all 'secondary schools'.

Schools 'recognised as efficient'

The term 'recognised as efficient' spans all three parts of the timeline and refers to educational institutions providing a 'minimum of staffing and accommodation' as specified by the state. The Inspectorate of Schools had the authority to visit these schools to ensure the standards were being met.

All state schools were in this category, as were some independent (public) schools. If in addition certain other financial, curriculum and management conditions were met and the school was eligible for grants, they were referred to as 'schools on the grant list'.

Special schools

Children deemed to be ESN (educationally sub-normal) attended special schools. Thankfully, this term has now been replaced by 'special needs' or children with 'educational difficulties'. In the absence of an ESN school place the child was likely to attend a secondary modern. In 1956 some 12,000 children who ought, by current medical opinion, to have been in these schools attended secondary moderns.

Technical schools

The 1938 the Spens Report recommended that the name technical school be used to describe the junior technical schools that recruit pupils at the age of 13-plus and provide a course of two or three years' duration.

Technical high schools was the name given to those junior technical schools where children entered at the age of 11-plus and received a five-year course of training.

Voluntary schools

This was the generic name for schools operated by the church. In 1930 the Church of England was responsible for more elementary schools than local councils, although they educated fewer pupils. Many of these schools were small and in rural areas.

Birth and death

All-through comprehensives

All-through comprehensive schools educated children from the age of 11 to the end of their school life.

Bilateral schools

A bilateral school was organised so that it could provide, in clearly defined parts of the school, for any two types of tripartite education. Mostly they were divided into a secondary modern and technical school side.

Campus schools

This was the term given to a collection of schools (usually a secondary modern and a grammar) that shared the same 'campus' and some of their facilities, but were located in separate buildings with their own headmaster or headmistress. I expect another reason for this configuration was that it could assist (theoretically) the movement between schools of pupils who were wrongly assigned by the 11-plus exam.

Common school

This name has a variety of meanings. It is most often used as a term that describes both multilateral and comprehensive schools.

Comprehensive school

The word 'orthodox' was sometimes used to preface the title comprehensive school. These schools provided secondary education for all the children from a local area who would have attended a grammar, secondary modern or technical school. Located in the same facility, these schools were not divided into separate streams or sides.

County colleges

There was a section of the 1944 Education Act devoted to providing 'further education' for children once they left school. LEAs were supposed to establish 'county colleges' that would provide one day a month of 'cultural' and 'recreative' activities for under-18s. This idea was never implemented – the same fate as when it was proposed in the Lewis Report (1917).

County schools

The 1944 Education Act used the term 'county schools' to refer to primary and secondary schools that were maintained by a local education authority, as distinct from those operated by the church (which were called voluntary schools).

Grammar school

The most academically able children (at the age of 11) attended these schools. At their height grammar schools were educating 27% of the country's children. The availability of places was uneven because each LEA controlled the availability of schools in their geographic region. In some parts of Wales over 60% of children attended these schools, while in England some LEAs provided spaces for as few as 10%.

Most of these schools disappeared as the result of the move to comprehensive education.

Junior school

Junior schools are the institutions that now deliver Key Stage 2 education for children aged seven to 11 years. The Hadow Report (1926) referred to this phase of education as the 'upper stage of primary education'.

Multilateral school

The terms 'multilateral' and 'comprehensive' school were often used interchangeably. The difference between the two was made clear with this definition from the Ministry: 'A multilateral school is one which is intended to provide the secondary education of all the children in a given area and includes all three elements [grammar, technical and secondary modern] in clearly defined sides.' The comprehensive school was one that was intended to provide the secondary education of all the children in a given area without being organised into three sides.

Primary schools

Primary schools provide education to children between the ages of five and 11. Usually this is divided into two phases, with infant schools for five to seven year olds and junior schools for seven to 11 year olds.

Technical schools

Technical schools were the third leg of the tripartite system. Like secondary moderns their purpose was ill-defined. As the name suggests they were intended to provide, from the age of 11, a secondary education with a scientific and engineering bias. In practice their status was somewhere between a grammar and secondary modern school. They were often situated in buildings that were unsuitable for providing a technical education and not given the funding to deliver a high-quality technical syllabus.

In 1960 there were approximately 100 technical schools in operation. This number halved in the following decade.

Secondary modern

Following the 1944 Education Act the large majority of LEAs implemented some form of the tripartite system of secondary education. The type of school children aged 11 attended was determined by a combination of exams and their past school performance. Those who were thought to be the least academic continued their studies at a secondary modern.

For the first decade of their existence the schools were encouraged to 'experiment'. This resulted in many different types of school being established. Some were little changed from the elementary schools they replaced, with others attempting to mirror the grammar school's academic model.

The comprehensive era

Academies

In 2000 the New Labour government announced that city academies would replace seriously failing schools. Academies were established by partnerships between the government and voluntary sector, church and business sponsors. The concept was similar to the city technology college programme.

They were publicly funded independent schools with private and voluntary sector sponsorship and management, and had greater freedom than other state schools.

Academies and specialist schools had much in common but differed in two important respects. Specialist schools were partly funded by third parties, but they remained embedded in the state school system.

Academies required a much higher level of investment from their 'promoters', amounting to 20% of the initial and ongoing capital costs. For this investment the promoters were outside the state system, owning and running the schools and receiving grants from central government that were equivalent to the cost of educating pupils in specialist schools.

Beacon schools

The Beacon school initiative was launched in 1998. Through a competitive process, schools could apply for 'Beacon Status', an accolade that implied they were 'among the best in the system'. Their reward was additional funding that could be spent on teaching resources, equipment and administrative support. In return for the award they worked closely with partner schools to disseminate their good practice. In other words, good schools got more money to help improve the not-so-good.

The number of Beacon schools reached a peak of 1,145 in September 2002 but the scheme was discontinued in 2004.

City technology colleges

City technology colleges were launched in 1988. As the name suggests they specialised in teaching technology and were part-funded by central government and private sponsorship. The scheme was later broadened to include schools that specialised in the languages, arts and sports.

Although the colleges operated outside LEA control, they still required their cooperation – something that was often not forthcoming. Only 15 colleges were opened but they provided the blueprint for academy schools that later became a major part of the education system.

Community schools

The 1998 Education Act announced that county schools would become known as community schools. This renaming was first mentioned in New Labour's *Diversity and Excellence* paper in 1995. It proposed that existing comprehensives, which were originally secondary moderns, be re-christened as community schools. In most other respects, nothing changed. Instead of the admissions policy being dictated by the LEA it became 'based on parental preference agreed by the LEA'.

Foundation schools

The 1998 Education Act announced that grant-maintained schools were to become foundation schools. The governing body of a foundation school had ownership of and was responsible for the school buildings.

Grant-maintained schools

Grant-maintained schools were announced in the 1988 Education Act. Because these schools received their funding from central government they were not controlled by the LEAs. By January 1998 there were 1,261 grant-maintained schools; just over half were secondary schools, with the remainder being primary and 'special' schools.

Specialist schools

The origin of the term 'specialist school' goes back to the city technology colleges. The 1998 Education Act permitted existing specialist schools to continue and enabled new schools to select 10% of their pupils by 'aptitude'. When Labour came to power there were 225 of these schools and over the next couple of years a further 160 were opened.

By 2004 the number had increased to 2,000, two-thirds of all secondaries. Many of them specialised in technology, a generic term that included maths, science and design technology.

Specialist schools were a clear demonstration of the move away from the 'one size fits all comprehensive school'.

Voluntary aided and controlled schools

The distinction between these schools has changed over time. Both are faith schools. In the voluntary aided (VA) schools, capital expenditure is grant aided and the responsibility of the governing body. In voluntary controlled schools (VC) the capital work is paid for by the local authority.

The governors in the two types of school have different responsibilities. In the VA school, a majority of the governing body are appointed by the faith group. There are faith-appointed governors in VC schools but they are a minority.

In VA schools the governing body is the employer of the staff. In VC schools the governing body has delegated powers in relation to the staff, but all members of staff are employed by the LEA.

NOTES

Prologue

1. *This I Know*, Kindle Direct Publishing, 2017.

1. The truth is what we want it to be

1. *This I Know*, Dick Stroud, Kindle Direct Publishing, 2017.
2. 'School leavers debate', House of Commons debate, 29 March 1976.
3. *The Daily Telegraph*, 26 September 2019.
4. *Pensions at a Glance 2019*, OECD, 2019.
5. 23 April 2017.
6. *Internet Strategies*, Dick Stroud, Palgrave Macmillan, 1999.
7. *Marketing Week*, 4 May 2017.
8. https://en.wikipedia.org/wiki/Echo_chamber_(media) (accessed 11 January 2021).
9. Allen Lane, 2016.
10. 'Two friends who change what we think about what we think', *The New Yorker,* 7 December 2016.
11. *The Undoing Project*, Michael Lewis, Allen Lane, 2016.
12. The average percentage of secondary pupils educated in secondary moderns and all-age schools between 1949 and 1969, from multiple government statistics.
13. Ratio of education spending in 2014–2015 and 1968 in constant value pounds, Education Spending, IFS, 29 September 2015.
14. https://en.wikipedia.org/wiki/Secondary_modern_school (accessed 11 January 2021).
15. The number of pupils aged 11 in 1960, *Education in 1960*, HMSO, July 1961.
16. 'Availability cascades and risk regulation', Timur Kuran and Cass R. Sunstein, October 2007.

2. George Gascoigne Secondary Modern – a personal view

1. https://youtu.be/hMsXordUPp4 (accessed 11 January 2021).
2. *George Monoux's school,* C. Pond, Walthamstow Antiquarian Society, 1977.

3. A consistently negative image

1. *The Stakes of Diplomacy*, Walter Lippmann, H. Holt, 1915.
2. https://www.english-corpora.org/hansard/ (accessed 11 January 2021).
3. Secondary Modern Blog, http://secmod.blogspot.co.uk (accessed 11 January 2021).
4. https://en.wikipedia.org/wiki/Secondary_modern_school (accessed 11 January 2021).

5. Wikipedia on secondary modern schools, referenced 'Date of birth, family background, and the 11 plus exam: short- and long-term consequences of the 1944 secondary education reforms in England and Wales', Stirling Economics Discussion.
6. https://en.wikipedia.org/wiki/Secondary_modern_school (accessed 11 January 2021).
7. *A History of Modern Britain*, Andrew Marr, Picador, 2009.
8. *The costs of education*, John Vaizey, George Allen & Unwin, 1958.
9. 'Does Failing the 11-plus Really Damage your Future?', *HuffPost*, 18 September 2012.
10. *The Daily Telegraph*, 3 July 2014.
11. *Posh and Posher*, Andrew Neil, BBC TV, 19 February 2011.
12. Theresa May, speech about grammar schools, 9 September 2016.

4. A condensed history of secondary moderns

1. *The Graduate Premium*, The Intergenerational Foundation, August 2016.
2. *Participation rates In Higher Education: Academic Years 2006/2007–2014/2015*, Department of Education, 15 September 2016.
3. 'School leavers debate', House of Commons debate, 29 March 1976.
4. *The Struggle for the History of Education*, Gary McCulloch, Taylor and Francis, 25 February 2011.
5. *People's history of education: Brian Simon, the British Communist Party and Studies in the History of Education*, Gary McCulloch, History of Education, 23 April 2010.
6. *Higher Education Quarterly*, May 1963.
7. By Brian Simon, 13 February 1995, the *Independent*, http://www.independent.co.uk/news/people/harold-dent-1572842.html
8. *Brian Simon*, Anne Corbett, *The Guardian*, 22 June 2002.
9. https://hansard.parliament.uk
10. http://www.educationengland.org.uk/history
11. *Human Capital in Britain, 1790 to 2009*, Jan Kunnas, Nick Hanley and others, Economic History Society Annual Conference, 2013.
12. *Educational Documents for England and Wales*, Stuart Maclure, 1979.
13. *Education in 1949*, report of the Ministry of Education for England and Wales.
14. *Education in 1966* and *Education in 1969*, reports of the Ministry of Education for England and Wales.
15. House of Commons Library Educational Statistics, SN/SG/4252, 27 November 2012.
16. https://en.wikipedia.org/wiki/List_of_recessions_in_the_United_Kingdom (accessed 11 January 2021).
17. Population estimates for England and Wales by sex and quinary age (mid-1911 to mid-1960) and by sex and single year of age (mid-1961 to mid-2015).
18. *British Historical Statistics*, B. Mitchell, Cambridge University Press, 2011.
19. *British Historical Statistics*, B. Mitchell, Cambridge University Press, 2011.
20. *Occupations of the people of Great Britain*, Guy Routh, Palgrave Macmillan, 1987.
21. *Social class mobility in modern Britain*, Dr John Goldthorpe, Nuffield College Oxford, 15 March 2016.
22. Multiple reports from the Institute of Fiscal Studies.

5. Between the wars

1. *Departmental committee on juvenile education in relation to employment after the war*, His Majesty's Stationery Office, April 1917.
2. *The Lewis Report on juvenile education in relation to employment after the war*, HMSO, 1917.
3. *Report of the Board of Education 1927–1928.*
4. *Report of the Board of Education for 1916–1917.*
5. *Report by the Board of Education for 1911–1912.*
6. Longman Green, 1965.
7. Routledge, 1976.
8. *Youth's Opportunity*, HMSO, 1946.
9. Charles Trevelyan, president of the Board of Education, *Hansard*, 21 March 1924.
10. These three extracts are taken from the charts discussed in Chapter 4 ('A condensed history of secondary moderns').
11. *The Politics of Educational Reform*, Brian Simon, Lawrence & Wishart, 1974.
12. Available at https://archive.org/details/secondaryeducati00tawnuoft (accessed 11 January 2021).
13. https://www.statista.com/statistics/289987/expenditure-on-alcoholic-beverages-in-the-united-kingdom-uk-quarterly/ (accessed 11 January 2021).
14. https://www.ukpublicspending.co.uk/education_budget_2017_2.html, (accessed 11 January 2021).
15. 'The "school masters' parliament": the origins and formation of the Consultative Committee of the Board of Education 1868–1916', K. Brehony, *History of Education*, 1994.
16. J.R. Brooks, *Journal of Education Administration and History*, 1987.
17. *Agriculture: historical statistics*, House of Commons Library, 25 June 2019.
18. *Report of the Board of Education 1927–1928.*
19. *Report of the Board of Education 1929–1930.*
20. http://www.bl.uk/learning/timeline/item107595.html (accessed 11 January 2021).
21. *Education and policy in England in the 20th Century*, Robert Aldrich, Woburn Education, 1991.
22. *Education and Labour Party Ideologies 1900–2001 and Beyond*, Denis Lawton, Woburn Education Series, 2004.
23. *The Spens Report on Secondary Education with Special Reference to Grammar Schools and Technical High Schools*, HMSO, 1938.
24. Routledge, 1976.
25. Lawrence Wishart, 1974.
26. Routledge, 1949.
27. https://www.historic-newspapers.co.uk/blog/sunday-newspapers-in-the-1940s (accessed 11 January 2021).
28. *The Audit of War: The Illusion and Reality of Britain as a Great Nation*, Faber & Faber, 1985.
29. *The Last Lion: Winston Spencer Churchill: Defender of the Realm 1940–1965*, William Manchester and Paul Reid, Pan Macmillan, 2015.
30. *Education After the War* ('The Green Book'), Board of Education, HMSO, 1941.

31. *The Norwood Report on the Curriculum and Examinations in Secondary Schools*, HMSO, 1943.
32. *Journal of Educational Psychology*, November 1943.
33. *Education in 1928–1929*, Board of Education and Statistics Public Education in England and Wales, HMSO.
34. *Education in 1938–1939*, Board of Education and Statistics Public Education in England and Wales, HMSO.

6. Birth and death

1. Routledge, 1976.
2. *Problems of Social Policy,* R. Titmuss, HMSO, 1950.
3. Debate about evacuation, House of Commons, 14 September 1939.
4. In this video, for example: https://youtu.be/0Hd_fQLAEXw (accessed 11 January 2021).
5. https://hansard.parliament.uk/lords/1939-11-01/debates/3513b00f-3a10-462b-961d-aaf63fe2e04b/EvacuationProblems (accessed 11 January 2021).
6. *Secondary education for all*, H.C. Dent, Routledge, 1949.
7. *Education and the Second World War*, Routledge Library Editions, 1992.
8. http://www.iwm.org.uk/history/how-childrens-lives-changed-during-the-second-world-war (accessed 11 January 2021).
9. Board of Education report, 1947.
10. *Schools building and capital funding (England)*, House of Commons briefing paper number 07375, 2017.
11. *Report to Education (General) Sub-committee,* 13 September 1943.
12. Macmillan, 1988.
13. *Education in 1938*, HMSO, 1939.
14. *Political Quarterly*, 1943.
15. *Oxbridge 'elitism'*, House of Commons briefing paper, 5 September 2016.
16. http://www.ibiblio.org/pha/policy/1943/1943-03-21a.html (accessed 11 January 2021).
17. HMSO, 1943.
18. *Educational reconstruction debate*, House of Commons, 29 July 1943.
19. *Woman in Parliament and Government*, House of Commons Library, 25 February 2020. http://researchbriefings.parliament.uk/ResearchBriefing/Summary/SN01250
20. Meeting of the War Cabinet, 28 March 1944.
21. *The making of the 1944 Education Act*, Cassell Education, 1994.
22. *The Evolution of the Comprehensive School: 1926–1972*, Taylor and Francis, 1969.
23. *Labour and the Wartime Coalition: from the diaries of James Chuter-Ede*, Kevin Jefferys, Historians' Press, 1987.
24. *The art of the possible,* Lord Butler, Penguin Books, 1971.
25. *The British Economy 1945–1955*, chapter on social services, edited by G. Worswick, Oxford University Press.
26. 'The Education Act of 1944', https://www.parliament.uk (accessed 11 January 2021).
27. *Ellen Wilkinson,* Paula Bartley, Pluto Press, 2014.
28. *Red Ellen,* Laura Beers, Harvard University Press, 2016.
29. *Education in 1947*, HMSO.
30. *School Workforce in England*, Department of Education, 2016.
31. *Citizen Clem: A Biography of Attlee*, Quercus, 2016.

32. http://archive.spectator.co.uk/article/24th-august-1945/5/miss-wilkinson, *The Spectator*, 24 August 1945.
33. *http://www.bbc.co.uk/programmes/b08zc6fs, Great lives: Maxine Peake on Ellen Wilkinson,* BBC interviewer Matthew Parris, 4 August 2017.
34. Ministry of Education, HMSO.
35. *Education and the social order*, Brian Simon, Lawrence & Wishart, 1999 edition.
36. *Education in 1947*, HMSO.
37. *Challenge and Response – pamphlet number 17*, HMSO, 1950.
38. *Proposed Postponement of the Raising of the School Leaving Age*, memorandum by the minister of education, 14 January 1947.
39. Conclusions of the Cabinet meeting, 16 January 1947.
40. *The Battle for Output 1947*, HMSO, 1947.
41. National Archive folder ED 136/788 The Secondary Modern Schools: Draft and Comments.
42. *We Want Winns!*, Walthamstow Forest Oral History Workshop, 1993.
43. HMSO, 1947.
44. A minute of the 'toned down' headings of the speech Ellen Wilkinson would have made about an early draft of *The New Secondary Education* had she been in opposition; no date provided.
45. *Education in 1938*, HMSO.
46. *Education in 1947*, HMSO.
47. Routledge, 1949.
48. *British Historical Statistics*, B.R. Mitchell, Cambridge University Press, 1988.
49. ONS, https://visual.ons.gov.uk/birthsanddeaths/ (accessed 11 January 2021).
50. Population estimates for England and Wales by sex and quinary age (mid-1911 to mid-1960) and by sex and single year of age (mid-1961 to mid-2015).
51. *The Royal Commission on Population*, HMSO, 1949.
52. *Education in 1952*, Ministry of Education, HMSO.
53. Bloomsbury, 2007.
54. *Schools, pupils and their characteristics*, Department of Education, January 2016.
55. Reports titled *Education in [year]*, HMSO, 1947–1954.
56. New Towns Act of 1946.
57. HMSO, chancellor of the Exchequer, March 1949.
58. Minister of education, Parliamentary debate, 4 May 1950.
59. National Archive E417/416.
60. Memo to School Inspectors, Ministry of Education, National Archive ED 147/415, February 1946.
61. National Archive folder E147/415, 19 February 1946.
62. National Archive folder E147/415, 7 July 1948.
63. National Archive folder E147/415; not dated.
64. Circular 90, draft reviewed by the Association of Education Committees, National Archive ED 147/415, March 1946.
65. Routledge, 1969.
66. *English Education: 1946–1952*, H.C. Dent, Routledge, 1954.
67. Routledge, 1980.
68. George Allen & Unwin, 1966.
69. *Organization of Secondary Education*, Ministry of Education Circular 144, 16 June 1947.
70. *Education in the post-war years*, Routledge, 1988.

71. Reports titled *Education in [year]*, HMSO, 1947–1956.
72. Richard Aldrich, Dennis Dean and Peter Gordon, Woburn Education, 1991.
73. *Secondary Education Survey*, January 1952.
74. *Capital Funding for Schools*, National Audit Office, 22 February 2017.
75. *Secondary Education Survey*, Joan Thompson, Fabian Society, January 1952.
76. *Education for all*, H.C. Dent, Routledge, 1949.
77. *The Last Lion: Winston Spencer Churchill*, William Manchester and Paul Reid, Pan Macmillan, 2015.
78. *The Audit of War: The illusion and reality of Britain as a great nation*, Correlli Barnett, Faber & Faber, 1985.
79. Election broadcast, 4 June 1945.
80. Conservative Party manifesto, 1945.
81. *Michael Young: Social Entrepreneur*, Asa Briggs, Palgrave, 2001.
82. Labour Party manifesto, 1945.
83. Meeting of the Cabinet, 22 January 1952.
84. *Covid-19: deficits, debt and fiscal strategy*, Institute of Fiscal Studies, July 2020.
85. Labour Party manifesto, 2017.
86. 'Jobless falling to 1950s level', *The Times*, 6 May 2018.
87. Annual publications of the Ministry of Education, supplemented by other sources.
88. Reese Edwards, University of London Press, 1960.
89. National Archive folder ED 136/861, 10 April 1955.
90. ED 136/861, 14 April 1955.
91. ED 136/861, 21 April 1955.
92. ED 136/861, 18 April 1955.
93. *British general election manifestos 1900–1974*, F.W.S. Craig, The Macmillan Press, 1975.
94. *British general election manifestos 1900–1974*, F.W.S. Craig, The Macmillan Press, 1975.
95. Taylor and Francis, 2005.
96. *A policy for secondary education,* The Labour Party, 1951.
97. *The Political Quarterly*, Wiley Online Library, October 1951.
98. *Education and the social order*, Brian Simon, Lawrence & Wishart, 1991.
99. https://ukpressonline.co.uk (accessed 11 January 2021).
100. Sixty years of daily newspaper circulation trends, Communications Management, 2011. Supplemented with data from Wikipedia.
101. https://www.britishnewspaperarchive.co.uk (accessed 11 January 2021).
102. https://hansard.parliament.uk
103. *British Labour Party education policy and comprehensive education*, 2015. http://discovery.ucl.ac.uk/1475747/ (accessed 11 January 2021).
104. *Examinations in secondary schools*, Ministry of Education, Circular 289, 9 July 1955.
105. https://www.gov.uk/government/news/chief-inspector-sets-out-vision-for-new-education-inspection-framework (accessed 11 January 2021).
106. Museum of the History of Education, 1982.
107. *Secondary Technical Schools*, ED 147/207, 20 December 1954.
108. Eccles' use of grammar didn't always follow the usual conventions. These are his words, not my typing mistakes.
109. Secondary Technical Schools, ED 147/207, 24 January 1955.
110. *Secondary Education*, National Archive reference ED 147/207, January 1955.

111. *The New Secondary Education*, Ministry of Education, Pamphlet No. 9, 1947.
112. National Archive reference ED 147/207.
113. *Technical Education*, HMSO, February 1956.
114. National Archive ED 46/1001, 22 December 1955.
115. The Crowther Report was not published for three years (August 1959) and is covered later in the chapter.
116. G. Bell and Sons, 1956.
117. The Labour Party, July 1956.
118. National Archive Reference ED 147/636.
119. Ministry of Education annual report, 1960.
120. Victor Gollancz, 1956.
121. Interview Memorandum, ED 147/636, 18 October 1956.
122. *Secondary Modern Schools – an interim report*, Routledge Library Editions, 1958.
123. Data taken from the 1957 (or whichever year) Ministry publication.
124. *Secondary Modern*, Harold Loukes, Harrap, 1956.
125. Ministry of Education annual report, 1957.
126. Ministry of Education annual report, 1957.
127. 'Secondary Modern', *The Times Educational Supplement*, 19 October 1956.
128. 'Incentives for Moderns', *The Times Educational Supplement*, 13 January 1956.
129. *Secondary Modern Schools*, Political and Economic Planning, 1956.
130. *Secondary Modern Schools 1955–1959*, National Archive Folder, ED 147/639.
131. 'Secondary Modern Schools' debate, House of Commons, 12 June 1956.
132. *Class sizes up in 'two-thirds of secondary schools'*, BBC News website, 8 March 2018.
133. *Standards of Reading 1948–1956*, Ministry of Education, Pamphlet No. 32, 1956.
134. *Literacy scores by gender at age 15*, OECD Family Database, http://www.oecd.org/els/family/database.htm (accessed 11 January 2021).
135. National Foundation for Educational Research in England and Wales, Newnes Educational Publishing, 1957.
136. *Secondary School Selection: A British Psychological Society inquiry*, Methuen & Co, 1957.
137. *Early leaving (The Gurney-Dixon Report)*, The Central Advisory Council for Education (England), 1954.
138. *Early leaving (The Gurney-Dixon Report)*, The Central Advisory Council for Education (England), 1954.
139. *Occupation of the people of Great Britain*, Guy Routh, The Macmillan Press, 1987.
140. Floud, Halsey and Martin, Central Advisory Council for Education, 1956.
141. *Cabinet Paper: A further advance in education*, National Archive, 10 December 1956. http://filestore.nationalarchives.gov.uk/pdfs/small/cab-129-84-cp-56-278-28.pdf, December 1956.
142. *Minutes of Cabinet meeting*, National Archive, 7 February 1957.
143. Government white paper, December 1958.
144. Letter to C.D. Hamilton, Kemsley Newspapers, National Archive ED 136/942, 3 December 1958.
145. ED 136/942.
146. *Post-war policies and the state of the schools to-day*, ED 136/945, January 1958.
147. Draft memorandum by the Minister of Education, ED 136/945.
148. National Archive, ED 136/943.
149. Minister's brief and statistics, National Archive, ED 136/943.

150. External examinations, National Archive, ED136/945.
151. The minister's press conference notes to launch the white paper, ED 136/943.
152. H. Gaitskell, press statement of his speech to the Co-operative Society, 5 July 1958.
153. *British General Election Manifestos*, F. Craig, The Macmillan Press, 1975.
154. Memorandum from Harold Macmillan and Geoffrey Lloyd's response, ED136/945, May–June 1959.
155. *External examinations in secondary s*chools, T.R. Weaver, ED 147/304, 1/3/1957.
156. *The Crowther Report – 15 to 18,* Vol. 1 Report, Vol. II Surveys, Central Advisory Council for Education, HMSO, August 1959.
157. *The Beloe Report – Secondary school examinations other than the GCE*, Secondary School Examination Council, July 1960.
158. *External examinations in secondary schools in England and Wales,* Peter Fisher, University of Leeds, 1982.
159. Question asked in Parliament by Mr Owen and answered by Sir Edward Boyle, 31 July 1958.
160. *Secondary school examinations*, Ministry of Education Press Office, 27 September 1960.
161. National Archive, first published in the November 1960 issue of Education *Today and Tomorrow*, ED 147/309, January 1961.
162. National Archive, ED 147/309, 14 January 1961.
163. National Archive, ED 147/310, 4 July 1961.
164. This references the 1998 film starring Gwyneth Paltrow.
165. *Failing the ordinary child*, Open University Press, 1998.
166. Education Statistics, Department of Education and Science, 1969.
167. Minutes of the Secondary Schools Education Council, March 1964.
168. Institute of Education, National Archive, ED 146/30 Part B, 22 March 1960.
169. Between the ages of 18 and 26 almost all men were liable to spend 24 months training with one of the armed forces.
170. Crowther's definition: 'a fifth-year course given in a school where not all are expected to make use of it. Thus a fifth-year course in a grammar school is not an extended course; in a modern school it is.'
171. *The Crowther Report and Further Education debate*, House of Lords, 23 March 1960.
172. *Journal of Educational Administration and History*, July 2006.
173. Notes taken from ED146/46, CACE Newsom Report papers 1961–1963.
174. *Half our Future*, Central Advisory Council for Education, August 1963.
175. *Analysis of Evidence*, CACE meeting 129/2/62, National Archive ED 146/46.
176. *Percentage of secondary school pupils with free school meals in England*, Local Government Association, 2019–2020.
177. Reporting of the debate in the House of Lords, 20 November 1963.
178. Palgrave Macmillan, 2013.
179. Permanent secretary at the Ministry of Education, Herbert Andrew, note to Mr Cocker-ill, 1 November 1963; Ministry of Education papers, National Archives ED 147/513.
180. *Educating for uncertainty*, David Downes & Fred Flower, Fabian Society, October 1965.
181. *Children and their Primary Schools (The Plowden Report)*, Department of Education and Science, 1967.
182. 'The politics of secondary school reorganisation: some reflections', *Journal of Educational Administration and History*, 1972.

183. *The Making of Tory Education Policy*, Christopher Knight, The Falmer Press, 1990.

184. *Good Learning*, Angus Maude, Michael Joseph, 1964.

185. The 1964 Education Act, HMSO, 1964.

186. *The politics of education (Maurice Kogan in conversation with Boyle and Crosland)*, Penguin, 1971.

187. 'The politics of secondary education', Edward Boyle, *Journal of Educational Administration*, 1972.

188. *British Labour Party education policy and comprehensive education*, History of Education, Taylor and Francis, 2016.

189. Conducted by Research Services Ltd, a sample of 400 parents (aged 30–39) with children aged 5–16.

190. Labour Party, June 1958.

191. *The Secondary Modern School*, William Taylor, Faber & Faber, 1963.

192. *The backbench diaries of Richard Crossman,* Richard Crossman, Hamish Hamilton and Jonathan Cape, 1981.

193. *Daily Mail, Daily Express* and other lower circulation titles.

194. *The Plowden Report (Research and Surveys),* Department of Education and Science, research conducted during June–July 1964.

195. *Annual Civil Service Employment Survey,* March 2017.

196. *Educating the Nation*, RHS presidential address, November 2013.

197. The provisions of the London Government Act 1963 had increased the number of LEAs.

198. *Inside Comprehensive Schools*, Tyrrell Burgess, HMSO, 1970.

199. Mr Michael Stewart, House of Commons, 12 November 1964.

200. Report created by M.L. James and sent to Mr V.H. Stevens and Miss Heart, Ministry of Education and Science, ED 147/826, 27 October 1964.

201. *Trends in British Society since 1900*, A. Halsey, Macmillan, 1972.

202. Education Statistics, HMSO, 1969.

203. Minster's brief for the white paper, National Archive, ED 136/943, 1958.

204. *Commission on Inequality in Education*, The Social Market Foundation, June 2017.

205. Appendix A.

206. Figures compiled from multiple sources.

207. *The Secondary Modern School*, William Taylor, Faber & Faber, 1963.

208. Education statistics, Department of Education and Science, 1969.

209. *British general election manifestos 1900–1974*, F.W.S. Craig, Macmillan Press, 1975.

210. *British Labour Party education policy and comprehensive education*, Gary McCulluch, History of Education, 2016.

211. *Life and Labour*, Michael Stewart, Sidgwick & Jackson, 1980.

212. Notes from Miss W. Harte, ED 147/827A, 1 January 1965.

213. Undated note, ED 147/827A.

214. *Whip to Wilson*, Edward Short, Macdonald, 1989.

215. Minutes of the Cabinet meeting, 19 January 1965.

216. *The organisation of secondary education,* Circular 10/65 (1965), 12 July 1965.

217. Letter to Anthony Crosland from Lady Plowden, ED 147/827A, 27 April 1965.

218. D.H. Leadbetter note to H.F. Rossetti, ED 147/827A, 3 May 1965.

219. *Children and their Primary Schools (The Plowden Report)*, Department of Education and Science, 1967.

220. Meeting between Crosland and his officials with the Association of Education Committees, the Association of Municipal Corporations, County Councils' Associations and the

Inner London Education Authority, ED 147/827A, 14 May 1965.

221. This comment was made at the same meeting.

222. House of Commons debate, 21 January 1965.

223. Note from M.L. James, ED 147/827A, 16 December 1964.

224. Circular 10/66 – Schools building programmes, 10 March 1966.

225. *Ten days that changed the nation*, Simon & Schuster, 2009.

226. *Towards a new education system*, RoutledgeFalmer, 1989.

227. *Anthony Crosland*, Kevin Jefferys, Richard Cohen Books, 1999.

228. 'Circular 10/65 Revisited: The Labour Government and the "Comprehensive Revolution" in 1964–1965', *Paedagogica Historica*, Dennis Dean, 1998.

229. *The Times Educational Supplement*, 23 July 1965.

230. 'Circular 10/65 Revisited: The Labour Government and the "Comprehensive Revolution" in 1964–1965', *Paedagogica Historica*, Dennis Dean, 1998.

231. *The Castle Diaries,* Barbara Castle, PaperMac, 1990.

232. 'Unanimous vote to reject integration of public schools', *The Times*, 3 October 1968.

233. 'Schools report is attacked', *The Times*, 23 July 1968.

234. 'Circular 10/65 Revisited: The Labour Government and the "Comprehensive Revolution" in 1964–1965', *Paedagogica Historica*, Dennis Dean, 1998.

235. *A Plan for Polytechnics and Other Colleges,* HMSO.

236. *A Century of Fiscal Squeeze Politics: 100 Years of Austerity, Politics, and Bureaucracy in Britain*, Christopher Hood, OUP Oxford, 2017.

237. *Negotiating Credibility: Britain and the International Monetary Fund 1956–1976*, Ben Clift and Jim Tomlinson, Contemporary European History, November 2008.

238. Account of the Cabinet meeting according to Susan Crosland, Tony Crosland, Jonathan Cape, 1982.

239. *The Crossman Diaries 1964–1970*, Richard Crossman, Hamish Hamilton, 1975.

240. 52nd meeting of the Inspectorate Secondary Panel, ED 158/22, 28 March 1969.

241. Circular 7/65, HMSO, 1965.

242. *Schools, pupils and their characteristics: January 2017*, Department for Education.

243. National life stories annual lecture 2017, British Library, https://youtu.be/ ZLfRlnATXKs (accessed 11 January 2021).

244. *Rethink the '60s*, British Library lecture, 19 August 2019.

245. '10/65 and non-streaming in comprehensive schools', *Forum*, Autumn 1966.

246. 'Labour and Education: Secondary reorganisation and the neighbourhood school', N. Rao, *Contemporary British History*, 2002.

247. 'Towns swing right', *The Times*, 13 May 1967.

248. Secondary Education reorganisation debate, House of Commons, 1 November 1968.

249. *Going Comprehensive in England and Wales*, Alan Kerckhoff, Ken Fogelman, David Crook and David Reeder, Taylor and Francis, 1996.

250. *Statistics of Education: Schools Edition*, HMSO, 1979.

251. *Education and the Social Order*, Brian Simon, Lawrence & Wishart, 1991.

252. ED 147/647, National Archive, February 1965.

253. Alan Kerckhoff, Ken Fogelman, David Crook and David Reeder, Taylor and Francis, 1996.

254. Notes of meeting with the secretary of state, Ministry officials and educational advisers, ED 147/644, February 1965.

255. ED 147/828, 12 April 1965.

256. ED 147/829.

257. Debate in the House of Commons, Edward Short, 28 November 1968.

258. *Comprehensive Education in Action*, T.G. Monks, National Foundation for Educational Research, 1970.

259. *A Critical Appraisal of Comprehensive Education*, J.M. Ross, National Foundation for Educational Research, 1972.

260. *Half Way There: Report On the British Comprehensive School*, Penguin Books, 1970.

261. *Children and their Primary Schools (The Plowden Report),* Department of Education and Science, 1967.

262. *The politics of educational change*, Manchester University Press, 1978.

263. *1968 Education Act,* 10 April 1968.

264. Ministry of Education archived files, ED 207/69, ED 207/45, 1967.

265. Ministry of Education archived file ED 207/22, 1967.

266. *Education Bill 1970 proposals for legislation*, ED 207/151/Item 1.

267. *The Times*, 7 August 1969.

268. Peter Gregson (private secretary to Harrold Wilson) to D.W. Tanner, ED 2017/19, 24 November 1969.

269. *Critical Quarterly* archive, https://archiveshub.jisc.ac.uk/data/gb133-cqa (accessed 11 January 2021).

270. William Collins, 2017.

271. Obituary, *The Guardian*, 10 May 2012.

272. *The Death of Progressive Education*, Roy Lowe, Taylor and Francis, 2006.

273. Rhodes Boyson, debate in the House of Commons, 6 May 1975.

274. *Whip to Wilson,* Edward Short, Macdonald, 1989.

275. Taylor and Francis, 2005.

276. 'A case-history of Labour Failure'*, New Statesman*, ED 207/151 – ITEM2, 11 April 1970.

277. *Margaret Thatcher official biography volume 1*, Charles Moore, Penguin Books, 2014.

278. Circular 10/70, Department of Education and Science, 1970.

279. 28 June 1970.

280. 'The Tory Style', 25 October 1970.

281. Edward Short's speech, House of Commons, 'The second reading of the Education (Milk) Bill', June 1971.

282. July 1971.

283. *The Trend of Reading Standards*, K.B. Start and B.K. Wells, National Foundation for Educational Research, 23 March 1972.

284. *The Times*, 17 June 1972.

285. 'A case of overkill', 13 February 1976.

286. 'Alan Bullock, 1914–2004', Amikam Nachmani, *Diplomacy & Statecraft*, 7 August 2005.

287. 6 December 1972.

288. https://www.margaretthatcher.org/document/102233 (accessed 11 January 2021).

289. 9 March 1972.

290. 7 December 1972.

291. 14 December 1972.

292. *A Century of Fiscal Squeeze Politics*, Christopher Hood, OUP, 2017.

293. Meeting at Chequers between Thatcher and Heath, 13 January 1972, National Archive.

294. *The Times*, 12 November 1970.

295. *The Road to Serfdom*, Friedrich Hayek, Routledge, March 1944.

296. https://www.margaretthatcher.org/document/102304 (accessed 11 January 2021).
297. 'Margaret Thatcher and secondary reorganisation', Roger Woods, 1981.
298. Edward Heath, John Campbell, 2013.
299. *Margaret Thatcher official biography volume 1*, Charles Moore, Penguin Books, 2014.
300. *Education: Historical Statistics*, House of Commons Library, 2012.
301. *Raising the school leaving age to 16*, HMSO.
302. *Change and Response – the first year's work*, The Schools Council, 1965.
303. 'Discussion at Chequers on Education', https://www.margaretthatcher.org/document/109464, 13 January 1972 (accessed 11 January 2021).
304. Circular 8/71 stipulated that the LEAs had to submit 'short reports on their state of preparedness' by December 1972.
305. *The Guardian*, 10 January 1972.
306. *Statistics of Education*, HMSO, 1969.
307. S. Cowan, G. McCulloch and T. Woodin, *History of Education Journal*, 15 August 2011.
308. *Inspectorate of secondary education panel meetings*, ED 158/22, 1966–1971.
309. 'Most local preparations for new school leaving age are "superficial"', *The Times*, 15 September 1972.
310. S. Cowan, G. McCulloch and T. Woodin, Palgrave Macmillan, 2013.
311. Tim Devlin, education correspondent, *The Times*, 14 March 1974.
312. Multiple reports from the Institute of Fiscal Studies.
313. Population estimates for England and Wales by sex and quinary age (mid-1911 to mid-1960) and by sex and single year of age (mid-1961 to mid-2015).
314. *Social class mobility in modern Britain*, Dr John Goldthorpe, Nuffield College Oxford, 15 March 2016.
315. *British Historical Statistics*, B. Mitchell, Cambridge University Press, 2011.
316. *British Historical Statistics*, B. Mitchell, Cambridge University Press, 2011.
317. ONS, 2018.

7. The comprehensive era

1. Department of Education and Science, 16 April 1974.
2. Public Schools Commission – Second Report, HMSO, 29 January 1970.
3. The secretary of state for education and science, House of Commons, 11 March 1975.
4. Miss Joan Lestor, House of Commons, 26 January 1976.
5. This number is derived from the Donnison Report's figure of 20,000 pupils having their fees payed by LEAs.
6. *Education and the Social Order*, Brian Simon, Lawrence & Wishart, 1991.
7. *Prime Minister: Conduct of Policy under Harold Wilson and James Callaghan 1974–1979*, Bernard Donoughue, 1987.
8. Department of Education statistics, HMSO, 1975.
9. *Circular 7/75 (Phasing out of direct grants to grammar schools), Department of Education and Science, 1975.*
10. Education Act 1976.
11. *The Fight for Education: Black Paper 1975*, J.M. Dent, April 1975.
12. 'Black mark for progressives', *The Times*, 21 April 1975.
13. *Teaching styles and pupil progress*, Neville Bennett, Open Books, 27 April 1976.

14. *Daily Mirror*, 26 April 1976.
15. *The Observer*, 25 April 1976.
16. *The Times*, 27 April 1976.
17. *Education Guardian*, 4 May 1976.
18. 'Teaching styles and pupil progress: a re-analysis', M. Aitkin, *Journal of Educational Psychology*, June 1981.
19. *A Chapter of Errors: Teaching Styles and Pupil Progress in Retrospect*, J. Gray and D. Satterly, Education Research, 9 July 2006.
20. *William Tyndale Junior and Infants Schools Public Enquiry*, Robin Auld QC, Inner London Education Authority, July 1976.
21. 'William Tyndale – Collapse of a school – or a system', J. Gretton and M. Jackson, *The Times Educational Supplement*, 1976.
22. Fred Mulley, Thameside (Secondary Education) debate, House of Commons, 3 August 1976, https://hansard.parliament.uk
23. *The Crown*: Series 3, Netflix, 2019.
24. *Downing Street Diary Volume Two*, Bernard Donoughue, Random House, 2009.
25. *Towards A New Education System: The Victory of the New Right?* Clyde Chitty, Taylor and Francis, 1989.
26. *School education in England: problems and initiatives*, secretary of state for Education and Science, July 1976.
27. Ruskin College Oxford provided education for those lacking academic qualifications and educated many trade unionists.
28. *The Heat of the Kitchen*, Bernard Donoughue, Politico's Publishing, 2003.
29. 'Mr Callaghan calls for improved education standards', *The Times*, 19 October 1976.
30. 19 October 1976.
31. 19 October 1976.
32. Falmer Press, 1998.
33. *Education and Labour Party Ideologies*, Denis Lawton, Woburn Education Series, 2005.
34. *Education Policy*, I. Abbott, M. Rathbone and P. Whitehead, Sage, 2013.
35. 'Cabinet accused of leak', 11 July 1977.
36. *Climbing the bookshelves: The autobiography of Shirley Williams*, Shirley Williams, Little, Brown Book Group, 2009.
37. Circular 11/76 – Education Act 1976, 25 November 1976.
38. Circular 12/87 – Support by LEAs in non-maintained schools, 25 November 1976.
39. 'Special Schools' in *Education: the Wasted Years? 1973–1986*, P. Rowan, Falmer Press, 1988.
40. Various datasets, ONS.
41. *A Century of Fiscal Squeeze Politics*, Christopher Hood, OUP Oxford, 2017.
42. *When Britain Went Bust – The 1976 IMF Crisis*, OMFIF Press, Richard Roberts, 2016.
43. A motion passed at the Labour Party Conference, May 2019.
44. Labour Party manifesto, November 2019.
45. Conservative Party manifesto, May 1979.
46. Education Act 1979, 26 July 1979.
47. Education Act 1980, 3 April 1980.
48. *Industrial Relations in Schools*, Roger Seifert, Taylor and Francis, 1995.
49. *Downing Street Diary Volume Two*, Bernard Donoughue, Random House, 1987.
50. *Prime Minister: Conduct of Policy under Harold Wilson and James Callaghan 1974–1979*, Bernard Donoughue, 1987.

51. *Climbing the Bookshelves: The autobiography of Shirley Williams*, Shirley Williams, Little Brown Book Group, 2009.
52. *Radical Educational Policies and Conservative Secretaries of State*, P. Ribbins and B. Sherratt, Cassell, 1997.
53. *Class War*, Chris Woodhead, A Little Brown Book, 2002.
54. Harry Hudson, *The Times*, 30 December 2020.
55. *Whatever happened to progressivism?*, Institute of Education – University of London, 2005.
56. *Educating for the Modern World,* CBI, June 2019.
57. Review (1979) LEA arrangements for the school curriculum, Circular 14/77, HMSO, November 1979.
58. Education statistics, HMSO, 1979.
59. *Aspects of secondary education in England: A survey by HM Inspectors of Schools*, HMSO, December 1979.
60. *A framework for the school curriculum*, HMSO, January 1980.
61. *The School Curriculum*, HMSO, March 1981.
62. *Towards A New Education System: The Victory of the New Right?* Clyde Chitty, Taylor and Francis, 1989.
63. *The School Curriculum,* Circular 6/81, HMSO, October 1981.
64. Obituary of Lord Carlisle of Bucklow, *The Times*, June 2005.
65. *Kinnock – the biography*, Martin Westlake, Little, Brown and Company, 2001.
66. The *Observer*, January 1970.
67. *Radical educational policies and Conservative Secretaries of State*, Cassell, 1997.
68. A television comedy series about the struggles of a government minister to formulate and enact policies that are opposed by his civil service officials (1980–1984).
69. *Kenneth Baker – the turbulent years*, Kenneth Baker, Faber & Faber, 1993.
70. *Standards in English Schools*, C. Cox and J. Marks, NCES, 1983.
71. C. Cox and J. Marks, The Claridge Press, 1988.
72. *The Daily Telegraph*, 29 November 1983.
73. *The Times*, 20 March 1985.
74. Lady Warnock obituary, *The Guardian*, 21 March 2019.
75. National Education Union, https://www.teachers.org.uk
76. *The New Teacher in School – a report by Her Majesty's Inspectors*, HMSO, 1982.
77. *White Paper – Teaching Quality*, HMSO, 1983.
78. *Secondary School Examinations: A Single System at 16 Plus*, HMSO, October 1978.
79. *Better Schools*, HMSO, March 1985.
80. *Towards a new education system*, Clyde Chitty, RoutledgeFalmer, 1989.
81. *The Observer*, 19 June 1988.
82. 'Teachers must bite the GCSE bullet', *The Guardian*, 2 June 1986.
83. *The Times*, 30 December 2014.
84. *Value-added analysis of GCSE, http://www.bstubbs.co.uk/gcse.htm*
85. *The Times*, 20 November 2019.
86. *Hansard*, 12 November 1982.
87. *Hansard,* 12 November 1982.
88. 'The implementation and development of the TVEI', National Audit Office (HMSO), 22 October 1991.
89. House of Commons debate, 26 March 1991.

90. http://technicaleducationmatters.org/2011/11/12/the-technical-and-vocational-education-initiative-tvei-1983-1997/ (accessed 11 January 2021).
91. *Education and the social order*, Brian Simon, Lawrence & Wishart, 1999.
92. 'The "Patron Saint" of comprehensive education – an interview with Clyde Chitty', *Forum* Volume 60, 2018.
93. Joseph's speech to the North of England education conference, 6 January 1984.
94. *The Guardian*, 11 June 1987.
95. *Daily Mail*, 13 July 1987.
96. *Education in a post welfare society,* Sally Tomlinson, Open University Press, 2005.
97. *Education statistics,* Institute of Fiscal Studies, September 2015.
98. HMSO, 29 July 1988.
99. *Towards A New Education System*, Clive Chitty, Taylor and Francis, 1989.
100. *Education and the social order*, Brian Simon, Lawrence & Wishart, 1991.
101. M. Flude and M. Hammer, Falmer Press, 1990.
102. *The Times Educational Supplement,* 24 April 1987.
103. *National Pupil Projections – Future Trends in Pupil Numbers: July 2014*, Department of Education, July 2014.
104. The Election Centre, http://www.electionscentre.co.uk (accessed 11 January 2021).
105. Labour MP Gerald Kaufman's description of their 1983 election manifesto, Oxford Reference.
106. *Councils in Conflict: The Rise and Fall of the Municipal Left*, S. Lansley, S. Goss and C. Wolmar, Palgrave Macmillan, 1989.
107. The Rates Act 1984 enabled central government to limit the increase in rates that each LEA could levy.
108. https://www.margaretthatcher.org/document/105799 (accessed 11 January 2021).
109. *Hansard,* House of Commons, 1 December 1987.
110. Roy Jenkins, David Owen, Bill Rodgers and Shirley Williams formed the SDP in March 1981.
111. The SDP–Liberal Alliance achieved 73% as many votes as Labour.
112. Labour Party manifesto, 1997.
113. Tony Blair, Launch speech of education manifesto for the general election, 1997.
114. Queen's speech to Parliament, 14 May 1997.
115. *Value for Money at Grant-Maintained Schools: A Review of Performance*, National Audit Office, 20 July 1994.
116. Documentation catalogue for CRDA/36/DD, National Archive, last updated 2000.
117. *Self-Government for Schools*, HMSO, June 1996.
118. 'Local management of schools in England: Results after six years', Rosalind Levačić, *Journal of Education Policy*, 1998.
119. 'Standards In English Schools Part I: The introduction of the National Curriculum and GCSEs', 27 January 2015, https://dominiccummings.com
120. Progressively Worse – the burden of bad ideas in British schools, Robert Peal, Civitas, 2014.
121. *Radical educational policies and Conservative Secretaries of State*, Cassell, 1997.
122. *The National Curriculum and its Assessment,* Sir Ron Dearing, HMSO, September 1993.
123. *Trends in standards of literacy in the United Kingdom, 1948–1996*, Greg Brooks, NFER, September 1997.
124. *Opening Doors to a Learning Society*, Labour Party, 1994.

125. *Tony Blair: Prime Minister*, John Rentoul, Warner, 2001.
126. 27 July 1994.
127. Labour Party Conference, 6 October 1994.
128. *David Blunkett*, Stephen Pollard, Hodder & Stoughton, 2005.
129. *Peter Mandelson: The Blair revolution revisited*, Peter Mandelson, Politico's, 1996.
130. *Tony Blair: A Journey*, Random House, 2011.
131. *Diversity and excellence: A new partnership for schools*, Labour Party, 1995.
132. Labour's big, bad idea. 25 June 1995.
133. 22 June 1995.
134. 'Blair attacks Tory "policy of rejection"', the *Independent*, 28 April 1997.
135. Research Papers in Education, 2004.
136. Tony Blair, speech at Ruskin College, 16 December 1996.
137. John Prescott, speech at Ruskin College, 13 June 1996.
138. *The Sunday Times*, 11 February 1996.
139. *The Daily Telegraph*, 28 February 1996.
140. The *Independent*, 25 January 1996.
141. 1997 Education Act, HMSO, 13 July 1997.
142. HMSO, 24 July 1998.
143. *New Labour and Secondary Education*, C. Chitty, Palgrave, 2013.
144. BBC News website, 19 May 1998.
145. BBC News website, 24 September 1999.
146. Memorandum from the National Union of Teachers, October 1999.
147. *Excellence in Cities and Education Action Zones*, Ofsted, 2003.
148. 'A Fresh Start for a "failing school"? A qualitative study', 2009.
149. Answer to a question from Bercow, House of Commons, 24 November 2000.
150. *Evaluation of the Beacon School Initiative*, NFER, December 2004.
151. House of Commons, 22 March 1999.
152. *Excellence in Cities,* Research Report No 675B, Department for Education and Skills, 2003.
153. *Evaluating the effectiveness of specialist schools in England*, School Effectiveness and School Improvement, September 2006.
154. *Daily Mail*, 13 July 1987.
155. *Evaluation of the National Literacy Project*, NFER, December 1998.
156. As reported in *The Guardian*, 17 January 2000.
157. David Blunkett speech to the Social Market Foundation, 15 March 2000.
158. The Learning and Skills Act 2000, July 2000.
159. Department for Education and Employment, May 2000.
160. 'Labour abandons campaign against grammar schools', interview by David Blunkett, 12 March 2000.
161. *Education Policy in Britain*, Clyde Chitty, Macmillan, 2014.
162. *Losing Labour's Soul?,* Eric Shaw, Taylor and Francis, 2007.
163. *The Blair Years*, Alastair Campbell, Random House, 2007.
164. *The Blair Years*, Alastair Campbell, Random House, 2007.
165. HMSO, February 2001.
166. 13 February 2001.
167. *Instruction to deliver*, Michael Barber, Politico's, 2007.
168. Tony Blair speech outside Downing Street, 22 June 2001.
169. BBC website, June 22 2001.

170. The *Observer*, 23 June 2002.
171. *Schools achieving success*, government white paper, 23 November 2001.
172. Education Act, 24 July 2002.
173. 23 June 2002.
174. *The Guardian*, 25 June 2002.
175. Amendment to the Education Act, House of Commons, 6 February 2002.
176. 'Bishops warn Blair over the dangers of creationism', *The Observer*, 7 April 2002.
177. *Ofsted report of Emmanuel College City Technology College*, 26 March 2006.
178. *A five-year strategy for children and learners*, Department for Education and Skills, 8 July 2004.
179. 'Clarke aims to lure back "despairing" middle class', *The Guardian*, 9 July 2004.
180. 'A return to tradition in schools', *The Daily Telegraph*, 9 July 2004.
181. *Specialist schools operation in September 2003*, DfES, 2003.
182. *A five-year strategy for children and learners*, Department for Education and Skills, 8 July 2004.
183. *Academies, the School System in England and a Vision for the Future*, A. West and D. Wolfe, LSE, June 2018.
184. *Statistics of Education 2004 Edition*, Department of Education and Skills, 2004.
185. Audit Commission, October 2003.
186. *Education and Skills – Fourth Report*, House of Commons, 14 July 2004.
187. 'Parental school choice "naïve"', BBC website, 2 August 2006.
188. *Institute of Fiscal Studies* (September 20
189. *Has Labour delivered on the policy priorities of 'education, education, education'?* S. McNally and R. Vaitilingam, LSE, 2007.
190. *United Kingdom Education 1997–2001*, Howard Glennerster, LSE, 2001.
191. Parliamentary answer by question asked by D. Laws, 26 February 2004.
192. *From Baker to Balls: The foundations of the education system,* House of Commons Children, Schools and Families Committee, 24 March 2010.
193. *Achievement in public examinations,* School Curriculum and Assessment Authority (SCAA), 1996.
194. *Education and Training Statistics for the United Kingdom (2004),* Department of Education and Skills, 2004.
195. 'Some thoughts on education and political priorities', Dominic Cummings, *The Guardian*, 11 October 2013.
196. *Class War: The State of British Education,* Chris Woodhead, Sphere, 16 January 2003.
197. *Chalk and sleaze,* Martin Bright, *The Guardian*, 16 March 2002.
198. 'Lessons well worth learning', P.D. James, *The Daily Telegraph*, 17 March 2002.
199. *Commenting to a question from R. Beggs MP.* Steven Timms, minister of state for school standards at the Department for Education and Skills, House of Commons, 7 February 2002.
200. 'The other "c" word', *The Guardian*, 17 February 2004.
201. 'Why Big Sister's plans spell doom for your children', Chris Woodhead, *The Times*, 7 March 2004.
202. 'Lessons in class warfare', Polly Toynbee, *The Guardian*, 6 December 2002.
203. 'Education Policy, 1997–2000: The effects on top, bottom and middle England', S. Tomlinson, *International Studies in Sociology of Education*, November 2001.
204. Debate about specialist schools, House of Commons, 11 March 2003.
205. 'Academies "will create two-tier school system"', *The Guardian*, 19 February, 2005.

206. *14–19 Curriculum and Qualifications Reform*, The Working Group for 14–19 Reform, 18 October 2004.

8. Much maligned or monstrous mistake?

1. *A review of the TV programme 'That'll Teach 'Em'*, 5 August 2004. This TV series took children from 2004 and put them into a reconstructed secondary modern school. In 2020 it was available on YouTube.
2. Bridges to the future webinar, RSA, 23 July 2020.
3. *Education in 1928–1929*, Board of Education and Statistics Public Education in England and Wales, HMSO.
4. *The Audit of War,* Correlli Barnett, 1986.
5. *Oxbridge 'elitism'*, House of Commons briefing paper, 5 September 2016.
6. November 1943.
7. http://www.iwm.org.uk/history/how-childrens-lives-changed-during-the-second-world-war (accessed 11 January 2021).
8. *Social Welfare and Health Care in World War II: Problems of Social Policy*, Richard Titmuss, HMSO, 1950.
9. *Standards of Reading 1948–1956*, Ministry of Education Pamphlet No. 32, 1956.
10. *The British Economy 1945–1955*, chapter on social services, edited by G. Worswick, Oxford University Press.
11. 'Party Gains and Losses', 3 November 1945.
12. *Schools, pupils and their characteristics*, Department of Education, January 2016.
13. *Education in the post-war years*, Routledge, 1988.
14. National Archive folder E147/415, 7 July 1948.
15. Print Resources, 2019.
16. *International Survey of Adult Financial Literacy Competencies,* OECD, November 2016.
17. *Public Understanding of Economics and Economic Statistics*, ONS, November 2020.
18. 'Numeracy skills: what's not adding up in the UK?', *Financial Times*, 30 October 2020.

9. Half a century on – what lessons can we learn?

1. *Do schools kill creativity?,* Sir Kenneth Robinson, 2006.
2. The Technical and Vocational Education Initiative, 1982.
3. *The Comprehensive School*, Robin Pedley, Penguin, 1969.
4. Briefing paper: Secondary modern schools, SESC, October 2017.
5. Notes of meeting with the secretary of state, Ministry officials and educational advisers, ED 147/644, February 1965.
6. ED 147/829, National Archive.
7. Civitas, 2014.
8. Taylor and Francis, 2014.
9. *Juvenile education in relation to employment after the war,* HMSO, 1917.
10. *Educating for the Modern World,* June 2019.
11. *The University Admissions Officers Report*, IBSCA, 2017.
12. Frances Ryan, 3 May 2018.
13. *IFS presentation*, 12 November 2020.

14. *Post-18 Education,* Centre for Vocational Education Research, September 2020.
15. Beloe Report, HMSO, 1958.
16. *Pointless GCSEs should be scrapped*, BBC News, 11 February 2019.
17. 'I introduced GCSEs in the 1980s – but now it's time to scrap them', Kenneth Baker, the *Independent*, 11 February 2019.
18. Investigation into university technical colleges, Audit Office, 30 October 2019.
19. Penguin Books, 2020.
20. *The rise of the meritocracy*, David Young, Transaction Publishers, 1994.
21. *The coming of post-industrial society*, Daniel Bell, Basic Books, 1976.
22. *Coming Apart*, Charles Murray, Crown Publishing Group, 2013.
23. *Student loan statistics*, House of Commons Library, October 2020.
24. *Education at a glance*, OECD indicators, OECD, 2018.
25. *Percentage of employed graduates in non-graduate roles*, ONS, April 2018.
26. *Non-continuation summary: UK Performance Indicators,* HESA, February 2020.
27. 'Too many students take courses that don't benefit them or the economy', Paul Johnson, *The Times*, 2 March 2020.
28. *Business Barometer,* The Open University, 2018.
29. *Graduates' reflection on activity by subject area of degree*, HESA, July 2020.
30. *The state of the adult social care sector and workforce in England*, Skills for Care, October 2020.
31. *Over-qualification and skills mismatch in the graduate labour market*, CIPD, August 2015.
32. *Post-18 Review of Education and Funding*, HMSO, May 2019.
33. *The Class Ceiling*, Sam Friedman, Policy Press, 2019.
34. *The Economist*, 11 November 2020.
35. *Independent*, 30 October 2017.
36. *Washington Times*, 29 September 2020.
37. *2019 general election: the demographics dividing Britain*, YouGov, October 2019.
38. World Education Blog, UNESCO, December 2015.
39. *The Breakaway*, Perry Anderson, *The London Review of Books*, 21 January 2021.
40. Policy report, CIPD, November 2017.
41. Social background of MPs 1979–2019, House of Commons briefing paper, March 2020.
42. British Policy and Politics blog, LSE, February 2015.
43. *Ages of Discord: A Structural-Demographic Analysis of American History*, Peter Turchin, Beresta Books, 2016.
44. Penguin Books, 2002.
45. HMSO, 2011.
46. *Heading for the precipice*, Kings College London, 2015.
47. '"One Size Fits All" – A Default Policy that is Serving No One Well', *European Review*, August 2020.
48. *Review of Post-18 Education and Funding*, HMSO, May 2019.
49. 'The Augar report on higher education has a sting in its tail', *The Guardian*, 4 June 2019.
50. *Higher Education Student Statistics: 2018/19,* HESA, 29 January 2020.
51. 'Master's degrees on rise as graduates seek to stand out', 8 April 2018.
52. *Graduate wellbeing recorded in the Graduate Outcomes survey*, ONS, December 2020.
53. *The Labor Market for Recent College Graduates*, Federal Reserve Bank of New York, 2020.
54. *2020 Annual Report on Education Spending in England,* IFS, 3 November 2020.

55. *The Impact of Selective Secondary Education on Progression to Higher Education*, HEPI, 2019.
56. *Prisoners of the Blob*, Toby Young, Civitas, April 2014.
57. Hodder & Stoughton, 2018.
58. *Identity: the demand for dignity and the politics of resentment*, Profile Books, 2018.
59. 'Before society can "level up", the ruling Eton-Winchester clique needs levelling down', Fiona Millar, *The Guardian*, 10 March 2020.
60. 'The battle for Britain's education', Melissa Benn, *Socialist Worker*, 27 September 2011.
61. Andrew Adonis, Twitter, 17 August 2020.
62. *Financial Times*, 22 December 2020.
63. Book review of *The Charity School Movement*, R.H. Tawney, *The Economic History Review*, May 1939.
64. *Left behind white pupils from disadvantaged backgrounds*, House of Commons Education Committee, December 2020.
65. 'The ethnic question we're too scared to ask', Trevor Phillips, *The Times*, 2 November 2020.
66. *7 truths about social mobility*, HMSO, May 2012.
67. *Underachievement in Education by White Working Class Children*, HMSO, 2014–2015.
68. 'Sociogenomics is opening a new door to eugenics', *MIT Review*, October 2018.
69. *Permanent and fixed-period exclusions in England 2016 to 2017*, NAO, April 2019.
70. *Anatomy of Britain today*, Anthony Sampson, Hodder & Stoughton, 1965.
71. 11 January 2007.
72. *Whitehall's black box: accountability and performance in the senior civil service*, 2006.
73. John Gray, Harper Collins, 1992.
74. Speech to Britain's venture capitalists, 6 July 1999.
75. *Deliverology 101*, Michael Barber, Corwin, 2010.
76. *Civil service shake-up: Rewiring the government machine or blowing a fuse?*, BBC Westminster Hour, 26 September 2020.
77. *PM's latest hire signals desire for Whitehall reform*, Laura Kuenssberg, BBC, 12 January 2021.
78. 'Britain's failing state apparatus', *The Daily Telegraph*, 17 December 2020.
79. *All Change: Why Britain is so prone to policy reinvention*, The Institute of Government, 2016.

Appendix B

1. 'Grammar schools: back to the bad old days of inequality', *The Guardian*, 4 May 2017.
2. 'Why grammar schools are not the answer to our economic and social problems', *The Daily Telegraph*, 20 August 2016.
3. 'Technical Hitch', *The Spectator*, 11 September 2106.
4. 'Meritocracy and its discontents', *The Economist*, 7 October 2006.
5. 'A new syllabus', *The Economist*, 17 September 2016.
6. 'Does Failing The 11-Plus Really Damage Your Future?', *HuffPost*, 18 September 2012.
7. *Fair Enough? Schools admissions: the next steps*, Comprehensive Future, September 2007.
8. *History lesson best forgotten*, Tes, 13 August 2004.
9. *Time for an end to the lazy assumptions about secondary moderns*, Tes, 22 October 2016.

ACKNOWLEDGMENTS

Part of the reason I wrote this book was to 'put the record straight' about the quality and commitment of secondary modern teachers. Against all the odds they did a terrific job.

The pupils of George Gascoigne Secondary Modern owe a massive debt of gratitude to Mr Wolfe, Mr Jones, Mr Acres, Mr Williams, Mr Hughes, Mr Foster, Mrs Wright and Mr Dixon, the school's remarkable headmaster. I know that without their help my life could have gone in a very different direction. Above all, I have written this book for them.

I would like to thank all my friends, especially Malcolm and Brian, for their encouragement and for believing that the book would ever get finished.

This is the third book for which Suzanne Arnold has helped transform my writing into readable text. More than that, Suzanne has ensured the consistency of language and logic throughout the book.

Finally, I want to thank my wife, Stella, for putting up with a partner who has been obsessed with a single subject for the past three years.

INDEX

Printed in Great Britain
by Amazon